A Companion Website accompanies MANAGEMENT, 2nd edition, by John Naylor

Visit the *Management* Companion Website at www.booksites.net/naylor to find valuable teaching and learning material including:

For students
- Study material designed to help you improve your results
- Comprehensive learning objectives detailing what you need to know
- Multiple choice questions to test your learning
- Glossary of terms
- Weblinks to sites relevant to chapter cases and also others of topical interest

For lecturers
- A secure, password-protected site with teaching material
- A downloadable version of the full *Lecturer's Guide*
- Downloadable PowerPoint slides of figures from the book
- Additional articles to support material in each chapter
- Weblinks to sites relevant to chapter cases and also others of topical interest

Also: This site has a syllabus manager, search functions, and email results functions.

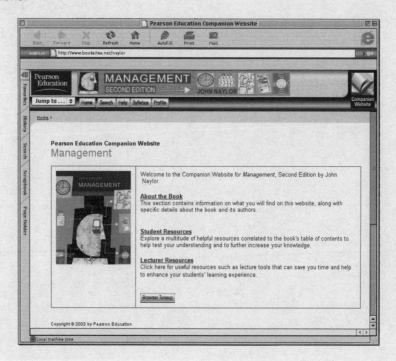

PEARSON
Education

We work with leading authors to develop the strongest
educational materials in business and management,
bringing cutting-edge thinking and best learning practice
to a global market.

Under a range of well-known imprints, including
Financial Times Prentice Hall, we can craft high quality print
and electronic publications which help readers to
understand and apply their content, whether studying or
at work.

To find out more about the complete range of our
publishing, please visit us on the World Wide Web at:
www.pearsoned.co.uk

Second Edition

MANAGEMENT

John Naylor

Principal Lecturer in Management
Liverpool John Moores University

FT Prentice Hall
FINANCIAL TIMES

An imprint of **Pearson Education**
Harlow, England • London • New York • Boston • San Francisco • Toronto
Sydney • Tokyo • Singapore • Hong Kong • Seoul • Taipei • New Delhi
Cape Town • Madrid • Mexico City • Amsterdam • Munich • Paris • Milan

Pearson Education Limited

Edinburgh Gate
Harlow
Essex CM20 2JE
England

and Associated Companies throughout the world

Visit us on the World Wide Web at:
www.pearsoned.co.uk

First published 1999
Second edition published 2004

ISBN 978-0-273-67321-1

British Library Cataloguing in Publication Data
A CIP catalogue record for this book can be obtained from the British Library.

Library of Congress Cataloging-in-Publication Data
A catalog record for this book is available from the Library of Congress.

10 9 8 7 6 5 4
08 07

Typeset in Century 10/12pt by 30
Printed by Ashford Colour Press Ltd., Gosport

The publisher's policy is to use paper manufactured from sustainable forests.

BRIEF CONTENTS

CONTENTS

PREFACE

■ Aims of the book

This book aims to offer excellent value to students taking courses in management. These may be part of an undergraduate programme or postgraduate courses for those who come to management for the first time. The book is comprehensive and thorough, yet flexible, readable and interesting. Theory is explained and applications are discussed. From this source, students can both learn about, and develop skills in, management.

The complexity of management as a field of study is reflected in the range of approaches taken to its presentation. Among these, we can pick out four:

Management as a process

Variants of the sequence of planning, organising, implementing and controlling can be found in management thought from the earliest days. In this book, Parts 3 to 6 represent stages of this process. The constraints of book design inevitably lead to a sequential presentation. Yet, the management process should really be seen as a number of loops. In practice, not only is there neither beginning nor end, but also managers are engaged in several stages simultaneously. As we shall see in Chapter 1, the process model of management does not constitute a descriptive theory, even less a prescriptive one. It simply offers a way to sort and examine ideas.

The division of chapter topics among the process stages is always somewhat arbitrary, for the sequence and elements could be changed. For instance, control could be discussed much earlier than in the last two chapters. Furthermore, most readers will not follow the book from begining to end. Therefore, the chapters are written as a set of self-contained units, with cross-references as appropriate.

Themes in management

A less structured approach is to use current themes and controversies as the basis of book design. The starting point is to examine what questions are of greatest concern to the modern manager. In this book, we select four: globalisation; ethics and social responsibility; quality; and enterprise. This selection does not mean that other issues are ignored. Questions such as diversity, e-commerce, gender and governance could have warranted their own chapters. The limited space, however, kept the list to four and other issues are included at appropriate points.

The book is designed to relate the chosen themes to the management process. They are, therefore, set out in Part 2 and referred to again at appropriate points throughout.

Management skills

It has been recognised that knowing *about* management is not enough. Most learners want to enhance their skills. These can lie in administrative or interpersonal aspects of the managerial role or in the ability to manage oneself or one's career. In recognising the importance of skills, the book takes many opportunities to demonstrate how things are done. Examples include: appraising the state of an organisation and environment; choosing appropriate forecasting techniques; preparing a mission statement, objectives and plans; examining the ethics within a decision; using techniques to assess and improve quality; avoiding decision traps; designing an organisation structure; recruiting; communicating and making a communications plan; working out a payment scheme; setting up control systems; anticipating and coping with cultural differences; nurturing enterprise; and learning.

Summarising and presenting ideas are important skills. For instance, through its use of hundreds of examples, the book encourages students to use diagrams as support for investigation, thinking and presentation. Styles vary from the formal flow and block diagrams to the apparently less formal mind maps and rich pictures. The book shows that they all have their place.

Critique

With the overwhelming weight of material about management that exists, there is a danger of not standing back and taking a detached, critical look. Without this perspective, one might conclude that the only controversies in the field were about the efficacy of one theory compared to another. A critical perspective, on the other hand, sees through what is so often taken for granted. For instance, in discussing communication in Chapter 13, we might assume that the problem is to identify the best way to transmit information from one person to another. Yet, a more detached view asks whether this assumption is sustainable. It may be that managers do not want to tell the whole story. While espousing openness and sharing, they may practise obfuscation and manipulation.

The discussion of theory is developed in Chapter 1. Nevertheless, the book is not a comprehensive critique of management. In referring, however, to alternative perspectives on processes such as communication and control, and practices such as marketing, it points out that there are alternative viewpoints. Students are encouraged to question basic assumptions, theory and actions. Then they can resist swallowing simple dogma such as, 'Managers have the right to manage'.

A combination of approaches

The design of the book combines the above approaches. Having established a context for management in Part 1, and set out the four themes in Part 2, the book follows the stages of the management process. Readers may follow a different sequence. It is possible, for instance, to start with organising and study planning and control later. To assist with alternative routes, each chapter has been set out in a standard way, introduced by clear objectives showing the material that is to be covered.

■ Student learning features

While fitted into the sequence explained above, every chapter stands on its own. Key features are as follows:

- learning objectives immediately establish the purpose of the chapter;
- the opening case study provides a context for discussion and draws attention to the practical implications of key concepts;

- these concepts are laid out in sections with clear headings;
- there are numerous examples and references, including useful website addresses;
- the conclusion of each chapter draws the themes together;
- a 'Quick check' test challenges the student to assess whether learning objectives have been met at a basic level;
- chapter questions are structured to test knowledge, explore practical applications and stimulate further investigation;
- the closing case builds on the work covered in the chapter and raises points for discussion;
- the opening and closing cases use real-life examples. They are short enough to be digested quickly yet are especially written to focus on relevant issues;
- other examples and illustrations are highlighted in text boxes or, if sufficiently brief, incorporated in the text;
- the cases and examples are deliberately varied to cover different perspectives and nations, and organisations of different sizes and types.

Support material for lecturers

This book comes as part of a teaching package and the following supplementary material is available:

- *Website support* A regularly updated website can be found on **www.booksites. net/naylor**. This contains downloadable versions of diagrams from the book and extra OHTs to aid preparation and presentation of classes on the password-protected section of the website.
- *Lecturer's Guide* A resource manual containing lecture notes and suggestions for tutorial work and assignments.

GUIDED TOUR

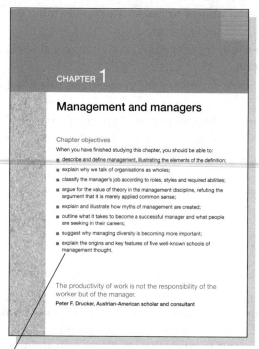

Each chapter is introduced with a list of **chapter objectives**.

An **opening case** sets the themes in context.

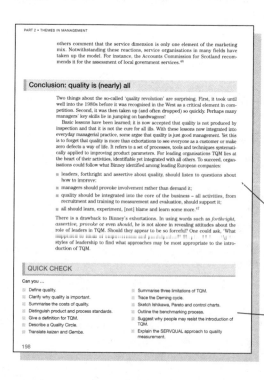

A narrative **conclusion** is followed by a **quick check** feature to ensure the learning objectives for the chapter have been achieved.

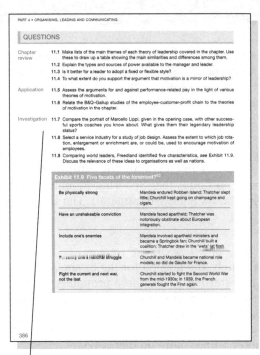

A range of short and longer answer **questions** encourage critical reflection on the chapter as a whole.

At the end of each chapter, a **closing case** with questions examines the application of theory to a practical context.

A short annotated **bibliography** suggests relevant further reading. This is followed by a more comprehensive list of **references**.

A NOTE ON WRITING STYLE

Students often ask about style in management writing. Although oral communication predominates among managers, writing is an important skill. Chapter 13 discusses features of good communication, including adopting an acceptable written style. Without it, recipients take messages less seriously than they deserve. Here are some common issues.

Singular or plural

In grammar, names of organisations are singular. Good examples are: 'France Telecom *has* a map of the next three years. *It is* committed to cutting costs'; 'DT *has* targets only for this year'; 'There is no doubt that Schering-Plough *is* sick ... with a debilitating patent expiry on Claritin, *its* allergy treatment'; 'The US administration *considers* further action'.[1]

Gender

Writing should avoid gender bias. Fortunately, the fashion for 'he or she', 'he/she' or even 's/he' seems to have died out. It is better not to use these pronouns. Using plurals allows the use of 'their'. Otherwise, articles (*a* or *the*) often work. The use of 'their' to refer to one person has spread, although many do not accept this usage.

Rewording often helps in handling pronouns and other words, such as 'seamstress', that suggest gender roles. Chapter 13 has more on this issue.

Contractions and possessives

Contractions, such as *don't, isn't, we've* and *they'll*, should not be used in formal writing. One exception applies to possessives, where the apostrophe signals ownership. Examples are: 'Gillette's boss led it back to the cutting edge'; 'The SEC's case against firms ...'; '... under last week's settlement ...'; '21 employees' partners'.

The apostrophe is often used to refer familiarly to companies, especially retailers or employers. People say they shop at Tesco's, drive for Stobart's and watched the fall of Baring's. We write about Tesco, Eddie Stobart or Baring Brothers.

The apostrophe is not used to form plurals, even if numbers or abbreviations are used. For instance, 'In the 1990s, he ran Kraft foods ...'; 'The company had a succession of CEOs ...'; 'They topped up their pensions with AVCs.'

Possessive pronouns, such as *my, his, her* or *its*, have no apostrophes: 'Baring Brothers did not report *its* heavy exposure.' Note that *it's* is a contraction of 'it is'. Therefore, if you find yourself writing it, you are probably wrong.

References

Students often ask which method to use. Although publishers' practices vary in detail, only two main styles are in use.[2] Each has its advantages. The Vancouver

---

1 Examples are taken from *Financial Times* 7, 14 and 16 May, 2003.

2 Many guides appear on the Internet. For example, Monash University (2003) *Guide to referencing*, www.lib.monash.edu.au/biomed/referenc.htm; Thames Valley University (2003) *Guidelines on reference listing – the Harvard system*, www.tvu.ac.uk/lrs/guides/harvard.html#1; Norwegian School of Management (2003) *Citations and references*, www.bi.no/library/siteringfact.htm; all accessed 17 May 2003.

system, used in this book, allows multiple entries and further comments under each endnote. Word processors keep numbered lists up to date. On the other hand, the Harvard system (e.g. Smith, 2004) allows multiple references to the same source. They are listed alphabetically, also at the end.

Checking your style

Improvement comes through practice and using good sources. If word processing, use spelling and grammar checkers. Ensure they are set to the appropriate version of English and remember that grammar checkers have faults. Finally, reading your work aloud will often reveal lapses in style that you may not have noticed.

ACKNOWLEDGEMENTS

Many people have contributed to this work. In particular, I would like to thank present and past members of the management teaching team at John Moores University. They have supported and guided my ideas over many years. An especial debt is owed to colleagues who commented on improving the first edition: Alastair Balchin, Alex Douglas, Mike Kennedy, and John Meehan. Bernard Beatty and Bob Woods, from the University of Liverpool, offered critique, encouragement and guidance.

At Financial Times Prentice Hall, Matthew Walker was a valuable point of contact and encouragement. My thanks also goes to others in the team who worked behind the scenes. Seven reviewers commented anonymously as the first edition of the book was being written. Their details appear below. Although always interesting and constructive, I was not able to incorporate every suggestion. On the other hand, I hope each reviewer found something of themselves in the ideas and the way they are expressed:

Professor William Conradie, Rand Afrikaans University, South Africa

Professor Peter Kähäri, Swedish Institute of Management, Stockholm

Dr F.J. van de Linde, Erasmus University, Rotterdam

Benny Loke, Temasek Polytechnic, Singapore

Louise McArdle, Department of Organisation Studies, University of Lancashire

Dr John Mackness, The Management School, Lancaster University

Chris Prince, Director of Programmes, Nottingham Business School, Nottingham Trent University

My thanks also to the reviewers of this second edition:

Dr Anuradha Basu, Department of Management, University of Reading

John Prior, Business School, Oxford Brookes University

Mike Orton, Buckinghamshire Business School, Buckinghamshire Chilterns University College

Dr Alex Douglas, Department of Management, Liverpool John Moores University

Professor Peter Kahari, Swedish Institute of Management

I have two personal acknowledgements. Once again, I offer warm thanks to my wife, Maureen. She again cheerfully added an extra share of domestic duties to the responsibilities of her career. Finally, the book is dedicated to my mother, Mary Naylor, who was always an inspiration.

John Naylor
Summer 2003

Plan of the Book

Part 1 Management in context

Chapter 1
Management and managers

Chapter 2
Outside the organisation: understanding the environment

Chapter 3
Inside the organisation: adapting to change

Part 2 Themes in management

Chapter 4
Global business: bridging nations and cultures

Chapter 5
Social responsibility and ethics

Chapter 6
Managing for quality

Chapter 7
Enterprise

Part 3 Planning and decision making

Chapter 8
Planning and strategic management

Chapter 9
Decision making: choosing from alternatives

Part 4 Organising, leading and communicating

Chapter 10
Organising: principles and design

Chapter 11
Leadership and motivation

Chapter 12
Groups and teams

Chapter 13
Communication in management

Part 5 Implementing policies and plans

Chapter 14
Human resource management

Chapter 15
Operations management

Chapter 16
Marketing: managing relations with customers

Chapter 17
Innovation: from ideas to customer benefits

Part 6 Control and change

Chapter 18
Control of management processes

Chapter 19
Control, learning and change

Management in context

The three chapters of Part 1 provide the foundation, background and context for the study of management. It is defined in Chapter 1, which considers a range of descriptions based on roles, styles and abilities. The function of theory is also investigated, showing that practising management is more than merely the application of common sense. The chapter also offers a historical context. It outlines the development of management ideas, mainly through the twentieth century. Students who have already met these ideas may prefer to skip this material, although they may benefit from the extra historical detail.

Chapters 2 and 3 use the open systems idea of the organisation in a complex environment. They promote the idea of the organisation achieving a 'fit' if it is to succeed. Chapter 2 presents the environment as layered and shows how managers interpret and forecast its behaviour. In Chapter 3, these changes are presented as challenges to which the organisation must adapt. Whether and how the adaptation occurs is strongly influenced by the prevailing culture.

CHAPTER 1

Management and managers

Chapter objectives

When you have finished studying this chapter, you should be able to:

- describe and define management, illustrating the elements of the definition;

- explain why we talk of organisations as wholes;

- classify the manager's job according to roles, styles and required abilities;

- argue for the value of theory in the management discipline, refuting the argument that it is merely applied common sense;

- explain and illustrate how myths of management are created;

- outline what it takes to become a successful manager and what people are seeking in their careers;

- suggest why managing diversity is becoming more important;

- explain the origins and key features of five well-known schools of management thought.

The productivity of work is not the responsibility of the worker but of the manager.

Peter F. Drucker, Austrian-American scholar and consultant

Education, education, education[1]

How a school is managed makes a difference. Claremont Junior School is in Moss Side, Manchester, one of the United Kingdom's most run-down areas. The district, having many dilapidated terraced houses with no gardens, has a reputation for crime and drugs. The pupils are mostly poor: 60 per cent take free lunches; 82 per cent are from ethnic minority families; many live with one parent in rented housing or units for the homeless; many are refugees; 89 per cent speak English as an additional language. According to those who cite poverty and class as the main reason for educational failure, the place is bound to be a dump. Not so. The 2000 inspection report found, 'Claremont Junior is a good school with some excellent features'. The 243 pupils had a positive attitude and were well behaved.

About a mile away, in a similar neighbourhood, stood Princess Primary School. In 1996, inspectors found its hitherto separate junior department to be a 'failing' school. It required special measures to counteract the unacceptable standard. Some staff were seconded to other schools to improve their skills; experienced teachers replaced them. The junior and infant schools were amalgamated. The head of the infant department, which had received a more favourable report, took charge. After a year, a return visit recognised 'considerable gains' in teaching quality. Yet they had come too late. Manchester City Council wielded the axe. In spite of progress, standards remained unsatisfactory. Furthermore, finances were seriously in the red, enrolments were down to 30 per cent of capacity and parents were sending their children elsewhere.

Figure 1.1 shows how achievement differed between the two schools. While Claremont's leavers showed achievement below the national average, the 1999 inspection found the school to be improving and doing better when matched against schools in similar situations. Pupils at Princess clearly underachieved. Differences appeared across the curriculum. Standards at Claremont in art, drama and music were high; the school's choir and steel band are well known.

Teachers' organisations and others argue for more money, small classes and new buildings to resolve such problems. Yet the two schools suggest otherwise. Claremont has a two-storey Victorian building, although in good condition; Princess's smart new one replaced another burnt down a few years previously. Claremont spends less than the national average on each child; at the end, Princess was spending 50 per cent more.

Could the explanation be lazy teachers? At Princess the report found, 'The teachers work hard and have an adequate knowledge of the subjects ... but their expectations of the pupils are often too low'. Low achievement was blamed on an overall lack of structure. There was no clear curriculum and little monitoring of what pupils were learning. At Claremont, the 1999 report found, 'Teachers work hard and so do the pupils'. They give all pupils, from the brightest to those

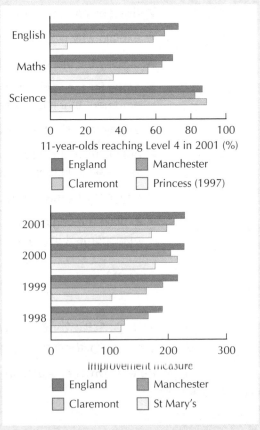

Figure 1.1 **Standards, spending and sizes – three Manchester schools**

with learning difficulties, suitable work, including regular homework. Teachers planned lessons carefully, keeping detailed records for each child; assessment was used very well to plan work. All were clear about discipline policies, ensuring a consistent approach. Pupils had very good attitudes towards school. Over at Princess, crises had been common. Teachers spent much time keeping order and were tempted to give easy work to avoid child frustration and misbehaviour. They gave homework only if parents asked for it.

When Princess Primary closed, pupils transferred to Claremont and other local schools. Other changes in the neighbourhood included a regeneration project and an influx of refugees. Despite these challenges, Claremont continued to raise its level of achievement. Leadership and management were both important and 'very effective'. Their impact was also shown at another school in the area, St Mary's. As the graph of Improvement

Measures shows, it seemed to be failing in 1999 despite good accommodation and adequate resources. The 2000 report criticised poor teaching and low expectations of older pupils. It also recognised the leadership and management skills of the new head teacher and support of the governors. Clearly, these had an impact on performance.

Low expectations often dog failing schools. Overall, teachers, pupils and parents at Princess believed that improvement was impossible. Community relations were distant; many parents showed little concern about development so long as their children seemed happy. Parents were more involved at Claremont and most were keen for their children to do well. Continuity of leadership strengthened such links. Destruction of the old building had caused great disruption for Princess; yet the school had also had eight heads in twelve years. In the same period, Claremont had experienced one change at the top.

Introduction

Management makes a difference. Claremont Junior shows how inner-city schools can offer a good education. Both St Mary's and, in its last years, Princess Primary showed that recovery is possible. Whether schools succeed depends on good leadership, a clear curriculum, sound planning and monitoring and realistic expectations.

Picking a few examples to make a point is easy. The comparison may be harsh on Princess Primary. The fire that destroyed the previous buildings may have had more impact than we could guess; the neighbourhoods, all in central Manchester, may be very different in detail. We have just part of the story and should take Tomlinson's advice warning against reducing complex social, political and educational issues to the 'demonisation' of one school and its staff.[2] Yet Ofsted reports are consistent in stating that well-managed schools do better. Is this because the inspectors simply attribute good performance to good management? Perhaps, but there is evidence, too, from other fields. Dorgan and Dowdy[3] studied 100 manufacturing companies in four countries. They found that productivity is linked to use of three management approaches – lean manufacturing to minimise waste, attracting and retaining high-calibre staff and rewarding people who meet clear goals. Openness to pressure from a demanding environment helps to set standards and keep managers on their toes. Those that respond do better. These essentials of management are represented in this book by the core themes of planning, organising, implementing and controlling. This chapter begins our study by exploring definitions of management, finding out what makes managers and setting out some of the antecedents of present-day management thinking.

What is management?

A broad view of management presents it as a process – the planning to controlling cycle we mentioned above. This, however, involves all members of the organisation. So we must ask what distinguishes management from other organisational activities. A definition brings out its main features:

> *Management is the process of achieving organisational objectives, within a changing environment, by balancing efficiency, effectiveness and equity, obtaining the most from limited resources, and working with and through other people.*

The five key elements can be explained as follows:

■ *Achieving organisational objectives*

An objective is a target or aim to be striven for. As we see in later chapters, individuals and organisations are more successful if they seek outcomes that are both challenging and achievable. They enable the individual to plan and co-ordinate work with others. Through objectives, leaders communicate their broad plans and so mobilise effort.

School inspectors' reports stress the value of objectives. For instance, at Claremont Junior, they noted that matching targets to the ability of each child was a significant element of success. Doing this consistently throughout the school meant that each teacher could provide good quality learning linked to what had gone before.

■ *Within a changing environment*

We shall see in Chapter 2 how the changing world outside an organisation imposes new demands and problems, whether they concern shortage of raw materials, rising energy prices, new customer requirements or tougher competitive policies of rivals. A key part of the management function is to maintain an awareness of such changes and prepare responses to them. Senior managers spend a great deal of their time learning about, and interpreting, the environment. While saying that rival organisations may face a common environment is easy, this notion of interpretation is important. The Manchester schools served similar catchment areas. Yet they interpreted and responded to the educational needs of their pupils in different ways.

■ *Balancing efficiency, effectiveness and equity*

Trying to achieve the three Es of the management balance (*see* Figure 1.2) is a dilemma. Success against one criterion is often at the expense of another. Efficiency is a measure of how well resources are transformed into outputs. We are encouraged to compare results in terms of how much resource is used in producing them. We can see this among the things we buy: washing machine suppliers state the energy consumption per cycle; car manufacturers state fuel consumption in litres per 100 kilometres. In these cases, efficiency is being assessed by comparing an output with the use of a key resource or input. But what if the washer does not wash very well or the car is too small? They may be very efficient but incapable of doing what we want. We have overemphasised efficiency at the expense of effectiveness.

Effectiveness is an assessment of how far a stated objective is achieved. Often, a focus on 'getting the job done' is important, for example when managing a crisis.

War, the ultimate crisis, requires leaders who believe in 'winning at all costs'. Yet, even in such dire circumstances, good generals consider how to conserve and deploy their resources. A leader's overemphasis on effectiveness leads to a loss of efficiency. Resources are wasted. On the other hand, too much stress on efficiency may mean that the task does not get done at all. The right balance is a management decision.

Equity is the third ingredient of the mixture of Es. This concerns the fair distribution of outputs among recipients. Many public sector and not-for-profit organisations place equity at the core of their objectives. In principle, hospital staff or social workers ensure that they treat all clients according to their needs, no matter how well off they are. Managers in the private sector are not always so concerned with treating everyone the same, although they must not discriminate unfairly. If goods are expensive and some people cannot afford them, that is not normally a reason to withdraw them. Yet private companies are involved with questions of equity. Many accept they must consider the interests of those affected by their activities. For instance, they must not abuse monopoly positions. Sometimes, regulators such as OFGEM strive to maintain equitable energy prices to protect the budgets of poor families. This is an element of *social responsibility*, a theme picked up in Chapter 5.

The blend of the three Es is a changing choice for all organisations. This is illustrated in primary schools. When controlled closely by local authorities, their mission was clear. They were expected to achieve the best results for the children in a defined district using resources, such as staff levels, set down by the authority. More recently, as management powers have been devolved to them, schools have become engaged in competition. They sometimes abandon the notion of clear catchment areas; they try to avoid admitting difficult children; heads are tempted to appoint inexperienced (yet cheaper) teachers; there is competition for resources. Such decentralisation has shifted the balance among the three Es towards efficiency.

■ *Obtaining the most from limited resources*

Recognising that resources are limited is more than a question of using them most efficiently. Managers have to recognise that they have to be found and obtained. Where

Figure 1.2 Balancing the three Es

materials are scarce, innovation may be needed. This means adapting products and processes to use fewer or alternative resources. Concerns over raw materials mean more emphasis on less wasteful processes, recycling and improved product designs. Rising labour costs, especially when compared with competitors in developing countries, press managers into finding ways of deploying staff more efficiently.

Squeezing more from resources is not the only route to success. Another way to offer value for money is to increase value. We can see the music at Claremont as just one way a school can increase the value of its education and hence its popularity.

■ *With and through other people*

Management is primarily a social process, often defined as 'getting things done through people'. There is always a danger of presenting management as a set of techniques, such as for optimising plans or controlling production rates. Yet people put all plans into effect. In the primary school, teachers co-operate in developing the curriculum. In this way, they learn about what happens in classes and departments other than their own. At the same time, they build a shared commitment to the plans which makes it easier to make them work. This is why the staff at Claremont Junior were so positive about their planning. They saw that it avoided the wasteful work incurred in a crisis. We shall find throughout the book many examples of work that require co-operation to make it happen. This takes us back to one element of the management cycle – organising. Texts on management stress this area because organising both huge enterprises and small work groups presents such difficulties yet offers so much potential.

■ Talking about organisations...

We noted the danger of presenting management as a set of techniques independent of the people involved. Similarly, we often talk of organisations behaving with a life of their own. A typical example is the quotation shown in Exhibit 1.1.[4]

Exhibit 1.1 Organised behaviour

'Tesco also happens to be the undisputed world leader in Internet grocery sales. Its on-line home delivery service is now profitable, Tesco says, and it has struck a deal in the United States with Safeway, which will use Tesco's system for a home-shopping service. Underpinning Tesco's success is excellent management and an obsession with operational efficiency and productivity gains, which the company uses to keep prices low or to improve service rather than to increase its operating margins.'

Reification

Some experts object to discussing organisations in this way, pointing out that words such as *system*, *Tesco* and *company* are abstractions. Although defined in law and vested with legal powers, organisations can only act through the behaviour of managers and members who make individual responses to, say, environmental stimuli or instructions received from others. Extending the argument, the same experts say that the idea of the 'interests of the organisation' is a falsehood. What is really meant is the interests of whichever individual, group or coalition happens to wield power.

Talking of an organisation as 'undisputed world leader' or striking a deal with another is called reification. This means giving a reality to abstract notions that they do not possess. In this argument, organisational behaviour is nothing other than the collection of members' actions. This is what Margaret Thatcher meant in her famous remark, 'There is no such thing as Society. There are individual men and women and there are families.'[5]

There is, however, a justification. Speaking of the attributes and behaviour of organisations is a useful way to summarise observations, make comparisons and develop new ideas and theories. We could hardly make progress if we ruled offside any discussion of organisations in general, or of named ones, such as the BBC or the European Commission. Furthermore, there is some sense in which organisations act as wholes. As we see in Chapter 3, the notion of collectivity is expressed in culture. A little like bees in a hive, individuals feel bonded through sharing common values and ways of doing things. The fact that they work *together* shows that organisations have meaning. Studying the behaviour of wholes, known as *holism*, is a feature of systems thinking, outlined later in the chapter.

Organisations, like systems, tend to be nested. That is, within a large one we find smaller ones, and, within each of those, there may be smaller ones still. Curiously, Thatcher's remark allowed one level, the family, yet not another, society. We see levels linked in a hierarchy with managers as bosses and subordinates lower down. This, however, is but one way of arranging relationships. For example, many have noted the advantages to be gained from subcontracting, the pattern that tends to prevail on building sites. Now, new organisational forms are emerging to try to reap these advantages. We shall return to these in Chapter 10. Meanwhile, we shall introduce three further ways of understanding management – roles, styles and abilities.

■ Managerial roles

Here we examine *what* managers do. It turns out they fulfil a variety of functions that we call roles. One study that has become well known was carried out by Mintzberg in the 1960s. He was concerned that 'classical' descriptions of management in terms of functions did not correspond to what happened in practice. So while we might *think* of management as the ordered sequence of planning, organising, doing and controlling, it seemed to him to be much more interactive and complex than this. So Mintzberg shadowed managers, keeping detailed records of what they did. From the observations, he identified ten roles that most managers appeared to occupy from time to time.[6] Grouped into three classes, they are set out in Figure 1.3.

In his list, Mintzberg generalised about all managers, especially senior ones who formed the subjects of his research. Others have narrowed the perspective to look at the roles of those carrying out named functions, such as Human Resource Management or Marketing, or at different levels. Middle managers are a group that have come under scrutiny. For instance, many enthusiasts for 'downsizing' as a cost-cutting measure sought to remove the middle layers. We may imagine that these mainly link decisions at the top with actions at the bottom. Much of this activity of communication and co-ordination, said the cost cutters, could be substituted by information systems. This, however, left many organisations lacking a critical resource as other important roles came to the fore. Dauphinais found that middle managers:[7]

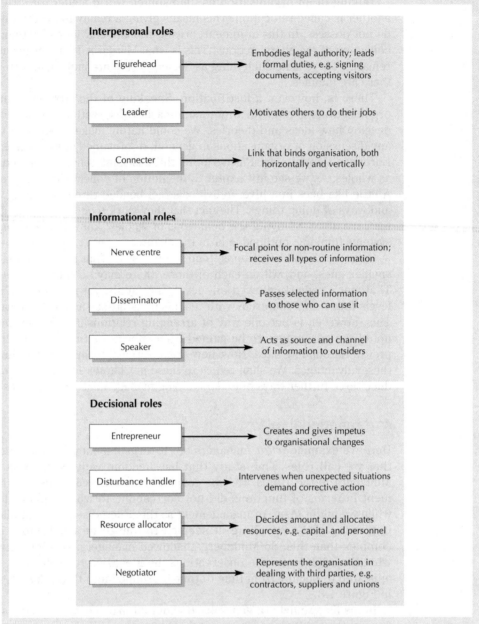

Figure 1.3 Interpersonal, informational and decisional roles

- *Create and implement strategy* through recognising and quickly responding to changes.
- *Influence* people at all levels to follow goals and plans.
- *Offer stability* to consolidate and integrate the improvements that change may bring (although they may resist needed change).
- *Drive continual change* through participating in, and controlling the output of, project teams.

◾ Management styles

For our second perspective on management, we shall look at *how* managers carry out their jobs. This is the area of management style often called the 'softer' aspect of the job. It contrasts the 'harder' facet concerned with formal structures and systems. Style helps us understand why managers, faced with situations which appear identical, act in such different ways. Rowe and Mason,[8] for example, identified four decision styles:

- ◾ *Directive* – practical, authoritarian, impersonal, power centred;
- ◾ *Analytical* – intellectual, impersonal, control oriented;
- ◾ *Conceptual* – insightful, enthusiastic, personal, adaptive, flexible;
- ◾ *Behavioural* – sociable, friendly, supportive.

Other authors have studied leadership style, often setting out two independent dimensions to form a grid. For instance, Hersey and Blanchard[9] proposed scales representing task orientation (goal setting, planning, organising, scheduling and controlling) and relationship orientation (supporting, communicating, enabling interaction, listening and giving feedback). The former scale assesses commitment to the managerial process forming the core of this book, while the latter covers motivation, leadership, teamwork and communication that we discuss in Part 4.

The scales of Blake and Mouton[10] are even better known. The two dimensions of concern for production and concern for people form the managerial grid, shown in Figure 1.4. It contrasts, for example, the impoverished manager, who does as little as possible with production or with people, against the team manager, who works to satisfy individual needs through commitment to the organisation. There is more on the grid in Chapter 11.

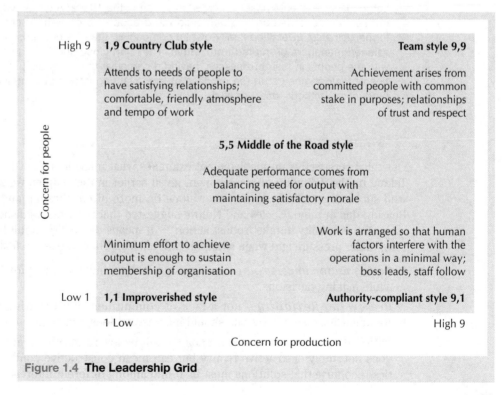

Figure 1.4 **The Leadership Grid**

Ideal-types

There is another lesson in such work. Setting out stereotypes (often referred to as *ideal-types*) is a common practice in behavioural science. If you objected that many people display mixed characteristics, you would be right. Experts recognise this but use the ideal-types to set up scales to compare one person or group with another. The scales or grids then allow managers to display a mix of styles. For example, Blake and Mouton's middle-of-the-road manager is neither fully concerned with people nor fully concerned with production.

Different cultures

Setting up scales and placing different managers (or groups of managers) on them is a useful way of unravelling questions of why managers behave so differently. Thinking in terms of the above grids may yield useful insights when comparing, say, British and French styles. Yet there is a trap. Such scales have been developed from research carried out in the West, in these cases in the United States. Take the case of Japan. Exhibit 1.2 draws on work by Morikawa, a Japanese economic historian.[11] After a first read, we may conclude that, compared with Europeans, the new Japanese managers were more concerned with relationships and people. Yet such notions may have no meaning in that country. We are using a theory whose applicability is untested. The most important differences may arise from other attributes – such as traditions of group loyalty. The question of checking theories adequately before using them is considered later.

Exhibit 1.2 The rise of the Japanese managerial enterprise

Large managerial enterprises emerged in Japan in the 1930s. After the war, they were critical in reconstruction and achieved rapid economic growth. In contrast to the former *zaibatsu*, diversified family-owned companies, the new enterprises were run by salaried managers promoted from within. They had close and trusting relationships with the people in their businesses, having a particular understanding of the capabilities of their engineers. In the process of transplanting and improving leading-edge production methods, this was vital.

Management abilities

Our third perspective on management examines what managers should be capable of. Taking up the definition of management given earlier in the chapter, we see that those who succeed get things done, either alone or, more often, through and with others. Bearing this in mind, Eccles and Nohria suggested that what distinguishes good managers is their ability to take 'robust action'.[12] It means the ability to fulfil management roles under pressure and when situations are unclear. There are seven features:

- *Acting under uncertainty* – recognising and coping with the gaps in knowledge while making decisions.
- *Preserving flexibility* – not a lack of commitment but ensuring that there is room left for change. Actions should increase options, not reduce them.
- *Political awareness* – a good manager will be aware of others' agendas. Politics does not imply destructive rivalry but can mean constructive conflict, where parties recognise that solutions must be found among different interests.

- *Timing* – decisions, say, to enter new markets must be neither too early nor too late; announcing good or bad news to several people and groups must be carefully sequenced.
- *Judgement* – interpreting and using qualitative information involves subtle judgement as opposed to formal calculation.
- *Using rhetoric effectively* – communication in organisations is more than sharing information. Managers, for example, have to both inform others of decisions and persuade them that the decisions are justified. Using appropriate rhetorical skills, *see* Exhibit 1.3, helps in persuasion and builds flexibility.
- *Running multiple agendas* – keeping 'several balls in the air' enables a good manager to use a sense of timing to take opportunities and allow several decisions to fall into place at once.

Exhibit 1.3 Understanding the world through talking about it

Rhetoric is concerned with how language is used to influence the ways people think and act. We often use the term to mean trickery, as in empty, mere, inflammatory or powerful rhetoric. Scholars, however, are concerned with what happens, not whether it is good or bad.

*... management has a lot to do with the use of language, both in the sense of how language is used in organisations and in the sense it is used in ways – such as business books and journalism – that span organisations ... In a nutshell, managers live in a rhetorical universe – a universe where language is constantly used not only to communicate but also to **persuade**, even to create.*[13]

Studying management

The study of management involves an interplay between theory and practice. Yet, the mixture makes many students uneasy, especially if they already have experience of being a manager. 'After all, it's practical, not theoretical,' one might say, 'and isn't it all applied common sense?' In reply, we can consider two aspects of these concerns – the value of theory and the seemingly obvious nature of management ideas.

The value of theory

To talk about theory and practice suggests a separation of the two that does not really exist. No successful practical person, from farmer to film maker or painter to politician, can proceed without a framework of theory. Sometimes this is explicit – the things they learn when being trained – while at other times they develop the theory intuitively. We all build on experience and, as we advance, we consolidate it into a personal theory of our world. This helps us to understand things without having to remember the details of every case.

The trouble is that some of it can be wrong. If we never take the trouble to learn from others, we will believe the earth is flat. Take the tale of the inductivist turkey, originally told by philosopher Bertrand Russell, shown in Exhibit 1.4.[14] The turkey in the story asked the wrong question. Just as we often do from our limited perspective, it asked the narrow, 'When does feeding happen?' instead of the broad, 'Why does feeding happen?' If the turkey had shared its theories with others long since on the dinner table, it might have thought again.

Exhibit 1.4 Turkey talk

Feeding on the first morning was at nine. A cautious inductivist, the turkey drew no conclusion. It collected data and studied variables. At the weekend or in the week, on warm days or cold, whether rain or shine, feeding occurred at nine. Satisfied at last, the turkey drew the inductive inference, 'They always feed me at 9.'

Then came 24 December. The turkey was no more. With true premises and inductive inference, it had reached the wrong conclusion.

We can draw out two broad points about good theory and the way it is formed. First, a good theory makes a proposition, builds on observations, explains something and is *shared*. Only by presenting our theories of the world, and comparing them with others, do we develop useful, robust ones that work. Second, there is nothing wrong with induction. Billsberry explains that the theories we meet in management books are all inductivist in nature.[15] For example, we can take the well-known theory of motivation developed by Herzberg, explained in Chapter 11. Adding to existing knowledge, it allowed him to explain the satisfaction of workers. The ideas having been shared, work by others has strengthened the theory so we know it can be applied in many cases. Yet, we can never prove it right for all cases. Christmas Eve may come.

So how could we, as managers, use theories such as Herzberg's? The answer is to do so cautiously. Every situation is unique. So avoid the trap of blindly applying a theory developed in one set of circumstances to another. We must understand the theory, understand our circumstances and check that the theory can be applied. Variations require us to take a critical view. This is not to praise one and denigrate another, but to learn to compare theories and situations to see where they can come together. That is why good managers, and a good management course, blend theory and practice.

Description and prescription

Another way to look at theory is to compare two types, descriptive and prescriptive:

- Descriptive theories refer to the world as it is. Based on observations, they may say things such as, 'Multinational enterprises usually have decentralised personnel functions'.

- Prescriptive theories make statements about the world as it ought to be. They may say things such as, 'Multinational enterprises should decentralise their personnel functions'.

While you may think that the statements amount to the same in practice, the differences are important. The former makes no judgement and recognises that there is never a best way that applies in all cases. The latter tells all organisations in a particular category what is best. Many managers prefer prescription. Would it not help if they could be told what to do? – 'Have you a problem with one of your staff? Then reach for the *Universal Guide to Personnel Management*.'

Although what are sometimes called 'airport books' offer guidance like this, Mintzberg and colleagues warn against it. To them, '... no prescription works for all organisations. Even when a prescription seems effective in some context, it requires a sophisticated understanding of exactly what the context is and how it functions. ... one cannot decide reliably what should be done in a system as complicated as a contemporary organisation without a genuine understanding of how that organisation really works'.[16] They then point out that a science student is interested in how a molecule works, not in knowing how it *ought* to work. Why should a management student want something so different?

In the main, the theories presented in this book are of the descriptive type. Along the way, however, there are examples of the prescriptive, for example in Chapter 15. Some operations planning processes are so well established that it is sensible to say, 'This is the way things should be done'. Even in such cases, however, we should follow the warning given above. Always check that a theory does apply before applying it!

Are management ideas obvious?

The comment that statements about management are obvious often follows a reading of research studies. For example, the conclusions of Chapter 11 on motivation may seem trite: 'People work better if the work is interesting'; 'They are driven to satisfy meaningful goals'; or 'People's perceptions of a reward are influenced by their prior experience'. Aren't these statements so self-evident that going through lengthy studies to arrive at them is a waste of time? To examine this problem, we can draw on a neat argument presented by Vecchio, given in Exhibit 1.5.[17]

Illusions

Through giving erroneous, yet plausible, results, Vecchio cleverly destroys the idea that behavioural phenomena are obvious. How does this confusion happen? It comes from being human. When someone tells us something about behaviour, we often respond with a defensive reaction similar to, 'Naturally, I could have guessed that'. It is common in daily life. We hear, 'June and Jack are getting a divorce', 'Telecom shares have fallen again', or 'The washing machine's broken'. We reply, 'I knew it couldn't last'. This is the advantage of hindsight. Hindsight is logical. Survival is helped by persuading ourselves that we are so much in control of our surroundings.

As humans, we are clever at rationalising, that is building *post hoc* explanations. Buckley and Chapman draw on social anthropology, which reveals how groups 'reorganise' their history. They attribute present successes to forethought in the past. It is common among managers, who make random events seem planned or recast good luck as strategic thinking.[18]

Mintzberg's myths: what management is not

The relevance of delusion to management becomes clearer when we realise how the subject is full of myths. Summarising many studies including his own, Mintzberg points to four widely held notions of managerial work that do not withstand scrutiny.[19]

Exhibit 1.5 Obvious ... isn't it?

During the Second World War, the research branch of the United States War Department conducted several studies on soldiers' attitudes, morale and feelings of frustration. In total, some 600 000 servicemen were interviewed. So extensive were the results that the final summary, which appeared in 1949, occupied four volumes. On publication, the report was much criticised in the popular press. One charge dwelt on the obvious nature of the findings, citing the conclusion that many soldiers were unhappy during the war. Questions were raised over whether such surveys were justified.

One review listed typical findings. How novel do you find the following results? And would you make comments similar to those on the right?

Results	Comments
1 During the fighting, servicemen were more desirous of returning home than they were after the fall of Germany.	1 Would anyone be surprised to find that soldiers wanted to avoid being killed?
2 Soldiers from the southern states stood the tropical climate of the south Pacific better than northerners.	2 This could be easily predicted by differences in upbringing and climate.
3 Less well educated men adjusted better to army life than did the better educated. This was especially shown by the incidence of minor psychological disorders.	3 Of course, the army requires obedience and unquestioning acceptance in its harsh daily life. Low intelligence aids adjustment.
4 Black soldiers from the South preferred to serve under white officers also from the South than under northerners.	4 Naturally, under the rigid social divisions of the South, both parties would know where they stood.
5 Those who had been brought up in rural areas adjusted better to army life than those from urban areas.	5 Clearly, rural recruits would have experienced a rougher life, including sleeping in the open.

Two points follow. First, if we go along with the comments, we are agreeing with the 1949 critics. The results were obvious and the whole enterprise a waste of time. Second, if these are the basic data to be used for developing principles in, say, how to manage an army in the field, then normal officers already have enough expertise to go ahead.

The snag is that these statements are precisely the opposite of the published findings. These showed that: soldiers preferred to remain abroad while the war was on but were most anxious to return once it had ended; southerners were no better at adjusting to the heat of the south Pacific than were northerners; poorly educated men found adjustment more difficult, and so on. In each case, however, we can immediately reach for new explanations. For instance: patriotism and commitment were motivators during the war, but, once it was over, homesickness was the strong emotion; urban life, with its pressure on personal space and freedom, was a better preparation for being in the army than was a rural upbringing. Had we listed these true results and comments first, we would also have said they were obvious.

■ *Managers engage in reflective, systematic planning*

The work pace for all is unrelenting. In the European Union, about a quarter take work home several times a week with another third staying behind after normal hours. In Japan, annual hours seem stuck at around 2100; working late has been a traditional way of displaying loyalty to boss and company.[20] During the working day, one study found half of managers' activities lasted less than nine minutes.

Another reported that working for half an hour without interruption happened only every other day. 'Free' time is immediately grabbed by subordinates. For supervisors, one study found an average of 48 seconds per encounter. Managers do plan but do so implicitly, during the framework of daily work; it is no wonder that many plans stay in their heads.

■ *Managers have few regular duties to perform*
Figure 1.3 includes some roles, such as figurehead, connecter, nerve centre and negotiator, that many managers perform routinely. A chief executive is expected to receive dignitaries, officiate at Christmas parties and hand out retirement watches. Much external, 'soft' information only comes to them because of their access to business and social networks. To support the work of others, they must pass it on regularly. These are all regular duties.

■ *Senior managers need plenty of information provided by a formal information system*
Typical results show that managers spend between 66 and 80 per cent of their time in oral communication. Most managers skim periodicals and do not reply to all correspondence. Only about one-sixth of the mail they receive is important. Senders know this so may send email, follow with a letter and ring to check it has arrived! Another research result is that managers cherish gossip, hearsay and speculation. They build broad pictures which they use to anticipate the behaviour of others. Unfortunately, the extensive use of verbal, informal information makes delegation of many tasks difficult. There is no dossier of data ready to be passed to subordinates.

All in all, most managers see written material as a burden. It is, however, worth noting that the French seem to be an exception. In France there is emphasis given to written communication using correct and elegant language.[21]

■ *Management is a science and a profession, or, if not, it is rapidly becoming one*
Observations of managers at work show this to be untrue. True they make decisions *about* new technology or about the application of science to new products. Yet the way they make decisions is complex, fragmented, often superficial and rarely recorded or followed up.

Sources of myth

How do myths like these grow? Ignorance is a critical factor. Adopting the general view of management as applied common sense means that many organisations do not spend on anything but limited management training. One report on United Kingdom graduate recruitment (not necessarily for management positions) showed that employers look for people with suitable personal and interactive attributes.[22] Rarely do such studies mention the advantages of learning about management, although reports that are more recent have begun to call for awareness of enterprise. Additionally, many employers prefer their managers to learn through specific on-the-job training and in-company courses rather than through broad studies of the management discipline. This further restrains any interest in management as an object of serious study. Essentially uneducated, with only about 20 per cent in the United Kingdom having degrees,[23] managers are prey to the fad, the quick fix and the myth.

Becoming a successful manager

Management is a complex job. It is no surprise to find that managers come from many backgrounds and display a wide range of personal attributes and abilities. Given the complexities of theory and the difficulties of accumulating experience, we may ask how managers reach their positions. The answer is that they come by many routes.

■ The school of hard knocks

Learning from experience is important, whether one has 'risen from the ranks' or entered a fast-track training scheme after graduation. Unfortunately, such experience can be bruising to the individual and wasteful for the organisation. Snell's study among United Kingdom managers identified what they had found to be 'hard knocks'. We list examples in Exhibit 1.6.[24] Although these traumas meant that managers learned to avoid making the same errors twice, they involved unnecessary psychological distress. Consequently, Snell argued for better learning practices both on and off the job.

Exhibit 1.6 Classes at the school of hard knocks

- Making a big mistake
- Becoming overstretched by a difficult task
- Feeling threatened
- Finding oneself stuck in an impasse or dilemma
- Being treated unjustly at work
- Losing out to another
- Being attacked personally.

■ Seeing oneself as a manager

The many abilities required of a manager present serious challenges. Whether one chooses to take them on depends on what Schein calls a 'career anchor'.[25] This is the self-concept we all have, consisting of three elements: talents and abilities that we perceive; our basic values; and, most important, an evolving set of needs and motives related to our career. Although the anchor develops and changes with experience, we can also see it as a stabilising element. It represents the values and motives that we will not give up when making a career choice. An important point with all anchors is that we are usually unaware of them until confronted by a career decision such as, 'Shall I move home for a job with more money or stay in my present occupation, knowing that it fulfils my need for autonomy?'

Students have their career anchors changed by their university experience and the companies and brands they meet in their studies. This is indicated by the annual study by Universum, a leading Swedish recruitment consultancy.[26] In 2002, the top five preferred employers among a large sample of European business students were McKinsey and Company, Boston Consulting Group, Goldman Sachs, Accenture and

L'Oréal. Among engineering and science students, the list was BMW, Nokia, Siemens, IBM and Sony.

Universum notes how anchors change with time. Perceptions of tough times ahead made new British graduates more concerned with job security than ever. For them, this was the third most important characteristic of a new employer behind international career openings and a variety of assignments. Ranked top among early career goals was a balance between career and personal life. The BBC was the most-preferred employer.

Cultural differences

As with other aspects of management, we must beware of assuming that career anchors and attitudes are universal. For instance, respondents to a Universum study of graduates from eight East European business schools placed competitive salary much more highly than did their counterparts in the West. Further, they were interested in specialisation, while Westerners wanted to be generalists. They did not favour careers with consulting firms.[27]

Further afield, becoming a top manager in Japan is very different from the experience of most Europeans. Storey and colleagues compared the origins and development of managers in the United Kingdom and Japan.[28] Firms in the former are not alone in holding a 'sink or swim' attitude to early managerial development and stick to the notion that individuals are responsible for their own careers. In Japan, employers accept more responsibility for development and direction of careers. Being a successful European manager probably means gathering a wide range of role experiences, frequently with different employers. The convention in Japan is to change roles less often and stay with the same organisation for life.

■ Managing diversity

Coping with cultural differences has become one of the most difficult problems for managers. There are two reasons. First, as explained in Chapter 4, the world is experiencing a new wave of globalisation. This means not only more trade but also increasing integration of business through the growth of the multinational corporation. It used to be that distant branches of such enterprises were managed by expatriates on short-term development assignments. Now, leading companies, such as Unilever, want to recognise the aspirations of all their staff and draw on the global pool of talent.[29] Second, migration has created significant minority groups in many countries. At the same time, some long-settled minorities, whose aspirations have until now been suppressed, are asserting their rights to being different.

Taken together, these trends mean that managers are faced with an increasingly diverse workforce. Staff and colleagues do not come from the same cultural background as themselves. Adler noted three possible responses to this pressure:[30]

■ *Parochial*
This is the most common response, captured by the phrase, 'Our way is the only way'. The organisation does not recognise differences and therefore makes no provision. Any problems that occur are attributed to other causes.

■ *Ethnocentric*
Here, 'Our way is the best way.' Managers recognise diversity but try to minimise its effects by maintaining a single corporate culture. Usually this means domination by

people from the original country. Others are admitted provided they accept this ascendancy.

■ *Synergistic*

The least common of the three, this organisation trains its managers to recognise cultural differences and use diversity to advantage. The idea is to combine the best.

This classification can explain the different attitudes between West and East European graduates. Accepting the increasingly diverse nature of the people they will work with, Westerners stress the importance of some international experience in the development of their careers. In the East, attitudes are more parochial. Aspirations are limited to gaining good positions in local firms or local branches of multinationals. There is, therefore, more emphasis on salary and specialised competence with little mention of international experience.

Using a historical perspective

We have, so far, outlined a range of ideas, theories and principles. How can a manager, or a student of management, make sense of it all? We each carry with us a set of attitudes and beliefs about the subject. These lead to generalisations and hypotheses that enable us to say, 'Such and such an action will have the following consequences'. In turn, theories guide our practical actions. The two are inseparable. Yet where do these theories originate?

An important source of theory is experience, both our own and that of others. We may have learned by being employees or clients, from novels, plays or films, or through informal contact. Yet there are also those authorities who have conducted systematic studies of management. As we discussed earlier, studying their work takes our understanding of management beyond the level of applied common sense. It provides a rich framework within which we can criticise and develop our own ideas and, in turn, improve our practice.

Studying the history of management and the development of management theory is fruitful. While we do not engage in studying the past for its own sake, a historical perspective helps us because:

■ it clarifies our view of the present;

■ it allows us to explain the way things are;

■ it instils a sense of causation;

■ it underlines the importance of interpretation in social science.

Studying management is like studying history in that both are processes going beyond the gathering of facts. There is interaction between the facts and the practitioner. As Carr argues, 'To enable man to understand the society of the past, and to increase his mastery over the society of the present, is the dual function of history'.[31] The history of management, combining facts and interpretation, contributes to our ability to understand, and therefore succeed, in the present. Further, in recognising how the present is a product of the past, the idea that the future is strongly influenced by current decisions also becomes embedded. This notion of causation or teleology, events being connected as a series through time, is as basic to the study of history as to the practice of management.

We must be cautious, also. We tend to interpret past events through current attitudes. Historical patterns may now seem logical although events were not connected at the time. Therefore, while we present a time-line covering the past hundred or so years of management thought, the selections of important trends and events and the connections that are made among them are to some extent arbitrary. In each era, scholars and practitioners have asked new questions and faced new problems and have proposed new (or recycled) approaches to their resolution. Further, there have been other ideas, authors and events whose significance we have yet to recognise.

Understanding the background to current theory should not be left to historians. Management is an interdisciplinary field. It draws on the work of, among others, anthropologists, economists, engineers, geographers, information scientists, lawyers, mathematicians, political scientists, psychologists, sociologists and statisticians.

The history of management thought starts from a search for a universal theory. Today, however, we see that no single theory is accepted. Instead, we have theories devised and developed at different times with applications to different aspects of the management role. We shall discuss five approaches that have become well known and accepted:

- Classical
- Human Relations
- Management Science
- Systems
- Contingency.

The classical perspective

One can trace reference to management principles and problems back to medieval times or earlier. For instance, authors refer to Confucius[32] or Machiavelli.[33] From their writings on government, servants, leadership or the conduct of war authors pick out statements about questions of management today. This is unsound. Authorities of the distant past were discussing the government of city-states, directing armies or the running of traditional enterprises. We are separated from that era by the Industrial Revolution, a period that transformed everything. The context of management changed considerably. Business developed from small cottage industries to large industrial organisations employing many thousands of staff at one site. With its scale, the factory system posed challenges that, apart from military activities, had been little experienced in earlier generations. Problems arose in areas such as operational co-ordination, organisation structure, communication and control. The ideas that emerged were responses to these problems and many remain relevant today.

The views that we now call the classical perspective really developed about the end of the nineteenth century. They resulted from attempts by proponents, mainly American engineers, to establish general principles upon which management practice could be based. We can identify three important categories, namely scientific management, bureaucracy and administrative principles. They sought means of improving management practice in different areas, namely operations, organisational structure and the general processes of management.

▦ Scientific management

In their search for ways of improving business performance, advocates of scientific management focused on operations. These are the many routine tasks that any large organisation finds itself engaged in. Pioneers conducted detailed investigations and experiments to discover the best ways of carrying them out. Further, they argued that such an approach was rational. The benefits from even minor process improvements outweighed the costs of the studies.

Exhibit 1.7 F.W. Taylor: the father of scientific management

Frederick Winslow Taylor (1856–1915) was born into a Quaker family in Philadelphia. Although it was intended that he follow his father into the law, an eye problem prevented him from attending Harvard University. Instead, he became a labourer in a machine shop, where he took four years to learn the trades of pattern maker and machinist. Having recovered from the eye condition, he took a part-time degree in mechanical engineering while rising quickly to chief engineer of the Midvale Steel Works.

Taylor observed the inefficiency and lack of co-operation that characterised large plants. Restrictive practices (Taylor's 'systematic soldiering') were rife. Poorly trained and ill-equipped workers decided for themselves how tasks were carried out. Taylor became committed to stamping out such inefficiencies.

At Midvale, and later at Bethlehem Steel, measurement and experiment became Taylor's watchwords. He changed the role of supervisor, issuing each with a stopwatch and details on how to break down tasks into measured work elements. Scientific study sought to match each worker to the most suitable job. Payment was to be by results; Taylor wanted to raise the living standards of workers who co-operated in the new ways.

In the highly influential *Principles of Scientific Management* (1911), Taylor was the first to publish about the detailed processes of manual work. His inventiveness also applied to engineering, and he took out more than one hundred patents. Beyond this, Taylor was an accomplished sportsman, becoming United States tennis doubles champion in 1881. He invented a spoon-shaped tennis racquet and persuaded the baseball authorities to switch from under-arm pitching to the more efficient over-arm style.

At the end of the nineteenth century, many industrial plants were mechanised. Yet they still employed thousands of staff to feed and unload the machines, shift materials and so on. It was in such a context that scientific management was born. The movement's pioneer was F.W. Taylor, *see* Exhibit 1.7.[34] Taylorism was founded on six key ideas:

▪ *Observation*

Systematic observation and stopwatch timing enabled analysis of every aspect of the production process. Studies showed the inefficiency of allowing each worker to decide the way tasks were carried out. For instance, in the ironworks yard, labourers unloading wagons brought their own shovels. Yet, a shovel full of iron ore weighed some 15 kg compared with 2 kg for loose coal. Taylor saw that using the same shovel for each task could not be the best way of working.

▪ *Experiment*

From observations, often many thousands, Taylor developed a science of work and devised experiments to discover optimal methods. Studies ranged from eliminating unnecessary movements to varying the frequency and length of breaks. In the ironworks, for instance, he found the optimal shovel load for sustained work to be 10 kg. This implied that, for each grade of material to be shovelled, the supervisors had to provide a matching size of shovel.

■ Standardisation

Having established optimal working methods, managers had to publish instructions for the workers. Taylor's machining expertise helped him establish optimal cutting speeds and depths as well as best sizes and shapes for the cutting tools. Using the correct cutter under the right conditions caused productivity to increase. Standardisation meant that managers had to provide the proper tools and ensure they were used effectively.

■ Selection and training

Taylor argued for care in matching of staff to tasks. In the famous 'pig-iron study' at the Bethlehem Steel Corporation, Taylor investigated the job of loading railway wagons with 42-kg blocks of iron. A group of 75 men was employed to carry the 'pigs' up a 12-metre incline. Each made some 300 trips in a ten-hour day, loading some $12\frac{1}{2}$ tonnes. Selecting one of the strongest and fittest, and instructing him in correct techniques of lifting and carrying, Taylor showed how output could be increased to $17\frac{1}{2}$ tonnes. Others were then selected and trained, although only one in eight could achieve the top rate. Taylor reported how the labourers preferred this remarkable four-fold increase; the new methods left them feeling less fatigued and enabled them to earn 60 per cent more pay.

■ Payment by results

Taylor believed that workers were primarily motivated by pay. Therefore, piecework was central to scientific management schemes. Traditionally, piecework rates were figured out by rule of thumb and negotiation between supervisor and worker. Instead, Taylor and his followers experimented with differential piecework plans. For example, having established the best method, they would match the rate to the average worker. Output higher than this might be rewarded with an enhancement of, say, 20 per cent. Thus, the standard rate might have been 10 pence per unit up to 20 units and 12 pence after that.

■ Co-operation

Taylor felt that co-operation was vital if the fruits of success were to be shared equitably. In Perrow's[35] summary, the argument between labour and management, over how to divide any surplus between higher wages and profits, should be replaced by constructive discussion about increasing the size of the surplus itself. In short, it was rational for both sides to co-operate in applying scientific principles to the study of work.

While Taylor is often called the 'father' of scientific management, he was hardly alone in innovation and publication of new ideas. A colleague, Henry Gantt, gave his name to the Gantt Chart – a bar graph widely used to plan and sequence events along a time-line. Frank and Lillian Gilbreth (*see* Exhibit 1.8) were also innovators, working on the idea of 'motion study'.

The legacy

Although scientific management showed how to improve productivity, its failings quickly became apparent. It did not consider the social context of work and the workers' psychological needs for attachment to the work process itself. Feelings of exploitation contrasted with the rational harmony advocated by Taylor. Less scrupu-

> **Exhibit 1.8** The Gilbreths: time and motion and psychological studies
>
> Following a successful career in building, Frank Gilbreth (1868–1924) turned to consultancy, becoming converted to scientific management. Using films and special charts to build on his experience, he identified 17 basic human motions which he called *therbligs* (coined from his surname). These were used in the training of bricklayers and soldiers and the rehabilitation of the disabled. The focus was less on times than on the elimination of unnecessary movements.
>
> After her husband's death, Lillian Gilbreth (1878–1972), although more interested in the psychological aspects of work, carried on Frank's studies and seminar programme. She eventually became professor at Purdue University.
>
> Two of the Gilbreths' 12 children published *Cheaper by the Dozen*, which describes how both family and household were organised for maximum efficiency.

lous managers focused on work measurement, using the notorious 'time and motion man' to beat down workers' pay. A strike at Watertown Arsenal led to a House of Representatives investigation. This led the Senate to ban Taylor's methods from United States defence establishments.

As students, however, we should not deride the approach. It was developed in an age of manual mass production with emphasis on the quantity, as opposed to quality, of output. The stress on detailed management control of every aspect of a job now looks old fashioned. Yet, the attention to work design, worker development, fair rewards and co-operation has echoes in much modern management literature. What has happened since is that definitions of ideas of development, fairness and co-operation have shifted from narrow managerial rationality towards broader ideas of equity.

Bureaucracy

Whereas scientific management gained by making a detailed analysis of production processes, the study of bureaucracy looked at the problem of managing the organisation as a whole. Advocates, led by Weber (*see* Exhibit 1.9), took up the scientific management notion that there is one best way to do a job: they argued that there must be one best way to run an organisation.

Weber argued that the most efficient organisation paralleled a machine, its rules and controls corresponding to the shafts and rods of the mechanism. This was the *rational-legal* model of organisation, distinguished from the *charismatic* (dominated by the leader) and *traditional* (run on custom and practice) models. Weber worked at a time when many organisations were managed by families with their practices serving personal rather than organisational goals. He saw the need for impersonal, rational management in charge of his ideal organisation, the *bureaucracy*.

The elements of a bureaucracy are:

- *Division of labour* – definitions of authority and responsibility as official duties.

- *Organisation of positions into a hierarchy* – each position under the authority of a higher one.

- *People assigned to positions* – based on qualifications, assessed by examination or training and experience.

- *Decisions and actions are recorded in writing* – files provide continuity and memory.

Exhibit 1.9 Max Weber and the ideal-typical bureaucracy

While best known as a sociologist, Weber (1864–1920) lectured in law, then economics, before obtaining a chair in sociology. He was an evolutionist who saw man in society moving towards greater reasoning based on acquired knowledge. Rationality would replace blind faith or unquestioning assumptions based on tradition.

Weber developed the difficult concept of the *ideal-type*. This is a pure model of part of social reality with which some element of that reality could be compared. It is a sort of lens used to focus and clarify the area under study. While Weber was not the first to use the term *bureaucracy*, he discerned its qualities in terms that we can recognise today. Some followers have taken Weber's discussion as prescriptive, a statement of the way organisations ought to be. For instance, a bureaucracy must be hierarchical, with clear and comprehensive rules. This contrasts with his intention of the concept being a starting point for debate and comparison.

- *Separation of management from ownership.*
- *All subject to rules and procedures* – applied impersonally and equally to ensure predictable behaviour.

Weber believed that the rational-legal organisation would be both more efficient and more adaptable to change than any other. The system was rational in that competent managers made decisions according to clear criteria; it was legal because they had been appointed by legitimate processes. Yet the notion of bureaucracy has become discredited in modern times. It is associated with stifling rules and red tape. As with Taylorism, however, we should not be too critical. The emphasis in Weber's time was on improving efficiency and consistency whereas for some modern organisations the stress is on innovation and flexibility. Furthermore, many modern organisations incorporate most of Weber's elements. For instance, applying rules impersonally is fundamental to dealing with personnel issues. It is in complex, rapidly changing market environments that zealous adherence to rules leads to a downfall.

Management principles

A different, yet related, approach to the question of running whole organisations examined the practice of management itself. Perhaps the best known among the advocates of general principles applied to practice was Fayol, *see* Exhibit 1.10. Others such as Follett made contributions that we shall include in this discussion.

In the short *General and Industrial Management*,[36] Fayol examined three themes: the abilities required of managers; general principles of management; and elements of management.

Abilities required of managers

Fayol's first theme is analysis of the abilities required of personnel at different levels and in different types of organisation. His intention is to show that while many people are engaged in the process called management, they are involved to different degrees. He distinguishes management from other abilities required of people in organisations, concluding with the following definition:

> *To manage is to forecast and plan, to organise, to command, to co-ordinate and to control.*

Exhibit 1.10 Henri Fayol: general principles of management

Fayol (1841–1925) graduated in mining engineering from the École Nationale in St. Éti-enne at the age of nineteen. The first years of his career were devoted to resolving mining problems, especially fire hazards. Then, on promotion, he worked on geological questions, publishing a theory of coal deposition. In 1888, Fayol was put in charge of the ailing Commentry-Fourchambault mining and ironmaking group which he saved and developed into Comambault, one of France's most successful companies. Retiring in 1918 at the age of 77, he devoted his last years to spreading his manage-ment theory.

The classic *Administration industrielle et générale* appeared in 1916, although the book had little influence in the English-speaking world until translations appeared. Although a few copies were available in the United Kingdom in 1929, it was not until 1949 that Pitman published it throughout the Anglophone world. It was based on his broad experience.

Fayol saw his work as complementing Taylor's. He argued that his five basic func-tions and fourteen principles of management were applicable in any organisational setting. For him, these basic ideas of management were waiting to be discovered and elaborated. They appear in developed and adapted form in much modern manage-ment teaching.

By identifying abilities, and defining management as stages of a process, Fayol indi-cated the need for, and the possibility of, teaching management as a discipline. The principles would naturally form a framework for the curriculum.

■ *General principles of management*

Fayol set out as principles the ideas that he said he had had to apply most frequently, *see* Exhibit 1.11. In studying the list, we should focus less on the detail, and more on two features. First, there is generalisation. Fayol sought to extract from the manager's job common features to be studied and, for example, used as the basis of selection, training and assessment. This is the start of a long tradition leading to what we now call management competences. Second, to be universal, the principles are couched in very general terms. Fayol intended them to be flexible, adaptable to every need. In being so general, however, they can be criticised for not being *operational*. This means they cannot readily be converted into practical action in any particular case.

■ *Elements of management*

The elements are drawn directly from Fayol's definition of management. He gives details of: good planning on a business and national scale; organising materials and personnel at all levels, including the use of organisation charts, defining jobs and training people to fill them; the knowledge and personal qualities needed to give commands; means of achieving co-ordination; and the timeliness of control with related sanctions.

Fayol's writings now seem old-fashioned and can be criticised for being grounded in the experience of someone whose career was confined to one organisation. As with others of his era, however, we should recognise the originality of the ideas and the different context in which they were developed. Many can be traced through to today, although the ideas have frequently been reinvented and re-labelled.

Mary Parker Follett,[37] *see* Exhibit 1.12, was another who saw management as a generic function to which can be attached general principles. Her work can be seen as part of the classical tradition yet it provided a bridge to later ideas. She investi-

Exhibit 1.11 Fayol's fourteen principles of management

Division of work	To produce more and better work with the same effort.
Authority and responsibility	Authority is the right to give orders and have them followed. It matches responsibility, the accountability for exercise of authority.
Discipline	Maintained by good superiors, fair agreements and appropriate sanctions.
Unity of command	Dual command causes disorder and is a perpetual source of conflict.
Unity of direction	Established by sound organisation with plans coming from one person.
Subordination of individual to group interest	Good leadership, fairness and supervision ensure that people follow the organisation's goals and not their own.
Remuneration	Pay should be fair and encouraging yet not excessive.
Centralisation	Both centralisation and decentralisation are necessary; the question is how to establish the proportions to optimise the use of people.
Scalar chain	The path followed by authority up and down the hierarchy can be too long in large organisations. Fayol showed how horizontal links could be maintained.
Order	Everyone and everything should be in its place. Beyond tidiness and discipline, this also means staff selection to match abilities with jobs.
Equity	Fair treatment of all employees encourages loyalty.
Stability of tenure	Instability of tenure is both the cause and the effect of inefficiency.
Business strength	Is combining everyone's initiative. Managers should encourage initiative among subordinates.
Team spirit	Despite unity of command, personnel must not be arbitrarily split up; contacts within and between departments should be encouraged to avoid misunderstandings and disputes.

gated questions of power and responsibility but also recognised the needs, abilities and aspirations of employees.

The management task is to integrate all the specialist functions of the bureaucracy. Echoing Taylor, Follett stressed the need for systematic record keeping and learning

Exhibit 1.12 Mary Parker Follett: looking forward with new ideas

Follett (1868–1933) was born near Boston and educated at Radcliffe (now part of Harvard) and Cambridge. She started in political science and social work and it was only when she was in her fifties that she began lecturing and writing on business administration. She never worked in business but applied her ideas on the health of society to the task of creating healthy organisations. She wrote on conflict, power and leadership, explaining how the former should not be hidden within the rational organisation but be resolved through processes aimed at joint accommodation rather than imposed solutions.

Follett knew Taylorism well, having joined the Taylor Society. Yet she did not see workers as hired hands to be optimised. For her, managers and workers all had reason, feelings and character.

In 1926, grieving for the loss of a friend, Follett moved to London. Her 1933 lecture series at the London School of Economics was on *The Problem of Organisation and Co-ordination in Business*. She died later that year, during a brief visit to Boston.

from experience. Simultaneously, she criticised the inhumanity of hierarchical structures, arguing that people were more important than machines. Follett saw conflict not as something to be avoided but as a 'fact of life'. Conflict was based on difference and, without difference, there would be no progress. She argued against the conventional idea of power, which is the idea of one person having it 'over' another. Instead, Follett argued that power should be pooled, built around transactions and mutual influence. She continually interpreted situations as wholes, taking the broad picture and examining the linkages between the elements. In taking the humanist stance and also looking at the broad picture, Follett foresaw future trends in management thought.

The human relations perspective

We have seen how the emphasis in the classical approach was on principles, science and structure. The human aspects of work and organisation had not been ignored but relegated to a secondary issue in the campaign to increase the efficiency of enterprises. It was during the 1920s that scholars and innovators turned their attention more towards the behaviour of employees within organisations. They became concerned with human relations.

Three factors brought about this change:

■ *The rising influence of trade unions in many countries*

The scale of mines, manufacturing plants and service industries meant that unions could readily organise. Many governments had granted them the necessary freedoms. Meanwhile, workers became angry with both the 'time and motion' studies imposed by unreasonable employers and the boom and bust cycles affecting many industries. Some enlightened employers became attracted by human relations ideas. More contentment among workers would make them less likely to support trade union activities.

■ *Industrial humanism as a philosophy*

Industrial humanism began among philanthropic employers such as the Rowntree family, *see* Exhibit 1.13.[38] They did not approve of merely paternalistically caring for welfare, a view that justified managers deciding what was in the workers' best interests. Following Follett, they held that all employees had rights, aspirations and needs

Exhibit 1.13 Seebohm Rowntree: industrial humanist

Rowntree (1871–1954) attended the Friends' School in York and Owen's College, now the University of Manchester. His chemistry degree benefited his family's York Cocoa Works, yet he spent much time on social issues. When made labour director he worked on improving democratic relations, an attitude many regarded as risky. All factory rules had to be approved by managers and workers; there were elected shop stewards whose chief was paid by the company; foremen appointments followed consultation; on appeal, disciplinary cases went to a joint committee. There were welfare and training departments and, in 1906, the company introduced a generous pension scheme.

Rowntree constantly argued that workers were more than hired hands. They were citizens and, because of this, they were entitled to demand that industry should be conducted in the interests of the whole community. Scientific management methods could only be justified if they generated surplus to share with employees.

and these should be a major concern. The manager's role was to engage with the worker in making decisions. Work should flow from motivation, not from command.

■ *Studies that challenged the assumptions of scientific management*

The best-known example is the series of studies beginning with the illumination experiments conducted from 1924 to 1927 by engineers at the Hawthorne Plant of the Western Electric Company. Lighting manufacturers, seeking to promote their products as productivity aids, proposed the experiments in the true tradition of scientific management. At Hawthorne, four selected groups underwent tests while three acted as controls. In one case, the illumination level was increased. As expected, output went up. Then, illumination was put up again. Productivity rose once more. So far, the results tallied with expectations.

To check on the results, the lighting was cut, first to the intermediate level and then back to the basic. Productivity continued to rise. In similar trials, work-rates rose whether the work conditions were made better or worse. Curiously, the output of the control groups also tended to rise when the experimental rooms were made brighter. In addition, when the illumination was cut, the control groups performed even better. The experiments seemed to lead nowhere. Mayo commented later:

> The conditions of scientific experiment had apparently been fulfilled – experimental room, control room; changes introduced one at a time; all other conditions held steady.[39]

These inconclusive results prompted further experiments and studies lasting until about 1933. Together, they are known as the Hawthorne Studies.

■ The Hawthorne Studies

The follow-up studies were initiated by the company's own managers with advice from staff at the Massachusetts Institute of Technology. Elton Mayo, of Harvard Business School, became involved in 1928. It is often said that the main guidance over the following years was given by Mayo and another Harvard professor, Fritz Roethlisberger, although there is some doubt as to Mayo's direct involvement in all phases.[40] These numbered three: the relay assembly test room; the interview programme; and the bank wiring observation room.

The relay assembly test room (RATR)

The boring, repetitive work of relay assembly involved women who put together telephone relays from many small parts. Two women friends were asked to select four others for a trial. The six worked in a special room where observers could watch the process, listen to and consult with them and keep them informed of progress. During the 13 periods of the experiment, lasting from 2 to 31 weeks, the researchers evaluated changing conditions. These were patterns and times of rest breaks and length of the working day. Simultaneously they monitored factors such as diet, physical health and sleep habits.

The experiment was designed so that the last two periods meant a return to the nominal conditions experienced earlier. Period 12 resembled Period 3, which was similar to the conditions measured before the experiment began, that is, without morning and afternoon rest breaks. Although there was a slight dip at the start of Period 12, production rose to a new record, from less than 2500 units at the start to more than 2900. Periods 7, 10 and 13 also had similar nominal conditions, this time with breaks. Output figures were 2500, 2800 and 3000 respectively. Overall, apart from the dip in Period 12, output rose steadily throughout the two years of the trials.

Mayo later explained the results as follows:

> I have often heard my colleague Roethlisberger declare that the major experimental change was introduced when those in charge sought to hold the situation humanly steady ... by getting the cooperation of the workers. What actually happened was that six individuals became a team and the team gave itself wholeheartedly and spontaneously to cooperation in the experiment. The consequence was that they felt themselves to be participating freely and without afterthought, and were happy in the knowledge that they were working without coercion from above or limitation from below...
>
> Here then are two topics which deserve the closest attention ... – the organisation of working teams and the free participation of such teams in the task and purpose of the organisation.[41]

Mayo's discussion has the advantage of hindsight, as we discussed earlier in the chapter. Yet, at the time, the result was puzzling. Even today, authors dispute how the RATR results should be interpreted. What was so special about the RATR? How did it compare with the work outside? To try to answer such questions, the interview programme began.

The interview programme

The RATR outcomes seemed to point to the influence of supervision. Interviews were aimed at eliciting workers' feelings about their supervisors and their conditions of work. More than twenty thousand were conducted during this period, ended by the onset of the Great Depression. Interviews followed a prepared schedule, which was later changed when responses showed some questions to be irrelevant. The style became less directive and more open-ended. Subjects were encouraged to talk about any aspect of their work.

Information on many aspects of working life was gained. Further, many welcomed the opportunity to talk to a sympathetic listener in a friendly atmosphere. This finding pointed the way to the development of personnel management and associated counselling services. According to Mayo, however, the most important outcome was the recognition of the power of groups.

In one case, group members talked about fatigue. They reported doing most work in the morning and 'taking it easy' in the afternoon. In contrast, the boss thought the group worked hard all day. Although well respected, he knew nothing of the practice. The researchers organised engineers to quietly measure the electric current, which would indirectly measure activity. The results supported the women's statement. This was just one of many observations showing how, in Mayo's words, 'the working group as a whole actually determined the output of individual workers by reference to a standard that represented the group conception of a fair day's work. This standard was rarely, if ever, in accord with the standards of the efficiency engineers.'[42]

The bank wiring observation room

The researchers again used experiment to continue their investigation of groups. Here, 14 men – wiremen, solderers and inspectors – connected telephone cables to switchgear. The men formed their own informal subgroups with leaders emerging by consent. The group set norms, including output standards. In spite of pay inducements, the men decided to produce much less than their full potential. Social pressure upon individuals was much stronger than the financial incentives of management.

Overview of Hawthorne

Taken as a whole, the Hawthorne Studies generated new ideas. The interpretation of the results remains controversial. For instance, it has been pointed out that the RATR workers were all young unmarried women living, bar one, with their parents. The bank wiring group was male. Responses have been explained, therefore, by traditional power differences between the sexes.[43] In another interpretation, Greenwood and others challenged those who ignored money. Interviewed many years later, one participant acknowledged how joining an experimental group meant a substantial rise in income.[44] One theme, however, dominates the difficulties with interpretation. It is impossible to conduct experiments or make detailed enquiries without influencing the attitudes and behaviour of those being studied. This is widely known as the *Hawthorne effect*.

■ The human relations movement

The human relations movement gathered momentum from the Hawthorne Studies. Additionally, the Depression stimulated people's humanitarian efforts. At work, it was believed that the search for increased productivity was held back by ignoring workers' concerns and needs for job satisfaction. The naive view was that contented staff would produce more.

Deeper insights came from Maslow and McGregor. Maslow drew insights into human behaviour from psychology practice, proposing that human motivation is driven by a hierarchy of needs. We shall discuss this further in Chapter 11. Douglas McGregor (1906–64) used his own psychological training and management consultancy experience to extend Maslow's ideas. His *Theory X and Theory Y* were not theories in themselves, but ideal-types describing typical management attitudes, *see* Exhibit 1.14.[45]

Exhibit 1.14 Douglas McGregor: Theory X and Theory Y managers

Theory X managers believe

- The average person inherently dislikes work and will avoid it if possible.
- Therefore, most people must be coerced, directed or threatened to get them to put in adequate effort.
- The average person prefers direction, avoids responsibility, is unambitious and desires security above all.

Theory Y managers believe

- The expenditure of effort, both physical and mental, is natural.
- Control and direction are not the only means of stimulating effort; a person will exercise self-control and self-direction when committed to the task.
- The average person is prepared to both accept and seek responsibility.
- Many can demonstrate imagination, ingenuity and creativity in the organisational context.
- In most industrial jobs, employees' intellectual potential is only partially tapped.

McGregor used his theories to challenge both the classical and the early human relations perspectives. To him both were coercive, the former seeking to systematise incentives and punishments, the latter looking for other variables to push up output. Neither Taylor nor the managers at Western Electric started by recognising that the worker might have at least as much to contribute as the manager. In contrast, Theory Y managers seek to enrol employees in a wider and deeper range of questions. Under the right conditions, Theory Y managers could rely on staff to exercise self-direction and control and apply their intellect to problems as they arise. In advocating training policies aimed at creating Theory Y conditions, McGregor was taking both a pragmatic and a moral position.

■ Organisational behaviour (OB)

The OB, or behavioural science, perspective has linked the practical concerns of the human relations movement with all the behavioural sciences, for instance: anthropology, medicine, political science, psychology and sociology. Although set in organisations, OB is not necessarily managerial in its orientation. Many who work in OB have as their goal what many would regard as the core purpose of science, the gathering of knowledge for its own sake. The benefits of this work may not become apparent until much later. At the same time, leading researchers have influenced modern management practice and we shall draw on their work throughout the book.

The management science perspective

Whereas OB covers the application of social sciences to enterprise, management science draws on the natural sciences. Scholars in fields such as physics and mathematics began to see that management problems had many features related to their own. Applications were therefore stimulated by the development of new techniques as well as new problem situations. We mentioned earlier in the chapter how the problems of scale arose with the growth of business enterprises themselves. This ignores any learning that may have taken place, for example from military experience. Many leading figures in management and consultancy, such as Lyndale Urwick (1891–1983), had experience in the services that they transferred to the civilian sphere. It was in wartime that the two grew closer.

During the Second World War, groups of scientists, especially mathematicians, were assembled by governments to solve military problems. These frequently included, for example, *logistics*. Warfare demands the rapid movement of large quantities of personnel, weapons, equipment and stores. It is not surprising that successful solutions readily found application to large-scale business. The approach, named *operations research* (*OR*), requires the expression of a problem in mathematical terms, the manipulation of the data to produce a result and the translation of the result back into management practice.

Further explanation and examples are left to Chapter 15. Operations management applies a wide range of OR techniques that have been developed to optimise the supply of goods and services. They range from forecasting to stock control and queue management to scheduling. While many mathematical techniques have been known for a long time, OR had to await the development of computers for its major impact.[46] Exhibit 1.15 describes how a classic OR problem was solved at the dawn of the information era; this would nowadays take seconds on a moderate computer.

Exhibit 1.15 OR applications had to await the computer

Transportation studies were carried out by the UK National Coal Board from the mid-1950s. Solutions required desk-top calculators and much effort; a 60 colliery to 60 customer problem took three days to solve! The Central Electricity Generating Board conducted similar studies at around the same period. Efficient movement from pit to power station was the focus. A regional model with 135 mines and 32 stations needed 71 iterations even though the most efficient numerical procedures were used.

Such problems were ready made for the nascent computing facilities. By the late 1960s, British Petroleum was one of the largest computer users in the country. Most of its usage was devoted to OR, working on forecasting, marketing, supply and so on.

As mentioned above, management science has been applied to many aspects, especially operations. We should also recognise, however, that the approach traditionally focuses on quantitative aspects, playing down the significance of attitudes and behaviour and the problems of implementing solutions in complex organisations.

Integrating perspectives

The perspectives we have considered grew out of problems and attitudes of their time. They differ not only in their diverse origins but also in their concerns with distinct aspects of the management problem. Scientists call this *reduction*. This process suits those interested in the advancement of knowledge. It enables them to establish general truths about elements of the world. *Reductionism*, however, is not so good for managers faced with coping with complex, interrelated problems. They want the world to be fitted together rather than taken apart. The systems approach promises this integration.

▦ The systems approach

The systems debate began when scholars in different fields recognised common patterns that could be investigated with similar techniques. For instance: the flow of traffic on a busy road resembles the flow of water along a channel or waves up a beach; networks, from telephone companies to the connections in the brain, have fascinating commonalities; political instability can be analogous to the weather. Such insights led pioneers, such as von Bertalanffy,[47] to search for a general systems theory. This would be applied in many spheres, from economics to ecology or biochemistry to business. Despite much effort and some success, notably in work on complexity and control, the goal of an overarching model to describe patterns in different fields has not been reached.

The approach is built around the idea of *system*. When we observe something we call a system, we tend to speak of it as a whole. Although remaining wary of reification, discussed above, we notice in the whole system attributes that cannot be attached to any particular element. It is as though the system behaves in a way that is different from simply a sum of the behaviour of all its parts. It is said to have *emergent properties*. Therefore, we talk about the whole. Examples are: the band; the crowd at the match; the United Nations; the flock of sheep; Rome; and so on. The idea that the whole is greater than the sum of the parts is called *synergy*. This gives the study of systems its importance.

> *A system is a set of connected parts that behave together in significant ways.*

Central to the idea of system, captured by this definition, are the significant connections or *relationships* among the components. It is as though the arrangement of these parts, and the way they work together, are at least as important as the parts themselves.

For the manager, what are the key features of systems thinking?

■ *Holism*

The whole of the system behaves in a way which is greater than the sum of its parts.

■ *Open system*

The system interacts with other systems in order to survive and succeed. In the above example, we cannot understand the band without knowing about the audience, the venue and so on. Similarly, the match crowd interacts with the teams.

This is an antidote to the classical perspective. It frequently saw organisations as closed systems where all behaviour could be accounted for by events that took place within the plant, office, business or whatever. Open systems thinking, however, recognises that interactions with external factors, the *organisation's environment*, are very important. This is the basis for Chapter 2.

■ *Hierarchy*

Each system consists of parts that are themselves systems. This goes beyond Weber's notion of bureaucratic hierarchy to see it as 'systems within systems'. The elements of these smaller systems may be people or other elements, such as plant to patents or inventory to instructions. When we see that the elements themselves are made up of systems, we may call them *subsystems*.

■ *Boundary*

The boundary separates the system from its environment. For a business organisation, what is owned by it and who is employed by it are usually easy to define. Modern organisational forms, however, break down firm boundaries between single hierarchies into much more flexible networks, *see* Chapter 10. While they bring advantages by improving responses to changing situations, there can be problems of responsibility when things go wrong.

■ *Significance*

The word *significant* in the definition is important. Systems definitions are subjective, depending on the purpose of the observer. Just as a marine biologist sees a shoal as part of a wider ecosystem, so the captain of a trawler sees it as profit and the European Union official as an excuse to write regulations in 23 languages. Awareness of the effect of different viewpoints helps us to understand ideas such as that of stakeholders, developed in Chapter 5.

Figure 1.5 gives an example of the systems view of a business in the form of a *rich picture*. In this format, we capture our initial impressions of a nursing home before we proceed to analyse it. The figure picks out features of the system such as the home, its staff and its patients. It also suggests the boundary and key elements in the environment. We can see, within the boundary, various subsystems (departments) that interact with each other. Together they make up a *transformation system*, so called because it transforms inputs (resources) into outputs (patient care). We shall cover formal representations of transformation systems in Chapter 15.

We noted that the search for general systems theory has been only partially successful. Instead, different thinkers have taken the idea of system and used it in different ways. We shall summarise four lines of thought: socio-technical systems, systems and control, systems and chaos and systems as methodology.

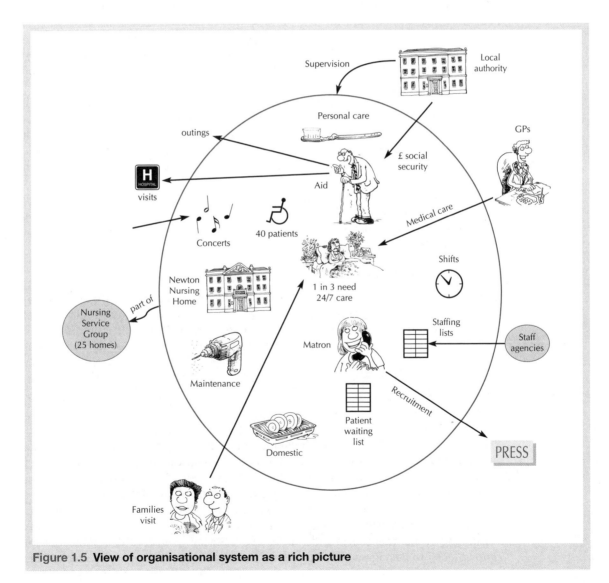

Figure 1.5 View of organisational system as a rich picture

Socio-technical systems

Trist and Bamforth, with others at London's Tavistock Institute, carried out a series of studies into the relationships between the social and technical subsystems of an organisation. Their famous studies in the UK coal-mining industry of the late 1940s coincided with the change from traditional methods to large-scale mechanisation.[48]

The customary method of coal getting involved teams of about four miners working together. They hewed coal from a short section of the face and loaded it into wagons for transport to the surface. It was sometimes known as the 'tub and stall' method. Typically, the group selected itself, rotated tasks between members and shared bonus payments. The quiet, the confined spaces, the risks to health and mortal dangers meant that there was a high degree of mutual dependence among members. Social ties were strong and these tended to be replicated above ground, where miners lived close to the pit.

New equipment, longwall seam cutters, conveyors and hydraulic roof supports, demanded great change in the way mining was organised. The work pattern was changed to three specialised shifts – preparation, cutting and loading. Forty or more miners were dispersed along the face rather than confined in the short faces or stalls. Supervision and communication were difficult because of the noise and dust caused by the new machines. Productivity levels that had been planned for were not realised.

The Tavistock researchers helped to relieve some negative features of the longwall method. They devised the 'composite longwall' arrangement under which specialisation was reduced. Responsibility was returned to multi-skilled work teams. The work was found more satisfying and more efficient than with the earlier version of longwall.

The important lesson from the Tavistock Studies is the strong interaction between the social and technical subsystems. Combining these, the *socio-technical systems* approach recognises that any work system has these key components. When the technical system is changed, for example in an attempt to increase efficiency or safety, there will be social consequences and reactions. Good managers will look at these before the change is introduced.

Systems and control

Cybernetics is the study and application of the idea of control. As we shall see in Chapter 18, control systems include regulators to maintain them at their desired states. They work according to Wiener's recognition of feedback: 'the difference between the pattern [goal] and the actually performed motion is used as a new input to cause the part regulated to move in such a way as to bring the motion closer to that given pattern'.[49] Feedback returns information about output to cause the system to reduce any output gap.

Systems and chaos

The control approach has been challenged because it suggests that organisations should continuously strive towards equilibrium. Feedback loops help them to correct deviations from the chosen path. Belief in cause and effect interactions among system elements suggests that managers, having predicted the future, can take steps to control it. But is the search for stability justified? What if feedback control is so strong that the organisation cannot change?

Building on the theoretical work of Gleick,[50] Stacey pioneered the application of *chaos theory* to management.[51] He argues that most organisations are *chaotic*. This means they operate in a zone of bounded instability. It is a region between being stable and predictable and being unstable and falling apart. The future of an organisation is bounded and it will display regular patterns of behaviour. Yet the detailed outcomes of these patterns cannot be predicted. This implies that, with the long-term future essentially unknowable, any manager's attempts at close and rational control are likely to flounder. 'Muddling through' is likely to be a more effective approach. A more detailed discussion of chaos theory is given in Chapter 19.

Systems as methodology

The term methodology refers to a way of approaching questions or problems. It is broader than a technique, which is a specific process to be applied once a problem or task has been clearly specified. Managers are familiar with techniques for scheduling vehicles, finding optimal stock levels or assessing the health of a balance sheet. Yet managers quickly find that real problems are not so well defined. No one is saying, 'Hey! Solve this!' In reality, they are told, 'Customers are uneasy about the delivery schedules,' or, 'The quality of our service seems to be suffering'. To proceed, managers have to select and define problems as well as resolve them. This is aided by a methodology which, if appropriate, gives pointers to the way through the complexity.

Methodologies have been matched to problem settings. On the one hand, there are relatively clear-cut (called 'hard') situations characterised by agreed goals and clear data. OR techniques have been extended to cope with these circumstances.[52] On the other hand, Checkland's methodology[53] is focused on 'soft' systems where the goals are unclear and there are few quantitative data to go on. More specialised methodologies are designed for tasks such as information systems planning.[54]

The attempted integration of relevant disciplines under the systems banner, followed by the spawning of several new directions, reflects one theme of our history. As with the classical view, systems set out to be universalistic. Yet, in delving into the complexity of each case, they recognise its uniqueness and act accordingly. This tension between the universal and the particular is the basis of the contingency view.

The contingency perspective

The universalists saw management ideas and skills as transferable across all sorts of organisation. Once one had found the 'one best way', all could learn from it. In contrast, others pointed to the special nature of each case and how it differed. This view, which has been matched by the 'case method' in management education, says that there are no universal principles. The way to learn is to study and experience as many circumstances as possible.

The contingency perspective comes to terms with these opposing views. It recognises both commonality and uniqueness but proceeds with care in the way both are interpreted. General principles can only be transferred from one case to another once it has been established that the cases are sufficiently similar. The contingency approach is well established in many aspects of management. For instance, links between organisation structure and other variables have been studied by Burns and Stalker, Lawrence and Lorsch, Woodward, Williamson and Mintzberg. As detailed in Chapter 10, these scholars sought to find the best structure to match different factors whether within the organisation or its environment.

Conclusion: looking backwards and forwards

We began by showing that management is important. The difference between good and failing schools, or between successful and ordinary companies, is often due to factors outside their control – schools have catchment areas and companies face powerful external forces. Given reasonable parity, however, the best-managed organisation will succeed.

To understand what management is, it is tempting to rely on a definition. Ours develops from the idea of 'getting things done through people' to clarify aspects such as the 'things' that mangers do. Yet to define management in this way is to use only one angle. Other approaches look at how managers behave. Studying roles, styles, capabilities and what managers do, or do not do, also helps us to understand.

We seek more than understanding. Studying management is also about seeing ourselves as managers and improving our chances of success. While many learn most of their skills at the school of hard knocks, studying the discipline has its place. It helps us avoid the worst mistakes and enhances our rate of learning at that hard school. Theory and practice are complementary. Good theory is practical. It helps us look ahead and avoid or mitigate errors. At the same time, practice develops theory. It allows testing and refinement and a deeper understanding of how it can be used. Becoming a successful manager involves personally integrating the two.

Diversity means that managers have to become more sensitive to cultures other than their own. Happily, graduates increasingly value international experience. Not only does this stimulate understanding of differences, but also it reveals how different people think about management. In other words, both practice and theory are grounded in culture.

We end the chapter with a diagram. Figure 1.6 lays out the key points roughly along a time-line representing the past century. It both provides a useful summary and makes a valuable teaching point. As a summary, the diagram refers to main trends of management thought. It identifies key actors and events referred to throughout the chapter. Lines suggest the main influences among these various elements. Note that the start and finish dates for the major 'movements' are somewhat arbitrary. This particularly applies to their termination, for it is clear that all have an influence down to the present day.

The teaching point concerns the discipline of drawing the diagram itself, for in doing so, we go beyond summarising. We are made to recognise the way we choose, group and interpret historical events, trends and figures and the weight we give to each. In expressing the complexity of history in this form, it shows our selectivity in what we have covered and hints at what is missing.

What is missing? We have not covered some themes that have had a strong influence on management. For example, modern management wrestles with issues of culture, globalisation, quality, information, ethics and enterprise. Furthermore, this history has been ethnocentric, focusing on the development of thought in one, predominantly Anglo-Saxon, culture. The other issues, and how the best companies and managers are learning from wider sources, are discussed in later chapters.

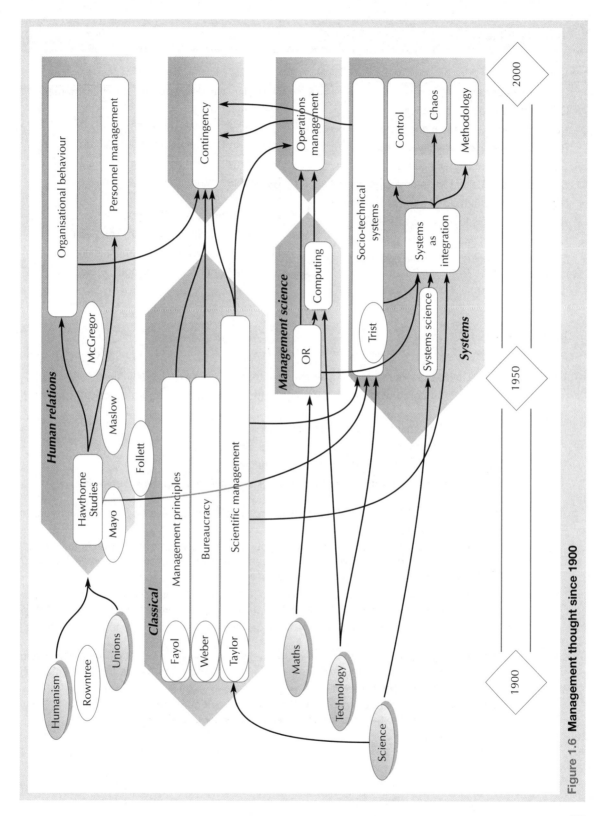

Figure 1.6 **Management thought since 1900**

QUICK CHECK

Can you ...

- Define management.
- Outline the purpose of objectives.
- Name the three Es of the management balance.
- Recognise reification, identifying its uses.
- List Mintzberg's managerial roles.
- Summarise the Blake–Mouton managerial grid.
- Distinguish descriptive and prescriptive theories.
- Refute Mintzberg's four management myths.
- Explain career anchors and how they develop.
- Show why managing diversity is becoming more important.

- Name five well-known schools of management thought.
- List six key ideas of Taylorism.
- Identify the six elements of bureaucracy.
- State Fayol's definition of management.
- Name three trends that led to the rise of the human relations movement.
- Define Theory X and Theory Y.
- Outline the operations research process.
- List the key features of systems thinking.
- State the principles of contingency theory.

QUESTIONS

Chapter review

1.1 Define management, giving an example for each phase of the definition.

1.2 Do you agree with Lewin's statement that there is nothing so practical as a good theory?[55]

1.3 Is management just applied common sense?

1.4 Why should managers be aware of the origins of ideas?

1.5 What is classical about the classical perspective?

1.6 Explain why the Hawthorne Studies were so significant and remain so today.

Application

1.7 From your knowledge of head teachers in schools, assess how good they were in occupying Mintzberg's roles.

1.8 Given that, in a management career, you will occupy each of Mintzberg's managerial roles, which do you think you will be good at and which others are your weak points? Explain the implications of your analysis for career choice.

1.9 What do the developments in management thought during the second half of the twentieth century tell us about the possibility of developing a universal theory of management?

1.10 Analyse the opening case from the classical, human relations and systems perspectives.

Investigation

1.11 Conduct interviews with a few fellow students to investigate their career anchors and preferences. Start by listing names of favoured employers before trying to establish why they have been chosen.

1.12 Prepare a short paper on the writing of one key figure mentioned in the text. Show how it related to the time it was written and how far it is relevant today.

Overdose of managers?[56]

Managers within the United Kingdom National Health Service (NHS) have found themselves under increasing pressure. Not only have they had to respond to reforms directed by the government but they have been pressed both by others within the service and by the public to justify what they do. They are expected to make the service 'ever more efficient, rational and controlled [while] at the same time ... caring and people centred'.[57] The rational approach is supported by data being compiled on all aspects of activity. Many argue that if patients have doubts about the service they are receiving, there should be the possibility of comparison based on independent assessment. Hence, as with schools in the opening case, we have league tables and other comparisons.

There are now as many managers in the National Health Services a nurses. In Leeds, for example, the teaching hospitals St James's and Leeds General Infirmary have 387 senior managers. They, in turn, are in charge of 2674 administrators and clerks. Are so many managers really necessary? Several studies have shown that good management improves medial care. One found a strong relationship between good personnel practice and mortality; this was more significant than the number of doctors per one hundred beds.

Wall argues that the middle manager occupies 'The most uncomfortable position in the NHS'.[58] They feel that their role is unrecognised by patients, colleagues, the public and the government. The Department of Health makes their jobs more difficult by issuing a stream of initiatives and targets leaving managers struggling with paper and distracting all from important tasks. One survey sent to senior mangers was to confirm the accuracy of a previous one!

What is it like to be a manager under these circumstances? Preston and Loan-Clarke[59] interviewed 39 managers working in two community hospitals and related units. Their feelings of lack of sympathy were captured by one respondent: 'I think that Joe Public doesn't have a very good opinion of us, I think the media portray us very badly – that there's far too many of us'. Another complained about ministers grumbling about the people they employ, while a third said, '... I don't know how they think the NHS workforce gets organised'. A senior manager pointed out that the NHS is a major organisation, with more than a million people, and evidently needs to be managed.

Pressure arises internally, too. Many staff complain of managers never revealing the story behind changes. One said, 'I think people always think there is something going on ... some people have this perception of managers up there plotting'. Middle and junior managers, seeing themselves as implementers of strategy, feel they lack the information they would like although their staff think that they withold it. They have less autonomy and decision involvement that their staff assume. And they are subjected to increasing control. Introducing a new code of conduct, the NHS Chief Executive said, 'We decided to introduce this Code in order to have a means for holding managers to account for their own professional behaviour. It will be used in that way and breaches of this Code will be taken very seriously indeed.'[60]

Several respondents regretted how the notion of management had become divorced from clinical practice, even though many managers were doctors or nurses who had taken on the role to try to make a difference. To them, what was now called management was just an extension of the profession. Calling a sister or matron a ward manager had not been helpful.

Another difficulty for the NHS manager is the need to manage professional staff with equal or higher status. The organisation is very complex. Managing professional staff who have a high degree of autonomy means that an autocratic style does not work. Yet middle managers find they act as buffers between the professions and senior managers who look at 'black and white statistical information that's their version of the reality'. Preston and Loan-Clarke conclude, 'Amidst this constant negativity it may be easy for managers to lose sight of their role in the wider scheme of bringing more accountability and effectiveness to NHS organisations'.

Questions

1 Why is the middle manager 'The most uncomfortable position in the NHS'?

2 Do rationality and efficiency conflict with a service that is 'caring and people centred'? And what about equity?

3 How do NHS management jobs fit into Mintzberg's framework of managerial roles?

4 Combine the case with your own experience to identify the abilities required of a good NHS manager.

5 What theories of management are implied in the statements of this case?

Bibliography

In *The Effective Manager* (London: Sage, 1996) Jon Billsberry extends and broadens many of the issues raised in this chapter. Laurie Mullins (2002) *Management and Organisational Behaviour* (6th edition, Harlow: FT Prentice Hall) covers the history in more detail. Leading thinkers Peter Drucker, Charles Handy and Henry Mintzberg have produced both popular and serious works on management that you should find in the library. For classics, your library may have one of the many editions of works by Fayol, Follett, Mayo or Taylor. To read one is rewarding. Founded by Drucker, the Leader to Leader Institute is a good on-line source at **www.pfdf.org/**.

References

1 *Inspection Report: Princess Junior School*, 30 April–3 May 1996; *Inspection Report: Claremont Junior School*, 13–17 January 1997; School inspection reports for Manchester are on: **www.open.gov.uk/ofsted/htm.pri352.htm**; 'Moss Side Story', *The Economist*, 22 November 1997, 32–3; 'Ask me my three main priorities for Government and I will tell you: Education, education, education', Future Prime Minister, Tony Blair, Oxford, 16 December 1996.

2 Tomlinson, Sally (1997) 'Sociological perspectives on failing schools', *International Studies in Sociology of Education*, **7(1), 81**.

3 Dorgan, Stephen J. and Dowdy, John (2002) 'How good management raises productivity', *The McKinsey Quarterly*, **4**.

4 Child, Peter N. (2002) 'Taking Tesco Global', *The McKinsey Quarterly*, **3**, www.mckinseyquarterly.com, accessed 21 November 2002.

5 Thatcher, Margaret (1993) *The Downing Street Years*, London: HarperCollins, 626.

6 Mintzberg, Henry (1971) 'Managerial work: analysis and observation', *Management Science*, October, B97–110.

7 Dauphinais, G. William (1996) 'Who's minding the middle managers?' *HR Focus*, **73(10)**, October, 12–13.

8 Rowe, A.J. and Mason, R.O. (1987) *Managing with Style*, New York: Jossey-Bass.

9 Hersey, P. and Blanchard, K.H. (1988) *Management of Organisational Behavior*, Englewood Cliffs, NJ: Prentice-Hall.

10 Blake, R.R. and Mouton, J.S. (1964) *The Managerial Grid: Key Orientations for Achieving Production through People*, Houston, Tex.: Gulf Publishing; Blake, R.R. and McCanse, A.A. (1991) *Leadership Dilemmas – Grid Solutions*, Houston, Tex.: Gulf Publishing.

11 Morikawa, Hidemasa (1995) 'The role of managerial enterprise in post-war Japanese economic growth: focus on the 1950s', *Business History*, **37(2)**, April, 32–43.

12 Eccles, Robert G. and Nohria, Nitin with Berkley, James D. (1992) *Beyond the Hype*, Boston, Mass.: Harvard Business School Press, 40–4.

13 *Ibid.*, 8.

14 Russell, Bertrand (1957) *The Problems of Philosophy*, London: Williams and Nogate.

15 Billsberry, Jon (1996) 'There's nothing so practical as a good theory: how can theory help managers become more effective?' in Billsberry, Jon (ed.) *The Effective Manager*, London: Sage, 1–5.

16 Mintzberg, Henry, Quinn, Brian and Ghoshal, Sumantra (1997) *The Strategy Process*, revised European edition, Hemel Hempstead: Prentice Hall, xi.

17 Vecchio, Robert P. (1995) *Organisational Behaviour*, 3rd edition, Fort Worth, Tex.: The Dryden Press, 22–3.

18 Buckley, Peter J. and Chapman, Malcolm (1996) 'Wise before the event: the creation of corporate fulfilment', *Management International Review*, **36**, Special Issue, 95–110.

19 Mintzberg, Henry (1997) 'The manager's job' in Mintzberg, Quinn and Ghoshal, *op. cit.*, 23–7.

20 Jack, Andrew, Rich, Motoko and Terazono, Emiko (1995) 'Daily grind of the 7 to 9 – The working week is becoming longer', *Financial Times*, 18 January, 16.

21 Barsoux, Jean-Louis and Lawrence, Peter (1991) 'The making of a French manager', *Harvard Business Review*, **69(4)** July–August, 58–67.

22 Harvey, Lee, Moon, Sue and Geall, Vicki (1997) *Graduates' Work: Organisational change and students' attributes*, Centre for Research into Quality, University of Birmingham, 63–73.

23 Taylor, Robert (1995) 'Only 20 per cent of managers have degrees', *Financial Times*, 19 June, 11.

24 Snell, Robin (1989) 'Graduating from the school of hard knocks', *Journal of Management Development*, **8(5)**, 23–30.

25 Schein, Edgar H. (1996) 'Career anchors revisited: implications for career development in the 21st century', *The Academy of Management Executive*, **10(4)**, November, 80–8.

26 Universum International (2002) *The European Graduate Survey 2002*, www.universum.se/; accessed 21 November 2002.

27 Universum International (1997) *The European Graduate Survey 1997*, www.universum.se/international/surveys/ces-96/8.html, accessed 1 November 1997.

28 Storey, John, Edwards, Paul and Sisson, Keith (1997) *Managers in the making: Careers, development and control in corporate Britain and Japan*, London: Sage.

29 Interview with Richard Greenhalgh, head of management development at the Anglo-Dutch company Unilever, in Jackson, Tony (1997) 'Perspective: The myth of the global executive', *Financial Times*, 8 October.

30 Adler, Nancy J. (1983) 'Organisational development in a multicultural environment', *Journal of Applied Behavioural Science*, **19(3)**, Summer, 349–65.

31 Carr, E.H. (1964) *What is History?* Harmondsworth: Pelican, 55.

32 Dawson, Miles Menander (1932, ed.) *The Wisdom of Confucius*, Boston, Mass.: International Pocket Library. This is one of the many pocket books of sayings available

33 Machiavelli, Nicolo (c.1505) *The Prince*. A translation by W.K. Marriott is available at: http://daemon.ilt.columbia.edu/academic/digitexts/machiavelli.

34 Nelson, Daniel (1980) *Frederick W. Taylor and the Rise of Scientific Management*, Madison, Wis.: University of Wisconsin Press.

35 Perrow, Charles (1979) *Complex Organisations: A critical essay*, New York: Scott, Foresman and Company, 64.

36 Fayol, Henri (1916) *Administration industrielle et générale*; English translation, *General and Industrial Management* (1967), London: Pitman.

37 Graham, Pauline (1995, ed.) *Mary Parker Follett – Prophet of Management: a celebration of writings from the 1920s*, Boston, Mass.: Harvard College.

38 Urwick, L. and Brech, E.F.L. (1959) *The Making of Scientific Management: Volume 1, Thirteen pioneers*, London: Pitman, 58–70.

39 Mayo, Elton (1975) *The Social Problems of an Industrial Civilisation*, London: Routledge & Kegan Paul, 61.

40 Smith, J.H. (1975) 'The significance of Elton Mayo', foreword to Mayo, Elton (1975) *op. cit.*, xvi.

41 Mayo (1975) *op. cit.*, 64.

42 Mayo (1975) *op. cit.*, 70.

43 Stead, B.A. (1978) *Women in Management*, Englewood Cliffs, NJ: Prentice-Hall, 190.

44 Greenwood, Ronald C., Bolton, Alfred A. and Greenwood, Regina A. (1983) 'Hawthorne a half century later: relay assembly participants remember', *Journal of Management*, **9**, Fall/Winter, 217–31.

45 McGregor, Douglas (1960) *The Human Side of Enterprise*, New York: McGraw-Hill, 33–48.

46 Ranyard, J.C. (1988) 'A history of OR and computing', *Journal of the Operational Research Society*, **39(12)**, 1073–86.

47 von Bertalanffy, Ludwig (1950) 'An outline of general systems theory', *The British Journal for the Philosophy of Science*, **1(2)**.

48 Trist, E.I. and Bamforth K.W. (1951) 'Some social and psychological consequences of the longwall method of coal getting', *Human Relations*, **4**, 1–38.

49 Wiener, Norbert (1948) *Cybernetics or Control and Communication in the Animal and Machine*, Cambridge, Mass.: MIT Press, 6.

50 Gleick, J. (1988) *Chaos: The making of a new science*, London: Heinemann.

51 Stacey, Ralph D. (1996) *Strategic Management and Organisational Dynamics*, 2nd edition, London: Financial Times Pitman Publishing.

52 Pidd, M. (1996) *Modelling in Management Science*, London: Wiley.

53 Checkland, Peter (1981) *Systems Thinking, Systems Practice*, London: Wiley.

54 Partanen, Karl and Sovalainen, Vesa (1995) 'Perspectives on executive information systems', *Systems Practice*, **8(6)**, December, 551–76.

55 Lewin, Kurt (1945) 'The research centre for group dynamics at Massachusetts Institute of Technology', *Sociometry*, **8**, 126–36.

56 'Guide to breast cancer treatment' (2002) *Observer*, 29 September; 'Revealed: one in four health employees is now a bureaucrat' (2002) *Observer*, 13 October; 'Why HR is such a life or death issue' (2002) *Sunday Times*, 3 November.

57 Learmouth, M. (1997) 'Managerialism and public attitudes towards UK NHS managers', *Journal of Management in Medicine*, **11(4)**, 214–21.

58 Wall, A. (1999) 'Courtin' the middle', *Health Service Journal* **109**, 4 February, 22–5.

59 Preston, Diane and Loan-Clarke, John (2000) 'The NHS Manager: A view from the bridge', *Journal of Management in Medicine* **14(2)**, 100–8.

60 Department of Health (2002) *Press release* PR Newswire, London, May 23. The code is available at www.doh.gov.uk/nhsmanagerscode/code-code.htm.

CHAPTER 2

Outside the organisation: understanding the environment

Chapter objectives

When you have finished studying this chapter, you should be able to:

- explain why and how managers filter environmental information and focus their attention on key factors;

- model the environment in its operating and wider layers;

- describe the main components of the operating environment, demonstrating how they continuously interact with the organisation;

- use the PEST categories to describe the wider environment;

- show how the international environment adds complexity to scanning;

- summarise the main methods of forecasting and their contribution to making sense of change.

The best architects always design a thing by considering it in its larger context – a chair in a room, a room in a house, a house in an environment, an environment in a city plan.

Eliel Saarinen, Finnish architect

EMI's exacting environment[1]

The recorded music industry is polarised between multinational media groups and independent labels, such as the tiny Viper of Liverpool or the nightclub chain, Ministry of Sound, which publishes dance compilations. The big five, Bertelsmann, Sony, EMI, Warner Brothers and Universal, control about 72 per cent of the global market. They grew quickly during the CD boom in the ten years to 1996. Then came a recession and the rise of P2P (person-to-person) transfer technology. *See* Figure 2.1 for more details.

Nowadays, listening to music is as popular as ever, but the recycling of hits from the 1960s and 1970s dampens demand for new material. The large firms hesitate to invest in new talent without the certainty of international sales. Artificially created artistes, targeted at a mass audience, are heavily promoted – for example the winners of the Popstars and Pop Idol competitions. These acts sell few copies outside their home nations and buyers are unlikely to be significant music consumers.

Risks are high. In 2001, EMI had to pay $20 million to Mariah Carey to leave its label after poor CD sales. The following year, however, it renewed its contract with Robbie Williams for an estimated £35 million. The deal gave the company a share of touring and merchandising revenue and further revenues if the star's career took off in the United States.

Major companies spend heavily on advertising; £10 million is the typical annual spend in the United Kingdom. Yet these sums are spread thinly across many labels and artistes. Sales are dominated by pop, rock and dance music (70 per cent) while classical accounts for just 4 per cent.

The average drop in the 2001 European market of 2.3 per cent hid considerable differences among nations; large falls in Germany, Portugal and Eastern Europe outweighed gains in France, Sweden and the United Kingdom. Growth in France, despite its high Internet penetration, supported arguments that investment in new acts pays off. Seventeen of the top twenty albums were from French artistes. Other markets, from Japan and South East Asia to North America, also fell. Acute economic difficulties affected demand in Latin America, especially Argentina, which slumped 24 per cent.

Piracy, both physical and digital, remains a serious problem. Legitimate recordings account for 75 per cent of the world market, publishing takes some 16 per cent and pirate music recordings 9 per cent. Now, a whole generation thinks that music should be free. More than 3 billion music files a month were downloaded from the top four Internet sites in 2001, compared with 2.5 billion CDs sold worldwide. According to the industry trade association, Greece (50 per cent of

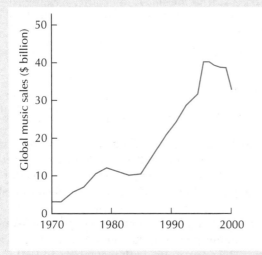
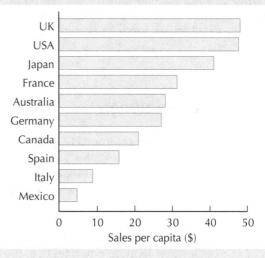

Figure 2.1 Music sales

sales) and Spain (35 per cent) are among the leading territories for music piracy. Taiwan has the capacity to press 8 billion CDs but 'legitimate demand' for only 200 million. About 90 per cent of sales in China are counterfeit. Manufacturers co-operate with governments to enforce anti-piracy legislation. New technology helps in the battle. EMI is using copy protection in Asia and Latin America. In Europe, it is testing a method to prevent stealing, while permitting legitimate personal copies. Yet digital technology also represents an opportunity. Music companies have joined to launch two online services, MusicNet (Bertelsmann, EMI and Warner Music) and Pressplay (Sony and Universal).

There have been many suits, mainly under copyright law, in recent years. In 2002 EMI both won damages from MP3 and sued AOL Time Warner for unauthorised use of its music in films. Bertelsmann was threatened by other major producers over its $90 million investment in Napster, through which, in its heyday, millions of songs were exchanged. United States copyright law allows damages up to $150 000 for every infringement. Also in the United States, the big labels had to pay $146 million to settle charges of price fixing during the 1990s. They admitted that they had been trying to avoid price wars.

Ranked third in the industry, EMI Group is the exception. Unlike the other conglomerates, it depends almost entirely on music. Turnover for 2002 fell 8.5 per cent to £2445.8m, while profit was down 43 per cent to £190.9m. The Recorded Music division, more than four-fifths of the business, accounted for the decline. Sales were down 11 per cent in a global market, which fell some 6 per cent.

The top album was Robbie Williams' *Swing when you're winning*, with 5.4 million sales in the year; in 2001 the Beatles' *I* album had retailed 22 million. EMI handles about 1500 artistes through both world brands – Capitol, Virgin Records and EMI Classics – and some 70 specialist labels such as Abbey Road Studios, Blue Note and Parlophone. Angel, which distributes EMI Classics in the United States, is the oldest trademark in the industry.

The division follows a strategy of using many channels to reach as many people as possible. It licenses its music widely, having agreements with over 70 different companies. Examples include the Internet jukeboxes of Ecast and the streaming technology of Listen.com. EMI also tailors CDs to markets. A David Bowie hits compilation was released in 20 versions. Each nation received the track listing matching Bowie's biggest hits.

The Music Publishing division, the world's largest in this field, produced good growth from its list of hit songwriters and back catalogue. Through offices in 30 countries it trades rights to more than one million compositions from *You are the Sunshine of My Life* to the music from *The Wizard of Oz*. Built on sales of sheet music and piano rolls, business income now comes from: mechanical royalties (55 per cent) paid each time a record is sold; performance revenue (24 per cent) for live and broadcast performances, including the Internet; and synchronisation (13 per cent) when tracks are used in television, films and advertising. Toys, ring-tones and game soundtracks are also becoming important revenue sources. The division's reputation means that artistes and writers who record under non-EMI labels use it for royalty collection.

Introduction

We define the environment of an organisation as *all those elements that lie outside its boundary with which it interacts.*[2] Examples range from trade in the marketplace, where there are exchanges of products for money and pressures of competition, to less tangible influences within, say, the political arena. The number of factors that could be involved is huge.

What happens to an organisation in this complex and ever-changing environment? Is it tossed like a blade of straw among powerful currents or steered like a majestic ship more powerful than the tides? We can apply both metaphors to EMI. In recorded music, it struggles with an onslaught from diversified competitors, technological change and pirates. In publishing, it is the powerful force. Yet recording is most of the business. Will the music industry, and hence the company, thrive again? We cannot tell. Yet, we can see that the powerful forces of falling demand and rising competition for the customer's money pose serious questions. This is the business environment. It presents the organisation with a context in which to succeed, often expressed as a set of *opportunities*. Simultaneously, it poses challenges that must be faced and coped with. Without appropriate responses, these *threats* may lead to the organisation's downfall.

We begin to examine how organisations respond to these external forces in Chapter 4. First, however, we must look at how managers scrutinise and interpret them.

Sensing the environment

We noted that the number of environmental factors is huge. As Kourteli points out, '… managers who recognize the importance of the external environment and, as a result, try to collect as much data as possible, are faced with a strong contradiction, which is the uncertainty of the fast changing environment. This uncertainty relates to all those external events that affect the organization, and evolves from the dynamic and complex relations of all those variables which make up the environment.'[3] To succeed, must managers continually study a vast quantity of external information? No, just as human sensory organs are designed to *both* collect *and* filter out information, so must managers. Their approach is selective; they habitually study only those aspects of the environment that are relevant to them.[4]

Aguilar[5] pioneered studies of managers' environmental scanning. He wanted to know how they gain relevant information, what kinds of information they look for and how they improve their scanning. Figure 2.2 is based on this perspective.

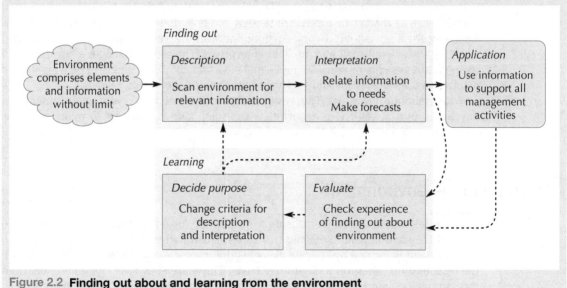

Figure 2.2 Finding out about and learning from the environment

The upper half of the diagram shows the process of finding out. It has two phases related to a manager's need to say:

- this is the way the environment is; and
- this is the environment's impact on the organisation.

Therefore, we see both description and interpretation. First, managers *identify* what they need to know and collect the appropriate information. Second, managers *interpret* the information by relating it to the needs of the job and the organisation. Also, since good management is forward looking, interpretation includes an element of forecasting. More than knowing about the effect of the environment now, managers want to know what it will be.

The lower half of the diagram concerns learning, a theme we shall return to in Chapter 19. The learning process controls the way managers find out. Either formally or informally, they assess how effective their selection has been and consider how to improve it. This is how each organisation develops a view of what is important and not important, and hence finds itself in a unique environment. This is an example of contingency theory mentioned in Chapter 1.

What and how managers scrutinise

Lozada and Calantone[6] compared managers' perceptions of the operating environment with how they collected information. They showed that frequency of scanning was contingent on uncertainty, high rate of change and strong competition. Uncertainty is a common theme. For instance, Sawyerr and others [7] showed that businesses operating in developing countries attend more to the wider, unpredictable economic and political sectors than those in developed nations, who pay more attention to the operating environments of markets and competition. In another study, Tyler and others[8] found that rich information sources, such as discussions with workers, customers or suppliers, were used more than less rich ones, such as financial statements and letters, when conditions were unstable or unpredictable. This extends Mintzberg's observation, *see* Chapter 1, that managers generally emphasised informal, oral information gathering. Such processes are quick yet incomplete. However, they help in deciding when formal studies, such as market research, are needed and ensure they yield the greatest benefit. Reaching for a normative theory, Analoui and Karami[9] recommend the use of formal scanning systems in small and medium enterprises. The senior manager's 'awareness of the potential benefits of considering formal environmental scanning will be a significant determinant of the success and survival of the firm in long term'.

Where should one start? The systems view of organisations and environment has developed into a well-tried, descriptive approach that enables us to make progress and helps comparison with the work of others.

Describing the environment

We have just noted the value of using a framework for our description. It is useful to think of the environment as having two zones, illustrated in Figure 2.3. The *operating environment* is formed by specific elements that have clear and direct interactions with the organisation, often on a day-to-day basis. These are shown as customers, distributors, suppliers, competitors, investors and regulators. Remember that the list is typical, but may be longer or shorter, depending on the organisation and the manager's purpose in studying the environment. Successful organisations understand well their operating environments and collect information on all elements so that they can respond quickly to changes. The *wider environment* contains the broader factors that establish the context within which the operating environment exists. We refer to it as wider because its influence is often indirect, occurring gradually over a long period. We can also refer to a third zone, outside the wider environment. This contains, so to speak, everything else. Nevertheless, managers perceive these elements as so remote as to be irrelevant. In practice, the boundaries around the environments will be neither clear nor fixed; the diagram shows this with irregular edges.

Figure 2.3 also includes the international environment, drawn as a third dimension. Shown this way, it illustrates how international issues permeate all aspects of the environment. In the music industry, for example, both the operating and the wider environments are global. There are few differences between technology and piracy problems throughout the world. Yet, as we saw in the opening case, trading environments in different countries are so different that EMI and competitors run different businesses in these locations. The layers in Figure 2.3 remind us that managers' mappings will be contingent on which region they are operating in.

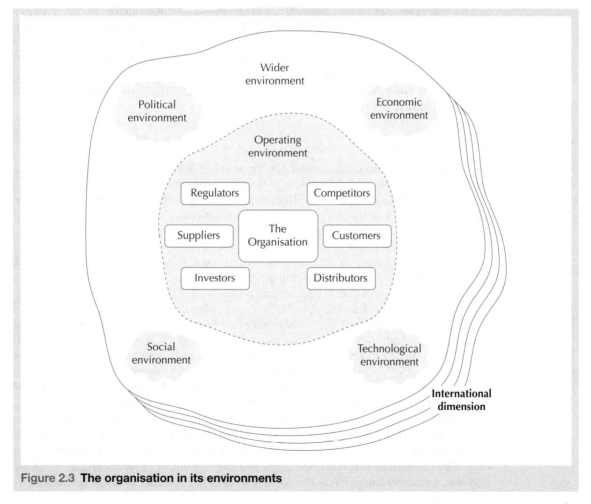

Figure 2.3 The organisation in its environments

The operating environment

■ Customers

'First, know your customer' is a valuable adage for the market-oriented organisation. Serving the needs of customers is its key purpose and if they are not satisfied, the organisation will fail. Usually, the identity of the customer is clear. For example, retail clothing shops deal with individual shoppers whose money is exchanged for goods. Other relationships are more complicated. If I buy Coca-Cola from a supermarket, I am a customer of that store yet what is my link to the Coca-Cola Company? The product will almost certainly have been supplied to the store by a bottling company with a licence to mix the special syrup with water, sugar and gas. Cadbury-Schweppes performs this function in the United Kingdom. Further, I may have bought the drink for consumption by someone else. The Coca-Cola Company is faced with a difficult problem. Many consumers are not customers. Where should it focus its marketing effort? It needs to make sure that sufficient bottlers and distributors make Coca-Cola available while, simultaneously, co-operating with them in persuading individuals to consume it.

The difference between customers and consumers is highlighted in many public and personal service organisations. Here the latter become clients, patients or students, who often do not pay for the services they receive. For the supplying organisation, the problem is to show that the needs of the clients are being satisfied while the paying authority is receiving value for money.

Getting to know who customers are and what they want is the core task of marketing, explained in Chapter 16.

■ Competitors

The competitors of an organisation are those other organisations that vie with it for resources. The most obvious contest is over winning customers and gaining the revenue that they bring. While the price of products is an important factor, there are few cases where it is the only element in the customers' choice. For a firm to succeed in price competition there must be enough customers sensitive to prices and the firm must show that it is among the cheapest sellers.

Among United Kingdom supermarkets, Asda uses its buying power as part of the Wal-Mart group to follow a price policy. In offering keen prices every day, extended to non-food items, it concentrates on customers who do not trust continually changing promotions, *see* Exhibit 2.1. Many companies do not engage in direct price competition; there has not been a serious price war in food retailing since the early 1970s. Poor results have shown the low-price strategy of Somerfield (merged with Kwiksave in 1998) to be vulnerable to pressure from both leaders and newcomers with lower costs.[10] Competition from these *limited assortment discounters* intensified from the 1980s, especially in the north of England. Entrants from other EU countries include Aldi (Germany), Netto (Denmark) and Ed (France).

Winning customers depends on more than price. Customers' perceptions of value are important. Depending on the industry, value means a balance among quality, reliability, responsiveness to needs, service and speed. In the music business, for example, the name of the artiste plays the major role in determining a purchase decision, provided the price is not far out of line. A customer may be influenced by

Exhibit 2.1 Asda: competing on price?

One of the features of the past 12 months has been the out performance of Asda, the third-largest supermarket.

'Many analysts attribute this to its huge strength in non-foods. "They have shown everybody a clean pair of heels in the UK for the past year," said one. "They have made an enormous breakthrough in non-food."

'... it is thought to be showing high double-digit sales increases. ... while a few years ago it was selling non-food products to one in six of its customers, that figure has now changed to one in three.'[11]

price, however, to prefer one distribution channel. This accounts for the rise in online shopping for commodities such as CDs and books.

Competition is not restricted to profit-making businesses. For instance, we see that universities compete with each other to attract students who, in most European countries, either pay a fixed price or do not pay fees at all. Course content, location and reputation are important in applicants' decision making.[12] Further, competition for all organisations is not confined to gaining customers. Other resources, from raw materials to capital investment and from personnel to ideas and innovations, have to be contended for.

Given the importance of the competitive environment, it is not surprising that companies spend effort in gathering information on rivals' behaviour. Some is easy to obtain. The leading chain of department stores, John Lewis Partnership, claims to be 'Never knowingly undersold'. It employs 'Undersold Officers' to regularly scan all other local shops to check that no one is beating its prices. Similarly, it is good practice for manufacturers to buy competing goods, for hotel managers to stay at rivals' premises, for editors to read opponents' publications and even for chefs to eat out.

Regulators

Regulators have power to control, legislate or directly influence an organisation's policies and practices. Industry regulators, the so-called 'watchdogs', became well known in the United Kingdom as utility companies were transferred from state to private ownership. OFGEM,[13] for example, seeks to balance the interests of customers and companies in an industry where competition is limited. Yet, there are many more regulators than these and we shall look at some examples. They can be placed into three groups: statutory and voluntary regulators and self-appointed advocates.

Statutory regulators are set up by governments to ensure that legislation is followed, the rights of individuals are protected and the interests of the nation as a whole are advanced. Most aspects of organisational life are affected. Examples covering most organisations include: the Equal Opportunities Commission, which oversees the application of legislation in personnel management; the Health and Safety Executive, which supervises products and work practices; Trading Standards departments, which act upon breaches of consumer protection legislation. Many countries have equivalent establishments. Other bodies have roles within particular industries: the Civil Aviation Authority, the Independent Television Commission and the Nuclear Inspectorate. Yet others have international jurisdiction. These exist within trading blocs, such as the competition monitoring offices within the EU, or under wider international agreements. IATA, the International Air Transport

Authority, regulates many aspects of its industry from safety to routes and prices; the International Organization for Standardization brings together national standards offices; the International Telecommunication Union works on technical standards and regional interconnections.

Voluntary regulators are those established by groups of firms in certain fields or industries. Trade associations may perform this function although they are frequently formed to share information and exert pressure on governments. In most countries, concerted action to, say, control supplies or prices is illegal so these voluntary regulators cover other issues. The United Kingdom Press Complaints Commission was established by newspaper companies to study complaints and apply moral pressure to non-compliant publications. The intention was to forestall the setting up of a statutory body. One role of professional associations, for instance in accounting, engineering, law and medicine, is to regulate the behaviour of members.

Self-appointed advocates are outside interest groups whose power or influence is so great that they constrain an organisation's actions. They do not have official status, but are often perceived by managers as *stakeholders*, *see* Chapter 5. Not only do associations such as Greenpeace call for changes in business practice, but also they increasingly expect to be consulted when organisations such as Shell seek licences to exploit natural resources. Groups of customers, such as the Post Office Users' National Council, exert pressure over prices and service standards. The verdicts of consumers' associations, now co-operating across Europe, influence the sales of products and indirectly set standards. Trade unions have often succeeded in regulating employment practices.

Given the importance of regulators to many organisations, many respond by appointing managers with the responsibility of dealing with them. In firms from financial services to utility companies, for example, there are compliance departments whose role is to ensure that there is no breach of rules and codes of practice. Health and safety and equal opportunities questions are often dealt with by specialists in the personnel department.

Many industries do not have regulators dealing regularly with firms. We would then not include them in the diagram (Figure 2.3). The music industry, for example, has seen states bringing actions for unfair commercial practice. These actions are uncommon, however, and managers would perceive governments to be part of their wider environment.

■ Suppliers

Suppliers provide resources of all kinds. For retailers, the cost of goods bought for resale can amount to more than three-quarters of all costs. Consequently, the buying department occupies a significant role. Being able to source the best goods at the keenest prices is a key success factor. This applies especially to those relying on the ability to put the lowest-priced goods on the shelf. Supplies cover more than raw materials, however. The organisation needs capital goods, from vehicles and equipment to land and buildings; other organisations supply the funds to finance these acquisitions; yet others provide personnel, either as employment agencies or as direct employers of subcontract staff.

Many organisations argue that it is best not to rely on one supplier of whatever resource is being obtained. Either use several simultaneously or, in major purchases, make each contract the subject of open tender. Having a sole supplier brings with it the risk associated with too much dependence and severe problems if that company goes out of business. Motor assemblers, such as Volkswagen, had a tradition of sourcing key electrical components from two or three manufacturers, so-called *multiple sourcing*.

The trend in modern supply chains, however, is to integrate and deepen the supplier–organisation links. Sharing information, often through direct computer connections, leads to savings in stock levels and improved service through just-in-time deliveries. Common efforts in product improvement are also being fostered. Therefore, the trend in industries such as car assembly is towards *single sourcing*. In aircraft, it may seem less risky to buy from more than one manufacturer, but buying from more than one entails extra internal costs in pilot training, maintenance, scheduling and so on. British Airways and easyJet, for example, keep with Boeing jets to avoid these *switching costs*.

Distributors

Distributors handle the organisation's products and ensure that they reach the customer. Their function is to add value to the product by ensuring that it is available at the right place and in quantities that the customer wishes to buy. In some industries, such as cars, manufacturers have built networks through granting exclusive dealerships. They are justified by reference to the need to supply spares and after-sales service. The European Commission has challenged the practice because it restricts others from supplying new cars and creates barriers for new manufacturers. In the UK, Daewoo bypassed entry problems by setting up sales outlets in very small premises and contracting servicing to the specialist repairers, Halfords.

Access to crowded distribution channels is a constraint on the growth of small and medium-sized companies with good ideas. In service industries, franchising is one way of overcoming this problem. An innovator can achieve rapid exploitation of a new idea before imitators enter the market. Many restaurants, hotels, film processors, printers and household service companies are franchise operations. Each business is owned and managed locally, paying fees and royalties to the franchisor in exchange for supplies, technical support, marketing and so on.

The transport and warehousing of products, usually known as logistics, is often a critical part of an organisation's operating environment. Mothercare, retailer of baby and maternity goods, found this out when its new distribution warehouse at Daventry, run by Tibbett and Britten, went wrong. Not only did the building turn out to be too small, but also poor sales data meant that the new stock holding system did not work. Restricted flows hurt Christmas sales. The company's logistics costs for 2001 were reported as £18.3 million, or 8 per cent of turnover.[14]

Deepening of linkages with suppliers was mentioned in the previous section. The same can be seen in distribution. Partners set up supply chains, often to manage every stage of the flow of a product from source to the customer's basket. Through integration of information and management systems, the chain behaves as a single organisation even though each stage consists of separate businesses. The closing case in this chapter presents a good example.

Investors

The final element of our model of the operating environment is the group of investors. These range from banks providing short-term finance to sustain the business on a daily basis, to shareholders and lenders of long-term capital whose commitment may last for years. Governments are often willing to provide grants and loans if it is in their national interest to do so. EU membership restricts such action, however, if it can be shown to damage businesses elsewhere.

For sources of long-term capital, national differences are clearly seen. The United Kingdom and United States have well-developed stock markets with ready flows of funds for new investment. On the other hand, different traditions and the illiquid stock markets in Germany and Italy mean that banks provide more long-term finance as loans. Loans among business groupings are also common in Japan and South Korea.

■ Managing the operating environment

A summary of the operating environment is shown in Figure 2.4. This develops the centre of Figure 2.3 by adding examples of links representing flows of products, cash, operating information and influence. Operating information, being the day-to-day flows of data related to the exchange of products and cash, is separated from 'influence' to suggest that the latter is different in kind. Besides the formal links among elements of the system, there is much unstructured, informal information passing among them. Examples range from advertising by competitors to political pressure exerted by regulators. In combination, all the flows of Figure 2.4 represent the dynamics of the system, enabling it to 'operate'.

Organisations handle links with their operating environments by allocating specialists to roles from marketing to investor relations. These *boundary-spanning roles* usually focus on one aspect of the environment. This gives us clues as to how the vast quantity of information is coped with. The perspectives of the distribution manager or the financial accountant are purposeful; they are based on a key principle of management – the value of specialisation. Together, these managers handle the complexity faced by the organisation every day. In systems terms they map the complexity of the environment. The more complex the environment, the greater is the number and variety of such roles.

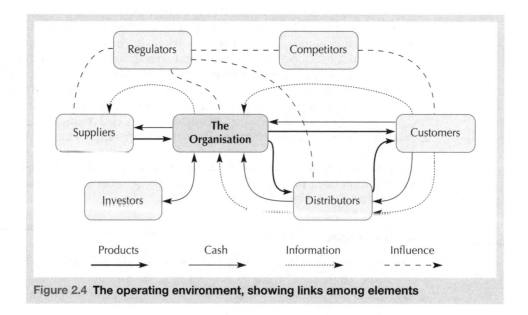

Figure 2.4 The operating environment, showing links among elements

Focus on the operating environment has its dangers. What if it changes unexpectedly? To anticipate this possibility, and prepare responses, managers need to develop an understanding beyond the immediate. They must take a view of the world over the horizon. Such broader and deeper understanding comes from investigation of the wider environment, which sets the context in which operating activity occurs.

The wider environment

Elements in the wider environment influence the organisation in ways whose scope differs from the behaviour we have discussed. While the boundary between the two environmental layers is rather arbitrary, we can separate them by the following ideas:

■ *Operating environment*
The organisation is engaged in regular, two-way interaction with other elements of its operating environment. There are exchanges of products, money, information and influence as shown in Figure 2.4.

■ *Wider environment*
The organisation is influenced by elements in the wider environment, either directly or through changes in its operating environment. Influence is usually one-way, that is inwards. Only the largest organisations can exert much sway over the wider world and, even then, the effect will be limited.

The music industry illustrates this point. Tiny Viper records publishes tracks of local bands, distributes them through several local shops and hopes occasionally to have examples played on local radio stations. The emphasis is on local. Customers, distributors and advertisers are concentrated in the city where the bands have a following. Viper competes only indirectly with the major labels. These, and all other elements of the music industry, lie in its wider environment. In contrast, EMI, as one of the majors, would paint a different picture. Its rivals, with whom it also co-operates in distribution and dealing with governments on anti-piracy work, now lie within its operating environment. Similarly, it works with broadcasting media to promote music and develop new shows or other products. A sketch of the differences between these perspectives is shown in Figure 2.5.

How do we identify and make sense of the wider environment? We made a start in constructing Figure 2.5 by recognising markets and the effects of incomes and tastes. We could continue in this *ad hoc* way but, rather than list items as they occur to us, we could use one of several classifications. Their advantage is that they act as checklists, ensuring a comprehensive view. One well-known method is known by its PEST acronym. It is valuable to think of the environment as made up of political, economic, social and technological factors. (Others use STEP, or add more elements, to give PESTLE. We include such extra elements within the PEST categories.)

■ The political environment

The political environment of organisations comprises both the formal legal framework established by governments to regulate behaviour and the often more complex and subtle relationships among governments and organisations involving power,

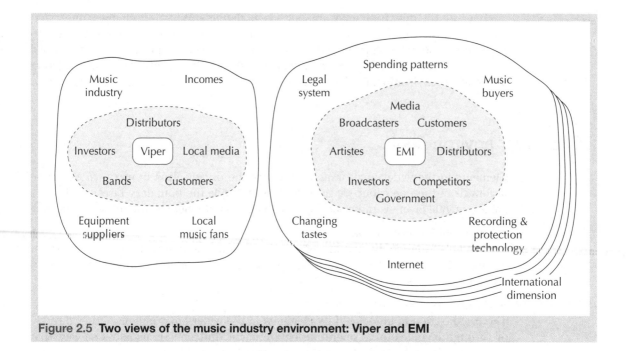

Figure 2.5 Two views of the music industry environment: Viper and EMI

pressure and influence. Especially for large organisations operating in more than one country, awareness of and sensitivity to these influences can be very important in achieving success.

Before looking at the international dimension, let us note three aspects of government–organisation links in one country:

■ *The legal system* establishes a framework for operations. Even in nominally 'free' markets, there are many controls on behaviour. Some laws state what organisations must do: paying taxes and minimum wages; recruiting fairly; meeting safety standards. Other laws prescribe limits, stating what they must not do: banks must not allow balances to fall below defined levels; effluent producers have toxicity limits; publications of all kinds are censored; charitable and religious organisations have the scope of their activities restricted.

■ *Governments encompass attitudes* that either favour or hinder different types of organisation and organisational behaviour. When *laissez-faire* views prevail, companies may find it easier to pursue policies such as growth by merger without the state mounting an investigation. Interventionist governments, on the other hand, press the national interest upon companies. In France of the 1990s, President Chirac's government followed Gaullist habits of intervention by creating large national groups. For instance, fearing the impact of international competition, Chirac forced the 1996 combination of the defence companies Aerospatiale and Dassault to form a group larger than British Aerospace or DASA. This merger was against the wishes of the profitable, privately owned Dassault.[15]

■ *Governments seek to create a favourable economic and social environment.* This raises business confidence and, consequently, the willingness to invest and grow. For example, the favourable economic environment of the United Kingdom, coupled with efforts to welcome and integrate visiting managers and their families, are seen as the main reasons why the United Kingdom has received up to half the investment into the European Union by companies from South-East Asia.

Since governmental influences vary from country to country, international businesses face extra problems compared with those operating within one state. They must bear *political risk*. This is the threat of loss of assets, income or control through political actions of host governments, or indeed others. Revolutionary governments seize assets of companies and individuals associated with previous regimes; sanctions are sometimes imposed by leading powers, often the United States. The Iran and Libya Sanctions Act was enacted by the US congress in 1996 and renewed in 2001. It penalises foreign companies that provide large new petroleum investments or violate existing UN prohibitions in those countries. The sanctions can be waived if doing so is in the US national interest. US companies are barred from transactions with Iran or Libya.[16]

The effect of political risk can be seen in Eastern Europe. After the 'velvet revolution' of 1989, Czechoslovakia was quick to establish a market economy and a central bank and remove exchange controls. It established or extended its legal code covering company activities including a formal framework for joint ventures. Internal tensions were alleviated by a peaceful split between Slovakia and the Czech Republic. The former underwent a shift to the political left and began to lag, while the latter proceeded to 'Westernise' its institutions more rapidly and receive inward investment. Both nations were among those planning to join the EU in 2004.

International alliances

A notable change in the international political framework is the growth of international trade alliances. The two most important are the EU and NAFTA:

- With 15 member nations in 2002, and a further 13 expected to join, the European Union is the most developed and integrated grouping in the world. Common decisions cover agriculture, economics, energy, fishing, trade, transport and the physical environment. Beyond economic co-operation, members have agreed to work together in foreign policy and aspects of justice and home policy. At the time of writing, all except the UK accept the 'Social Chapter' on workers' rights. The single market, formally completed for 1993, means that there are few constraints on moving products or assets among members. Some other countries, such as Norway, Iceland and Liechtenstein, are in the economic zone but not the EU.

- The North American Free Trade Agreement was signed in 1992 by Canada, Mexico and the United States. Its initial policies cover: phased abolition of tariffs on agricultural products and cars; access to Mexican operations for other road hauliers; and the raising of many standards in Mexico, including legal protection for patents and copyright.

Other groupings either exist (such as the Economic Community of West African States) or are proposed. Few have been successful. In some cases, member governments are rivalrous and unstable and the community's purpose is limited by stagnation of intra-regional trade. The ECOWAS countries, for example, rely on exporting agricultural and mineral products to the industrialised countries in exchange for manufactured goods. Furthermore, they suffer from poor infrastructure. Sub-Saharan Africa, excepting South Africa, has some 10 per cent of the world's population and less than 1 per cent of its telephone lines.[17]

Blocs can be welcomed by companies and other organisations as ways of reducing risk for those who operate within them. Yet there are two dangers. First, economic competition may develop into greater tension between the alliances. Such difficulties have shown themselves in disputes between the EU and the United States over subsidies to both agriculture and new aircraft. In 2003, a contract to power the new A400M military transport was awarded by Airbus Military to the EuroProp International consortium (EPI). A spokesman for the United States engine maker Pratt & Whitney complained that, although it had submitted the lower bid, 'We didn't have a chance anyway'. To justify backing EPI, European governments referred to the policy of supporting industrial integration and to their wish to place defence contracts at home.[18] The second danger is that alliances may further develop into three powerful trading blocs – America, Europe and the Pacific Rim. Whatever their form, they will have profound effects on the management of international operations.

Many organisations have to cope with a political environment rendered more complex by the overlapping and conflicting responsibilities of different authorities. SNCB, the Belgian state railway, is encouraged by the EU to plan and invest in high-speed lines as part of the development of the European transport infrastructure. Such investments are to cut travel times between Brussels and Amsterdam, Cologne, London or Paris by more than an hour. Simultaneously the national government seeks to rein in public spending while trying to satisfy regional aspirations. Railway investments in competing Flanders and Wallonia have to be balanced in spite of marked differences in costs and benefits of investment in the two parts of the country.[19]

■ The economic environment

The economic environment influences both the costs and the revenues associated with operating in different locations. Within a national economic system, we can examine the general health and stability of the economic system using measures such as: general demand; per capita income; inflation; interest rates; and employment. When interest rates are high, for instance, consumers are less willing to borrow to make purchases and demand falls. This has strong effects in house buying markets, in turn influencing demand for goods and services associated with moving house. Examples range from removal services themselves to sales of interior decorating and other materials.

Advantages of different nations

There is more to the economic environment, however, than general measures of the economy. Porter presents a framework for comparing the characteristics of nations.[20] He argues that competing firms with different home bases have different advantages, summarised by the four factors shown in Figure 2.6. A home base in the right nation does not guarantee success since it is up to firms to seize opportunities. On the other hand, being based in the wrong nation raises problems. Firms seeking to build new strategies, engage in new activities, establish regional headquarters or make acquisitions in other countries should look for nations that present a favourable pattern. Rather than seek quiet backwaters, Porter argues that ambitious companies should base themselves in national environments where standards are high. Figure 2.6 enables us to pick out the special national factors behind the success of Italian shoe manufacturers. Throughout the industry, there are medium-sized family companies with a history of vigorous competition; local support comes from world-class leather suppliers and designers, enhanced by the mutually supportive industries such as gloves and handbags.

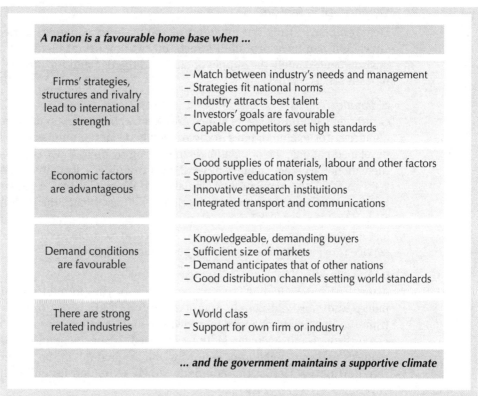

Figure 2.6 **Factors behind the relative advantages of nations**

As with the political environment, study of the economic environment becomes more complex and risky for international transactions. The missions of many charities, including the International Red Cross, Médecins sans Frontières and Oxfam, take them into areas where the 'business' infrastructure is weak. In 1994, conflict in Rwanda caused the displacement of refugees into neighbouring countries, Tanzania or Zaire, whose governments were themselves facing economic difficulties. Regional offices of the charities in these border areas had often relied for international links on the dependable banking and communication systems within Rwanda. After the collapse, even taken-for-granted activities such as transferring money became very difficult. The only way to pay local staff was to send messengers from Europe with sufficient United States dollars to be exchanged through informal markets.

The Rwandan example, though easily recognised by managers with similar field experience, is atypical. Government policies, especially within blocs, aim towards stable exchange rates and converging economic indicators. It is believed that business investment and growth will be helped by calm economic conditions. Advocates of European monetary union, for instance, make this case.

The social environment

Sometimes called *societal* or *sociocultural*, the social environment refers to the elements that make up and give unique identity to what we broadly call society. A general description is helped by looking at demographic, geographic and cultural factors.

Demographic factors

Demographers study the make-up of populations. Changes generally take place slowly but can have profound effects on two important elements of the operating environment, namely the supply of staff and the demand for products. The most significant are as follows:

■ *Population*

Clearly, demand for products will be affected by changes in population. Most European countries, for example, have static or slowly declining numbers while, in some less-developed nations, the population is increasing by up to 3 per cent per annum. Within the national average, changes at local level can differ substantially. For instance, from 1991 to 1995, the population of England and Wales rose by 1.4 per cent. Yet some districts grew at more than five times this rate: Forest Heath, the Suffolk district around Newmarket, recorded 13 per cent and Bracknell, 9 per cent. In contrast, Scunthorpe lost 4.6 per cent of its people with Ipswich next at 4 per cent.[21] The implications for service providers from schools to supermarkets are clear.

■ *Age structure*

After birth rates decline, the age structure of the population shifts. With fewer babies and more old people, the demand for all kinds of products changes. Apart from the immediate changes in midwifery and geriatric care services, other trends come through more slowly. Mothercare used to specialise in clothes for expectant mothers and young children. Following the seminal fall in the United Kingdom birth rate during the 1970s, the company slowly extended its childrenswear range to cover ages up to 12 years old.

The increase in the numbers of healthy retired people creates new markets for holidays and leisure activities, especially at off-peak periods. The 2001 census confirmed, for the first time, more people aged over 60 than under 16. Further, as Table 2.1 shows,[22] a further rise in the numbers of very old people is expected. Japan's population is ageing more quickly. The 15 per cent now over 65 is expected to reach 26 per cent by 2025. Japan's largest cosmetics company, Shiseido, finds its fastest growing lines are lotions to smooth wrinkles and resist baldness.[23]

Changes in age structure compound population shifts to influence the supply of labour. Shortage of skilled and experienced people has led many companies to recruit or retain older staff, *see* Exhibit 2.2.

Exhibit 2.2 Advantages of age

Nationwide, Britain's biggest building society, offers its 15 000 employees the option of working until 70, subject to attendance and health checks. The idea is to reduce staff turnover and retain experience and talent. It had suffered from losing older employees, its corporate memory, after the 1987 merger with Anglia Building Society.

In 1999, Nationwide looked to the often-ignored under-25s and over-50s for its IT recruitment. Turnover among these segments is just 4 per cent compared with averages of 10 per cent for Nationwide and 17 per cent in the financial services industry. Over-50s comprise 10 per cent of the society's staff, compared with 1 per cent in 1989. Many people at 60 still have children at university.[24]

■ *Income distribution*

In democratic countries, shifts in income distribution are part of the battleground of party politics. There are many countries, however, where differentials are much higher than in Europe. Brazil is among the world's richest countries yet has many of its poorest people. Egypt, a nominally poor country, is a leading market for exported Mercedes-Benz cars.

Table 2.1 **The ageing population of the United Kingdom**

	1901	1931	1961	1991	2001	2011
Total (millions)	38.2	46.0	52.8	57.8	58.8	61.2
School (5–15)	n.a.	n.a.	17.2%	13.6%	14.2%	13.5%
65–74	3.3%	5.3%	7.5%	8.8%	8.4%	8.8%
75–84	1.2%	1.8%	3.6%	5.4%	5.6%	5.4%
85+	0.2%	0.3%	0.7%	1.6%	1.9%	2.4%
Total 65+	4.7%	7.4%	11.8%	15.8%	15.9%	16.6%

Geographic factors

In examining geographic factors, the manager is trying to find out whether operating at one location is superior to operating at another. Relevant questions are: location of raw materials; sources of energy and labour; location of markets; transport infrastructure; availability of sites; and climate. Different factors matter to different firms. When planning a new store, a supermarket chain evaluates accessibility, competition, the cost of land and the local population. Many firms are attracted to London because of the large numbers already there, especially in the financial sector. One survey of European locations ranked the city first on the most important factor – the availability of qualified staff. London is also seen as having easy international access; high quality telecommunications; most free office space; and is the top city for the range of languages spoken. Another study, on e-business, added reliable electricity supply and fibre bandwidth to this list.[25]

Cultural factors

Under the heading of culture, we examine the values and attitudes of people – especially as customers or employees – and how these affect the organisation. One difficulty is that these issues are so much part of the taken-for-granted that we fail to recognise them. To overcome this, we can start by examining how values and attitudes are changing in our society and then move on to study others. Learning about other cultures leads to reflection on our own. Here we shall note some main changes, leaving intercultural comparisons until Chapter 4.

It has become commonplace to argue that society is changing at a pace never seen before. In these dangerous, 'turbulent times',[26] everything in society is challenged and transformed. New realities do not fit the old order. Some offer assistance through predicting where we are going, others tell us how to cope. Yet, whether our age is any more irregular, erratic and discontinuous than any other is doubtful. Social change is normal. And, since all parts of social and cultural life are interconnected, change is widespread. Exhibit 2.3 lists some areas where our attitudes and values change.

Exhibit 2.3 Challenging cultural changes

- *The individual* – the nature of self; gender; notions of responsibility; privacy; housing; health; ageing.

- *The social person* – one's behaviour and others; attitudes to smoking, drinking, driving; leisure; mass behaviour – concerts, crowds, trade unions; the structure of society – wealth, place, race; religion; the law.

- *The family* – definition of family; single parents; role of grandparents and care for them; parenthood and the 'housewife'; children's rights.

- *Employment* – attitudes to work and employment; women as employees and leaders; pressure for equal opportunity; retirement.

- *Organisations* – function and power of organisations; privatisation; employers or exploiters?

- *Mankind and the environment* – attitudes to: animal rights; the purpose of the countryside; pollution and waste; the function of cities; congestion.

- *Intellectual life* – the function of education – training or enlightenment? The arts; media; control of science and technology.

- *The nation* – political system; attitudes to monarchy, presidency, etc., nationalism.

- *Europe* – economic fortress; integrated harmony; centralisation versus sovereignty; currency.

The technological environment

Technology is the application of knowledge to products and processes. Clearly, advances can affect both aspects. For example, the development of scanning systems, using light or ultrasound, has applications in fields as diverse as medicine and retailing. The processes of diagnosing heart problems or counting groceries at the checkout have been transformed. Suppliers have been able to offer new products to support these innovations, both in the equipment itself and in associated machines from couches and conveyors to computers for processing the information.

It has been argued that one benefit of large scale is the ability to develop technology more quickly. This comes from more spending on research and the faster accumulation of operating experience. Companies from pharmaceutical manufacturers to innovative service providers have followed this policy. Yet it is important to distinguish between transferable and embedded knowledge.[27] The former, incorporated in products, publications or even the minds of individuals, can move quickly. A rival can buy and dismantle a machine to discover its parts and method of operation; information on innovations appears in publications from patent applications and learned journals to instruction books; technologists with needed expertise can be recruited. Embedded knowledge, on the other hand, is neither written down nor possessed by individuals; it is embedded within teams or even whole organisations. While it is easy to buy a Toyota car, dismantling it will yield few clues about how its production has been organised.

Recognising the transferable nature of much knowledge, organisations draw on the technological environment as a source of product and process innovation. They maintain close contacts with equipment suppliers and research organisations.

Woollen carpet weavers, for example, have access to process innovations through both the Wool Industry Research Association and loom manufacturers such as Cobbles. Since the knowledge is shared, each does not require large scale to benefit from the developments. There is more on technology and innovation in Chapter 17.

Technological innovation does not stand around, so to speak, awaiting ready applications. Winning firms are those that recognise the possibilities presented by new ideas and apply them both quickly and in imaginative ways. The bar coding of consumer products began for improving the management of retail stocks. Leading companies, however, soon saw the opportunities presented by collecting detailed information on each customer. Hence the creation of loyalty cards. Their dual functions are to reward customers according to how much they spend and to capture detailed information on what each is buying. Therefore, promotions can be targeted and stores can ensure that more of the goods bought by high-spending customers are on display. Personalisation and improved service levels are keys to customer retention. This race to apply innovations does not stop. Extensions of self-service to self-billing have been pioneered by Albert Heijn, in The Netherlands, and Safeway in Britain. Even the bar code may not survive. Its one-dimensional form limits the information to one serial number. It may be replaced by new patterns containing up to 2000 characters, or by cheap radio-sensitive chips.[28]

The international dimension

Through the examples of operating and wider environments, we have seen different issues that must be confronted when the organisation has interests in more than one country. The international dimension is best seen not as yet another environment but as a number of layers suggested in Figure 2.3. Each layer represents a nation or region and contains all the PEST factors. Therefore, there are multiple political, economic, social and technological environments. Their similarities and differences have implications for all organisations.

A first glance at the PEST factors may suggest that technology displays the greatest uniformity across the world and hence fewest problems in its global management. Harmonisation of products is a trend picked out by authors such as Levitt.[29] He saw large-scale production of standardised items as so cheap that it is better to treat the world as a single market than as many separate ones. Levitt went beyond recognising the harmonisation of products and production systems. For him, differences in cultural preferences, national standards and tastes, and even business organisations themselves, were remnants of the past.

Levitt cited as evidence changes in automatic washing machines in Europe from the 1960s. Hoover, a United States owned company with a strong market share in the United Kingdom, sought to increase its sales in other countries. It analysed carefully each national market and tried to adapt its products to match local preferences. For instance, German and Swedish consumers were used to tall, wide and strong-looking casings, stainless steel drums, 6 kg capacity and high spin speed. In Sweden, water heating was not normally required. In Germany, however, it was demanded as users preferred to wash at temperatures higher than available from the domestic system. Italians, on the other hand, expected smaller, brightly coloured casings, enamelled drums with only 4 kg capacity and lower spin speed. The effect on Hoover's policy was that it had to bear extra costs to meet just some variations in preference. To these had to be added trade tariffs, as the United Kingdom did not join the EEC until 1971. In retrospect, Levitt argued that there was already ample evidence of the 'cheap and cheerful' Italian models, including Indesit and Zanussi, making headway in all markets, including Germany and Sweden. Hoover ought to have standardised production on a simple model and used promotion to overcome previously apparent differences between markets. Today, the European market for automatic washers displays much greater homogeneity.

To counter Levitt's convergence argument, we can point to its narrow focus on a few manufactured goods. Rugman[30] mounts a challenge by arguing that markets are not integrating globally but forming into clusters, especially the triad of Europe, the United States and Japan. Companies, and trade, operate on a regional level. We can also note that many differences in processes occur throughout the world. For example, the technology of cultivation, from the hand-held hoe to the deep plough, is deeply embedded in local factors from physical conditions and labour costs to family structures and cultural patterns. Differences in other of the PEST environments are perhaps more obvious. Whether they are converging or diverging, and how international organisations cope with trends, are questions raised again in Chapter 4.

Interpreting the environment

Interpretation is the second stage shown in Figure 2.2. Successful organisations display the ability to link the gathering of information to their purposes. This can be done by focusing attention on key success factors. How are they selected?

Key factors have the following characteristics:

- they have *continuing influence* on the project, department or organisation;
- they affect the *relationships* between the organisation and others in the environment;
- their influence is *substantial* – they are worth much money.

Examples vary from manager to manager, firm to firm and industry to industry. We can illustrate the need for identifying key success factors by referring to a case that went wrong. Gilad and others[31] describe a pharmaceutical company project. The managers were considering whether to conduct a large-scale pilot production run of a new nutritional product. Judgements had to be made on market potential and competitors' strategies. Exhibit 2.4 lists items of environmental information thought by managers to be relevant.

Exhibit 2.4 New product pilot project: relevant environment information

Market
Who are the competitors? *
Market size, present and future *
Competitors' prices *
Who might enter the market?
Substitutes and competing products
Competitors' track records
Competitors and our customers
Consumers' views of new product
v. rivals

Technical
Total costs for rival products *
Raw material supplies *
Competitors' development efforts *
Competitors' costs for new products *
State of technology *

Other
Links between competitors and parent companies

Asterisks identify the most important.

The study brought out several problems with collecting information in the lists: it was difficult to learn about competitors' technologies; managers were more satisfied with their marketing intelligence than their technical intelligence; senior managers were more likely to find gaps in information, reflecting the filtering that often takes place in hierarchies. Overconfidence about their firm's technical competence meant that the managers were surprised when competitors launched low-cost products or dropped prices. Furthermore, access to the United States market was hampered by restrictions imposed by the Food and Drug Administration, an environmental question that did not figure in the original success factor list.

■ Forecasting

Noting that key factors have a continuing influence over a long period, managers need to go beyond descriptions of the present environment towards anticipation of the future. There are various forecasting methods depending on whether data are quantitative or qualitative.

Quantitative methods

These models use numerical techniques with historical data. We divide them into causal and time-series modelling.

■ *Causal models attempt to establish patterns of relationships that decide the behaviour of the variables in question.*

For instance, many believe that sales from DIY stores are closely linked to the numbers of people who move home. Then, since house purchase data are readily available, and moves precede the spending on carpets, curtains, finishes and furnishings, this approach gives a better forecast. A feature of the wider environment (house moves) explains how sales, in the DIY stores' operating environment, behave. Or does it? *See* Exhibit 2.5.

Exhibit 2.5 Forecast-it-yourself

Curiously, DIY is an example of a 'common sense' trap discussed in Chapter 1. Leaver and Al-Zubaidi[32] show the close correlation of house moves and DIY sales during the boom of the 1980s. Growth in both variables reinforced beliefs in the causal link, especially among the leading retailers who were consolidating their hold on the market during this period. Yet, from 1989 to 1993, the two variables displayed negative correlation; that is, higher DIY sales related to fewer house moves. Either consumer behaviour changed around 1988 or the common sense was wrong in the first place!

After examining a range of variables, the authors show that DIY sales over the whole period can be linked to four factors: house *prices*; number of owner-occupiers; level of car ownership; and superstore floor space. Together, these four variables explain more than 90 per cent of the variation in DIY sales and make a reliable forecasting model. Why car ownership? This increasingly aided access to out-of-town DIY retailing and allowed the carriage of bulkier goods. Of course, this is obvious ...?

Planners look for causal variables that can be predicted reliably. Purchasers of television advertising time are buying a predicted audience. They buy in advance using clips, programme outlines and schedules. Adjustments to prices are made after showing, but this is unsatisfactory from the advertiser's point of view, for budgets will have been allocated. Accurate forecasts are especially difficult for new programmes. Recognising the habit of viewers sticking to one channel, Napoli[33] notes the influence of the lead-in (previous) and lead-out (following) programmes. Further, if these are returning programmes, that is not new, they can be predicted more accurately. Audiences for the lead-in and lead-out can therefore be used as inputs to a causal model. Napoli also shows the higher errors that occur when there are new programmes on rival channels and the lower predictability on channels with older audiences.

■ *Time series models are based on the simple notion that the future depends on the past.*

Lacking known relationships that could be built into a causal model, historical data are combined to make the forecast. For example, sales of a national newspaper for the next three months can, in the absence of significant changes in policy such as a price war, be predicted by examining recent trends. Those whose sales are growing should continue to grow, and so on.

Sometimes, trends are masked by seasonal and random variations. To illustrate these issues we can look at peak demand for electricity in England and Wales. It is an especially important parameter because it must be matched by power station and grid capacity. The first pane of Figure 2.7 shows a typical December weekday, in this case during a spell of mild weather. The peak, about 50 000 MW, is reached in the early evening. The second pane shows how demand relates to the seasons; it uses mean temperature values in the forecast. The randomness of the weather cannot be included in demand predictions more than a few days ahead. The effect of taking out the weather is also shown in the seven-year demand forecast, pane 3. The weather-corrected history clearly shows the mild winters of 1992–3 and 1994–5. This series is then extended to make the time series forecast.

Electricity forecasting also uses causal ideas. The annual forecast incorporates the expected impact of holidays and planned shutdowns among major consumers. Furthermore, operators are aware of not only the weather effect but also our domestic habits. Consumers wait for television breaks before switching on kettles or lights. The highest 'TV pickup' of the past 25 years occurred on 4 July 1990. The 2800 MW surge followed the end of extra time in the World Cup match between England and Germany. Match progress can be traced in the fourth pane of Figure 2.7, which also shows the normal profile for a summer Wednesday. Demand can also be depressed through television watching. During the 1997 funeral of Princess Diana, there were falls of more than 1000 MW in a few seconds as many of the 31 million viewers simultaneously turned off appliances. To cover such events, operators must respond rapidly to stabilise the grid system.

Qualitative methods

Qualitative methods bring together the experience, intuition and value systems of experts to forecast the long-term future. We can mention three here:

■ *Delphi method*
The Delphi method is named after the Greek oracle, *see* Exhibit 2.6. A series of surveys draws together expert opinion. The experts, about ten in number but not necessarily assembled in one place, are asked to speculate on questions about their field in (say) ten or more years' time. If there is no accord after this first stage, all are circulated with each other's responses. Then follows a second round in which a

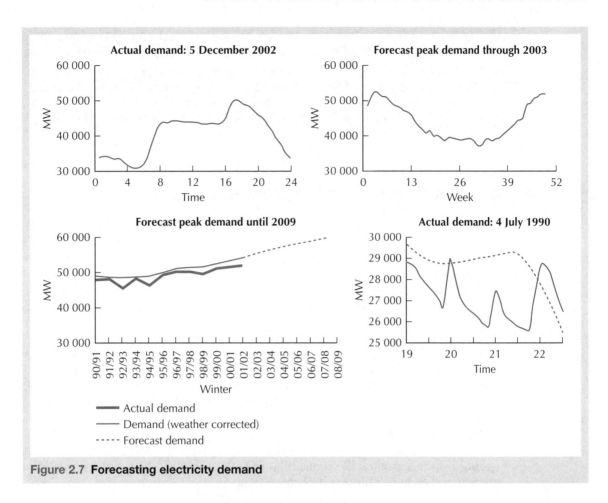

Figure 2.7 Forecasting electricity demand

move towards consensus is anticipated. Rounds continue as necessary. Questions asked may be, for example, 'What do you think the average size of long-range passenger aircraft will be in 2020?' or 'What changes will there be in steel production methods before the middle of the next decade?'

Delphi methods are part of the family of jury methods gathering expert opinion. A related approach invites senior managers to forecast the business environment. They meet in a workshop setting away from the normal workplace with support from background data, statistical trends and so on.

■ *Sales force surveys*
Using the opinion and contacts of sales people themselves can enrich quantitative forecasts. Representatives spend much time with customers, hear about developments and gain a feel for the actions of competitors. Data are assembled using jury methods, general meetings or questionnaires.

■ *Customer surveys*
While many customer surveys gather quantitative data, approaches using customer panels are used to give an early feel for changes in attitudes or the likely acceptance of new product ideas. This is one of the functions of market research, discussed in Chapter 16.

Exhibit 2.6 Consulting the oracle

In ancient Greece, enquirers about personal issues or affairs of state visited sacred sites, or oracles. Here answers, often ambiguous, came via priests from the utterances of priestesses of the deity. Delphi, whose shrine was dedicated to Apollo, was the most celebrated. Here, a conical stone, the *omphalos*, marked the centre of the Earth.

Conclusion: interpreting the changing environment

This chapter has covered two parallel themes: the nature of the changing environment and how managers can make sense of it. People do not relate to the environment haphazardly. They use intuition and experience to select, investigate and interpret.

The problem for managers is that reliance on past sources of information is no guard against the unexpected. Key success factors change. Hence, a manager needs to review whether the right information is being obtained. The wider environment yields important clues.

The layered model of the environment, shown in Figure 2.3, helps in understanding and coping. The operating environment contains elements with which there is continual interaction. Yet, everyday pressure may prevent anticipation of upheavals. Warnings often can be found in the wider environment. Furthermore, for firms that have interests in more than one nation, the international environment adds extra layers of complexity.

Whatever the data, managers must use them to anticipate. Many methods of forecasting help this process. Both quantitative and qualitative, their purpose is to give predictions and hence support decision making.

QUICK CHECK

Can you ...

- Define environment.
- Distinguish between operating and wider environments.
- List six main elements of the operating environment.
- Give instances of boundary spanning roles.
- Name the four PEST elements.

- Outline how managers select key environmental factors.
- Identify two classes of quantitative forecasting model.
- Give examples of three qualitative forecasting methods.

QUESTIONS

Chapter
review

2.1 What elements of the operating environment are identified in the text? Suggest another that may be relevant in various industries.

2.2 How can one distinguish between the operating and wider environments?

2.3 Outline the types of forecasting set out in the chapter and suggest a role for each.

Application

2.4 What are the main elements of the operating environment for a hospital, a furniture retailer or a local newspaper? Use a diagram to sketch the key flows.

2.5 Suggest some key success factors in relation to the environment of EMI.

Investigation

2.6 Investigate how a manager finds out about the business environment. Find out what types of information are collected and from what sources.

Going bananas[34]

CLOSING CASE

Co-operation among food industry firms has grown in recent years. The 1990 Food Safety Act requires due diligence with respect to food supplies. Sharing information with suppliers allows every product to be tracked from source to shelf and hence reduces risks such as contamination. Further, customers expect fresh supplies of a wide product range all year round; this requires all stages to work to rapid and regular schedules. Just-in-time deliveries promise lower wastage rates and more regular revenues compared with the traditional, unscheduled spot market system. Distributors and suppliers, therefore, are attracted by the security offered by membership of supply chains.

Retailer power has led to replacement of intermediate markets with contracts. Bananas have long been transported to Europe in special 'banana boats'. Vertically integrated companies, such as Chiquita, Del Monte and Fyffes, are expert in growing, shipping, ripening and distributing the product. Over the past two decades, however, retailers have become more involved in managing the supply chain. They seek lower costs, more consistent quality and, of course, traceability.

One supply chain involves three companies. Noboa is the largest grower, and second-largest business, in Ecuador, which in turn accounts for a third of the world's exports. Mack Multiples is the largest privately owned fresh fruit importer and distributor in the UK. It acts as an intermediary between many importers and retailers. J Sainsbury, the supermarket, retails about a fifth of fresh fruit and vegetables in the UK. The supply chain was developed by Sainsbury, which prefers to deal with good private businesses. Noboa, recommended by Mack, had not previously traded in Europe in this way. The arrangement started with a trial at one Ecuadorian farm and built up after experience.

The banana market

The banana is a staple food of producer countries. They export about a fifth of their annual 60 million tonne production, of which the European Union consumes about 35 per cent. Traditional sources were countries with duty-free agreements, such as the Lomé convention or the contract between Britain and Geest (now part of Fyffes) to guarantee a market for Caribbean suppliers. However, growth and trade liberalisation over two decades have meant an increasing share for the so-called 'dollar' bananas from Latin America. They now comprise two-thirds of the flow, although the UK market remains largely sourced from the Caribbean. Bananas are important in the UK. The £631 million at retail prices represented 22.4 per cent of fresh fruit sales in 2001. Having doubled in ten years, per capita consumption reached 10 kg per annum, that is a banana a week. Fruit consumption varies throughout the country, from 45 kg in the south east to 31 kg in Scotland. It is highest among older people, although growth among the young is stimulated by the snacking culture. In 2000, the banana overtook the apple as the nation's favourite fruit.

With about 60 per cent of the total, the leading EU importers are Chiquita, Dole, Del Monte and Fyffes. In UK, Fyffes leads with 30 per cent followed by Chiquita, Jamaica Producers and Del Monte at 15 per cent each. Among UK retailers, the multiples sell about 75 per cent. Demand is steady throughout the year, with a slight decrease in the summer when local fruit is on sale.

Three factors have caused falls in real prices: the dominance of the multiples; the fruit's presence in many 'shopping basket' comparisons; and the limited opportunities to differentiate the product. Although bananas from different regions and root stocks taste different, retailers have concentrated on finding the one or two varieties that consumers want to buy rather than a range of named varieties as with apples or potatoes. Sainsbury, for example, combines the results of customer taste tests in its stores with opinions of its central appraisal panel. This and other quality information is returned to the growers. Standardisation is being challenged by Costa Rican growers trying to develop a national brand and fair trade companies such as Oke.

Banana supply

From planting to harvest takes about a year. Quality management begins early with site selection and drainage. Growing fruit are wrapped in plastic to prevent scarring and insect damage. When the bananas are harvested, the wrappers are twisted into packaging to protect the fruit in transit. Bananas for the European market are cut when three-quarters mature, with the rest of the ripening controlled during transit.

Each stage of the supply chain is managed by one of the partners. Noboa controls packing stations, haulage, quayside storage and handling, and shipping to Zeebrugge. Mack transfers consignments via its ripening rooms at Paddock Wood, Kent, to Sainsbury depots. In the supermarket, the 'sell-by' date allows two days on the shelf. Reordering is automatic using EPOS data from checkouts. Central computers aggregate this data to forecasts sales trends, adjusted for the seasonal variations.

Sainsbury plans to streamline the supply chain by improving information flows among the partners. It will become more responsive to customer needs. The company sees competition in groceries as not simply between retailer and retailer but between supply chain and supply chain.

Questions

1 Sketch diagrams, following Figure 2.3, to show views of the environment before and after the development of supply chains. Comment on what these maps show.

2 Draw a diagram, based on Figure 2.4, to show the main flows through the banana supply chain.

3 What are the key environmental factors for the banana merchandiser at Sainsbury? How would you expect the manager to collect information about them?

4 According to Key Note, recent market trends are likely to continue over the next few years. What does this imply for market forecasting methods?

Bibliography

As well as the texts on the business environment mentioned in the references, the following give broad views of the business environment: Richard Lynch (2002) *Corporate Strategy* (3rd edition, Harlow: Financial Times Prentice Hall) and Will Hutton (2003) *The world we're in* (London: Abacus). The Office for National Statistics has data on many aspects of British society, **www.statistics.gov.uk**.

References

1 Sanghera, Sathnam (2002) 'Rock 'n' Roll suicide: how Napster, TV-created pop acts and a dearth of talent are killing the record business,' *Financial Times*, 15 November, 17; Sanghera, Sathnam and Burt, Tim (2002) 'EMI takes big gamble on £60m Robbie deal: record label hopes to make UK singer a star in US', *Financial Times: Companies & Markets*, 3 October, 1; Key Note (2002) *UK Leisure and recreation*, London: Key Note, September; *Financial Times* (2002) 'Music groups pay $143m to settle suit', 1 October, and 'Piracy set to hit global music sales,' 11 November; Thal Larsen, Peter (2003) 'They're playing our tune – charge them', *Financial Times*, 24 February, 8; *The Times* (2002) 'Bertelsmann faces big Napster lawsuit', 28 September, 'Music giants turn tables on the internet pirates', 14 September; EMI (2002) *Annual Report 2002*, www.emigroup.com/index.html.

2 Some authors refer to this as the *external environment*. This enables them to use *internal environment* to refer to elements inside the organisation. These extra labels are muddled and are not used here.

3 Kourteli, Liana (2000) 'Scanning the business environment: some conceptual issues', *Benchmarking: An International Journal*, **7(5)**, 406–13.

4 Smart, C. and Vertinsky, I. (1984), 'Strategy and the environment: a study of corporate responses to crises', *Strategic Management Journal*, **5**, 199–213.

5 Aguilar, F.J. (1967) *Scanning the Business Environment*, New York: Macmillan.

6 Lozada, Héctor R. and Calantone, Roger J. (1996) 'Scanning behavior and environmental variation in the formulation of strategic responses to change,' *Journal of Business and Industrial Marketing*, **11(1)**, 17–41.

7 Sawyerr, Olukemi O., Ebrahimi, Bahman P. and Thibodeaux, Mary S. (2000) 'Executive Environmental Scanning, Information Source Utilisation and Firm Performance: the case of Nigeria', *Journal of Applied Management Studies*, **9(1)**, 95–115.

8 Tyler, B.B., Bettenhausen, K.L. and Daft, R.L. (1989) 'The use of low and high rich information sources and communication channels in developing and implementing competitive business strategy', Annual Meeting of the Academy of Management, quoted in Analoui, Farhad and Karami, Azhdar (2002) 'How chief executives' perception of the environment impacts on company performance', *Journal of Management Development*, **21(4)**, 290–305.

9 Analoui and Karami, (2002) *op.cit.*

10 Voyle, Susanna (2002) 'Little sign of end to Somerfield's turmoil: Increasing competition has made a long job of turning around the supermarket group even longer', *Financial Times: Companies & Finance*, 15 October.

11 Voyle, Susanna (2002) 'Supermarkets Feel Competitive Heat: Talk of consolidation in an increasingly tough sector continues', *Financial Times: Companies & Finance*, 16 September.

12 Moogan, Yvonne J., Baron, Steve and Bainbridge, Steve (2001) 'Timings and trade-offs in the marketing of higher education courses: a conjoint approach', *Marketing Intelligence and Planning*, **19(3)**, 179–87.

13 Office of Gas and Electricity Markets, *see* www.ofgem.gov.uk.

14 Politi, James (2002) 'Supply Chain Headache for Mothercare's New Broom', *Financial Times: Companies & Finance*, 23 November.

15 Milner, Mark and Duval-Smith, Alex (1996) 'Divine right of Chirac leaves aircraft firms cursing union', *Guardian*, 31 August, 24.

16 United States Department of State (2001) 'Bush Signs Extension of Iran and Libya Sanctions Act', Press Release, 3 August; http://usinfo.state.gov/topical/pol/terror/01080303.htm, accessed 2 December 2002.

17 Holman, Michael (1995) 'A continent in transition', *Financial Times*, Survey of International Telecommunications, 3 October, xxxviii.

18 Migault, Philippe (2003) 'Airbus retient le moteur européen pour son avion militaire', *Le Figaro: économie*, 7 May, I; Done, Kevin (2003) 'Europeans beat P&W to Airbus engine deal', *Financial Times*, 7 May, 23.

19 Southey, Caroline (1995) 'Controversy threatens rail network', *Financial Times*, 28 June, iii.

20 Porter, Michael E. (1998) *The Competitive Advantage of Nations*, 2nd edition, London: Macmillan Business.

21 Office for National Statistics (1996) *Monitor PP1*, London: ONS.

22 Central Statistical Office (1996) *Annual Abstract of Statistics*, HMSO, 8; Office for National Statistics (2002) *2001 census results*, www.statistics.gov.uk, accessed 3 December 2002.

23 Dawkins, William (1995) 'Gold streaks highlight Japan's grey waves – Shiseido's fastest growing products are aimed at the aged', *Financial Times*, 7 January, 11.

24 Maitland, Alison (2002) 'A fresh start for older employees: Companies that hire workers close to retirement age are finding that it brings bottom-line benefits', *Financial Times*, 22 January.

25 London First Centre (2002) *London Voted Europe's Best Business City*, News Release, 17 October, www.lfc.co.uk/press_centre/newsreleasedetail.asp?L2=40&NewsReleaseId=1710; … Sector Briefing: e-business, www.lfc.co.uk/key_sectors/EBusiness.asp?L2=29; both accessed 4 December 2002.

26 Drucker, Peter (1981) *Managing in Turbulent Times*, London: Pan, 10.

27 Badaracco, J. (1991) *The Knowledge Link: How firms compete through strategic alliances*, Boston, Mass.: Harvard Business School Press.

28 Gooding, Claire (1995) 'Bar codes get high-tech links', *Financial Times*, 4 October, vi; Foremski, Tom (1995) 'Supermarkets checkout systems', *ibid.*, v.

29 Levitt, Theodore (1983) 'The globalisation of markets', *Harvard Business Review*, May–June, 92–102.

30 Rugman, Alan J. (2001) 'The myth of global strategy', *International Marketing Review*, **18(6)**, 583–8.

31 Gilad, Benjamin, Gordon, George and Sudit, Ephraim (1993) 'Identifying gaps and blind spots in competitive intelligence', *Long Range Planning*, **26(6)**, 107–13.

32 Leaver, David and Al-Zubaidi, H. (1996) 'Challenging conventional wisdom: a reappraisal of the UK DIY market', *International Journal of Retail & Distribution Management*, **24(11)**, 39–45.

33 Napoli, Philip M. (2001) 'The unpredictable audience: An explanatory analysis of forecasting error for new prime-time network television programmes', *Journal of Advertising*, **30(2)**, 53.

34 Wilson, Natasha (1996) 'Supply chain management: a case study of a dedicated supply chain for bananas in the UK grocery market', *Supply Chain Management*, **1(2)**, 28–35; Liddel, Ian (2000) *Unpeeling the Banana Trade*, London: Fairtrade Foundation, **www.fairtrade.org.uk/unpeeling.htm**, accessed 8 December 2002; Key Note (2002) *Fruit and Vegetables*, London: Key Note, April.

CHAPTER 3

Inside the organisation: adapting to change

Chapter objectives

When you have finished studying this chapter, you should be able to:

- identify types of environmental change and the problems they pose for organisations;

- outline the population ecology perspective on adaptation and how it applies to organisations;

- present and illustrate the ways that small or large organisations achieve fit with their environments;

- define organisational culture and show how it can be seen as having visible and invisible layers;

- demonstrate how artefacts can be used as a route to holistic understanding of culture;

- comment on the application of categories of culture;

- show why cultural change may be needed and explain why this change is difficult to achieve.

Notice that the stiffest tree is most easily cracked, while the bamboo survives by bending with the wind.

Bruce Lee, actor, writing on Kung Fu

Lego: the toy of the twentieth century?[1]

Lego is the only European toy company in the world's top ten and one of the best known of all brands. Fourteen billion plastic pieces are produced each year and few of the 330 billion supplied since 1949 have been thrown away. With 300 million miniatures, Lego is the world's largest tyre maker. The owning family is one of Europe's wealthiest.

The story started when founder, Ole Kirk Christiansen, and his son switched from wooden toys to injection moulded plastic bricks. The early design, a close imitation of the British Kiddikraft, was improved in 1955 when the hollow bricks had the familiar tubes moulded inside. This one innovation allowed better interlocking and ensured future success. Having given up bricks because they did not sell, Kiddikraft claimed no trade infringement when exports to the United Kingdom started in 1960. The final breakthrough in the acceptance of Lego System as an educational toy came in 1963 when the cellulose acetate specification was changed to the superior acrylic, ABS. Fundamentals have not changed since. Now, most patents have expired and Lego attracts copies. None lasts long because the company has such a lead in marketing, design and manufacture. Bricks are made to 5-micron tolerances (0.005 millimetres). Furthermore, Lego vigorously defends its intellectual property of trademarks, designs and remaining patents.

The secretive family company, registered in Switzerland, released few figures until 1995. For 20 years, annual profit grew by over 10 per cent. Then it oscillated. Falling 34 per cent to €102 million in 1995, it steadied before turning into the first loss of €38 million in 1998. A range of Star Wars figures brought a recovery in 1999, but 2000 again saw Lego losing, this time €135 million on sales of €1265 million. 2001 saw another recovery, with a profit of €71 million on €1430 million sales.

Lego has 70 per cent of the construction toy market. Possibly matching different ways of bringing up children, construction accounts for 8 per cent of toys sold in Germany, 5 per cent in the United Kingdom and 1.5 per cent in Spain. Yet, parents who favour educational toys accept that electronics and personal computers help expand their children's skills. No longer raised on conkers

and tag, children prefer Playstations and video machines. In this fierce competition, especially at Christmas, Lego has lost market share.

'Age compression' describes how children, especially in smaller families, grow up faster than previously. One study showed children wanting more sophisticated toys after the age of nine. The 2002 product Spybotics, for nine-year-olds, involves constructing a motorised robot. Advertising began on Internet sites used by children and driver software can be downloaded. The 1998 Mindstorms, for children 12 and over, requires some computer programming. Lego has never cracked the gender problem. Recognising that two-thirds of sets are bought for boys, the company introduced Scala in 1997 and continues to search for solutions.

Lego is diversifying. It aims to expand in regions where it is weak, such as Asia and the United States. About a quarter of sales are from 'non-core' products using licensed characters, such as Bob the Builder and Harry Potter. Not wanting, however, to become dependent on other companies for ideas, Lego launched in 2002 its own fantasy figures – Bionicles. An animated feature film based on these toys was planned for 2004.

Product diversification risks weakening brand identity. The company wants Lego to be the world's strongest brand among families with children. Consequently, it is rebuilding its range, introducing a new slogan and developing new shops. Except for the pre-school group, Lego has dropped age themes in its designs, preferring themes such as Make & Create, Stories & Action and Next. The 'Play on …' slogan replaces 'Just imagine …' because it captures better the five brand values: creativity, imagination, learning, fun and quality. The new shops will carry only Lego merchandise and aim for excellence in design and service.

There are to be more theme parks. Starting with a few models on a patch of waste ground, the original Legoland followed requests to see the Billund factory. Some 33 million people have visited the site. Other parks opened at Windsor in 1996, San Diego in 1999 and Munich in 2002. Costing more than £50 million to build, Windsor received more than 1.5 million visitors in its opening year. Many cities have written asking for their own versions.

The slow development, with several false starts, shows reluctance to move away from the business the company knows best. The family atmosphere among the 9000 employees is underscored by the private ownership and the fact that the present chief, Kjeld Kirk Kristiansen, is the founder's grandson. The family, and company, focus on doing the right things for children. While models of knights and pirates are sold, there are no modern military references. This non-violent theme dates to the 1940s when Kristiansen's mother stopped the company from selling a wooden toy pistol.

Mr Kristiansen concedes that the company had been guided too much by the success of the past. He recognised that quicker response was needed.

Change included bringing in new talent so that, by 2002, half of the senior managers were outsiders, including the chief operating officer, Poul Plougmann. Cost reductions included removing layers of middle management and shifting manufacture to low-cost sites such as Kladno in the Czech Republic. A change project encouraged senior managers to halve their time in formal meetings, spend less effort on control and more time on coaching employees. Managers in key markets would be more autonomous, deciding the mix of products to be pushed and choice of packaging. Product development, concentrated at Billund, was decentralised and accelerated. Marketing staff worldwide will contribute to plans at an early stage.

Introduction

The question posed in the opening case – can Lego adapt? – is faced by all organisations. For some, it is permanently on the agenda while, for others, it is asked only intermittently. How often depends on changes in the environment. In general, more changes mean that more adaptation is required.

Lego was founded by people who had the insight and drive to pick and develop a winning formula. For more than fifty years it has built on that same formula, entering new geographic markets, broadening the product range and improving quality. With success leading to success, it never had to question if there might be an end or when the end might be. Recent signs, however, are of threats to Lego's hegemony. Parents begin to value imaginative, as opposed to manual, skills. Construction toys face information technology. Software arrives in the kindergarten.

Naturally, the Kristiansens and the Lego company do not have to take any notice of this. The business, after all, is a private one. It does seem that, for several years, belief in the 'winning formula' caused them to resist change. They were not asking the adaptation question. Taking up a point from Chapter 2, we see that it is not the *fact* of environmental change that is important. Instead, it is the way the managers recognise and interpret the change and incorporate it into their business. At one extreme, they can ignore it and run the risk of following into oblivion the makers of Bayko, Kiddikraft bricks, Meccano (almost) and Trix. At the other extreme, they can seek to match every whim and fad, risking the loss of focus suffered by almost all of Lego's rivals in the top ten. Lego has to find the balance. It has to understand the shifts to which it chooses to respond. Then it must match them with appropriate actions.

The chapter considers two features of this discussion. First, we study how organisations cope with the dynamic environment. Second, we probe more deeply into the organisation to investigate how they respond, or do not respond. This is the effect of organisational culture.

Coping with the uncertain environment

The organisation without problems exists within a stable environment. With regular customers, no new competitors, fixed technology, quiet social conditions and so on, this fortunate organisation can hone its internal processes to maximum efficiency and achieve its budget every year. Problems come from changes. If these are small, taking place *within limits*, the organisation will cope through various operational mechanisms. It will maintain flexible operating capacity, switch resources, carry stocks, allow queues to form, regulate demand and so on. With fluctuations as variations around a mean, operating procedures are sufficient. On the other hand, if the change is permanent or in large steps, routine responses will not work. Major surgery is called for.

Types of change

Rhenman[2] distinguished between the two types of environmental change using the terms reversible and irreversible.

- *Reversible changes* are the cyclical or random disturbances mentioned above. They mostly arise in the operating environment. For instance, a hospital plans its outpatients' surgeries through estimating the average time required per patient and issuing appointments to them. Disturbances arise from patients arriving early or late, or not showing up at all. Furthermore, each treatment lasts for a different time. The department, therefore, uses queues to even out the flow. Visitors do not like queues, but will accept them provided they are well managed and not too long.

- *Irreversible changes* are permanent shifts in the environment requiring more fundamental responses within the organisation. Their source can usually be traced to developments in the wider environment. Frequently, new and unknown conditions occur of which there is no previous experience. Then the organisation cannot rely on standardised responses. Over recent years, for example, capacity planning for United Kingdom hospital maternity units has been subject to many such changes. They include examples of all the PEST categories referred to in Chapter 2: decentralisation of planning and control structures in the Health Service with a rise in competition among units; shifts in resources allocated to midwifery services; steady decline in the birth rate accompanied by changed attitudes towards home deliveries; and new techniques in gynaecology.

Rhenman's categories encourage us to relate each disturbance to origins and possible effects. A broader view of the totality of changes was taken by Duncan.[3] He suggested two dimensions to assess the overall impact of the changes faced by an organisation. These were:

Simplicity versus complexity

A simple environment contains a few important factors and has little variety. In contrast, a complex environment is made up of many factors and displays greater diversity. We can illustrate these factors by comparing schools. Let us say, for a moment, that each child is seen as an element of the environment, a customer so to speak. Looking at no other factors, we say that larger classes are more complex just because there are more children. Smaller classes are simpler. In addition, we can consider diversity. In a selective school, or one with streaming, the teacher is faced with pupils with a narrow ability band. The teacher faces a simpler environment. Some claim benefits from more efficiency under this 'simpler' selective system. We should, however, note that others point to disadvantages from a wider, societal perspective.

■ *Static versus dynamic*

The degree of environmental stability is the second cause of uncertainty. Few environments are unchanging, although there are often managers that treat them this way. We can see great differences in the dynamics of nations, markets, industries and companies. For instance, in suburban areas with stable population, enrolments in primary schools vary little from year to year. Short of any other information, a good predictor is to use last year's registrations. One could not rely on a similar approach in countries with fluctuating rates of birth and infant mortality or considerable migration.

Duncan proposed that uncertainty arises from the combination of these dimensions. The most uncertain environments are those that are both complex and dynamic. If either comes into play, there is moderate uncertainty. Figure 3.1 summarises these relationships.

When conditions are uncertain, the following tasks become more difficult:

■ identifying key factors in the environment;

■ forecasting the environment;

■ evaluating the impact of potential changes;

■ knowing the costs of making the wrong choices.

For some managers, the last point is reassuring. Even though a decision is wrong, no one will ever suspect! The foggy environment hides both successes and mistakes. Information has value associated with the quality of decisions that it supports; it also has costs linked to the effort expended in obtaining it. Uncertainty hampers good estimates of these values and costs.

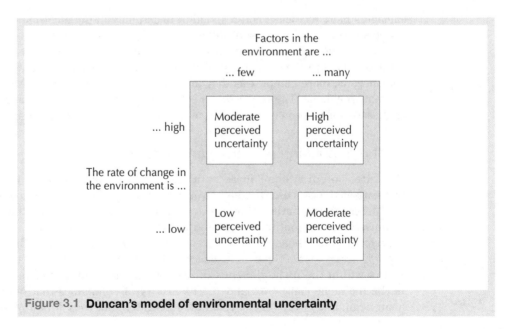

Figure 3.1 Duncan's model of environmental uncertainty

It is useful to link the views of Rhenman and Duncan. Organisations must respond to environmental changes if they are to survive. The easiest problems arise from reversible changes in relatively static and simple environments; irreversible changes in dynamic complex situations pose greater problems.

The Lego case illustrates these issues. The company is gradually diversifying from dependence on plastic brick technology. In so doing, it is facing greater complexity and dynamism, that is greater uncertainty. The above ideas help us to analyse the case in more detail.

Table 3.1 presents a set of notes prepared from the case study. Naturally, there will be more issues in practice, but space is restricted and the table will suit our purposes. The first column of the table lists, in order of appearance, the environmental changes mentioned. The second places the issues among the environments of Figure 2.3. Then we see interpretation of each for reversibility and uncertainty. Comments on suggested action complete the table. Study of the entries suggests that, for Lego, deeper problems arise in the wider environment. It has become used to managing its operating environment. For instance, it knows a great deal about the construction toy market: managers are familiar with competitors, customers and the monthly sales pattern leading up to Christmas. They can cope with fluctuations there. Similarly, the company faces infringements of its property rights each year. Such matters are mostly routine to the legal department. On the other hand, the irreversible changes mentioned demand more fundamental responses based on watching societal developments and innovating new products. In facing these changes, Lego is moving into untested territory. Uncertainty, rated at moderate or high in the fourth column, means that the company must find new ways of relating to the new opportunities and threats.

Organisations and environments

Managers must recognise and respond to uncertainty in the environment. Drawing on systems theory, Ashby's Law of Requisite Variety[4] suggests that, to survive, a system must match the variety of the environment within itself. As the variety (or uncertainty) increases, so must the complexity of the organisation. This implies that most organisations become more complex as they grow, for they have to cope with more factors in their environments. The processes of selection of environments and adaptation of the organisation have been encapsulated in the *population ecology perspective*.[5]

■ The population ecology perspective

This extension of systems ideas parallels Darwin's theory of evolution. Figure 3.2 summarises the process of creation of new organisations and the 'natural selection' that determines whether they are to survive. *Mutation* means that unique new organisations are continually created out of what has gone before. The process of *selection* favours those that can mirror the environment, often by finding a suitable opportunity or *niche*. Success leads to *survival* and, perhaps, growth. Whether this occurs within the niche depends on its size and the number of other occupants. Maybe the niche can be expanded. The history of companies that have grown from small beginnings over recent years demonstrates that they found niches that were

Table 3.1 **Appraisal of Lego's environments**

Item mentioned in study	Environment category	Reversibility	Uncertainty	Action
World's Top Ten	Operating – competition	Reversible	Moderate	Watch key competitors
Copies	Operating – competition	Reversible	Moderate	Monitor
Intellectual property law	Wider – political	(Static)	None	
Swiss company law	Wider – political	(Static)	None	
Oscillating demand	Operating – market	Unclear	Moderate	Monitor carefully
Culture and toy market (D, GB, E)	Wider – social	Slow change	Moderate	Scan
Parents' preferences	Wider – social	Irreversible	High in long term	Scan
Electronic toys	Wider – technology	Irreversible	High	Watch closely
Christmas	Operating – market	Reversible	Low	Stock control
Age compression	Wider – social	Irreversible	Moderate	Innovate
Internet	Wider – technological	Irreversible	High in long term	Innovate
Asia & United States	Operating – market	Irreversible	Moderate	Market development
Licensors	Operating – suppliers	Reversible	Low	Seek opportunities
Franchisees	Operating – distributors	Reversible	Moderate	Seek expansion
Theme park industry	Wider – economic	Irreversible	Moderate	Steady expansion
Cities' requests	Wider – economic	(Static)	Low	
Key markets (D, J, GB, USA)	Operating – market	Reversible	Moderate	Decentralise control

large, unoccupied or expandable. IKEA, Lego, easyJet, Ryanair, Microsoft, Tesco and Virgin are but a few examples.

The perspective takes us on into later development. The third stage, *survival*, is never guaranteed. An organisation must continue to fight to achieve everlasting life. It may outgrow its niche, or predators may enter and force it out. Some fail at this stage. Therefore, managers must be prepared to adapt, to ward off predators and to find and develop new niches. Examples range from the corner grocer threatened by the predator supermarket, to Lego, which in turn outgrew the Danish, the Nordic and then the European construction toy markets.

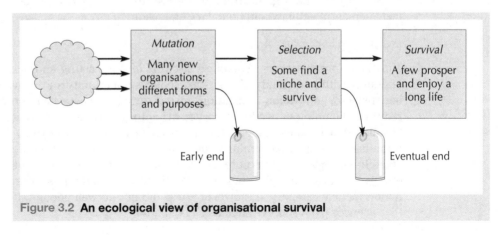

Figure 3.2 **An ecological view of organisational survival**

Developments discussed here have focused on growth through time. More important to the population ecologists are emerging patterns of chronological and spatial distribution. Rather than look at individual location decisions, such as where a plant, bank or shop may decide to set up, they observe the developing patterns of whole industries. Actions of each individual firm are clearly affected by the choices of those who have come before. Just as we see clusters of development through time, as in 'Industrial Revolutions', so they appear geographically. From the Potteries to the Ruhr, or the Po Valley to Silicon Valley, firms cluster in emerging networks. Lomi noted how photographs of Europe taken at night show concentration patterns that give no clue to political frontiers.[6]

The danger with analogies

We gain insight from thinking of organisational change as a continual response to pressure. There are, however, dangers in using natural systems as analogies of organisations. In noting parallels between systems, we apply knowledge about one to explain something about the other. Analogies use one system as a likeness of another. Problems arise when, seeing the first as having *some* features in common with the second, we carelessly assume that other features are also similar.

Drawing conclusions from connections must be done with care. A more rigorous comparison between two systems should discover important differences. The Darwinian perspective is a subtle and plausible picture of *some* aspects of organisational development and change. Living and organised systems display important differences. For example, the organisations are abstract, designed, possibly fast changing, and can have indefinite life. Living things are the opposite.

We can also note that the ecology perspective is a descriptive theory. It provides insight but is hardly useful in answering managerial questions such as, 'What shall we do next?' Notwithstanding these difficulties, it supports an important idea that has become embedded in the managerial way of thinking. Success follows establishing a suitable *fit* between the organisation and its environment. This implies internal adaptation or, if the power exists, action upon the environment to make it fit the organisation's needs. We shall consider each in turn.

■ Achieving fit by internal adaptation

There are several internal actions available to managers to counter the effects of uncertainty on the organisation. These are: forecasting and planning; information management; flexibility and boundary extension.

Forecasting and planning

Most large organisations expend great effort on forecasting and planning as means of coping with uncertainty. Forecasting reduces uncertainty and provides the breathing space for innovation, relocation, restructuring or whatever internal changes are required. Planning is needed in larger firms to ensure not only that change occurs but also that it takes place at the necessary rate and in the right direction. If an organisation sees a particularly uncertain future in which it could not adapt fast enough, managers may prepare a *contingency plan*, which could be enacted if necessary. Lego, for example, could rely on Bionicles to extend its sales in the Stories & Action fantasy category. If, however, these did not go well enough, it could seek further licences from sources such as Harry Potter.

Another problem arises from unwanted events leading to a crisis. Effective organisations plan for such occasions through *crisis management*. Just as they do with fire drills, they rehearse responses to failures in information systems or supplies of raw materials, sabotage, loss of key personnel and so on.

Information management

Information management is vital both when managers are forming an initial appraisal of an environment and when they scan to look for signs of change. Just as forecasters try to improve techniques to give early warnings, so managers strive to obtain both accurate and early information. This can yield great advantages. The story of Rothschild making a fortune, although probably exaggerated, illustrates the point, *see* Exhibit 3.1.[7]

Exhibit 3.1 First with the news from Waterloo

Throughout the Napoleonic wars, Nathan Mayer Rothschild (1777–1836) ('NM') implemented the British government's banking commitments. NM had a network of agents with tasks such as funding the French opposition and paying Wellington's army. Family connections criss-crossed Europe. His communications were known to be good. For instance, contractors at Dover and Calais kept speedy vessels at the ready with post-boys making the land connections.

The Battle of Waterloo occurred on 18 June 1815. There are many conflicting accounts of Rothschild's subsequent actions. Writers talk of NM being present at the scene or of carrier pigeons bringing back news; others suggest that, in London, he either pretended that Wellington had lost so as to depress securities prices, or started to sell so as to suggest that he knew of disaster.

Cowles' official biography has NM receiving the news through a *Gazette Extraordinary* published in Brussels and sent post-haste to arrive early on the 20th. He went with a companion to rouse Lord Castlereagh, the Foreign Secretary, with the news. Foreign Office officials, however, were sceptical because they had just heard of the English defeat in the minor battle of Quatre Bras on the 17th. Frustrated, NM left immediately for the stock exchange and began to buy large quantities of bonds. Wellington's official despatches arrived some forty hours after Rothschild's copy of the *Gazette*.

Flexibility

The structure of an organisation should allow it to make the required responses to external change. In a well-known study, Burns and Stalker[8] compared the flexibility required of a successful organisation with the uncertainty of the environment:

- *Organic structure* – an organic structure is characterised by few rules and regulations, stresses teamwork and decentralises decision making to the level of employees doing the work.

- *Mechanistic structure* – a mechanistic structure features clearly defined tasks, has many rules and regulations, requires little teamwork and tends to centralise decision making.

They found that in conditions of rapid change, the organic structure is more successful; the mechanistic structure, corresponding to Weber's bureaucracy, works best in stable environments. As with other models, note that Burns and Stalker are describing ideal-types. These establish a scale or continuum along which real organisations can be placed. For instance, one of Lego's responses to market change is to decentralise Billund's marketing decision-making processes. This means a shift towards the organic type. For more on the work of Burns and Stalker, *see* Chapter 10.

Many tactics respond to operating environment uncertainty. Production managers carry stocks and maintain spare capacity. Finance managers use insurance to guard against some bad debts and hedge to cover foreign currency movements. Incorporating such flexibility is costly and is often not called into play. Yet, it guards against the unexpected.

Mergers

One way of reducing external uncertainty, especially in the operating environment, is to take direct control. Facing the risk of loss of supplies, the organisation can buy the source; fearing loss of outlets – buy the distributor; threatened by competition – buy the rival; spotting a new technology – buy the licence; finding an opportunity overseas – buy a local company. Control through ownership is attractive for the certainty it imposes upon the uncertain. Although such practices are sometimes banned by governments because they are anti-competitive, they are permitted if they appear to be in the national interest. From the government's point of view, home industry consolidation can dampen down uncertainty in domestic business and enable firms to face international competition more effectively.

The terms merger, takeover and acquisition describe three variants on the theme of boundary expansion although distinctions are often blurred.

- Merging firms usually combine to form a new one. Each party to the merger may join because it seeks to cut uncertainty in its environment.
- In a takeover, one firm buys another in order to absorb it.
- After an acquisition, the target company often maintains its identity as a subsidiary company.

All three processes have been seen as the United Kingdom clearing banks have passed through waves of consolidation from the 1960s. By 1970, three of the 'Big Four' British clearing banks were in the world's top twenty – Barclays (4), NatWest (7) and Midland (20). By 1995, however, mergers and growth elsewhere meant that their rankings fell. Barclays (22) and NatWest (26) remained independent while Midland had been absorbed into HSBC. In 2002, HSBC was the world's fifth largest bank. By then, Royal Bank of Scotland Group (8) and Lloyds TSB (12) were the results of further UK consolidation, while the independent Barclays stood at 13.

Japanese banks are often parts of large conglomerates called *keiretsu*. These form huge internal markets, producing, trading and distributing a wide range of goods and services. Many transactions are internal to the *keiretsu*, therefore avoiding the uncertainties of the market. Mitsubishi is one such example whose branded goods are well known in many countries. Its bank, having been number six in 1995, ranked twenty-fifth in 2002.[9]

Achieving fit: adapting the environment

The alternative approach to fit comes through shaping the environment. After all, to fit a square peg in a round hole, either the peg or the hole, or indeed both, can be worked on. To dampen external uncertainty, managers can try to steer events along planned courses or at least fight to resist unfavourable outcomes. The possible countermeasures are advertising and promotion; public relations; lobbying; bargaining; boundary extension; and supra-organisational groups.

Advertising and promotion

Advertising has now become a central plank of many organisations' attempts to manage, that is limit the uncertainty of, their market environments. As in many developed countries, spending on advertising in the United Kingdom is dominated by detergent, cosmetic, beer and car companies. Their production is characterised by high start-up or fixed costs and low variable costs per unit. This means that it pays suppliers to run plant as close as possible to full capacity and use advertising to push the product towards consumers. In such mature markets, advertising is less about attacking than defending. That means that maintenance of sales at planned levels is the overall objective. Advertising reduces uncertainty in the production and distribution environment.

Promotion refers to the final steps in the selling process. In its early days, Toyota's production workers were sent out to sell door to door during times of slack demand. Rather than produce more cars, the company put its efforts into managing the environment.

Public relations

Public relations processes are similar to those found in advertising and promotion except that the goal is to influence public opinion about the organisation rather than directly manage demand for products. Clearly, the two are connected, as people will be more willing to deal with companies with good reputations. British Telecom's operating licence requires it to compete fairly. Yet, the Consumers' Association found that BT's staff were giving misleading information about rivals' costs and services. In response to resulting criticism from the industry regulator, BT established a special compliance department to ensure that its performance was above reproach. Tasks include checking of all advertisements, training of staff and setting up procedures to be followed in cases of doubt. BT feels it will gain through being seen publicly to meet standards.[10]

Lobbying

Lobbying can be seen as public relations focused on a narrow section of opinion. Usually the targets are groups in authority such as Members of Parliament or local authorities. Many organisations, often in combination, employ professional lobbyists to ensure that their view is heard. A combination of public relations and lobbying can be a powerful factor in persuading governments to accept arguments from interest groups. Much of this process, sometimes called *politicking*, is legitimate although, many would say, misguided. Tobacco companies throughout Europe have spent many years persuading governments against more stringent controls. They have argued, for example, that advertising has little to do with total consumption but merely persuades existing consumers to try other brands. There are also benefits for employees and some sports, especially Formula 1. In 2002, however, the European Commission and Ministers directed companies to increase the size of health warnings, ban terms suggesting safety, such as 'light' and 'mild' and stop broadcast advertising.[11]

Bargaining

An important outcome of a bargain is the removal of uncertainty, especially if the result is some kind of long-term contract. For instance, during periods of high inflation, unions are unwilling to enter into wage agreements lasting more than one year. When inflationary expectations are low, two- and three-year agreements become acceptable. Managers concede a little extra in return for being able to plan for labour costs. Other forms of bargain with similar effects cover long-term supplies of raw materials or undertakings to purchase outputs. Supply chains in some industries have developed in recent years into complex networks of long-term bargains. They include single-sourcing agreements and undertakings to exchange operational information. A key benefit for managers is the removal of uncertainty.

Benefits of such bargains tend to be undermined if basic assumptions prove to be wildly inaccurate. Ghana's Volta Dam project,[12] *see* Exhibit 3.2, was guaranteed by the construction of a foreign-owned aluminium smelter to take most of the electric power. In retrospect, the government's political needs made it blind to the risks it faced.

Exhibit 3.2 The Volta Dam scheme: subverted by the volatile environment

Construction of the Volta Dam began in the 1960s. It was part of a scheme to stimulate rapid industrialisation. Desperate for both foreign investment and exports, the Ghanaian government needed a guaranteed market for electricity to make the project work. An aluminium smelter, with capacity of 200 000 tonnes per annum, would provide this guarantee and consume local bauxite ore. Yet the reduction of uncertainty has proved dear. First, the electricity tariff was fixed before the global rise in energy prices. Then it was found that local ores were too expensive to work and the Volta Aluminum Company (a subsidiary of Texas-based Kaiser Aluminum) imported richer bauxite from North America. Then, a 1983 drought shut the plant for two years. Finally, weak demand meant that Kaiser had too much capacity worldwide. Production in Ghana during the 1990s was little more than half of capacity. It recovered to 80 per cent in 2000, but electricity rationing in 2002 cut it again to 60 per cent.

Boundary extension

Mergers were identified as a means of adapting to uncertainty through internalising an important part of the environment. There are more subtle means of exercising some controlling influence without ownership. One means is to establish favourable links with other organisations through individuals occupying *boundary-spanning roles*. Representatives of important constituencies, such as major customers or banks, can be co-opted on to boards of directors. In the outward direction, senior managers may take up roles on other company boards or community groups. Through such *interlocking directorships*, individuals reduce uncertainty by sharing and spreading common interests and learning of board-level strategies such as acquisitions.[13] The practice is more common in France, Germany and Japan than in the United Kingdom or United States.

Strategic alliances are long-term agreements among organisations, which can take many forms. One of their functions is to exchange resources or information. Again, as with other forms of agreement, alliances can serve to cut uncertainty. A joint venture in a developing country can combine the local knowledge of the home partner with the technical knowledge of the foreign firm. Each avoids risks in its partner's environment. This is a common way for foreign firms to establish business in China.

Supra-organisational groups

Supra-organisational groups are formed among organisations with interests in common. They recognise that members can achieve more through working in concert than by acting on their own. At one end of the scale are international organisations such as the International Maritime Organization, the Organization of Petroleum Exporting Countries, the International Labour Organization, or the World Council of Churches. They help in regulation, price fixing, information sharing or spreading the word. Echoes exist at a smaller scale in local communities. Chambers of Commerce and Trades Councils bring firms and unions together to discuss local issues, although their influence varies according to tradition and official support. The voluntary sector is characterised by small organisations that gain from group membership. The National Association for Special Educational Needs conducts research, produces publications and sets up events and courses; sports 'governing bodies' are usually committees elected by member organisations.

Groups use many of the tactics already mentioned: advertising and promotion; public relations and lobbying; bargaining; and boundary extension. They prosper when members see continuing membership as being in their own interests and wither when the motivation for joining fades. Among small firms, some of the strongest voluntary organisations bring direct operating benefits. Buying and market groups in retailing, such as the Spar network of food wholesalers and retailers, bring scale economies to members. Membership of the Wool Industry Research Association gives access to innovations in process technology. The strength of Chambers of Commerce, on the other hand, has declined in the United Kingdom. Their moderate budgets limit their functions to lobbying, information sharing and social events. In France, chambers do have important local functions. They raise levies and offer financial incentives for training and development.

■ Adaptation and size

Not all the adaptation strategies are available to every organisation. Size is a major factor deciding which is most applicable. Rather like David against Goliath, the small firm prospers through its internal flexibility, a feature that larger ones find difficult to replicate. Instead, giant firms rely more on modelling and forecasting the future. Reliance solely on forecasting creates a difficulty explained in Exhibit 3.3.

Lacking internal flexibility, can large organisations rely on the combination of forecasts and countermeasures? The problem with reliance on the latter is that even they have to be part of the forecast. The organisation has to know the kinds of gaps that might arise before it can be sure it is ready with responses. Of particular concern are events with immediate impact arising in the operating environment. Lack of flexibility requires the large organisation to combine forecasting and countermeasures against these events. At the same time, as problems in the wider environment unfold more slowly, it adapts either by internal change or by evolving new countermeasures. If it behaves as though it can permanently cope with change through forecasts and *planned* countermeasures, it will be doomed. Kaiser's investment in

Exhibit 3.3 Bridging gaps between forecasts and outcomes

To predict the future, a forecaster must, following Ashby's Law, have a model that matches the complexity of the environment. This is not a reasonable prospect. Complexity is always going to be too great and, moreover, it is impossible to test the model.

The complete model is unnecessary if the forecaster has countermeasures powerful enough to control the environment. In other words, when a gap emerges between the forecast and 'reality' then the organisation changes the latter! For this to work, the planner needs to know what sort of change is possible so that the countermeasures can be put in place.

The future, then, is partly predicted by the model and partly adjusted to fit the model.

Ghana failed through being unable to predict or control a key environment, the river flow, and having no alternative source of energy.

Adaptation strategies are summarised in Figure 3.3. Here each is placed according to whether it is concerned with internal or external adaptation and whether it is relevant to small, medium or large organisations. There is no fixed rule. For example, advertising is available to all but, from the point of view of attempts to *manage* the environment, it is only relevant to those who can commit vast resources to it. At the other end of the scale, flexibility is most appropriate to small firms whose only hope of influencing the environment is through supra-organisations such as industry

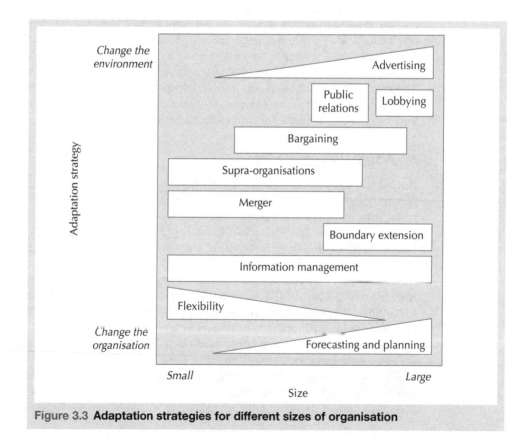

Figure 3.3 Adaptation strategies for different sizes of organisation

associations. In between, merger and boundary extension have aspects of both internal and external change.

The organisation's culture

So far, we have discussed methods of coping with uncertainty and avoided, except for a mention of scale, a search for reasons why one path or another is followed. Such reasons lie in the organisation's culture, which pervades all other aspects – people, resources, structure and processes – to give it its identity. Culture can be defined as follows:

> *Culture is the set of policies, values, beliefs and attitudes learned and shared by the organisation's members.*
>
> *Values are fundamental principles that people have regarding what is right or wrong, important or unimportant, and so on.*
>
> *Attitudes are persistent inclinations to feel and behave in a certain ways towards people or objects.*

To define culture in such an analytic way tends to lose some of its holistic meaning. Mullins is one who suggests that we all have an intuition of what it is and it is better to use the phrase, 'How things are done around here'.[14] The story in Exhibit 3.4 illustrates the point. Note how the neighbour showed a sense of how culture is formed and diffused. I was reminded not only of the rules but also of how to pass them on. The neighbour was expecting an equally polite response that, in other districts, might not have been given!

Exhibit 3.4 Haughty culture

One afternoon a few days after moving into our new house, I made a bonfire of a heap of garden waste that had accumulated while the place was empty. After an hour or so, a neighbour, a resident of long standing, arrived to complain. 'You know, you shouldn't be making all that smoke,' he said, politely. 'We don't do that sort of thing in Queen's Park.'

▣ Investigating

Quite what forms organisational culture is a difficulty. In this, it compares with the problem of the archaeologist collecting information to describe a prehistoric society. A century ago, the focus was on monuments and objects that had deliberately been left behind by our forebears. Now, with the development of technique, every scrap is analysed. Fish bones tell us about early imports to Britain from the Mediterranean, for example. In this view, knowing more of the Roman army's eating habits can be as important as reading Caesar's *Gaul*.

Denied access to the people, however, the archaeologist cannot interpret discoveries through the producers' eyes. We need, instead, to follow the social anthropologist, who proceeds to both observe and interpret. What is important in an organisation, and is captured by the 'Way we do things round here' definition, is the way people in the workplace understand the world. Linstead argued, 'The point is not simply to explain as an external observer what is happening, but to understand what the group members think is happening as an insider'.[15] It is, after all, the way group members interpret the world that leads to their unique response to it.

To make a start, we can recognise levels of analysis based on what we can see. Close to the surface are those elements that can be observed, the artefacts of the 'organisation society' under investigation. These include symbols, language, stories and activities. They can be observed, compared and assembled into a description of the organisation. Although easy to see, they are difficult to interpret. An example can be taken from the widespread introduction of single-level lunch rooms at workplaces:

A casual observer of such a change may applaud, 'This is a welcome representation of democratisation.' Note how the observer sees the act not only as an event but also as a symbol of a shift in values. Additionally, personal views on democracy are tossed in for good measure. Yet is it evident that the change symbolised this? It could have been forced by the canteen losing money; it may have been part of a settlement of a wider dispute; it could be the stated policy of a new parent company. In any case, the decision to reorganise the lunch arrangements had to be taken by managers. Making the 'concession' can also be interpreted as an expression and reinforcement of managerial control; 'They did this to demonstrate that they could.'

Beneath the 'culture visible' at the surface, there is the invisible layer of beliefs, values and basic assumptions, *see* Figure 3.4.[16] Values were incorporated, for example, in the 'that sort of thing' statement of Exhibit 3.4. Certain types of behaviour, including making smoke when the neighbours may have their washing out, were not tolerated generally and especially in this neighbourhood. Beliefs are created by combining

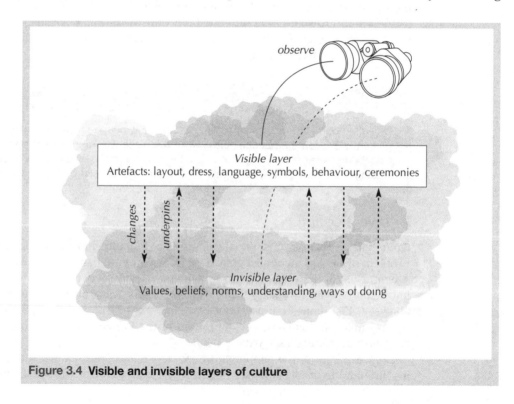

Figure 3.4 Visible and invisible layers of culture

values with experience of the organisation to establish 'facts' about the way processes work. For example, experience may suggest that closing an hour or two early on the day before a holiday does not affect work output. In planning to make this concession next time, a manager is combining belief in its limited cost with the value that it is a good idea to treat staff in this way if possible. Other managers may not agree; in other words, they either have different experiences or do not share the same values.

Underlying assumptions are the unconscious premises that are learned by the organisation's members and taken for granted. All have world views that act like personal lenses through which they perceive what goes on around them. To some extent, membership of an organisation causes them to share these world views. Being part of the group, therefore, affects not only the way they perceive the world but also how they think about it.

■ Artefacts: the culture visible

The process of recognising and interpreting culture can start from identifying its special artefacts, symbols, language, stories and activities.

Symbols

Symbols are articles, actions or events that convey meaning. We noted in the above example of the lunch room how the same action could have different meanings. Therefore, to enrich our understanding of the 'way things are done round here', we must go beyond finding out the important symbols, to investigating the interpretations people put on them. In his wry observation of institutional life, Parkinson compared chaotic departments such as publishing and research, which flourished in shabby and makeshift surroundings, with the splendid headquarters. Here you sit in a chromium armchair consoled by a receptionist 'with a dazzling smile for any slight but inevitable delay ... A minute later you are ankle deep in the director's carpet, plodding sturdily towards his distant, tidy desk. Hypnotised by the chief's unwavering stare, cowed by the Matisse hung upon his wall, you will feel that you have found real efficiency at last.'[17]

Note the artefacts mentioned by Parkinson – chromium chair (*chic* in the 1950s), receptionist, delay, carpet, distant and tidy desk, stare, Matisse! It may be that the director does not mean to intimidate, to express power, but these symbols are taken by lesser mortals as expressions of that lofty position in the hierarchy. What is more, to the extent that subordinates replicate the same imagery (within their budgets) suggests they accept the relationship that is somehow captured by the thickness of carpet, area of office, tidiness of desk, number of secretaries and so on. In other words, the status symbols at the workplace serve a function akin to the organisation chart in maintaining the *status quo*.

Effective managers can be good at using symbols positively. Richard Branson, of the Virgin Group, regularly joins in the activities of his businesses, meeting crew aboard aircraft or trains, or driving a courier motorcycle. Michael Eisner, when chief executive of Disney, joined with fellow managers in entertaining all staff to Christmas parties at the theme parks. Other mass-service organisations use symbols, uniforms, badges and photographs to reward staff who have performed good service. To the outsider, these activities may seem trivial. Yet their importance lies in their meaning inside. Note also the likelihood of unintended signs and symbols. What is your response to empty desks or others stacked high with paper, untidy signs and notices, or rubbish lying around?

Language

Pehr Gyllenhammar, when president of Volvo, wrote the description of leadership given in Exhibit 3.5.[18] We can examine what he wrote in two ways. At one level, we can use it as a definition. It states, in five categories, what leadership is and then explains why it is needed. Taken as a rational exposition to someone who is interested in knowing about the subject, this is useful. But is that all? No, the message contains more than explanation. It is full of symbolism conveying meaning at deeper levels. Possibly, he thought of the Volvo employees in his audience. This elaboration, designed to persuade, justify and legitimise, is rhetoric.

We can comment on a few of the instances in the quotation. These fit in with three common uses of rhetoric by managers identified by Gowler and Legge.[19] They are hierarchy, accountability and achievement.

Exhibit 3.5 Plain speaking and rhetoric

In 22 years at the top of Volvo, Pehr Gyllenhammar became one of the best-known and admired figures in Sweden. He developed the company's international reputation both for products and for worker-friendly production techniques. Long-term resentment over his autocratic style came to a head when Gyllenhammar announced a plan to merge with Renault. Lacking widespread support among institutional shareholders, the project became a fiasco and he was ousted at the end of 1993. Years earlier, Gyllenhammar had written:

Leadership is giving support, explanations, and interpreting information so employees can understand it. Leadership is developing consensus. Leadership is sometimes the ability to say 'stop', to draw a line, to take the heat out of a conflict, to conclude a debate and get down to negotiations. Leadership is having the courage to put a stake on an idea, and risk making mistakes. Leadership is being able to draw new boundaries, beyond the existing limits of ideas and activities. Only through this kind of leadership can we keep our institutions from drifting aimlessly, to no purpose.

■ *Hierarchy*

Relationships within many organisations tend to be less formal than outsiders think and insiders may want. With their position subject to erosion, managers often use rhetoric to reinforce their roles in the hierarchy. Note how Gyllenhammar's 'giving support, explanations and interpreting information' can be interpreted ambiguously. On the one hand, actions of training and nurturing can only be regarded as good for all. On the other hand, leaders are there precisely because of their superior ability, especially at simplifying information so the (less able) employees can understand it. By referring to hierarchical ideas in this matter-of-fact way, the rules of, and indeed existence of, hierarchy are re-established.

■ *Accountability*

Extending the notion of accountability throughout the organisation creates and sustains a culture of responsible conduct and legitimates sanctions against those who do not follow the rules. This idea is contained within phrases such as 'interpreting information', 'developing consensus' and 'keeping our institutions from drifting aimlessly'.

■ *Achievement*

This theme concerns the duty of managers to achieve results. Within the capitalist system, varying degrees of achievement are rewarded differentially according to a rough and ready share-out. The notion of achievement is fundamental to risk, opportunity and inequality. By embedding ideas such as 'having the courage to put a stake on an idea', the quotation applauds the person who is prepared to seize a chance in spite of having to 'risk making mistakes'. Going 'beyond the existing limits of ideas', which is innovation, is also a trait to be rewarded.

We noted in Chapter 1 how managers spend most of their time communicating and how a greater part of that communication was oral. Courses in interpersonal skills espouse plain speaking as the ability to communicate efficiently about management matters at the surface level. Yet, as Exhibit 3.5 illustrated, many messages contain rhetoric that works at a deeper level. Put another way, the message has both intentions and implications. It both instructs and persuades.

Figure 3.5 sets out the plain speaking–rhetoric scale. It suggests that, as intentions and implications are usually combined, most of us operate somewhere in the middle. We also move about on the scale, depending on the needs of the circumstances. There are many more interpretations of the implied content of language. For example, the use of jargon or 'group speak' enables one to express membership of a group and prove expertise and commitment. More on the content and context of communication is given in Chapter 13.

Stories

Besides illustrating a point about quality, the story in Exhibit 3.6 tells us something about the development of organisational myth. I have heard it in presentations and conversations with buyers who were sure that similar events happened in their own organisation. I took to asking them to give more details and learned that they never knew but could refer me to someone who might. From these observations, I do not know whether such incidents are common or never happen. It hardly matters. They tell a simple story to audiences ready to believe. It symbolises the time when many had to change their shared views about quality. Truth and myth are indistinguishable.

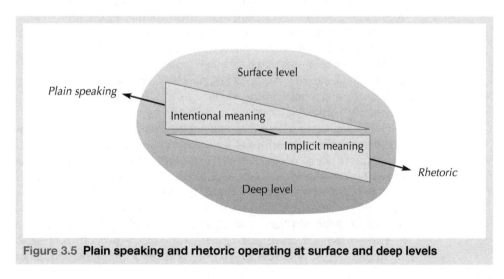

Figure 3.5 Plain speaking and rhetoric operating at surface and deep levels

Exhibit 3.6 Quality as a story

A European company ordered some semiconductor components from a Japanese supplier. The order stated something like, '10 000 items required, with a defect rate of 0.02 per cent'. The consignment duly arrived in two containers. The larger carried 9998 good components and the smaller held the two defects, clearly labelled. The supplier could not understand why the customer wanted the defects but they were sent all the same.

Organisations abound with stories. Along with the language with which they are told, their many functions include: confirmation of the role of management; clarification of how to deal with aspects of work from awkward customers to fiddling expense accounts; and understanding of what it takes to be a successful manager within the particular organisation. Lego's story of the wooden gun is significant in that it was a mother figure, combining notions of family-as-producer and family-as-consumer, who vetoed its sale. This myth has a continuing influence on the company's product policy.

Heroes and villains are identified in stories. Sometimes a hero who falls from grace turns into a villain as news filters out about mistakes and the good times are forgotten. Volvo, after the fall of Gyllenhammar, is one of many companies that have had to reinterpret their past after the end of a leader and a shift in policy. Stories about the old and new are elaborated in their retelling during such times.

Activities

Managers' actions are a form of communication and, just as language has both intended and implied meaning, so do actions. Of particular interest in understanding culture are rituals. These can be deliberately planned events, or ceremonies, designed to influence an audience. Otherwise, there can be informal activities that take on significance because they are often repeated and become part of the 'way things are done'.

Ceremonies are special events that display and reinforce an organisation's values. They may occur regularly, as in the annual staff awards (the 'Oscars') or presentations to people with long or meritorious service. University awards ceremonies combine the two in acknowledging graduates and giving honorary degrees for service to university or community. The ritual, pomp, music and formal speeches stress the university's power over its members. In other cases, ceremonies are used to launch new initiatives or to mark turning points.

Rituals are more mundane than ceremonies. They are patterns of repeated behaviour that are not especially designed but, nevertheless, convey layers of meaning. Sometimes they become elaborated into ceremonies as shown by the process of initiation. At the Université Catholique de Mons in Belgium, new students as a group have to spend a week of humiliation before their seniors before they are accepted into student life. Other organisations have less formal initiation rituals where new members are subjected to jokes and tricks to demonstrate their *naïveté*. As in many workplaces, apprentices at Crewe Locomotive Works were sent to the stores with notes for 'Red oil for a red lamp' or 'A left-handed screwdriver'. Naturally, the storekeeper would make them wait a long time, telling other callers what they were waiting for, and eventually send them to another department where what the victim was looking for was sure to be in stock.

These examples show that rituals, while often difficult to understand, should not be thought of as pointless (as in 'empty ritual'). Initiations and regular habits, such as 'the office always goes out for lunch on a Friday', test new members and sustain bonds among the team. Managers also incorporate ritual into routine, cyclical processes such as budgeting.

Difficulties with interpretation

The focus on artefacts brings with it three dangers:

Confusing artefacts and culture

Artefacts are elements that are relatively easy to observe and compare between organisations. It is tempting, therefore, to treat them as 'data' in the same way as figures on a balance sheet or pie charts in a market report. The data then becomes a description of the culture. We should guard against this trap, reminding ourselves of the aim to understand what the group members think is happening as insiders. Artefacts are not the culture. Seeing through them enables us to understand the deeper levels.

Artefacts as a screen

The surface and deeper layers were presented here as simplifications. Having to use artefacts as a route to investigating deeper levels should not mean their value is discounted. They are not just manifestations or symbols of a 'real world' beneath the surface layer. We should not dismiss the totem pole as a mere representation of something more profound. Understanding culture means understanding culture as a whole; values, beliefs and their symbolic representation are all parts of the same system.

Interpreting espoused values

Why, we may say, is there such a puzzle over values when so many organisations express them formally? Examples of these so-called *espoused values* can be found in codes of practice (Chapter 5), quality and service policies (Chapter 6), mission statements (Chapter 8) and many other places. Since they are documented, we could treat them as artefacts or, as Schein proposed, a third cultural layer between the others of Figure 3.4.[20] Either way, they could offer a crucial guide to an organisation's culture. Yet, are they clues or false trails? Do they reveal or mask the invisible layer? The answer depends on the extent to which the espoused values express the wishes of the managerial group or are shared by all members. Many recognise that an organisation, especially a large one, has not one culture but many.

How to investigate

Our purpose should be to reach the underlying assumptions held by the group and its sub-groups. As our discussion shows, it would be naive to expect to gain answers merely by administering a questionnaire! The approach should be to study:

- symbols and how they are used to convey information;
- the value placed on artefacts;
- the relationships between language and concepts such as hierarchy, control and motivation;
- stories and the development of myths, heroes and villains;
- how communicative media are used;
- mental processes such as interpretation and understanding;
- social processes such as initiation, development and change.[21]

Table 3.2 **Analysis of artefacts and espoused values**

Observed feature	Clue to culture invisible	Managerial action?
Visitors must check in at security office, although employees are not checked in or out	Safety and security are important but employees are trusted	None
All must don clean overalls before entering the plant	Hygiene is a core value reinforced by the provision of new kit every day	None
All must wash hands when entering any building from the yard, but some wash areas are untidy	Some employees do not value the need for high standards	Improve wash area design and equipment. Emphasise hygiene in induction, training and, where necessary, discipline
Employee on mixer: 'A few raisin bags are torn. Does it matter?' Supervisor replies: 'Check them as you put them in'	Neither employee nor supervisor fully buys in to 100% standards on food safety. (Damaged consignments should never be accepted)	Urgent action to reinforce quality values in this work area

A practical approach to observation and interpretation lists observed artefacts, including espoused values, in tabular form. Table 3.2 shows how observations at a food processing plant began to give clues to the culture invisible and suggest managerial intervention.[22]

■ Classifying organisational culture

Various proposals for classifications of culture have been put forward. In a populist approach, Handy suggested four ideal-types, summarised in Table 3.3.[23] He proposed a quick diagnosis based on the question, 'What do you do for a living?'

Table 3.3 **Types of culture proposed by Handy**

Type of culture	'What's your job?'	Explanation of response
Power – Central source of power connected to all members. Often in small enterprises. Few rules and procedures; decisions on hunch and influence	'I work for Dr Forster'	Job seen as being employed by an individual. Power/dependency relationship
Role – Based on rationality, as in Weber's bureaucracy. Roles are defined and people, who are 'slotted' into them, gain psychological and contractual security. Stability is a watchword	'I am Head of Data Security at Megabooks Limited'	Using the job title within a large corporation indicated a role culture
Task – Management is seen in terms of action. The purpose of the organisation is to bring together groups to work on problems. Membership depends on expertise and not on formal position	'I'm working on new product development at the Long Division'	The individual does not mention role but activity, suggesting a task culture
Person – Individuals are the central concern. Professionals, such as solicitors or surveyors, gather in a practice to share resources, but work independently and often have their own clients	'I'm a solicitor (monk, pilot, opera singer)'	Such organisations are made up of people who are what they do

Such models of culture, combined with quick tools for diagnosis, are helpful for those who seek a snap analysis or want to draw general conclusions across a broad swathe. The problem is that they present ideal-types that are rarely matched in practice, as a university example shows:

Handy suggests that university departments are person cultures. He paints a picture of individuals committed to scholarship and drawn together by common interest. This ignores the 'reality' of many departments where, for example, financial stringency has led to tight control on resources by officials. This implies a swing towards a task culture as specialist staff become responsible for budgets, resources and so on. Meanwhile, some professors, skilled at winning external funds, create projects with teams of researchers dependent on them for advancement.

In this example, we have a mix of Handy's types. We can try to get by with statements such as, 'It's mainly a person culture but it does have aspects of ...'. Far better, when studying one organisation, to avoid general models and approach with an open mind.

Strong cultures

Investigation that is more robust has been conducted into the idea of a 'strong' culture. This extends our original definition by referring to values, beliefs and attitudes *widely* shared and *strongly* held throughout the organisation, which is consequently more unified than otherwise. Measures, based on the degree of sharing strong attitudes, have been developed. Using them, Sorensen related performance, cultural strength and the rate of environmental change.[24] In stable environments, firms with strong culture show both superior and steadier performance. Their commitment to an established view of the world enables better exploitation of known opportunities. However, when environments are more volatile, the advantages of the strong culture disappear. Such firms find it difficult to develop new skills to exploit openings caused by new conditions.

Culture change

Should and can culture be changed? A look on consultants' websites shows many firms offering to do just this. There is a tension between such rapid interventions and what we know of the gradual accumulation of culture from shared experiences. Yet, the environment changes and the organisation must change with it. Change creates gaps, shown in Figure 3.6, between values and the rest of the organisation and the environment. This brings out internal and external problems.

Internal gaps

Of many reasons for organisational inefficiency, among the most intractable is misfit between the deep and surface layers or between culture and other organisational elements. For instance, a firm may undergo rapid expansion. The 'way things were done' when output was lower may not suit the new requirement for mass production. Employees may have been brought up to value widespread personal contact with colleagues and customers, yet the new order may require specialisation in small teams. Internal inefficiency may show up as waste, frustration, soured relations and unrest.

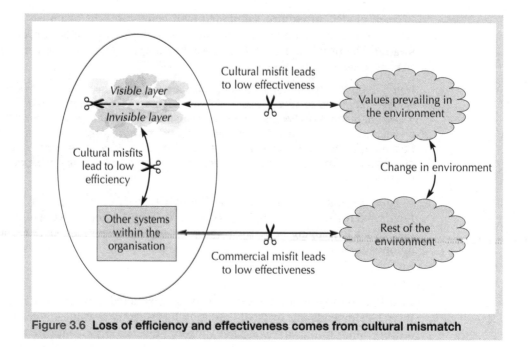

Figure 3.6 **Loss of efficiency and effectiveness comes from cultural mismatch**

External gaps

External gaps appear when an organisation no longer fits its environment. Figure 3.6 points out two issues. First, there is a problem in the commercial relationship between the organisation and the environment. It could be that the products are no longer required or the firm persists with the wrong supplies. These difficulties can be resolved by innovation in products and processes and we shall deal with these in Chapter 17. The second, probably more difficult, problem results from a cultural gap between the organisation and the region or nation where it operates. For instance, just as 'Westernisation' of business has been resisted in some nations, so have some aspects of 'Japanisation' been resisted in European manufacturing. In retailing, Toys "Я" Us experienced a long dispute in Sweden when it decided to stick to its global no-union policy. The campaign became a national cause. Questions of how closely an international firm should fit in with the local 'scene' are raised again in Chapter 4.

We see from these examples that match between system and environment goes beyond finding appropriate markets and products. It requires that an organisation's value system matches both its own policies and its environment. Culture gaps can be large, especially after takeovers or mergers. We frequently see rapid turnover of senior managers after such changes, not because of their incompetence but because they do not like the new ways of doing things. After the 2000 recruitment of Bob Nardelli from General Electric, Home Depot, the huge United States DIY retailer, ran into difficulties. The new chief replaced highly decentralised store operations with a top-down approach based on accountability, discipline and structure. Service quality slumped.[35]

◼ Changing culture

Clearly, cultures change and, unless there is a major disturbance, they will change slowly. Rapid environmental change, however, means that this may not be sufficient. Matters are too pressing. Burnes reports a survey showing that, in one five-year period, a quarter of the United Kingdom's leading companies had been involved in a deliberate culture change programme through shaping the beliefs, values and attitudes of employees.[26] A common example is the introduction of 'customer care' programmes in firms that were reorganising or, during this period, undergoing privatisation. These programmes included training in the processes of dealing with customers as well as attempts to implant the notion that the customer comes first.

Without any follow-up studies, we cannot know how effective the culture change programmes are. They run the risk of developing widespread cynicism and direct resistance. In any case, have managers the right to try to act in such a manipulative way? Should employees' attitudes be directed towards favouring particular economic ends? The answer is surely negative. Not only is the managers' right questionable, but also they are unlikely to succeed. This illustrates the danger of regarding organisational culture as a variable like technology or structure. These can be changed to suit circumstances. Culture is different; it is best regarded as the 'way things are'. Understanding is required not so that culture can be manipulated directly but so that the impacts of other changes can be recognised and evaluated.

Conclusion: change is necessary but difficult

Misfit between organisation and environment leads to problems. Depending on the type of change, reversible or irreversible, the problems can be handled by routine processes or adaptations that are more fundamental. Uncertainty, arising from change and complexity, compounds the problems because managers find it difficult to recognise and interpret what is happening.

Essentially, the fit between the organisation and its environment is maintained by adapting either the environment or the internal structure. Large firms seem to have a choice. If, however, they rely solely on assumed perfect information and a battery of countermeasures against change, they will eventually fail. All firms, and small ones in particular, must continuously change themselves or disappear.

Culture, or 'the way we do things round here', is a powerful subsystem of every organisation. It may be the source of direction, innovation and change but so often it develops to reinforce existing ways of doing things and hence resists change. Lego, among Europe's most successful family businesses, illustrates both the benefit of a strong culture in providing direction and unity and the danger of being guided by successes of the past when conditions change.

Managers may be attracted to the idea of manipulating culture. Like tearing down statues, they may work on changing the artefacts of a culture where they want radical remodelling. We should recognise that culture is more than the artefacts; it is a powerful, integrated system of artefacts, values, beliefs and fundamental assumptions. To improve the business, managers should work directly on altering processes and practices and not attempt to manipulate these values, beliefs and assumptions. Understanding culture gives clues as to the best ways to introduce and nurture changes so that they will be sustained.

QUICK CHECK

Can you …

- Name Rhenman's categories of change.
- Use a diagram to show Duncan's change dimensions.
- Summarise the population ecology perspective.
- Distinguish four ways of adapting to the environment.
- Illustrate six ways of adapting the environment.
- Match the means of adaptation to organisational size.
- Compare formal and informal definitions of culture.
- Identify four types of artefact.
- Give examples of each of Handy's cultural types.
- Relate the notion of strong culture to success.

QUESTIONS

Chapter review

3.1 What are the main sources and types of change originating in the environment?

3.2 Outline the population ecology perspective on growth and change. What use could it be to someone who advises small firms?

3.3 Explain Handy's categories of organisational culture, naming an organisation you know which fits each case.

Application

3.4 Use the layout of Table 3.2 to explain the artefacts described in the Lego case. What is the cultural significance of Legoland to staff, customers and others?

3.5 In what ways would a culture that accepts change differ from one that resists it?

Investigation

3.6 Many websites carry statements of codes of practice, charters or similar expression of values. Select and compare several of these and suggest reasons why these statements have been made. What clues can you find as to how they will influence the deeper levels of culture?

CLOSING CASE

Creating a new culture[27]

Heinz International operates two successful food processing plants at Hastings, New Zealand. The first, King Street, was built in 1934, while the second is a brand new plant at Tomoana, opened in 1996. This occurred after a period when the UK's accession to the European Union had devastated New Zealand's agricultural export market and new competition generated pressure to raise productivity. The Employment Contracts Act of 1991 enabled businesses to switch from national agreements to local, departmental or even individual contracts. Seeking to use their new staff most effectively, managers at Tomoana viewed the new location as chance to pursue a different human resource strategy. This went beyond merely avoiding the unionised constraints at King Street. An alternative culture would be the basis of worker participation, innovation and multi-skilling.

King Street was part of a business established by Sir James Wattie in 1934. He was known for his open office door, humility, friendliness and genuine interest in his staff. Two sons continued the business after the founder's death and, until their retirement in the 1980s, the values and culture followed Sir James's ideas. Several international mergers, restructurings, splits and redundancies followed until Wattie's New Zealand plants were sold to Heinz in 1992.

Although the two plants were to be run from King Street, senior managers agreed to manage them in different ways. This was reflected in new employment practices. The contract at King Street has 146 very detailed and prescriptive pages, including 110 job classifications. The document at Tomoana, with 23 pages, is more a statement of intent, underpinning the desire to establish teams. Rewards are based on competence, not length of service, and trust replaces rules. Flexibility is shown in arrangements for sick leave, an hours bank and skill-based pay based on achieving training standards. With 87 per cent representation, unions are parties to the King Street contract; at Tomoana, where participation is 50 per cent, they do not have this status.

When recruiting for the new plant, senior managers were personally involved. They sought people who had literacy and numeracy skills higher than norms for the industry and could play team roles in small manufacturing units. For example, any of the 15 staff on the jam line will also clean up or drive a fork lift, jobs done by specialists at King Street. Following recruitment, local managers continued to build the new culture around the concept of 'Team Tomoana' with its greater freedom and challenge built on partnership.

Using the Organisation Culture Inventory to compare culture between the two plants, Hursthouse and Kolb found significant differences. Tomoana, which had 43 staff at the time of the survey and grew to 250 by 2002, was rated more highly as a constructive culture. This indicates that members interact and work so they can achieve higher-order satisfaction needs, such as achievement, self-actualising, humanistic-encouraging and friendship norms. On the other hand, King Street, with some 300 staff, scored more heavily on the other two OCI scales: the passive/defensive culture, where members believe they must interact with people so as not to threaten their own security, manifests approval, conventional, dependent and avoidance norms; the aggressive/defensive culture, whose members approach tasks forcefully to protect their status and security, is marked by oppositional, power, competitive and perfectionist norms.

Clearly, the efforts of the management team had created a different culture, although they still regarded it as in its infancy. It may not be able to survive beyond the tenure of the founder-managers. Further, a new government in 2000 promised to repeal the Employment Contracts Act and restore some of the powers of the unions.

Questions

1 What features of the business environment contributed to the management search for lower costs at the new site?

2 The case has two examples of the development of organisational culture. How do they compare with Schein's sources of culture – founders, selection and learning?

3 How can the 'trust' contract between management and workers be reconciled with an employment contract for the managers based on a philosophy of 'deliver or go'? What risks can you envisage for the 'trust' philosophy as time passes?

4 What does the Tomoana experience suggest for managers seeking to change the culture at King Street or elsewhere?

Bibliography

Bernard Burnes (2000) *Managing Change* (3rd edition, Harlow: Financial Times Prentice Hall) includes useful chapters on culture and managing change. The works by Handy and Schein given in the references are among the more important works in the field. Stephen Linstead and Lynn Fulop (2002) *Management: A critical text* (London: Palgrave) supply a critical view of current orthodoxy.

References

1 Brow, Christopher (2002) 'A universe beyond the plastic bricks: Lego has returned to profit by adapting to a world of increasingly sophisticated children', *Financial Times*, 24 May; Inside Track (2002) 'The generation game', *Financial Times*, 24 May; (2002) 'Lego returns to basics to rebuild brand', *Financial Times*, 12 May; 'Lego revamp to axe sub-brands', *Marketing Week*, 17 October 2002; Marsh, Peter (1996a) 'Lego builds its future: the Danish toy maker is expanding its empire', *Financial Times*, 16 March; Marsh, Peter (1996b) 'Management: one step ahead of the pack', *Financial Times*, 13 May; Bowen, David (1996) 'The house Kirk built: this is the toy that charmed the kids that pestered the parents that bought the bricks that built the firm that made the Danes a billion', *Independent on Sunday*, 24 March; Lawson, Mark (1996) 'The brick gets slick: once the bastion of educational values, even Lego has succumbed to the theme park', *Guardian*, 30 March; Luger, Fritz (1996) 'Lego will in 15 Landeren Themenparks bauen', *Der Standard*, 20 March; Castello, M. (1997) 'Lego estudia un parque tematico en el area de Barcelona', *Expansion*, 15 April; Richards, Hale (1997) 'Business Portrait: master builder and his wall of Lego: Kjeld Kirk Kristiansen', *European*, 24 April; Barnes, Hilary (1997) 'Lego looks at girl power to spice up sales', *Financial Times*, 23 January; **www.lego.com.**

2 Rhenman, Eric (1973) *Organisation Theory for Long Range Planning*, London: Wiley-Interscience, 16.

3 Duncan, R.B. (1972) 'The characteristics of organisational environments and perceived environmental uncertainty', *Administrative Science Quarterly*, **17**, 313–27.

4 Ashby, Ross (1956) *An Introduction to Cybernetics*, New York: John Wiley.

5 Sharfman, M. and Dean, J. (1991) 'Conceptualising and measuring the organisation environment: a multidimensional approach', *Journal of Management*, **17**, 749–68.

6 Lomi, Alessandro (1995) 'The population ecology of organisational founding', *Administrative Science Quarterly*, **40(1)** March, 111–44.

7 Cowles, Virginia (1973) *The Rothschilds – A family of fortune*, London: Weidenfeld & Nicholson, 47–9.

8 Burns, Tom and Stalker, G.M. (1961) *The Management of Innovation*, London: Tavistock.

9 Ranking data from Business Week (2002) *Business Week Global 1000*; **http://bwnt.businessweek.com/global_1000/2002/index.asp**, accessed 12 December 2002.

10 Bannister, Nicholas (1996) 'Rebuke stings BT's sentinel', *Guardian*, 10 September, 18.

11 Black, Ian (2002) 'Tobacco giants lose EU fight over labelling', *Guardian*, 11 December, 9.

12 Morse, Laurie (1994) 'Drought threatens Ghanaian aluminium smelter', *Financial Times*, 1 September, 3; 'Kaiser averts Ghana smelter shutdown', *Financial Times*, 17 September, 11; Kaiser Aluminum Corporation (2002) *Smelter in Ghana curtails one potline*, Houston, Tex., 5 March.

13 Haunschild, Pamela R. (1993) 'Interorganisational imitation: the impact on corporate acquisition activity', *Administrative Science Quarterly*, **38(4)** December, 564–92.

14 Mullins, Laurie J. (1996) *Management and Organisational Behaviour*, London: Financial Times Pitman Publishing, 711.

15 Linstead, Stephen (1996) 'Understanding management: culture, critique and change', in Linstead, Stephen *et al.* (eds) *Understanding Management*, London: Sage, 14.

16 Schein, Edgar H. (1985) *Organisational Culture and Leadership: A dynamic view*, New York: Jossey-Bass, proposes two hidden layers – values and beliefs, and basic assumptions – but space does not allow such a detailed discussion.

17 C. Northcote Parkinson (1957) *Parkinson's Law, or the Pursuit of Progress*, London: John Murray, 84.

18 Gyllenhammar, Pehr G. (1977) *People at Work*, Reading, Mass.: Addison-Wesley, 161–2.

19 Gowler, Dan and Legge, Karen (1996) 'The meaning of management and the management of meaning', in Linstead *et al.* (eds) *op. cit.*, 34–50.

20 Schein, Edgar H. (1997) *Organisation Culture and Leadership*, 3rd edition, New York: Jossey-Bass, 17.

21 Based on Linstead (1996) *op. cit.*, 19.

22 Tabular presentation based on: Buch, Kimberly and Wetzel, David K. (2001) 'Analyzing and realigning organizational culture', *Leadership and Organization Development Journal*, **22(1)**, 40–3.

23 Handy, Charles B. (1986) *Understanding Organisations*, 4th edition, Harmondsworth: Penguin, 188; (1978) *Gods of Management*, London: Pan, 44.

24 Sorensen, Jesper B. (2002) 'The strength of corporate cultures and the reliability of firm performance', *Administrative Science Quarterly*, **47(1)**, 70–94.

25 *Atlanta Journal And Constitution* (2002) 'Home Depot's Painful Transition: Nardelli's GE-type policies reverse freewheeling style', 8 December.

26 Burnes, Bernard (1996) *Managing Change*, 2nd edition, London: Financial Times Pitman Publishing, 116.

27 Hursthouse, Paul and Kolb, Darl (2001) 'Cultivating culture in greenfields' *Personnel Review*, **33(3)** 317–30; Competenz (2002) *A recipe for success*, Auckland, NZ: Competenz, **www.competenz.org.nz/heinz_case_study.pdf.**

Themes in management

P art 2 introduces four themes frequently encountered in the study and practice of management. Awareness of the issues, and competence at coping with them, are important to every manager. Chapter 4 shows how the forces promoting globalisation of business seem, in the past half-century, to have overcome those resisting it. In the 'second global economy', commerce is dominated by multinational enterprises. Their emergence raises questions of how they should organise and operate as well as problems for the individual manager. How can a person work well in different cultural environments, making the necessary adjustments?

Whatever the size of the organisation, the issue of social responsibility has become important. The view of businesses as private enterprises is being modified as stakeholders increase their influence. Chapter 5 investigates the question of corporate social responsibility from a manager's viewpoint, setting it in its ethical context. Ethical concepts assist managers to recognise and resolve dilemmas.

Thanks to the work of pioneers such as Deming and Juran, who cultivated their ideas in the fertile ground of the post-war Japanese economy, the importance of quality has been recognised by leading organisations. Chapter 6 shows how concern with quality means more than ensuring that products meet standards. It is both a philosophy, illuminating all management practice, and a set of techniques with wide application.

The dominance of multinational organisations overshadows the role of entrepreneurs in building businesses. Willing to take risks and innovate, entrepreneurs often create tomorrow's success stories. Although entrepreneurs are often to be found in small organisations, their contribution to large ones is also vital if stagnation is to be avoided. Chapter 7 studies what it takes to be an entrepreneur and how they can succeed.

CHAPTER 4

Global business: bridging nations and cultures

Chapter objectives

When you have finished studying this chapter, you should be able to:

- compare the forces promoting and resisting the globalisation of business activities;

- show how the presence of multinational enterprises makes the second global economy differ from the first and debate what sorts of world groupings might emerge;

- name some leading MNEs, outlining where they are based and where they operate; link MNEs to the process of globalisation;

- explain key features of MNEs, showing why and how they have grown and, in particular, why they engage in foreign direct investment;

- illustrate how managerial attitudes within MNEs can differ;

- address the problems of managing in different cultures, explaining the benefits and limitations of cross-cultural research applied to management;

- outline the key issues in cultural adjustment for a manager being posted abroad and how a firm can improve the rate of success.

The new electronic interdependence recreates the world in the image of a global village.

Marshall McLuhan, Canadian sociologist

Exports keep up Scotch distillers' spirits[1]

Few United Kingdom manufacturers have a greater need to export than distillers of Scotch whisky do. Of total sales exceeding £2 billion, 90 per cent is sold abroad. Annual output exceeds one billion bottles, mostly blends from several distilleries. Johnny Walker Red Label, J&B Rare and Ballantine's are the world's leading whiskies. The smaller-volume, expensive 'single malts' are identified by source and year of distillation. They are matured in oak casks and bottled some 10, 12 or even 20 years later. Leaders are Glenfiddich, Glenlivet and Glenmorangie. Balancing supply, demand and stock over decades is a major problem. To cut risk, some diversify into other spirits or products. Highland Distilleries has Gloag's Gin, while Glenmorangie is among those operating a visitor centre and a top-class hotel.

Many distilleries are small by world standards. Some 80 per cent of capacity, however, is owned by groups with other interests. These provide international distribution without which the brand would not survive. William Lawson, in the Bacardi group, exports 90 per cent of its £22 million turnover. Morrison Bowmore, part of the Japanese drinks company Suntory, exports 60 per cent. Highland Distilleries has a cross-shareholding with Rémy-Cointreau.

The industry jealously guards its name. To qualify as 'Scotch', a whisky must be distilled in Scotland, although it can be bottled elsewhere. Smaller companies have long relied on leaders, such as Diageo, to promote the idea of Scotch as a drink. Eighty-nine per cent of Diageo's £7.7 billion turnover comes from premium drinks, which include Johnny Walker, J&B and Bell's, as well as Guinness, Smirnoff and other spirits and wines. It spends some 25 per cent of turnover on marketing.

Sales of Scotch in the United States have fallen by 60 per cent since 1980. Failure to continually recruit new, younger drinkers meant that Scotch has increasingly borne the burden of an 'oldie' image in its traditional markets. Some 70 per cent of the UK's 55–64 age group drink it, compared with 6 per cent of the same group in Spain. Gin, sherry, port and Dutch jenever also suffer, although to a lesser extent. Young people often choose a different drink from their parents. In expanding markets, such as France, Greece, Italy and Spain, it is easier to present Scotch as a more fashionable product. Women, who consume about 30 per cent of all worldwide sales, are especially important in these markets. Recent television advertising has dropped the 'kilts and castles in misty glen' image. Worldwide sales of single malts have grown rapidly, although this luxury market was affected by the terrorist threats from 2001. Falling demand for up-market hotels, restaurants and bars affected sales; duty-free and other travel-related turnover also fell.

Overseas markets are reached through international distributors with strong local networks. There can be difficulties, however. Macallan-Glenlivet's dispute with its Italian distributor caused a loss of one year's sales in a key market for 'The Macallan'. A feud between William Grant and its French agent Marie Brizard was settled in court.

Glenmorangie is a family-controlled company with 295 employees. Most work at Broxburn, near Edinburgh, site of the bottling plant and warehouse, with about 50 at three distilleries, Tain, Elgin and Ardbeg. Some 30 per cent of the company's £59 million turnover comes from the Glenmorangie brand, leader in Scotland, second in the United Kingdom and third in the world. Other malts include: Ardbeg, made in a reopened distillery on the Isle of Islay; Glen Moray, a middle brand also in the UK top ten; and the prestigious Martin's 20-year-old. The last is particularly strong in Portugal, where it is known as the top people's drink. During the 1990s, multiple export markets and distributors had led to a proliferation of products. A new management team refocused the strategy to emphasise strong brands, new premium variants and reaching new international markets.

Operations were improved. In the mid-1990s, there were 9 brands, 41 bottles, 27 closures, 40 packages, 73 labels and 74 shipping cases! Halving the range simplified production and cut overheads. In 2000, Glenmorangie formed a cost-saving partnership with Drambuie. The latter is blended and bottled at Broxburn and economies are gained in supplies of blending whiskies, packaging and logistics.

Wooden casks, of finely grained Kentucky oak, are used during maturation despite evaporation of the 2 per cent 'angels' share'. Glenmorangie has excellent wood selection and management skills.

Its 15 000-cask sampling programme enabled it to relate taste to the way the oak is treated. This knowledge was used in the development of new luxury finishes that command a 25 per cent price premium. The malt is moved to former port, sherry or Madeira casks for the last two of the 12-year maturation period. Thus, sub-brands are created quickly. Some Glen Moray, for example, is mellowed in used Chardonnay or Chenin Blanc casks. Glenmorangie Malaga spends the last of its 25 years in sweet wine casks and is only available to members of an online club.

Many customers buy small quantities and are difficult to reach. During the 1990s, Glenmorangie served its mature international markets through agents: Brown-Forman in the USA; Kokubu in Japan; and Bacardi-Martini or Moët Hennessy for Europe and elsewhere. By 2002, however, it had consolidated its distribution through one strategic sales and marketing partner. Kentucky-based Brown-Forman, the world's seventh-largest drinks company, is renowned for Jack Daniels and Southern Comfort. It brings a global sales and distribution network and, having bought 10 per cent of Glenmorangie's share capital, has a seat on the board. Glenmorangie company sales increased 52 per cent from 1996 to 2002.

While concentrating on its key markets, especially Western Europe, Glenmorangie foresees growth in new ones. Small volume sales in Eastern Europe and elsewhere are intended to 'seed' these markets. Further afield, the early 1990s saw joint ventures in India and China, exchanging technical advice for bottling capacity. Loss making and not fitting the new focus, both projects were terminated by 2002, although some sales continue. Entering developing countries is a high-risk strategy with unknown rewards. Consumption of Scotch in China is lower than in Stirling, the Scottish town of 28 000 inhabitants.

Introduction

International business is simply that which takes place across national boundaries. At first we may think just of trade, as with the exporting of whisky from Scotland. Then, however, we recognise the presence of foreign firms in most countries. These companies, often among the largest in the world, have made investments in foreign operations that go beyond simply trading from their home base. Foreign investment tends to be handled by the large multinational enterprises. Of these, the top 500 are responsible for about 80 per cent of the flow of capital for investment.

Although almost all of the largest companies are international, to operate across frontiers is not the preserve of this group. Many Scotch distillers, with sales of perhaps £10 million, sell their products to fans and collectors in many countries. In service industries, small specialist companies, from courier services to publishers, operate and have offices or outlets in more than one country. One popular method of development is the international joint venture. This combines, for instance, the local know-how of one company with the technical know-how of another. Glenmorangie followed, then withdrew from, a typical joint-venture strategy in China. Its link with Brown-Forman combines the international marketing reach of the American company with the unique product and technical skills of Glenmorangie.

Is Scotch a 'global' product? Broadly speaking, it is not changed from market to market. That is part of the product's appeal. Yet there are differences of detail, of tradition, of brand image, of competition, of distribution and so on. These affect demand in different markets. For example, the Japanese government has been criticised by the World Trade Organization for protecting local 'shochu' producers. Taxes on imported whisky and brandy are seven times the rates on the potato-based spirit whose 1996 market share was 74 per cent.[2] In India, Bagpiper whisky, number four in the world, provides stiff competition. We can, therefore, see similarities among Scotch markets and consumers as well as differences. Which come into play when companies face decisions on international operations?

This chapter provides answers to these questions. It starts by investigating *globalisation*, the trend towards increased integration of business activities throughout the world. Then we look into the companies that have both stimulated and benefited from this trend to examine why and how they become international and why they go beyond trading to investing in foreign countries. Finally, in spite of global trends, substantial differences between countries remain. The question of managing in different cultures must be addressed.

Globalisation

The term globalisation refers to the process of integration on a world scale. Some authors define it solely as a business policy. For example, Rugman and Hodgetts saw it as:

> *The production and distribution of products and services of a homogenous type and quality on a worldwide basis.*[3]

As discussed later in the chapter, this policy is a response to the needs of large companies to both gain economies of scale and take opportunities throughout the world. In contrast, other authorities see globalisation as either a much broader cultural trend or at least the convergence of multiple forces. McCluhan, quoted at the start of the chapter, studied the cultural effects of media. Even before the Internet, he foresaw electronics stimulating the emergence of the global village. Perlmutter is among many who have identified forces, summarised in Exhibit 4.1. He argued that they are 'but the first steps on a rocky road to building a global civilisation'.[4]

Exhibit 4.1 Convergent forces support global harmonisation

- *Accommodation among political systems*
  - openness and transparency among nations,
  - willingness to co-operate.
- *Open world economy*
  - recognition of interdependency,
  - reduction of trade barriers.
- *Increased awareness and respect for other cultures*
  - sharing of ideas,
  - convergence of consumer tastes.
- *Developments in communications*
  - investment in freight and passenger systems,
  - growth of the digital world.
- *Common concerns for consequences*
  - ecological effects,
  - rich versus poor.

The reference to a rocky road underlines that it is not clear what kind of civilisation is emerging. There are many difficulties and paradoxes. For instance, we know of the Westernisation of tastes in many countries of Asia, the Middle East and Africa. Rashly, we may see these as 'harmonisation'. At the same time, however, we recognise the assertion and reassertion of ethnic, religious and cultural differences. These are manifest within and between nations and also on a wider scale. Western industrialism and commercialism meet Islamic fundamentalism and Confucianism. The obstacles to harmonisation are powerful, *see* Exhibit 4.2. The two effects go side by side. Isolationism, tried by countries such as Albania, Burma and North Korea, does not work. Autonomy and difference can only be sustained within a framework of worldwide co-operation. Countries, companies and individuals increasingly accept the need to do business with each other.

Exhibit 4.2 Divergent forces oppose global harmonisation

- *Geography*
  - uneven distribution of natural resources,
  - different and shifting climates.

- *Income*
  - contrasting stages of economic development,
  - rich and poor within nations.

- *Education*
  - difficulties of catching up,
  - flows of the brightest out of poorer countries.

- *Culture*
  - conflict among ethnic and cultural groups,
  - rejection of dominant values.

- *Language*
  - rising divergence *within* languages such as English.

The second global economy

Making known, and extolling, the scale and scope of worldwide business has become common. The point is often made that the turnover of leading companies matches the output of leading nations. The leaders are crudely compared with nations ranked around twentieth in terms of gross national product (GNP), close to Austria or Belgium. The phenomenon of vast international business is regarded as new. Yet, as Kobrin points out, the world economy was at least as open and convergent between 1870 and 1914 as it is today.[5] Levels of international trade and investment before 1914 – measured both relatively and absolutely – were only recently surpassed. It could be said that recent growth in world business has been simply a return to the state of affairs before the calamities of the two world wars.

This somewhat rosy view is tempered by those who point to uneven development and the advantages that protectionism brought to some countries. Protectionism often arises through different regulations and standards that hinder exporters. The Agreement on Technical Barriers to Trade aims to prevent regulations, standards, testing and certification procedures creating such obstacles.[6]

In any case, history is not repeating itself. This 'second global economy' differs greatly from the first. Obviously, there are now many more national markets and the flows of goods and money are broader and deeper. Most important, however, is the change in organisation of international transactions. A century ago, the mechanism was the market; goods were traded through markets and foreign investments made directly by share and bond holders. Nowadays, these mechanisms are being supplanted by the international business that uses internal supply channels to replace trade and transfer of funds to replace investment markets. Internationally planned and controlled production has become a key characteristic. Some 65 000 international businesses employ some 54 million staff in their 850 000 foreign affiliates. The affiliates' 2001 worldwide sales, about $19 trillion, were twice as high as total world exports; in 1990 the figures had been equal. They account for about 10 per cent of the world's GDP and a third of all exports.[7]

> The terms multinational and transnational, enterprise and corporation are used interchangeably when referring to organisations operating across frontiers. Hence, we have MNE, TNE, MNC and TNC. This text sticks to MNE.

The integrated international business, often called the *multinational enterprise* (*MNE*), has advantages within the second global economy that parallel those possessed by the international trader in the first. In his classic article 'The Globalisation of Markets',[8] Levitt argued that the global corporation wins by harnessing *technology*. This 'drives consumers relentlessly towards the same common goals – alleviation of life's burdens and the expansion of discretionary time and spending power'. The truly global company is reluctant to adjust to local differences, only doing so after testing consumers with standardised products of the highest quality. Standardisation allows for low-cost supply at huge scale. Therefore, we have standard products: aero engines from Rolls-Royce; shoes from Nike; chips from Intel; globally marketed pharmaceuticals, pesticides and agrochemicals; and drinks from Guinness to Glenmorangie.

Who are the multinational enterprises?

The introduction mentioned that a business does not have to be huge to be multinational. On the other hand, most of the largest are multinational. Table 4.1 lists the top 25 businesses measured by 2002 results.[9] Almost all are heavily committed internationally.

What does Table 4.1 tell us? Looking first at the industries, we can see companies that fit into the picture of the second global economy. They supply products whose demand is high in many corners of the world and have built their size through the internalisation of markets: the petroleum companies control all stages from oil wells to the service station; the motor and engineering companies work by exploiting their technical innovations and process skills on the world stage; the service providers – telecommunications, retailing and insurance – match the high demand for these functions in and between the world's major economies. Four of the 25 are Japanese trading companies. These firms act as the distribution ends of combines of manufacturers, each of which can be a huge company in its own right. Commanding such a large proportion of trade both within and between Japan and other states, these companies are typical organisations of the second global economy.

Turnover is but one measure of size. It overstates the importance of trading companies that combine high turnover with small margins. Other assessments are based on employment or capitalisation. After all, for many observers, 'a big company' is one with many staff and huge facilities. Looking at turnover and employment, four appear in the top ten for both. Three are motor manufacturers – General Motors, Ford and Daimler Chrysler. With between 300 000 and 400 000 employees in many countries, and also highly capitalised, it is no wonder that these are frequently seen

Table 4.1 The world's 25 largest corporations by turnover

Rank	Company	Nation	Industry	Sales $ bn
1	Wal-Mart Stores	USA	Retailing	241
2	Exxon Mobil	USA	Oil and gas	213
3	General Motors Corporation	USA	Motor vehicles	175
4	BP	UK	Oil and gas	174
5	Ford Motor Company	USA	Motor vehicles	162
6	Daimler Chrysler	D	Motor vehicles	136
7	Royal Dutch/Shell Group	NL/UK	Oil and gas	135
8	General Electric Company	USA	Electronics; electrical equipment	126
9	Toyota Motor Corporation	J	Motor vehicles	122
10	Mitsubishi Corporation	J	Trading	113
11	Citigroup	USA	Banking	112
12	Mitsui & Co., Ltd	J	Trading	105
13	TotalFinaElf	F	Oil and gas	98
14	ChevronTexaco	USA	Oil and gas	98
15	Itochu Corporation	J	Trading	98
16	Nippon Telegraph & Telephone	J	Telecommunications	94
17	Philip Morris	USA	Tobacco and food	90
18	IBM Corporation	USA	Computers	86
19	Volkswagen	D	Motor vehicles	83
20	Siemens AG	D	Electronics; electrical equipment	81
21	Sumitomo Corporation	J	Trading	78
22	E.On	D	Electric utility	74
23	Allianz	D	Insurance	73
24	Verizon Communications	USA	Telecommunications	67
25	Carrefour	F	Retailing	65

as the archetypal MNEs. Topping both lists, however, is Wal-Mart with about 1.2 million staff (many part-time) attached to over 4000 stores.

There are many European enterprises in the leading turnover list. Table 4.2 includes the ranking and nation of registration of the EU leaders. Of Forbes' Top 500, 132 are registered in an EU member state.

Table 4.2 **EU corporations in the world's top 50, by turnover**

Rank	Company	Nation	Industry	Sales $ bn
4	BP	UK	Oil and gas	174
6	Daimler Chrysler	D	Motor vehicles	136
7	Royal Dutch/Shell Group	NL/UK	Oil and gas	135
13	TotalFinaElf	F	Petroleum	98
19	Volkswagen	D	Motor vehicles	83
20	Siemens AG	D	Electronics; electrical equipment	81
22	E.On	D	Electric utility	74
23	Allianz	D	Insurance	73
25	Carrefour	F	Retailing	65
28	Koninklijke Ahold	NL	Retailing	62
33	RWE	D	Diversified utility	59
37	Fiat Group	I	Motor vehicles	54
39	Vivendi Universal	F	Media	54
45	Unilever	NL/UK	Food	48
48	Peugeot	F	Motor vehicles	47
49	Metro	D	Retailing	46

Among these leaders, commitment to international activities and investments varies. UNCTAD calculated a 'transnationality index'. This is the average of three ratios: foreign assets to total assets, foreign sales to total sales and foreign employment to total employment. Swiss companies Nestlé, ABB and Roche score over 90, petroleum companies average 70, while General Motors, Ford and Toyota are in the 30s. Wal-Mart's low index of 26 indicates its home market strength.[10]

Location of multinational enterprises

Tables 4.1 and 4.2 suggest some geographical distribution of the leading MNEs. It is hardly surprising that their headquarters are to be found, for the most part, in the nations with the strongest economies. This spread is illustrated in Figure 4.1, showing how 86 per cent of the Top 500 companies have their homes in the European Union, Japan or the United States.[11] Trade and investment among these regions dominate world commerce and are, in turn, dominated by MNEs. Figure 4.2[12] illustrates export flow between regions; there are similar strong links for investments. Heaviest flows are typically among countries that are part of a cluster, that is in the same region. Some authors see the clusters crystallising into the three members of

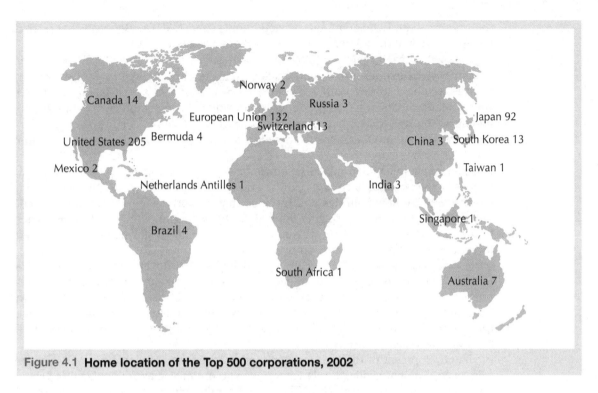

Figure 4.1 Home location of the Top 500 corporations, 2002

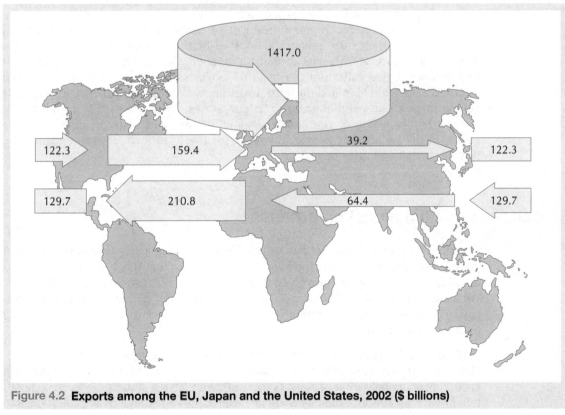

Figure 4.2 Exports among the EU, Japan and the United States, 2002 ($ billions)

the *triad*[13] – the EU, Japan and its neighbours, and NAFTA. Between them, triad countries account for 80 per cent of all foreign investment flows.

Links within each region are strengthening. Some 61 per cent of EU and 49 per cent of NAFTA exports are to countries within the cluster. Japan's foreign investment is weighted towards other countries in South-East Asia. For instance, 60 per cent of Matsushita's overseas production is in neighbouring countries; a tenth of this output is exported to Japan, a proportion that is rising. Japan is a key source of foreign investment in China and its foreign aid programme is focused on poorer countries in the region.[14]

Governments display a mixed response to such developments. On the one hand, they seek the benefits of foreign capital and technology and frequently offer incentives to capture new facilities and the jobs that go with them. On the other hand, they fear the threat to sovereignty implied by the ceding of control of key industries to foreign owners. Therefore, we see the United Kingdom government welcoming investments by Ford, General Motors, Honda, Nissan and Toyota while simultaneously watching the sale of the locally owned Jaguar and Rover. Ambiguous attitudes to trade blocs are part of the same dilemma. On the one hand, the EU single market offers the possibility of scale economies to producers in many of its industries. On the other hand, EU members, both separately and in unison, sometimes try to use trade barriers to protect key industries, such as agriculture or aircraft manufacture, from worldwide competition.

The development of the triad clusters underscores the point that we do not know what sort of global civilisation is emerging. The optimist may follow Levitt's view[15] that, led by the most efficient MNEs, trade barriers will continue to be dismantled and the benefits of the best technology will be spread among all countries. The pessimist will fear that the richer blocs will be satisfied with less than optimum performance in their own industries, boosted by the removal of internal barriers. Rugman argues that this has already happened; MNEs pursue not global but regional strategies matching the triad of 'Fortress Europe', 'Fortress Asia' and 'Fortress America'.[16] Limited outward investments from these economic strongholds will be targeted on neighbouring or 'client' states. Latin America will look north, Eastern Europe will look west and the Pacific Rim will look to Japan and China. The effect, in the pessimistic scenario, will be for the triad fortresses to consolidate, leaving weaker countries outside.

Features of multinational enterprises

The MNE is an enterprise that has its headquarters in one place (the *home* country) but has operations in others (the *host* countries). Note that this is a form of international business in that it is involved in both trade and investment across frontiers. We have seen that the MNE harnesses the twin forces of globalisation and technology to achieve its ends. From this statement, we can derive three key characteristics of these organisations:

■ *MNEs must respond to environments in both their home and host countries*
Many aspects are replicated from country to country. For example, in the operating environment, globalisation of markets means that an MNE will meet the same competitors in each nation or region. This applies as much to Sony and Toshiba as it does to

BP and Royal Dutch/Shell. Yet, different traditions and histories of competition, combined with the presence of local competitors, can have subtle or substantial effects. The malt whisky market is hardly uniform. We noted the varying strengths of each Scotch in different countries and how they face diverse competitors. Figure 4.3 sketches these ideas. It shows an MNE with operations in two foreign countries. All share the same raw materials sources; headquarters and country A operations use the same distributors; and HQ and country B have common customers and competitors.

The wider environment also has a variable influence. For instance, the way products are used varies from place to place. Germans prefer to wash clothes in very hot

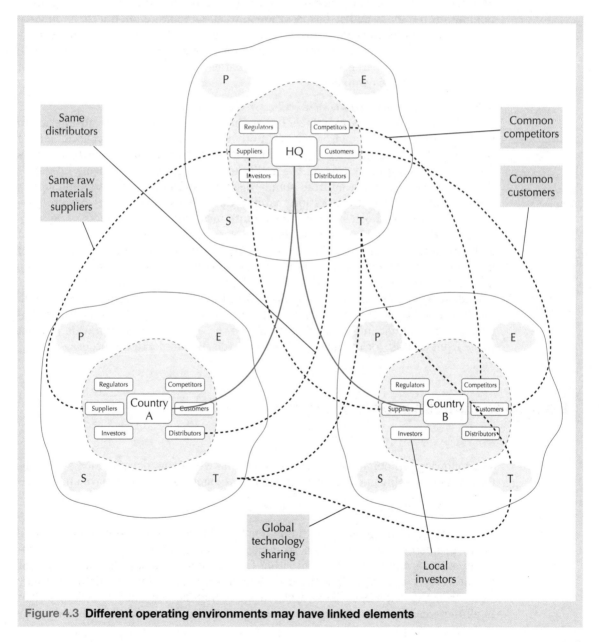

Figure 4.3 **Different operating environments may have linked elements**

water, while Brazilians wash their clothes (and themselves) in cold. This distinction, with variations in water quality and other factors, means that the soaps and detergents on sale are not the same.

■ *The strength of the MNE is drawn from its pool of resources*

These range from the tangible assets of plant and facilities to the intangible assets of information, trademarks, patents and designs. Capital can be made available for projects and, given the general strength of the business, funds can be obtained at advantageous rates. Furthermore, there are the knowledge and skills of the personnel. They know how to supply and make things, how to buy and sell. Many international developments are based on applying the knowledge in new markets. Pilkington, the glass maker based in north-west England, gained a technological advantage from its float glass process. It used a system of licensing, followed by direct investment, to ensure rapid and widespread application of its knowledge while it was protected by patents. The flow of royalties enabled it to become one of the world's leading glass companies.

■ *The MNE can plan and control all its resources*

Sometimes it can do this in a decentralised manner, allowing local subsidiaries to work closely with their environments. In other cases, it is very centralised, setting targets and making detailed plans from headquarters. If there is a trend, it is towards *glocalisation*, based on the ability to 'think globally, act locally'. Despite the cost reductions resulting from standardisation, McDonald's has adopted such a *glocal* strategy. Product adaptation matches differences in consumer preferences, tastes and customs. Kosher restaurants require meat and dairy products to be separated, so Big Macs come without cheese in Israel. Indian outlets sell the Mutton Maharajah. In Malaysia, the chain has a *halal* certificate indicating the absence of pork. In China, the employment policy focuses less on efficiency savings and more on the need to interact with customers.[17] Many firms use advances in operations management to support *mass customisation*, the offering of product variations in different regions, markets or even to different customers. At a very small scale, finishing Glenmorangie in flavoured casks allows the company to offer a wide product range from what is, for the most part, a standardised manufacturing process.

Becoming a multinational enterprise

■ Why become an MNE?

The following six points summarise the reasons why firms become MNEs. Clearly, they do not all apply in each case although more than one will often have an effect.

Avoid reliance on home base

There may be difficulties in the home country. For example, the market could be highly competitive or subject to constraints imposed by government controls or difficulties in distribution. Other operating factors such as lack of human and other resources may also mean that the prospects are not good. Finally, the market may suffer from the nation's business cycle, meaning that income and profits vary widely. In all these cases, entering a new country is a form of diversification. The company will look for an operating environment whose characteristics differ from those of its home base and are more favourable. Throughout the 1990s, the British government followed a policy of developing competition in telecommunications. This implied a cap on the growth of BT, which responded by increasing its unregulated overseas business interests.

Take opportunities abroad

In contrast to the *push* away from the home environment, the *pull* factors of foreign opportunities draw businesses to particular regions. The strength and long-term growth of the United States' economy has made it attractive to firms from other countries. Involvement ranges from exports of all types of goods to direct investments. More recently, opportunities have begun to be taken in Japan and countries whose size and growth rates suggest that long-term benefits will flow. In the 1990s, more than half of all investment in developing countries was occurring in Brazil, China, Hong Kong, Mexico and Singapore.

Improve competitiveness

Firms become MNEs in response to threats from international competitors. This behaviour may be in retaliation against a rival entering the home market or as a pre-emptive move to forestall a challenge. In response to increased demand for worldwide travel, leading airlines such as British Airways have been building global networks, often in co-operation with operators with complementary and linking route structures. This development has forced rivals to form other multinational groups to defend business on their routes.

Respond to creation or removal of trade barriers

Trade barriers are designed to protect national markets from overseas competition. Until 1995, the textile industries in both the EU and the NAFTA were protected by a special policy outside the normal rules of GATT (General Agreement on Tariffs and Trade). Export quotas imposed on fibres and clothing from developing countries are to be abolished under a 10-year transitional programme of the World Trade Organization.[18] The change has accelerated the trend among manufacturers in developed countries to shift their operations to low-cost countries.

Improve operations

Direct control of operations in a foreign country can result in service improvements and reduced costs. This is the advantage of the MNE compared with trading in the market or using agents. Provided business is of sufficient scale, direct control enables more rapid response to customers, selection of the most efficient pattern of production and distribution and elimination of intermediate traders and inventory holders.

Apply knowledge

Innovative firms have the potential to reap benefits from their developments. These can be in all aspects of business from products to processes. One way of rapidly exploiting these inventions on a world scale is to allow others the right to use them in their own regions. The licence is a contract to exchange expertise for royalties. In the short term, the licensor gains cash flow while the innovation is still fresh and has not attracted imitators. The problem in the longer term is that the licensee can build its own business strength and learn too much about the innovation. Quick service restaurants, such as McDonald's, are based on a particular kind of process knowledge – knowing how to deliver good service every time. They have spread across the world by issuing franchises. Market share in each target country is built quickly by this method, a move that forestalls competitors. Yet, the continuing success of the leading companies means that it is now better for them to invest directly in the restaurant facilities. In manufacturing, the case of Pilkington was mentioned above. It eventually found its glass process to be so successful that it was better to make investments in foreign ventures than merely issue licences.

■ The internationalisation process

There are four main methods of engaging in international business – trading, licensing, co-operating and investing. These are sometimes presented as a set of stages through which most home businesses develop into MNEs.[19] As some of our examples will show, however, an organisation may start with any of the methods and proceed by using others. Figure 4.4 shows some of these routes. The business may not start out with the intention of becoming an MNE. Yet, as Figure 4.4 shows from left to right, this is a likely development if the initial forays pay off and the business gathers strength and experience in international affairs. The four main policies are listed in the left margin of the figure. Their sequence represents an increased degree of control over foreign operations. Given the need of large corporations both to control their activities and strongly to influence their operating environments, the expanding MNE moves towards the lower right-hand corner of the diagram.

Trading, or export-import

A home company will frequently make a start in international business through trade, either exporting or importing. Exporting may result from push or pull factors in the

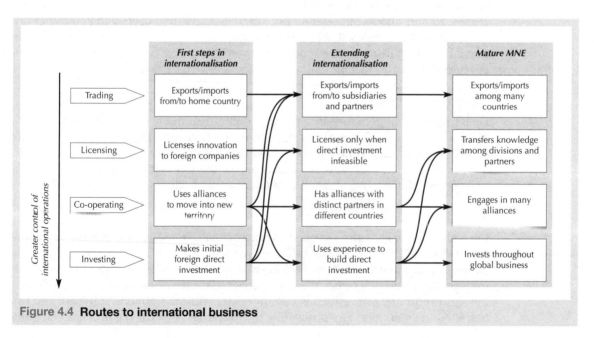

Figure 4.4 **Routes to international business**

home or target environments. Since net prices obtained in export markets are often lower than those at home, selling abroad will be attractive only if it can be done at low cost. Scotch whisky producers, for example, find that their revenue from exports is around 25 per cent lower than that at home. There are, in addition, many risks and difficulties facing the exporter. A small firm in Liverpool manufactures battery-powered locomotives that can haul loads along metre-wide passages in mines and other excavations. The owner's fluency in Spanish and local knowledge enables him to gain export opportunities in Bolivian silver mining. This is, however, an erratic industry in a volatile country so there are risks from currency fluctuations and payment delays or defaults.

Importing reflects exporting in that the company acts as a foreign agent or customer for the exporter. The activity could be to exploit an opportunity in the home market, such as the rising demand for foreign wines, clothes or authentic 'ethnic' products. On the other hand, the stimulus may be to reduce operating costs through a search for cheaper raw materials or semi-finished goods.

Once an enterprise has become an MNE, its operations in different countries will themselves engage in international trade. The ability of the MNE to rationalise and co-ordinate these activities, and use them to avoid trade restrictions, is one of its strengths.

Grönroos points out that electronic marketing offers new opportunities for suppliers of both goods and services.[20] Indeed, many services can be offered without the supplier and customer coming into direct contact. Examples include design, insurance, entertainment and education.

Licensing

As we have seen, licensing involves trade in intellectual property. This includes items recognised in law, such as patents, designs, works of art and trademarks. Knowledge can also go beyond this if it consists of skills and experience that the purchaser of the licence would otherwise take too long to acquire. Some organisations, from research arms of universities to the entertainment conglomerates of Hollywood, trade almost entirely in intellectual property, looking to worldwide exploitation for their profits. A notable example is the Victoria and Albert Museum, which has entered international business via the licensing route, *see* Exhibit 4.3.[21]

Exhibit 4.3 *Inspiring Design* brings licence income to the V&A

The Victoria and Albert Museum is constantly on the lookout for extra revenue to pay for the care and display of its five million artefacts. The museum's name is famous, especially in the United Sates and Japan. Recognising this, the V&A set up, in 1994, a licensing project *Inspiring Design* intended to generate revenue and further spread awareness of its collection. It is a world leader in licensing, issuing more than 80 in little over a year.

More than 80 per cent of the licensed goods are sold abroad. They include textiles, gifts, wall coverings, jewellery, china and glass. In a typical three-year rolling agreement, V&A Enterprises allowed the Welsh tie-maker Frank, Theak and Roskilly access to its William Morris archives to reproduce patterns. The initiative coincided with the centenary of Morris' death when a large exhibition was being held. FT&R supplies silk ties and accessories for sale through the V&A's shop and mail-order catalogue. A different range is sold through Marks & Spencer and other leading fashion shops. The link has helped FT&R to recover from a decline. Sales rose from £7.5 million in 1992 to £11 million four years later.

A franchise is a form of licensing in which the core organisation provides its franchisees with detailed support. This ranges from materials to marketing, products to processes and trade marks to training.

Co-operating, or forming strategic alliances

A strategic alliance could be an agreement between two firms to exchange technical expertise for other resources. It would then be similar to a licence agreement. In general, however, strategic alliances involve all types of co-operation between two or more partners for mutual benefit. Applied to international business, a frequent arrangement is for one party to offer product and process expertise and, possibly, capital, while the other is a local company, bringing with it relevant political, market and management experience. Alliances are generally for experienced companies willing to commit themselves to long-term links. Through a 2003 partnership with Mobilkom Austria, Vodafone, with 108 million customers, filled a blank spot in its European coverage. The Mobilkom group had about 4.3 million customers in Austria, Croatia and Slovenia. For Vodafone, further co-operation in central and Eastern Europe, where Austrian companies are strong, could follow. The attraction for Mobilkom was integration into a global network, including economies of scale, without loss of independence.[22]

Joint ventures are special types of alliance where the partners establish jointly owned facilities. Political restrictions and high risks mean that they are a common method of joining the race to set up business in China. The Chinese government has encouraged MNEs such as Shell, BP, General Motors and Wal-Mart, to provide up-to-date technology and management skills in exchange for access to its large and growing market At the end of 2002, Shell and China National Offshore Oil Corporation agreed to develop a petrochemicals complex in Guandong province. At $4.3 billion, it was both the largest foreign investment and the largest petrochemical project in the country, overtaking BP's $2.7 billion joint venture near Shanghai. Market growth attracted General Motors. Having established a joint venture with the bankrupt South Korean company Daewoo, it planned to take the brand into China with its partner the Shanghai Automotive Industry Corporation. Interest also grew in the retail industry in anticipation of liberalisation following China's entry to the WTO. Wal-Mart agreed with local utilities company Citic to open new stores in Shanghai and other cities on the booming east coast where Carrefour is well established. During the transition period, the government restricts ownership, growth and location of foreign retailers.[23]

Investing

Joint ventures span the co-operating and investing categories because they involve international flows of capital. The current surge of such projects is fuelled by MNEs' urgent desire to achieve global coverage while also limiting risk. Beyond the joint venture, however, is the establishment of a wholly owned subsidiary. This gives the MNE complete control and may bring cost savings, for example through shortening of distribution channels. Local awareness is achieved not through partnerships but by direct employment of local managers.

Investments can be to buy current businesses or to build new facilities on green-field sites. Ford Motor Company has displayed both policies. It built its European business through investment in new plant over some 70 years and acquired Jaguar during the 1990s. In services, hotel groups demonstrate both direct investment and franchising to achieve global expansion. European leader Accor employs 109 000 staff in its 3700 hotels in 90 countries. It covers the market with brands from the budget Formule 1 and ETAP to the prestigious Sofitel. In contrast, most of the 3200 properties in the Six Continents Hotels group are owned and operated independently. Brands include Holiday Inn, Crowne Plaza and Inter-Continental.[24]

Foreign direct investment

It is important to distinguish between foreign direct investment (FDI) and other forms of overseas financial holdings. For the latter, an organisation may purchase bonds or financial securities in the expectation of gaining a profit when they are sold. It may also hold currencies in cash to simplify trade and hedge against rate fluctuations during the life of a sale or purchase contract. FDI, on the other hand, means active management of foreign facilities. Why should firms engage in such investments as opposed to exporting and importing? To answer this question, Dunning compared firm-specific and location-specific advantages.[25] Firm-specific advantages (FSAs) are those 'knowledge' factors that the firm can protect and use to resist the establishment of rivals. Location-specific advantages (LSAs) arise from the country's geographical position – for instance, distance from resources and markets – and its endowment in terms of infrastructure, information, skilled labour, cheap power and so on. The interplay of the two types of advantage suggests the best development policy for each firm.

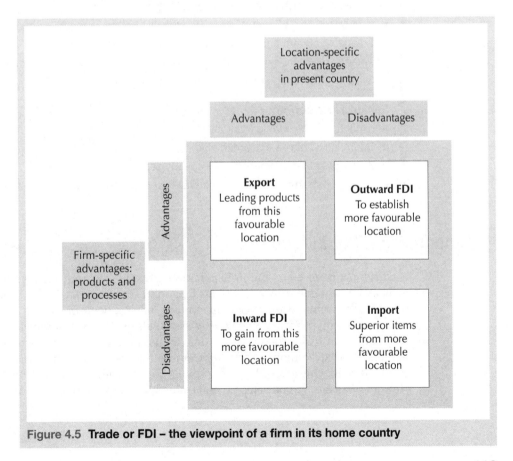

Figure 4.5 **Trade or FDI – the viewpoint of a firm in its home country**

Figure 4.5 shows how Dunning combined the ideas. Let us say that a firm has an FSA, such as a patent, yet its home country is not well suited for its exploitation. It may lack sufficient skilled labour or other costs may be too high. This places the firm in the top right-hand cell of the diagram, suggesting that outward FDI may be the best policy. If, on the other hand, home firms have no FSA, or there are simply no firms, then inward FDI is likely when the location is favourable. Furthermore, FSAs and LSAs together imply exporting; having neither means importing will be successful. A weakness of the model is that it takes no account of licensing or joint venturing. Dunning saw these as second-best policies for firms that are prevented from trading or exercising full control. Yet, their advantages, especially in terms of the speed with which they can bring results, should be recognised.

Exhibit 4.4 pulls together the above discussion, summarising why firms undertake FDI. LSAs explain the waves of investment from East Asian firms into the United Kingdom. The 1996 decision of Hyundai to build a £1 billion semiconductor plant at Dunfermline, Scotland, is a typical example. Reasons given were: the threat of trade barriers; market benefits from being close to customers; and production costs lower than Korea, considering government regional assistance grants.[26]

Exhibit 4.4 Summary of FSAs and LSAs leading to foreign direct investment

Using and strengthening firm-specific advantages
- Increasing scale of operations to grow profits and reduce costs.
- Defending current home market by opening in a rival's backyard.
- Defending current export market by becoming 'home' company there.
- Acquiring knowledge by purchase of existing business.

Seeking location-specific advantages
- Exploiting fast-growing markets.
- Operating within an economic bloc.
- Being close to customers means speedy service.
- Cutting costs in new location: materials, labour, energy, transport.

Managing in different cultures

A consequence of engaging in international business is that managers are immediately faced with colleagues and rivals from different cultures. Unfortunately, they are often badly prepared for these encounters, having been presented with racial and national stereotypes from when they were children. The rest of the chapter examines two aspects of this difficult area. First, there is the field of cross-cultural research, looking at what is known about differences and how relevant they are to management. Second, there are the implications for staffing of international operations. How are managers to be selected and trained for these 'outposts' of MNEs?

■ Cross-cultural research

As we saw in Chapter 3, cultural studies attempt to find out about individuals within organisations. Extending the approach, *cross-cultural studies* look for the similarities and differences between people in different cultures. Vecchio warned of the difficulties of this work and hence the danger in placing great reliance on many of the results.[27] These arise from two issues: defining cultures and measurement. Comparisons are often made between managers in different nations, taking for convenience the national boundary as a basis for defining culture. Yet, as Denfeld Wood points out, differences between individuals within one culture may be greater than shown by those from different ones.[28] Variations arise from gender, social class, education, age, religious background and so on. Given that culture is a *shared system of meaning*, this begs the question of what a national culture is!

Vecchio's second concern is with the application of theory to measurement. He is concerned with the use of theories and techniques that had developed in the West for the study of Western workers. 'It is probably incorrect to assume that ideas and constructs ... are equally appropriate for explaining the behaviour of workers in all other countries.'[29] More specifically, Riordan and Vandenberg report on two scales developed in the United States to assess self-esteem and satisfaction with supervision. They concluded that Koreans used different frames of reference when responding to the scale items and, therefore, different scores could not be interpreted.[30]

In spite of these difficulties, studies continue. They parallel the continuing problem of managing MNEs, especially if formed by merger or acquisition. Diverse cultural approaches to handling conflict can lead to failure unless shared meanings are achieved quickly.[31] Furthermore, managers are less concerned with research than with action. Consequently, they often see divergence as a source of learning as well as an obstacle to be overcome. For example, German and United Kingdom companies each now invest huge sums in the other nation. Marsh reports on how interaction among managers is leading to a *rapprochement* between the German industrial perspective and 'long-termism' and the British emphasis on finance and the short term. German managers are conscious of technical competence and position in the hierarchy while their British counterparts prefer less structure and the freedom to use initiative.[32] In summary, we can quote Hofstede: 'There is something in all countries called management, but its meaning differs to a larger or smaller extent from one country to the other, and it takes considerable historical and cultural insight into local conditions to understand its processes, philosophies, and problems.'[33]

■ Management attitudes

Perlmutter was concerned with assessing the degree of multinationality of an enterprise. How could one tell whether a firm was 'truly' multinational as opposed to one having a few overseas operations? He concluded that there were no feasible operational or financial measures, such as the proportion of activities or investment that takes place outside the home country. The striking difference among firms lay in another direction – in the state of mind of the managers. 'The attitudes men hold are clearly more relevant than their passports.'[34]

Perlmutter identified three states of mind: ethnocentric, polycentric and geocentric. They are never seen in pure form; some measure of each is present in all organisations. Their characteristics, as ideal-types, are set out in Exhibit 4.5 and explained overleaf.

Exhibit 4.5 Orientation of headquarters to subsidiaries in three types of MNE

Organisational feature	Ethnocentric	Polycentric	Geocentric
Complexity	High in HQ, which makes main decisions; low in subsidiaries	Varies among subsidiaries	Complex and interdependent
Authority	HQ	Local	Collaborative
Monitoring and control	Home standards applied throughout	Local	Agreed universal standards applied locally
Rewards and incentives	High in HQ; low in subsidiaries	Wide variation	Matched to worldwide and local objectives
Communication	Downwards from HQ	Little	Many paths among subsidiaries
Identification	Home country	Host country	International and national interests
Continuity	Home-country recruitment for foreign postings	Local people developed for own-country management	Best people for key positions throughout the world

◼ *Ethnocentric, or home-country alignment*

Regarding one's culture as superior to others is an ethnocentric attitude. For instance, although a manager may assert, 'Of course I don't think like that!' the firm orders basic components from overseas subsidiaries, leaving the trickier finishing to be done at home. Explanations suggest that foreign staff are neither ready nor reliable. Within this firm, business follows home-country practices and uses the home language. 'Outposts' are run by expatriates on temporary postings. Finding it difficult to deal with foreign managers, headquarters places its own in key positions.

There are many ethnocentric MNEs, perhaps the majority. The proportion of foreign-born board members of the United States' Top 500 companies is about 2 per cent, while, in France, 50 per cent of chief executives of large companies come from six *grandes écoles*. Few have international experience.[35] As for companies, McDonald's *knows* the best way to run quick-service restaurants. Therefore, it appoints and trains its staff according to headquarters standards and rules. Training includes a visit to the McDonald's University. Operations in the United Kingdom owned by Brother, Nissan, Sharp and Toyota typically have Japanese nationals both in overall charge and running the production and engineering functions. The advantage of having the same procedures throughout the world should not be underestimated.

◼ *Polycentric, or host-country alignment*

Polycentric firms incorporate the notion that host-country cultures are difficult for the outsider to understand and local people know best. Therefore, the branch should be allowed as much local character as possible. Rarely are home-country managers placed in top positions in overseas subsidiaries. The polycentric MNE is, therefore, a group of companies that have a high degree of operating autonomy. Such an approach can have its problems if conflict is allowed to develop. When in 1995, the British end of Royal Dutch/Shell, having obtained clearance from the government, began to tow the obsolete Brent Spar rig towards its planned dumping point in the Atlantic Ocean, the strongest public protests arose in Germany. There were attacks on petrol stations and a consumer boycott. The company's German and United Kingdom subsidiaries became involved in a public row.[36]

■ *Geocentric, or world orientation*

Perlmutter argues that a geocentric attitude is beginning to emerge. Its ultimate goal is a worldwide approach both in headquarters and in the subsidiaries. Collaboration is important, creating worldwide standards for the company products with local variations where agreed. Local managers are expected to manage their operations effectively but always within the total context. Promotion of managers is done on merit, not nationality.

Simon argues that the modern MNE no longer produces in one country and trades with another.[37] It has become an integrated system, capable of sourcing products from many sites while passing funds between semi-independent business operations in many countries. For many, the international transactions are less to do with goods and more to do with transfers of advanced technology. In this view, cultural diversification of large MNEs is inevitable. The question for the geocentric organisation is not whether loyalty to the business overcomes ethnicity or nationality. Instead, managers in such MNEs should learn to tolerate diversity and come to terms with conflicting loyalties. Such comments echo those of Adler, noted in Chapter 1.

■ Cultural differences

Having noted Perlmutter's analysis of ways for MNEs to consider differences, we can go on to ask what they are. Cross-cultural research has identified many issues relevant to managers and organisations. A few are noted here.

Attitudes to time

We can look at two aspects: the pace of life and temporal style. First, we observe that the pace of life seems to vary from nation to nation, many jokes being based on national stereotypes. To measure pace, Kirkcaldy and colleagues combined observations of rate of walking, speed of service at the post office and the accuracy of bank clocks in a selection of major cities. They placed the results into three groups, shown in Table 4.3. The fastest pace was found in European nations along with Japan and Hong Kong (observed while a colony). The intermediate group included some North American and European nations as well as Singapore and Taiwan. The slowest pace was observed in less economically developed countries from Latin America, Europe, Asia and the Middle East.

Searching for explanatory factors, the authors compared these observations with attitude measures such as competitiveness and achievement orientation. Common sense (see the discussion in Chapter 1) may suggest that these would be higher in the faster-paced countries. Yet, the opposite was seen. Surveys among fully industrialised nations show *lower* scores on these scales. This matched previous studies, which 'found that cooperativeness becomes more important in sustaining economic successful communities once the threshold of "healthy" national wealth is reached'.[38]

Table 4.3 Nations with fast, intermediate and slow pace of life measures

Fast	Intermediate	Slow
Switzerland	Poland	CSSR
Germany	France	China
Ireland	Netherlands	Greece
Japan	Singapore	Bulgaria
Italy	Taiwan	Romania
Sweden	Canada	Jordan
United Kingdom	United States	Syria
Austria	South Korea	Brazil
Hong Kong	Hungary	Mexico

The second aspect of attitudes to time concerns Hall's separation of temporal frames into monochronic and polychronic.[39]

■ *Monochronic, or linear time*
When time is conceived monochronically, it is a measurable, objective standard having equal units. Time passes by the tick of the clock and without reference to events. Activities are arranged linearly. People concentrate on the job, and stress the completion of tasks, schedules and procedures. They are accustomed to short-term relationships. They believe in the superiority of this habit of thought, which is prevalent among northern Europeans and North Americans, members of large organisations and males.

■ *Polychronic time*
With a polychronic style, people pay attention to several things at once, interspersing activities as and when needed. They are subject to distraction and change of plan and regard time commitments as objectives. The need for promptness depends on the significance of the relationship, each of which is potentially for life. They also believe in the superiority of their habits, which are found in southern European, Amerindian and many Asian cultures, smaller organisations, and among women.

We should remember that these explanations concern ideal-types, most people displaying a mixture. Bluedorn and colleagues developed a scale to measure polychronicity; they found differences not only among nations but also among companies, departments and individuals.[40] As Exhibit 4.6 suggests, the juxtaposition of two incompatible assumptions leads to difficulties! Within the MNE, these include the problems of trying to get people from different backgrounds to work together on time-constrained projects.

Communication context

In some groups, known as *high-context* cultures, people are very aware of the context of communication. Social setting, social status and non-verbal behaviour are recognised and understood as part of the message. Each part of a business transaction is seen as a step in building the relationship. Trust and the harmony of the group are valued. In a *low-context* culture, on the other hand, business correspondence and other messages will focus on the exchange of facts and data. Meaning is derived from words. Clarity and brevity are important for the transaction; relationship building takes place outside the immediate context. During the preparations for the Gulf War in the 1990s, for example, the United States General Schwarzkopf learned to spend many hours in philosophical discussion with members of the Saudi royal family, realising that it was the way the group came to decisions.[41]

Exhibit 4.6 Monochronic meets polychronic time

Scene: Jones' general store in Llanarmon-yn-Lal

Mrs Jones: Good morning, here again for the weekend? What can I get you?
Mrs Ledger: Good morning. I'll start with two pounds of carrots and four of potatoes.
Mrs Jones: Good morning Mr Roberts, what can I do for you?
Mr Roberts: I'll have two pounds of potatoes with my paper.

Mrs Jones brings enough potatoes for both, weighs them and takes Mr Roberts' money. Begins to weigh carrots ...

Mrs Jones: [*In Welsh.*] Hello, Mrs Evans. Nice to see you again. How's your daughter? Just be wanting your paper is it?
Mrs Ledger: I thought you were serving me.
Mrs Jones: I am, dear, I am. [*Puts carrots in bag and takes coins from Mrs Evans.*] Now what else would you like?

Scene: Bank in same village
Cashier: Who's next?
Mrs Ledger: Will this bill be settled by Tuesday if I give you cash?

Attitudes to rules and legal agreements

Managers of MNEs frequently comment on different attitudes showing themselves in situations such as contract negotiation and enforcement. We can look at two examples:

■ *The buying process*
Managers from Europe and North America are used to the legal notion of *caveat emptor* – let the buyer beware – applied to buying real estate. When considering a business acquisition, they conduct a thorough investigation before completing. The target company is expected to co-operate. In Japan, the onus of diligence is on the seller who must show good faith and satisfy all reasonable expectations that the buyer would have. *Caveat emptor* is not followed in Asia and Latin America, so detailed investigations can be seen as insulting.[42]

■ *Contract enforcement*
Western managers view contracts as the basis of all transactions and seek to formalise those of significant value. Their enforceability through the courts or arbitration provides security. Choi contrasts this with East Asia where the reputation of the individual or the organisation plays a much more important role. 'Losing face' is to be avoided and the sense of personal obligation is strong.[43]

Management policy in different cultures

Many organisations espouse standard policies for issues such as the welfare and safety of staff. Janssens and others compared perceptions of safety at three plants of a United States MNE.[44] They found that it was perceived differently in Argentina, France and the USA. In the last two countries, the individualist culture was reflected in the expectations for managers to take control. They were seen as responsible for finding the balance between production and safety. In the collectivist culture of Argentina, however, blue-collar workers saw production and safety as everyone's responsibility. MNE policies need to recognise local cultural differences.

The above paragraph mentions an important idea in cross-cultural studies – individualism versus collectivism. It is among the dimensions established in one of the most ambitious and famous pieces of research in this field, that carried out by Hofstede.

■ Hofstede's cultural dimensions

Many studies have been limited in scope because they have compared two or three nations along a predetermined dimension such as attitudes to time, space, rules, control and so on. When differences were found, since these were the only ones that were looked for, assessment of whether other factors might be more important was not possible. In contrast, the Dutch scholar Geert Hofstede applied a wide-ranging questionnaire to 116 000 IBM employees in some 70 countries.[45] He then used statistical methods, especially factor analysis, to find patterns among the data.

> *Factor analysis looks for patterns of answers that suggest relationships among the questions. Hence if those who answer Question 25 positively tend also to answer Question 37 positively and 51 negatively, and vice versa, we can infer that these three questions refer to aspects of the same underlying factor.*

Such methods led Hofstede to discover four such underlying factors, or *cultural dimensions*, later extended to five after studies from China were included.[46] These factors are summarised in Exhibit 4.7, which also shows countries that scored high or low on each scale. The lists pick out patterns among countries. While some may be similar on one or two dimensions, they may diverge on others.

Hofstede's work is a touchstone for those investigating cultural differences; it marks a switch from the descriptive case orientation of previous work to analytical methods based on surveys and statistics. He is among the social scientists most frequently cited by others. Tenth among Europeans referenced in 2000, he ranked below Freud and Foucault but above Marx, Kant and Keynes.[47] Many have adapted and used both the theoretical model and research method while also finding limitations in their application. We must note some of these:

■ *Interpreting the results*
When looking at the results, we should remember their origin. IBM staff between 1966 and 1973 were mostly men. Having one company reduced other sources of difference and brought out the culture effect. The effect of male dominance is difficult to judge, but would tend to mask issues such as gender bias that have come to the fore more recently. Such limits make generalisations risky. We must avoid stereotyping statements like, 'People in West Africa ...'

We should also beware of taking Hofstede's results as describing a fixed and general state of affairs. This is the 'permanent present' trap exemplified by anthropologists' habits of writing in the present tense.[48] Although we readily recognise cultural differences and changes in our own society, our ignorance of others makes us think of them as much more uniform and stable. For instance, Rugman and Hodgetts noted that, although Japan's score for *individualism* was not so high

Exhibit 4.7 Hofstede's dimensions of cultural differences

Power distance
How far is unequal distribution of power, and hence distance between people, accepted?

Low power distance
- Independence is valued
- Managers consult staff
- Organisations have flat pyramids

Austria, Israel, Denmark, New Zealand, Ireland, Norway, Sweden

High power distance
- Subordinates follow instructions
- Control is close
- Hierarchies have many layers

Malaysia, Panama, Guatemala, Philippines, Venezuela, Mexico, Ecuador, Arab countries, West Africa

Uncertainty avoidance
How much do people feel threatened by ambiguity and seek to minimise or avoid it?

Weak uncertainty avoidance
- Activities tend to be unstructured
- Managers take risks
- Dissent is acceptable
- Initiative encouraged

Singapore, Jamaica, Denmark, Sweden, Ireland, United Kingdom, Malaysia

Strong uncertainty avoidance
- Dependence on rules
- Means found to avoid risk
- Decisions based on consensus
- Security is important

Greece, Portugal, Guatemala, Uruguay, Belgium, Japan

Individualism
How far do people look after themselves and their immediate family only?

Individualist
- Stress on self and self-sufficiency
- Focus on initiative and leadership
- Individual security

Australia, United States, United Kingdom, Netherlands, New Zealand, Canada, Italy

Collectivist
- Group affiliation and decision making
- No one wants to be singled out
- Belongingness

Guatemala, Ecuador, Panama, Venezuela, Colombia, Indonesia, Pakistan

Masculinity
How far do 'masculine' values dominate society?

Masculine
- Growth seen as important
- Achievement = wealth and recognition
- Challenge important

Japan, Austria, Venezuela, Mexico, Ireland, Jamaica, Germany, United Kingdom

Feminine
- People and environment important
- Co-operation is valued
- Quality of life

Sweden, Norway, Denmark, Netherlands, Costa Rica, Yugoslavia, Finland, Chile, Portugal

Long-term orientation
(Also called **Confucian Dynamism**.) *Do people favour a pragmatic, future-oriented perspective?*

Short-term
- Analytic – interest in 'how'
- Present and recent are important
- Concern with stability

Australia, Canada, East Africa, Germany, Philippines, United Kingdom, United States, West Africa

Long-term
- Pragmatic – interest in 'what'
- Perseverance
- Thrift

China, Japan, Taiwan

as in the West, it was high among countries in the Orient. Further, it has become more pronounced in that country since 1970.[49]

■ *Using the dimensions*

Others have found difficulties of replicating and interpreting Hofstede's dimensions. Trompenaars, while acknowledging a debt to the groundbreaking work, argues that Hofstede has hardly added to his model. The four (then five) dimensions rely on 30-year-old data collected for different purposes. Dimensions, such as long-term orientation originally, could be missed because they were not looked for. These might include showing emotions, perception of control over one's environment and the depth of relationships.

Trompenaars also notes the ethnocentric nature of the model; it uses questions written from a Dutch point of view, representing how many Western scholars would think. This is shown, for example, in the selection of exclusive categories such as individualist-collectivist. Do they mean that an individual cannot join in a collective venture?

Another problem of interpretation is illustrated by Schramm-Nielsen, who contrasts the position of Danish and French managers on uncertainty avoidance scales. Does the low score revealed in Denmark mean fundamentally greater tolerance of ambiguity than suggested by the high scores in France? It may. On the other hand, the Danish employment environment, with a habit of high job mobility, good social security and recognition of professional qualifications, is much more certain than the French. In France, managers experience more stress through greater personal dependence on superiors, lower job mobility and a less certain environment. Schramm-Nielsen summarises, 'the scores should be understood in the light of the fact that Danes already have a high degree of certainty, and therefore have less reason to feel insecure. It is no doubt an expression of their great need for security that they have built a society which provides it!'[50]

■ *The impact of the model*

Many have responded to Hofstede's theory by replicating the research, to either confirm it or seek new dimensions. Although most studies do not produce the same results, their cumulative effect has been to reinforce the underlying paradigm. This risks leaving intercultural studies stuck with a plausible yet superficial model. Others, such as Trompenaars and Hampden Turner, have developed their own scales, shown in Exhibit 4.8.[51] Yet, even these suffer from trying to summarise the whole of culture into a few variables.

Exhibit 4.8 Seven dimensions of culture

(Trompenaars and Hampden-Turner)

■ Universalism versus Particularism	■ Stressing rules or relationships
■ Individualism versus Communitarianism	■ Functioning alone or in a group
■ Specific versus Diffuse	■ Depth of involvement
■ Affective versus Neutral	■ Displaying emotions
■ Achievement versus Ascription	■ Status gained or given
■ Sequential versus Synchronic	■ i.e. Monochronic or polychronic
■ Internal versus External control	■ Control environment or work within it

■ *National differences*

Others have examined the question of how similar countries are to each other. Although it was stated above that countries varied widely, analysis can show that each is more similar to some and more distant from others. Cluster analysis looks for groups who tend to have similar scores on the underlying factors. For instance, Ronen and Shenkar[52] found that countries fell into eight clusters with four misfits. The clusters were labelled: Anglo; Arab; Germanic; Far Eastern; Latin American; Latin European; Near Eastern; and Nordic. The four fitting no group were: Brazil; India; Israel; and Japan.

While cross-cultural research raises as many questions as it answers, it does awaken us to the notion of cultural similarities and differences. Generalisation, as with clustering, is useful as a starting point yet we must be aware of its dangers. For example, Luce reported:

> *Viewed from afar south-east Asia strikes many as a relatively homogenous group of countries. Moves to integrate the region through the seven-member Association of South East Asian Nations (ASEAN) have reinforced the view ... Companies with direct experience in more than one Asian country, however, take a strikingly different view. South-east Asia is in fact probably one of the most diverse regions in the world ...* [53]

■ Developing global managers

The growth of MNEs has increased the demand for international managers. Yet, many report on the shortage of people with transportable skills and the frequent failures where postings are cut short or the manager performs ineffectively.[54] Adler and Bartholomew explain these problems in terms of the lag between firms' global strategies and the human systems required to carry them out.[55] They argue for improvements both in the skills of individuals and in the management of human resource systems.

Many of the problems associated with taking up international posts apply equally to managers changing jobs within or between organisations inside one country. Black, Mendenhall and Oddou divide the process of adjustment into two phases – preparatory and on-location.[56]

■ *Preparatory adjustment*

Selection is critical. The organisation must choose managers as much for their adaptability as for their technical competence. Training builds on experience to ensure accurate expectations about the job and its environment. Managers with previous overseas experience are more likely to succeed again.

Training will include substantial cross-cultural work. This is particularly relevant for managers, who, as noted in Chapter 1, spend so much time communicating. Fluency means more than language skills; it involves acknowledging cultural differences and building the capacity to send and receive messages in 'other-culture' terms.

■ *On-location adjustment*

Despite preparatory effort, the manager faces adjustment on arrival. This has two aspects – mode and degree. Mode refers to coping with the gap between expectations and requirements, hopefully limited by preparation. The gap can be spanned either by changes in the manager's behaviour or by adaptation of the role to suit the existing capability. The degree of adjustment refers to three facets: work, relating to host-country people and the general environment outside work. The manager will succeed if there is a response to all three.

■ Differences at work

Differences in attitudes to management can be profound. Nowhere might they create more urgent problems than on an aircraft flight deck. Helmreich and colleagues surveyed more than 13 000 pilots employed by 25 airlines in 16 countries.[57] They were interested in values and attitudes related to work, such as teamwork, leadership, response to stress and organisational culture. The results showed commonality in communication, teamwork and attitudes toward stress but strong cross-cultural differences when it came to command interactions, and tolerance for rules, routines and procedures. Exhibit 4.9 lists first the 'universals' – items endorsed by at least 85 per cent of pilots from all airlines in all countries. Then follow the differences among the groups of pilots according to country. The percentages show the range of agreement.

The pilots varied dramatically in their preference for an egalitarian versus a hierarchical command style, and for flexibility and autonomy versus adherence to, and compliance with, rules and set procedures. The study alerts airline managers to doubts over the value of operating procedures and the question of how to best deploy pilots from different nations. Note also the relationship to Hofstede's dimensions.

Exhibit 4.9 Pilots agree and disagree

Attitudes universally endorsed

- Good communication and crew co-ordination are as important as technical proficiency for flight safety.
- The captain's responsibilities include co-ordination between cockpit and cabin crews.
- The pre-flight briefing is important for safety and for effective crew management.
- The pilot flying the aircraft should verbalise plans and be sure the information is understood and acknowledged.
- Pilots should monitor each other for signs of stress and fatigue.

Attitudes varying by national culture

- Crew members should not question the decisions or actions of the captain except when they threaten the safety of the flight (15 per cent – 93 per cent).
- If I perceive a problem with the flight, I will speak up, regardless of who might be affected (36 per cent – 98 per cent).
- Written procedures are required for all in-flight situations (15 per cent – 84 per cent).
- The organisation's rules should not be broken – even when the employee thinks it is in the company's best interests (22 per cent – 76 per cent).

Conclusion: managing the global corporation

For better or worse, the business world is dominated by MNEs. In contrast to earlier times, the MNE gains its strength from bypassing markets and replacing them with internal transactions. This trade is in goods, services and, increasingly, the transfer of technical knowledge to be applied throughout the world. Information technology is very important. Its role in processing and communications has made the MNE ever more efficient. At the same time, it has spawned new worldwide industries to satisfy demands for both hardware and software. Computer systems are powerful homogenising forces.

In many ways, MNEs are agents for good. They can contribute to economic development of poor regions and the spreading of education, health and so on. At the same time, we have seen how these global corporations possess great economic power. This has come to worry national governments who fear the MNEs' ability to switch technology, to form joint ventures or to close down operations without significant constraint. Liberalisation of trade may continue, or the world may crystallise into blocs, each with its proportion of giant MNEs, protected by barriers against the others.

As it develops, the MNE retains its ethnocentric character or develops along lines that are more diverse. The true geocentric organisation is rare although some companies are beginning to adopt this perspective. Whatever attitude prevails, the organisation has to face and cope with cultural diversity. The ethnocentric organisation has to make bridges between expatriate managers and local employees; the polycentric business has to link national divisions to headquarters. The world view within the geocentric firm is perhaps the most problematic. Are managers expected to 'forget' their backgrounds and adopt the new company culture? Perhaps this is both meaningless and impossible. Managers of such companies have to find their own ways of coming to terms with bridging the cultures across which they function.

The failure rate of managers posted abroad imposes unnecessary costs on international companies and their staff. Increased cultural sensitivity is needed if managers are to succeed. Cross-cultural research suggests agendas for programmes of training and other activities that can contribute to successful adjustment.

QUICK CHECK

Can you ...

- Define globalisation.
- Identify five convergent and five divergent forces.
- Recall the industries in which the world's largest corporations operate.
- Explain triad.
- Name six reasons why firms become MNEs.
- List four routes to internationalisation.

- Distinguish LSA from FSA.
- Name Perlmutter's three states of mind.
- Separate monochronic and polychronic time.
- Outline Hofstede's dimensions of cultural difference.
- Name two phases of a manager's international adjustment.

QUESTIONS

Chapter review

4.1 Discuss the forces that, it is suggested, are pushing the world apart or pulling it together. Can you add to the list? What is your conclusion about the balance?

4.2 Explain how an MNE responds to a combination of firm-specific and location-specific advantages.

4.3 What are the main types of cultural difference identified in the text? Can you think of other factors or examples that could be valuable?

4.4 Compare Perlmutter's classification of MNEs with Adler's set of managerial attitudes given in Chapter 1.

Application **4.5** Return to Mrs Ledger's experience in Exhibit 4.6. Apply the ideas of time and context to each stage of the transactions to build a cultural interpretation of the events.

4.6 Review Glenmorangie's FDI policies in the opening case in the light of the ideas in the chapter.

Investigation **4.7** Study an MNE, from Fortune's Top 500 or elsewhere, to assess the extent to which it 'thinks globally and acts locally'. Use a range of sources to examine factors such as integration, location of operations, nationality of senior managers and dealing with customers. Why does it act as it does?

CLOSING CASE

Tesco's glocal growth[58]

In 2003, Tesco was, with 17 per cent of the market, the United Kingdom's biggest grocer. Its ambitious overseas plans placed it among the fastest-growing international retailers. Since its launch in Hungary in 1994, its foreign floor space has increased to 40 per cent. New, fast-growing countries offered opportunities not available in Western countries where problems include shortage of sites and union issues. Tesco focused on just eight countries, becoming market leader in six, *see* Table 4.4. Deputy Chairman David Reid referred to strong home cash flow funding this expansion, but most overseas operations had become profitable.

Table 4.4 Tesco's markets

	Number of stores	Sales area (million sq.m)	Store openings 2001–3
United Kingdom	729	1.88	130
Ireland	76	0.17	5
Hungary	48	0.21	12
Poland	46	0.18	11
Thailand	35	0.38	27
Czech Republic	15	0.15	6
Slovakia	13	0.11	7
South Korea	13	0.14	16
Taiwan	3	0.03	3
Total overseas	249	1.37	87

To use its cash resources well, Tesco relies on strengths of location research, supply chain management, own label development and innovation. Since many aspects are transparent, and therefore imitated, competitive edge is won with the 'soft' factors of how a store relates to its customers. And these depend on how the staff are treated. Through such care, Tesco produces a better, more local offer than rivals.

Tailoring a brand formula to local needs is important. For instance, in a country where customers are more interested in price than range, spending on extending the latter will not be fruitful. Loyalty cards help in identifying such customer wants. Tesco quickly saw that vast quantities of data are useless without interpretation. Data-mining skills are valued so highly that Tesco bought the company it engaged for the analysis. The same approach was being applied overseas to uncover customers' habits and tastes.

With sales of €33.6 billion, Tesco was small compared with Wal-Mart (€247.6 billion) and Carrefour (€69.3 billion). It did not see scale as being as important as operational capability and customer relations. With more than 85 per cent of food sourced locally, global scale had little effect in groceries. There is an effect, however, with some non-food items, such as textiles and durables, but Tesco did not see it as significant.

Human resources had been a constraint overseas, especially as rapid domestic growth also required more managers. Tesco needed good people abroad to translate Tesco values into the local environment, but, as Reid pointed out, most did not join Tesco to be posted, say, to Thailand. In each Asian country, Tesco relied on about six expatriate employees to establish key processes and show how to manage and motivate people. Local managers ran the customer side. This policy was based on the plentiful supply of well-educated local people with retail experience. In Central Europe, however, there had been no real retailers, just government stores. This meant more expatriates, but only until new managers came through.

Interested in growth markets, Tesco had research teams in several countries. Since 1999, Tesco had been looking for a suitable local partner in China. The United States growth was also attractive, despite the strong competitors. To build on one of its strengths, Tesco forged an e-commerce deal with Safeway, permitting the latter's use of the home shopping system. With its profitable online service, Tesco was already world leader in Internet grocery sales.

Although it had entered some markets, such as Ireland, by acquisition of existing chains, Tesco had used partnerships elsewhere. It sought to repeat this model in Japan, where the cost of starting from scratch is prohibitive. The company's growing reputation led to approaches from potential associates in this and other nations.

Despite no domestic experience of the format, many overseas Tesco stores were hypermarkets selling about 50 per cent of non-food items. Competition from strong consumer goods retailers in the home market had held this proportion to about 10 per cent. However, Tesco planned to increase its non-food business in the UK at twice the rate for groceries. Managers applied the company's overseas learning to developing new hypermarkets at home.

Questions

1 Is Tesco becoming global, glocal or what?
2 Explain Tesco's development in terms of FSAs and LSAs.
3 Compare the benefits of expanding by direct investment, acquisition or partnership in food retailing.
4 How should the company prepare an experienced UK store manager to run a hypermarket in Asia?

Bibliography

Ohmae, Kenichi (2001) *The Invisible Continent: Four strategic imperatives of the new economy* (London: Nicholas Brealey) and Alan Rugman (2002) (first published 2000) *The End of Globalisation* (Random House) capture many questions surrounding MNEs today. For current debates on aspects of international business, try the working papers published at **http://knowledge.wharton.upenn.edu** mentioned in the references. On diversity, a good addition is Trompenaars, Fons and Hampden-Turner, Charles (1997) *Riding the Waves of Culture: Understanding diversity in global business* (2nd edition, London: Nicholas Brealey).

References

1 London Stock Exchange (2002) *Preliminary results, Glenmorangie plc*, **www.uk-wire.com**, 22 May; Glenmorangie plc (2002) *Annual Report and Accounts 2001–2002*, Broxburn; Symon, Ken (2000) 'Whisky duo are prefect blend', *Sunday Times*, 19 November; Cochrane, Lynn (2000) 'Shot of sex equality', *Sunday Times*, 15 October; Oram, Roderick (1996) 'Glenmorangie changes the blend', *Financial Times*, 15 May; Laforce, Marguerite (1996) 'Marie Brizard prévoit des bénéfices cette année', *Les Echos*, 3 June; Wright's Investors' Service (2002) *Corporate Information* **www.corporateinformation.com**, accessed 18 December 2002; **www.glenmorangieplc.com**, accessed 18 December 2002.

2 Nakamoto, Michiyo (1996) 'WTO's liquor tax ruling unsteadies Japan', *Financial Times*, 8 October, 7.

3 Rugman, Alan M. and Hodgetts, Richard M. (1995) *International Business: A strategic management approach*, New York: McGraw-Hill, 433.

4 Perlmutter, Howard V. (1999) 'On deep dialog', *Knowledge@Wharton Newsletter*, 19 July, **http://knowledge.wharton.upenn.edu**, accessed 1 September 2002.

5   Kobrin, Stephen J. (1995) 'Beyond symmetry: state sovereignty in a networked global economy', *Working Paper*, 95–8, Wharton School: University of Pennsylvania, **www.gsia.cmu.edu/afs/andrew/gsia/bosch/kobrin/ kobrin.html**, accessed 1 June 1997.

6   World Trade Organization (2003) *Technical barriers to trade*, WTO, **www.wto.org/english/tratop_e/tbt_e/tbt_ e.htm**, accessed 17 January 2003.

7   United Nations Conference on Trade and Development (2002) World *Investment Report: Transnational Corporations and Export Competitiveness* Geneva: UNCTAD, 1.

8   Levitt, Theodore (1983) 'The globalisation of markets', *Harvard Business Review*, **61(3)**, May–June, 92–102.

9   *The 2002 Global 1000 Scoreboard*, *Business Week Online*, **bwnt.businessweek.com/global_1000/2002/ index.asp**, accessed 19 December 2002.

10 United Nations Conference on Trade and Development (2001) *World Investment Report: Promoting Linkages*, UNCTAD, 95–112.

11 'The Forbes International 500' (2002) *Forbes Magazine*, **www.forbes.com/2002/07/03/internationals.htm**, accessed 20 December 2002 (uses mainly 2001 data).

12 World Trade Organisation (2002) *International trade statistics 2002* WTO, **www.wto.org/english/res_e/ statis_e/statis_e.htm#stats**, accessed 16 January 2003.

13 Ohmae, Kenichi (1995) *The Evolving Global Economy*, Boston, Mass.: Harvard Business School Press.

14 Stopford, John M. (1994) 'The impact of the global political economy on corporate strategy', *Working Paper*, 94–7, Wharton School: University of Pennsylvania, **www.gsia.cmu.edu/afs/andrew/gsia/bosch/stopford/ stopford.html**, accessed 1 May 2003.

15 Levitt, *op.cit.*

16 Rugman, Alan (2001) 'The myth of global strategy' *International Marketing Review*, **18(6)**, 583–8; *see also* his (2000) *The End of Globalization*, New York: Random House Business Books.

17 Vignali, Claudio (2001) 'McDonald's: "think global, act local" – the marketing mix', *British Food Journal*, **103(2)**, 97–111.

18 World Trade Organization (2003) *Textiles Monitoring Body (TMB): The Agreement on Textiles and Clothing*, WTO, **www.wto.org/english/tratop_e/texti_e/texintro_e.htm**, accessed 22 January 2003.

19 For example, Daft, Richard L. (1994) *Management*, 3rd edition, Fort Worth, Tex.: Dryden Press, 94.

20 Grönroos, Christian (1999) 'Internationalisation strategies for services', *Journal of Services Marketing*, **13(4/5)**, 290–7.

21 Oldfield, Clare (1996) 'The V&A ties up classic deals with licensing', *Sunday Times*, 12 May.

22 *Financial Times: Companies & Finance* (2003) 'Vodafone signs Austrian partner', 8 January.

23 *Financial Times: Companies & Finance* (2002) 'Shell and CNOOC to start $4.3 billion project', 2 November; 'GM to sell Daewoo cars in China', 29 October; 'Wal-Mart signs up for China venture', 11 October.

24 **www.sixcontinents.com/investors/overview.htm** and **www.accor.fr/sf/groupe/default.htm**, both accessed 1 February 2003.

25 Dunning, J.H. (1979) 'Explaining changing patterns of international production: in defence of the eclectic theory', *Oxford Bulletin of Economics and Statistics*, **41**, 269–96.

26 Burton, John and Buxton, James (1996) 'Scotland wins £1 billion Korean factory', *Financial Times*, 8 October, 9.

27 Vecchio, Robert P. (1995) *Organisational Behaviour*, 3rd edition, Fort Worth, Tex.: Dryden Press, 625.

28 Denfeld Wood, Jack (1995) 'Culture is not enough', *Financial Times*, 8 December, II.

29 Vecchio (1995) *loc. cit.*

30 Riordan, Christine M. and Vandenberg, Robert J. (1994) 'A central question in cross-cultural research: do employees of different cultures interpret work-related measures in an equivalent manner?' *Journal of Management*, **20(3)**, Autumn, 643–71.

31 McKenna, Stephen (1995) 'The business impact of management attitudes towards dealing with conflict: a cross-cultural assessment', *Journal of Management Psychology*, **10(7)**, July, 22–27.

32 Marsh, David (1995) 'Positive effects of a culture clash', *Financial Times*, 15 May, 11.

33 Hofstede, G. (1993) 'Cultural constraints in management theories', *Academy of Management Executive*, **7**, 81–94.

34 Perlmutter, Howard V. (1969) 'The tortuous evolution of the multinational corporation', *Columbia Journal of World Business*, **4**, 9–18.

35 Woolridge, Adrian (1995) 'Survey of multinationals – from multilocal to multicultural – this way for the rainbow corporation', *The Economist*, 24 June, 70.

36 Summers, Diane (1995) 'PR consensus finds Shell at fault. Opting for a U-turn over Brent Spar only made the nightmare worse say the publicity experts', *Financial Times*, 23 June, 11; Southey, Caroline and Corzine, Robert (1995) 'Gummer attacks Brent Spar U-turn: European partners are accused of "caving in"', *Financial Times*, 23 June, 18.

37 Simon, Herbert A. (1994) 'Is international management different from management?' Carnegie Mellon University Working Paper; **www.gsia.cmu.edu/afs/andrew/gsia/ bosch/simon/simon.html**, accessed 12 May 2003.

38 Kirkaldy, Bruce, Furnham, Adrian and Robert Levine (2000) 'Attitudinal and personality correlates of a nation's pace of life', *Journal of Managerial Psychology*, **16(1)**, 20–34.

39 Hall, Edward T. (1969) *The Dance of Life*, New York: Anchor-Doubleday; Hall, Edward T. and Hall, M.R. (1990), *Understanding Cultural Differences*, Yarmouth, Maine: Intercultural Press.

40 Bluedorn, Allen C., Kalliath, Thomas J., Strube, Michael J. and Martin, Gregg D. (1999) 'Polychronicity and the Inventory of Polychronic Values (IPV)', *Journal of Managerial Psychology*, **14(3/4)**, 205–30.

41 Dumaine, Brian (1992) 'Management lessons from the general', *Fortune*, 2 November, 104.

42 Chu, Wilson (1996) 'The human side of examining a foreign target', *Mergers and Acquisitions*, **30(4)**, January–February, 35–9.

43 Choi, Chong Ju (1994) 'Contract enforcement across cultures', *Organisation Studies*, **15(5)**, 673–82.

44 Janssens, Maddy, Brett, Jeanne M. and Smith, Frank J. (1995) 'Confirmatory cross-cultural research: testing the viability of a corporation-wide safety policy', *Academy of Management Journal*, **38(2)**, April, 364–72.

45 Hofstede, Geert (1980) *Culture's Consequences: International differences in work-related values*, New York: Sage.

46 Hofstede, Geert and Bond, Michael Harris (1988) 'The Confucius connection: from cultural roots to economic growth', *Organisation Dynamics*, **16(4)**, 4–21.

47 Social Sciences Citation Index (2000) Thompson, Institute for Scientific Information.

48 Carrithers, Michael (1992) *Why Humans Have Cultures*, Oxford: Oxford University Press, 8.

49 Rugman and Hodgetts (1995) *op. cit.*, 135.

50 Schramm-Nielsen, Jette (2000) 'How to Interpret Uncertainty Avoidance Scores: A comparative study of Danish and French firms', *International Journal of Cross Cultural Management*, **7(4)**, 3–11.

51 Trompenaars, Fons and Hampden-Turner, Charles (1997) *Riding the Waves of Culture: Understanding Cultural Diversity in Business*, 2nd edition, London: Nicholas Brealey.

52 Ronen, Simcha and Shenkar, Oded (1985) 'Clustering countries on attitudinal dimensions: a review and synthesis', *Academy of Management Journal*, **28**, September, 449.

53 Luce, Edward (1995) 'SE Asia – singularly different', *Financial Times*, 4 December, 12.

54 Houlder, Vanessa (1995) 'Cultural exchanges – roving executives with truly transportable skills are in short supply', *Financial Times*, 5 April, 19; Marquardt, M.J. and Engel, D.W. (1993) 'HRD competences for a shrinking world', *Training and Development*, **47(5)**, 59–65.

55 Adler, Nancy J. and Bartholomew, Susan (1992) 'Managing globally competent people', *Academy of Management Executive*, **6(3)**, 52–65.

56 Black, J. Stewart, Mendenhall, Mark and Oddou, Gary (1991) 'Towards a comprehensive model of international adjustment: an integration of multiple theoretical perspectives', *Academy of Management Review*, **16(2)**, 291–317.

57 Helmreich, R.L., Merritt, A.C. and Sherman, P.J. (1996) 'Human factors and national culture', *ICAO Journal*, **51(8)**, 14–16., www.psy.utexas.edu/psy/helmreich/nasaut.htm.

58 Child, Peter N. (2002) 'Taking Tesco global', *McKinsey Quarterly*, **2**; Vignali, Claudio (2001) 'Tesco's adaptation to the Irish market', *British Food Journal*, **103(2)**, 146–63; Child, Peter N., Heywood, Suzanne and Kliger, Michael (2002) 'Do retail brands travel?' *McKinsey Quarterly*, **1**; Wrigley, Neil (2002) 'The landscape of pan-European food retail consolidation', *International Journal of Retail and Distribution Management*, **30(2)**, 81–91.

CHAPTER 5

Social responsibility and ethics

Chapter objectives

When you have finished studying this chapter, you should be able to:

- explain why social responsibility has emerged as an important issue for organisations;

- identify stakeholders; compare arguments for and against recognition of their interests;

- describe and illustrate four main social responsibility strategies;

- summarise deontology, utilitarianism and virtue ethics; show how these apply to management decisions;

- resolve ethical dilemmas through the application of these principles;

- outline how organisations should plan their approach to managing social responsibility and ethics programmes;

- assess your own views on social responsibility and ethics.

A task becomes a duty from the moment you suspect it to be an essential part of that integrity which alone entitles a man to assume responsibility

Dag Hammarksjöld, United Nations Secretary-General, 1953–61

Being socially responsible and staying in business[1]

With 13 per cent of the market, Norske Skog is the third largest producer of paper for newsprint and magazines. Having grown strongly beyond its Norwegian base since 1995, it has 24 mills in 15 countries in all continents. Management of this diversification is based on a common code of conduct and shared values. Strategies include sustainable development, minimal waste discharges to air and water, recycling of materials and energy and safe working conditions. Norske Skog accepts that its presence influences developments wherever it operates, especially as mills are frequently located in ecologically sensitive areas. The company reports on eco-efficiency targets for process performance from forest production through to final delivery. These include raw materials and energy consumption, and discharges such as dissolved organic materials, gases such as CO_2 and SO_2, and general waste. Sustainability of forest sources is measured and certified under ISO14001 and Paper Profile.[2]

A cubic metre of spruce produces about 1000 copies of a 68-page broadsheet newspaper. Recycled material saves wood but, since fibres break down after the fifth use, the maximum proportion of recycled content is about 80 per cent. This fraction of collected paper is now recycled, but much is lost in the loop. The European paper recycling declaration requires re-use of 56 per cent of consumption by 2005, with much of the responsibility placed on producers. New mills have been built close to population centres to simplify this process. Many countries do not produce paper, so there is a developing trade in waste for recovery, especially from North America to Asia. Since many papers, especially magazines, contain impurities from staples to ink and pigments, recycling requires large investments in equipment to remove them.

Norske Skog believes that business value goes hand in hand with wide social responsibilities. Thus it recognises employees' rights to training and involvement in decision making as well as freedom to organise. Beyond the plants, policies cover the rights of local communities to basic needs and maintenance of their cultural heritage. Half of the staff at a New Zealand mill is of *Tangate whenua* (Maori) descent and there is a special council to assist in Maori matters. Staff at a Brazilian plant enjoy company housing, medical insurance and childcare.

Pressure does not abate. While leading paper companies accept targets for sustainability and incorporate social responsibility issues into their policies, standards are rising and pressure groups launch new campaigns. Although many European forests have recovered their tree populations after the reckless felling of the nineteenth century, they have not regained their biodiversity. A farmed forest does not contain the original range of species from birds to lichens and mosses. Therefore, companies, including Norske Skog, need to invest continually in research, planning and training.

Introduction

Few managers these days fail to acknowledge the wide societal impact of business. Hence, few refuse to face questions about how they should influence, control and restrain it. We have seen, since the growth of large corporations at the end of the nineteenth century, gradual shifts away from reliance on the unfettered economic market. In most European countries, companies have come to be seen as public property with non-owners having a legitimate interest in influencing the decisions that their managers make. As illustrated by the opening case, governments regulate corporate behaviour in many ways and there are numerous groups who press their viewpoints upon organisations.

Organisations, therefore, are engaged in a continual interaction with an environment that is wider than the market. Harvey[3] calls this an 'influence market', populated by all sorts of interest groups, lobbyists, quasi-judicial regulatory bodies, government officials and ministers and other organisations. It is more complex and uncertain than the classical market, varying from firm to firm, time to time and country to country. These variations appear in the paper industry; the political framework within which the industry operates is changing rapidly and each firm is affected differently depending on its scale, location, technology and so on.

Recognising at least that governments will take greater measures to control business unless it 'puts its house in order', the question for managers moves on from *whether* they should admit to having a social responsibility to *how much* they have. Answers to these questions influence managerial action. At one end of the scale, the statements of free market economists such as Milton Friedman are well known – being socially responsible is to follow a fundamentally flawed doctrine. Firms should do the minimum they are required to do and no more. 'Business is business.'[4] At the opposite end, those favouring greater responsibility, such as Harvey, argue that firms could, and should, do much more. Investors increasingly express this view; in the United Kingdom, ethical investment funds grew 18-fold during the 1990s. Consumers, too, feel they have a growing influence.[5]

Social responsibility is grounded more deeply than simply doing good business within the influence market. In their decision making, managers face ethical issues. Frequently these are so implicit that they are not recognised as such but, in choosing one course of action against another, managers are making moral judgements. They are, moreover, displaying leadership which, since managers occupy positions of influence, must bring with it moral responsibility. Therefore, ethical choices are important for individuals and groups within the organisation. The second part of the chapter is devoted to a discussion of ethics in business.

Social responsibility

Social responsibility is the obligation of managers to choose and act in ways that benefit both the interests of the organisation and those of society as a whole.

While this definition has the advantage of brevity, a closer look shows that it is not, on its own, a means of answering the question, 'Are we a socially responsible organisation?' We can raise three issues for clarification:

■ *Who is included?*
While there is a growing consensus that all organisations should do their best to avoid detrimental impacts on the natural environment, there is less agreement about who and what else ought to be included in the 'society as a whole'. Consumer rights have become well established in advanced economies, taken seriously by leading companies and underpinned by legislation. On the other hand, few companies concern themselves with disadvantaged people even though the disadvantage may be an indirect outcome of their own activities. We can give two instances. First, a supermarket may drive local shops out of business. Although many gain from the switch,

some customers will find difficulty in reaching the new store. This is not seen as the company's problem. Second, there are congestion costs to which all contribute and for which people are only beginning to feel responsible. Only the private aspects of these costs, that is delays to one's own fleet, are built into company transport policies. The social costs, delays to other people, are left for others to worry about.

■ *Complexity of decisions*

As we shall see in Chapter 9, it is often difficult for managers to select the best course of action for an organisation. Given that assessing the impact of any action upon the wider society is a far more exacting task, what chance do managers have of getting it right? A firm may decide not to close a plant in a region where unemployment is high, deciding that community interests demand that it be given 'a last chance'. Such action may save jobs in the short term but may put other areas of the business at risk. Furthermore, it may reinforce a local habit of reliance on outdated skills and employment patterns. Then, when the plant is eventually closed, the catastrophe is worse.

■ *Winners and losers*

Part of the decision-making problem is the choice of who is to benefit from its outcomes. Social programmes, for instance, do not come free. In 2002, Littlewoods, Britain's second largest home shopping business, was sold by the Moores family to David and Frederick Barclay for about £750 million. To reduce costs, the new owners immediately withdrew Littlewoods from the Ethical Trading Initiative and closed its ethical trade operations, dismissing the staff involved.[6]

Companies respond to these questions in different ways. The opening case was set in the context of the protection of our physical environment. The Body Shop,[7] *see* Exhibit 5.1, pursues a social policy extending far beyond ecological issues. It tries to make a real difference to the lives of people it deals with throughout the world. Central to its themes are a belief in trade with developing countries, rather than aid, and recognition that money is rarely the sole motivator of people. These values have their basis in the outlook of the organisation's founder, an outlook that has developed and changed with her experience of leadership. Successful socially responsible leaders manage to transmit their ideals to others. This binds organisation members into a cohesive, recognisable whole.

Although The Body Shop stands out as an example, in other cases the benefits are not clear-cut. Many maintain that business should not encompass social responsibility at all. The debate is nicely balanced, with four main arguments on each side.

■ Arguments for social responsibility

The arguments in favour of social responsibility stem from the power and importance of organisations in modern society. This means that they are repositories of power and skills that can make a difference. The four arguments are presented as though spoken by a proponent.

■ *Potential to do good*

'Modern businesses have high technical, managerial and financial capability. Indeed, many multinational companies have more resources than the governments in whose territories they operate. Therefore, since their actions could have a decisive impact upon social problems we should require them to behave responsibly.'

Exhibit 5.1 The Body Shop: building on ideals

More than 40 countries host the 1200 outlets of The Body Shop. It sells a range of cosmetic products inspired by traditional manufacture using natural ingredients. Formulations are not tested on animals. Packaging is simple and recycled; marketing is low key with very limited advertising.

The company expresses the ideals of its founder Anita Roddick and the many franchise holders and employees who have, since 1976, enjoyed its growth within a culture that has taken more and more interest in the natural environment, sustainable development and the lot of fellow humans. According to Tom Peters, Roddick stands out as a visionary thinker. She has 'A set of beliefs that really are the essence of what she's about. ... She really does live that set of beliefs, and it happens to have been tremendously effective commercially in a very, very difficult industry.' In the late 1970s, the industry had come to be seen by some as exploiting women, torturing animals, damaging the environment and self-promoting on the basis of huge exaggerations.

The Body Shop seeks to create bonds with its employees, franchisees and customers through deeper links than the commercial or employment contract. It aims to create a sense of passion about world issues and encourages people to join in action. Staff are assisted to join in community work and have been given paid breaks to work in Romanian orphanages.

Companies that espouse high levels of social responsibility invite criticism from new directions. An example was the report in August 1994 by the American journalist Jon Entine which criticised The Body Shop's relations with its franchisees and third-world suppliers. Unused to defending itself against such attacks, The Body Shop had some difficulty in refuting the claims that Entine made. Later, it reported that the controversy had had little effect on sales. Slackening of growth around this period was attributed to increased competition in the company's largest division, the United States. Imitators of the successful formula included Body & Bath Works which, taking advantage of low store opening costs, expanded rapidly.

■ *Anticipation of emerging problems*

'If organisations had displayed greater responsibility in the past in areas such as equal opportunity, safety, quality and financial probity, there would have been less need for the tight regulation that many governments feel obliged to apply nowadays. It follows that more socially responsible behaviour now, such as in respect of ethical advertising, tax and duty payment and information security may avoid government intervention in these problem areas.'

■ *Investment should yield benefits for all*

'Profitability in the long term depends on a favourable social, economic and physical environment. Policies from conservation to training mean that extra spending now can lead to more riches later, including *benefits for the organisation itself*. Good values mean good business.'

■ *Unavoidable responsibilities linked with rights*

'Notwithstanding whether businesses ought to show responsibility, there is no doubt that business is intimately involved in any society. Society grants rights and privileges to organisations, such as legal protection or the freedom to open or close facilities within established constraints. A civilised society requires rights to be exercised responsibly.'

■ Arguments against social responsibility

Arguments against tend to start from the classical economic model but can also be broadened into expressions of fear about the power of businesses managed by a self-appointed elite. Again, the cases are put as though spoken by a proponent.

■ *Purpose of business*

'The purpose of business is to make profit. Markets work because the sum of individual transaction decisions between buyers and sellers is the best way to allocate resources. The needs of groups from local residents to third-world suppliers should only be considered by business managers when such action yields clear improvements in business efficiency and effectiveness. Unless an organisation is established with explicit social goals – for instance an arm of government or a charity – it should not become involved with them.'

■ *Capability of managers is limited*

'Since businesses are economic institutions, they should develop the competence to pursue economic goals. Social goals take them into fields where they have no particular capability. They only sidetrack managerial attention.'

■ *Power should be restricted*

'Business already has too much power. If harnessed for good ends, use of this power can be beneficial. Yet, there have been many cases where businesses have manipulated weaker groups and governments. In a democratic society, it is better, in principle, if power is not concentrated in the hands of a few.'

■ *Legitimacy is confined to the organisation's legal purposes*

'Owners and managers are unelected. How can managers be held responsible for the allocation decisions that they make? The market system is the ultimate test of the enterprise's economic performance but, without elections, there is no sanction on the societal performance. Without a political process, where managers are subjected to tests of public opinion, how would conflicts of interest be resolved?'

■ Stakeholders

For those organisations that accept some degree of social responsibility, there are two central questions: whose interests are to be served and how far should the organisation go in serving them?

If managers are to consider the interests of parties other than those formally owning or placed in charge of an organisation, there must be a mutual recognition that these parties stand for something that is important. This legitimacy, which is the right to a stake in the organisation, comes from a variety of sources. These are: economic necessity; the legal framework in which the organisation operates; and the values espoused by the organisation and its members. Managers can, therefore, exercise some choice over whom it recognises as a stakeholder, that is, whose interests are to be taken into account. We can summarise these points in the following definition:

> *A stakeholder is an individual or group, inside or outside the organisation, who has a meaningful stake in its performance.*

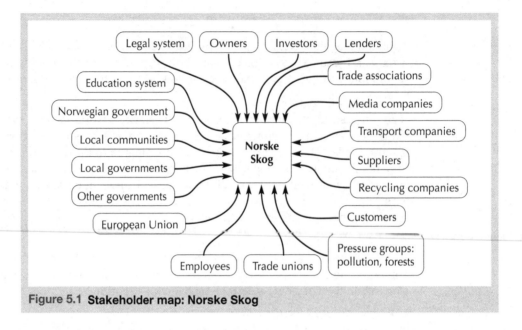

Figure 5.1 Stakeholder map: Norske Skog

Figure 5.1 represents the important stakeholders in the home country of Norske Skog. Each stakeholder has interests that sometimes conflict with the interests of other groups. Managers serve the economic interests of investors by aiming for a satisfactory return on investment while maintaining long-term stability. Employees expect good pay as well as work satisfaction, job security and good prospects. Recognising that a few employees have reading difficulties, the company subsidises literacy courses at adult education centres, open to outsiders.

Other stakeholders join with the company in creating its value chain, which is the system of processes through which products are made, distributed and sold to the customer. With the increasing integration of these chains, *see* Chapter 15, the dependency of each component on the progress of all the others becomes more apparent. They are each stakeholders in the other. Customers are also stakeholders to the extent that they depend on the company products. If, for example, Norske Skog makes a special paper for a customer, then the latter becomes dependent on the paper company for the supply. The more difficult it is for the customer to switch, the greater the economic dependency.

The legitimacy of local and national government interests in the many countries in which Norske Skog operates has two foundations. First, there is the legislation covering areas from fair trade practices to product and process safety. Only fool-hardy companies do not take such responsibilities seriously. Second, governments take an interest in the progress of major companies because they are significant components of national economic performance and, through employment, location and purchasing policies, can aid or hinder development in different regions. Although Norske Skog has grown into a global corporation, its scale in Norway means that relations with the Norwegian government remain close. For example, the company will expect the government to maintain a transport infrastructure appro-priate to its needs while the government will expect to be briefed on strategic plans and decisions affecting the nation. We saw in Chapter 4 how MNEs maintain such relations in all countries in which they have a presence. Norske Skog has mills in 15 countries and customers in more than 100.

Beyond the strict legal and economic frameworks, companies are subject to pressures from groups advancing causes ranging from product safety and environmental protection to equal opportunity and fair trade. The case study identifies recent pressures over the interlinked issues of biodiversity and forest management. Its strength is such that it is as if the trees themselves have become stakeholders. Norske Skog responds by going beyond eco-investments in its own plant to pay for fish ladders to benefit salmon stocks and to lead a scheme ensuring all Norway's forests receive sustainability certificates. To some extent, these actions conflict with the interests of investors.

The last stakeholders we can consider achieve recognition not from any claims they advance, but from the discretion of the owners or managers themselves. The Co-operative Bank supports the publication of the *Big Issue*, a newspaper sold by the unemployed. Other examples are: Coca-Cola, supporting many social programmes around its home city of Atlanta, Georgia; and Pilkington, well known for similar activity in St Helens in north-west England. Although some would claim that this is merely 'good business', there is an element of philanthropy in such gifts. The companies do not necessarily see them as economic investments and do not demand analysis of any direct return.

In the basic presentation of Figure 5.1, a *stakeholder map* is little more than a listing of the groups having an influence on Norske Skog. Clearly some influences are two way, such as between the company and other parts of its value chain. Additionally, some groups exercise direct or indirect influence, and occasionally both. Employees relate directly to the company as individuals as well as collectively through trade unions. Further, when the interaction has a legal framework such as the employment contract, influence can be exerted through that framework. We can develop our stakeholder map to aid a deeper understanding of such linkages. Figure 5.2 suggests how two of the areas could be presented. The left-hand half explores the relationships between the company and administrators in Norway. The right-hand half covers the link between employee and trade union and suggests how interactions can be usefully labelled.

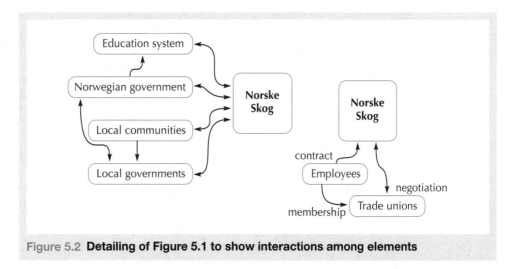

Figure 5.2 **Detailing of Figure 5.1 to show interactions among elements**

■ Social responsibility strategies

Whatever conclusions we could reach on the social responsibility arguments, it is clear that organisations are increasingly committing themselves to act responsibly.[8] We can classify these actions into four types, recognising that they really form a continuum of behaviour from obstructive to proactive, *see* Figure 5.3. Since the actions are deliberate, they can rightly be called *social responsibility strategies*.

Obstructive

An organisation following an obstructive strategy will tend to deny responsibility for its actions and resist change that it can only see as disadvantageous. The policy is also known as *stonewalling* or a *reactive* policy.

In March 1993, Volkswagen recruited from General Motors a team led by José Ignacio Lopez, head of global purchasing. He had a high reputation for reducing supply costs. Later, Lopez and others were accused of taking with them confidential documents. VW spent many months suggesting that the evidence had been planted. It also argued that the secrets were of no use to VW! GM brought a civil action for damages in a Detroit court while prosecutors pursued the criminal investigation in Germany. VW spent time arguing that the civil case should be heard in Germany but, rather than take its chances in Detroit, it eventually agreed to settle the civil action. Announced in early 1997, this meant a payment of more than $100 million and a VW commitment to buy at least $1 billion worth of components from GM over 7 years. Lopez resigned in 1996 and was indicted by a federal grand jury in Michigan in 2000.[9]

Another back-to-the-wall campaign was fought by tobacco companies for many years. It ended in the United States in 1998, when the manufacturers agreed to pay the 50 states $250 billion over ten years and accept advertising controls. Companies switched their attention to developing countries where, according to the World Health Organisation, about 70 per cent of smoking-related deaths will occur. The 190-country tobacco control treaty aims to make a big difference.[10]

Now we see skirmishes over obesity. The case of Pelman v. McDonald's, in which two young plaintiffs, one 135Kg, sued the fast-food giant for making them fat, may seem just 'typically American'. Nestle[11] argues, however, that a disproportionate amount of the food industry's marketing budget is spent on less healthy products. Furthermore, it is directed at children.

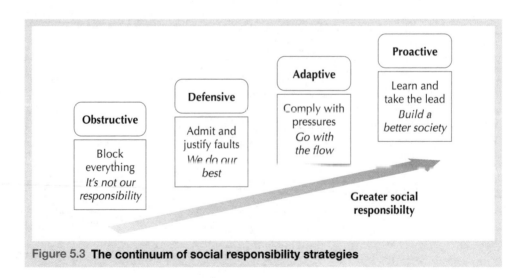

Figure 5.3 **The continuum of social responsibility strategies**

When state lunch budgets were cut back, McDonald's and Pizza Hut were allowed to sell on school premises. Pepsi and Coca-Cola offer exclusivity agreements for vending machines, paying bonuses to schools if sales targets were reached. Companies are also increasing portion sizes and bundling meals to persuade customers to eat more. The McDonald's meal of the 1950s had 590 calories; now an 'extra value' meal has 1550.

Although blaming obesity on food producers is unlikely to succeed, others point to deceptive marketing. Just as Philip Morris persuaded smokers to think of 'light' cigarettes as healthy, so labels such as 'low-fat' or 'healthy-eating' are coming under scrutiny. The industry may do better than blame overweight on unhealthy lifestyles and accept some responsibility. This would lead to changes in the way food is marketed.[12]

Defensive

Using a defensive strategy, a company proceeds not by denial but by manoeuvring to justify its position and avoid being saddled with extra responsibility. The stance is to do everything that is legally required and no more. The strategy uses legal actions and public relations campaigns to prove compliance.

In November 2002, the Burma Campaign launched a worldwide effort to force British American Tobacco to withdraw from that country. Kenneth Clarke MP, once Chancellor of the Exchequer, was chair of BAT's CSR committee. He wrote to a constituent, 'I must admit that I do sometimes feel uncomfortable about investment in that country . . . The problem in Burma arises when companies start collaborating with an extremely unpleasant regime which is totally contrary to our notions of civil liberties and democracy.' This note contrasted with company policy to press on with a joint venture with Union of Myanmar Economic Holdings, owned by the Burmese military regime. Clarke defended the apparent confusion by arguing that the arrangement had been inherited in the merger with Rothmans in 1999. Furthermore, he proposed that a foreign company could not reform the politics of every country where it operates; about a third of the world was run by dictatorships. The 400 employees in Burma would not gain if they pulled out. The Burma Campaign pointed out that a year's redundancy pay would cost six minutes' profit; the factory site had been upgraded using child labour and democrats within the country opposed further investment.[13]

Adaptive

Under an adaptive social responsibility strategy, the company accepts that it is accountable for its actions, although this acceptance is often the result of pressure brought by external groups.

When Shell's Brent Spar oil production platform reached the end of its useful life, the company carried out detailed studies of the best means of disposal. It received a licence from the United Kingdom government to sink it in the North Atlantic. It was only after strong pressure from environmental groups, led by Greenpeace, and a customer boycott and political pressure felt most strongly in Germany, that the company abandoned the scheme and had the rig towed to a Norwegian fjord to await a decision on its dismantling. Shell's approach had focused on a technical optimisation of the decision within economic and regulatory constraints. It had failed to consider the emotional and violent response, including fire bombing of filling stations, that occurred once the disposal got under way. In the end, the company decided to have the 14 500 tonne platform cut into pieces to form the foundations for a new quay near Mekjarvik in Norway.[14]

Proactive

The proactive company takes the lead. It looks carefully at the relationships between its activities and the interests of its stakeholders. Then it responds to these interests without pressure being applied.

Building on its traditions, the Co-operative Bank serves seven 'Partners' – shareholders, cus-tomers, staff, suppliers, local communities, national and international society and past and future generations of co-operators. It wants to deliver value, defined by Partners, in a socially responsible and ecologically sustainable manner. Its ethical policy was launched in 1992. It is revised regularly after consultation with customers. In the Human Rights section, for exam-ple, the bank supports the principles of the Universal Declaration of Human Rights. It will not invest in any government or business that fails to uphold basic human rights within its sphere of influence; nor will it finance any business whose links to an oppressive regime are a con-tinuing cause for concern.

The bank estimated that its ethical stance had contributed about £20 million to 2001 prof-its. Among reasons given for the rejection of financing opportunities were environment, 41 per cent, and animal testing and sustainability, 15 per cent. Up to a third of customers said they had joined because of the ethical stance.[15]

The four responsibility strategies, summarised in Figure 5.3, represent organisa-tions whose attitude varies from 'the business of business is business'[16] to 'we are responsible for all the consequences of our actions'. Why do they choose one or other, or even a mix of these strategies?

■ Altruism or enlightened self-interest?

Does social responsibility mean that businesses should be motivated by altruism, the selfless commitment to the benefit of others? Our examples suggest that such cases would be rare. If social responsibility was defined narrowly as corporate altruism, most firms could not claim to be responsible at all. Motives are the keys to under-standing altruism. Yet, since most business leaders use their political skills to present a decision to different stakeholders in different ways, we are left to specu-late what these motives are.

It is more realistic to consider business decisions taken for the benefit of wider stakeholders stemming from *enlightened self-interest*. We have looked at many exam-ples that can be interpreted in this way. Many senior managers admit to the change of emphasis. David Buzzelli, environment director at Dow Chemical, pointed out that no one in the 1970s chemical industry could have built a career on environmental friend-liness. Now the company, the world leader in chlorinated compounds, is leading discussions of the role of chemicals in a greener world. Dow produces many com-pounds with benign, valuable applications but others are: raw materials for napalm, widely used in the Vietnam war; bleaching agents, applied in textiles and paper but producing harmful dioxins; and solvents that are both toxic and not biodegradable. Greenpeace argues that Dow's environmental policies are not proactive but merely methods of marketing, public relations and keeping on the right side of officials.[17]

Enlightened self-interest is much more than using sponsorship to build public images. Green policies yield business opportunities and powerful active companies have begun to persuade governments to pass relevant legislation, which, incidentally, favours their business prospects. The Montreal Protocol is an intergovernmental agreement banning the use of CFC aerosol propellants and refrigerator gases because of their harmful effect on the ozone layer. The policy was backed by the major suppli-ers Du Pont and ICI, partly because they were already well advanced in the development of substitutes. Since the ban, the number of suppliers of suitable refriger-ants in the EU has fallen from more than 20 to 4.

Examples from Germany show that there are many business opportunities. More than 2500 companies gain more than half their income from recycling and green technologies. There is also restriction. From 1991, drinks for the German market had to be supplied in refillable bottles. This helped to protect small local brewers.[18] In 1995, the government announced it was banning imports of textiles containing Azo dyes. These dyes have caused cancer in the workers who use them but there is no evidence of any harm to wearers. They are widely used in India whose large export industry sees Germany as second only to the United States as a customer. Trade-based quotas are being phased out under the rules of the World Trade Organization, but restrictions on safety grounds will remain lawful.[19]

These examples suggest the range and variety of potential benefits for the socially responsible organisation. Here is a brief round-up:

- creating markets for environmentally friendly products or process technologies;
- supplying products and programmes for disadvantaged groups;
- influencing governments through direct lobbying or swaying public opinion;
- recruiting, motivating and retaining good employees;
- staff training assignments in community programmes;
- enabling owners and managers to see funds diverted to their favourite organisations;
- providing a favourable image as a defence against possible accusations of malpractice;
- creating or sustaining an impression of having high ethical standards in business dealings;
- attracting ethical investors.

While we can readily observe action, we cannot easily sort out the reasons why organisations choose their policies. If we return to our definition of social responsibility, we can see that, in situations of choice, it identifies *obligation both to the organisation and to society*. The obligation may have become more accepted and the balance between organisation and society may be shifting. Understanding why, however, requires us to get inside the hearts and minds of every manager. This alters the focus from corporate social responsibility to the choices made by individuals.

Ethics

The study of ethics centres on choices facing the individual. Further, to the extent that the individual participates in a group whose members have the same views, we can speak of the ethics of the group. As we shall see in Chapter 17, the relationship between a person and a group is two way. The person joins with others in forming the group and brings his or her individuality to it. Simultaneously, membership of the group changes the individual, shaping values and therefore stimulating or restraining behaviour. To the extent that there is cohesion among members, we can speak of group values and behaviour. The groups may be very large, such as when we speak of religious ethics as sets of moral principles, which guide the lives of millions.

The connection with corporate social responsibility follows. In the first part of the chapter, we saw how responsible behaviour can be seen as a rational reaction to external pressures – the influence market as mentioned in the introduction. But arguments based on adaptation to the business environment can never explain why one firm turns out to differ from another. Why managers, individually or as a group, choose one action or another is answered by examining the ethical principles to which they adhere. Studying ethics in management, therefore, means we must study both the basis of individual choice and how a group or organisation ensures that its standards are followed in decision making.

What is ethics?

Of many possible definitions, we shall use the following:

> *Ethics is concerned with the code of values and principles that enables a person to choose between right and wrong and therefore select among alternative courses of action.*

It follows that an ethical issue is one where there is a choice between alternatives and these alternatives will bring benefit or harm to others. One response to this line is to ask, 'Doesn't this apply to most issues, since real choices mean at the least giving benefit to some as opposed to others?' To answer this point we need to draw a boundary to cut out cases where ethics is not relevant. First, there are personal decisions that have no impact upon other people. Generally, the books I read, the time I waste and the dreams I dream have no effect upon others and are purely independent choices. It is only when they have consequences for other people that these choices become ethical. Second, influences on others must be neither remote nor trivial. It is possible to draw chains of cause and effect from almost any human action to any other in the future. One could argue, for example, that if I buy a new washing machine I may be joining others in representing an increase in demand leading to, say, rising prices and eventual disadvantage for others. On the other hand, if I do not buy the model, someone loses a little income. Clearly, no one is saying that I should follow this reasoning but there are other more significant circumstances that echo this choice. Should people campaign for the retention of the corner shop while shopping at the supermarket? Should I drive into town or take the park-and-ride? Should companies support suppliers through lean times? Should firms buy nationalistically?

The third limitation looks to the law as a codification of the ethics of the society as a whole. The law is part of the framework set up by the state that enables society to function. Furthermore, it underpins the role of government in its many activities carried out for the common good. As Argandoña[20] points out, business and markets would be impossible without the rights and duties given to individuals and agents, the establishment of 'rules of the game' and so on. The law sets out what to do in many circumstances and, in so far as the law is just, it must be obeyed.

There is an argument that following the law is all that one has to do, and no more. Yet, this may be inadequate for two reasons. In the first place, there are many areas of life in which the government chooses not to legislate, because of unenforceability, a desire to 'roll back the boundaries of the state' or because change has made previous laws go out of date. Doing only what one is forced to do, which might be called 'yuppie ethics',[21] springing from extreme notions of personal freedom, would lead to a breakdown of many social processes. Something more than law is needed.

The second problem is that legal systems differ in different countries. Argandoña distinguishes between legality and morality:

If the legislation ... is different but is just, it must be followed because, by so doing, one contributes to the common good. If there is no law, or if it is not in accordance with moral criteria, one must always follow the moral criteria.[22]

For instance, German and Portuguese companies operating in both Germany and Portugal follow the relevant national environmental legislation. This is true except when, with greater permissiveness in Portugal, they find in all conscience that they should not observe it. Then they should apply moral criteria.

The difference between law and morality is important. Many human actions are subject to law, and therefore to ethics, since adherence to the law is a moral duty. Others are subject to ethical rules and not to laws as the latter are absent. Additionally, there are those private, free choice acts that are subject to neither. Figure 5.4 labels the three domains of action, suggesting ill-defined boundaries that tend to change in time.

■ Ethics in management

Ethics is about: norms; values; rights and responsibilities; sharing; fairness; obligation and exchange. It is more than just understanding the rules and how they apply to cases. It includes study of the origins of the rules and how they are developed and elaborated through experience of their application. Therefore, being part of a community that both establishes and maintains a set of moral rules is a matter of concern. An organisation is such a community, one of whose purposes is to establish rules by which its members make decisions. Whether this happens formally, through the setting out of codes of conduct, or informally, through the gradual diffusion of the principles of the leaders, depends on the organisation itself. Establishing such controls will be discussed at the end of the chapter. First, we must check to see whether and how managerial decisions have ethical implications. We take the line that management ethics is not a separate branch of ethics. Managers face different applications from those faced by other people, for example in advertising, recruitment, international trade and industrial safety, but the moral questions they face are fundamentally the same. They have to decide what is right according to a set of principles.

The organisation context is important. As we saw in Chapter 2, one school of thought analyses the organisation as a bureaucracy. This functions most efficiently when carrying out clear rules. Once these have been established at the top, the role of members is to implement them. If the rules are found to mutually conflict, the problem goes up the chain for resolution. From the point of view of ethics, it is as

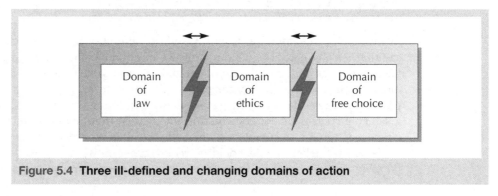

Figure 5.4 Three ill-defined and changing domains of action

though the law/ethics boundary of Figure 5.4 has moved towards the right so that the whole domain of action is covered as far as possible by written rules. These enable people in the organisation to avoid ethical dilemmas. A social security office is an example that aims to cover most of its choices by reference to rules. Even here, however, some instances are referred to adjudicators who have to judge whether individuals qualify for this or that benefit.

At the other extreme, we can conceive of a very 'loose' organisation, full of entre-preneurial spirit, whose members are encouraged to treat each deal as it comes according to their personal judgement. Of course, the law is not broken but, besides that constraint, the 'law of the jungle' prevails. In Figure 5.4, this is equivalent to pulling the ethics/free choice boundary to the left to shrink the domain of ethics.

Yet, neither of these perspectives is realistic. The ideal bureaucracy is impractica-ble and the loose organisation, if it is to be an organisation at all, must have some common code governing practice. Anyhow, both have implied moral positions – 'Follow the rules' or 'Follow the market'.

Ethical dilemmas

Most managers recognise that they wrestle with ethical dilemmas. Dilemmas arise because the interests of different parties involved in, or affected by, decisions are in conflict. One finds that benefiting one party cannot be achieved without disadvan-taging another. At this point, the manager has already made the first moral decision, that it is right to include the interests of the selected parties in the decision at all. In the loose organisation discussed above, following the market implies that no one has rights beyond those either implied by market transactions, as buyers and sellers of property, labour and so on, or as contained in the law, for instance, third parties cov-ered by safety legislation. The bureaucratic organisation can go almost to the other extreme, stating that, in the interests of equity, all decisions affect all members and clients. They must be applied to all in the same way.

A further difficulty for managers, as for other people such as doctors and lawyers who take on responsibilities that affect others, is that they are acting as agents for the organisation. They are carrying out organisational rules and decisions that may have personal implications that they have to resolve. The following case illustrates:

You are in charge of a section of an office. In your spare time, you play in a band, both relax-ing and earning good money. Heavier work responsibilities have meant you have had to gradually reduce your band commitments. At the year end, your manager tells you that you are a valued, vital member of the team who performs well above average but there is to be no pay rise because of a government freeze. In recognition of your efforts, however, the manager offers to help you spend more time with the band by 'looking the other way' if you want to leave early on Fridays to travel to out of town bookings.

At first sight, this situation would pose little difficulty for many people. They may say that leaving early breaks the contract of employment, the manager should not make this offer and, therefore, you should not accept it. Others would appeal to the moral implications of the contract of employment, a fair day's work for a fair day's pay, and suggest that the manager is simply correcting the harm done by not giving a salary increase. Yet others would argue against the unfairness of granting a spe-cific exception for one employee when all should be treated even-handedly.

Naturally, further details would be required before we could explore the case fur-ther. We can see, however, the general point that there is no single principle that can be applied in this setting. Some appeal to equity, others to strict rule adherence. Generalising, we can suggest that using a single principle is rarely satisfactory. More likely is the sort of questioning, 'If I were to follow this rule, then I might recommend this course of action. On the other hand, if I were to follow ...'. We can picture the process as something like Figure 5.5. It is the process of fitting principles and lessons from similar cases to the case in question. In developing a view of the case, people start by looking for principles that may have a bearing upon it. They then assess the extent to which the principles match the situation, possibly by referring to cases that are similar – 'Oh it's rather like ...', or, 'They had something like this in XYZ the other day ...'. There is, therefore, a triangular judgement to be made, between the principles, cases that display similarities but are not the same and the case in question. Having weighed the arguments generated by this process, a person makes a decision and moves to action.[23]

In contrast to the goal-oriented decision processes explained in Chapter 9, this appears to be a messy process. Although outlined as a series of steps, there is no suggestion that a person can slavishly follow a formula, as a bureaucrat might, to reach a decision. On the contrary, the result emerges as a process of subtle judgement among the forces unique to the circumstances and may indeed involve several people.

▣ Ethical principles

We now reach what most see as the core of ethics, coming to grips with the principles themselves. What is their nature? There are many traditions and classifications of such principles, the two dominant being *deontology* and *utilitarianism*.[24] A third approach, *virtue ethics*, concentrates on the type of person one ought to be rather than on establishing a set of rules. All have applications in management.

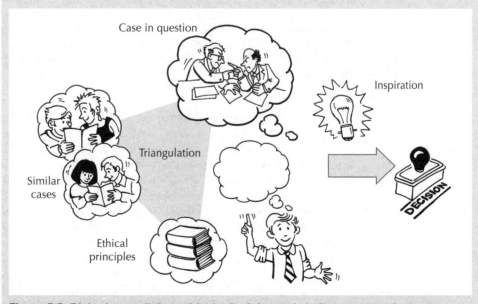

Figure 5.5 Rich picture: fitting ethical principles and similar cases to the case in question

Deontology

By its origin, deontology is the science of duty. It now refers to the method of directing our thinking according to basic ideals that are almost universal in character. This caveat of 'almost' is included because, while rules, when set out, are intended to apply always, it may be that exceptions are discovered. For instance, one may willingly support a principle that pharmaceutical companies should not produce drugs that could harm people. Yet, there are many products that carry a risk of harmful side effects for some users. In these cases, it is up to the producers to post warnings on packets and advise doctors and pharmacists how to avoid supplying the drugs to those who would be at risk.

Exhibit 5.2 Immanuel Kant: one of the great contributors to the study of ethics

Immanuel Kant (1724–1804) is held by many to be the most influential thinker of modern times. A German born in what is now Kaliningrad in Russia, Kant studied and worked at the local university first in classics, then in science and mathematics. He became professor of logic and metaphysics in 1770, continuing to teach until retirement in 1797. The *Critique of Pure Reason* (1781) set out Kant's views on the basis of how humans come to know things. Truths are either *analytic*, based on pure logic, or *synthetic*, based on observation. 'This red cup is a cup' is an example of the former, while 'This cup is red', being an observation, is in the latter category. From these beginnings, Kant created a structure of categories of knowledge.

Metaphysics of Ethics (1797) explained Kant's system of ethics, which is again based on reason. Since we are rational, we must do our duty out of respect for the moral law. Kant identified two types of moral law: the hypothetical imperative, which decides the method of reaching a desired outcome; and the categorical imperative, which determines action because it is right and necessary. The latter is the universal basis of morality. It can be summarised as: 'One should never act unless one is willing to have the principle behind the act become a universal law.'

Kant wrote in other fields, notably astronomy, politics and religion. Because of his controversial religious views, the King of Prussia banned him from teaching the last subject for five years from 1792.

One of the greatest philosophers, Immanuel Kant, created much of the foundation of deontology. His *categorical imperative, see* Exhibit 5.2, can be used as a guide for moral choice. We can illustrate its application by looking at bribery. Is it right to pay a bribe to gain a business contract? The purpose of the bribe is to gain preferential treatment, putting others at a disadvantage. If such action is right for one, then it is right for everyone, a conclusion that the person offering the bribe would not support. Justification for offering bribes cannot be universalised. They are, therefore, unethical.[25]

Deontology has appeal in its simplicity and universality. Difficulties arise when people discover exceptions or when a case appears to be subject to conflicting principles. To illustrate the former we may suggest that 'Always tell the truth' is a good rule. Yet, there are plenty of circumstances, from contract negotiation to playing poker, where such behaviour is not expected. For the latter, we can contrast 'Follow the just law' with 'Respect life'. Is it justifiable to break the speed limit when taking a sick person to hospital? These examples point to weaknesses in deontology. It does not consider consequences of actions, focusing only on foregoing principles.

Utilitarianism

In contrast, the utilitarian approach does look at consequences. The *moral course is the one that provides the greatest good for the greatest number*. This reasoning has been widely accepted in administration and business. It offers grounds for capitalistic market systems and the existence of business organisations themselves. These, according to economists, combine to provide the greatest good for the greatest number, at least when measured in money terms. In government there has been the development of cost–benefit analysis, first concentrating on money value and then extended to measure social costs and benefits of public projects and investments. All these find their ethical foundation in utilitarianism.

Criticisms of the utilitarian approach are threefold. First, there is the possibility of unfair distribution of the benefits of any action. It could be that minor advantages for many are hidden by major disadvantages for a few, the latter having to 'bear the brunt' of whatever is proposed. In response, the rule could be adapted to prevent anyone being worse off, either by not allowing any action that disadvantages anyone or by ensuring that the losers are fully compensated. This is *distributive ethics*, the basis for many management polices, for instance redundancy payment schemes. Yet, as seen in the notorious Ford Pinto case,[26] *see* Exhibit 5.3, a general policy of resolving difficulties by compensation payments is questionable.

Exhibit 5.3 The Ford Pinto: $11 for a product improvement, $200 000 for a life

Ford launched the Pinto in 1970 as an urgent response to rising competition from imported small cars. In rear-end crash tests shortly before the launch, engineers found that the petrol tank could fail easily, although its design met the prevailing safety standards. The defect was discovered after assembly line tooling had been made. Senior managers decided to proceed with manufacture even though the company had a patent on a much safer design. Change would have cost millions through retooling and delays.

A new safety standard had been under discussion since 1968. Realising that the Pinto design would not meet this standard, Ford lobbied hard to have its introduction delayed. In this it was successful, 'Standard 301' was adopted in 1977. Another controversial aspect of the case was a cost–benefit study carried out inside the company and presented to the National Highway Traffic Safety Administration. It showed that introducing an $11 dollar improvement to prevent tank rupture was not economical. The total cost of $137 million far outweighed the benefit of fewer deaths and injuries estimated at $49.5 million. In the latter figure were included 180 deaths at $200 000.

Critics challenged both the calculation and the principle behind it. They asserted that between 500 and 900 extra people suffered death by burning in Pinto crashes because of avoidable tank failure. Ford settled many cases out of court. The Pinto sold at the rate of 500 000 units each year.

The second criticism is that utilitarianism addresses itself to separate acts and does not yield general guidance about what is right and wrong. Times and circumstances change the morality of actions. Further, it may be possible to imagine some wrong actions that, resulting in no apparent losers, must be right. This is the equivalent of the so-called 'victimless crime'. Is it wrong to run unregistered software on my computer when I only do it as a pastime and I wouldn't buy it if I had to? Is it ethically wrong to make false claims in advertising when one can show that nobody suffers? Is it wrong to use inside information to buy or sell a very few shares on the stock exchange? If there are truly no sufferers from each of these acts, the utilitarian is in difficulties. The deontologist, on the other hand, would say, 'You must not use unregistered software unless you were prepared to have a world where registration had no meaning. Then there would be little software supplied!'

The third criticism of utilitarianism is its complexity. While having the great advantage of putting forward a single principle, it suffers from difficulties with 'the greatest good'. How is it to be measured and who is to decide what is good? While the approach seems both democratic and practical in principle, it breaks down when confronted by the extent and depth of real circumstances. Consequently, many managers use judgement, checklists and rules of thumb to simplify issues and therefore cope. How they make choices under these conditions depends on what sort of person they are.

Virtue ethics

Rather than looking at moral principles, virtue ethics asks the question: 'What sort of person ought I to be?' Stretching back to the Greek Aristotle, the virtue tradition has the advantage of seeing morality as a set of attitudes and behaviour established among groups or societies. Further, it underpins and justifies the idea of moral education, which is training people to behave according to a society's views of what is right and wrong. Training in virtue is possible if there are a role model, motivation and the opportunity to perform in practice. This is as important in parenthood. Disciplining children serves many functions from protecting them from danger to guiding their moral development. In organisations, those who see management as a professional practice require all managers to accept common goals and ideals of good behaviour. Codes of practice and other policies, covered later in the chapter, follow from this line.

There are two reasons why a person might behave virtuously. First, there are practical advantages in being seen to be honest, fair, strict, friendly, dependable, upstanding and so on. If nothing else, being known for virtue reduces transaction costs. One can close deals quickly, gain credit and have promises accepted without other parties seeking guarantees or carrying out investigations. Further, one is accepted into a club or community of like-minded people that operates both efficiently and pleasurably. Therefore we note, 'The banker's word is the banker's bond', and the expressions of shock when someone is found to have betrayed trust. Nowhere was this more sharply illustrated than in the series of company failures in Japan at the end of 1997. On 17 November, Hokkaido Takushoku, a big commercial bank, went under with huge debts. Pictures of tearful directors, apologising for their breach of faith with depositors, were broadcast around the world.[27]

The second reason relates to the sort of person one wants to be. Self-perception, say of being a loyal friend, a good parent (or faithful child), a sound team-player, a clear thinker and so on, accounts for much of what people think they are. Self-esteem amounts to regard for a set of virtues.

These examples immediately raise problems with virtue ethics. They point to the relativist nature of good and ill, in the first case allowing it to be determined group by group and in the second putting the burden on the shoulders of the individual. Another difficulty arises when two virtues conflict. I may be part of a society that condemns certain behaviour as wrong, for example making a disturbing noise in the park. Simultaneously I may see myself as a tolerant person. Does my tolerance prevent me from condemning minor noise infractions by others? Such problems abound in business. There are problems in reconciling empowerment and control, personal development and getting the job done. We return to these points in Chapter 12.

Illustration

We can briefly illustrate how ethical thinking brings issues together. The question is the thorny one of whether we should tell the truth, this time in business. Hamilton and Strutton[28] explain that two fundamental problems connected with honesty in business are preventing violations of standards and being uncertain about what the standards are. For instance, firms sign contracts promising to pay invoices within 30 days. Yet they do not settle until later. Since such a breach is common, do the standards apply? If 30 days is 'merely a guide', then no standard is breached.

The guidelines that are offered are that honesty is required either when the other party expects it or when it supports the firm's known reputation for honesty. Details of the possibilities are set out in Figure 5.6. They are based on a mix of ethical approaches. The deontologist would look for maxims to be generalised. For instance, it would be possible to say, 'In situations where recipients of our information (such as advertising) will depend on the truth of that information, then we must tell the truth'. The utilitarian position is illustrated by a realisation that dishonesty may result in costs, say in litigation and compensation for breach of contract. The

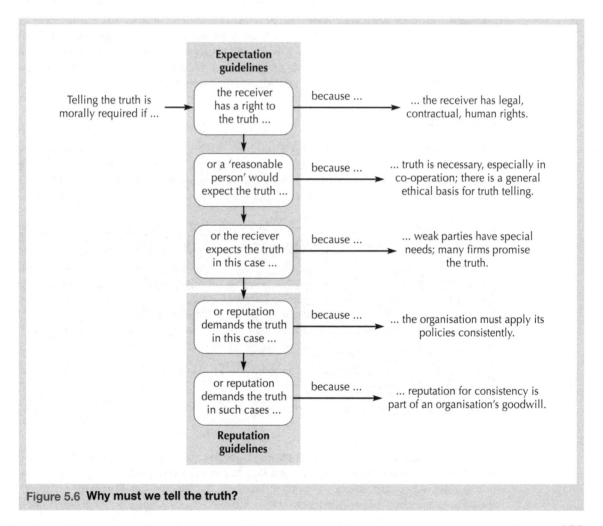

Figure 5.6 Why must we tell the truth?

155

virtue view is, 'We must do what we said we would do', or, 'The reputation of the organisation depends on consistently telling the truth'.

Managing social responsibility and ethics

Clearly, exhorting managers to recognise the wider picture or behave virtuously will not do. Behaving consistently in these areas is as important to many organisations as the continuing pursuit of financial targets. Compliance with standards can be achieved through the following methods: training; advocacy; codes of practice; and encouraging whistle blowing.

▣ Training

Training is covered in detail in Chapter 14 so we will merely outline its function here. Two outcomes of training programmes are relevant – the appropriate skills to recognise and analyse problems in the field of responsibility and ethics and the changed attitudes towards these issues. If nothing else, training programmes may sensitise managers to the implications of their decisions and therefore convert them from *amoral* (blind or indifferent) attitudes to moral ones. As with the accomplishment of all such proposals, training programmes need to be related to managerial jobs and be backed up with motivation from senior management.

▣ Advocacy

An advocate in the domains of ethics and social responsibility is a specialist in the study of such problems. Many organisations appoint an ethics officer to guide the resolution of difficult questions or challenge current thinking and practice. Attaching the role to senior management is seen as good practice, *see* Exhibit 5.4.

Exhibit 5.4 The ethics officer at Suez[29]

Suez is a global energy, water and waste management committee employing about 180 000 staff. To ensure excellent standards in these sensitive areas of business, the group board has an Ethics, Environment and Sustainable Development Committee. It establishes procedures and ensures that subsidiary companies abide by their codes of conduct.

Every subsidiary has an Ethics Officer, appointed from among senior management, who:

- oversees ethical issues related to business;
- creates and distributes codes of conduct;
- monitors compliance;
- reports on implementation and recommends changes.

Furnham[30] supports the notion of expert analysis. He notes that, drawing on the conventions of the medical and human science professions, ethics committees are being established to consider everyday business situations. Yet Furnham criticises these because their main purposes are to diffuse responsibility for awkward decisions and to stave off, avoid or deaden the impact of legal actions. Few have had an impact on the sense of responsibility of individual managers.

■ Codes of practice

Codes of practice have long been common in professions, being applications of the virtue ethics tradition. Exhibit 5.5 summarises key points from the code of the Chartered Institute of Purchasing and Supply in the United Kingdom. Many companies have similar, or even stronger, rules for their purchasing staff. Breaches attract heavy penalties.

Exhibit 5.5 Code of Practice for purchasing managers: key points of the CIPS code of ethics[31]

- *Declaration of interest* – members should declare any personal interest in any transaction.
- *Confidentiality and accuracy of information* – information gained in the course of business should not be used for personal gain; information given should be true and fair.
- *Competition* – arrangements with suppliers, which prevent the operation of fair competition, should be avoided.
- *Business gifts* – gifts, other than small tokens such as diaries and calendars, should not be accepted.
- *Hospitality* – mutual hospitality is an accepted courtesy yet the member should not be put in a position where the hospitality itself influences a business decision.

Farrell and colleagues caution against expecting too much from ethical codes. In an Australian study, they found little association with behaviour, concluding:

> *Many purposes have been proposed for codes. Some top managers may consider codes are useful for reasons of staff morale, team building and idealism; as restatement of community values; for public relations; as part of an ethics education program; or other grounds.*[32]

■ Whistle blowing

What should you do if you see that a colleague or superior is involved in misconduct? The formal position might be that it is your duty to report it. Yet the realities of organisational life mean that, faced with pressures to conform and with the fear of loss of earnings or job, many employees ignore the symptoms of trouble. The inquiry into the 1988 explosion on the Piper Alpha oil platform, when 167 lives were lost, reported that workers feared for their employment if they raised safety issues that might embarrass their superiors. A sales manager with Colonial Mutual Insurance was dismissed after repeated attempts to interest senior managers in his reports of breaches of regulations.[33]

In the end, those who complain may feel forced to reveal unethical behaviour to authorities or other outsiders. Whistle blowing refers to this action.[34] As has been suggested, the cost and risk to the individual make whistle blowing very difficult. Recognising its value in stemming malpractice, however, both enlightened companies and governments have made moves to encourage it. Companies such as Esso and NatWest Bank have set up confidential 'hot lines'. Public Concern at Work is a British charity set up to give advice to those who feel compromised. The main United Kingdom legislation is the Public Interest Disclosure Act 1999. The following summarises a case brought under it:

In 1997, a finance officer of a subsidiary of a United States company told his headquarters contact that he suspected his Managing Director of making false expense claims. He was advised to turn a blind eye. Then, in late 1999 when the expenses had exceeded £300 000, the officer reported his concerns to the US Board. The outcome was that he found himself under pressure to resign, and when he refused, he was dismissed for authorising the expenses. He brought a claim under the Act. The MD was not dismissed until after the interim hearing, which the officer won. The tribunal at the full hearing found that the officer had been dismissed for whistle blowing and complaints about him were a diversion. As he was 58, compensation of £293 000 took into account his inability to find similar employment.[35]

Conclusion: social responsibility and ethics

Corporate social responsibility and the ethics of managers meet at several points. The organisation is the means by which stakeholders, both internal and external, achieve their aims. Their influence is reconciled by managers' interpretation of the validity of those aims and the pressures that the stakeholders are able to exert. Clearly, managers' individual ethics play their part in this process.

Another aspect of the interaction is that managers' values both shape, and are shaped by, their organisational experience. Founders and leaders are important. Beyond these, however, there is a complex web of culture, people and events among which the manager learns and develops. This growth can be haphazard or the deliberate diffusion of consistent management practice. Whatever the means, we should not be surprised that the resulting social responsiveness is one aspect of the unique face that an organisation presents to the world.

Why bother? Aside from saintliness, there is the practical value, which Connock and Johns, among others, stress. Ethics makes for effective organisations and good management. Acknowledging that there is a measure of self-interest on behalf of managers, they conclude that ethical leadership:

- is good for business;
- makes organisation members feel good about what they do;
- helps senior managers pursue the organisation's interests and shape and guide its destiny;
- reflects growing societal desires not to harm others and engage with the problems of the disadvantaged;
- matches emerging societal expectations of how organisations should conduct themselves.[36]

EXERCISE: A manager's ethical dilemma – the mailing list

The information given in Exhibit 5.6 comes from real events.

Exhibit 5.6 Thomas's doubts

For many years Thomas has run his own import–export business. He depends on his ability to create and spot opportunities and build trust with both suppliers and customers. One of Thomas's clients told him that he had been approached by an acquaintance recently made redundant as senior sales manager of a main competitor. He offered to sell the client the firm's mailing list.

Thomas had advised his client not to buy on the grounds, 'Knowing the way the competitor works, I would be surprised if a comprehensive up-to-date list would be available, even within the company.'

I pressed Thomas, arguing, 'That's an easy way out. You advised rejection for practical reasons.'

Thomas continued, 'Very well, if he is prepared to sell a list so readily, he is not the sort of person I would want to deal with.'

Again, I argued that this was hardly a moral position. Pressed, he would not concede that one should appeal to contractual, legal or moral arguments.

Questions for discussion

1 Summarise the ethical issues in the case of the mailing list.
2 Was I correct in suggesting that Thomas had not taken a moral position?
3 Should the manager's old organisation be informed? Or anyone else?

ETHICS TEST: Marketing

What is your response to the practices outlined below? Think about each and note your response.

a A supermarket is using a hidden camera to observe shoppers' behaviour. The camera is directed by the observer, working in another part of the building. From time to time, the store layout is modified to try to see what factors influence buying decisions.

b You have found that your boss is cheating on travel expenses. You suspected this for some time but recently came across a copy of a claim left on the photocopier. You know that some journeys were not made at all and overnight stays did not take place in the hotels stated.

c Your agency is placing advertisements that use women dressed in underwear. There are three accounts, for:

(i)   lingerie, placed in a women's magazine;

(ii) motorcycles, placed in a trade journal;

(iii) bed linen, placed in daily newspapers.

d Your firm sells financial products from life insurance to personal pensions. It generates sales leads by telephoning or stopping people in the street. Staff pretend to be conducting a survey.

Turn to page 163 to see how you compare with other students.

159

QUICK CHECK

Can you ...

- Define social responsibility.
- Outline four arguments for social responsibility...
- ... and four against.
- Define stakeholder.
- Summarise four corporate responsibility policies.
- Define ethics.
- Illustrate deontology, utilitarianism and virtue ethics in management.
- List four means of encouraging compliance to ethical standards.
- Give five benefits of ethical leadership.

QUESTIONS

Chapter review

5.1 Summarise the arguments for and against social responsibility.

5.2 What are the classes of ethical ideas that can be brought to bear on a management dilemma?

5.3 What benefits are available to the socially responsible organisation?

Application

5.4 What connections can you draw between ethics and social responsibility?

5.5 What do you think is the best method of encouraging whistle blowing, if indeed it should be encouraged?

5.6 Return to the opening case to analyse its dilemmas from an ethical position.

Investigation

5.7 Many organisations publish social responsibility and ethical policies on the Internet. Select one and check the degree to which it reports on performance and whether the report is independently checked. Use this knowledge to place it on the continuum of social responsibility, *see* Figure 5.3.

5.8 Use a few interviews to gain insights into how far managers tell the truth at work. Summarise and explain their views of cases when they feel they need not.

CLOSING CASE

Irresponsible advertising from Benetton?[37]

Established in 1965, and run by three brothers and a sister, Benetton is one of the world's most successful clothing companies. It buys more raw wool than anyone, knits, stitches and dyes in highly automated owned and subcontractor factories in Italy and sells through thousands of franchised agents and retailers. Operations in this 'virtual' manufacturing and distribution system are both flexible and tightly controlled as needed in the high-volume fashion industry. Benetton has succeeded by separating this internal culture of efficiency and hard work from the external image of an exciting company where things happen.

Luciano Benetton is responsible for advertising. Rather than display typical products or stores, campaigns have increasingly used issues such as life and death, war, genocide, race, poverty, religion, homosexuality and AIDS. 'Every theme we choose has to be recognised all over the world by a single image. There's no point in choosing an image that means something only in Italy and nothing anywhere else...By itself, the theme of news is not new but what is new is that it's used like this by a company... this approach certainly has raised our visibility.'[38]

Benetton spends a modest 4 per cent of turnover on communications. Yet the outrage created by the shock tactics of the campaigns adds much more. There were 800 complaints to the UK's Advertising Standards Authority about a poster featuring a new-born baby. The theme is issue-led brand recognition, used less controversially by The Body Shop. Luciano argues, 'Not showing the product will become more and more common'. With masterful pictures that have won many prizes, the campaigns were directed by photographer Oliviero Toscani, given freedom to express his conscience by his friend Luciano.

Throughout the 1990s, Benetton had been declining in the United States and sought to recover its position through a multi-million dollar in-store concession agreement with the retailing giant Sears. In 1999 however, Toscani negotiated access, possibly by deception, to several Missouri prisons.[39] Although he intended to highlight the plight of those on death row, families of victims were appalled at the resulting posters. Displaying no Benetton clothing, they sought to arouse compassion for the inmates. The families launched a powerful campaign of picketing stores, sending protest messages and tearing up Sears cards. Sears cancelled the agreement in February 2000 and, within three months, Benetton and Toscani had parted.

By 2001, Benetton was back on form. Its Year of Volunteers campaign included pictures of young prostitutes. The 2003 theme was 'United Colours of Benetton and World Food Programme'. The new material differed from the old in carrying text to explain what each picture was about. Toscani was said to be working with the World Health Organisation on a global anti-smoking drive.

Most who wear Benetton are under 25 years old. They like the feeling of disapproval, of authorities making the company take posters down, of media refusing to accept some images. Benetton customers receive high-quality products from world-class factories. Yet wearing Benetton is chic rebellion.

Questions

1 Who are Benetton's stakeholders?

2 What arguments can be assembled for and against Benetton's publicity policy? Would different stakeholders take different views?

3 Explore the decision to campaign this way using ethical perspectives.

Bibliography

Comprehensive and accessible discussions of the issues in this chapter are to be found in: Alan Lovell and Colin Fisher (2002) *Business Ethics and Values* (Harlow: Financial Times Prentice Hall) and Chris Megone and Simon Robinson (eds) (2001) *Case Histories in Business Ethics: Virtues and moral decision making in business* (London: Routledge). See also companies such as the Co-operative Bank, **www.co-operativebank.co.uk**/, Suez, **www.suez-lyonnaise-eaux.com/ indexuk.htm**, and the pressure group Public Concern At Work, **www.pcaw.co.uk/index.html**.

References

1 Norske Skogindustrier SA (2002) *2001 Environmental Report*, Norske Skog; **www.norske-skog.com**, accessed 27 February 2003.
2 Environmental product declaration for paper products; see **www.paperprofile.com/what.html**, accessed 1 March 2003.
3 Harvey, Brian (1994) *Business Ethics: A European approach*, Hemel Hempstead: Prentice Hall, 3.
4 Eighteenth-century proverb. See also Henderson, David (2001) *Misguided Virtue: False notions of corporate social responsibility*, Hobart Paper, 142, London: Institute of Economic Affairs.

5 Mazur, Laura (2001) 'Time for brands to don a mantle of respectability', *Marketing*, 27 September, 16; Bishop, Linda (2002) 'Building social contracts', *Brand Strategy*, July, 30.

6 Barber, Brendan *et.al.* (2003) 'Littlewoods' CSR Record Undermined', letter to *Financial Times*, 12 February; this letter, challenging the new policy, was sent by Mr Barber, General Secretary elect of the TUC, other union leaders and directors of international aid organisations.

7 Ward, Stephen (1993) 'You must be green – and squeaky clean', *Independent*, 23 August, 15; Franssen, Margot (1993) 'Beyond profits (The Body Shop Canada's social policy)', *Business Quarterly*, **58(1)**, 14–20; Romano, Gerry (1993) 'Crazy times call for crazy organizations: Management analyst Tom Peter's management restructuring scheme', *Association Management*, **45(11)**, 30 November; Buckley, Neil (1995) 'The Body Shop warning hits shares', *Financial Times*, 3 May, 24.

8 Pizzolatto, Allayne Barrilleaux and Zeringue, Cecil A. II (1993) 'Facing society's demands for environmental protection: management in practice', *Journal of Business Ethics*, **12(6)**, June, 441–7.

9 'Why José's dream-car matters: General Motors and Volkswagen', *The Economist*, **328(7821)**, 24 July 1993, 65–6; 'Pistols at dawn: General Motors and Volkswagen', *The Economist*, **328(7822)**, 31 July 1993, 64; Flint, Jerry (1993) 'Der Zuricher', *Forbes*, **152(5)**, 30 August, 80; Tran, Mark (1997) 'Carmakers settle the espionage dispute', *Guardian*, 10 January, 22; *Financial Times* (2000) 'Lopez indicted over GM material', 23 May, 2.

10 Williams, Frances (2003) 'Final talks on global tobacco control start', *Financial Times*, 18 February, 10; WHO (2003) *Framework Convention on Tobacco Control*, World Health Organisation, **www5.who.int/tobacco/page.cfm?pid=40**, accessed 18 February 2003.

11 Nestle, Marion (2002) *Food Politics: How the Food Industry Influences Nutrition and Health*, Berkeley, Cal.: University of California Press.

12 Buckley, Neil (2003) 'Unhealthy food is everywhere, 24 hours a day, and inexpensive', *Financial Times*, 18 February, 19.

13 *Financial Times* (2002) 'Clarke Facing Embarrassment Over Burma Link', 12 November.

14 Corzine, Robert and Dempsey, Judy (1995) 'Shell stunned by Brent Spar anger', *Financial Times*, 17 June, 2; Lascelles, David, Dempsey, Judy and van der Krol, Ronald (1995) 'Brent Spar dents oil giant's pride rather than profit', *Financial Times*, 20 June, 13; Boulton, Leyla (1995) 'Shell seeks temporary berth for Brent Spar in Norway', *Financial Times*, 29 June, 10; Corzine, Robert (1995) 'Shell and that sinking feeling', *Financial Times*, 5 July, 14; Ostrovsky, Arkady and Burt, Tim (1998) 'Brent Spar: Oil rig to be rebuilt as ferry quay', *Financial Times*, 30 January.

15 Business in the Community (2003) *Co-operative Bank – Managing impact on society*, **www.bitc.org.uk/resources/case_studies/co-operative_ban.html**; Co-operative Bank (2003) *Our Revised Ethical Policy*, **www.co-operativebank.co.uk/ethics/ethicalpolicy_**

policy_revised.html, both accessed 17 February 2003; *Financial Times* (2002) 'Ethics proves big draw for Co-op Bank', 15 May.

16 Attributed to John Calvin Coolidge, whose United States presidency spanned the boom years 1923–9.

17 Boulton, Leyla (1995) 'A delicate balancing act – Dow Chemical benefits from making green issues a business concern', *Financial Times*, 28 June, 18.

18 Editorial (1995) 'How to make lots of money and save the planet too', *The Economist*, **335(7917)**, 3 June, 75.

19 Murthy, R.C. (1995) 'Germany slams the door', *Financial Times*, Supplement: India, 17 November, 9.

20 Argandoña, Antonio (1994) 'Business, law and regulation: ethical issues', in Harvey (1994) *op. cit.*, 124.

21 An example of *psychological egoism, see* Hoffman, W. Michael and Frederick, Robert E. (1995) *Business Ethics: Readings and cases in corporate morality,* New York: McGraw-Hill, 17. Broadly, this view focuses on what is, that is people are self-interested, whereas ethics is concerned with what ought to be.

22 Argandoña (1994) *op. cit.*, 129.

23 This discussion is developed from van Luijk, Henk (1994) 'Business ethics: the field and its importance', in Harvey (1994) *op. cit.*, 12–31.

24 For an application in retailing see Uusitalo, Outi and Takal, Tuome (1995) 'Retailers' professional and professio-ethical dilemmas: The case of Finnish retailing business', *Journal of Business Ethics*, **14**, 893–907.

25 There are other arguments against bribery. This one is picked out to illustrate the categorical imperative. For a full discussion and criticism, *see* Hoffmann and Frederick (1995) *op. cit.*, 28–33.

26 Hoffman, W. Michael (1995) 'The Ford Pinto' in Hoffman and Frederick (1995) *op. cit.*, 552–9.

27 'And then there were 19', *The Economist*, **345(8044)**, 22 November 1997, 125.

28 Hamilton, J. Brooke III and Strutton, David (1994) 'Two practical guidelines for resolving truth-telling problems', *Journal of Business Ethics*, **13**, 899–912.

29 Suez (2001) *Company Rules on Organisation and Conduct* and *Ethics Charter*, December; **www.suez.com/group/english/index.htm**, accessed 12 January 2003.

30 Furnham, Adrian (1995) 'Of business ethics and litigation', *Financial Times*, 6 February, 12.

31 Chartered Institute of Purchasing and Supply (1999) *Code of Ethics*, CIPS; **www.cips.org**, accessed 1 March 2003.

32 Farrell, Brian J., Cobbin, Dierdre M. and Farrell, Helen M. (2002) 'Can codes of ethics really produce consistent behaviours?' *Journal of Managerial Psychology*, **17(6)**, 468–90.

33 Norton-Taylor, Richard (1995) 'Corporate whistle blowers set to receive protection they deserve', *Guardian*, 6 December, 20.

34 Loeb, Marshall (1995) 'When to rat on the boss: the costs of snitching can be high. Here are some guidelines for when you should – and shouldn't – speak up', *Fortune*, **132(7)**, 2 October, 183; Norton-Taylor, Richard (1995) *op. cit.*

35 Public Concern At Work (2002) *Policy Into Practice*, PCAW, 26; **www.pcaw.co.uk/index.html**, accessed 2 March 2003.

36 Connock, Stephen and Johns, Ted (1995) *Ethical Leadership*, London: Institute of Personnel Development, 222–3.

37 BBC (2001) *Blood, Sweaters and Tears*, January, **www.bbc.co.uk/business/programmes/trouble_top/arc hive/benetton.shtml**, accessed 20 February 2003; Sullivan, Ruth (1995) 'Dropping the shock for the new', *Marketing*, 20 April, 12; Wright, Robin (1994) 'Benetton's "shock" tactics only irk the moral minority', *Campaign*, 25 March, 23; Tomkins, Richard (1995) 'Risk and reward (Benetton Sportsystem's controversial advertising campaign)', *Financial Times*, 27 July, 14.

38 Quotations from Rocco, Fiammetta (1995) 'Woolly thinking', *Telegraph Magazine*, 2 December, 24–32.

39 Nixon, Jay (2000) *Nixon sues Benetton for prison trespassing and fraud in ad campaign that features death-row inmates*, Press release, Office of Missouri Attorney General, 9 February.

How did you score on the marketing ethics test? (see p. 159)

The questions are based on Lane, J.C. (1995) 'Ethics of business students: some marketing perspectives' *Journal of Business Ethics*, **14**, 571–80. Lane surveyed 412 Australian business students, noting means and significant differences among sub-groups.

a Customers are unknowing subjects of a research experiment. Such experiments should not occur but 73 per cent of the students approved. Marketing students were more likely to approve.

b You should blow the whistle. Only 42 per cent of the sample would do this; 25 per cent would not; 2 per cent would resign and the rest were undecided.

c Depending on the details, using women models is justified in lingerie advertisements but not in the other cases. Ninety-six per cent of students agreed for lingerie; 39 per cent approved for motorbikes (with 52 per cent against and the rest undecided); 68 per cent approved for bed linen (with 21 per cent against and the rest undecided). Males were significantly less critical of the last two cases.

d Fifty-one per cent approved of 'sugging' – selling under the guise of market research. It is unethical and against the professional body's code of practice. Thirty-one per cent were against and the rest didn't know. Males aged 22–26 were significantly less critical.

CHAPTER 6

Managing for quality

Chapter objectives

When you have finished studying this chapter, you should be able to:

- define quality, recognise the range of definitions in use and show how meanings differ between buyers and sellers of goods and services;

- clarify the importance of quality – its impact upon both costs and market advantage;

- identify the costs of quality; show how an organisation can gain by changing the balance among them;

- outline the contributions made over the past 50 years by some leading advocates of the quality message;

- evaluate the role of product and process standards and suggest why the latter have gained ground at the expense of the former;

- explain Total Quality Management as a mix of philosophy, processes and techniques; outline its limitations;

- demonstrate the use of charts and other forms of data presentation in the investigation and communication of quality issues;

- summarise the key features of benchmarking for establishing standards and evaluate the associated benefits and problems;

- explain the issues involved in establishing and monitoring service quality performance.

Quality has to be caused, not controlled.

Philip Crosby, American author and practitioner

Perfecting the Big Mac[1]

McDonald's mission includes delivering operational excellence. At the heart of its effort to increase sales and profits lie policies on food and service quality designed to make the firm stand out from its rivals. While the Big Mac is not to everyone's taste, the company was cited by Fortune as the world's most admired food service company. It aims for zero defects, that is to serve hot, fresh, tasty food of good value to customers on every occasion. About 45 million visit the 28 000 restaurants every day.

Achievement means high standards at every link in the supply chain, from dairy herds to lettuce seedlings and flour to chicken rearing. McDonald's sets exacting requirements for quality and safety. It will only use ingredients whose source can be traced and which satisfy all regulations. Quality assurance staff carry out audits and site visits to verify the supply chain. They also co-operate with suppliers to improve product quality. For instance, lard was replaced by vegetable oil in buns, fat levels in sauces were cut and saturated fats in the cooking oil were reduced.

To disseminate its commitment to quality among its 4000 suppliers, the company introduced the Sweeney Award in 1990. Judging takes place every two years. Criteria are based on those used for the Baldrige Award (*see* below). The 2000 winner, Sunny Foods (Thailand), supplies chicken products to more than 200 outlets in Hong Kong. Another company in the same group, Sunny Fresh Foods, gained the Sweeney in 1998 and the Baldrige in the following year.

Standardisation of the product range helps to assure quality. Staff training is simplified by the limited range and process development, including the provision of computer-controlled cooking facilities. Chicken McNuggets are shaped into uniform sizes from breast and thigh meat to ensure cooking consistency. Like all meat, the chickens are traceable, in this case to their grandparents. Their food and water, medication and litter are also traceable to source. Fish products use cod whose origins can be matched to the vessel and day of catch. Boning is a matter of great concern and 23 checks occur during fish product manufacture. McDonald's prefers to use free range eggs in the United Kingdom.

Food quality and safety policies are closely linked to concerns for the environment. Pressed to improve its wasteful practices in food packaging and serving, the company works on reducing its use of materials and energy. Operations, purchasing and training policies all include a strong theme of waste reduction including distribution in reusable containers, using recyclable packaging and installing heating and lighting controls.

Introduction

The success of McDonald's is based partly on its record on food quality, the hygiene standards of its outlets and the speed and style of service. In the case study, we see many aspects of good quality practice. Processes are designed to 'build in' quality and then standardised; company requirements complement and exceed legal minima; training concentrates on customer safety; inspections take place at critical points; traceability allows rapid response to problems; and all aspects are continually reviewed with an eye to improvement. In Crosby's words (*see* above), quality is caused, not controlled. Such policies are not created in isolation. We can relate them to forces in the environment, from competition and law to customer preferences and pressure group issues. They also relate to notions of good corporate citizenship.

During the last quarter of the twentieth century, the critical significance of quality became clear as industry after industry was challenged by innovation and international competition. Organisations that could not keep up suffered in the new climate; those that absorbed the quality message prospered. Success bred success as customers responded to rising standards and had their demands satisfied as never before. In the transformation of the fast food outlet of the 1970s into the quick service restaurant of today, weaker establishments were left behind.

Companies whose products fall below the new specifications and do not carry industry standard warranties have only themselves to blame. Quality, as we shall see, requires good management to mobilise the whole organisation in its achievement.

Our discussion of quality begins with definitions and further views on why quality is important. Then we examine the emergence of ideas and standards, working towards the notion of total quality management. Finally, since quality is about making things better, we look at techniques used to control and improve it.

What is quality?

Let us start by referring back to the story of Exhibit 3.6. The supplier sent two containers, one with 9998 good items and the other with the 2 defects. The story was used to make a point about the development of myth. Yet it also brings out one aspect of quality – *conformance to specification*.

Conformance is, however, only one interpretation of quality. For instance, people may say the quality of cheese bought from the supermarket is inferior to Carron Lodge, a Cheshire cheese sold only through specialists. The latter regularly wins prizes at county shows. Yet, if used for cooking, both perform equally. This introduces the notion of suitability, or *fitness for purpose*, an alternative idea to conformance. If you want to make a sauce for plaice Florentine, then a mass-produced mild Cheddar will do. On the other hand, when served after the dessert, something better, possibly served on a decorated plate, is required. The cheese, in other words, must be fit for the purpose.

Other aspects of quality are included in Exhibit 6.1. All items are equally relevant to goods and services. This is even true of the penultimate item, quality of service, that at first seems to apply only to the service encounter.[2] Yet, service is often central to customers' opinions of the quality of manufactured goods. For instance, Williams showed that Australians and Japanese judge seafood differently. For the latter, business and personal relationships were a significant component of the perceived quality of fish supplied by an Australian exporter.[3]

One feature of the items in Exhibit 6.1 is their apparent incompatibility. For instance, tailoring a product to suit a customer's requirements in terms of special use or aesthetic values runs up against the benefits of uniform standards required by large-scale production and marketing. Further, as the last item suggests, quality is defined differently by customers and producers. The latter spend much effort on tracking what their customers think, as shown in Exhibit 6.2.

Quality defined

The above ideas are common and frequently mixed. We need, therefore, a more usable definition of quality combining attributes and standards with the purpose to which the product is to be put. Crosby has been influential in this argument. 'Quality has to be defined as conformance to requirements, not as goodness... The setting of

Exhibit 6.1 Dimensions of quality

Quality in use
- Performance – will it do the job?
- Safety – with no hazards?

Quality as features or grade
- Zanussi FJ1093 Jetsystem RS: rinse sensor; half-load; child security …
- Ballantine's £250 sweaters from the *finest cashmere wool.*

Quality as reliability
- Reliability – risk of failure in use.
- Serviceability – easy attention.
- Durability – life before wear-out.

Quality as conformance
- Are agreed specifications and imposed standards met?

Quality as aesthetics
- The sensory attributes – 'That is a very good design/piece of music/ book/ …'

Quality of service
- Reliability – precise and dependable.
- Responsiveness – prompt attention to individual needs.
- Service environment – facilities and the appearance of staff.
- Confidence – manner, knowledge and trustworthiness of staff.
- Empathy – caring staff, offering personal attention.

Quality defined by the customer
- Does it match the customer's personal requirements?

requirements may simply involve only answers to questions. Requirements, like measurements, are communications.'[5]

In stressing *conformance to requirements*, Crosby emphasises two features. First, quality is about matching, that is conforming to, some standards. Secondly, these standards, or requirements, have to be established and communicated in some way from their origin, be it customers or some other external source. If we are talking about individual service, it may be possible to adjust operations for each client. On the other hand, mass production within competitive markets works because standards exist across whole industries.

Exhibit 6.2 J.D. Powers reveals the consumer's perspective[4]

J.D. Powers conducts customer surveys in many markets and industries. Its car hire customer satisfaction survey was begun in 1996. In a 2001 study, Powers reported that satisfaction among leisure travellers depends on: the reservation, pick-up and return processes; price and value; and cleanliness and features of the cars.

Quality is, therefore, about using information to set standards and then conforming to them. These ideas are captured in the definitions within the international standard, ISO 9000, listed in Exhibit 6.3.[6]

Exhibit 6.3 Quality defined

Quality is the degree to which a set of inherent characteristics fulfils requirements.

A *characteristic* is a distinguishing feature. It can be: physical (such as the strength of a material); sensory (smell, taste, etc.); behavioural (honesty, courtesy, truthfulness); temporal (reliability, punctuality, availability); ergonomic (physiological or safety related); or functional (such as maximum speed).

Requirements are needs or expectations that are stated, implicit or mandatory. They can have many sources, including those indirectly affected by a transaction. Therefore, an aircraft design should consider the interests of passengers and crew, users of other aircraft and all who may be affected by its flight. Implicit, or *generally implied*, requirements are based on common practice among the organisation, its customers and others.

Why is quality important?

The story of a supplier sorting defects from good items emphasises how Japanese companies gained competitive advantage from supplying quality goods. The remarkable progress of the Japanese consumer goods manufacturers is further, more solid evidence. Quality is a strategic factor that works through virtuous cycles to build market share and reduce costs. Figure 6.1 illustrates some key relationships. The *quality improvement* area of the diagram has two zones, one related to product improvement, making it more suited to customers' needs, and one related to process improvements, ensuring better conformance to standards. Improved quality increases demand and enables the firm to charge higher prices for the value differentiation that it offers. An important second-order effect is the way customers learn about quality and continue to feed back their demands into product design. Achieving customer satisfaction is not, therefore, a one-off process; rising standards create demand for even higher standards in the competitive marketplace. Within the organisation, process improvements have a direct impact on costs and also show feedback as the habit of continual development is self-reinforcing. Lastly, the increased profits both provide the funds for, and justify policies devoted to, quality improvement.

Managers in Japanese firms have recognised these interactions since the 1950s.[7] It may be difficult, initially, to accept that improving quality will lead to improved productivity but the fewer delays, mistakes and reworking more than pay for themselves in terms of rises in net output.

Deming used a simple example to make the point.[8] He referred to a production line running with 11 per cent defective output, a level of which the management was unaware. The line was well controlled, showing consistent performance over time. The main cause of the defects was that neither operators nor inspectors understood sufficiently the kind of work that was acceptable or unacceptable. To them, 11 per cent was normal. The manager and two supervisors made a special study and, in seven weeks, came up with a practical definition of work standards. They displayed

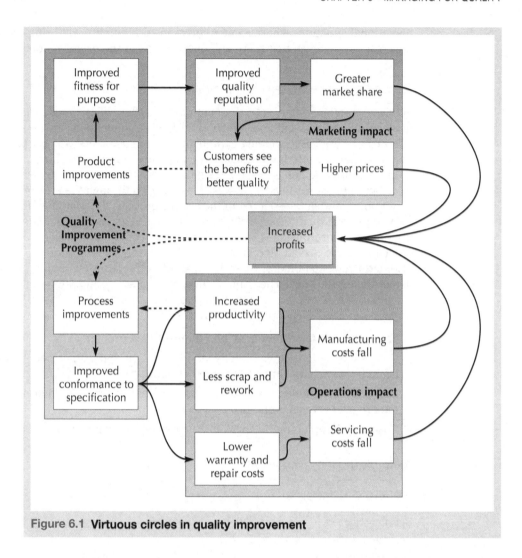

Figure 6.1 **Virtuous circles in quality improvement**

this for everyone to see. Defects fell to 5 per cent. The corresponding benefits, shown in Table 6.1, were achieved at very little cost. Productivity rose 6 per cent and, as Deming noted, 'Customer happier. Everybody happier.'

Defects are not free. Someone is paid to make them, resources are used and, as Deming's example shows, opportunities of making saleable products are lost. There is a danger if this argument is over-stressed. Problems are not always so serious that, in Crosby's words, *quality is free*.[9] We should recognise that there are many

Table 6.1 **Quality up, costs down**

	Defects before change: 11%	Defects after change: 5%
Total cost	100	100
Number of good items	89	95
Cost per item	1.12	1.05

operational situations where some improvement in quality will bring reduced operating costs, so much so that there will be net gains to the organisation.

Importance of service quality

Service operations often echo the manufacturing line of Deming's case. Quality standards are ill defined and consequently difficult to implement. At the same time, their effect can be critical in winning and holding on to customers. As cost pressure reduces the firm's service-offering capacity, so competitive forces and the experience of good quality intensify demands, as in Figure 6.1. The solution is not to spend more and do more but to be more effective. Quality must be seen through the eyes of customers, who only recognise what they *get out* of the service process, not what the firm *puts in*.

Why provide quality service? There are good reasons. The satisfied customer will not only do more business in the future but recommend the firm to others. On the other hand, the dissatisfied customer will not only reduce profitability directly but also deter new customers. In addition to the effects on customers, poor service is demoralising for staff. They spend time coping with complaints and are frustrated when nothing seems to be done to relieve them. Lister referred to data on the effects of poor service.[10] Depending on the industry:

- For each complaint there may be 26 unresolved problems.
- Of those who do complain, between 50 per cent and 70 per cent will do business again if their complaints are handled effectively.
- Dissatisfied customers will tell between 10 and 20 people whereas satisfied customers tell between 3 and 5.
- Customers stop doing business for the reasons shown in Table 6.2.

Table 6.2 **Reasons for quitting**

Reason given for quitting (%)	
Upset at treatment	68
Become dissatisfied	14
Move to competitors	9
Find substitutes	5
Move away	3
Die	1

The importance of quality is to recognise that, although 'everyone is doing his best', the 'best efforts are not sufficient'.[11] Without leadership focused on consistently improving quality, these best efforts cause a random walk; such a walk takes you an unknown direction and distance from your starting point.

Costs of quality

The costs of quality include those flowing from poor quality as well as the efforts taken to prevent defects. We can split them into three categories, failure, appraisal and prevention, as set out in the following list:

Failure – waste that could be avoided

This category includes failures that occur within the process and those that occur, or become apparent, after the product is supplied to the customer. In both cases, failure means that the product has not reached intended standards.

■ *Internal failure costs*
  - Producing items scrapped or downgraded to be sold as second quality.
  - Rectification of defects to raise items to the specified standard.
  - Waste of time and materials incurred at all stages including design and planning as well as manufacture and supply.
  - Re-inspection and investigation of causes.

■ *External failure costs*
  - Repair, extra servicing and replacement under warranty.
  - Extra handling of returned items.
  - Loss of goodwill through any of the above and customers' complaints in general.
  - Consequential losses risking litigation and damages.
  - Financial compensation paid to customers outside litigation.
  - Further inspection, investigation and administration.

Appraisal – stopping defects going further

This group relates to the assessment of all incoming materials, components and services and all processes to ensure achievement of standards:

■ Inspection of all materials whether bought or produced by intermediate processes.

■ Final inspection of products and services.

■ Quality audits to assess whether the quality control system is operating satisfactorily.

■ Vendor rating, including auditing suppliers' standards and procedures.

■ Equipment and processes used in inspection.

■ The costs of quality appraisal, control systems and organisation.

Prevention – eliminating waste

Prevention costs are incurred before production begins. They refer to processes preventing failures and limiting appraisal costs. Frequently called quality assurance, the prevention costs cover:

■ Identification of customers' quality requirements.

■ Producing specifications for all components, assemblies and services.

■ Creating the system to optimise prevention, appraisal and failure costs.

■ Building in quality to all products. The cost of quality research, good design and prototyping is included.

■ Training staff to appreciate their contribution to quality, especially failure prevention.

■ Administration of quality programmes.

Failing to plan and manage quality means too much expenditure on the total of these quality costs. Almost certainly, the excess will lie in the *failure* category. An example comes from Tennant, the world's largest manufacturer of floor sweepers and scrubbers.[12] A steering committee of six senior managers was set up to redirect corporate culture towards quality and productivity. As shown in Figure 6.2, the change resulted in a substantial reduction in quality costs and a shift in the balance of these costs towards prevention and away from correction. In Figure 6.2, Tennant shifted from A to B and then to C. This is an example of a general relationship between the ability to match quality to customers' expectations and the direct quality costs. Where the quality capability is low, as at A, failure costs are high and dominate the total. With improving capability, both failure and appraisal costs can be cut, resulting in better performance overall. Whatever the starting point, advocates of continuous improvement argue that improvements are always possible. The costs of quality should continue to fall as the organisation learns new approaches in an ever more exacting environment. Yet enthusiasm may wane. A cost of quality programme at Xerox achieved excellent savings over seven years. By then, however, the big improvements had been achieved and its protagonists had moved on.[13]

In other cases, quality improvements can pay for themselves quickly. Whirlpool found that a sticking bearing in a dryer was accounting for 2.33 per cent of its calls for service under warranty. These annual costs were running at $1.3 million. A study found that improving the bearing material cost just half a cent per machine or less than $5000 a year.[14]

The two main thrusts of a quality plan are, therefore, prevention and appraisal. We have seen that failures must be avoided. This is the so-called ZD or zero-defects policy. It should be recognised, however, that the *cost of avoiding all failures may*

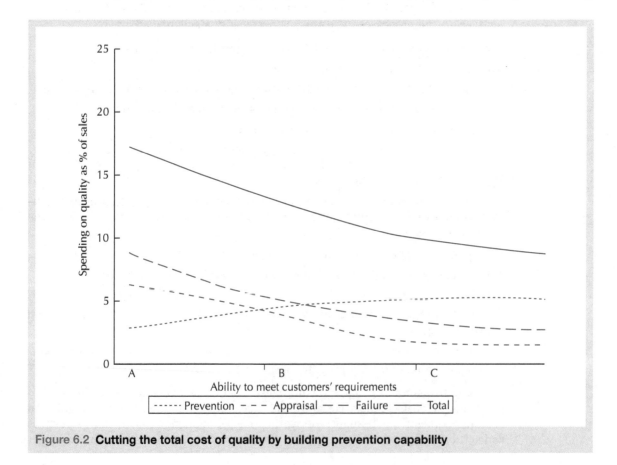

Figure 6.2 **Cutting the total cost of quality by building prevention capability**

be prohibitive and the technology to do so may not be available. If failures do occur, the organisation must make an effective response, especially if the problem occurs after the product is supplied to the customer.

Sources of quality ideas

Perhaps more than in other fields of management, the move of quality to the top of the operations agenda has been associated with the names of experts. The quality 'gurus' have moulded the attitudes of a generation of managers. Interest in quality as a competitive weapon took root in the West with the tide of imports of Japanese consumer products. The ideas then spread from the factory into all organisations from service businesses and non-profit organisations to government operations and administration. We shall pick out the names of a few advocates of this slow process.

■ W. Edwards Deming

In the late 1930s, Deming was responsible for mathematics and sampling at the United States Bureau of Census. His methods of statistical control achieved great improvements in the productivity and quality of the 1940 census. This work led to invitations to train industrialists and military personnel and he worked with many thousands of US military engineers and technicians to improve quality. In 1947, he was in Japan with the government of occupation to prepare a census there. At that time, the Japanese business community became so impressed by the standards of American military equipment that it invited Deming, in 1950, to advise on industrial recovery. While Deming based his work on advanced statistical methods, his contribution lay in presenting the ideas in a simple way. The results were both impressive and influential, so much so that eventually the Deming Prize was created. It remains Japan's leading quality prize.

Deming's main argument against traditional quality control was that it focused on the product rather than the process. Keeping down the number of delivered defective products typically meant high expenditure on inspection and reworking and, in any case, many defects slipped through. Deming advocated the use of statistics to measure process variability, which was the chief culprit of poor quality. He then argued for continual investigation and fine-tuning to incrementally improve the production system. He proposed a framework for this continuous improvement, the PDCA cycle, to which we shall return later in the chapter. Participation of everyone in the process was, at the time, a revolutionary notion.

It was not until the early 1980s that Deming's work was recognised in his own country. He spent the last part of his life spreading his message to large audiences throughout the United States and setting up the Deming Institute, in 1993, to continue his work.[15] He died the same year at the age of 93.

■ Kaoru Ishikawa

A professor at the University of Tokyo, Ishikawa advocated quality ideas before the Second World War. He founded the Union of Japanese Scientists and Engineers, which became the focus of Japan's quality developments as its economy recovered. The UJSE was responsible for Deming's 1950 invitation. Ishikawa advocated the notion of customers being both internal and external to the organisation and popularised the fishbone diagram as a problem investigation tool as well as other techniques.

Ishikawa saw that Western management practices could not be grafted on to Japanese habits. He was a pioneer of quality circles, which emphasised the role of the group in working and learning. His first circles were at Nippon Telegraph and Cable in 1962; by 1978, there were more than one million quality circles in Japanese manufacturing industry.

Joseph M. Juran

Like Deming, Juran had a background in statistics. He also had strong influence on Japanese managers, being linked to Ishikawa's UJSE. Many Japanese workers were illiterate, this problem being a serious hindrance to the introduction of quality processes. Juran took advantage of this situation. Large businesses had already started 'reading circles' led by supervisors and others with the necessary skills. Juran had his ideas published in forms suitable for learning materials for these groups. The pamphlets were even sold through newspaper kiosks. For the reading circle using Juran's material, it was a short step to the quality circle.

In 1979, Juran founded a training consultancy, the Juran Institute,[16] and through this, spread his ideas about partnerships and teamwork, internal customers, problem-solving techniques and application of Pareto analysis to quality issues. He was concerned about fitting quality improvement programmes into a company's current strategies and plans to minimise the risk of rejection. For him, quality was fitness for purpose, a wider definition than conformance to specification, which he regarded as very limiting. In this approach, he differed from Deming's more conservative adherence to the idea of matching specifications. Like Deming, however, Juran continued to speak on quality into his nineties.

Genichi Taguchi

Japan's Ministry of International Trade and Industry (MITI) awarded its Purple Ribbon to Taguchi for his contribution to the development of industrial standards in that country, the award being presented by the Emporor of Japan. Taguchi's strength has been in the application of statistical methods, not to quality control where they had already found wide application, but to improving products and processes. He applied methods in novel ways to: making products less sensitive to variations in their components and in the environment in which they are made; improving reliability; and improving testing procedures. A family of techniques, called 'Taguchi methods' has grown up. Yet Taguchi himself did not like the use of the term, especially when it was used to describe standard statistical methods. Moreover, while many acknowledge his contribution to the engineering design of experiments, they criticise his use of statistics as being inefficient and cumbersome.[17]

Philip B. Crosby

Author of *Quality is Free*, Crosby began his career as a manager in ITT, where he developed the Total Quality Management programme. From this experience he went on to become a quality advocate. With credibility founded on his experience and well-documented examples of uncovering the costs of waste, scrap and reworking,

Crosby has become well known in the field. He argues that *getting it right first time* is an achievable goal. This zero-defects strategy (ZD) is important because the costs of poor quality are seriously underestimated.

ZD is part of the 'four essentials' of quality management:

■ Quality is conformance to requirements. To Crosby, either a product conforms or it does not. There is no such concept as 'good' quality and quality has nothing to do with notions such as elegance.

■ Prevention is the route to achieve conformance, not appraisal.

■ Zero defects is the only acceptable performance standard.

■ Quality is assessed by the cost of non-conformance.

Compared with the work of the other authorities described above, Crosby's change programme is more behavioural. It stresses management and organisational processes rather than the application of statistical methods. While this enables a fit with current cultures and hierarchies it gives little detail of the practical tools of analysis that are essential in quality improvement.

Quality standards

Behind the 'stated or implied needs' of our quality definition are standards. How are these discovered and incorporated into trade? It could be that every contract included a detailed specification but for most products in most applications this would severely restrict free trade. Most buyers and sellers are content to use common standards that have grown from local and industrial customs through national agreements to international conventions. The European Union, for example, has made common standards one main plank in its construction of the single market.

Assay offices represent an early attempt by governments to regulate a trade. Then they were established to prevent unscrupulous traders from diluting gold with base metals. Gradually, national organisations emerged, such as the British Standards Institution (BSI), Deutsche Institut für Normung (DIN) and the American National Standards Institute. This made it possible for commonly manufactured goods to be interchanged and for users to know in advance details of product properties. British structural engineers, for instance, used BS 4 to specify rolled steel I-beams. Nowadays, standards cover products as diverse as film speeds, flame proofing, pencils and paint.

While often formalised in national and international organisations, industry standards and norms emerged by several routes: agreement between suppliers and users, such as the emerging specifications for digital television; success of a leading design or brand, IBM's PC being notable in this respect; or almost by chance, as evidenced by the dimensions of wallpaper, cloth, railway track and vinyl records. Product standards are frequently backed by statute, often at the international level. There are many EU regulations covering product specifications from the strength of vehicle seat belts to the noise emitted by domestic lawn mowers.

Several drawbacks with product standards can be noted:

■ *Limited scope*
Technical constraints and change mean that they relate to only a limited range of products in circulation.

■ *Limited applicability to assemblies*

Standards can apply to some components but not to complete assemblies. It is, for example, hardly of interest to know that the bolts inside a washing machine are made to BS dimensions.

■ *Applied only to some properties of a product*

BS 476, for example, specifies testing methods for fire resistance of building materials. The attachment of this label to a batch of, say, decorative panels will say nothing about their acoustic or other properties.

■ *Complexity*

The historical multiplicity of standards almost denies the point of having them. Although BSI and similar organisations aimed to provide national coverage, many purchasers continued to issue specifications based on their special needs. Government purchasing, especially of military equipment, became subject to rules such as the 05 standards of the Ministry of Defence and NATO's Allied Quality Assurance Publication.

Since many items of military hardware were very complex and had to have quality built into every component, procurement agencies required suppliers to be open to external audit. From the frustration and costs of this system, and the burgeoning number of standards, grew a new approach, concentrating on the processes themselves.

■ Process standards: from BS 5750 to ISO 9000

The first major process standard, BS 5750, was published in the United Kingdom in 1979. It responded to the need to externally validate those many situations where product certification was not practicable. A national standard usable by organisations of all sizes, it was built around basic quality disciplines. It ensured that procedures could consistently meet the specifications set out by the company. Quality in every process had to be evidenced with relevant documentation. Compliance with the provisions of the standard, validated by an inspection organised by the BSI, led to certification and an inclusion in the *QA Register*.[18] Unannounced checks were made up to four times a year.

Recognising the benefits of BS 5750, the International Standards Organisation, ISO, adopted it as the core of the first version of ISO 9000 in 1987. Its formal title

---

Exhibit 6.4 Benefits of quality management registration

Internal
■ Clearly defined responsibilities
■ Procedures form a point of reference for all staff
■ Reduced costs of failure
■ Strengthened morale and motivation.

External
■ Enhanced marketability to customers buying only from registered suppliers
■ Greater customer confidence
■ Enhanced image and reputation.

BS EN ISO 9000 identifies it as the national, European and international quality process standard.

At first, some companies found the registration effort very onerous. Yet, certification spread. By 1998, 127 000 organisations had joined, with 54 000 in the United Kingdom.[19] The need to assure process inputs meant that companies began to require suppliers to register. International sourcing was facilitated by the common approach. Nowadays, many recognise the range of benefits listed in Exhibit 6.4.[20]

Experience of ISO 9000

The International Standards Organisation approves amendment to all standards, undertaking major reviews about every five years. Experience with the 1987 and 1994 versions identified several deficiencies. These were:

Weak links between product and process standards
Assessors focused on how well internal procedures matched standards set by the company. The source of these standards was not questioned. Moving away from products was intended to promote both widespread registration and innovation. Yet it meant that the ISO 9000 label did not guarantee any particular product. Makers of lead balloons could be certified as long as they made them according to declared procedures.

Narrow definition
Attention on process consistency meant that ISO 9000 ignored other dimensions of customer satisfaction that many would include in a broad quality definition. Possibilities are speed of response, customisation and continuous improvement. The service element of manufacture is very important in achieving customer satisfaction.

Universality meant average
Through establishing norms achievable by a wide range of organisations, excellent companies were hardly affected. Apart from recognition, ISO 9000 was valuable to neither them nor their customers. They simply registered and continued unchanged. On the other hand, as Dickson noted, there was a 'fuss over European-wide certification – notably complaints by small and medium-sized suppliers about the time and money spent on acquiring the quality standard ISO 9000 to appease their demanding customers'.[21]

Improvement
The universal approach looked for achievement of standards but said little about how these standards were to be raised. Lessons from the best companies, however, were that standards of themselves did not lead to good and improving quality and gave no guide to where any changes should be made.

The ISO 9000 series

Responding to such comments, new versions of ISO 9000 were published in 2000. There are three main documents:

- ISO 9001 specifies a quality management system for use internally by an organisation, or for certification, or as the basis of contracts with customers.
- ISO 9004 offers guidance on the wider objectives of a quality management system, especially for continual improvement. It is not used for certification or

contracts but is for those organisations that want to go beyond the requirements of ISO 9001;

- ISO 9000 provides an introduction and vocabulary.[22]

We can see that registration is achieved using ISO 9001. A summary of its main requirements appears in Exhibit 6.5.

Exhibit 6.5 Main provisions of ISO 9001:2000[23]

Quality management system
Registered organisations are required to 'establish, document, implement and maintain a quality management system and continually improve its effectiveness'.

Management responsibility
'Top management shall provide evidence of its commitment to ... the quality management system.' To achieve this they should establish a clear quality policy with focus on customer satisfaction, and plan, organise, communicate and review performance.

Resource management
The competence of staff shall be maintained together with infrastructure and the work environment to assure quality in the products.

Product/service realisation
Design and development of all products should centre on meeting customers' requirements along with standards set by regulations. Purchasing should ensure that inputs conform to specified requirements and their origins can be traced.

Measurement, analysis and improvement
Management should 'plan and implement the monitoring, measurement, analysis and improvements processes' needed to establish conformity, ensure that the quality system is effective and continually improve the system.

Figure 6.3 is a process diagram showing the links among these elements.

Convergence of approaches

In its stress on two themes, customer focus and continual improvement, the ISO 9000 series presents a model of Total Quality Management. Figure 6.3[24] shows how the requirements of Exhibit 6.5 are set out as a transformation process. The process converts customer requirements into both products and customer satisfaction. There are two control loops. First, we see the control within the quality management system, ensuring that defined quality standards are achieved all the time. Second, we see the wider loop, highlighting the importance of review and continual improvement. This second loop passes beyond the first system because it involves change; it interacts with all aspects of managing the organisation.

The broadening of quality ideas beyond process standardisation has led to convergence among sponsoring organisations. The European Foundation for Quality Management (EFQM)[25] was established in 1988 by 14 leading businesses. It adopted its 'Excellence model' as a framework based on nine criteria. Five are 'Enablers', representing what an organisation does, and four are 'Results', what it achieves. They are listed in Exhibit 6.6.

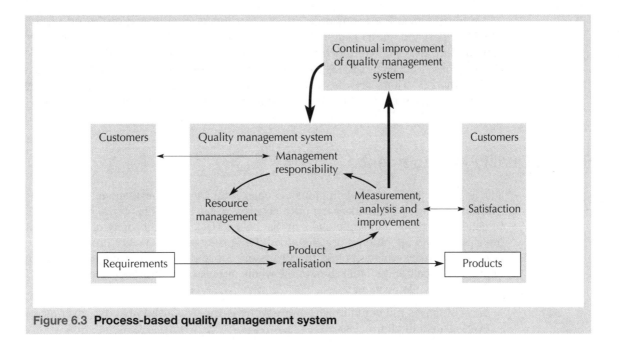

Figure 6.3 Process-based quality management system

Promoting quality through awards

By including society results among its criteria, the EFQM model acknowledges how improved quality benefits more people than the parties to the immediate transaction. This perspective is also present in ISO 9004, where the broader 'interested parties' replace the 'customers' of Figure 6.3. Having recognised the benefits, governments and business organisations have made quality a plank of industrial policy and have sponsored awards both to promote interest and disseminate best practice.

Among the best-known awards are the European Quality Award (based on the EFQM model) and, in the United States, the Baldrige Award. Both focus on customer satisfaction and quality improvement and results are disseminated widely. The Deming Prize (*see* page 173) is narrower, stressing problem prevention using statistical methods.[26] There are also many industry and company honours; the Sweeney award, offered among the suppliers of McDonald's, was noted in the opening case.

Total Quality Management

Just as quality has various definitions, so does Total Quality Management. In essence, TQM brings together the ideas we have covered so far in this chapter and links them to detailed methods and techniques. In that sense TQM is a philosophy of quality that links policy and operational practice. Identifying the need for quality products in the competitive marketplace is just the first step. More difficult, however, are setting appropriate goals and mobilisation of the whole organisation towards achieving them.

Of the three elements of TQM:

- *Total* suggests full commitment of everyone in the organisation and a coverage of every aspect of all processes.
- *Quality* means continuously meeting customers' requirements.
- *Management* implies an active process led from the top.

For our discussion, therefore, we shall use the following definition:

> *Total Quality Management is a process of involving everyone in an organisation in continuously improving all products and processes to achieve, on every occasion, quality that satisfies customers' needs.*

The definition has four key implications that we shall examine further. They are:

- involving everyone in the company through teamwork, trust and empowerment;
- continuous improvement;
- identification of customers and their needs, and then focusing on them;
- using tools and techniques to jointly resolve quality problems.

▨ Teamwork, trust and empowerment

The holistic approach of TQM distinguishes it from conventional approaches where the responsibility is assigned to a 'quality department'. For some, it even goes beyond the Quality Circle (QC), *see* Exhibit 6.7, which can be seen as a means of management delegating some quality responsibilities while retaining most of the control. The holistic goal is commitment and sharing of the quality issue among all employees so that the contribution of each is both recognised and influential. Although some Japanese workers see QCs as coercive, managers among leading companies, such as Matsushita and Kansai Electric, do not see such TQM practices as other than normal management of the business.[27]

Exhibit 6.7 Quality circles

Quality Circles have made major contributions to the success of Japanese companies. Conventionally, staff are organised into groups of, say, 6 to 12. Training and guidance in the concepts of quality and problem-solving techniques are given by middle managers. At regular meetings a group selects problems to work on and solve. It sets its own targets, not only for quality improvement but also for related issues such as production flow, planned maintenance, working conditions and safety.

Among many variants, QCs may:

- have people from one or several work groups;
- have people from one or several levels in the organisation;
- have a nominated leader or decide to rotate the leadership role;
- be stimulated by a scheme offering rewards for suggestions.

From the first QC in Japan in 1962, the number has expanded to, perhaps, 100 000 registered with the Union of Japanese Scientists and Engineers. (There are an estimated 1 000 000 further circles not formally recorded.) In the early 1990s, Yamaha had 700 circles, Toyota 6700 and the medium-sized Toppan Printing 150 among a mere 2000 workers. More than 13 million Japanese people participate, always voluntarily and usually outside working time. Each QC generates about 50 suggestions a year. The movement is seen as a driving force behind the continuous improvement of products and processes.

The QC fits well into the Japanese organisational culture with its emphasis on the group, as opposed to the individual, its lifetime loyalty (at least in major firms) and lack of serious demarcation of job roles. Although QCs have been tried in the West with some success, the different context makes the idea difficult to transfer. Organisations face either the struggle to create favourable conditions or the temptation to remove or dilute some of the key principles that make QCs work.

Empowerment can only occur when people are well trained, given access to relevant information, know and use the best techniques, are involved in the decisions and receive appropriate rewards. Many quality problems relate to materials, designs, specifications and processes and have little to do with poor employee performance or organisation. Yet these same employees are usually well aware of the shortcomings of the production system and can be valuable in finding solutions.

■ Continuous improvement

Many programmes for change are based on the notion of restructuring the system and moving it from one state to another. Large changes are difficult to install and are frequently resisted by those most affected by them. Furthermore, in the uncertainty of complex operating systems, it is not always clear in which direction great steps ought to be made. To cope with these problems, advocates of continuous improvement, or *kaizen*, see striving for quality as an endless journey rather than a trip to a known and fixed destination. Actions involve experimentation, adjustment and minor improvement to every detail. In the *kaizen* philosophy, employees expect small developments and do not see them as challenges to existing working practices and relationships. Continuous questioning of the status quo means that no one stays happy with it for long.

According to Imai, every person's work should comprise two parts – continuation and improvement.[28] The former, which Imai calls maintenance, refers to the current work. People must know what to do and follow the standard. The second part is improvement. This means finding a better way of doing the job and raising the standard. It sometimes happens that people find new ways of doing jobs without raising the standard. Imai argues that this behaviour should be seen as deviation rather than improvement because the key factors of quality, cost and delivery have not been affected. For improvement to take place, the standard must be raised. *Kaizen*, then, implies continuous challenges to the standards in every job.

Imai noted that most of the work at shop floor level is directed towards continuation. The role of managers, however, is to take on more responsibility for improvement. Imai suggests a set of questions to act as guide when problems occur. Did it happen because:

- There was no standard?
- The present standard was inadequate?
- Staff did not follow the standard?
- Staff were not trained to follow the standard?

When problems arise, managers must find out what happened, using the above questions. A better standard or method can be worked out. This, in Imai's view, is most important. For him, standards guide both continuation and improvement and there can be no quality without them. Standards prevent recurrence of problems and limit process variability.

Closely associated with this commitment to involvement in the detail of standards and their improvement is *Gemba*. *Gemba* means the place where the activity takes place. It can refer to: the shop floor; a customer's offices; a customer's site; a design engineer's screen; or a hotel reception area, bedroom, restaurant or sauna. Imai sets out the improvement process based on five *Gemba* principles, *see* Exhibit 6.8.[29]

Exhibit 6.8 The five principles of *Gemba*

1 When an abnormality occurs, go to *Gemba* first and right away!
2 Check with *Gembutsu*. *Gembutsu*, in Japanese, means something you can touch, such as machine, material, failures, rejects, unsafe conditions, etc.
3 Take temporary countermeasures on the spot.
4 Find and remove the root cause.
5 Standardise for recurrence prevention.

Many solutions can be made in the first two steps. Yet the real solutions are achieved only after the last ones are taken. Otherwise, managers not using the discipline remain fire-fighters. The principles have implications for the roles of senior managers. They should be there to remove restraints on *Gemba*, that is to help people lower down the hierarchy to investigate and solve problems without excessive constraints. Since managers are ultimately responsible for everything that happens in *Gemba*, they need to stay in touch and become involved when problems arise. Hence the opening maxim, 'Go to *Gemba* first and right away!' To Imai, the problem with most managers is that they believe their workplace is their desk.

■ Being customer centred

We have seen how Ishikawa and Juran both advocated the notion that, in the TQM organisation, everyone has customers. These may be internal or external. Internal customers are other members of the organisation who rely on the individual next along the quality chain for the inputs to get their work done. When it comes to quality, the internal customer is very much like an external one. The difficulty of the customer's work, and the quality of the output, are strongly affected by the quality of the input.

As for external customers, it is obvious that the TQM company will require *all employees* who deal with them to be committed to satisfying their needs. Being customer focused entails:

■ appreciating situations through customers' eyes so that needs, especially hidden ones, are anticipated;

■ listening to customers, especially the detail of what they want;

■ understanding possible ways of satisfying customers' wishes;

■ providing the appropriate response.

Exhibit 6.9 illustrates how leadership, when customer focus is concerned, can be so negative. The point of the tale is that it represents customer service failure.[30] Any discussion of who is responsible for the problems is put on one side. Further, the manager does not see the impossibility in a mass service organisation of a small elite of managers dealing with customers. The TQM business acknowledges this and, rather than criticise the inadequacy of recruits, develops its people to achieve high standards. This means leadership, training, standards and rewards.

Exhibit 6.9 The blaming trap

A senior railway manager once told me, 'The trouble is that the people in this organisation who deal with the public are the people at the bottom'. We went on to discuss something else. Later, I thought about the implications of the assertion. The critical points of contact between travellers and railway staff are not at ticket sales or general enquiries but when a passenger has a difficulty or complaint. Then, the manager is implying, 'the sort of people we employ' on the shop floor (porters, train crew and so on) are ill-equipped to handle the problems. If only the complaints were immediately handled by intelligent and articulate staff (like the manager himself) passengers would be better satisfied.

In many organisations, the front-line people have low status and pay.

Leading retailers can teach a great deal about customer orientation. Writing on excellence, Peters likens retailing, in the classroom or the showroom, to a performance art. True, to locate, build and stock a store, or to organise a management seminar, require skills from purchasing to project management. Yet, when everything is in place, and the shop opens or the class begins, success is down to personal delivery. Just as there are good and bad actors and actresses, so there are good and bad shopkeepers, receptionists, ticket collectors and teachers. Being good means giving the customer the best of what they want every day. 'You are the absolute master, ruler, tsar,' says Peters. 'You alone bring that space, or those five restaurant tables, to life. Ninnies or saints, fearful or fearless, management can't hold you back.'[31]

Tools and techniques

Later in the chapter we shall survey some important tools for solving quality problems. Imai warns, however, that too much stress can be laid on techniques.[32] He believes that resolving most quality problems needs simple steps. Imai advocates the following:

■ *Go to Gemba*
This is the most important rule.

■ *Standardisation*
Standards are the basis of both continuing activity and improvement. If there are no standards they should be introduced. If the standards are failing, they should be modified.

■ *Don't get it, don't make it, don't send it*
Based on the premise that quality is everyone's job, this says that one should be determined not to receive rejects, create them or pass them on.

■ *Speak with data*
Collecting data is the starting point of analysis. People should be prepared to measure before changing anything.

■ *Ask why*
Problem solving means asking why as often as necessary to find the root cause. Only then can the problems be eradicated.

Others argue that quality cannot be sustained without quality measurement techniques. This is clearly true, but the focus of the TQM organisation is less on the measurement and more on the use of simple approaches to support continuous improvement. Rather than use detailed recording and statistical analysis at the end of the production process, it may be more effective to enable a process worker to take some simple measurements earlier on. Immediate corrective adjustments are possible. Matching the complexity of quality tools with the training and experience of the users is a vital part of involving people at all levels. Tools are clearly a necessary but not sufficient basis for a TQM programme.

Limitations of TQM

At its core, TQM is a simple idea. The search for competitive advantage through quality is best sustained by applying basic ideas right across the organisation. Yet to the simplicity have been added a great deal of jargon and extra techniques. This is one reason why European firms may not have committed themselves to TQM as much as Japanese ones. We can examine this further by looking at costs and people.

Costs

When examining the costs of quality and changing the balance among them, we saw that quality programmes would eventually pay for themselves. 'Quality is free' because the total costs of prevention are less than the costs of failure. This begs two questions. First, what of the firm that has cut its costs of failure to a low level? Gains will become more difficult to achieve. Then, further quality investments may not be supported when managers have other problems on the agenda. Second, quality programmes are an investment. This means spending early to gain benefits later. Figure 6.4, which uses the same data as Figure 6.2, shows how the quality spending may change during a five-year improvement programme.

The graph tracks cash flow to cover all spending, both expenses and investments. Note how, over the first two years, there will be a bulge in prevention spending before it settles to a new level higher than before. Costs relate to reorganisation and initial training. The benefits come later. Failure costs reduce as the programme begins to take effect and, as confidence in the new system rises, appraisal systems can be scaled back.

Human resources

Dawson sounds several warnings when discussing changes in technical and social processes during the introduction of a TQM programme.[33] He first points out that TQM is not a panacea. Many plants have problems that need to be resolved either as a prerequisite of a quality programme or separately from it. Further points concern social issues:

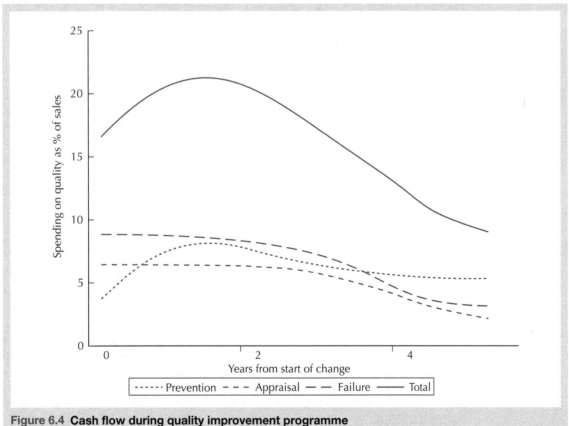

Figure 6.4 Cash flow during quality improvement programme

■ There may be problems within the work groups. To participate in TQM, through Quality Circles for example, is voluntary. Yet to work under the restructured operating system is mandatory. Those unwilling to join in will not support the change. The TQM development may, therefore, make current social tensions worse.

For the employee, non-involvement could be rational. A factory worker with a dull job may make reaching the end of a shift the prime aim. Work is then forgotten until the morrow. Why staff adopt these attitudes, and whether they can be changed, is a subject for Chapter 11.

■ Mobilising employee involvement may be difficult and be put off until later. Cultural, language and structural constraints create barriers:

  – *Culture and language*. A Pirelli plant in Adelaide, Australia, employed many recent immigrants. Language differences among workers hindered the complex communication which co-operation requires. This problem would not arise in the remarkable homogeneity of Japanese society.

  – *Structure*. The relevant structures at shop floor level include plant layout and the shift system. Both may hinder participation in TQM, through either physical or temporal separation. Workers will rely on supervisors for co-ordination and they are likely to see TQM in the same light. Night shift workers, usually fewer than day staff, often perceive themselves as semi-independent of management and are reluctant to make strong personal commitment.

■ Beyond cultural and language diversity, employees may be hampered by poor education. Although the value of TQM techniques, especially statistics, has been exaggerated, participation requires fair standards of literacy and numeracy. Again, those left out of the discussions by such barriers are expected to go along with any decisions made by the group.

There remains a further question, that of seeing the above points as 'problems' to be solved by omniscient, homogeneous and rational management. Yet TQM, as with other management programmes, is often introduced in an atmosphere of contradiction among managers and uncertain relations with the shop floor. In short, its introduction is a political process.[34]

In a wider context, it may appear that the emphasis on individual and group development, backed up by training, would provide great opportunities for the development of personnel policies and practices generally. Yet personnel functions are not heavily involved. TQM accomplishment is very much an operations activity, often established under a project leader who is a line manager. The stress in many Western companies will be on immediate business results rather than long-term development of employees.

Paradoxically, while several American engineers, scientists and statisticians worked with their local counterparts during the rebuilding of Japan after 1946, their work did not become recognised in their home country until much later. By this time, American and European business had seen Japanese imported products climb from the cheap imitations of 1950 to the outstanding quality of the 1980s and beyond. Belatedly, the teachings of pioneers were recognised and they have moulded the attitudes of a generation of factory managers followed by those in service businesses, government and non-profit organisations. We noted earlier the work of Deming, Juran, Ishikawa, Teguchi and Crosby. Yet the outstanding contribution came from Deming.

Spreading the word: the work of Deming

In the 1950s, when scientific management perspectives on control were common in the best companies, ideas of participation were revolutionary. Western industrialists thought that they could not be applied in their concerns. Quality Circles, invented in Japan in the early 1950s, did not reach the United States until 1974. Deming's ideas were ignored in the West for all that time. Yet, fifty years on, many have become incorporated in conventional management training and practice. Nowadays they seem less surprising and, perhaps, rather quaint. In proposing his famous 14 points, *see* Exhibit 6.10, Deming emphasised that they are the permanent obligations of top management, none of which is ever completely fulfilled.[35]

Exhibit 6.10 Deming's *14 points*

1 *Create constancy of purpose.* Take the long-term view; innovate; invest in research, education and equipment.

2 *Learn the new philosophy.* Be dissatisfied with defects, unsuited materials, poor training and management.

3 *Ask for evidence of process control along with incoming parts.* Inward inspection is futile.

4 *Be prepared to reduce the number of suppliers.* More vendors means more costs. Buyers should buy for quality–price value.

5 *Use statistics to find the sources of trouble.* Judgement always gives the wrong answer when looking for a fault.

6 *Institute modern aids to training on the job.* Use statistics to identify training needs. A fully trained person can do no better.

7 *Improve supervision.* Supervisors should lead and use statistics to improve the production system.

8 *Drive out fear.* Insecure people ask no questions, report no difficulties, discuss no improvements.

9 *Break down barriers between departments.* Barriers hinder achieving the common goal: customer satisfaction.

10 *Eliminate numerical goals and slogans. Tear down pictures and posters urging people to increase productivity, sign their work as an autograph, etc.* 'ZERO DEFECTS' posters have no effect. Numerical targets frustrate; they show management lazily trying to convert budgets into action.

11 *Look carefully at work standards.* Do quotas and targets bring the claimed benefits? They make people forget quality.

12 *Train staff in simple, powerful statistical methods.* Statistics should be part of everyone's training. Experts should guide the rest.

13 *Vigorously retrain people in new skills.* Match developments in models, processes, materials, machinery, rules, etc.

14 *Top management must push every day on the above thirteen points.* Development is everyone's job. Leaders must take full responsibility for change.

Eventually, Deming was listened to because of his experience of Japan and the simple rigour of his problem-solving approach. He pressed for the adoption of informed decision making based on good quality data. He advocated the plan–do–check–act (PDCA) cycle, *see* Figure 6.5.[36] He called this the *Shewhart*

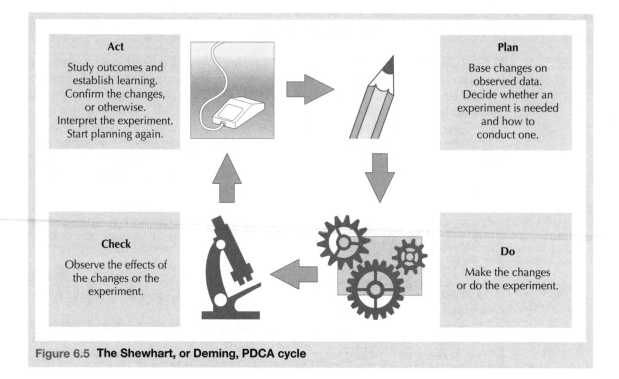

Figure 6.5 The Shewhart, or Deming, PDCA cycle

cycle in recognition of the founder of statistical quality control but the Japanese, and others, call it the *Deming cycle*. It is an example of a family of learning cycles developed in different contexts.[37]

Using the PDCA cycle, managers are encouraged to start with small changes about things that are really important. Through making these changes and reflecting on the process, they both improve quality and *learn how to improve it more*. This approach is set in the tradition of research and experimentation. Actions and reflections are grounded in observed data.

The cycle is not original. As with many of his ideas, Deming's contribution was to draw them together and apply them both rigorously and vigorously to the quality question.

Techniques for quality investigation

Deming argued that data are vital to improving quality. Yet the temptation to use advanced statistical techniques must be resisted if participation is to be encouraged. To avoid the trap, several simple tools and charts have been devised to stimulate problem awareness and breakdown, and act as valuable records of group discussion.

■ Cause and effect diagrams

As an aid to the communication of complex ideas, a well-designed chart is difficult to beat. The cause and effect diagram is a good example. It helps when starting an

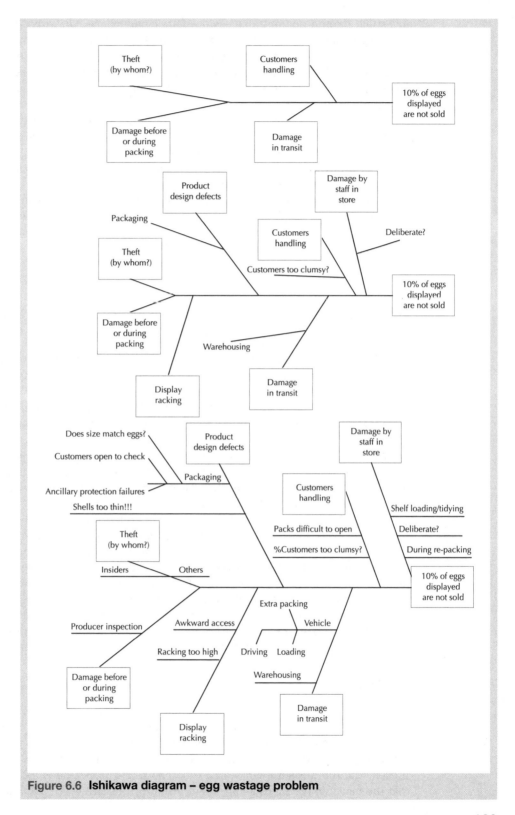

Figure 6.6 Ishikawa diagram – egg wastage problem

investigation and opening discussion. Other names are *Ishikawa diagram*, after the pioneer, and *fishbone diagram*, after its form. While often drawn to suggest a fish, it has no conventional method of presentation. Mind maps or spider diagrams do equally well.[38] The essence of the diagram is to record discussion and ideas. Since it is a practical aid to thinking, not restricted to quality questions, it is a valuable study skill.

Figure 6.6 shows how a chart builds up during a session. Egg damage in a supermarket is on the team's agenda. This is noted on a board and ideas, as they emerge, connect to it. The top diagram starts with four suggestions for causes. The centre shows how further ideas are added as the discussion proceeds. The bottom diagram records yet more thoughts and tidies the arrangement. An informal convention uses boxes to represent main limbs where causes may lie while the small bones suggest detailed sub-reasons. Therefore, the diagram summarises ideas of cause and effect in a hierarchical way. It records the outcome of the meeting. The team uses the diagram to plan further investigation, collect data and so on.

Pareto charts

Although there is a role for advanced statistics, it is remarkable how much understanding can be gained from simple records and summaries. This is what the Japanese call *speaking with data*.

To illustrate, let us imagine we are concerned about faults in sheet steel destined for consumer goods. Asking around, we may be told, 'We get many surface markings because …', or, 'It's quite common to find …', or, 'Sometimes it's as though …'. Staff will be aware of many issues but are unlikely to agree on the main causes. For instance, they will stress the most recent problems. Their estimates of the most common faults over, say, a twelve-month period would be unreliable.

The next step is to collect data. Before recycling scrap material, good procedure would examine each piece. The point is to look more closely at the reasons for failure. Juran was one who taught how Pareto charts can be used at this stage. This form of presentation shows the frequency of events in ranked order.

Figure 6.7 gives the results for the mill in two surveys a year apart. We can see that strides were made in the reduction of failures, especially those caused by roll marks in the steel. Yet pock marks in the surface remained the most serious problem, dominating the others in terms of material spoiled. The Pareto presentation helps to focus the problem-solving effort. In the TQM firm, it is normal to record critical parameters, not merely to appraise whether products are acceptable, but also to continually understand and improve the process. Kobe Steel Company combined such internal appraisal with an external comparison with rivals' products to focus its efforts on improvement.[39]

Control charts

Setting out results on time charts is a common approach to process quality control. Let us say we have a sanding machine that finishes timber furniture components. We need a consistent thickness. One way of tracking the process is to take samples of five components every 15 minutes. How can we speak with this data? Figure 6.8 presents all the measurements on a time chart. We do not need calculations to see that the machine produces a consistent group of samples each time but its setting is

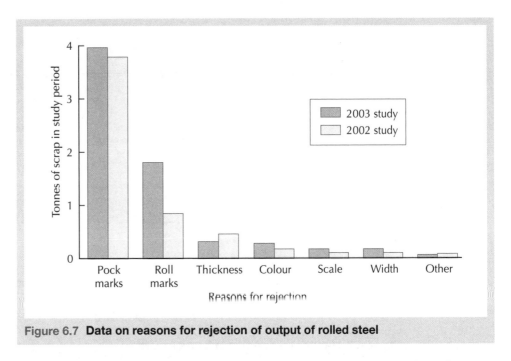

Figure 6.7 **Data on reasons for rejection of output of rolled steel**

drifting slowly. The impression is confirmed when we summarise the data: the mean line shows the downward drift while the range, representing minor process variation, lies between 0.05 and 0.06 mm. The results do not tell us why the panels are getting thinner. Someone may be adjusting the machine or one of its parts may be wearing. The graph tells us the process is capable of consistent quality but its setting needs investigation.

We have omitted the question of whether the sanding or spraying machines actually produce quality products. Study of this aspect requires targets and limits to

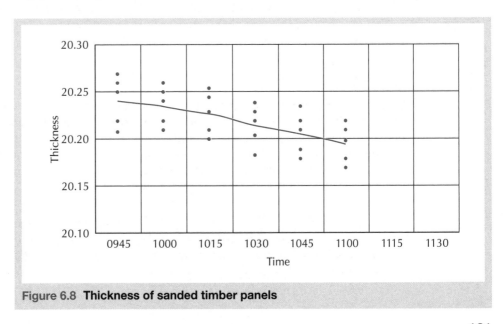

Figure 6.8 **Thickness of sanded timber panels**

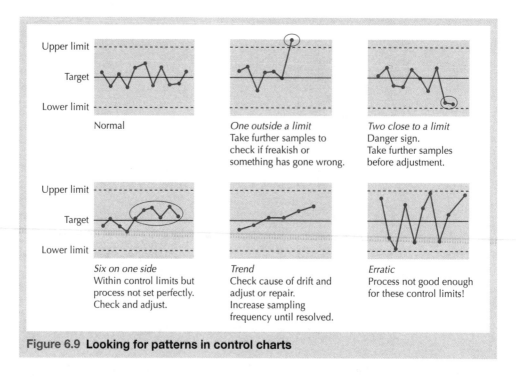

Figure 6.9 Looking for patterns in control charts

have been set in advance. These boundaries form the framework for *control charts*, proposed first by Shewhart in 1924. Deming acknowledged that this formed the basis of much of his later work.

Control charts are used to set out process variables in a standard form. The horizontal axis shows time and the vertical axis represents a variable. This could be any property such as length, weight, electrical resistance, viscosity and so on. Lines across the chart show the target value and two *control limits*, upper and lower. These are usually set well within the *specification limits* outside which the product would be unacceptable. Typical control chart patterns are shown in Figure 6.9. As with other charts, visual inspection can reveal a great deal and suggest the actions shown.

■ Setting standards

Process control requires the setting of targets and control limits. Where do these originate? We have already examined how standards were established to mediate between customers' varied wishes and the need of many companies to achieve economies of scale. Inside organisations, however, there are many activities hidden from the market's view whose performance has a significant impact on overall results. How does an organisation know how well it is doing?

> *Benchmarking is the practice of recognising and examining the best industrial and commercial practices in an industry or in the world and using this knowledge as the basis for improvement in all aspects of the organisation.*

One answer lies in the growth of *benchmarking*. This is not mere imitation. It is about taking the best features from all other organisations and combining them in improved ways. Encompassed in the definition are two modes. The more straightforward one is done within the industry. The organisation monitors rivals' products and processes to enhance its own. Outside the industry, imaginative comparisons can be made between corresponding functions. For instance: Fujitsu measured its training methods against those of the Royal Mail; a United States regional airline compared its aircraft turnarounds with motor racing pit stops; the United Kingdom government has compared its tax and benefits office practices with the successful telephone-based insurance company Direct Line.[40]

Beyond quality itself, benchmarking can produce ideas across all aspects of management: internal and external *products*; *processes* used in the production and distribution of these products; *infrastructure* including people, capital assets and other resources and how well they are used; *management processes*, especially strategy and the management of change.

Exhibit 6.11 The benchmarking target

Target organisations	Advantages	Disadvantages
Other in-house organisations	Ready access to information	Insufficiently convincing; biased
Domestic and foreign competitors	Much information accessible; very convincing	New information not easy; resistance; concern over leaks
'National class' of excellent organisations	Innovative; co-operation most likely	Different operating environments
'World class' of excellent organisations	Highly informative and innovative	Cultural differences hinder transfer; costly; time consuming

A key issue is picking the target or partner for a study. Exhibit 6.11 summarises some selection criteria.[41] The process can run into problems with other companies, particularly fierce rivals. Yet much information is available from three sources: it is published; products can be examined or experienced; and customers are often willing to compare rivals' offerings. Main gives some advice for use when approaching other organisations:[42]

- *Don't go fishing* – limit scope to areas that need improvement.

- *Send out the people who face the problems* – let people see for themselves.

- *Consider exchange* – the target may be involved in its own benchmarking.

- *Steer away from legal problems* – avoid price, market share and new product development.

- *Keep shared information secure* – a partner will be alarmed if it is passed on.

Benchmarking can be both an eye-opener and a stimulus to action. When studying engine repair processes, British Airways found that technicians on Japanese Airlines took 40 minutes to turn round a 747 while its own people took 3 hours. The process also has its limits, however. It works well for high-performance companies. Yet for moderate performers, the exercise may generate only confusion and low morale. There are plenty of basic actions such organisations can take, from team building to improving links with customers, before they start to worry about becoming world class.

We can also note that benchmarking has an internal orientation. Yet, as ISO 9000 tells us, *see* Figure 6.3, the key task is to match standards to the needs of the customers. Nowhere is this more clear than in the provision of services.

Service quality

Quality in use

Each transaction includes an element of service. Its quality is affected by the way the service is provided. Although we should not support the staff member's attitudes expressed in Exhibit 6.12, we can recognise that service is vulnerable at its weakest point, the moment of interaction with the customer. This is the *moment of truth*. In the restaurant, good food can be spoiled by indifferent service, while in the supermarket the checkout can be a positive or negative experience. The TQM service organisation pays attention to four interconnected factors that contribute to quality – organising and staffing, process, facilities and monitoring.

Exhibit 6.12 An awkward customer?

I visited the snack bar of a ferry on a Holyhead to Dublin sailing. Having bought tea, I settled at a table in a quiet corner. After a moment, a staff member came over to tell me I should not be sitting there because the area had just been cleaned. I replied that it seemed to be an excellent reason for sitting there and refused to move. I suppose I went down in the log as an 'awkward customer'.

Organising and staffing for service quality

The nature of the service will, largely, determine how it is provided. We can distinguish *personal service*, delivered in the presence of the customer, from *isolated service*, produced away from contact with the customer. Isolated service needs a 'front office' to make this contact. It can gain from high efficiency, using 'factory style' processes. Yet, the separation can be a retrograde step if the organisation loses its orientation towards service quality. Solutions include quality circles, training, job rotation and appropriate controls.

Service delivery is full of uncertainty. We often forget that even shopping is an acquired skill. Things go well when suppliers and customers have common expectations. In other situations, uncertainty can be the result of genuine unpredictability of outcomes or the customer not knowing what to do. Does one help oneself or wait to be served? Can one sit anywhere? May one make a noise?

The TQM organisation recognises that customer satisfaction depends on narrowing the perception–expectation gap and requires the commitment of all to achieving it.

The service process

Imai's arguments about standardisation apply equally to manufacture and service. The specification of quality standards in service functions, however, is difficult and tends to concentrate on quantifiable elements, especially the time taken for various stages of delivery or the frequency at which certain tasks are carried out. The non-quantifiable aspects, such as the overall impression of the helpfulness and politeness of the staff, are more difficult to assess, although they can be observed by supervisors and monitored using sample surveys. Vandermerwe distinguishes between 'hard' and 'soft' capabilities, arguing that customers evaluate the service they receive on what they *get out*, while firms, using conventional quality measurement and control, concentrate on what they *put in*.[43] The contrast between the capabilities is shown in Table 6.3.

Facilities, equipment and materials

Facilities, equipment and materials have differing degrees of importance depending on customer expectations and the nature of the service. In food retailing for example, they are all very important whereas professional advisers make little use of materials and equipment.

Development of information systems has enabled more services to be provided through self service. In these cases, ergonomics and the study of human–machine interaction play a significant role in the design of equipment. The quality of such equipment will itself have an impact on the customer's perception of the service

Table 6.3 Hard and soft thinking about service attributes

Hard thinking		Soft thinking	
Minimise variation	*Deviation avoided*	Maximise adaptation	*Be able to respond*
Get it right first time ...	*... without fail!*	Ensure relevance over time	*Make it work for the customer*
Measure attributes	*Assess the facts of the service*	Measure customer experience	*How the service functions*
Zero defects	*No faults at any time*	No breaks	*Do not interrupt the flow of service*
Fitness for purpose	*Build value in*	Ease of application	*Getting value out*
Standards...	*... and adhere to rules*	Resilience	*Adaptation, renewal*
Uniformity	*Everything the same*	Consistency	*Can provide the customer's needs each time*
Durability	*Product lasts*	Reliability	*Things work*
Cause and effect	*Clear links*	Interactions	*Solutions in complex situations*

package as a whole. Its reliability is critical, as witnessed by any customer who has been let down by a cash machine when trying to obtain £10 for a late night taxi.

Quality monitoring in services

Effective quality control requires the establishment of clear standards and the ability to measure conformance to these standards. Only then can action be taken to ensure compliance and also decide where standards themselves can be improved. The example from P&O European Ferries, given in Exhibit 6.13, is typical of leading companies. It monitors both objective and subjective measures. But note that the effectiveness of the audit will depend on its covering characteristics important and relevant to the customer. Furthermore, the way the information from the survey is used will have a strong influence on whether quality levels are maintained and improved.

Exhibit 6.13 Customer survey card: P&O European Ferries

The two-sided comment card uses a combination of yes/no, four point and open ended scales to solicit comments on accommodation, catering, bar, service and general points.

Cabin accommodation

Was your cabin ready for you?	*Yes*	*No*	(Please circle)	
	Excellent	*Good*	*Average*	*Fair*
How was your cabin in terms of cleanliness and maintenance?	❑	❑	❑	❑

Catering

Quality of the food	❑	❑	❑	❑
Taste of the food	❑	❑	❑	❑
Temperature of the food	❑	❑	❑	❑
Appearance of the food	❑	❑	❑	❑
Choice of the menu	❑	❑	❑	❑
Efficiency of the service	❑	❑	❑	❑
Level of courtesy	❑	❑	❑	❑
Appearance of the catering staff	❑	❑	❑	❑

Any other comment _____

The question for service quality monitoring is how to combine hard data with the much more difficult soft data. After all, the latter may say a great deal more about the customers' responses to the service.

SERVQUAL

One approach to capturing the soft variables was developed by Parasuraman, Zeithaml and Berry.[44] It measures the gap between what customers expected and their perceptions of the service experience. The size of this gap would indicate areas for improvement. They developed the SERVQUAL questionnaire containing 22 pairs of questions derived from a larger survey. They are grouped into five categories, called the dimensions of service quality, as follows:

■ *Reliability*: dependable and accurate performance as promised.

■ *Responsiveness*: responding promptly to customers' needs.

■ *Assurance*: competence and courtesy of staff, coupled with their ability to show trust.

■ *Empathy*: caring attention to each individual.

■ *Tangibles*: appearance of facilities, equipment, personnel; environmental factors such as noise and temperature.

Table 6.4 illustrates the questionnaire layout with just two questions on tangible dimensions of a library service.[45] Taking each in turn, the scores on the Likert scales are subtracted to yield the satisfaction measure.

Table 6.4 Extract from SERVQUAL questionnaire applied to a library

	My expectation of the library service is:	My perception of the library service is:
When it comes to:	Low————High	Low————High
1 Having physical facilities that are visually appealing	1 2 3 4 5 6 7	1 2 3 4 5 6 7
2 Having staff who give users individual attention	1 2 3 4 5 6 7	1 2 3 4 5 6 7

To allow for the varying importance of the dimensions in different settings, the questionnaire often asks subjects to weight the categories by sharing 100 points across them. The results of the weighted survey are then assembled in a report such as Table 6.5. We can see that, although the respondents reported the greatest gap in empathy, they found that dimension less important than assurance. The weighted score ranked the latter more highly.

Criticism of SERVQUAL has been based on the importance of expectations and questions on the general application of the five-factor structure. In detail, interpreting the meaning of the (P – E) gap is difficult. In the wider, marketing context,

Table 6.5 SERVQUAL scores with weighting

	SERVQUAL score (P – E)	Weights %	Weighted SERVQUAL	Rank
Tangibles	−0.37	18.7	−0.31	5
Reliability	−0.41	23.8	−0.44	4
Responsiveness	−0.48	23.3	−0.51	3
Assurance	−0.67	19.8	−0.60	1
Empathy	−0.82	14.5	−0.54	2
Overall	−0.53	100	−0.48	

others comment that the service dimension is only one element of the marketing mix. Notwithstanding these reactions, service organisations in many fields have taken up the model. For instance, the Accounts Commission for Scotland recommends it for the assessment of local government services.[46]

Conclusion: quality is (nearly) all

Two things about the so-called 'quality revolution' are surprising. First, it took until well into the 1980s before it was recognised in the West as a critical element in competition. Second, it was then taken up (and often dropped) so quickly. Perhaps many managers' key skills lie in jumping on bandwagons!

Basic lessons have been learned; it is now accepted that quality is not produced by inspection and that it is not the cure for all ills. With these lessons now integrated into everyday managerial practice, some argue that quality is just good management. Yet this is to forget that quality is more than exhortations to see everyone as a customer or make zero defects a way of life. It refers to a set of processes, tools and techniques systematically applied to improving product parameters. For leading organisations TQM lies at the heart of their activities, identifiable yet integrated with all others. To succeed, organisations could follow what Binney identified among leading European companies:

■ leaders, forthright and assertive about quality, should listen to questions about how to improve;

■ managers should provoke involvement rather than demand it;

■ quality should be integrated into the core of the business – all activities, from recruitment and training to measurement and evaluation, should support it;

■ all should learn, experiment, [not] blame and learn some more.[47]

There is a drawback to Binney's exhortations. In using words such as *forthright, assertive, provoke* or even *should*, he is not alone in revealing attitudes about the role of leaders in TQM. Should they appear to be so forceful? One could ask, 'What happened to ideas of empowerment and participation?' Chapter 11 investigates styles of leadership to find what approaches may be most appropriate to the introduction of TQM.

QUICK CHECK

Can you ...

■ Define quality.

■ Clarify why quality is important.

■ Summarise the costs of quality.

■ Distinguish product and process standards.

■ Give a definition for TQM.

■ Describe a Quality Circle.

■ Translate *kaizen* and *Gemba*.

■ Summarise three limitations of TQM.

■ Trace the Deming cycle.

■ Sketch Ishikawa, Pareto and control charts.

■ Outline the benchmarking process.

■ Suggest why people may resist the introduction of TQM.

■ Explain the SERVQUAL approach to quality measurement.

QUESTIONS

Chapter review

6.1 Explain why there are so many definitions of quality and how a manager can respond to them.

6.2 What are the costs of quality and how would you explain these to a confectioner?

6.3 How can quality be free?

6.4 Assess the strengths and limitations of TQM.

6.5 Why was the work of Deming and Juran accepted in Japan some 30 years before its recognition in the West?

Application

6.6 How do 'cost of quality' ideas apply in a quick-service restaurant? How does McDonald's seek to minimse them?

6.7 What benefits do product and process standards bring to McDonald's customers? Should the company seek ISO 9000 registration?

Investigation

6.8 Examine the bid of a recent winner of the European Quality Award.[48] Compare the bid to the ideas on quality management set out in the chapter to identify the key features of its success.

Shering weighs it up[49]

Founded in 1946, Shering Weighing Group is a family-owned business making weighbridges and related equipment. Bucking the 1980s industry trend towards outsourcing of most components, the company retained design, manufacture and after-sales service in house. It opened a new headquarters and plant at Dunfermline in 1991 and has invested heavily in a stream of new products designed to solve customers' problems. It led the introduction of electronic weighbridges with tamper-proof instrumentation and telemetry communication; it developed extra long models up to 45 metres and extra wide ones up to 5.5 metres and 180 tonnes; its patented restraint post system protects the precision load cells from shocks and damage; and detailed design and surface coatings promote safety and durability.

Quality of products and service has been at the core of these innovations. Shering has ISO 9001 accreditation and is approved under the stringent European Weights and Measures standard EN 45501. The rules require annual calibration using standard test weights. The cost of hiring these is included in the full maintenance service, which also has a two-hour response target if problems arise. The latest installations have modem links to enable condition monitoring from Scotland; software upgrades are also installed by this means.

Shering's products have many applications. In quarrying, weighing is a critical component of the process. Without accurate equipment the quarry cannot function and goodwill is lost. One of Shering's customers, RMC Western Aggregates, had had three problems with a previous supplier: excessive wear and tear under the heavy traffic of some 1000 vehicles per day; reliability of maintenance service; and the wish to integrate data into its management information system.

Another customer, quarrying stone for distribution throughout Munster, added fraud prevention and safety to the list of solutions required of a quality weighing system. Now, as the driver enters a J.A. Wood quarry area, the Entry Driver Terminal (EDT) automatically recognises the vehicle through a secure link and matches it with the booking. The terminal prints a ticket and directions for the driver on where to collect the load and shows a green light. The EDT transmits corresponding instruction to the cabs of the loading vehicles. The mechanised loading shovels can

CLOSING CASE

measure the materials reasonably accurately. The driver then returns to the unmanned weighbridge, sometimes along a public road, where the load is checked and confirmed automatically. Detecting a full vehicle at the exit terminal, the system cancels the loading instructions, prints details of gross, net and tare weights for the driver and updates all records. Opportunities for fraud are reduced and, since the driver does not leave the vehicle, many accident risks are eliminated.

Questions

1 Select from the case study one example of each of the three costs of quality.

2 Shering is one of many companies that stress the benefits of a full after-sales service. What are these, and who gains from them?

3 Using the evidence in the case study, outline how well Shering matches the latest ISO 9000 standard.

Bibliography

Perhaps the most readable works by a leading advocate are by Philip Crosby (1995) *Quality without Tears: The art of hassle-free management* (New York: McGraw-Hill), and (1996) *Quality Is Still Free: Making quality certain in uncertain times* (New York: McGraw-Hill). Classics include Joseph M. Juran (1988) *Juran on Planning for Quality* (New York: Free Press) and W. Edwards Deming (1988) *Out of the Crisis* (Cambridge: Cambridge University Press). Both founded institutes: **www.juran.com** and **www.deming.org**. Other web resources include the ISO, **www.iso.ch/iso/en/ISOOnline.openerpage**, the EFQM, **www.efqm.org/welcome.htm**, the UK Department of Trade and Industry, **www.dti.gov.uk** and the Baldrige Society, **www.quality.nist.gov/**. Mindtools has useful techniques, *see* **www.mindtools.com**.

References

1 McDonald's (2000) *McDonald's Fact File 2000*, London: Corporate Affairs Department, July; McDonald's (2001) 'McDonald's Presents "Sweeney Quality Award" to Asian Cargill Subsidiary', Sun Valley Ltd: McDonald's Corporation, 13 February; **www.mcdonalds.com**, accessed 20 July 2001.

2 Zeithamal, V.A., Parasuraman, A. and Berry, L. (1990) *Delivering Service Quality: Balancing consumer perceptions and expectations*, New York: Free Press, 26.

3 Williams, Steve (1995) 'Cross-cultural contextual differences in perceptions of seafood quality', *Asia Pacific Journal of Quality Management*, **4(1)**.

4 J.D. Powers and Associates (2001) *Rental Car Companies Compete Fiercely to Satisfy Customers*, Press release, 10 April; **www.jdpa.com/studies/pressrelease.asp?StudyID=512&CatID=4**, accessed 2 July 2001; Ulrich, Lawrence (2001) 'Toyota, its Lexus division lead in car-quality study', *Detroit Free Press*, 18 May.

5 Crosby, P.B. (1984) *Quality without Tears*, New York: McGraw-Hill, 60.

6 British Standards Institute (2000) *ISO 9000:2000 Quality management systems – fundamentals and vocabulary*, London: BSI, 7–12.

7 Ho, S. (1993) 'Transplanting Japanese Management Techniques', *Long Range Planning* **26(4)**, 81–9.

8 Deming, W.E. (1981) 'Improvement of Quality and Productivity through Action by Management', *National Productivity Review 1.1*, reprinted as Reading 7 in Latona, J.C. and Nathan, J. (eds) (1994) *Cases and Readings in Production and Operations Management*, Needham Heights, Mass.: Allyn and Bacon, 223–36.

9 A best-seller that did much to bring quality ideas to a wide audience: Crosby, P.B. (1980) *Quality is Free: The Art of Making Quality Certain*, New York: Mentor.

10 Lister, Richard (1994) 'Beyond TQM...' *Management Services*, May, 8–13.

11 Deming (1981) *op.cit.*, 223.

12 Gador, Brad (1989) 'Quest for Quality – Tennant Company, Minneapolis, MN', *Target*, Fall, 27–9.

13 Carr, Lawrence P. (1995) 'How Xerox sustains the cost of quality', *Management Accounting*, **77(2)**, August, 26–32.

14 Swanson, Edward T. and Jambekar, Anil B. (1995) 'A technology choice for noise reduction: a quality management case study', *International Journal of Quality and Reliability Management*, **12(7)**, September–October, 44–56.

15 www.deming.org, accessed 24 January 2001; for further notes on Deming and the other quality gurus, *see* the site of the UK Department of Trade and Industry, www.dti. gov.uk/mbp/bpgt/m9ja00001/m9ja000011.html, accessed 7 July 2001.

16 www.juran.com, accessed 24 January 2001.

17 In a special issue of *Quality and Reliability Engineering International* 4(2) (1988) on Taguchi methods, a number of articles show how the statistical methods can be improved. A general evaluative paper is: Box, G., Bisgaard, S. and Fung, C. (1988) 'An Explanation and Critique of Taguchi's Contributions to Quality Engineering', *ibid.*, 123–31.

18 HMSO (2001) *QA Register*, London: HMSO; www.quality -register.co.uk/about.htm, accessed 16 May 2001.

19 British Standards Institution (2000) 'How much does registration to ISO 9001/2 cost?', www.bsieducation.org/ higher/sect3d.html, accessed 2 July 2001.

20 British Standards Institution (2000) 'How can an organization benefit from registration to ISO 9001/2?', www.bsi education.org/higher/sect3c.html, accessed 2 July 2001.

21 Dickson, Tim (1993) 'Management Quality street cred – TQM is struggling to make an impact in Europe', *Financial Times*, 20 October, 16.

22 British Standards Institution (2000) *BS EN ISO 9000:2000 Quality management systems – requirements*, London: BSI, vi–vii.

23 *Ibid.*, 2–13.

24 Based on Figure 1 – Model of a process-based quality system, *ibid.*, 3.

25 www.efqm.org, accessed 1 July 2001.

26 Izadi, M., Kashef, A.E. and Stadt, R.W. (1996) 'Quality in Higher Education: Lessons learned from the Baldrige Award, Deming Prize and ISO 9000 registration', *Journal of Industrial Teacher Education*, 33(2), 60–76.

27 Westbrook, Roy (1995) 'Organising for total quality: case research from Japan', *International Journal of Quality and Reliability Management*, 12(4), April, 8–25.

28 Imai, Masaaki (1992) 'Solving quality problems using common sense', *International Journal of Quality and Reliability Management*, 9(5), 71–5.

29 *Ibid.*, 72–3.

30 It should be noted that British Rail, and its successors, have worked hard to improve in this area in recent years. The change in terminology from 'passengers' to 'customers' is a minor symbol of the development of a retailing philosophy.

31 Peters, Tom (1994) 'Theatre on the retail stage', *Independent on Sunday: Business*, 6 March, 26.

32 Imai (1992) *op. cit.*, 74.

33 Dawson, Patrick (1994) 'Total Quality Management' in Storey, John (ed.) *New Wave Manufacturing Strategies*, London: Paul Chapman, 103–21.

34 McCabe, Darren (1996) 'The best laid schemes of TQM: strategy, politics and power', *Industrial Relations Journal*, 27(1), March, 28–38.

35 Deming (1986) *op. cit.*, 229–35. Various versions and interpretations of the points can be found. For example:

by Deming himself, (1985) 'Transformation of Western style of management', *Interfaces*, 15(3), 6–11, (1986) *Out of the Crisis*, Cambridge, Mass.: MIT Press, 23–96 and (1991) 'Philosophy continues to flourish', *APICS – The Performance Advantage*, 1(4); Aguayo, R. (1991) *Dr Deming: The man who taught the Japanese about quality*, London: Mercury, 121–2. Curiously, Aguayo has 16 points in his list of 14!

36 Deming (1986) *op. cit.*, 88.

37 Argyris, Chris and Schon, Donald A. (1978) *Organisational Learning: A theory of action perspective*, Reading, Mass.: Addison-Wesley, 20; Stacey, Ralph D. (1996) *Strategic Management and Organisational Dynamics*, 2nd edition, London: Financial Times Pitman Publishing, 398.

38 Buzan, Tony (1995) *Use Your Head: Revised edition*, London: BBC Books; Mind Tools Ltd (2001) *Improved note taking with mind maps*, www.mindtools.com, accessed 3 March 2001.

39 Dale, Barrie and Asher, Mike (1989) 'Total quality control: Lessons European executives can learn from Japanese companies', *European Management Journal*, 7(4), 493–503.

40 Trapp, Roger (1994) 'Benchmarking moves on to bench-testing', *Independent on Sunday: Business*, 9 January, 13.

41 Ohinata, Yoshinobu (1994) 'Benchmarking: The Japanese experience', *Long Range Planning*, 27(4), 48–53.

42 Main, Jeremy (1992) 'How to steal the best ideas around', *Fortune*, 126(8), 19 October, 104.

43 Vandermerwe, Sandra (1994) 'Quality in Services: The "Softer" Side is "Harder" (and Smarter)', *Long Range Planning*, 27(2) 45–56.

44 Parasuraman, A., Zeithaml, V.A. and Berry, L.L. (1985) 'A conceptual model of service quality and its implications for future research', *Journal of Marketing*, 49 41–50; Parasuraman, A., Zeithaml, V.A. and Berry, L.L. (1988) 'SERVQUAL: A multiple item scale for measuring customer perceptions of service quality', *Journal of Retailing* 64(1) 12–36.

45 Tan, Pey Lin and Foo, Schubert (1999) 'Service Quality Assessment: A Case Study of a Singapore Statutory Board Library', *Singapore Journal of Library and Information Management*, 28 1–23.

46 Accounts Commission for Scotland 2000, *Can't get no satisfaction? – Using a gap approach to measure service quality*, Edinburgh, May; available at www.audit-scotland.gov.uk, accessed 8 July 2001.

47 Binney, G. (1993) *Making Quality Work – Lessons from Europe's leading companies*, London: Economist Intelligence Unit.

48 European Foundation for Quality Management (2001) *European Quality Awards 2000*, Brussels: EFQM, www.efqm.org, accessed 15 June 2001.

49 Shering Weighing (2001) *Western Aggregates Case Study*, www.sheringweighing.demon.co.uk/pr2.htm, accessed 11 July 2001.

CHAPTER 7

Enterprise

Chapter objectives

When you have finished studying this chapter, you should be able to:

- define entrepreneur and distinguish between enterprise and small business;

- describe the scale and importance of the SME sector in the United Kingdom and outline comparisons with other countries;

- evaluate the extent to which entrepreneurs can be distinguished from the rest of the population and describe the usefulness and limitations of such studies;

- explain what makes an entrepreneur;

- analyse why and how government policies towards SMEs are shifting from stimulating start-ups to picking winners and encouraging growth among them;

- explain the function of intrapreneurs and how some firms succeed in stimulating their activity;

- identify key management problems faced by owner-managers, suggesting how they can be overcome.

If Enterprise is afoot, Wealth accumulates, whatever may be happening to Thrift; and if Enterprise is asleep, Wealth decays, whatever Thrift may be doing.

John Maynard Keynes, British economist

The rise of Intrason[1]

When Patrice Flippe and his wife set out in 1984, with a capital of FF20 000 (€3000), they could not have foreseen that within a decade their enterprise would have created the world's most advanced miniature hearing aid. At 29, Flippe had little business experience. After dropping out of medical studies, he had taken dental technician training more from interest than need. Meanwhile, he supported himself from street selling. After four years at the Fédération française de l'audition (Hearing Association), sporting an earring and unable to stand hierarchies, the aspiring entrepreneur founded Intrason. Producing conventional in-ear devices, the company thrived, reaching sales of €1.7 million by 1989.

From 1990, Flippe moved into top gear to create a new device. He transformed the business by bringing in new managers. They included his brother-in-law, Christian Friconnet, with experience at Moulinex and Bébé Confort, and a Briton, Desmond Greener, expert in the hearing aid business. Venture capitalist companies took up 49 per cent of the shares and a government technology fund loaned €670 000. In four years, the enterprise invested €1.8 million to create the 'Alpha'. During this time, Flippe took out a €1.8 million key man insurance policy on the life of his technical director, who was vital to the development.

Ready in 1994, the Alpha was true high technology applied to hearing. Eight parameters were matchable by computer to each patient's hearing. Smallest in its class, it was invisible once placed in the ear. Tiny power consumption gave the battery a twelve-day life.

The future is bright for such products. There are some 40 million aurally impaired people in OECD countries, of whom five million live in France. Yet high prices mean that only 700 000 have prostheses. The deafness market is growing as the population ages and many young people carelessly damage their hearing.

A unique product is not enough; distribution is vital. Intrason appointed distributors in 1992 in the United States, followed by Belgium, Italy, Germany, Spain, and a five-year agreement in Japan. Turnover in 1995 reached €5 million, expected to double the following year. Export orders were estimated at €68 million for the next five years.

Abroad, the Alpha was not sold made up. Intrason supplied kits containing the key technical components. Local agents made individual moulds for each patient. High retail margins, up to 200 per cent, reflected the added value at this stage. To avoid missing this potential profit, Intrason needed to quickly develop its own world network to really push its product in the market against competitors such as Starkey, Siemens and Philips.

Flippe needed €8 million to fund the network. Flippe was put off a stock market flotation by the rules on disclosure. He preferred to remain the sole boss and was careful to keep just below the 50-employee threshold at which a works council would be required under French law. Yet he wanted to realise the goodwill value of Intrason, which he estimated at €9 million. The Flippes dreamt, 'We can begin with a year or two's holiday sailing round the world.' Patrice's contradictory attitudes exacerbated dealings with the venture capitalists. In 1996, they were due to sell their investments, which had tripled in value.

The Flippes sold out. Intrason continued as an independent business with Friconnet as President and Chief Executive. After a few slow years, revenue in 2001 grew by 33 per cent to €11 million. Some 40 per cent of the 45 000 hearing aids made were exported. Investment in digital technology had paid off with the launch of the all-French Digison using 256 sound channels. Weighing just 1.5 grams, it fits into a mould of the ear canal. Three other digital models were due in 2003.

Introduction

In using the terms 'enterprise' and 'entrepreneur' in the story of Intrason, we have met two words that have come to preoccupy many politicians, managers and scholars. For governments throughout the world, a problem has been to kindle the 'enterprise culture', which is seen as both stimulating growth and generating new jobs. Often, the term 'rekindle' may be more relevant because of the common feeling that the spirit of enterprise has been lost. For the manager, enterprise has become associated with innovation and dynamic adaptability. In large organisations, leaders have sought how to reproduce the same lost spirit to revitalise their sagging hierarchies. For scholars, the words pose something of a puzzle. We seek answers to questions from 'Who are entrepreneurs?' and 'How are they created?' to 'What government policies encourage their activities and nurture their businesses?'

Popular books on enterprise fall into two categories. The 'How to do it' book focuses on setting up a small business, almost from scratch. Chapters cover initial market surveys, the first visit to the bank, the purchase of the basic equipment and so on. Clearly, many entrepreneurs establish small businesses but then what happens? Some businesses disappear, some remain small and a very few thrive to become the large corporations of the next generation. The second category is 'How I (or they) did it'. These represent *post hoc* descriptions with some attempts to draw general conclusions when several case histories are brought together. What these sources reveal is that entrepreneurs are involved in businesses of all kinds and sizes, not always small.

This chapter takes neither the 'how to do it' nor the 'how I did it' approach. We can learn from the experience of practitioners yet, as with so many other aspects of management, this must be enriched with the results of research and reflection. In aiming to blend and enrich these two aspects, the chapter draws on both the experience and the research traditions. It starts by examining the nature of enterprise and small business. Then it looks at their origins and how development can be stimulated through public policy. Finally, there is a review of entrepreneurs as managers.

What do *enterprise* and *small business* mean?

Reference is often made to the small firm and the enterprise as if they were the same. Indeed, this merging is bound up in the label *Small and Medium Enterprise* used to describe any business whose size is below a defined level. We shall begin by distinguishing between the two ideas.

Enterprise and entrepreneurs

Enterprise, and associated terms with the same root, are used in many ways. For example, when discussing the notion of 'enterprise culture' from a sociological perspective, Burrows points out the lack of an agreed definition; the idea slips between a movement and a petit bourgeois class label related to self-employment.[2] Others take enterprise to mean simply 'business' and entrepreneurs the people who perform that role. To many, however, entrepreneurs are more special than this. Deakins and Freel compare a range of views that are summarised in Exhibit 7.1.[3] While there is a consensus that the entrepreneur is a key element in the economy, divergence between two main lines of thought continues. One concentrates on willingness to accept risks while the other stresses the innovatory function. Putting these together, we can summarise by saying that entrepreneurs:

- Are agents of adjustment. This means that, in being flexible in their choice of business and the way they conduct it, they both lead and satisfy the adjustment needs of the whole economy.
- Apply innovative ideas, changing the way businesses convert inputs into outputs.
- Go beyond replicating the current processes in the market. They find new marketing processes to reach new customers or satisfy existing customers in new ways.
- Take risks.

Exhibit 7.1 What is an entrepreneur? Five perspectives

- *The intermediary* is alert to profitable opportunities for trade. The opportunity arises from information not possessed by others yet freely available. The intermediary's advantage is alertness, for otherwise there are no special skills required. (Kirzner)
- *The originator* goes beyond being alert to imagining opportunities. This is a special skill involved not only in finding openings amid uncertainty but in identifying their potential and assembling resources to exploit them. (Shackle)
- *The innovator* relies on aptitude to develop new technology. This gives a temporary advantage over other firms, which can eventually respond by extending or replacing the innovation. There is some difference from the intermediary, who may look to exploit the innovations of others, and the originator, whose function may equally lie in marketing as in technology. (Schumpeter)
- *The risk taker* gains profit as the reward for carrying risk. This person assesses the uncertain future and ventures in business according to that judgement. All business faces risk that cannot be covered by insurance. This is the risk of being in business itself. (Knight)
- *The co-ordinator* makes judgements and co-ordinates resources. Central to this view is access to resources without which the entrepreneur could not function. This means capital. As the economy changes, the co-ordinator is first to adapt, matching changing supply and demand. In fact, co-ordinators make the economy work. (Casson)

In each of these aspects, the entrepreneur breaks new ground, usually seeking incremental rather than great change. In this way the person is a calculative risk taker yet not an out-and-out gambler or fool. Yet many entrepreneurs lack formal skills in risk management. Deakins illustrates this in a study of how small firms insure aspects of the business. More than 90 per cent of a sample of 76 took out insurance to cover motors, property and public and employer's liability. There are, of course, statutory and contractual requirements in these areas. Fewer than 10 per cent, in contrast, had insurance for health and life, personal accident, travel, key persons, professional indemnity or patents and copyright.[4] This shows that they took risks that they could have insured against. It is, however, unclear whether the firms were unaware of the possibilities or had decided not to insure because the premiums were too high. The data, however, underline the point that the risk is real. The entrepreneur is investing personal resources, including taking chances on health and personal accidents, for economic gain. As one commented, 'Insurance is all very well, but the real risk is losing everything'.

Summing up:

> *An entrepreneur perceives opportunities, creates solutions and is willing and able to take reasonable risks to build something of value.*

> *Enterprise is the behaviour shown by entrepreneurs, which is taking reasonable risks for business gain.*

Note that the definitions say nothing about the size or type of business activity. Taking a broad definition of entrepreneurship, government data suggest that 18 per cent of the population is engaged in three categories of entrepreneurship: as employers in mainly small firms (41 per cent of entrepreneurs); self-employed (38 per cent); and as a sideline to main employment (20 per cent).[5] Whatever the role, being an entrepreneur involves using a wide range of management skills in a variety of sizes of business.

■ Small business

A small business is usually defined by some arbitrary criterion such as sales or number of employees. Unfortunately, such criteria, being established to cover all cases, ignore the firm's perception of size as compared with the norms for its industry. For instance, Hendry and others studied a sample of firms in which the one with most employees (355) saw itself as a small independent bakery, while a visitor bureau (44) and software company (130) each perceived themselves as large for the industries they were in.[6] In competitive terms, some nominally small businesses are large and vice versa.

Relativist definitions of size do not suit governments or other agencies seeking to develop policies favouring small businesses. Even discussing a sector such as that comprising *Small and Medium Enterprises (SMEs)* is inappropriate. There are two reasons. First, using 249 employees as the upper limit of the range, some 95 per cent of all firms are included. Second, the character and problems of a firm with several hundred staff will be very different from those of one with a handful. A more detailed taxonomy is needed. From 1997, the European Union has used three subcategories of SME, illustrated in Table 7.1. This gives data for the United Kingdom's 3.75 million businesses. With a roughly equal split among micro, small and medium, and large, the UK employment proportions are similar to those of other Western European nations.

Among firms in the micro, small and medium categories, there is a mixture of those owned and managed by the same people and others where ownership and management are separated, as is normal in much larger organisations. The essence of small business lies in the former, that is firms that are owned and run by the same people. We can expect them to require and develop entrepreneurial attributes. There

Table 7.1 **Firm size, numbers and share of employment: UK 2001**

Label	Number of staff	% firms	UK employment
Micro	1–9	94.6	28.9
Small	10–49	4.5	14.4
Medium	50–249	0.7	12.0
Large	250 or more	0.1	44.6

Data refer to private business and public corporations.

will be some small businesses, however, whose owners are not entrepreneurial or who take little active part in the business, employing professional managers instead.

Entrepreneurs, therefore, are concentrated among the large number of micro and small firms. Exceptions are twofold. Some grow their firms into large ones while others work within existing companies to bring innovation and change. The latter are the so-called *intrapreneurs* who are discussed later in the chapter.

Distinguishing SMEs that are unlikely to change from those that can grow has become important to governments. As our opening quotation from Keynes makes clear, enterprise creates wealth. Job creation comes from both start-up and growing firms. Evidence and policy are mixed. During the early 1990s, for example, policy in England and Wales shifted towards supporting firms with growth potential. Meanwhile, in 1994, Scotland announced a new programme to back company creation. By 2002, policy south of the border had refocused on start-up support.[7]

What makes an entrepreneur?

Some people are naturally more entrepreneurial than others are. Furthermore, they show the tendency more at different times of their lives and in different situations. Explanations vary from those concentrating on personality traits to those that examine the relationships between a person and the social environment. A further question is how much entrepreneurship can be learned, and therefore taught. For instance, it can be argued that one function of business training is to give people confidence to take on responsibilities, therefore removing a personal barrier to entrepreneurial action. We shall examine personal, social and situational factors.

Personal factors

Researchers have examined personal traits for clues to explain entrepreneurship. For example, Bolton and Thompson[8] use categories of talent, temperament and technique to list personal factors, shown in Exhibit 7.2.

In contrast to comprehensive listings, others have searched for key factors that distinguish entrepreneurs from the rest of the population. Deakins and Freel[9] list need for achievement, desire to be in control, willingness to take calculated risks and the desire to be independent as their top four items. Dalmar[10] proposes a parallel list of traits, also headed by need for achievement. Monetary gain is not the sole driving force, for entrepreneurs gain satisfaction from activities such as problem

---

Exhibit 7.2 Personal factors in the entrepreneur

Talent
Advantage orientation; courage; focus; creativity; networker; opportunity spotter; obtaining resources.

Temperament
Needs: competition; responsibility; performance orientation; urgency; opportunity taking.
Drives: ego; mission; activator; dedication.

Technique
Skills; ability to develop talents and manage temperament; experience.

---

solving and taking responsibility for outcomes. Dalmar also notes, however, that, apart from this one item, studies are inconsistent.

Some studies have searched for special traits that distinguish entrepreneurs from the rest of the population. Are they really different? Clearly, some factors are found among all successful managers, especially the important need for achievement and desire to be in control. Managers combine dependent roles, being responsible to seniors, with responsibility for other staff, use of discretion and taking risks.

A further question concerns whether entrepreneurs are born or made. If such traits are needed by managers and entrepreneurs, then entrepreneurial development should have much in common with management development. In other words, many aspects of entrepreneurial behaviour can be acquired through learning and experience. The rise in entrepreneurship among middle-aged people, noted later in the chapter, is evidence for this view. It could be that the ability to learn is the key skill.

Answers to these questions could be useful, for example, in predicting whether an individual is likely to succeed. The approach, however, has been criticised by Chell and others.[11] As with other aspects of human activity, it is inappropriate to pick out just one or a few factors when entrepreneurs are clearly characterised by their diversity. In addition, this approach ignores factors in the social and economic environments, which may have a much greater effect.

Social factors

Beyond personality, there is evidence that social factors influence the likelihood of a person becoming an owner-manager.[12] Evidence includes:

- peaks in the age profile of the self-employed;
- the best single predictor of self-employment is whether the family has included some form of the same;
- self-employment is more prevalent among married than among single people;
- self-employment follows from social marginalisation and is more common in some ethnic groups.

While such factors may be noted as more typical of entrepreneurs than others, they offer limited help with the question of what makes an entrepreneur. For instance, it can be shown that marriage and self-employment are correlated. But what is the link? Does being married encourage self-employment in some way? One can easily propose an explanation. The danger, however, is the same evidence supports the opposite argument – self-employed people are more likely to get married!

Age profiles

The interaction of personal and social factors is illustrated by data on the age of the self-employed. Surveys have identified two peaks in the age profile of entrepreneurs, namely 35–54 and over 65.[13] Compared with a mean of 18 per cent, a UK Household Survey found that, while many young people think about setting out on their own, it is the 35–54 year-olds (22 per cent) that do so.[14] Many older people turn to self-employment from necessity but some seek to apply experience, either full-time or as a sideline. Business survival rates are highest when the founders are 50–55.[15]

A different approach compared the growth rate of small privately owned companies with the age of their directors. The companies, with a minimum turnover of £2 million, were beyond the start-up phase. Figure 7.1 gives a growth index with 100 as the mean value. We can see that companies with younger directors grew more quickly. Other data show changes in directors' motivation. Hunt's scale compares drive for achievement with the drive for comfort, with zero meaning they are equally important. The tendency for older directors to prefer comfort can be seen in Figure 7.2.[16]

Although the measures and age groupings in such surveys do not correspond, they all point to changes with age. We can suggest that the peak among the 'thirty-somethings' depends on their having gained sufficient experience to set up in business while retaining the drive for achievement. The second peak among over 65s is explained by their minimal chances of formal employment. Small-scale self-employment supplements pensions.

Family businesses

Self-employment runs in families. This is not only because ownership is inherited but also because it seems to follow from values and skills that parents give to their

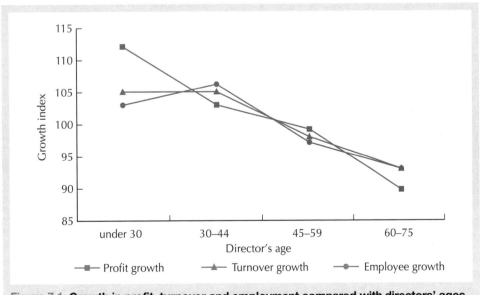

Figure 7.1 **Growth in profit, turnover and employment compared with directors' ages**

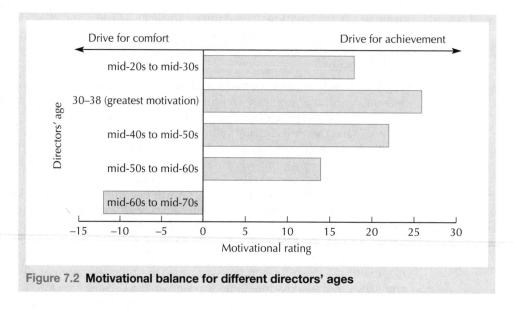

Figure 7.2 **Motivational balance for different directors' ages**

children. Inheritance may be a mixed blessing. There is evidence to support the adage, 'Rags to rags in three generations'. Abbott and Hay show that the growth rates of family firms tended to slow as second and subsequent generations took over, *see* Figure 7.3.[17] They conclude that offspring tend to 'harvest' the businesses more than the founders do. Costa makes the same observation. Just 8 per cent of family businesses reach the third generation. Decline in family businesses is not inevitable, however. Examples such as the Mogi family, engaged in making soy sauce since 1630, show how careful attention to strategic and succession planning is required.[18]

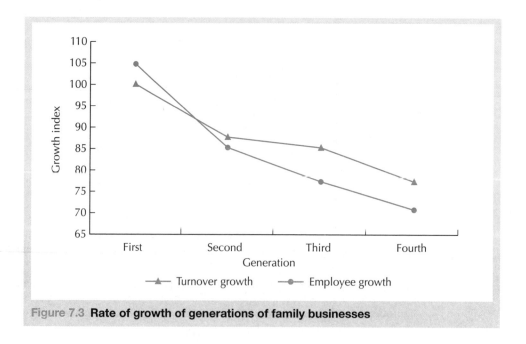

Figure 7.3 **Rate of growth of generations of family businesses**

Ethnic businesses

The family system as both a source of labour and a contact network is important for some ethnic minorities. Table 7.2 gives self-employment rates for groups in the United Kingdom in 2001.[19] Whites had relatively low unemployment (5 per cent) and self-employment (10 per cent), indicating a preference for, and easier access to, jobs. African-Caribbeans experienced high unemployment (13 per cent) but found few feasible business opportunities. Chinese and Pakistanis also faced high unemployment (16 per cent). Yet, their rate of self-employment suggested that small business did provide limited openings for many without jobs. In contrast, for Indians, self-employment seemed to provide enough openings to keep unemployment low (7 per cent).

Table 7.2 **Unemployment and self-employment rates for ethnic groups in the United Kingdom**

Average 10%		Self-employment rate	
		High	Low
Unemployment rate	High	Chinese 19%; Pakistanis 22%	African-Caribbeans 7%
	Low	Indians 14%	Whites 10%

Figures indicate percentage of working age population in self-employment in 2001.

Clearly, the British experience is of great diversity. South Asians, especially those coming from India and East Africa, typically used family and ethnic networks to provide flexible resources and market access, for example in the clothing and knitwear industries supplying international markets. African-Caribbeans, on the other hand, relied much more on product specialisation (for instance, record and fashion shops, hot bread) and local markets in urban areas. Their under-representation in self-employment is often explained by such cultural and location factors. Yet, Ram and Barrett point to other possibilities.[20] Immigrants from the West Indies were originally invited as a replacement workforce to take up unskilled jobs. Self-employment opportunities were thus confined to similar work. Such history leads to negative stereotyping of African-Caribbeans among bankers and other providers of business resources. Low levels of home ownership also make it difficult to accumulate funds.

Beyond the factors discussed here, other features can be noted. For example, those educated to at least degree level are more likely to be entrepreneurs (24 per cent against the 18 per cent average), although a significant minority of the unqualified are also included. Further, men (24 per cent) are much more likely than women (11 per cent) to be engaged in entrepreneurial activity, although the gap is closing. A quarter of male entrepreneurs are in construction, compared with one in twenty females. Women are common in service businesses, especially health and social work.[21]

■ Situational factors

The PEST framework, introduced in Chapter 2, reminds us of many other environmental factors that may influence the potential of a business. Drawing on the work of Mason,[22] the most important factors are:

- an industrial structure that favours small independent units;
- employees working in problem-solving occupations with close contacts with customers;
- clusters of technically advanced small firms;
- high awareness of small business activities;
- banks and financial institutions attuned to the needs of small businesses;
- available help and advice;
- an affluent population providing a market;
- social attitudes favouring individualism.

Based on the list, a variation among regions and industries would be expected. Service industries occupy about a half of all entrepreneurs, more in the south-east of England. Computing and 'other businesses', such as finance, property and professional services, are especially important in this region. In the north, however, the important sectors are construction, transport and distribution, retailing, and hotels and restaurants.

Ethnic minority entrepreneurs are also heavily concentrated in transport and distribution, as well as retail, and hotels and restaurants. Among minority owners in the last sector, Bangladeshis dominate.[23]

The effect of the social and cultural environment is clarified when international comparisons are made. The GEM survey[24] found entrepreneurial activity, using its own definition, averaged almost 10 per cent among adults, ranging from 5 per cent in Belgium and Japan to 18 per cent in Mexico. *Opportunity entrepreneurship*, taking advantage of clear openings, occupied almost 7 per cent. It was highest in Australia, Mexico, New Zealand and the United States. *Necessity entrepreneurship*, taking the best option available, was high in Brazil, India, Korea, Mexico and Poland.

Both types of entrepreneurship are more common in countries where there is greater income inequality and optimism about the economy. Opportunity entrepreneurship is associated with less manufacturing, fewer regulations, more informal investors and high respect for such behaviour. Necessity entrepreneurship is higher in nations with lower economic development and international trade, weak social security and less-empowered women. Beyond these generalisations, we have to study each country for insights into differences.

Business and social attitudes in Japan resist individualism, although this may be changing. The involvement of women is low. Few people invest in business start-ups and government tax policies do not favour SMEs. Financial difficulties among banks have reinforced their risk-averse attitudes.

Recent industrialisation in Mexico bred a new class of entrepreneur in urban centres. Their activity was supported by government incentives, trade protection and the policies of public and private monopoly industries to subcontract much of their work. Trade protection reduced after Mexico joined NAFTA, but access to the United States market offered further opportunities. Investors are ready to support business start-ups.[25]

Operating environment

The list of factors also points to the operating environment as favouring or hindering entrepreneurs. Since they find roles as agents of adjustment, innovators and risk takers, they will be more likely to succeed in situations that require these capabili-

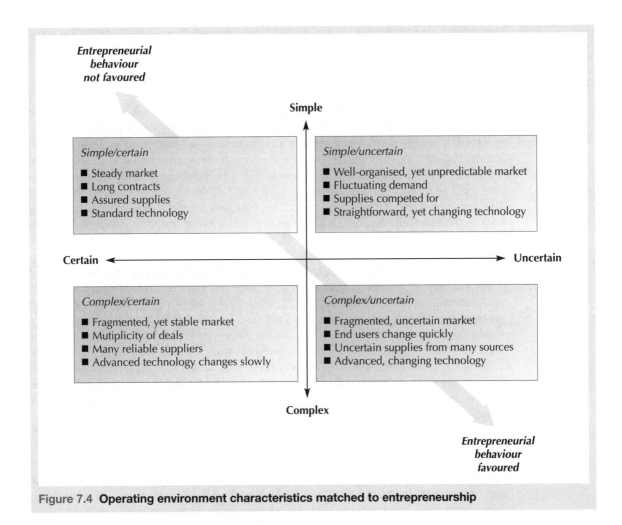

Figure 7.4 Operating environment characteristics matched to entrepreneurship

ties. This implies complex and uncertain supply markets, product markets and technologies. Larger, more stable organisations do better in simpler and more certain environments. These points are summarised in Figure 7.4.[26]

Encouraging the entrepreneur

In many countries since about 1980, there has clearly been an increase in self-employment. For example, SMEs in the United Kingdom increased from 1.8 million to almost 3 million during the 1980s. This measure of the stock of firms hides the important flows in and out of the sector during the period. We can say that births exceeded deaths by some 1.2 million. Because some businesses merge with others, however, not all deaths are failures. Furthermore, a few grow sufficiently to exceed the upper limit of the SME definition.

Typically, government policies have been focused on stimulating formation. Failures have been left to the market. Recently, however, governments have recognised that only a few SMEs grow quickly and provide the precious new jobs sought in the economy. We are beginning to see a shift in policy towards helping such firms.

■ Births and deaths

Many firms start small and remain so, struggling to survive on low turnover. Eventually, many cease to function. Although covering only 46 per cent of the 3.7 million UK enterprises, Value Added Tax returns are often used as indicators of trends. Figure 7.5, for example, uses VAT data to show how registrations exceeded deregistrations throughout the 20 years to 2002.[27] Numbers of VAT-registered firms rose by 2 per cent annually during the 1980s, fell during the recession and, from 1995, resumed growth of 1 per cent. These aggregate data hide variations among sectors. Numbers in financial and other services have more than doubled, whereas production, construction and transport were close to the average and two sectors, agriculture and retail, saw a fall.

Another way to examine the lifespan of companies is to compare the likelihood of death with the firm's age. Figure 7.6 again uses VAT data to present one- and three-year survival rates for firms in 2001.[28] While these were rising during the growth years of the 1990s, young firms have about a 9 per cent chance of deregistering within the first year and 35 per cent within three years. Non-survivors need not be failures. About a third are thriving at deregistration while a further few decline to below the turnover threshold.[29] The averages mask sector and regional variations. In Northern Ireland, for example, survival rates are high, but the start-up rate is low. This suggests a risk-averse culture with fewer people taking risks and a static stock of businesses.

High rates of new firm formation may look impressive as evidence of an 'enterprise culture'. Yet, many do not survive the first year and most fail within three. The preoccupation with start-ups has overlooked the consequent rise in failures with their effects on entrepreneurs, their families and their creditors. There is also the question of how far new, subsidised firms displace other enterprises that may themselves have been established only a few years earlier. Therefore, as important as the number of start-ups is their quality, that is their potential for survival and growth.

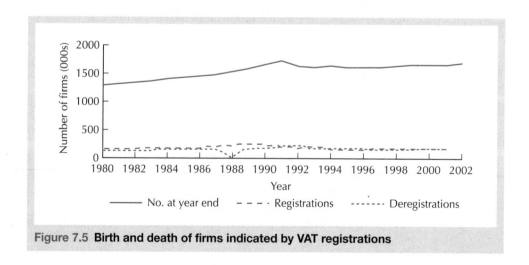

Figure 7.5 Birth and death of firms indicated by VAT registrations

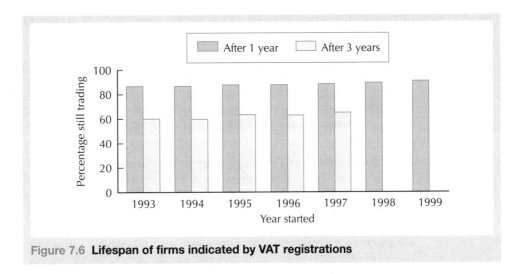

Figure 7.6 Lifespan of firms indicated by VAT registrations

Growth

Once any starting subsidies have been absorbed, SMEs can face higher costs than their larger rivals. Finance, for example, tends to be more expensive since SMEs have no access to the main equity markets and lenders charge premiums to cover their extra risk. The benefits of limited liability are often illusory as owners are required to cover loans with personal guarantees or secure them against family property. Furthermore, in industries with economies of scale in functions from purchasing and operations to distribution and marketing, the larger firm will again have the advantage. How, then, can the entrepreneur succeed?

Keasey and Watson identify four conditions where the small firm will gain advantage:[30]

Industries without economies of scale
From domestic repairs to high fashion, many industries lack scale advantages. This may be because of process technology or insufficient market demand. For example, car assembly has scale advantages yet small segments of the market are served by low-volume production. Here luxury, nostalgia or high performance niches provide work for Rolls-Royce, Morgan and TVR. Customising, restoring and rebuilding are niches populated by many small firms.

Opportunities favour entrepreneurial behaviour
As shown in Figure 7.4, complexity and change in the business environment means that flexibility within the firm will enable it to chase opportunities. Entrepreneurial behaviour is sometimes displayed by large firms with flexible systems and outlooks. Yet size is an obstacle to be overcome. The owner-entrepreneur, on the other hand, has the incentive and speed of decision making that are required. An example is the 'spin-off' contract based on research findings of large companies or other institutions that are unsuited to their own development plans.

Acceptance of lower returns
With many SMEs not having to provide detailed financial reports, it is not clear how their average financial performance compares with that of other firms. It is evident, however, that many SMEs, especially the very small ones, survive at the expense of poor working conditions, long hours and moderate pay and pensions. Involvement

215

of family, including children, is frequently seen in shops, restaurants, hotels and smallholdings.

Regulatory framework

The less stringent financial reporting rules, reduced taxes and non-applicability of some employment legislation mean a gentler legal environment for small businesses. In addition, governments attempt to counter the advantages of large companies in business transactions. These range from overseas sales promotions to penalising slow payers.

Given the possibility of exploiting entrepreneurial advantages, it is perhaps surprising that only 3 per cent of new firms show high growth and create many jobs.[31] There seem to be differences between the few firms that grow rapidly and the majority that remain small throughout their lives. A study by Barclays Bank[32] showed that fast-growth firms tend to be young and operate within emerging industries such as mobile telephony or low-cost aviation. Other sectors are business and personal services, and retail, including coffee shops but not restaurants. Fast growth is linked to high-growth regions, such as the south-east, especially 'hot spots' such as Cambridge, Milton Keynes and the Thames Valley. Improved transport, however, permits many to set up in lower-cost areas with pools of skilled labour. Owners or senior managers are younger than average, expert in their sectors and specialisation, better educated and experienced, and very likely to be from ethnic minorities. Financial management is rated as the most important skill and objectives focus on growth and profit as opposed to survival. High-growth firms are more likely to use the Internet, especially for market research and intelligence gathering; slow-growth firms use it more for e-commerce, possibly because many more are in manufacturing.

Results like these raise the possibility of picking winners, a policy that would be advantageous to the government and business advisers as well as the managers themselves. Unfortunately, failing firms frequently show the same characteristics as the very successful ones! Picking winners remains about as easy as in steeplechasing. Among the mix of personal and business factors, it is often persistence with a unique idea that makes the difference. At Intrason in the opening case, we saw that it was only after six years of trading that Patrice Flippe came up with his big idea and persuaded venture capitalists to join in. Without this product, he could not have been a 'winner'.

Harrison and Taylor studied some 200 high-growth medium-sized companies in Germany and the United Kingdom for the 15 years up to 1995.[33] Their results emphasised the importance of marketing and continued innovation. Successful medium-sized firms avoid taking on established rivals directly. Instead, they find market niches that are ready for innovative products and where entry is aided by speed, flexibility and customer service. Additionally, they protect these niches through patents, licences for distribution or long-term contracts with important customers. Following initial success, limited diversification avoids reliance on one product, one customer or one region. Finally, the entrepreneur must be prepared to pull out. As competitors come in and market growth tails off, it may be best to sell up and look elsewhere for innovatory opportunities.

Such studies support the view that medium-sized (in German, *Mittelstand*) businesses are often the engines of growth in the economy. In ten years, the 200 firms studied by Harrison and Taylor created between 50 000 and 100 000 jobs and invested more than £2 billion. Governments would like to encourage even greater success. Yet, whether their winning ways can be discovered in advance remains a problem.

■ Government support

We shall not detail government initiatives for stimulating the start-up and growth of SMEs. This is because they are continually changing, their impact is unclear and they vary so much between nations. There are, however, some common themes. The shift of focus from start-ups to continuance has already been noted. Non-sustainability is a problem encountered in many countries. For instance, commenting on the proposed sell-out of Intrason to a foreign rival, Le Parmentier noted, 'It's a story of a France that knows how to create high-tech products but is incapable of transforming such innovations into international winners'.[34] For France read Britain, Denmark, Sweden, the Netherlands and so on.

Encouraging, removing constraints and creating infrastructure

Governments offer support to starting and growing firms according to local perceptions of needs. They do this as part of their role in sustaining economic growth but also for wider social and environmental reasons. For instance, while much of the employment and regeneration focus in the United Kingdom is on areas of urban decline, others argue that the rural economy also needs help for diversification. According to the Countryside Alliance, this should be achieved through three policies: encouraging SME formation and growth by providing advice, opportunities and pump-priming finance; stimulating business integration, such as linking specialised food production with tourism and stimulating marketing co-operatives; removing constraints including excessive regulation; and developing infrastructure, including housing, communications and utilities.[35]

The same themes of encouragement, removing constraints and enabling through infrastructure are repeated throughout the nation and the world. Such policies are shown in sharp relief in South Africa where SMEs are a relatively small part of the formal employment picture and are, for the most part, in the hands of white owners. SME development is expected to be an instrument of social change for, as the government acknowledges, 'small business support will for a considerable time also have to focus on the particular needs of black enterprises and the ways to overcome the remaining consequences of that legacy [of big business domination and the uneven distribution of wealth]'.[36]

The SME scene in many countries is dominated by a collection of projects, schemes, clubs and institutions intended to offer support, advice and connections. Some are government agencies while others are local organisations sponsored by the state. Examples of the former are the United Kingdom Department of Trade and Industry and its equivalents in other nations. The latter are illustrated by the well-established Chambers of Commerce in France, Germany and Japan. It is often reported that one problem for SMEs is the diversity of sources of assistance and the skill required to find a route through the maze.

Despite the plethora of projects, governments usually have little power to directly create and sustain SMEs. Apart from budgetary constraints, they must avoid aiding new businesses at the expense of existing ones. Two recessions, marking the start and end of the 1980s, meant closure for many small businesses. Since entrepreneurs often operate at the margins of the economy, they are particularly sensitive to downturns. Furthermore, since many work through complex networks of contacts, they tend to fall when things go wrong like lines of dominoes. Hence the common plea, 'Government should remember that the best way it can assist small firms is by creating a stable macroeconomic environment'.[37]

Intrapreneurs

Intrapreneur is a term coined to describe employees who display entrepreneurial qualities while preferring to remain within the framework of an established organisation.[38] Unfortunately, there is little consensus on what these qualities are. Using a case approach to compare successful entre- and intrapreneurs, Jennings, Cox and Cooper identify the latter as those who have proved success at management by rising within major companies.[39] The range is wide. Richard Tait, *see* Exhibit 7.3, was recruited to be an intrapreneur; the aptitudes of scientist Art Fry emerged within a supportive environment, *see* Exhibit 7.4. Others, such as Peter Wood, are really *serial entrepreneurs*. He has built five international business ventures from the innovative Direct Line insurance business, sold to the Royal Bank of Scotland, to Esure, set up for the Halifax.

Exhibit 7.3 Microsoft® was intrapreneurial (once)[40]

Richard Tait spent ten years creating new products and business projects for Microsoft before leaving to set up his own businesses – an investment fund and Cranium, a fast-selling board game.

Tait joined Microsoft in 1988 when it had only 2400 employees. The company noted his first degree in computer science from Heriot-Watt, MBA from Dartmouth and entrepreneurial flair. It installed him in his own business unit, on the headquarters fifth floor, with the cream of the technical talent. During his 10 years, Tait and his team developed 16 award-winning products and 5 new business initiatives, as well as hundreds of other ideas. The unit aided the tenfold growth of Microsoft by the time Tait left in 1998.

Tait remembers, 'Everybody wanted to work on that floor. One way to cultivate intrapreneurs is to build an organisational structure based on product units which allows people to feel like it's a small business within a large organisation. You have to give people ownership so that they feel autonomy within the large business.' He says that bureaucracy will stifle the intrapreneurs, as happened at Microsoft when the management structure expanded. Businesses should use their intrapreneurs or lose their competitive edge. Without them, they will not evolve.

Intrapreneurs' qualities are especially needed in larger firms operating in the complex/uncertain environments of Figure 7.4. Large, established firms do not fit these environments well. They tend to:

■ make cumbersome plans;

■ possess rigid structures and systems;

■ limit personal autonomy and creativity;

■ use controls that hinder innovation.

Carrier defines intrapreneurship as *the taking in charge of an innovation by an employee or other individual working under the control of an enterprise.*[41] An innovation is any change leading to an improvement of performance.

Recognising how growth and change tend to stagnate, some companies have launched programmes to promote intrapreneurship. Pinchot defined three possible roles:

■ *The inventor* creates the new idea, whether it be for a product, process or other change.

■ *The product champion* helps with overcoming resistance to change through becoming committed to the idea and having the position and experience to press ahead with the project.

■ *The sponsor* is a senior manager who recognises the value of the idea and uses position and organisational politics to secure resources and give it a chance of survival.[42]

Although presented here as separate, the roles can be combined in one person. The product champion and sponsor, for example, do not have to understand technical details beyond being able to judge whether the idea has a chance of succeeding. These roles are vital, however, as difficulties of pushing ideas through hierarchies without sponsorship cause many inventors to either give up or leave.

Programmes to support intrapreneurship involve taking the long view, creating autonomous teams, allocating resources, tolerating lack of success and offering appropriate rewards.[43] Their purpose is to overcome barriers, including:

■ traditional corporate structure and culture;

■ large firm performance measures;

■ planning procedures;

■ diffused ownership;

■ lack of project commitment caused by management mobility.[44]

They have not always succeeded. Kodak dropped its attempts after disappointing results.[45] Others, such as Hewlett-Packard and 3M,[46] *see* Exhibit 7.4, have thrived over many years.

Exhibit 7.4 Success for 3M's intrapreneurship policy

Post-it Notes started in 1977 after Art Fry took advantage of 3M's policy of allowing scientists to spend up to 15 per cent of their time on self-selected projects. He applied a colleague's rejected discovery, a glue that was impermanent, to a problem that was frustrating him. At church, page markers frequently fell out of his hymnal!

Fry won the backing of 3M's Commercial Office Supply Division and became responsible for taking the idea to market. The product caught on in 3M's own offices but early sales were poor. After all, why should potential buyers pay for such pads when staff can use scraps of paper? The solution was to flood one market, Boise, Idaho, with free samples. Customers were hooked. Demand grew quickly. Now Post-it Notes are worldwide best sellers.

Fry was promoted in 1986 to corporate scientist, the highest technical grade.

■ Intrapreneurs and SMEs

The question of intrapreneurship arises in growing SMEs as innovators other than the owner-manager begin to emerge. Carrier[47] argues that distinctions between large and small firms are such, however, that the issues must be considered from a different viewpoint in each case. On the face of it, small firms' friendlier and more flexible structures, together with more personalised relationships, should enable better working partnerships to emerge. Yet the compatibility of the intrapreneur with the owner-entrepreneur becomes the key issue. If a trusting relationship is to be nurtured, the owner-entrepreneur must maintain a working atmosphere with matching strategies and rewards. The unwillingness of many to have their ideas challenged and to let go of controls can make matters difficult. Yet they need to be aware of the dangers of rejecting, and losing, the intrapreneur.

Managing the SME

Having compared the characteristics of entrepreneurs and intrapreneurs and outlined some government policies directed towards encouraging the success of SMEs, we shall complete the chapter by raising important management questions. These relate to management and technical expertise; information; international business; finance; and planning

▩ Management expertise

It is often argued that the most serious difficulty facing the SME is the shortage of skills. For instance, there is the observation that small firms make less use of information systems, including being unable to obtain and use software to suit their particular needs, and engage less in international business. These activities, it is stated, require management resources beyond those normally available. Compared with its larger rivals, the SME is also hampered by lack of other skills, especially in marketing and cash management. Some, however, are available under government sponsorship.

Entrepreneurs frequently apply expertise and experience gained in previous employment. They often set up in industries or markets in which they had been working. These 'technical entrepreneurs' are important since their SMEs often have substantial growth potential. Clearly, management requires technological expertise but success depends on how this is combined with business acumen. Jones-Evans identified four types of technical entrepreneur depending on their occupational background:

■ *Research*
Involved in scientific or technical development in a university or non-profit research centre.

■ *Producer*
Engaged in product or process development in a commercial environment, probably a large company.

■ *User*
Peripheral involvement in technological development through roles such as marketing or end-user applications.

■ *Opportunist*
Experience gained in a non-technical organisation, therefore no technical expertise.[48]

Jones-Evans found that few combined high technical and management expertise. *Users* showed high management expertise. The other groups had either good or high technical expertise but scored lower on the other scale. The small number of technical entrepreneurs who were also highly capable managers owned the firms with the greatest potential.

■ Using information systems

Expertise applies not only to setting up the business but also in coping with external innovation and change. Nowhere has this been more apparent than in information, where some SMEs establish an edge over their rivals. Naylor and Williams investigated the use of information systems (ISs) among 30 SMEs in Merseyside. Seven firms showed that even small firms can use ISs beyond basic transactional applications. Exhibit 7.5 gives two examples of firms that bought computers to carry out routine administration yet found, after installation, unplanned ways of using them. These more successful SMEs used their ISs to change operations and extend their markets. The study concluded that managers' ability to interact with the IS in creative ways was vital; success followed continual innovation to integrate applications into the whole business.[49]

Exhibit 7.5 Beyond basic IT applications in SMEs

Firm B, with 20 employees, distributed welding and related engineering equipment. It introduced a basic information system to monitor its operations yet the major gains were unplanned. Using the new spreadsheet facility, the sales manager saw how many customers were buying just one product from the wide range. Taking the twelve largest accounts, he aimed to increase their spending by selling them different lines. A discount scheme was offered. In one year, sales to these customers doubled.

Firm K, with 80 employees, is the leading United Kingdom manufacturer of shower surrounds. In a careful information system plan, it anticipated benefits in administration, sales and short-term forecasting. The greatest gains arose, however, from being able to introduce a five-day delivery guarantee throughout much of Europe, while at the same time increasing output and improving the control of stocks and work in progress.

While it is possible for SMEs to win in the IS application race, overall involvement in the sector is variable. In 2002, almost three-quarters of SMEs used PCs, with high levels in financial services and manufacturing and lowest use in agriculture, retail and personal services. More than half used email and the Internet, and about 20 per cent had some online sales.[50] Throughout Europe, the most important factor restricting SMEs in e-business is the feeling that it is not applicable to their products and would yield little benefit.[51]

■ International business

It is commonly thought that SMEs do not engage much in international business. Some 25 per cent sell outside the United Kingdom, with exports accounting for 6 per cent of their sales.[52] Yet experience is mixed. Westhead quotes surveys showing only 4 per cent of manufacturing firms in Merseyside export, compared with 70 per cent of small high-technology firms in south-east England. He found that exporting SMEs tended to be larger and run by more experienced people who felt that their local business environment was 'hostile'. They were pushed into seeking opportunities elsewhere.[53] This 'push' is one of the classical explanations for firms engaging in international business, *see* Chapter 4.

Apart from exporting, SMEs increasingly use joint ventures as the means of strengthening their position at home and penetrating developing overseas markets. Donckels and Lambrecht found alliances particularly frequent in building links between SMEs in industrialised and developing countries.[54] For the entrepreneur in the industrialised country, an alliance helps to overcome hurdles of market access, limited capital and political risk. The developing country counterpart, usually also an entrepreneur, gains technology, and technical and management skills. The authors go on to argue that, in such relations, entrepreneurs do best to team up with entrepreneurs rather than multinational enterprises.

Alliances between partners in nations at different stages of development can work very well. In business among developed countries, on the other hand, SMEs tend to be much more cautious. They prefer well-known partners and avoid co-operative agreements entailing high investments and risk. The latter point arises when partners are seen as potential competitors. Preferred alliances are, for example, with complementary firms that can share distribution channels to mutual advantage.[55]

◼ Managing finance

About 87 per cent of United Kingdom SMEs report few difficulties in raising the finance they need.[56] Those that do have problems, however, stated that growth was restricted or survival threatened. Manufacturing companies have most difficulty, probably because they usually need most capital. Many are undercapitalised and look to banks to provide a succession of overdraft arrangements. Compared with the average, small firms rely more on short-term loans, trade debtors and trade creditors. Their balance sheets show fewer fixed assets.[57] Almost the first business challenge is to find a way out of the cycle of high interest rates, lower profits and restricted growth. Under-capitalisation means not only exposure to sudden failure but also pressure to make poor decisions such as accepting barely profitable work or missing openings to purchase materials in bulk.

Banks

While banks are the first port of call for funds, it is often reported that entrepreneurs are dissatisfied with their service. Some can bypass restrictive or coercive lending rules by applying to initiatives such as the Loan Guarantee Scheme. These are, however, not available to all types of business and many are asked to provide personal guarantees or the backing of family property.

Chaston shows that differences in the *perceptions* of service quality, *see* Chapter 6, are important sources of dissatisfaction. In determining quality, banks stress accuracy and dependability while the SME would place willingness to help and prompt service at the top of the list. A further problem is the way that United Kingdom banks responded to the 'enterprise culture' by advertising and promoting service standards that were not, in practice, delivered.[58] Problems have abated as banks have improved. For example, they are now more likely to offer more stable 'term loans' instead of the unpredictable overdraft. They require collateral on only one-fifth of start-up loans.

A third of ethnic minority owners feel they have been discriminated against by banks.[59] Evidence is mixed. Deakins and Freel[60] report that Asians in the West Midlands can access commercial banks while African-Caribbeans experience problems. These perceptions could, however, arise from self-exclusion as black entrepreneurs assume that banks will reject their plans.[61]

Debtors

It is often reported that some large businesses obtain working capital by delaying payment to smaller suppliers. Depending on the survey, the average United Kingdom payment period is reported as being between 50 and 77 days. This compares with the 30 days widely accepted as the 'terms of trade' and a European Union average of 61 days. Other companies argue that deliberate delay is neither good business nor good ethical practice. Yet only 12 per cent of SMEs say they are paid within the 30-day period.[62]

There is a continual debate on a statutory duty to pay promptly and a right for creditors to charge interest. The 1998 Late Payment of Commercial Debts (Interest) Act, revised after an EU directive of 2000, means that all businesses can claim compensation and interest from all other businesses. The government remains, however, reluctant to establish penalties and face problems of enforcement. In any case, a small business needs its cash immediately, rather than awaiting a court order after it has folded. Therefore, good financial management practice is needed before problems arise. Initiatives such as the government-backed Better Payment Practice Campaign[63] are indicative of this trend.

Beyond these examples of banks and trade debtors, small businesses face many other problems of financial management. There is a lack of interest and awareness of finance among entrepreneurs, who, as we have seen, start out with the intention of exploiting innovations in technology or marketing. Improved preparation and training, combined with access to good, low-cost advice, may enhance the longevity of many micro and small businesses.

■ Planning

The role and value of planning in SMEs, especially for owner-managers, are a problem. On the one hand, it is evident that many small businesses do produce plans. This can be explained by their being needed when an SME is seeking funds from banks or venture capitalists or gaining a grant from a government agency. Deakins is not alone in seeing the necessity for at least elementary plans as a major advance over less formal discussions with bank managers.[64]

Producing plans because one has to convince a lender, however, is different from being committed to planning. As we will see in Chapter 8, planning is concerned with guiding and integrating the business and monitoring its performance. It is a process that must be both logical and flexible. We can see in Firms B and K of Exhibit 7.5 that they had planned their information systems to serve certain business needs yet could change as they learned that new possibilities became available.

In spite of the gains in performance available from planning, Richardson argues that many small firms are unable to overcome the following misconceptions and barriers.[65]

Misconceptions

- planning is for large firms with plentiful resources;
- relevant knowledge is to be obtained outside the organisation;
- the process requires special expertise and a structured, formal approach;
- benefits do not arise immediately;
- the output is a set of budgets spanning several years.

Barriers

- unwillingness of owner-managers to delegate and to learn and guide simultaneously;
- the pressure of the here-and-now;

▪ unavailability of current business information, especially financial. Obtaining regular flows requires a degree of analytical expertise that is often absent.

Progress is achieved by countering the misconceptions and overcoming the barriers, possibly through external training or other interventions. Given the apparent formality and inflexibility of it all, it is not surprising that many entrepreneurs intuitively resist planning, especially if it means making explicit written statements. Yet, if the firm is to grow successfully, it must face at some point the need to switch to using a wider group of professional managers. Formalising planning is part of this change.

Conclusion: the intertwining of enterprise and the economy

Starting from an examination of the nature of enterprise, we have studied what it means to become and be an entrepreneur. We saw that, while entrepreneurs were common in small businesses they could also be found in large ones. In the latter case, employers, recognising the need for flexibility in facing their environments, have policies to stimulate intrapreneurial activity.

Entrepreneurs and SMEs are needed by the economy both to make it work and to provide many innovations that will form the businesses and create the employment of the future. The need is reciprocal, because SMEs need, above all, a steadily growing economy. It continually generates openings and avoids recessions when these marginal businesses suffer. Government policy in stimulating the mystical 'enterprise culture' focused heavily on start-ups at the expense of high failure rates later. Now policy is becoming more discriminatory, seeking to back the few growing firms with high potential. Yet picking these winners is not easy.

Success is clearly linked to the competence of entrepreneurs. The problem for many companies is that they rely too heavily on the expertise of this one person. They score highly on flexibility and commitment yet fail on productivity, investment and continual innovation. SME investment in staff training, for instance, is often low.[66] From the nation's point of view, it may seem satisfactory to have a flexible business sector that can ebb and flow with the economic tide. Efficiency is also very important. Weak performance of SMEs hinders whole chains when they are heavily involved as subcontractors such as to the final assemblers of domestic appliances or vehicles, which compete globally.

QUICK CHECK

Can you ...

- Distinguish entrepreneur and intrapreneur.
- State the three SME categories used by the EU, giving key data on the sector.
- Summarise three classes of factors used to explain why people become entrepreneurs.
- Give four conditions under which small firms can gain advantages.

- Comment on government policies aimed at SMEs.
- State three important roles for the intrapreneur and show how they can be supported.
- Discuss common problems in the management of SMEs.

QUESTIONS

Chapter review	7.1	What are the similarities and differences between businesses run by entrepreneurs and SMEs in general?
	7.2	What are the arguments for and against the statement, 'Entrepreneurs are born and not made'?
	7.3	Explain the roles associated with intrapreneurs and suggest why they are so important in overcoming resistance to change.
Application	7.4	Using the information in the opening case, assess how far Flippe fits with the various models and categories of entrepreneur described in the chapter.
Investigation	7.5	Draw on sources such as the 'Enterprise' pages of serious newspapers, to investigate key factors in the business environment that help or hinder SMEs. Explain how far government policies have an effect on these factors.
	7.6	Draw up a brief schedule based on the 'What makes an entrepreneur?' section of this chapter. Use it to interview an owner-manager to build a picture of one person's reasons for being in business.

Storwell[67]

CLOSING CASE

For fifteen years, Storwell has specialised in the speedy delivery of high quality, keenly priced storage boxes. These are designed for stocking, filing and archiving of office materials, medical records and X-ray films. Recent additions to the range are bins for disposal of aerosols and broken glass. All products are made in tough corrugated board whose white, outer face carries the Storwell brand name and blank grids for lists of contents.

The business was founded in 1987 by its directors, Allan and Sandra Weddell. Neither had experience of small business nor was entrepreneurship running in their families. Allan had joined Lawton's office supplies company as sales representative in 1972. By 1982, he was divisional sales manager responsible for stationery and storage products. He found the job interesting at first. He cut the number of lines from 4500 to 300 while increasing the sales of higher-margin, branded lines. So, while volume began to fall, profit rose. Yet, by 1986 at the age of 40, Allan was dissatisfied. It was difficult to motivate and keep staff, especially as their numbers were reduced and territories expanded. Tight controls had become irksome. He felt the business should be launching new products but the directors were

reluctant to make the needed investments. There was no prospect of further promotion.

In 1986, Allan was invited, through a consultant, to be interviewed for a similar job at a rival company. On the way home he began to reflect on a question he had been asked: 'Why are you working?' At Christmas that year the family, the parents and two children in early secondary school, took stock. Sandra, who had worked in the Inland Revenue office before becoming a full-time mother, was finding it difficult to find good full-time employment. They wondered if they could set out on their own. The children were cautious. One observed how 'business seemed to make people unhappy'. After careful budgeting, however, the family agreed it could get by on half of the current expenditure if it needed to.

Storwell was registered in March. The business needed £30 000 to start, half from personal savings and half from an overdraft secured against shares inherited from Sandra's grandfather. Premises were to be rented at first. Allan resigned in June and started trading in September.

The Weddells' plan was to aim for national sales of a narrow product range. The boxes were stronger and cheaper than those offered by Lawton's, ▶

Eastlight and Fellows, makers of Bankers Box. Direct sales cut out the distributors' margin. Sales staff were to visit customers, supported by leaflets and mail shots. Two former Lawton's colleagues were brought in as commission-only sales representatives. Allan knew that the health sector had good potential so, from his prior experience, he wrote personal letters to buyers at each of the country's 380 major hospitals. About half the business now comes from the National Health Service. Schools, in contrast, were disappointing. Their orders were small and repeats slow. Mail shots to other markets used purchased mailing lists but these proved disappointing.

The business was launched at a good time. In spite of the first year sales being half of the budget, Storwell had three good years before the recession. While this slowed things down, a profit has been made every year. From 1990 onwards, growth was steady. The Weddells were able to buy the freehold of a larger warehouse, take foreign holidays and support the children through higher education.

Storwell's operations consist of buying in bulk from board manufacturers, storing and despatch. Each day, Allan makes up the consignments ready for collection by the parcel service. Sandra stays at home, also the office, to take calls and do the administration. Having budgeted for 80 days debtors, she is pleased that the average time for payment is around 45. Working hours for Allan and Sandra are reasonable as there is no business in the evenings or at weekends. During the day, however, someone has to be in the office all the time. Sales are now entirely by mail, telephone or fax.

In conversation, the Weddells claim little knowledge of designing and making corrugated cases. In this industry, it is normal for customers to discuss their needs with the board companies, which then produce prototypes. The X-ray and disposal boxes, added to the original range, were developed this way. There are no plans to move into other types of product.

Nowadays the Weddells recognise that their business gives them a satisfactory standard of living. They are planning retirement. 'Fifteen years ago we both needed interesting jobs. Now we have them and they provide a comfortable income. Will one or both of the children want to come in? Should we appoint a manager? Should we sell out?'

Questions

1 When asked about risk, Allan replied, 'There was little chance of it failing'. What does this tell you about the Weddells' attitude to risk? From the case and your wider knowledge, how could and can the business fail?

2 Comparing this case with theories in the chapter, how do you account for the Weddells' entrepreneurial behaviour? On what skills has success been built?

Bibliography

David Deakins and Mark Freel (2003) *Entrepreneurship and Small Firms* (3rd edition, Maidenhead: McGraw-Hill Education) and Sara Carter and Dylan Jones-Evans (eds) (2000) *Enterprise and Small Business: Principles, practice and policy* (Harlow: Financial Times Prentice Hall) give broad reviews of the issues covered in this chapter. The Small Business Service is a practical source, *see* **www.sbs.gov.uk/**. The BBC has a good series on starting business: **www.bbc.co.uk/business/work/issues/startingup.shtml**.

References

1 Le Parmentier, Arnaud (1996) 'Intrason, l'histoire d'une PME qui devrait passer sous contrôle étranger', *Le Monde*, 17 January, 14.

2 Burrows, Roger (1991) 'The discourse of the enterprise culture and the restructuring of Britain' in Curran, James A. and Blackburn, Robert A. (eds) *Paths of Enterprise: The future of small business*, London: Routledge, 29.

3 Deakins, David and Freel, Mark (2003) *Entrepreneurship and Small Firms*, 3rd edition, Maidenhead: McGraw-Hill Education.

4 Deakins, David (1996) *Entrepreneurship and Small Firms*, Maidenhead: McGraw-Hill, 24–5.

5 Shurry, Jan, Lomax, Steve and Vyakarnam, Shailendra (2002) *Household Survey of Entrepreneurship*, London: Small Business Service, Department of Trade and Industry, 18.

6 Hendry, C., Jones, A., Arthur, M. and Pettigrew, A. (1991) *Human resource development in small to medium sized enterprises*, Research Paper 88, Warwick Business School, University of Warwick, 6.

7 Storey, David (2002) 'Measuring the value of start-ups', *Financial Times: Inside Track Enterprise*, 22 August.

8 Bolton, Bill and Thompson, John (2000) *Entrepreneurs: Talent, Temperament, Technique*, Oxford: Butterworth–Heinemann, 11–47.

9 Deakins and Freel (2003) *op. cit.*

10 Dalmar, Frédéric (2000) 'The psychology of the entrepreneur' in Carter, Sara and Jones-Evans, Dylan (eds) *Enterprise and Small Business: Principles, Practice and Policy*, Harlow: Financial Times Prentice Hall, 140–5.

11 Chell, E., Haworth, J. and Brearley, S. (1991) *The Entrepreneurial Personality*, London: Routledge.

12 Keasey, Kevin and Watson, Robert (1993) *Small Firm Management: Ownership, finance and performance*, Oxford: Blackwell, 10–11.

13 Keasey and Watson (1993) *op. cit.*, 10.

14 Shurry, Lomax and Vyakarnam (2002) *op. cit.*, 20.

15 Armistead, Louise (2002) 'Grey-haired entrepreneurs lead the pack', *Sunday Times: Small Business*, 1 September.

16 Abbott, Steven and Hay, Michael (1996) *The 1996 Pulse Survey – survival of the fittest*, London: Arthur Andersen/Binder Hamlyn.

17 *Ibid.*, 6.

18 Costa, Shu Shu (1994) '100 years and counting', *Management Review*, **83(12)**, 32–4.

19 Office for National Statistics (2002) *Annual Local Area Labour Force Survey 2001/02*, London: ONS.

20 Ram, Monder and Barrett, Giles (2000) 'Ethnicity and Enterprise' in Carter, Sara and Jones-Evans, Dylan (eds) (2000) *op. cit.*, 188.

21 Shurry, Lomax and Vyakarnam (2002) *op. cit.*, 5, 25.

22 Mason, C. (1991) 'Spatial variations in enterprise: the geography of new firm formation' in Burrows, R. (ed.) *Deciphering the Enterprise Culture: Entrepreneurship, petty capitalism and the restructuring of Britain*, London: Routledge.

23 Shurry, Lomax and Vyakarnam (2002) *op. cit.*, 25.

24 Reynolds, Paul D., Camp, S. Michael, Bygrave, William D., Autio, Erkko and Hay, Michael (2001) *Global Entrepreneurship Monitor: 2001 Executive Report*, GEM, 4–5; **www.entreworld.org/gem2001**, accessed 1 February 2003.

25 Terazano, Emiko (1995) 'Daring to go it alone', *Financial Times*, 20 June, 18; Reynolds *et.al.* (2001) *op. cit.*, 42–3.

26 Based on Gibb, Allan (1988) 'The enterprise culture: threat or opportunity?' *Management Decision*, **26(4)**, 5–12.

27 Department of Trade and Industry (2002) *VAT registrations and deregistrations*, London: Small Business Service, DTI.

28 Department of Trade and Industry (2002) *Survival rates of VAT registered businesses*, Small Business Service, **www.sbs.gov.uk/statistics/**, accessed 1 February 2003.

29 £55 000 per annum in 2002.

30 Keasey and Watson (1993) *op. cit.*, 97.

31 Storey, D.J. (1994) *Understanding the Small Business Sector*, London: Routledge, 113–15.

32 Barclays Bank (2002) *Fast Growth Firms: Raising the bar*, Barclays Bank, September.

33 Harrison, John and Taylor, Bernard (1996) *Supergrowth Companies: Entrepreneurs in action*, Oxford: Butterworth–Heinemann.

34 Le Parmentier (1996) *op. cit.*, 14.

35 Countryside Alliance (2001) *Policy Handbook: The real rural agenda*, Countryside Alliance, 367 Kennington Road, London SE11 4PT; **www.countryside-alliance.org**, accessed 28 February 2003.

36 Government of South Africa (1995) *National Strategy for the Development and Promotion of Small Business in South Africa*, White paper, para. 2.3.3.

37 *Guardian* (1996) 'A lifeline for small firms – but they need macro-economic help even more', leading article, 12 March.

38 Pinchot, Gifford (1985) *Entrepreneuring*, New York: Harper & Row.

39 Jennings, Reg, Cox, Charles and Cooper, Cary L. (1994): *Business Elites: The psychology of entrepreneurs and intrapreneurs*, London: Routledge.

40 Masterson, Victoria (2000) 'Small price to hit the big time', *Scotsman*, 18 April.

41 Carrier, Camille (1994) 'Intrapreneurship in large firms and SMEs: a comparative study', *International Small Business Journal*, **12(4)**, April–June, 54–61.

42 Pinchot (1985) *op. cit.*

43 Jones-Evans, Dylan (2000) 'Intrapreneurship' in Carter, Sara and Jones-Evans, Dylan (eds) (2000) *op. cit.*, 247–51

44 Jones-Evans (2000) *op. cit.*, 252–4.

45 Hirsch, James S. (1990) 'Kodak effort at "Intrapreneurship" fails', *Wall Street Journal*, 17 August, B1.

46 Mitchell, Russell (1989) 'Masters of innovation: 3M keeps its new products coming', *Business Week*, 10 April, 58–63; for more examples from 3M, *see* **www.3m.com/about3M/innovation/firsts.jhtml**, accessed 1 March 2003.

47 Carrier (1994) *op. cit.*

48 Jones-Evans, Dylan (1996) 'Experience and entrepreneurship: technology based owner-managers in the UK', *Industrial Relations Journal*, **27(1)**, 39–54.

49 Naylor, J.B. and Williams, J. (1994) 'The successful use of IT in SMEs in Merseyside', *European Journal of Information Systems*, **3(1)**, 48–56.

50 Databuild (2001) *Regular survey of small business' opinions: First Survey – Final Report*, London: DTI, Small Business Service, August.

51 European Commission (2002) *Benchmarking national and regional e-business policies for SMEs*, E-business Policy Group, 28 June; **http://europa.eu.int/comm/ enterprise/ict/policy/benchmarking/final-report.pdf**, accessed 20 February 2003.

52 Databuild (2001) *op. cit.*, 32.

53 Westhead, Paul (1996) 'Exporting and non-exporting small firms in Great Britain – a matched pairs comparison', *International Journal of Enterprise Behaviour & Research*, **1(2)** 6–36.

54 Donckels, Rik and Lambrecht, Johan (1995) 'Joint ventures: no longer a mysterious word for SMEs from developed and developing countries', *International Small Business Journal*, **13(2)** January–March, 11–26.

55 Kaufmann, Friedrich (1995) 'Internationalisation via cooperation – strategies of SME', *International Small Business Journal*, **13(2)**, January–March, 27–33.

56 Databuild (2001) *op. cit.*, 8.

57 Storey (1994) *op. cit*, 215–16.

58 Chaston, Ian (1994) 'Rebuilding small business confidence by identifying and closing service gaps in the bank/SME relationship', *International Small Business Journal*, **13 (1)**, October–December, 54–62.

59 Databuild (2001) *op. cit.*, 10.

60 Deakins and Freel (2003) *op. cit.*, 93.

61 Guthrie, Jonathan (2002) 'Fair play and ethnic business: Access to finance', *Financial Times: Inside Track Enterprise*, 26 September.

62 Rapp, Roger (1996) 'Delays in payment fail to improve', *Independent*, 19 February, 18.

63 Better Payment Practice Group (2003) *A User's Guide to the amended late payment legislation*, **www.payon time.co.uk/**, accessed 12 March 2003.

64 Deakins (1996) *op. cit.*, 222.

65 Richardson, Bill (1995) 'In defence of business planning: why and how it still works for small firms and "corporations of small business units"', *Small Business and Enterprise Development*, **2(1)**, 41–57.

66 Marsh, Peter (1996) 'The ebb and flow that hampers Midlands: DTI says small companies suffer low productivity, investment and innovation', *Financial Times*, 11 July.

67 Thanks to Allan and Sandra Weddell, Directors of Storwell.

PART 3

Planning and decision making

Planning is the first stage of the cycle of planning, organising, implementing and controlling. This cycle forms the thread running through Chapters 8 to 19. To begin Part 3, Chapter 8 relates planning to uncertainty arising in the environment. Managers seek appropriate ways to handle what is frequently unknown. The result of the process is a statement of goals and objectives, together with the means by which they are to be achieved. We see how the plans of managers at various levels vary in scope and time horizon and consider how they should be fitted together. Strategic planning, usually conducted at a high level, implies a long-term perspective. We also see that plans go awry and see how managers can prepare for the worst.

Along with many other management tasks, making plans involves choices. Indeed, for many commentators, decision making is the core of management. Chapter 9 presents and compares two models that portray this process. Yet it is more than abstract calculation. The chapter examines the important roles played by individuals and groups and how they can so often go wrong. Finally, problems frequently require creative solutions. Therefore, managers face the question of how to simulate and harness creativity within the decision framework.

CHAPTER 8

Planning and strategic management

Chapter objectives

When you have finished studying this chapter, you should be able to:

- define a plan and explain the planning process, showing how it relates to the uncertain environment;

- explain levels of planning in the organisation and the links between them;

- classify the types of uncertainty faced by managers and outline how managers respond through forecasting and contingency and crisis planning;

- clarify the purposes of objectives and constraints, goals and mission statements, suggesting why each is needed;

- describe the main problems with, and barriers to, the use of objectives within organisations;

- describe and illustrate the main stages of the strategic management process for a strategic business unit;

- evaluate a mission statement;

- explain how SBUs fit into corporate-level strategy using the notion of portfolio management;

- summarise important limitations of the formal strategic management approach and their implications.

He's a real nowhere man,
Sitting in his nowhere land,
Making all his nowhere plans,
For nobody.

John Lennon and Paul McCartney, British musicians
(taken from *Nowhere Man*, © Northern Songs 1965)

Uncertain year for Halewood[1]

Employees at Ford's Halewood plant on Merseyside greeted 1997 with a feeling of uncertainty. In January, managers proposed to union representatives that, to cut costs, shifts should be cut from two to one. The company sought to remove more than 400 of the 4500 staff in assembly and 1100 on gearboxes. The move was part of a plan to turn round the company's European operations, which had lost £280 million in the third quarter of 1996.

The Escort model, built also at Valencia in Spain and Saarlouis in Germany, was in decline. Since quality problems at Halewood meant that its output served only the United Kingdom market, the plant was heavily dependent on home sales. Market share had halved from the peak of 12 per cent, when output had been 200 000. The previous two years, however, had seen short-time working as demand did not recover. Saarlouis was also in difficulties.

A new Escort model was due in 1998. In its highly competitive middle market, profit margins are always thin. Ford was considering whether to cut the number of plants to two, with Halewood switching to another model or closing. Low labour costs in Merseyside were insufficient to offset Halewood's low productivity, unfavourable location and militant workforce. A low-volume model with many variants, such as a people carrier, may suit a low-investment, low-labour-cost setting. To install equipment for a new Escort, and then operate one shift, would be wasteful.

Other stakeholders were involved. The government and local agencies had worked with Ford to persuade suppliers to establish facilities close to Halewood were the new Escort to be built. This would have been a *supplier park* with just-in-time deliveries following the rhythm of Ford's line. The government was concerned not only with local unemployment but also with the chronic unfavourable balance of trade in the automotive sector. Importing a further 125 000 Escorts would not have been good news.

Two weeks later, Ford announced that Halewood would not build the new model. About 1500 jobs were to go. For the rest, plans were incomplete and uncertainty over the Escort had been replaced with uncertainty over keeping any part of the site open. Unions organised a strike ballot among all 30 000 British workers. For European chairman Jac Nasser this move 'sharpened the mind' of managers. Within another fortnight, he named Halewood as the sole source for a new 'people carrier' from 2000. Short-term redundancies were scaled back from 1300 to 980 and made voluntary. Plans, insisted Nasser, had not been changed. Significant extra investment would attract, he hoped, a government grant of around £70 million.

By the end of March, the government announced £15 million of assistance to safeguard jobs. Jobs would be saved if the new vehicle output reached the planned 100 000 to 150 000. Yet, even this plan was changed. By January 1998, Nasser announced that Halewood was to build the brand new Jaguar X400 from 2001. The plant would become part of Ford's Jaguar subsidiary based at Coventry and had been chosen ahead of expansion in the Midlands or green field development elsewhere. The £300 million investment would safeguard the 2900 current assembly jobs, and create more opportunities once production started. Behind this good news for employees and the local district, some recognised the high risk. With its new models, Jaguar was moving into a very competitive market sector and would depend heavily on export success.

With the successful redevelopment of their Castle Bromwich site to take the new S-type, Jaguar managers had experience of operating in tough, traditional urban areas. They were confident they could reproduce this at Halewood. From producing poor quality Escorts, the £300 million would transform the plant to produce 100 000 X-types a year, more than doubling Jaguar's total output. Included in the scheme were measures to save energy and cut waste and emissions.

Transformation included training, occupying more than a million hours or 350 per person. 'It's not just about building a car, it's about integrating Jaguar into the community,' said Halewood's Operations Director. Jaguar needed 'a wholehearted commitment by the Halewood workforce to change the culture within the plant'. Everyone undertook: 10 days of basic skill training at the local college backed up by specific skills-training;

an intensive lean manufacturing week; a week of community service; and workshops on high-performance issues such as quality and teamwork, and adaptability.

Unions agreed that they had ceded some control, possibly seeing the change as their last chance. 'We see ourselves as working more in partnership rather than in confrontation. Jaguar's got a proud tradition and our people are buying into it.' Staff were responding to the call to engage brains and experience together with their hands. Nowadays, they stop the line to fix a quality problem. They time each other fitting a door trim and then fine-tune the process. They study videotapes to standardise methods and improve quality. Worldwide Jaguar sales rose sharply in 2002.

Introduction

The term *uncertain*, used in the case title, often refers to a future with gloomy prospects. Some at Halewood, and possibly all, were to lose their jobs. The opposite kind of future, with business booming and staff recruitment, gives employees a sense of certainty. These conditions mean they face the future with more optimism; they expect jobs to continue.

From the managers' point of view, however, prospects of growth or decline each present uncertainty. To cut production only to see sales pick up incurs unnecessary costs. To maintain output only to see the park fill with unsold models will soak up working capital for no extra revenue. Moreover, what should individual departments do? Should personnel stop recruiting, engineering delay new installations, or purchasing scale back its orders? Or should they all strive to squeeze that extra unit of production out of the lines?

While most managers do not want to spend time idly contemplating possibilities, they do need to decide where they want the organisation to be and how to get it there. Towards the end of the Escort years, output had been reduced through short-time working. When Ford confirmed the new levels, the scaling down was to be made permanent. Managers had to work together to make this happen. Dates and numbers had to be agreed both among the management functions and with the important stakeholders – trade unions, distributors and suppliers.

At a higher level, the case gives us hints of senior managers making decisions about a new model. With the launch less than two years away, development work would already have taken five; the decision on where to build which model was pressing. First, Halewood would get a people carrier, then a Jaguar. All these decisions were carried out and co-ordinated through plans. We pick up a sense of different time scales and different levels in the management hierarchy. Yet, this is not a planning machine, ticking away and co-ordinating activities as in the ideal bureaucracy. Organisations are seldom like this. At Ford, the threat of a strike knocked the plan off course. Long-range, strategic plans have to change to cope with uncertainty. Further, as Mintzberg observed, managers seldom engage in reflective, systematic planning, *see* Chapter 1. They do plan, but tend to do so 'on the fly', fitting it in amongst all their other activities and balancing a variety of pressures.

What is planning?

We are all planners. As individuals, we put together menus, make shopping lists, set out essays and revise for examinations, schedule our holidays and arrange for our retirement. With friends, we discuss where to go and what to do. We hope that someone has a sense of direction, and another a sense of time if there is a deadline. Often, plans are informal, including many in business. Whether formalised or not they give shape and purpose to our lives and enable us to gather resources and co-operate with others in achievement of ends. In larger organisations, plans are usually formal. A useful definition is:

> *A plan is an explicit statement of intention that identifies both objectives and the actions needed to achieve them.*

Note how the two aspects of this statement, objectives and action, must be integrated. Raffoni argues, 'The most creative, visionary strategic planning is useless if it isn't translated into action'.[2] The opposite, action without planning, matches many entrepreneurs, exploiting opportunities as they arise and planning intuitively, if at all. Large organisations cannot work like this.

The term *objective* presents some difficulty for the management student because it is frequently mixed with terms such as *goal, aim* and so on. Some authors offer shades of meaning while others, along with many managers, are less formal. At this stage, we shall stick to one term, objective. It is a statement of the future that the organisation wants to achieve. Good objectives identify both this state and *the time when it is to be reached*. In brief:

> *An objective is a defined, measurable result that can be achieved within a stated time.*

The planning process

Following from the definition of a plan:

> *Planning is the process of setting the objectives of an organisation and the means for their achievement.*

While some suggest that planning is the primary management function from which all activities follow, it is dependent on other managerial activities. For example, it goes hand in hand with control. The former sets the direction and points the organisation along its route; the latter ensures that the direction is maintained or, if that proves impossible, it warns of the need to choose a new direction. Together, planning and control form a cycle with four elements shown in Figure 8.1. While in practice it represents a continuous loop, we can start to read the diagram in a clockwise direction starting from *Formulate plans*. The planning process involves this stage and initiates the next – *Carry out plans*. Then follows control, with two elements – comparison and correction. Comparison requires observation of the out-comes of the action stage to discover how closely its results match the plan. The last stage, *Take corrective action*, depends on the mismatches between the plan and its achievement. Changes can be made to the way the plan is being carried out (*Review implementation*). Alternatively, if the gap is such that the plan itself needs review, then it can be adapted (*Review future plans*). This idea of a cycle of planning and control is a widespread, recurring one in management. In this chapter, we consider the planning aspects of the cycle. For the control elements that imply feedback to complete the loop, *see* Chapters 18 and 19.

Figure 8.1 also introduces the hierarchical nature of planning. To carry out plans at one level in the organisation usually means the creation of a series of more detailed planning and control cycles at the next lower level, and so on. The diagram illustrates this by proposing a set of nested loops. The *carry out plans* box contains a complete loop at the next level down, and so on. (The number is limited only by the printer's capability!) For instance, when rival mobile telephone companies, Vodafone and Cellnet, agreed a £42 million joint investment to upgrade communications throughout the Scottish Highlands, they began a series of nested planning and control loops. One team had to plan sites for up to 180 masts, working with local interest groups to optimise locations while minimising the impact on the natural environment. Others had to design the network, place construction orders and plan commissioning. Meanwhile, the two companies were developing their own competing marketing and service channels to reach the dispersed population. All this work had to be phased in as the geographical coverage spread.[3]

Levels of planning

It is common to identify three planning levels, although in practice there may be more or fewer. Typical terms are *strategic*, *intermediate* and *operational levels*.

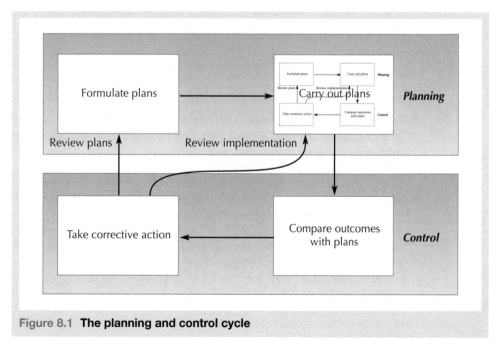

Figure 8.1 The planning and control cycle

They are shown in Exhibit 8.1, which also suggests the responsible managers and the time scale covered by each plan. Note that senior managers display a broader scope in their plans, in terms of both areas of the business and time span covered. The latter aspect is important. It is said they have longer *planning horizons* (also known as *time horizons*).

Exhibit 8.1 Three levels of planning

Planning level	Purpose	Managers	Time horizon
Strategic	Achieving business objectives through making long-term relationships between the organisation and its environment; obtaining key resources.	General managers and heads of functions.	One year to 10 years or more.
Intermediate	Giving direction to, and allocating resources among, sub-units and functions to give each clear objectives and to ensure co-ordination.	Middle managers working together and also with their departmental teams.	Six months to two years.
Operational	Accomplishing tasks with available resources to contribute to departmental objectives.	Operating unit managers, supervisors and individual staff.	A few hours to one year.

The planning horizon is the time that elapses between making and executing a plan.

Longer time horizons imply that strategic planners face greater uncertainty than intermediate or tactical planners do. Not only are forecasts likely to be less detailed over a longer period but also, put more simply, there is more time for unexpected events to occur.

The plans at the three levels have differing purposes. In general, senior managers are expected to face outwards, incorporating the uncertainty of the environment into their planning. Intermediate and operational plans can be more specific and concrete because they cover shorter periods and relate to the objectives given by the next higher level. In this way, agreement over objectives reduces uncertainty. The senior managers help to insulate the operating core of the organisation from the unpredictable environment. Another method at the operations level is that some linking, or boundary-spanning, roles are assigned to specialist departments. Examples are marketing or purchasing.

Links between levels

Effective planning is based on the co-ordination and linking of plans between levels. There are links that work both upwards and downwards:

- Downward links occur when managers at each level establish guidelines for their subordinates. As with other plans, these include statements of objectives and resources available for their achievement. Therefore, a *means–ends chain* is established in which each level provides the means to achieve the ends of the next higher one. This is illustrated by the mail-order film processing company of Figure 8.2. The operations director is responsible for the strategic objective to increase company profits over a period of three years. Figure 8.2 shows how the objectives of two other managers act as means to this end. The manager of the processing plant has, among others, the objective of reducing running costs. Another level below, a supervisor aims to find new ways of scheduling staff to reduce labour costs.

- Upward links are seen in the way managers apply information on the capacity and capability of their departments in formulating plans. Otherwise, plans would be unrealistic. For instance, the operations director of Figure 8.2 could not support

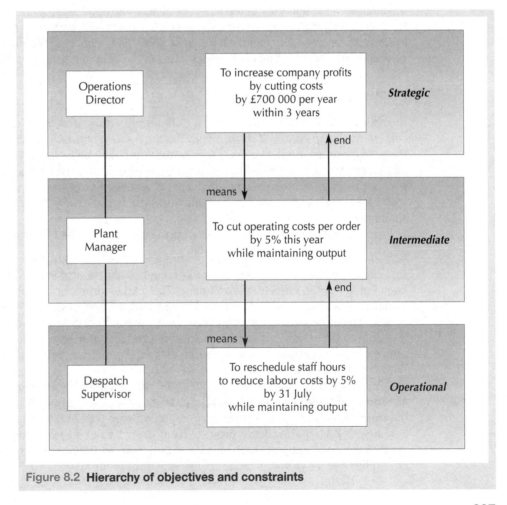

Figure 8.2 **Hierarchy of objectives and constraints**

an over-ambitious objective just to satisfy demands of external stakeholders, such as a holding company. There must be a test of feasibility, that is whether higher profits can be achieved within the time horizon.

Integration of planning involves both types of link. Senior managers provide leadership, setting out the directions the organisation should follow. This is known as *top-down planning*. At the same time they consult with their teams to find out what is feasible and what ideas the members have for change. This is called *bottom-up planning*. Integration of these styles can be achieved informally although, in large organisations, there may be formal planning cycles.

Planning under uncertainty

Lest we overstress the notion of planning systems running like clockwork, we should examine the relationship of uncertainty to planning in a little more detail. Organisations are continuously challenged to achieve success in spite of the actions of competitors, governments and other major influences in their environments. Planning does not to try to eliminate uncertainty, as in the five-year plans of Soviet economies, but to respond to it. In relatively stable environments, a single, integrated plan may be relevant and achievable. On the other hand, where great uncertainty abounds, the organisation must be prepared to adapt, using contingency plans in the light of emerging difficulties.

■ Types of uncertainty

Regarding the environment, Milliken defined uncertainty as *an individual's perceived inability to predict an organisation's environment accurately*. It arises from two sources. First, the necessary information may be lacking. This would affect all managers in the business in similar ways. Second, the person may not be able to sort out relevant and irrelevant data. This is a reflection of the individual's capability.[4] The opening case at Ford's Halewood plant illustrates both aspects, as we shall now see.

From her starting definition, Milliken proposed three types of uncertainty.

■ *State uncertainty: how things are and how they are changing*
Difficulties of both data collection and perception cause problems when it comes to knowing about the current environment. This makes prediction doubly difficult. For instance, Ford had good data on market share of the Escort model. Arising from car registrations, the data are shared throughout the industry. Yet, the company knows less about purchasers' attitudes towards its products and how such results suggest future buying decisions. These would be critical in predicting whether the downward sales trend was set to continue.

Sometimes state uncertainty is concerned with timing. The retraining programme at Halewood took place in the interregnum between two very different models. For the training to be most effective, its completion would fit in with the start-up of the new lines. Other parts of the project, from design to plant investment, would also require careful timing and all aspects would have to fit in with the model launch. Possibilities of delay in any aspect cause uncertainty for all.

■ *Effect uncertainty: how outside changes affect the organisation*

Global companies such as Ford have to cope with fluctuating exchange rates and government financial policies as well as the strategies of their competitors. While the company has experience of operating under these conditions, it will always be unsure of the effect of major changes.

■ *Response uncertainty: knowing neither choices nor their effect*

The manager does not know decision options in advance or cannot predict how various elements in the environment will respond. At Ford, despite intensive market research, managers could not be sure of how well customers would receive the new Jaguar. Prior experience of model launches would only be a rough guide as the 'baby Jag' was aimed at a new segment and volumes sought were high.

In any situation, perceptions of the different types of uncertainty surround the manager's decisions. In the last example, the managers could not predict demand very closely. Therefore, they would have alternative actions, such as making extra promotional efforts, to ensure a favourable reception by the market. This is one of the two choices for managers facing uncertainty

■ Forecasting to counter uncertainty

To counter uncertainty, managers can first try to reduce it, either by improving the quality of forecasts or, when doubt stems from their own lack of capability, through training in interpretive skills. Second, they try to absorb unexpected changes in the environment through a pattern of contingency plans. We shall study contingency later in the chapter but first we shall look at the role of forecasting. Exhibit 8.2 illustrates the need for a long-range forecast.[5]

Exhibit 8.2 How much runway capacity?

Aircraft passenger demand has grown at a steady 5 per cent for many years. Although events from price changes to outbreaks of war have had some effect on this figure, the upward trend has usually returned. Demand in south-east England, however, is expected to grow more slowly. For the period 2000 to 2030, the government growth forecast (from 114 million to 300 million) represents 3.3 per cent annually. Faced with this expansion, its options include permitting new runways at Heathrow, Gatwick or Stansted, or new construction at Cliffe. Such investment would be matched by expansion in connecting links. For example, two extra runways at Gatwick would require extra railway capacity and widening the M23 motorway. Protesters saw these plans as disastrous, challenging the government to constrain growth by removing tax concessions and other benefits.[6]

One snag is that a small error in the forecast, compounded over such a long period, would have a major effect on plans. If growth turned out at 5 per cent, demand would reach almost 500 million, while at 2 per cent, it would be 200 million.

Forecasts underpin all planning. They may be based on implicit thinking habits or on specially designed models that bring together streams of data into a program or algorithm. Usually the planner has a *time horizon* in mind. This relates to the period between making the plan and its coming into action. A forecast of passenger movements in 2030 differs from the supervisor working out today's route for a delivery van. Although varying in scope, two broad classes of forecast, qualitative and quantitative, still apply. They were discussed in Chapter 2.

Objectives, goals and mission

We noted earlier how the term *objective* is often used interchangeably with goal and aim, both in the literature and by managers. One distinction, however, is common and useful. Whereas objectives are specific statements with a time scale, goals refer more generally to desirable ends without measures of value or time.

> *A goal is a future state that the organisation is trying to achieve.*

Goals are useful when it is meaningful to express the desired state yet impracticable to suggest when it is to be achieved. The goal of New Zealand Telecom, for example, is to become 'the best performing, customer focused online and communications company in Australasia'.[7] Given the uncertain environment it would be rash to include a date in this statement. Usually, goals relate to broader ideas and higher levels of the organisation. They are often included in mission statements.

Mission statements

Although there are many views on what they should contain, mission statements summarise a hierarchy of intentions for the organisation to create a shared, clear sense of purpose. Drawing on the concept of *strategic intent*,[8] Denton[9] identifies these contents:

- A broad vision of what the organisation ought to be. This involves aspirations that appeal to the values, beliefs and emotions of members.
- An identity, represented by a statement of purpose, distinctiveness and core values.
- Goals and objectives.

While some organisations produce detailed mission statements covering the above factors, others prefer brief phrases. Matsushita, whose brands include Panasonic and Technics, does both. It includes: a brief statement of vision – *an electronic enterprise unlike any other in the world* – a summary of strategic intent; an exhortation to all employees to join in; and a slogan to capture the sense of mission.[10] Exhibit 8.3 picks out key details.

Why spend time crafting a short statement summarising the complexity of a large corporation? Advocates argue that the result is less important than the process used to achieve it. This can both be unifying and give direction. Yet, since the organisation is large and diverse, a mission statement should be couched in broad terms. This enables both inclusion of many stakeholders and creative interpretation. Tarnow proposes a practical model – a 'unifying action declaration' (UAD) – with three properties. It *suggests an action, identifies it only vaguely* and includes a *social categorisation*.[11] The latter links organisational membership back to the action. The model helps us

Exhibit 8.3 Matsushita's vision and mission

Matsushita will be an *electronic enterprise unlike any other in the world*. It will achieve this through:

- Business domain-based structure
- Creation of V-products (A ¥1,200 billion target for 90 new high value products)
- 'Black-box' technologies that cannot be copied easily
- Global strategy to earn 60 per cent of profits overseas
- Management focusing on cash flows
- Management quality innovation
- 'Flat & Web' organization
- Increased brand value

The company adopted the 2004 management slogan:

Each of Us Acting with the Spirit of a Founder.

deconstruct Matsushita's 2004 slogan: it suggests that everyone's contribution is necessary and valued; it invites entrepreneurial commitment; and, in stressing 'each of us', implies that being a member of this electronic enterprise is rather special.

Others warn against a formulaic approach to mission statements. The document 'gets tacked up on the wall and promptly forgotten'.[12] Mullane reports that mission statements do not transform behaviour by themselves. Yet, if developed with the intention of creating internal unity, and connected with other elements of the hierarchy of vision and objectives, mission statements are valuable. Similarly, Bart and colleagues stress that only when employees feel the sense of mission, through involvement in its development and execution, will it have a beneficial effect.[13]

■ What are objectives, goals and mission statements for?

Objectives, goals and a sense of mission, therefore, can bring important benefits within the organisation and send messages to wider audiences. Within the organisation, they provide:

■ *Unity of direction*

Objectives support a sense of direction. They focus members' attention on targets and give an opportunity to co-ordinate effort in achieving them. Without such clarification, each manager may interpret situations differently and find it difficult to act in unison.

■ *Basis of plans and decisions*

Good objectives help in the production of good plans. They help in choosing priorities, since some objectives will be more urgent or more vital to a company's success than others. Identification of these 'must-do' objectives separates them from others that can be postponed if resources are unavailable.

Objectives offer criteria that can be applied in decision making. Many techniques of operations management, for example, depend for their application on a framework of objectives. Cost is often the overriding criterion. For example, scheduling techniques seek to achieve delivery times at least cost.

■ *Motivation*

The process of objective setting includes encouraging employees to commit themselves to the ends of the organisation. Beyond building initial commitment, achievable objectives offer the individual a sense of personal achievement. As we shall see in Chapter 11, motivation needs more than a statement of objectives. Yet, without one, motivation would be worthless.

■ *Basis of control*

Through clarifying the performance that is expected, objectives become the basis for control. Used in the bottom right-hand cell of Figure 8.1, they are the criteria on which comparisons between outcomes and plans are made. They determine what is to be measured and set the corresponding performance standards.

Beyond these internal purposes, declarations of objectives and goals are often addressed to wider audiences. When incorporated into mission statements, they signify legitimacy to stakeholders from investors to customers and suppliers. It is intended that these interest groups then regard the organisation in a favourable light and accept its function. The Body Shop is a successful global business that incorporates the values of its founder, Anita Roddick. Strong, clear statements of the company's aims cover not only what business it is in but also how it wishes to carry it out and whom it prefers to recruit as employees or suppliers. Examples of Roddick's own business values, incorporated in the goals of The Body Shop, are given in Exhibit 8.4.[14]

Exhibit 8.4 Body *and* Soul

'... as far as I am concerned the business has existed for one reason only – to allow us to use our success to act as a force for social change, to continue the education and consciousness-raising of our staff, to assist development in the Third World and, above all, to help protect the environment.'

'We want to spark conversations with our customers, not browbeat them to buy.'

'One of our main responsibilities is to allow our employees to grow, to give themselves a chance of fulfilling themselves and enhancing the world around them.'

'I have never been able to separate The Body Shop from my own personal values.'

■ Good objectives

From our definition, we can see that a good objective should be couched in quantitative terms, both in measuring the outcome and in the length of time before achievement. Furthermore, since objectives represent formal agreements over means and ends, a written record is advantageous. In summary, the tests of a good objective are threefold:

■ Is the desired result clearly stated?

■ Is it possible to measure whether the result has been achieved?

■ Is the time scale made clear?

The examples given in Figure 8.2 all satisfy these tests. For instance, the plant manager is committed to reduce the ratio of operating costs to orders by 5 per cent. We can infer that the ratio is measured in control systems that collect costs and count orders. The time scale for the change is also set down.

Figure 8.2 brings out a further aspect related to objectives, namely *constraints*. From the example of the despatch supervisor, we see that the objective is 'To reschedule staff hours ... *while maintaining output*'. It would be easy for a line manager to cut staff hours if output was also permitted to fall. The italicised part of the statement, however, mentions a constraint on the cost cutting. Activity must remain at its previous level. Constraints such as this set the limits within which the objective must be achieved.

Constraints can be stated or implied. Explicit references are made to remove doubt in key areas; implied constraints arise from the shared understandings among managers, that is the culture and conventions of the organisation.

■ Problems with objectives

Conflict

In contrast to the examples of single objectives used so far, managers are usually faced with multiple objectives that may be in conflict. This is the managerial equivalent of jugglers 'keeping all the plates in the air'. Most can juggle with one, focusing attention and energy upon its movement. The task becomes more challenging with more plates. Keeping one going often means another's fall.

Conflict may be direct. For example, when choosing outputs managers have to balance efficiency and effectiveness, or work speed and quality, or profit margin and sales volume. On the other hand, conflict may be indirect, as when activities compete for a constraint. Examples are: two contracts requiring the same item of plant; several customers asking for delivery simultaneously; or too many deadlines for the manager to meet.

Measurability

The achievement of some managerial tasks is difficult to measure. Many managers have to combine such tasks as ensuring that short-term schedules are achieved with other aspects such as developing staff and work teams, improving quality and work processes, and so on. Having a mix of measurable and unmeasurable objectives creates the temptation of concentrating on the former in order to look good. There is the related problem of *measurementship*, where employees deliberately set out to agree low objectives so they can appear good at the period end review.

Means–ends confusion

Difficulties arise when the objective becomes an end in itself, forgetting its contribution to the wider effort. This is especially true if achievement is the basis of rewards. There have been many cases of stakeholders or leaders demanding improvements in one aspect while forgetting links with equally vital objectives or constraints. In extreme cases, much human ingenuity is devoted to reporting success and hiding failure. For example, in the public sector, policy accomplishment is often through special programmes or 'drives' that fail to incorporate a 'bottom-up' engagement of staff. With weaknesses in record keeping and income to their hospitals dependent on the results, the behaviour of some managers in Exhibit 8.5 is not surprising. Commenting on such cases, Duckworth said, 'So what's the problem with targets?

Nothing in principle. They are a well-tried means of creating organisational focus, mobilising people and providing a concrete measure of success. The problem arises when instead of the target being simply a way of calibrating the delivery of substance, meeting the target itself becomes the goal.'[15]

Exhibit 8.5 Playing a waiting game[16]

Credibility of government claims to be reducing waiting lists was put in doubt by a 2003 spot check of 41 National Health Service hospitals. Three had fiddled the figures, 19 had made mistakes and 15 had system weaknesses that increased the likelihood of misreporting. South Manchester University Hospitals Trust reported 6766 patients on its list, with none waiting longer than 18 months (the target maximum). Investigation revealed 7475 patients, with 27 waiting too long. Managers believed that failure to meet targets would lead to reduced funding and hence greater difficulty in achieving them.

Change

According to the formal description set out here, each objective contributes to the general plan of the organisation. This immediately raises the question of what happens when circumstances change. In stable environments, planning can be done with confidence but, if they are unstable, no sooner is the plan created than it is out of date. Therefore, the idea of a master plan for an organisation is a shaky one. Furthermore, at the individual level, detailed objectives lose their value if subject to change outside the manager's control. Pursuing an objective may become irrelevant. Such situations need continual review and a more flexible approach to setting objectives and plans.

▧ Problems with planning

Extending these points on problems with objectives, we can note common practices that hinder successful planning. These are:

▪ *Inappropriate use of planning specialists*
Given the complexity that planning can often involve, there is a temptation to delegate much of the activity to specialists. Only they, it is thought, can assemble and handle the range and quantity of data needed. This may be satisfactory as long as the specialists' role is to support those line managers who have to put the plans into practice. Often, however, a planning department becomes large, self-interested and distant from the line managers. Planning becomes an end in itself with a stress on technical expertise and use of techniques for their own sake. The plans, once delivered to the line managers, are immediately filed in their bottom drawers.

▪ *Lukewarm top management commitment*
Senior managers must not only provide the direction for the business, but also encourage and become involved in the process. It should be something that all managers do. Reasons for lack of involvement could be low morale, conflict among directors, a too powerful strategic planning group or the dominance of one charismatic leader.

■ *Lack of planning expertise*

Many managers have limited experience of collecting and interpreting data related to plans. To them, planning techniques may appear intimidating, or they may be content with simple recipes that give less than the best results. Line managers must, however, both co-operate with and lead planning specialists, ensuring that reality is brought to what would otherwise be abstract modelling of the company's future.

Contingencies and crises

Robert Burns wrote, 'The best laid schemes o' mice an' men gang aft a-gley'.[17] Even the best managed companies find that things go wrong because their environments change in unexpected ways, they do not achieve their targets or they simply make mistakes. The so-called 'Murphy's laws' capture the problem succinctly:

■ anything that can go wrong will go wrong;

■ some things that cannot go wrong will go wrong;

■ when things go wrong, they will do so at the worst possible times.

Good planners prepare as far as possible for these cases. For example, facing the diversion of shipping from the Suez Canal if war broke out, some European importers increased stocks as a buffer against longer delivery times. This is a *contingency plan*, often known as 'Plan B'. Clearly, cost and time prevent plans being made for every eventuality so they are only created for significant cases. IBM's

---

Exhibit 8.6 IBM's plans *gang a-gley*

Info '96 was the system provided by IBM for the Atlanta Olympic Games. It was a high-risk project: if it went well, few would notice; if badly, negative publicity would result.

In the first week of the games, the age of a 21-year-old athlete was given as 97, a French fencer was said to have run faster than Michael Johnson, one boxer seemed to be 60 cm tall while another topped 7 metres! Yet, these 'glitches' were minor compared with what happened behind the scenes. Twelve international news agencies, who had each paid $10 000 for the results service, were fed inaccurate and late data. Deadlines were missed; newspapers came out with incomplete results. Some athletes relied on the service to tell them starting times only to miss their events and be disqualified.

The IBM operations centre was a 1000-square-metre windowless hall in a location kept secret for fear of sabotage. There was no shortage of hardware including four mainframe systems, 80 mini computers and 7000 lap-tops. Many of the last were manned by volunteers whom IBM blamed for the initial errors. After these mistakes, the company flew in expert reinforcements with the effect of making the pressure cooker atmosphere worse. With no spare hotel rooms, the new staff had to put up on bunk beds in the centre.

In addition to its operations, IBM had paid $40 million to be an official Olympic sponsor. It had invited senior managers from client companies to the Games and had planned a tie-in media campaign. The advertising was dropped.

IBM saw that it had failed to run enough simulated tests on its ambitious exercise in integrated communications. Eventually things improved and there was barely a problem during the last week. Other problems at the Games, from an explosion to the chaotic transport system, overtook the negative publicity. IBM won the contract for Sydney 2000.

problems at the Atlanta Olympic Games in 1996 seemed to stem from hurried preparation and inadequate contingency plans, *see* Exhibit 8.6.[18]

Contingency plans can involve minor changes, such as devoting extra resources to activities that fall behind in a project, or altering schedules when a customer changes an order call-off. At the operational level, adjustments are commonplace, planners continually updating instructions as new information comes in. Other events can be more threatening to the organisation's survival and, while an organisation cannot prepare in detail for every eventuality, they rehearse *crisis management* procedures. British Airways has contingency plans for more than a hundred forms of crisis; Procter & Gamble has manuals on every desk in the marketing and communications departments and employs *agents provocateurs* to test its defences.[19]

Crisis plans may be well rehearsed for anticipated threatening situations. In general, however, good management involves centralising all control on a well-trained team. Their task is to obtain as much information as possible, act as the only spokespersons for the organisation and act quickly and decisively to bring the crisis under control. McDonald's learned from earlier experiences of Johnson & Johnson and Perrier when it responded quickly to the CJD crisis, *see* Exhibit 8.7. After an incident of sabotage, J&J withdrew its entire stock of the painkiller Tylenol from the shelves; Perrier did the same after benzene contamination of its water. Both explained in advertisements what had happened.

Exhibit 8.7 Customers beef about beef

In 1995, as the debate over 'mad cow' disease grew in intensity, McDonald's spent three months persuading customers its beef was safe. Like its main rivals, it used neither offal nor meat mechanically stripped from carcasses. Then, in March 1996, when the government belatedly admitted that there could be a link between BSE and Creutzfeldt-Jakob Disease (CJD) in humans, the company stopped its Big Macs. This response was not to 'scientific evidence' but to consumer emotion. It took five days to arrange for alternative supplies to be brought in from continental Europe. Its rivals Burger King, on the other hand, decided to wait until it had alternatives ready before switching sources. The outcome was a reported increase in McDonald's 70 per cent market share.

Compared with the normal loyalty of customers who are satisfied with products and service, if something goes badly wrong and the company handles it courteously and effectively, loyalty can rise substantially.[20] On the other hand, companies with a reputation for covering up face an uphill task when crises arise. Mercedes-Benz damaged its reputation with its reaction to the *moose test, see* Exhibit 8.8.

Responding, therefore, to the lessons of Murphy's laws, companies should, through planning:

- minimise the possibilities of things going wrong;
- minimise the impact if things go wrong;
- have alternatives available if things go wrong;
- have well-trained teams available if crises arise.

Exhibit 8.8 Mercedes' moose trap[21]

In September 1997, European journalists assembled to choose their 'Car of the Year'. The clear favourite, the new Mercedes A-class, did not behave well. Two wheels kept leaving the ground when swerving at normal speeds. Journalists then noticed how the test cars disappeared overnight and alleged that Mercedes-Benz was tinkering to get them through the test. On 21 October, a Swedish test included swerving manoeuvres to simulate avoiding wildlife. Four journalists were slightly injured when an A-class toppled at only 40 miles per hour, the first ever failure at that speed.

Desperate to make a good impression at the concurrent Tokyo motor show, Mercedes-Benz made no comment on these incidents, noting, on 23 October, that it was sending experts to investigate. By 29 October, Mercedes-Benz was citing German evidence that the A-class had been declared stable after 8 million kilometres of testing. Lacking details, correspondents began repeating the 'moose test' for themselves. By early November, they were sure that the car was unstable and the press was full of adverse comment. Forced at last to admit the defect, the company blamed it on the Goodyear tyres. Sales would continue with changed tyres and all cars would be fitted with the electronic stability programme reserved for the top models. This move, however, did not contain the crisis; critics pointed out that it was the assembler's responsibility to fit appropriate tyres. On 12 November, Mercedes admitted the fault and suspended production for three months. An Alfa-Romeo was the car of the year.

Strategic management

While focusing on the uncertainties faced by staff at one plant, the opening case offers insight into aspects of strategic management. We see managers making decisions on major issues including Ford's acquisition of Jaguar, the launch of the X-series, selection of the Halewood plant for assembly, transformation of that plant, new industrial relations policies, training strategies and shop floor organisation.

■ Strategic thinking

This is a picture of strategy in the making. Three themes can be picked out:

■ *The long term*

Thinking strategically means raising one's eyes from day-to-day problems to consider how the relationship between the organisation and its environment is shaping up for the long term. Chapter 2 showed how the environment changes in many directions. The strategist looks for patterns, which often at first comprise weak signals or 'straws in the wind'. Having formed a judgement on trends, the strategist begins the search for how the organisation should act for the best. In large organisations, internal change can be slow and costly, so being able to think as far ahead as possible is valuable.

We cannot define *long term* precisely. It depends on the speed of change, for 'A week is a long time in politics'.[22] Car assembly develops more slowly than the mobile telephone industry, for example, although we must not underestimate global competition, which imposes pressure to improve designs, raise quality and reduce waste in the manufacturing chain.

■ *Big issues*

Filtering issues of importance from the mass of detailed data is a skill possessed by good strategists. Many managers succeed through attention to detail, but strategic thinking means converting a deep awareness of trends into an overall picture of the world and how the organisation should relate to it. From being a volume producer of middle-range cars, Ford has shifted its focus towards premium brands, following the long-term growth of customers willing to pay more for their cars.

■ *Interdependency*

The strategist is able to place the big issues on a mental map. Understanding the way that each links to the others enables the manager to see the map as it changes. Nasser, at Ford, saw that the Escort could not sustain three plants and Jaguar had insufficient capacity for its ambitions. Linking these points with the 'wake-up call' of a strike threat, he cancelled that plan and placed the X-series at Halewood.

Interdependency also shows through when it is realised that different companies pursue different strategies. If they are well managed each will have studied the business environment and come to different conclusions about the best way to proceed. This stems from three factors: different perceptions of uncertainty; unique capabilities; and organisation cultures that support or resist relevant changes.

■ Strategic management

> *Strategic management is the systematic application of strategic thinking to the development of the organisation within its environment.*

Strategic management is important because it manages the basic issues that influence long-term success. We shall picture the process as having four stages: analysis, selection, implementation and control. They can be summarised as:

■ Strategic analysis is the stage of data collection and interpretation. The manager assesses how well the organisation is doing within its changing environment. Questions are asked about the value that the organisation offers to all its stakeholders. There is an appraisal of the resources available and how well they are arranged to provide this value.

■ Strategy selection involves the generation of possible choices for the future. Then, the chosen strategy will build on the capabilities or strengths of the organisation compared with the environment. It will look to develop and exploit relative advantages and sustain them over time.

■ Strategy implementation means taking the chosen pattern and ensuring that it is carried out through the organisation. This involves many aspects, from structure to leadership and innovation to communication. They appear in later chapters.

■ Strategic control is required, just as control is needed in any management process, *see* Chapters 18 and 19. Since every aspect of strategy is in a state of flux, managers need to continually monitor the outcomes of their choices to adapt the policies or the way they are carried out.

A sketch of the process is shown in Figure 8.3. This has much in common with the planning and control model of Figure 8.1 but is set out this way to emphasise the

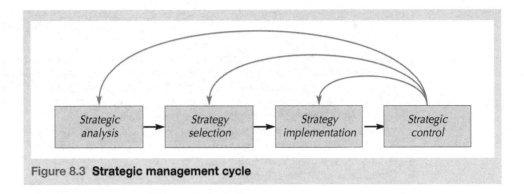

Figure 8.3 **Strategic management cycle**

details of strategic management. Before looking at the details, however, we need to set the process in the context of the whole organisation.

■ Corporate, business and functional strategies

Just as planning has interlinked levels, so does strategic management. Strategists think in terms of three levels, corporate, business and functional.

> *Corporate strategy is concerned with the question: What businesses should we be in?*

It looks at the business as a whole and considers the combination of businesses, seen in terms of products, markets, nations, technologies and so on that best suits the long-term aims of the stakeholders. Strategic thinking was formally applied first to the large, multidivisional corporations that lacked overall direction. Their divisions were spread across industries and nations. Each faced different challenges and each was presented with different opportunities. Planners had to decide where to invest funds for the best return, where to build or acquire new businesses and where to pull out if prospects were poor. They were managing a *portfolio* of businesses. An example appears in Exhibit 8.9.

While corporate strategy remains important, overemphasis led to dissatisfaction. First, better informed investors preferred to build their own portfolios; they could spread financial risk just as well as the managers of the portfolio businesses. Second, in their planning, managers ignored the details of each unit. There is an analogy with the remote general running a war, to whom military divisions are counters, pushed around a map. Meanwhile, what happens in the field, where experienced officers, integrated support and properly equipped troops are lacking, bears little resemblance to the grand strategies of headquarters.

Nowadays, strategists think of *strategic business units*, SBUs. These are businesses in their own right, responsible for a defined product range and market. While a function of headquarters is to integrate relevant SBU activities, each is semi-independent for the purposes of *business-level strategic management*.

> *Business strategy is concerned with the question: How do we succeed in this particular business?*

> **Exhibit 8.9 Hilton Group: attraction of opposites?[23]**
>
> After Hilton merged with Ladbroke, buoyant income from the former's hotels softened the impact of the National Lottery on the latter's betting business. Years later, the compliment was being repaid. Ladbroke was thriving after deregulation and tax changes in betting, while hotels were suffering. Decline in business travel since 2001 had accelerated through weak consumer spending and the threat of war.
>
> Analysts questioned the benefit of the relationship. With little chance of operating synergy, such as sharing marketing, resources or supplies, the Hilton and Ladbroke chains work independently. Investors build their own portfolios and see the Hilton Group as an unnecessary intermediary.

This question is asked of every SBU. For example, Ford has many SBUs such as Ford Europe, Volvo, Jaguar, Land Rover and Mazda. Each is required to plan new cars to succeed in its chosen markets. At the same time, they maximise the use of common components, and share supply chains and distribution networks.

Strategists often go down one more level, thinking in terms of functions. As with the means–ends chain of planning in general, *functional strategies* are the means by which business strategies are carried out.

> *Functional strategy is concerned with the question: How does this function contribute to the business strategy?*

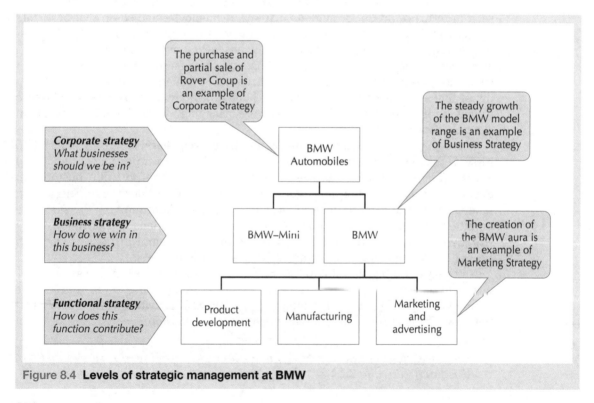

Figure 8.4 **Levels of strategic management at BMW**

Figure 8.4 summarises the three levels, using BMW as an example. This company has managed to capture the niche for cars for up-and-coming managers and professionals. Its products have the aura of being desirable and attainable. To achieve the transformation from a 1960s company making Italian bubble cars under licence, BMW has pursued consistent and steady product development, manufacturing and marketing strategies. It first pitched for the executive market below Mercedes with 2-litre saloons; the 7-series followed and took on its rival directly; then came the 3-series of smaller cars. Manufacturing has consistently focused on quality, at the expense of higher costs. Marketing has created an air of exclusiveness and desirability even though annual output has reached about 600 000 units.[24]

Depending on the level in the organisation, the focus of strategy ranges from achieving an overall balance in the business to optimising the contribution of each section. To examine the strategy management process in more detail we shall concentrate on the business level.

Business strategy

Figure 8.5 expands the sketch of Figure 8.3. It shows the elements of each stage of the strategic management process, how they link to form a chain, and how strategic control enables, through feedback of information about outcomes, the elements to be reviewed and changed.

Strategic analysis

This stage, sometimes called *situational analysis*, can be seen as a strategic check-up. Managers take a good look at their mission, the environment in which they operate and their organisation itself. While we start with mission, the analysis should be seen as a continual, integrated process and each element cannot be checked without awareness of the others. In other words, mission, environment and resources form a tightly interrelated system.

Mission, goals and strategy

We saw earlier how the direction of an organisation is expressed in terms of its mission. Now we consider a further aspect, how well it links with strategy, values and behaviour. The Ashridge Mission Model offers a benchmark for this assessment. It tests how far a strong sense of mission holds 'four elements ... tightly together, resonating and reinforcing each other'.[25] The elements are: mission, values, strategy and standards of behaviour. These are applied to the furniture retailer IKEA in Figure 8.6.[26] The founder of IKEA, Ingvar Kamprad, had a strong belief in the way any business should be conducted and this he incorporated in his 'testament', which guides the business today.

We can use the Ashridge model in two aspects of the check-up. First, are the elements of the model consistent? We see clues at IKEA, for example in the way that not only is low cost delivered at factory and store level but also designs are made for use throughout the world. There is little attempt at local variation. Another example is the way the Swedish identity is maintained. Informal working relationships, typical of Sweden, are reinforced by the leadership style of managers, dress codes and office layouts. Almost the entire design team is Swedish. All travel economy class.

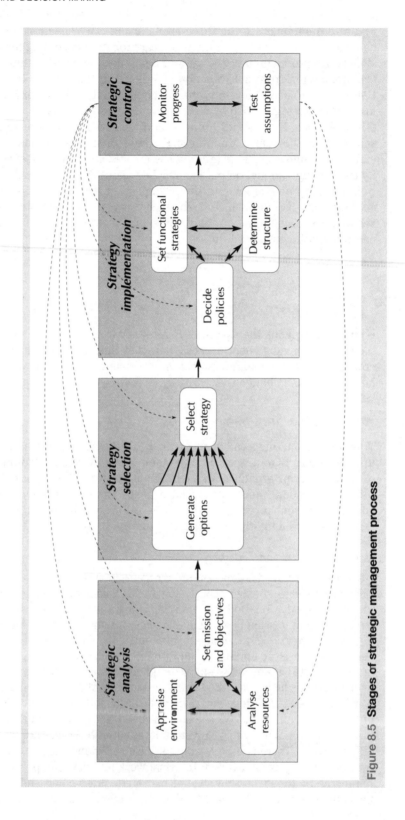

Figure 8.5 **Stages of strategic management process**

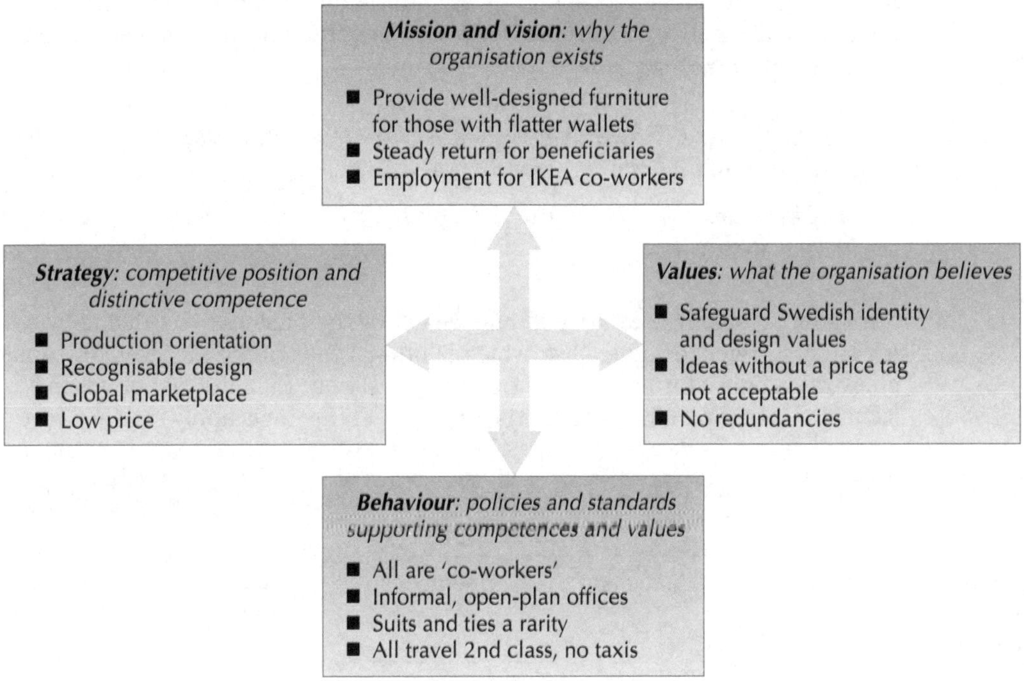

Mission and vision: *why the organisation exists*

- Provide well-designed furniture for those with flatter wallets
- Steady return for beneficiaries
- Employment for IKEA co-workers

Strategy: *competitive position and distinctive competence*

- Production orientation
- Recognisable design
- Global marketplace
- Low price

Values: *what the organisation believes*

- Safeguard Swedish identity and design values
- Ideas without a price tag not acceptable
- No redundancies

Behaviour: *policies and standards supporting competences and values*

- All are 'co-workers'
- Informal, open-plan offices
- Suits and ties a rarity
- All travel 2nd class, no taxis

Figure 8.6 **IKEA's mission, values, strategy and behaviour standards**

The second test looks at whether the mission is consistent with the two other elements in the appraisal stage – resources and environment. This is the mission–environment–resources test to which we return below.

Assessing the environment

In Chapter 2 we learned how the environment could be investigated and interpreted. From the strategic perspective, it can be categorised into opportunities and threats. These mean just what they say:

> **Opportunities** *are features of the environment that favour the organisation provided it is able to take advantage of them.*
>
> **Threats** *are features of the environment that will cause the organisation not to achieve its goals if it cannot resist or avoid them.*

The operating environment presents the most obvious opportunities and threats, say from the actions of a competitor or change at an important customer. Yet managers must also investigate the wider environment if they are to succeed in the long term, which is the purpose of strategic management.

Appraising the organisation

A practical and detailed check-up of the internal workings of the business is based on looking at its strengths and weaknesses. As with opportunities and threats, these mean just what they say:

> **Strengths** *are favourable internal characteristics that the organisation can apply to achieve its strategic goals.*
>
> **Weaknesses** *are internal characteristics that hinder or limit goal achievement.*

Strengths or weaknesses arise in any aspect of the business. A valuable way to get started is to refer to a checklist, which is often a tour of the business functions with an extra category for management and organisation. Exhibit 8.10 provides a typical example.[27] Although the checklist is long, not all the items apply in every case.

Exhibit 8.10 Checklist of strengths and weaknesses

Management and organisation	Finance	Marketing	Operations	Human resources	Research and development
Management quality	Profit margin	Market share	Location	Skills and qualifications	Basic research
Staff quality	Capital ratios	Advertising effectiveness	Capacity	Union relations	Development capabilities
Experience	Stock ratios	Channels of distribution	Age of facilities	Turnover	Research programmes
Structure	Credit management	Customer satisfaction	Purchasing	Absenteeism	New product introductions
Planning, information and control systems	Return on capital	Service reputation	Quality management	Job satisfaction	Process innovations
	Risk	Sales force turnover	Efficiency	Grievances	
	Costs				

How do we decide what is a strength or a weakness? There is no simple rule. Strengths and weaknesses need to be tested in two stages. First, we can see whether the organisation is truly strong in the area concerned. A good check is to compare performance with that of other organisations known to set a good standard. This is the process of *benchmarking*. Ideally, a comparison is made with a successful rival but, since they do not willingly share information, the measure can be against the standard of a firm engaged in a related activity. For instance, ICL compared its training methods with the Royal Mail and a United States regional airline matched aircraft turnarounds with motor-racing pit stops.[28]

Second, we can see whether the factor is strategically significant. A firm may pride itself on its excellent stock control. Unfortunately, it may be in an industry where rivals are 'good enough' and, in any case, stock control is not relevant to gaining advantage over them. Taking two extreme examples, it is crucial in food retailing but of less importance in banking or broadcasting.

■ Comparing mission, environment and resources

No analysis is complete without an assessment of how the mission, environment and organisation's resources interrelate. This *MER* test can be readily applied if strengths, weaknesses, opportunities and threats are set out in a single table, the well-known *SWOT* analysis. SWOT should be put to work. Many managers (and students) are satisfied if they can produce long lists in each category but this is to forget the advice given above. Three or four key factors in each stimulate a meaningful investigation of their interdependence. Figure 8.7 shows a SWOT layout for the furniture SBU of IKEA.[29]

The SWOT elements having been set out, comparison is made among them to answer questions such as: Does the company have the resources and willingness to

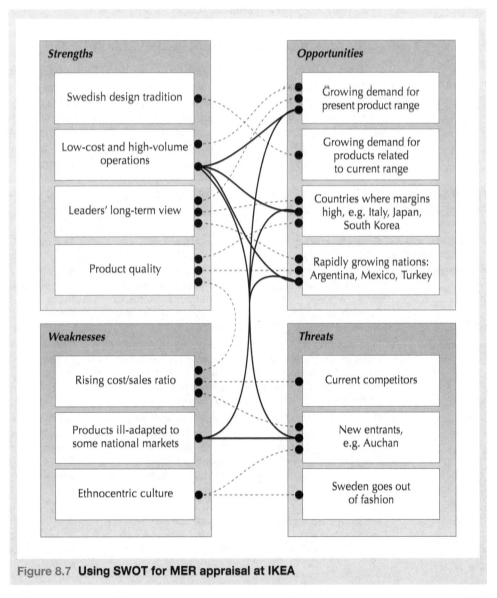

Figure 8.7 **Using SWOT for MER appraisal at IKEA**

take advantage of opportunities? Do threats pose risks against which the business is unguarded? Lines, as shown in Figure 8.7, can be drawn among elements of the SWOT as ideas about relationships grow. We shall pick out one set (shown as heavy lines) from the many that can be found. One of IKEA's strengths is its low operating cost, based on selling large volumes from a standard product range. Pushing costs down further enables further penetration of current markets and makes entry to new ones attractive. Possibilities are nations where current distribution is inefficient or where economic growth is rapid. Unfortunately, standardisation means poor adaptation to the needs of some markets. IKEA would sell more in Germany and the United States if its beds and seats were bigger, Austrians prefer corner settees in their arrangements. Local companies may exploit this weakness, matching IKEA's methods while offering more 'local' ranges. In spite of the threats, however, we can conclude that the expansion strategy implied in the company's mission is built on a realistic match between resources and environment.

■ Other tests of environment–organisation fit

Apart from this approach to fit based on the SWOT analysis, many studies have sought to understand why some strategies are more successful than others. The notion of suitable *generic strategies* is considered later. Miles and Snow[30] provide a further approach. They studied the links between the environment, organisations' value systems and the way they formulated their strategies. They named three active responses as *defenders*, *prospectors* and *analysers*. The last group, *reactors*, barely responded at all. Exhibit 8.11 sets out the key characteristics.

Exhibit 8.11 Responses to environmental uncertainty

Type of response	Environment sought	Internal features	Examples
Defender	Good at producing limited product range and serving a narrowly defined market. Openings beyond current market not sought.	Managers avoid uncertainty. Internal processes and structure change little. Concern over current efficiency and quality.	Many SMEs, once established. Building societies choosing not to convert to public companies.
Prospector	Produces stream of new products and constantly searches for new market opportunities. Challenges competitors.	Accepts fall of internal efficiency caused by persistent change of products and entry to new markets. Research orientation.	Direct Line until 1995, *see* Exhibit 8.12. Later, it became a defender.
Analyser	Operates in both stable and changing product/market sectors. Stays close to customers.	In stable sectors, aims for efficient processes and fixed structures. In changing sectors, studies competitors and imitates their best designs ('follow-my-leader').	Hastings Direct, set up in 1996 by one of Japan's leading insurers. It aimed not only at the UK direct market but analysed the process ready for its soon-to-be liberalised home market.
Reactor	Not a response. Does not actively make a choice.	Changes only under strong environmental pressure.	Ship building firms in the United Kingdom relied heavily on subsidy and military contracts.

Exhibit 8.12 Direct Line: a prospector enters

Direct Line, established in 1985, changed the way the British public buys insurance. Founder Peter Woods quickly developed his idea of telephone sales of car insurance into one of the country's most successful firms. Through aiming his business at low-risk customers, Woods cut prices. He became one of the nation's highest salaried people. By the early 1990s, Direct Line, with 40 per cent of the market and low costs, seemed unchallengeable. Success continued after takeover by the Royal Bank of Scotland. Profits reached £112 million in 1994–5. By this time, however, competitors with broader market bases had entered. Eagle Star and Norwich Union set up similar operations, eliminating the broker's commission. AA Insurance, which is a broker, cut its own costs and prices. By 2000 more than 60 companies offered direct insurance. As profits began to fall rapidly, Direct Line turned from prospector to defender, seeking ways of further reducing costs and improving customer retention.[31]

■ Strategy selection

Strategic analysis gives a picture of the capabilities of the SBU and the state of its environment. This forms a platform from which the process of strategy selection can begin. A classical decision model, covered further in Chapter 9, would present that as a choice from among alternatives and this is what happens in strategy. Further, as Chapter 9 goes on to explain, creating choices and choosing from among them are likely to be intertwined. For clarity, however, we shall look at them as though they were sequential – *grand strategy*, *directions* and *means*.

Grand strategy

The grand strategy represents the overall direction the business is going to follow. Three alternatives are presented in Exhibit 8.13. Many businesses, especially small ones, follow a *stability* strategy. This means that the business will follow the current pattern. If markets expand, so will the business, but it will not seek to expand faster than that. A stability strategy will pay off in stable conditions where the business can devote its efforts to improving its efficiency while not being threatened with external change. Finally, there are many organisations constrained by regulations or the expectations of key stakeholders. This is especially true of the public sector and many non-profit organisations. Schools, for example, usually serve their local community; charities are frequently set up to perform fixed purposes.

Growth strategies are followed by businesses that see themselves as strong and doing well. Their managers may prefer higher risks and be motivated to expand, for many equate business size with success. Furthermore, in a volatile environment, growth may provide a cushion against a downturn in fortunes or a barrier against the development of a rival.

Retrenchment means drawing back. Falling demand in main markets, pressure on costs through having a poor location, or the loss of key personnel may make it desirable for a business to *downsize*. Retrenchment may be the only means for the organisation to make the internal improvements necessary to face an increasingly competitive environment. In this light, it is often seen as a temporary expedient before the business adopts a growth or stability strategy starting at the new, lower level. Ultimately, however, retrenchment could lead to closure.

Exhibit 8.13 Selection of grand strategies

Grand strategy	What?	Why?
Stability, or consolidation	Continues with same products, markets, processes. Focus on steady all-round improvement.	Seen to be doing well. Prefers low risk and little change. Stable environment. Stakeholders constraints.
Growth, or building	Volatile environment. Seeks to add new products, markets and processes, or looks for major increases in current activity.	Wants to do much better. Prefers higher risk and change. Managers motivated to expand. Stakeholders have high expectations.
Retrenchment, or withdrawal	Recognises need to cut back on range of products or markets. Seeks to improve current processes through cutting back.	Recognises things are going badly. Threatening environment. Managers opt for survival policy. Stakeholders dissatisfied with current activities.

The use of retrenchment as an interim strategy suggests a further point about the three grand strategies: they can be used in combination. They can be sequenced, for instance growth followed by stability, or pursued simultaneously in different parts of the SBU. For example, stability in the current product line may be looked for while the company prepares to launch a replacement. The case of Ford replacing its Escort model is an example.

Directions: internal or external; product or market

The second basic question in considering alternatives is whether the change is to be internal or external. The internal direction means the firm does things itself. It implies change in the volume of output of current products or the introduction of new ones that it has brought forward. Gaining new markets is achieved by direct entry. The external direction, on the other hand, means joining with other organisations to achieve the strategy. Examples include merger, divestment and joint ventures.

These strategies can be presented on the product-market matrix that Ansoff introduced in 1965.[32] In the basic model, Figure 8.8, two growth directions from a stability strategy are shown – product development and market development. Compared with stability, product development means increasing the product range while continuing to serve current customers. Examples are BMW and Honda adding cars to motorcycles, the HSBC bank offering new types of insurance or supermarkets introducing newspapers, clothing or a pharmacy. Under market development, on the other hand, the organisation sticks to its product range, but offers it to new customers. Examples include new territories, such as exporting, or new segments such as the promotion of malt whisky to younger consumers. In either direction, the business builds from a base that it knows to be strong; it knows its customers or knows its products. They are sometimes referred to as *concentric diversification* since, although there is an element of moving away from the stable state, there remains a strong link to it.

Concentric development seeks to take advantage of *synergy*, the idea that the whole can be greater than the sum of the parts. It is sometimes referred to as the '2 + 2 = 5 effect'. Concentrically diversified companies seek synergistic relationships among units as follows:

- *Market synergy* – sales of one product reinforcing sales of another; sharing distribution channels; applying brand names across many products and so on.

- *Operating synergy* – filling out product ranges to occupy spare capacity; sharing infrequently used resources; recycling.

- *Technological synergy* – sharing product or process technology among divisions; exploiting patents throughout world markets.

- *Financial synergy* – allocating funds among units to gain the best return; using financial strength to raise new capital at low cost.

- *Management synergy* – applying core competences learned in one sector to another; transferring managers with special skills to areas where they are most needed.

In contrast, diversification (sometimes known as *conglomerate diversification*) means moving away from the current product-market base altogether. The business may find little opportunity in concentric moves and seeks completely new lines to which to transfer its competences. This is a riskier strategy because the number of unknowns is higher and there is an element of 'burning the boats'. Since the effect of such diversification is to set up a new SBU, this strategy really involves the corporate level. Perhaps the best known corporate conglomerate in the United Kingdom in

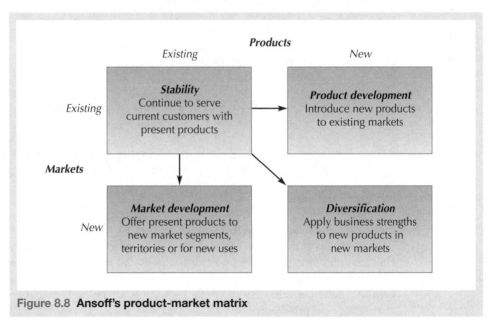

Figure 8.8 Ansoff's product-market matrix

recent years was Hanson Trust. The founders, who became Lords Hanson and White, saw their talent as acquiring and improving companies that had somehow lost their competitiveness. Links among SBUs were less important than turning each unit around. In the early 1980s, acquisition opportunities were cheap. By the 1990s, however, conglomerates were paying such high prices that gaining an easy return was no longer easy. After the founders' retirements, 1995–6 saw Hanson break up into four businesses – tobacco, coal, chemicals and building materials. The last was the only one to retain the Hanson name. By a circuitous route, it had become a concentrically diversified company.[33]

Means: how does the business compete?

In competitive environments, a company must make basic decisions about *how* it is to do battle with its rivals. Porter's work is well known here. Taking a perspective originating in economic analysis, he proposed three *generic strategies*: differentiation, cost leadership and focus.[34] Their characteristics are set out in Exhibit 8.14.

Exhibit 8.14 Porter's competitive strategies

Strategy	Features	Resources and skills
Differentiation	Distinguish products from rivals through superior quality, service, speed or response time, or strong brand image. Customers must value benefits more than the extra they have to pay.	Marketing stresses features as value. Effective operations. Design. Research and development. Reputation for providing superior standards.
Cost leadership	Attracts customers by operating more efficiently than rivals and hence charging low prices. Customers must be sensitive to price but standards must be acceptable.	Marketing stresses price as value. Tight cost control. Efficient process development. Product design focused on low costs.
Focus	Differentiation or cost leadership strategies aimed at limited target segment, usually a 'niche' market.	Marketing concentrates on chosen niche. Differentiation or cost leadership in operations as appropriate.

Differentiation

Following this strategy, the SBU offers distinctive value for factors that it expects its customers to appreciate. Examples are Savile Row suits, Aston Martin cars, Glenmorangie malt whiskey and Hilton hotels. All these are distinctive products that charge a higher price than cheap suits, cars, spirits or lodgings. Note that to be successful, the extra value offered must be valued by the customer more than the extra cost it takes to provide it.

Cost leadership

Cost leaders strive to offer lower-priced products than their rivals while keeping other aspects of value up to a sufficient standard. Some roadside restaurants, such as Little Chef, attract the traveller through offering attractive meals at low prices. Here the menu and service design, building construction and layout, and tight control systems concentrate on providing meals of acceptable standard at low prices. Budget motel chains such as Travellers' Lodge or Campanile keep costs down with small rooms and a reception area that doubles as a breakfast counter.

Focus

Using a focus strategy, a business concentrates on a sub-group of the market such as a district or buyer group. It tailors its offering to this group using either differentiation or cost leadership. SMEs often thrive by offering speedy service to particular buyers, *see* Storwell in the closing case in Chapter 7, or they may, through avoiding the expensive overheads of large firms, undercut their prices.

Porter argued that businesses ought to follow one of what he called these *generic strategies*. Failure to do so results in being 'stuck in the middle', having no advantage and eventual failure. Others have shown, however, that firms can combine cost leadership and differentiation and be successful.[35] Examples are McDonald's and Direct Line. We saw above how the latter sold car insurance by a new speedy and convenient method that, through focus on the low-risk market segment, turned out to be much cheaper than its rivals. Porter's arguments are not now taken as inflexible rules, but notions such as differentiation have entered the language of strategy and form useful aids to debate.

Strategy implementation and control

As Figure 8.5 showed, putting strategy into practice involves a mixture of: confirming or adapting the organisation structure; making detailed policies including those for each function; and ensuring there is a control system that allocates resources, motivates staff and provides timely information on deviations from planned progress. Putting strategy into action, however, will not happen of its own accord. Senior managers need to display effective leadership, bring together the above elements, persuade others of the benefits to be gained from change and ensure that all share the mission the organisation has set for the future. Topics such as leadership, structure and information systems are covered in later chapters. The last stage of the management process, strategic control, is discussed in Chapters 18 and 19.

Corporate strategy

At the corporate strategy level, organisations consider the mix of SBUs that they have under their control. The need to maintain a balance among these elements is a requirement of large multi-business companies. For instance, until it sold Rover Group to BMW, British Aerospace manufactured both cars and aircraft. Then BMW found it could not provide all the investment that the Group's brands needed and, having retained the Mini, sold Land Rover to Ford and the remainder to Phoenix.

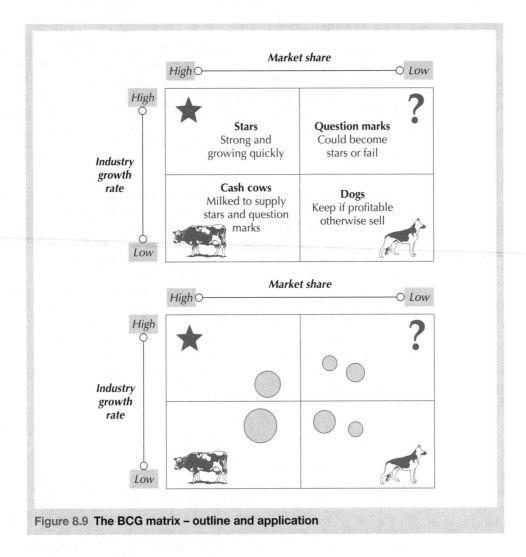

Figure 8.9 **The BCG matrix – outline and application**

The Boston Consulting Group matrix is the best known of a family of models that help to explore such problems.

The matrix, shown in Figure 8.9, presents the SBUs on an array whose scales represent industry growth rate and market share. Comparing SBUs that are in high or low growth industries, and possess high or low market share, creates four categories for classifying the corporate portfolio.

We can first refer to the upper grid of Figure 8.9. *Stars* have high market share in high-growth industries. They are important because they are doing well and have expansion potential. Since this needs investment in, say, larger-capacity plant or distribution channels, the star requires cash inflow. As its industry becomes more mature and growth slows, less investment will be required and the star transforms into a *cash cow*.

Cash cows are strong businesses in slowly growing industries. Low investment means not only that these SBUs should be profitable but also that they should generate surplus cash as they age. From the corporate point of view, cash cows can be 'milked' to provide funds for investment in stars and newer, riskier businesses, *question marks*.

These question marks have small shares of rapidly growing sectors. Risk means they can go either way. Investment can develop them into stars or they may make the wrong choices and fail. The business should not, however, shy away from having some question marks in its portfolio, for in them shine the glimmerings of future stars.

Finally, the *dog* is a weak business, having a small share of a slowly growing market. The BCG protagonists argued that, unless a quick recovery could be achieved, a retrenchment policy should be followed.

The lower grid shows how a business with six SBUs could be presented. Each circle represents one unit with its diameter corresponding to its size. The lone star SBU would be expected to become even brighter as it grows in future years. There is a healthy cash cow producing surplus cash for the star and question marks. Two dogs might be disposed of.

This plausible and beguiling model, with others in similar vein, has received both support and much criticism. Key points can be summarised as follows:

■ *Financial portfolios are not needed*
The notion that finance has to be balanced *within* the organisation has been challenged. Investors, many of whom are huge groupings such as pension funds, are able to build their own portfolios. They prefer not to leave decisions to the internal machinations of any one business. If a company is, in effect, a single star SBU, it can approach the market for investment. Alternatively, cash cows can return surpluses to shareholders.

■ *What do high and low mean?*
Defining and measuring growth and market share are difficult enough. Then come further problems of assessing whether a result is high or low. BCG suggested originally that a high growth be more than 10 per cent per annum and a high market share meant that the SBU was at least 50 per cent larger than any of its rivals.[36] This meant that only market leaders (and comfortable ones at that) could appear in the left-hand cells and, since 10 per cent is an uncommon growth rate, only a few of those would be stars. Ignoring the scales and using the BCG ideas qualitatively avoids this problem but weakens the analysis.

■ *Untested prescription*
Many, including some of the original advocates, have treated the model as prescriptive. That is they look to it for a view as to what should be done: 'Cash cows should be milked, dogs should be liquidated.' It is clearly inadvisable to base strategy on the rough calculation of two dimensions. The assumption that all businesses in all industries should receive the same treatment is groundless.

■ *Persuasive imagery*
Popularity of the model was enhanced by its simple, folksy imagery. Cows effortlessly produce milk while dogs are rather sad and useless creatures. Note that these dogs are American; the term in the New World has overtones of 'cur', unrecognised among European dog lovers. Yet, this imagery can be reversed. Farmers know that cows do not produce milk endlessly. They require an occasional visit from the bull. So cash cows need investment, too. Similarly, dogs have many functions. Rather than a mangy weakling, the dog in Figure 8.9 is a guard, preventing prospectors from trespassing on a weak segment as a prelude to a full-scale attack.

In spite of such weaknesses, the portfolio concept lives on. Yet, now it serves to aid debate rather than prescribe what should be done. This trend is not unusual. Many models familiar to strategists have been promoted as the 'one best way' to approach their task. After disillusion has set in, however, they may leave a ghost in the form of a useful idea or a piece of jargon. In any case, weak models do not invalidate the process itself. Strategic management has its stout defenders who, for instance, argue that it is better than 'no planning'.[37] Yet we must look at some other criticisms that point to the limits of its benefits.

Limits to strategic management

Criticisms of strategic management have ranged across both its practice and principles. For the former, for instance, follow-up studies based on models in use have shown that they have led to poor decisions. Weaknesses in portfolio models are but one example. The principles of strategic management have also been probed by those who found, for example, that many firms succeed without formal plans. We shall outline two of the main limits here.

Forecasting

We noted earlier that uncertainty presents managers with two choices. First, they can try to reduce it, by improving forecasting and interpretive skills. Strategic forecasting looks towards long time horizons, often obscured in a haze of incomplete information. Despite this difficulty, there is pressure to come up with firm statements about the future. These tend to be cautious, as shown by many economic forecasts. Kay noted that they have a tendency to cluster around a safe guess. When predicting inflation, for example, analysts pick a figure between the current rate and the long-term average. Furthermore, they persistently revise their forecasts. Economists could do better if they were invited to state the ranges within which they expected the outcome to fall. But clients and the media continually look for single 'headline' figures.[38] With analysts dithering so much in the short term, what hope for strategic forecasters?

The second approach is to generate a range of contingency plans. This means that if the first choice plan is thwarted for some reason, a second, 'Plan B', is available, and so on. Even here, however, there is a problem. How can the organisation be sure it has an alternative to suit any eventuality? Logically, not knowing the future means that it cannot. But many organisations find that testing plans against a range of possible futures helps to ensure they are robust.

Emergent strategy

Mainstream management thinking prefers a structured, analytical approach. Its advantages in fields from operations management to credit control are evident. Large businesses could not operate without the efficient procedures created by management scientists. In strategic management, however, many now recognise that analysis has been overemphasised at the expense of flexibility, insight and innovation.

Do senior managers produce single strategic plans? It seems not. Faced with uncertain environments, managers are constantly duplicating or adapting strategies.

Sometimes, as Microsoft famously showed, *see* Exhibit 8.15, a robust approach is to back many possibilities and see what happens. For adaptation, 'In a fast-changing environment, successful strategies tend to emerge from a series of decisions … There may well be no detailed written strategy at all'.[39] According to Mintzberg, chief executives are not systematic planners. They use information from many sources, often through *ad hoc*, oral interactions. They do not separate planning, implementation and control as stages suggested in models such as Figure 8.3. This does not mean that Figure 8.3 is wrong, rather that it is not a full description of what happens.

Exhibit 8.15 Microsoft emerges[40]

In 1988, Microsoft's DOS system, the dominant PC standard, was ageing. No one knew its replacement. At the Comdex trade show, suppliers from Apple to IBM, and consortia of names from Hewlett-Packard to Sun Microsystems, each focused on one new technology that they hoped would win. Microsoft's moderate stand looked a mess; it showed the latest DOS, updated Windows, OS/2 (with IBM) as well as versions of Word and Excel for Mac and a PC version of UNIX. Commentators wondered, 'What is Microsoft's strategy?' They should have asked, 'What are Microsoft's strategies?' While Bill Gates wanted Windows to win, he had a bet on every horse.

When there is uncertainty, some of the *intended strategy* is not put into effect, leaving the *deliberate strategy*. Events that were unexpected need new decisions and these form the *emergent strategy*. The middle managers come up with ideas that are generated by their learning about markets and technologies. The two streams of decisions come together to form what actually takes place, the *realised strategy*. Figure 8.10 summarises this complex flow.

Strategy emerges, therefore, in steps like a waltz on a crowded floor. There is an intention, to proceed around the room. But as paths open and close, each couple adapts. The emergent path traced by their feet depends on this changing environ-

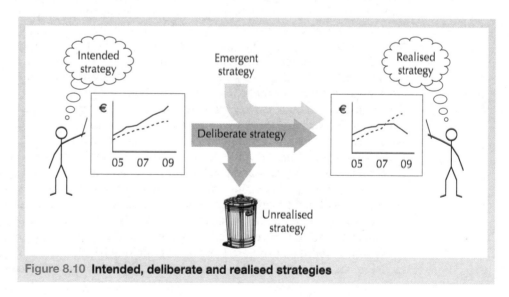

Figure 8.10 **Intended, deliberate and realised strategies**

ment interpreted through their own creativity. In strategic thinking, such proceeding by steps is known as *logical incrementalism*, a term coined by Quinn.[41]

The implication of this idea of emergence is that strategy is not the process of long-term management of an organisation. Instead, it represents the outcome of often complex social, technical and political decision making. It is simply another aspect of management. Does this mean that all the talk of vision, SWOT and directions is misplaced? Mintzberg argues not, for organisations pursue:

> *umbrella strategies: the broad outlines are deliberate while the details are allowed to emerge within them. Thus emergent strategies are not bad and deliberate ones good; effective strategies mix these characteristics in ways that reflect the conditions at hand, notably the ability to predict as well as the need to react to unexpected events.*[42]

Mintzberg goes on to argue that planners should be less concerned with perfecting plans in every detail and more involved with coaching managers in strategic thinking and to find originality where it has been hidden. The craft aspects of helping strategy to emerge need to be emphasised.

Conclusion: statements of ends and means

We began the chapter by showing that planning is an everyday activity in which we are all engaged. Things get more complicated in organisations, which require many people to pull in the same direction while remaining ready to change that direction. Many need formal, carefully worked out plans. Yet such plans will not suit others, especially the entrepreneurial firm whose advantage lies in its flexibility. The art of planning is to achieve a balance.

Three layers of planning were identified. The operating level needs objectives and plans to focus its stream of decisions on ordering, scheduling, task allocation and so on. These are framed in the context of higher-level plans that provide the operating level with enough stability to proceed. Strategic planning bridges the gap between the stability needed at the operations level and the changing environment.

At the heart of plans are objectives and goals. Making them explicit, in statements from departmental plans to organisational mission statements, offers important benefits. They provide unity of purpose and motivation, and form the basis of control. Furthermore, in linking levels in means–ends chains, they offer the opportunity to co-ordinate the work of the whole. We noted, however, the many difficulties in objective setting and planning. They explain why even the best laid plans go wrong. Many organisations protect themselves against failure through contingency and crisis plans that are prepared and tested by wise managers.

Strategic management involves analysis, selection, implementation and control. The context is the long term, dealing with big, interdependent issues. In a sense, this is the top of the hierarchy of planning. Yet it can be applied to all aspects of the business – corporate, SBU and function. Although we concentrated on business strategy in this chapter, we should note that managers will also talk of functional strategy, such as for personnel or operations. These must all be fitted into the jigsaw of plans.

We also noted the corporate level for the multidivisional business, using the BCG model to illustrate portfolio thinking. It is another illustration of the danger of simple, plausible prescriptive rules in management. One doesn't simply milk cash cows and dispose of dogs. We can, however, place our learning in context, as follows:

- Strategy must fit the environment.
- Successful strategies erode; what fits the environment one day may not do so the next.
- Effectiveness is more important than efficiency: doing the right thing is crucial.
- Speed is important; doing the right thing must happen early.
- Organisation and culture are more important than strategy.[43]

QUICK CHECK

Can you ...

- Define the terms plan and planning.
- Distinguish between an objective and a goal.
- Sketch the planning and control cycle, showing links between levels.
- Define uncertainty, listing three types.
- Suggest four internal benefits of objectives.
- Summarise the threefold test of a good objective.
- State what may be addressed in a mission statement.
- Name three problems with each of objectives and planning.
- Distinguish between contingency and crisis planning.

- Define strategic management and outline its cycle.
- Name three features of strategic thinking.
- Identify three levels of strategy.
- State what SWOT stands for.
- Explain the MER test.
- Summarise the four strategies from the Miles and Snow study.
- Name the steps of strategy selection.
- Draw Ansoff's product-market matrix.
- Distinguish Porter's generic strategies.
- Explain the BCG matrix and suggest four limitations.
- Suggest two limits to strategic management.

QUESTIONS

Chapter review

8.1 Define planning and explain the main components of the planning process.

8.2 With what aspects of uncertainty do managers have difficulties, and how do they respond?

8.3 What goes wrong with objectives and planning and how might these difficulties be overcome?

8.4 Define strategy and summarise the main components and tools of the strategic analysis and choice process.

8.5 Compare the main strategic directions available to an SBU.

Application

8.6 Suggest goals, objectives and constraints for an emergency service such as fire or ambulance.

8.7 Use a MER analysis to assess the position of an organisation with which you are connected. Does it suggest any problems?

Investigation   **8.8**   Examine the mission statements provided by several organisations in the private and public sectors. They appear in many annual reports on the Internet. Identify and comment on the stakeholders to whom the statements appear to be addressed.

8.9   Study an organisational crisis that has been reported in the newspaper recently. Assess how well the crisis was managed and how far contingency planning could be used to improve the response to future crises.

Nokia connects[44]

From its 1865 origins in forestry, Nokia grew and spread until, by the early 1990s it had become a sprawling, loss-making, conglomerate company. Paper products had grown downstream from the forestry; in the 1960s Nokia had entered rubber and cables; the 1980s saw electronics. There were costly moves into consumer electronics and computers, most of which were quickly disposed of.

Then, with a young team headed by Jorma Ollila, there came a dramatic transformation. The loss-making businesses were sold and the businesses refocused on telecommunications. By 1995, 90 per cent of revenues came from this industry; Nokia's mobile equipment, with a 20 per cent share, was second in the world to Motorola. By 2002, it had become number one with 37 per cent market share. Total sales were almost €30 billion, three-quarters in mobile handsets. The company's shares dominated the Helsinki stock market. Ollila and his team became important symbols of international success in an economy struggling to catch up with the rest of Europe.

Commentators attributed the success to the skill and vigour of the leadership, mostly in their 40s. Nokia had been the first to see that cell phones were consumer items and segmented its products by style. Margins were 18 per cent on handsets. There were, however, worrying signs. Nokia had not led the move to colour screens and cameras and it was weak in the Code-Division Multiple Access (CDMA) standard dominated by Samsung.

The 1992 reorganisation into three divisions – telecommunications infrastructure, mobile telephones and electronics and cables – had concentrated the business on growing markets. Numbers soared while the divisions tried to keep their structures as flat as possible. This maintained rapid decision making and enthused new staff with the open culture. 'The Nokia Way' had core values of high customer satisfaction, respect for the individual, achievement and continuous learning. By 2002, growth to 53 000 employees and developments in the environment meant it was time for another change. After a conference (Nokia does not use consultants for such matters), managers decided to establish nine SBUs, each with its own research, development and marketing:

Time-Division Multiple Access – to exploit Nokia's 50 per cent share of the market, especially in Latin America, which continues with this outmoded technology.

Code-Division Multiple Access – to build Nokia's 9 per cent of this technology, sweeping Asia, at the core of 3G phones.

Mobile Phone – the core of Nokia's business; could generate half of Nokia's profits.

Mobile Entry Products – low-cost versions for emerging markets.

Imaging – incorporating cameras, graphical software, etc.

Entertainment and Media – massaging and music.

Business Applications – smart phones and personal assistants to corporate clients.

Mobile Enhancements – accessories from cordless headsets to faceplates.

Mobile Services – Club Nokia clearing house for technical information, downloadable add-ins, etc. is popular with customers and builds brand loyalty.

By 2003, although markets in some countries were maturing, with per capita ownership around 50 per cent, the rate of change was not slowing. Overall, handset makers lost money in 2002. Half the mobiles sold in that year had built-in browsers. Many had cameras. More people used text messaging than email. Intel and Microsoft were looking to enter, the former with chips, the latter with an integrated version of Windows. The mobile would become smarter.

CLOSING CASE

Nokia's response to change had been to increase its spending on research and development from 7 to 9 per cent, two-thirds on software development. Along with Ericsson, Motorola, Samsung and Psion, it established Symbian, the London-based software company. So far, Symbian with its open operating system, had kept Microsoft at bay. The ten Symbian licensees accounted for 75 per cent of 2002 sales. They feared Microsoft's power and did not like the secrecy surrounding the Windows source code. On top of the Symbian code, Nokia's Series 60 software allows synchronisation with Microsoft products. It licensed Series 60 to other manufacturers.

Network operators were looking for higher margins to recoup the €100 billion they paid for 3G licences. They considered bypassing the branded handsets by going direct to low-cost manufacturers. This offered an entry to Microsoft. Handset manufacturers' brands, using Symbian software, may be replaced by network operators' brands powered by Microsoft. This is the story of the PC clone.

One cloud threatens the whole industry – health. Few electrical devices are held as close to the brain for any length of time as the transmitter in a mobile telephone. Studies have proved inconclusive, but research has fallen behind the rapid growth in use and doubts exist. Nokia and others claim that there is no danger from the tiny one-watt transmitters. Digital phones use less power and emit higher-frequency, less penetrative signals. Worried users can buy separate earpieces and microphones.

Questions

1 Use a SWOT analysis to identify the key factors and relationships to which Nokia managers should pay attention.

2 Position the SBUs on a portfolio matrix. What does this tell you about the future of Nokia?

3 'Our strategic intent, as the trusted brand, is to create personalized communication technology that enables people to shape their own mobile world.'[45] Evaluate this statement. You can obtain more from www.nokia.com.

Bibliography

Among many guides for starting a business are Brian Salter and Naomi Langford-Wood (1997) *The Essential Guide to Business Planning and Raising Finance* (London: Thorogood), and Matthew Record (2003) *Preparing a Business Plan* (4th edition, London: How to Books). Leading texts on strategy include Gerry Johnson and Kevan Scholes (2002) *Exploring Corporate Strategy* and Richard Lynch (2002) *Corporate Strategy* (both Harlow: Financial Times Prentice Hall). Stuart Crainer (1995) *Key Management Ideas* and Richard Koch (1995) *The Financial Times Guide to Strategy* (both London: Financial Times) may be in libraries. Journals, including *Management Today*, *Long Range Planning* and *Management Decision*, cover many aspects of planning and strategy.

References

1 Barrie, Chris (1997) 'Ford wields Halewood axe', *Guardian*, 13 January, 17; Milne, Seamus (1997) 'Ford lifts Halewood threat', *Guardian*, 8 February, 22; Halsall, Martyn (1997) 'Two key car plants rescued', *Guardian*, 28 March, 22; Wolffe, Richard and Simonian, Haig (1998) 'Ford: Jaguar's new baby brings joy to Halewood', *Financial Times*, 7 January; European Industrial Relations Observatory Online (1998) 'New Jaguar model to be produced at Halewood', European Foundation for the Improvement of Living and Working Conditions, 28 January, www.eiro.eurofound.ie/index.html, accessed 1 March 2003; Howes, Daniel (2002) 'Workers change ways, and Jaguar plant now ranks as Ford's best', *Detroit News*, 27 June.

2 Raffoni, Melissa (2003) 'Three Keys to Effective Execution', *Harvard Management Update*, Harvard Business School Publishing, 1.

3 Editorial (1996) 'Mobile phone firms plan masts in Highlands', *The Herald*, 11 November.

4 Milliken, Frances J. (1987) 'Three types of perceived uncertainty about the environment: state, effect and response uncertainty', *Academy of Management Review*, **12**, January, 133–43.

5 Manchester Airport plc (1993) *Runway 2: Planning Application Supporting Statement*, July, mimeo.; Cobham Resource Consultants and Consultants in Environmental Sciences Ltd (1993) *Runway 2: Environmental Statement – Non-technical Summary*, Manchester: Manchester Airport plc, July, mimeo; Naylor, John (1996) *Operations Management*, London: Financial Times Pitman Publishing, 288, 304–5.

6 Done, Kevin (2003) 'Two extra runways at Gatwick proposed' *Financial Times*, 28 February, 5.

7 New Zealand Telecom (2003) *About Telecom*, **www.telecom.co.nz/**; accessed 2 March 2003.

8 Hamel, Gary and Prahalad, C.K. (1989) 'Strategic intent', *Harvard Business Review*, **67(3)**, May–June.

9 Denton, D. Keith (2001) 'Mission statements miss the point', *Leadership and Organisation Development Journal*, **22(7)**, 309–14.

10 Nakamura, Kunio, President of Matsushita (2003) *Annual Management Policy for Fiscal 2004*, January, **www.matsushita.co.jp/corp/vision/president/amp2003/en/va001.html#p4**, accessed 1 March 2003.

11 Tarnow, Eugen (1998) 'A recipe for vision and mission statements', *The CEO Refresher*, **www.refresher.com/!recipe.html**, accessed 22 November 2002.

12 Goett, P. (1997) 'Mission impossible', *Journal of Business Strategy*, **18(1)**, 2.

13 Mullane, John V. (2002) 'The mission statement is a strategic tool: when used properly', *Management Decision*, **40(5)**, 448–55; Bart, Christopher K., Bontis, Nick and Taggar, Simon (2001) 'A model of the impact of mission statements on firm performance', *Management Decision*, **39(1)**, 19–35.

14 Roddick, Anita (1991) *Body and Soul*, London: Ebury Press, 24–5, 123 and 251.

15 Duckworth, Gary (1994) 'Meeting targets could knock you right off course', *Marketing*, 13 January, 6.

16 Carvel, John (2003) 'Spot check by auditors finds NHS waiting lists fiddled', and Ward, David (2003) 'Trust criticised for misleading public', both *Guardian*, 5 March.

17 [... *often go wrong*]; Burns, Robert (1759–1796) 'To a mouse'.

18 Garrett, Alexander (1995) 'No medals for Atlanta's corporate sponsors', *Observer*, 4 August; Carlin, John (1996) 'And you thought Britain had a bad Games', *Independent*, 5 August.

19 Cannon, Tom (1997) 'From the top', *Guardian: Jobs and Money*, 25 January, 29.

20 Armstrong, Stephen (1996) 'So much at steak', *Guardian: Media*, 25 March.

21 Puchan, Heike (2001) 'The Mercedes-Benz A-class crisis', *Corporate Communications*, **6(1)**, 42–6; Hammond, Andrew (1999) 'Roll model', *Business Review* **6(1)**, 24; Brierly, David (1997) 'Caught in a moose trap', *European*, 6 November, 28–9.

22 Attributed to Harold Wilson, 1965–6, United Kingdom Prime Minister, *Oxford Dictionary of Quotations*, 3rd edition, Oxford: Oxford University Press (1979), 574 (18).

23 Lex Column (2003) 'Hilton Group', *Financial Times*, 28 February, 20.

24 Simonian, Haig (1995) 'Survey of Europe's most respected companies (11). A desirable icon of the age – Profile, BMW', *Financial Times*, 19 September, IV.

25 Campbell, Andrew and Young, Sally (1991) 'Creating a sense of mission', *Long Range Planning*, **24(4)**, 10–20.

26 Carnegy, Hugh (1995) 'Struggle to save the soul of IKEA', *Financial Times*, 27 March, 12; Richards, Hale (1996) 'IKEA founder still part of the furniture – Ingvar Kamprad has built a dynasty that will survive his departure – when he decides it's time', *European*, 22 February.

27 Based on Daft, Richard L. (2000) *Management*, 5th edition, Fort Worth, Tex.: Dryden Press, 246.

28 Trapp, Roger (1994) 'Benchmarking moves on to bench testing', *Independent on Sunday*, 9 January, 13.

29 Villarno, Lalo Agustina y Pilar (1996) 'La distribucion tiembla ante el avance de los "category killers"', *Actualidad Economica*, 5 February; News item (1996) 'Un chiffre d'affaires en croissance de 8 per cent dans le monde', *Les Echos*, 27 September; Paine, Ines Garcia (1996) 'IKEA enciende la luz de alarma en las empresas del mueble', *Actualidad Economica*, 11 November.

30 Shortell, Stephen M. and Zajac, Edward J. (1990) 'Perceptual and archival measures of Miles and Snow's strategic types: a comprehensive assessment of reliability and validity', *Academy of Management Journal*, **33**, December, 817–32.

31 Brierly, Sean (1996) 'Red phone in dire need of a new line', *Marketing Week*, 28 June; Mortished, Carl (1996) 'Tempus; Insurance – Direct Line', *Daily Telegraph*, 30 November.

32 Ansoff, H. Igor (1965) *Corporate Strategy*, New York: McGraw-Hill.

33 Jackson, Tony (1996) 'Big can still be beautiful: Although the Hanson era is at an end, a new breed of conglomerates has prospered by adding value', *Financial Times*, 1 October; Bennett, Neil (1996) 'New Hanson will build on strengths', *Sunday Telegraph*, 29 December; Lex Column (2002) 'Hanson', *Financial Times*, 2 August.

34 Porter, Michael E. (1980) *Competitive Strategy*, New York: Free Press.

35 Miller, D. and Friesen, P.H. (1986) 'Generic strategies and performance: an empirical examination with American data. Part 1: Testing Porter', *Organisation Studies*, **7(1)**, 37–55; Miller, D. and Friesen, P.H. (1986) 'Porter's (1980) generic strategies and performance: an empirical investigation with American data. Part 2: Performance implications', *Organisation Studies*, **7(3)**, 255–62.

36 Henderson, Bruce (1984) *The Logic of Business Strategy*, Cambridge, Mass.: Ballinger, 56–61.

37 Richardson, Bill (1995) 'In defence of business planning: Why and how it still works for small firms and corporations of small business units', *Small Business and Enterprise Development*, **2**, 41–57.

38 Kay, John, quoted in leading article (1995) 'Economics as futurology', *Financial Time*s, 5 October, 23.

39 Barwise, Patrick (1996) 'Mastering Management 15(2): Strategic investment decisions and emergent strategy', *Financial Times*, 16 February.

40 Beinhocker, Eric D. (2000) 'On the origin of strategies', *McKinsey Quarterly*, **4.**

41 Quinn, J.B. (1980) 'Managing strategic change', *Sloan Management Review*, **21(4)**, 3–20.

42 Mintzberg, Henry (1994) *The Rise and Fall of Strategic Planning*, Hemel Hempstead: Prentice Hall, 25.

43 Doyle, Peter (1996) 'From the top', *Guardian: Management section*, 16 November, 23.

44 Hunt, Ben and Adams, Paul (2003) 'The lines are drawn in the battle to own the future of telephony', *Financial Times*, 26 February; Hunt, Ben and Adams, Paul (2003) 'Microsoft left out on a limb', *Financial Times*, 18 February; Reinhardt, Andy (2002) 'Nokia's next act', *Business Week*, 1 July, 24.

45 Nokia (2003) *Business Strategy*, **www.nokia.com**, accessed 3 March 2003.

CHAPTER 9

Decision making: choosing from alternatives

Chapter objectives

When you have finished studying this chapter, you should be able to:

- explain the causes of increasing complexity facing modern decision makers;

- compare risk, uncertainty and ambiguity in problem settings;

- describe the different types of decision made in organisations and match different styles to them;

- set out and explain the steps of the rational and administrative decision models, comparing the applicability of each;

- describe the main decision traps facing individuals – heuristics, framing, escalation of commitment and overconfidence; and show how these may be avoided;

- assess the value of having groups involved in decision making;

- identify the symptoms of groupthink and polarisation and how a manager may prevent them;

- recognise creativity and show how it can be cultivated in the organisational context;

- construct mind maps and decision trees as aids to decision making.

It is not always what we know or analyzed before we make a decision that makes it a great decision. It is what we do after we make the decision to implement and execute it that makes it a good decision.

William Pollard, American business leader and writer

Air traffic control: streams of complex, risky decisions[1]

The London Area Control Centre (LACC) at Swanwick controls most air space over England and Wales; it is supported by Terminal Control Centres for the lower altitudes around London and Manchester airports. Opened in 2002, it took over from the former LATCC the management of the air 'corridors' across the country along which civilian aircraft must fly. Each corridor is split into 30 flight levels separated by 1000 feet. LACC is Europe's busiest such operation, handling up to 6000 flights a day.

The 357 air traffic controllers (ATCs) work in pairs to cover each sector of air space. A tactical controller deals with current movements and a planner controller looks ahead to anticipate and resolve problems with flow. They follow movements on radar screens. Each aircraft is shown by a dot to which is attached its call sign and destination. ATCs cope with routine instructions and emergencies. The latter range from priority landings for planes with sick passengers to coping with dangerous incidents. For the two million commercial flights in British air space, air safety is the most important task for the controllers. An important feature is maintaining separation distances. International agreement sets the 1000 ft flight levels and lateral distances of five miles. Close to airports, these gaps may be reduced. As aircraft prepare for landing, they are given permission by the ATCs to descend from level to level as they approach. If traffic is heavy, the aircraft are directed towards a 'hold' or 'stack' where they circle, one at each level, until a landing slot becomes available.

Where aircraft come together, as in holds, there is an increasing risk of collision, especially through human error. Heathrow normally has two holding areas, Biggin Hill and Ockham. On 22 November 1996, a controller cleared a Boeing 757, circling at Biggin Hill, to descend from 11 000 to 9000 ft, having overlooked the presence of another that had been at 10 000 ft for 10 minutes. This may have been due to both planes being of the same type and airline. Fortunately, the crew of the descending aircraft saw the second below and were able to level at 10 400 ft before climbing back to 11 000 ft. Some 40 per cent of mistakes by controllers allow aircraft to get too close. Among pilots, non-compliance with

ATC instructions and deviations from set levels each account for 30 per cent of errors.

Improving the efficiency of flow is vital. In Europe, airport congestion is the greatest single threat to continued expansion in the region. Of Europe's 29 major airports, 25 will have a serious runway capacity shortage by 2005. Flight delays are increasing throughout Europe, especially as short-haul business increases. Ryanair, easyJet and bmibaby lead the way. Yet safety must remain paramount. LACC has automated many processes, but experts believe that future ATCs will still make the major decisions on speed, direction, height and separation. The controller must be kept 'in the loop' rather than pushed to one side as tasks are taken over by machine.

Controllers learn to make decisions based on a mental picture of a dynamic situation, presented visually and by voice. Although paperless systems have been tested, most centres keep written records. The familiarity of handwritten 'flight progress strips' reinforces the controllers' visualisations. Maintaining the skills is vital. Three times in the past 20 years power failure has hit LATCC. Controllers, having a mental picture of the traffic, stopped take-offs and entries from overseas and gradually emptied the skies until remaining flights could be routed without radar.

The following events show how vital human decision makers are in non-routine situations, in spite of their weaknesses. At 0720 on 10 June 1990, a scheduled flight, BA5390 with 81 passengers and 6 crew, left Birmingham for Malaga. At 0733, it was climbing through 17 300 ft when there was a bang as a windscreen panel blew out. The commander would have been sucked out had not a steward grabbed his legs and, aided by colleagues, held on to them until after landing. Having regained control, the co-pilot descended quickly to 11 000 ft before making a distress call.

Unfortunately, the noise on the flight deck meant that he was unable to hear the acknowledgement of the signal during the descent and there was some delay in establishing two-way communications. Several other pilots intervened, offering to relay the weak radio signals. Six minutes elapsed before the contact was clearly established. Then came this exchange:

▶

LATCC: *Speedbird 5390. London Control 132.8. I hear you strength five, sir. Go ahead now.*

BA5390: *Roger, sir, we have had an emergency depressurisation and er requesting radar assistance please for nearest airfield.*

LATCC: *Er Speedbird 5390. Roger. Can you accept landing at Southampton?*

BA5390: *Speedbird er 5390 I am familiar with Gatwick – would appreciate Gatwick.*

LATCC: *Er Speedbird 5390. Roger. If you make a left turn now, sir, direct to Mayfield.*

BA5390: *5390. If you can direct me into Southampton. Affirmative.*

LATCC: *OK, Sir. Would you prefer Southampton or Gat- er Gatwick? ... Er Speedbird 5390. Confirm you wish to route to Southampton.*

Untrained in, and unaccustomed to, emergencies because of their rarity, the ATC on duty mistakenly presented the beleaguered co-pilot in his chaotic, noisy cockpit, with choices of what to do. Yet the co-pilot needed firm directions to the nearest safe landing. These were given once the request came through. Several minutes were lost at a time when seconds were important.

Approaching Southampton, control was passed to the airport tower. It was only then that the co-pilot was able to report the extent of the accident:

TOWER: *5390. We've been advised it's a pressurisation failure. Is that the only problem?*

BA5390: *Er negative, sir. The er commander is half sucked out of the aeroplane. I understand ... I believe he is dead.*

Lack of preparedness may also have led to another problem, insufficient runway length. At 0746 this was the exchange:

BA5390: *... Could you please confirm the er length of your runway at Southampton is acceptable for a One-Eleven?*

TOWER: *Yes, it is acceptable for a One-Eleven and I'll give you the figures very shortly.*

BA5390: *Er as long as we have er at least two and a half thousand metres I am happy.*

TOWER: *Er I'm afraid we don't have two and a half thousand metres. Neither do Bournemouth. We have a maximum eighteen hundred metres.*

BA5390: *5390 that is acceptable.*

With the co-pilot unfamiliar with Southampton, the tower controller 'talked him down' until the runway was in sight. Landing occurred at 0753. The fire service pulled the commander back into the aircraft and took him to hospital. He had been on the aircraft roof for 20 minutes. Happily, despite wrist and arm fractures, frostbite and shock, he survived.

Introduction

Air traffic controllers make decisions that have an impact on the safety of travellers every minute of their working day. Co-operating with pilots in practised routines, they are used to the smooth flow of traffic through their air space. They cope with complexity through learning and rehearsal. It is when difficulties arise, however, that they are expected to show their mettle. Faced with extraordinary situations, they must make decisions whose accuracy and timeliness take on greater importance. Although acting in emergencies can itself be rehearsed, the very unfamiliarity of emergencies presents unusual challenges. Human judgement and discretion take over from formal routines. It is not surprising that some people cope better than others.

Simultaneously, other managers are making decisions about the future of the whole ATC system. Whether the focus is current economic performance or increased capacity or safety, planners have to study deeply how and why controllers choose from among alternative courses of action. This can then trigger the search for improvement.

This case study points us to some key issues confronting managers making decisions. They include complexity, risk and the fact that choices are often shared by several people who bring different skills, information and perspectives. Decisions, moreover, do not stand alone. Each forms part of a flow; it is affected by those that have already been made, and influences and constrains those that are to follow. The next section considers these issues from the manager's point of view. Then the chapter looks at decisions themselves, introducing two models that describe the process and the roles of individuals and groups within it. Finally, since it is often valuable to come up with original solutions to problems, the function of creativity is examined.

Managers making decisions

The word decision has appeared often during the preceding chapters. Sometimes it can be presented as a simple yes or no choice such as is presented in an algorithm. Another decision maker may have little information, and even less time, yet may be pressed into choosing from several courses that have not been tried before. Sometimes the consequences of error are small, at other times they are catastrophic. Another possibility is that the full effects are never established. How can we evaluate an entrepreneur spending a few hundred pounds on advertising, or the Irish nation voting in 2002 referenda first against, and then in favour of, the Treaty of Nice?

Whatever the scale, these actions are all decision making:

> *Decision making is the act of choosing from among alternatives.*

If it were as simple as a literal reading of the definition might suggest, there would be little more to be said. Yet, as we have already seen in planning, the act of choosing takes place in the context of a process. We recognise that a decision must be made and define it within its context. Then we set up alternatives to pick from, for a poor decision is often the result of being presented with just one proposal. A later section covers this *decision-making process* in more detail. We shall start, however, with its context to see the challenges presented to modern managers when faced with the responsibility for making decisions. The context includes complexity, risk, decision traps and managers' problem-solving styles. These issues are shown 'surrounding' the manager in the *mind map* of Figure 9.1. This is a tidy version of the one used to plan the chapter.[2]

■ Complexity

Decisions are rarely tidy. Frequently, as with the BA5390, they have to be made under just about the worst circumstances where complexity threatens to overwhelm the manager. The reasons for complexity are as follows:

■ *Many decisions*
Single decisions do not usually make systems work. They contribute to a flow, just like streams. Some follow others in regular order; others form parallel currents, backwaters and little eddies. Air traffic control functions because of teams of

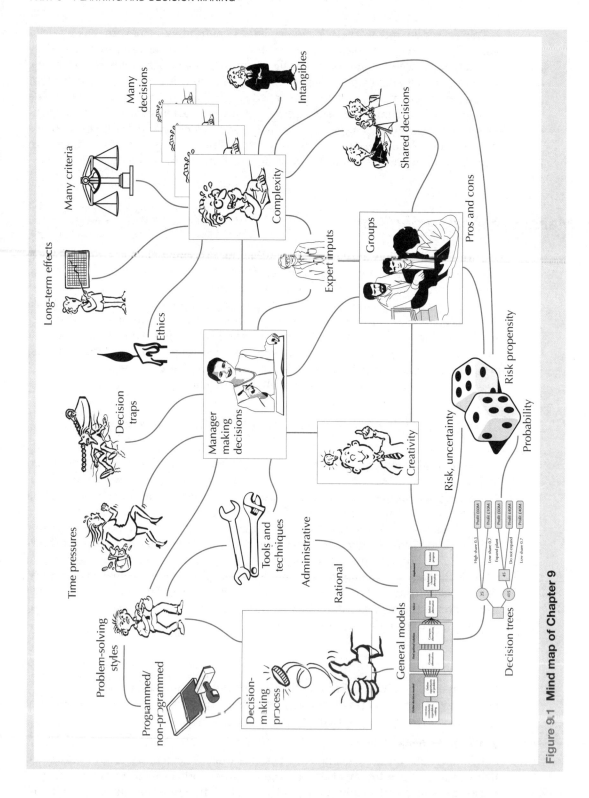

Figure 9.1 **Mind map of Chapter 9**

Exhibit 9.1 Mind maps

Sketching ideas and links in a mind map is a valuable habit for any student or manager. There are few rules. Words or pictures represent ideas. Lines, possibly weighted, show connections among the ideas. Some areas can be emphasised by outlining; in Figure 9.1 boxes pick out the main themes of the chapter.

Nothing is shown in detail. The aim is to start with a haphazard sketch and refine it to show the shape and relative importance of information and ideas. Since mind maps are more compressed than normal notes, the one-sheet picture helps us to pick out links and form new ideas.

Mind maps can be used for taking and consolidating notes from many sources. They work at an early stage before ideas have been sorted.

Stuck for somewhere to start? Put down a few ideas; link them; add a few more; leave it for an hour; think of some more links; make some tea; start again ... Try it!

operators exchanging information with pilots and other control centres, making decisions and issuing instructions based on them. The stream of ATC decisions relates both to each aircraft's movement and to the interrelated movements of other flights. Normally it runs smoothly but sudden changes create eddies when instructions have to be changed.

■ *Long-term effects*

It is not only the decisions that flow. Often a routine decision can create ripples that spread through an organisation and have a long-lasting effect. For instance, in a board mill, one supervisor came across two workers fighting in the cloakroom. Following agreed procedures, the supervisor immediately suspended the men and had them escorted from the premises. Subsequent investigation found that one had been bullying and the other had decided to 'sort him out'. Colleagues protested against the second's dismissal. The dispute rumbled on for months with output of a profitable line curtailed.

■ *Many criteria*

It is normal for decision makers to face multiple criteria, often imposed by different groups of stakeholders. Chapter 5, for example, pointed to the multiple influences over choices such as whether to expend more effort on recycling of materials or worn out plant. The manager's problem is that, in the end, a choice may well please some and annoy others.

■ *Shared decisions*

Yet another people problem arises from the sharing of many decisions. It is uncommon for one manager to act independently. Good leaders often share decision making to bring people along. Yet groups sometimes behave in unexpected ways when making decisions and usually slow the process down.

Slowness and confusion are seen acutely in international agencies. The European Space Agency decided to cancel a mission to land on comet Wirtanen after a test firing of an enhanced Ariane rocket failed. David Southwood, head of science, admitted, 'In the process of review and analysis, doubts arose about the procedures of verification – the rigour, so to speak – of the system. We think that the way things are done needs to be reviewed from the bottom up.'[3]

■ *Expert advice*

The complexity faced by managers is increased when they have to take advice from specialists. Not only can this be time-consuming but the manager also has to deal with contradictory advice. Referring to external guidance, a former finance director of ICI reported, 'When the peak of an economic boom or recovery is approached, the merry-go-round of advice rotates faster and faster, with more and more advisers climbing on board to tell companies what to do'.[4] Profits, dividends, target rates of return are either too high or too low depending on who is arguing.

■ *Intangibles*

Later in the chapter, we shall see how a rational decision-making process relies on stating both objectives and outcomes in consistent, measurable terms. Yet many decisions involve subtle judgements and have effects on intangible factors such as staff morale, company image or customer satisfaction.

■ *Ethics and values*

Chapters 4 and 5 illustrated many aspects of international business where conflict between values poses ethical dilemmas for the manager. For example, pharmaceutical companies have been criticised for conducting clinical trials in developing countries. For the company, the trial is a rational approach to mitigating risk; a few may suffer for the benefit of the many. Participants join knowingly, having had the benefits and risks explained to them. Pfizer was sued, however, after an emergency trial of Trovan during a bacterial meningitis epidemic in Kano went wrong. The drug had never been tried on United States children because the outbreaks do not occur in the West. Many of the Nigerian children either died or were left maimed. Critics questioned whether patients in such circumstances could be given 'full information' and reach a sound judgement.[5]

Holian is critical of managers who take a legalistic approach. They may not notice ethical issues and often condone unethical behaviour. She found judgement and integrity, supported by courage and humanity, to be primary requirements.[6]

■ *Risk propensity*

Risk propensity is the willingness of a decision maker to gamble when facing a decision. Some managers treat every decision cautiously. Their fear of making mistakes means that they will exaggerate the chances of failure and understate the chances and benefits of success. They avoid the big mistakes. Other managers are willing to take risks, often choosing courses of action intuitively and quickly. Entrepreneurs and intrapreneurs do achieve great successes from this approach but are also more likely to incur losses and ruin.

The culture and rules of an organisation influence risk propensity. This effect can be seen in City financial trading, illustrated in Exhibit 9.2.[7] The idea, and its companions uncertainty and ambiguity, are so important that it is worth looking at them in more detail.

■ Risk, uncertainty and ambiguity

Ideally, managers would have all necessary information to hand before making a decision. Yet, as always, the world is less than ideal. Figure 3.1 for example, showed that both change and complexity in the business environment combine to increase uncertainty in managers' perceptions of it. Since many aspects are unknowable, the manager has to accept that a decision may not resolve a chosen problem and future

Exhibit 9.2 Incentives encourage risk taking

Following the loss by NatWest Bank of £50 million through alleged unauthorised trading, an article by an economist at the Bank of England received wide attention. It suggested that bonuses paid to traders in the risky derivatives and futures financial markets might increase the business risk. A bonus system designed to motivate a risk-averse trader to take more risks may simultaneously encourage one who is risk tolerant to go too far. In some cases, lump sum bonuses tied to profit targets would push staff into taking chances to reach the target knowing that, if things went wrong, they stood to lose little personally.

In its supervisory role, the Bank of England has to ensure that banks can always cover their risks. It was considering whether to include details of bonus schemes in its future assessments of banks' policies.

events may follow unexpected tracks. Four conditions, shown in Figure 9.2, can be identified. These depend on the sort of information available and whether the decision is guided by clear objectives.

■ *Certainty*

A condition of certainty exists when *a manager has all the information needed to make a decision*. A distribution manager, for example, should know the number of vehicles, the location of warehouses and customers, running costs per kilometre and so on. From these data, and knowing that the objective is to minimise total cost for a given level of customer service, the manager has techniques to schedule the vehicles. Many operations research techniques depend on this level of certainty. Yet few decisions approach this ideal and most of these are confined to the operating level of the organisation. It is a mistake to treat decisions as though they were based on certainty whereas in reality they are not.

■ *Risk*

A condition of risk exists when *a manager has clear objectives and information yet knows that outcomes are subject to chance*. BMW, for example, measures the

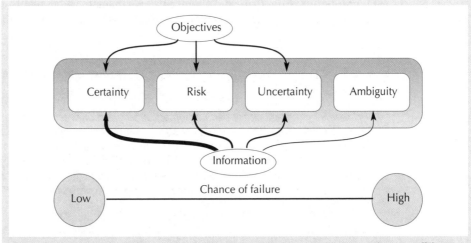

Figure 9.2 Decision making under different objectives and information conditions

risks arising from loss of production and insures them up to a realistic level. Flexibility in its manufacturing chains helps to mitigate the risk and reduce insurance premiums.[8]

Risks are stated in terms of probabilities, of which there are two types. *Objective probabilities* are odds that are worked out from reliable historical data or experiments. (Note that the term *objective* is used here as an adjective to mean detached or unprejudiced.) Before launching a new chocolate bar, for example, a manufacturer may use data from earlier products or test marketing in a limited area to provide relevant information. *Subjective probabilities* are estimates based on experience and judgement. Returning to the European Space Agency example, records may show that 1 in 20 launches goes awry. If there were no changes in rocket design and launch procedures, these data, 5 per cent, would represent the objective probability of failure next time. On the other hand, scientists change designs to increase rocket power and reliability. The effects of these changes cannot be measured exactly. Therefore, a 3 per cent failure risk might be a reasonable subjective probability estimate.

■ Uncertainty

A condition of uncertainty arises when *a manager has limited reliable information about choices and future outcomes*. For instance, Chapter 4 showed that, in international business, it arises from both unpredictable interactions among cultures and dealings with different governments. Scholars recognise that firms try to reduce or avoid uncertainty. Reduction is achieved commonly through imitative behaviour – 'Follow the leader'. Henisz and Delios showed how, when locating their first plant in a host country, firms would be more likely to mimic the past decisions of other home-country firms. Avoidance was seen in the way they shunned nations with political uncertainty.[9]

Plans and countermeasures also reduce uncertainty. Yet it cannot be eliminated for many decisions. Good judgement enables them to be successful with questions such as, 'Although it is impossible to assess the outcomes exactly, shall we go ahead anyhow?'

■ Ambiguity

A condition of ambiguity exists when *a manager faces an ill-defined problem, has unclear objectives and lacks information about choices and future outcomes*. This echoes uncertainty with added difficulties. In the normal run of events, such conditions do not present themselves (or managers choose to ignore them). If things are not going so well, however, managers may recognise they are facing a *mess*,[10] see Exhibit 9.3.

Exhibit 9.3 Ackoff warns that problems depend on perception

'Problems have traditionally been assumed to be given or presented to an actor much as they are to students at the end of chapters in text books. Where they come from and why they are worth solving is implicitly assumed to be irrelevant to consideration of how they should be solved or what their solutions are. Books dealing with the methodology of research and problem solving seldom give more than a polite nod to problem generation, identification and formulation. They move impatiently to problem solving.'

'... problems are taken up by, and not given to, decision makers. ...'

'What decision makers deal with, I maintain, are messes, not problems. ... A mess is a system of external conditions that produces dissatisfaction.'

Unclear and conflicting objectives, poor information, fuzzy problem boundaries and sudden change are characteristics of messes. Resolution often requires more than calculating optimum results, rather, fundamental organisational change.

◼ Decision traps

Ambiguity often arises when problems and objectives are unclear, suggesting great complexity and change in the situation. Yet personal traits can also affect clarity and hence lower the quality of decision making. Among the most common of these decision traps are heuristics, framing errors, escalation of commitment and overconfidence.

◼ *Heuristics*

Many people follow rules of thumb, or heuristics, when they make decisions. This is a realistic approach for, faced with a vast number and variety of decisions, we invent rules to simplify them. I mow the lawn every week, buy my shoes at Clark's, book flights through Airline Network, search the web with Google and never bid *no trumps* with a singleton. The notion of heuristics also includes learning. The rules are revised in the light of experience. Therefore, I mow the lawn more frequently in the spring and less in a dry summer.

Vecchio identifies two judgemental heuristics, or strategies, that people frequently rely upon.[11] Unfortunately, they often mislead people into making the wrong choices because the intuitive rules take them beyond the information they have been given. First, the *availability heuristic* reflects how accessible relevant information is to a person. For instance, asked to estimate the proportions of adult Americans and Germans who have passports, people in Stratford-upon-Avon will guess the former to be much higher. They generalise from unreliable perceptions of the numbers coming to their neighbourhood. In fact, about 10 per cent of United States citizens and about 90 per cent of Germans have passports. Similarly if asked to guess the proportion of British passport holders (50 per cent), answers will be biased by whether respondents have one themselves.

The second bias comes from the *representativeness heuristic*. This is based on one's sense of resemblance between events or objects. Ask a child to sort a tray of Lego and you will be surprised by the categories chosen. Would you use shape, thickness, colour, size, taste, number of studs, newness or who gave it as a present? In applying this rule of thumb, a person judges how well an object or event fits into a category and then makes decisions according to the category. This can be a basis of prejudice, as Exhibit 9.4 shows.

Exhibit 9.4 A test of representative heuristics

I have a friend who teaches in a university. He is small in build, rather shy and publishes poetry occasionally. Which is your best guess of his field of expertise – Chinese studies or psychology?

If your answer was Chinese studies, you have fallen into the trap of representative heuristics. You saw the personal profile as fitting more closely the stereotype sinologist than psychologist. Yet you ignored two critical items of statistical information. First, there are many more psychologists than sinologists. Second, someone who teaches in a Business School is more likely to come across the former. On either criterion, psychology is the superior answer. Put them together and the case is overwhelming.

On the other hand, if you saw the personal profile as fitting psychology ...

■ *Framing errors*

Framing errors arise from the influence on interpretation, and hence decisions, of the way information is presented. Nowhere is this more evident than in advertising. Product claims are framed carefully to influence consumers' choices. A disinfectant kills '99 per cent of all known household germs'. Or should one say, 'Domestos fails to eliminate 1 per cent of bugs and may miss any we don't know about'? In 2003, Halifax Bank pointed out that its current account paid 'thirty times more interest' than Barclays, NatWest and others.[12] The data were less exciting – 3.0 per cent at the Halifax; 0.1 per cent elsewhere – and there were conditions.

■ *Escalation of commitment*

Known colloquially as 'tossing good money after bad', escalation of commitment refers to people's unwillingness to change a course of action in spite of evidence that their decision has been incorrect. An organisation can become stuck with spending more resources hoping to achieve an outcome that is becoming less likely, *see* Exhibit 9.5.

Exhibit 9.5 Ferry story[13]

In the mid-1990s, government-owned BC Ferries decided to design and build three catamarans for the route between Vancouver and Nanaimo. The Premier of British Columbia promised that this faster travel could be achieved within a budget limit of $210 million. By the time of delivery, the project was two years late and costs had risen to $500 million. The first two vessels were so unreliable they were in service only half of the time. Then their wakes damaged the ecologically sensitive shoreline. Crew and fuel costs were higher than planned. Some had foreseen these problems but it was not until the fifth year that the government auditor censured the project, pointing out how BC Ferries' board had been pressed by the government into launching and continuing with the scheme. Six years from the first announcement, a new Premier cancelled the programme. His predecessor was among the few who disagreed with this decision.

Many individuals find that giving up is personally and socially difficult. Adding to these factors are those originating within the organisation. Summarised in Figure 9.3, they combine to provoke escalation. Yet continuation is sometimes almost unavoidable. Drummond and Kingstone Hodgson[14] point out that, while persistence often results from emotional factors and fear of failure, it is not always irrational. They caution against expecting too much. The British Columbia ferry case illustrates how politics may mean that reversing a decision is worse than carrying on.

■ *Overconfidence*

Overconfidence exposes people to unnecessary risks. We see this frequently in sport where some players develop reputations for taking more risks than others. Should the golfer drive over the hotel on the seventeenth hole at St Andrews or the poker player raise holding three knaves? When these 'long shots' pay off, legends are made; when they fail, they are soon forgotten.

Regular and familiar tasks encourage confidence, but not overconfidence, as each person develops a sound assessment of what is needed. Oddly, it is when tasks are less familiar and more difficult that overconfidence becomes a problem.

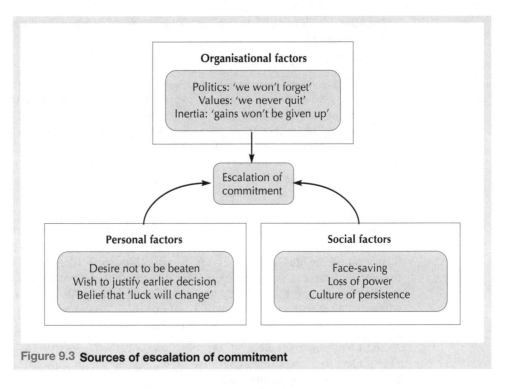

Figure 9.3 **Sources of escalation of commitment**

Inexperienced managers need to guard against the reassurance given to them by their qualifications when they move into unfamiliar territory. They should critically examine every element of their decision, from initial information through to implementation, to see whether they have overestimated their own capabilities.

Managing risk and overconfidence are also problems when decisions are made by groups. We shall, therefore, return to these later in the chapter.

■ Problem-solving styles

The different degrees of risk, uncertainty and ambiguity associated with decisions can be summarised by dividing them into two classes first proposed by Simon.[15] *Programmed decisions* occur in situations that have occurred often enough to enable managers to create decision rules to cover them. Many operating systems, from stock control to order processing, work almost entirely through decision rules. The operator's skill is to process routine material as quickly as possible while being on the lookout for anything unusual. As indicated in the opening case, air traffic control achieves high standards of efficiency and safety because almost all decisions are programmed.

Non-programmed decisions are required when conditions of uncertainty and ambiguity prevail. These decisions tend to be unrehearsed and infrequent and to have important consequences for the organisation.

Harrison and Pelletier relate decision types to hierarchy, showing that non-programmed decisions are the province of senior managers, while junior ones make the routine ones. They argue that managers should learn to avoid:

■ Treating non-programmed decisions as though they were routine.

■ Treating *ad hoc* or non-recurring decisions as though they were everyday occurrences.

■ Treating decisions with uncertain outcomes as though they had predictable, calculable results.[16]

Corresponding to the two types of decision, we can identify two problem-solving styles:

■ *Thinking*

Some managers prefer to approach problems using a thinking style. They look for precision, logic and objectivity. Clearly, these people will prefer routine tasks in which the ability to carefully assemble and weigh reliable information is an asset. Numeracy and the ability to break a problem down into elements are key skills. Such managers are most comfortable with programmed decisions although they could also work on non-programmed ones if they were not too ambiguous. The thinking style is that of the *technocrat*.

■ *Intuition*

In contrast, other managers approach problems with a predominantly intuitive style. They prefer complex and changing situations that offer opportunities to use judgement and follow 'gut feelings' about the way things will turn out. Rather than break problems down into workable elements, these people look at patterns to seek opportunities for intervention. They are comfortable with non-programmed decisions whereas, faced with colleagues who prefer to think, they may become frustrated and be accused of carelessness and imprecision.

As with many management ideas, these styles represent extremes of a continuum. This means that many managers use mixed styles, which they can adapt from time to time according to circumstances.

Decision making

Two models of decision making are frequently referred to by authorities – the classical and the administrative models. While they have superficial similarities, we must recognise that they originate from different traditions and were created for different reasons. We shall look at each in turn.

■ Classical model

The conventional approach to describing decision making, often called *classical decision theory*, makes certain fundamental assumptions that, as we shall see, have their limitations. These assumptions are:

■ objectives are clear and agreed;

■ problems are clearly defined;

■ the manager seeks full information on all possible alternatives before making any choice;

■ criteria for evaluation can be unambiguously drawn from the objectives and problem definition;

■ decision makers will make logical decisions to satisfy objectives as well as possible.

Figure 9.4 shows the steps set out according to classical decision theory. The approach in the model is to represent decision making as an optimal choice from an exhaustive list of alternatives. Implementation and monitoring follow as with all well-founded management processes. Here we see four stages in total, although the number can be varied according to the way they are broken down.

■ *Define decision need*

How does a manager know when to make a decision? Following the quotation from Ackoff in Exhibit 9.3, needs are rarely presented 'on a plate'. The early writer Barnard pointed out that there were three sources – instructions from superiors, reference by subordinates or the initiative of the manager.[17] All these result from someone 'taking up' the issue. Whatever the source, decision needs are defined according to the perception of those involved. If the paint is flaking off the door, that is only a problem to those who prefer doors to be nicely painted.

A further point concerns the basis of the decision need. It can lie in an *opportunity* when someone recognises that something positive could be achieved. Alternatively, it can come from a *problem*, that is someone is dissatisfied and wants something fixed. Therefore, a passing painter sees the door as an opportunity for employment, while the householder worries about a further drain on the budget. However it is defined, bringing out the decision need triggers the rest of the process.

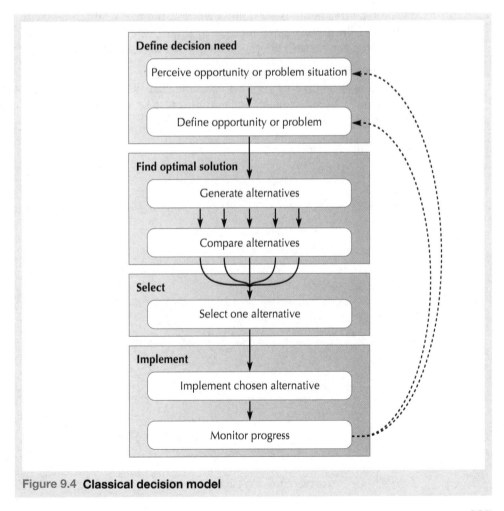

Figure 9.4 Classical decision model

■ *Find optimal solution*

The classical approach to finding an optimal solution relies heavily on the assumptions listed above. Rationally, one must explore all possible alternatives before coming to a conclusion about which is the best. Hence we can conceive of two stages, generation and comparison. They do not imply an infinity of choices for the constraints that surround the problem definition will usually mean that the number of possibilities is limited. A good example of rising numbers is the *travelling representative problem*.

The travelling representative problem can be stated succinctly. Given that a 'rep' has to visit several places during a tour, what is the shortest (or quickest) route? (*see* Figure 9.5). With 3 places there are just 6 routes, with 10 there are 3 628 800 and with 100 places the number soars to 10^{156}! Search methods proposing near-optimal solutions have been put forward but there is as yet no solution to all cases, save calculating every possibility! Apparently unreal with large numbers, this problem comes up often in business. A dispatcher may plan a lorry tour with 30 or 40 drops. Related problems come up in information network designs where hundreds of connections are made within and between silicon chips.[18]

■ *Select*

The selection stage is straightforward in the classical model. With clear objectives and full information about the problem, the choice of the best is automatic. Selection can be seen simply as an adjunct of the previous stage.

■ *Implement*

The chosen course of action is the one that will be put into effect. Note also that there must be subsequent evaluation to test its success in taking the opportunity or

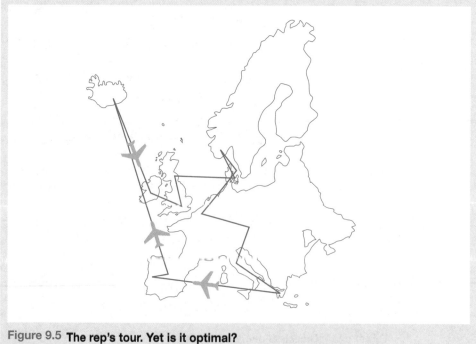

Figure 9.5 **The rep's tour. Yet is it optimal?**

solving the problem. This may cause changes to the process, especially in the way the decision need is identified.

Decision trees

To illustrate, a well-known method showing how the process follows on from a selected opportunity or problem is the decision tree. This is an aid in situations where a series of choices may be foreseen. A manager may make a decision, some events follow, another decision is required, some more events follow, and so on. The tree allows the manager to explore the consequences of the first choice through these anticipated events. Further, it is possible to build in allowances for chance, that is the risk that events may turn out differently.

Figure 9.6 shows a partly constructed decision tree. Our manager, looking for the best profit, has several strategies, labelled A to Z. Some have variants depending on future events. For example, Z has sub-strategies 1, 2, etc., although only Z2 is shown. The sequence runs from the left. Squares represent the decision points and lines the outcomes. Then we include the risks. For choice Z2, for example, the manager cannot tell what the outcome is to be but perceives three possibilities. A circle represents the uncertain event and the idea is to draw a line from the circle representing each possibility. The profits listed at the right correspond to each of them. Analysis continues until all branches have been explored.

The next stage is to evaluate the tree to find the series of decisions that are worth the most. This is done by working *from right to left*. That means assigning a cash value to each final result. At each circle, assign a probability to each chance at that point. The expected value at each circle can then be found by combining the estimated values and their probabilities:

$$Expected\ value = Probability_a \times Value_a + Probability_b \times Value_b + ...$$

Branches also emerge from squares. Since these depict decisions, the offshoot with the highest value is chosen.

A worked example is shown in Figure 9.7.[19] The mind map at the left sketches the starting point. The company is deciding the size of a new plant. After construction,

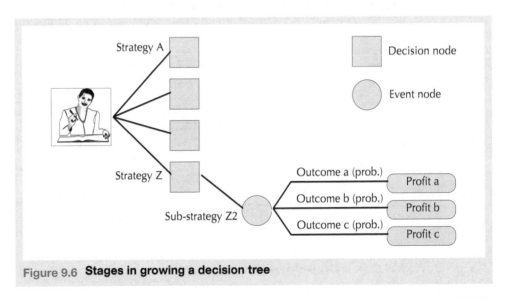

Figure 9.6 **Stages in growing a decision tree**

marketing effort will be increased but it is not clear what its impact will be. For simplicity, we shall say there is a 0.3 (30 per cent) chance of high revenue and 0.7 of little change, a low revenue. A small plant would satisfy the low market estimate but if sales did take off, a further problem would present itself: should the company expand the small plant? Building small and expanding later is more expensive than building large straight away.

The decision tree represents the choice and event nodes. At the right-hand side, the outcomes show the income for every combination of decisions and events. These are entered as shown. Then, working from right to left, the 'expected value' of each node can be calculated. Thus, for the large plant:

$$Expected\ value_{LP} = 0.3 \times 60 + 0.7 \times 10 = £25\ million$$

At the decision node concerning whether to expand the small plant in the light of rising sales, clearly the choice would be made to go ahead. The value of this node is £45 million and we can calculate the value of the small plant:

$$Expected\ value_{SP} = 0.3 \times 45 + 0.7 \times 40 = £41.5\ million$$

Clearly, the small plant would be favoured. Modelling this mind map into the form of a decision tree has enabled us to calculate the values of each option presented to the manager *in the light of subsequent decisions and risky outcomes*. Not only did the model aid in structuring the problem but also it provided a set of rules for finding the optimum systematically. These two features are to be found in many useful aids to decision making.

Problems with the classical model

The classical model has been popular with scholars and teachers partly because it is normative. This means it sets out how a decision should be made and does not necessarily conform to how managers actually make decisions in practice. The response of some scholars could be, 'What they should do is what matters. If only they followed the rigour of the model, their decisions would be improved!'

It is an uphill struggle. Improved modelling techniques, supported by powerful computers, have given a push towards reason and away from intuition. Yet examination of the assumptions underpinning the model shows its limited application. First,

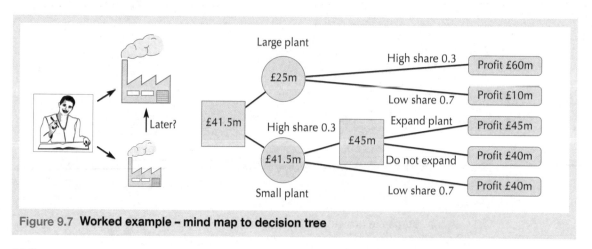

Figure 9.7 **Worked example – mind map to decision tree**

as Ackoff argued, there are many messes with ill-defined problems and unclear objectives. Second, it is almost impossible to consider all alternatives. Finding, and then evaluating, them would require too much effort. Information is not free so, in the end, the manager has to rely on limited and imperfect knowledge. Third, many cases go beyond the complexity that operations research techniques can cope with. Fourth, managers have neither the skills, nor the inclination, to perform heavy calculations. Fifth, social, cultural and political settings may restrict a manager's choice. Therefore, they may be unprepared to make the 'logical' decisions that the classical model demands.

We can conclude that managers are often unable to make rational decisions even were they inclined to do so. It is not surprising, therefore, that alternative models of the process have emerged. The behavioural theory of decision making contrasts with the normative classical approach in that it sets out to describe managerial behaviour. The *administrative model* is the product of this theory.

■ Administrative model

The administrative model describes how managers make decisions in the difficult settings we discussed earlier in the chapter. It recognises the limitations of the classical model. In summary, these are:

■ objectives are unclear and have not been agreed;

■ problems have not been clearly discerned;

■ managers' search for information on alternatives is limited;

■ decision criteria have not been established in advance;

■ the vagueness of criteria and information mean that managers are not committed to optimising decisions.

The model is based on the notion of *bounded rationality* developed by Simon and others in the 1950s and now an accepted part of decision theory.[20] Bounded rationality means that people set limits on how rational they can be. The boundary may arise from a stream of previous decisions. For instance, Simon pointed out that a doctor with seven years' training and ten years' practice does not ordinarily spend time thinking whether or not to be a physician.[21] Values pose another constraint. At The Body Shop, for instance, there is a policy of no redundancy. Others argue that ethics should be brought closer to the core of all decision processes and hence give focus and direction to them.

Because of the problems of processing vast amounts of information, namely attention, memory, comprehension and communication, managers will also *satisfice*. To satisfice is *to choose the first alternative that meets minimum decision criteria in spite of the possibility of there being others that are better*. For instance, a manager is looking for a convenient place to stay overnight in Brussels. A telephone call to the centrally located Ibis hotel establishes that there is a room and its price is within the company's budget. The manager makes the reservation. The decision is good enough.

Figure 9.8 lays out the stages of the decision process in the satisficing, bounded rationality mode. Having defined the decision need as before, the manager faces making a choice on incomplete information and with barely developed criteria. Therefore, looking for alternatives runs parallel with developing these criteria. The manager, so to speak, learns his or her way into the task. Uncovering alternatives suggests criteria and vice versa. Selection is also incorporated, for as soon as a satisficing alternative appears, it is chosen. If none emerges, the search is extended.

An example of the way decision criteria are allowed to emerge as the process evolves comes from investment decision making. For appraising new capital outlays, several procedures are well known. Generations of business students have been taught IRR (internal rate of return), NPV (net present value), payback period and ARR (accounting rate of return). They know that no technique is superior to the others in combining ease of understanding and use with validity in modelling the essence of complex problems. Wilkes and others[22] show how firms, especially larger ones, use several methods. Sometimes several were used on the same assessment, in other cases different approaches were used for different projects. Using several methods at once is a cautious way of avoiding major pitfalls. On the other hand, some techniques may be more suited to some types of problem, for example large or small, property or other assets. Furthermore, managers may choose methods that favour their own proposals. It appears that investment decisions are based on rational techniques. Yet, to the extent that the choice is a matter of judgement among the conflicting outcomes of these techniques, we see judgement and intuition come into play.

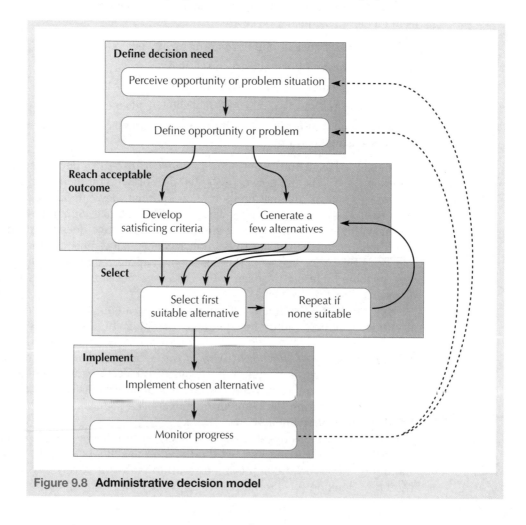

Figure 9.8 **Administrative decision model**

Groups in decision making

Chapters 11 and 12 look closely at the behaviour of groups and the role of the manager as leader. Clearly, this is a critical role since the manager can influence how much a group participates in the decision process. We can, however, look at groups from another angle. The question is less whether groups should be involved, but how and for what sorts of decision they are best suited. It is important, then, to understand the issues raised below so that a manager uses the group appropriately. Having compared their advantages and disadvantages, we shall comment briefly on how groups can be managed to best effect.

■ Advantages of groups

Exhibit 9.6 sets out the benefits and drawbacks of group decision making, matching the points roughly to the general pattern of the decision model. Some points could appear in more than one category, however. It can be seen that the group can gain at almost every stage although pitfalls, too, must be avoided.

Exhibit 9.6 Pros and cons of group decision making

Advantages of groups	Disadvantages of groups
Building a system of shared values:	
Pooling perspectives and values as part of cultural change.	Differences may be exaggerated.
	Status differences may limit sharing.
Defining decision need:	
Pooling adds to information base.	Confusing interpretations; overload.
Generating and evaluating alternatives:	
Specialisation; sharing skills in interpreting, modelling techniques, etc.	Higher cost if process inefficient or time wasted on routine tasks.
Choosing solution:	
Clarifying ambiguities reduces uncertainty.	Groupthink.
Sharing decision-making responsibility.	Polarisation.
	Diffusion of responsibility.
Implementing solution:	
Participation creates commitment to the outcome.	Escalation of commitment.
Motivation through the social process.	Poor processes can be demotivating.

When facing decisions, groups have advantages over individuals because they can bring wider perspectives to both the problem and the value framework that is to be applied to the selection of a solution. Drawing these together at an early stage forestalls later difficulties that could arise were the interests of certain stakeholders ignored, or important information forgotten. The sharing of ideas should also enrich the tasks of generating alternatives and modelling, evaluating and choosing among them. At the point of selection, it may be advantageous to share responsibility, especially if large sums or great risks are involved. Finally, the group's processes can increase the satisfaction of participants and help to build commitment to putting the result into effect.

Disadvantages of groups

Whereas a group with appropriate membership and organisation *may* bring with it great advantages, managers need to be wary of the corresponding drawbacks. Perhaps the most obvious is cost. Bringing people together for a couple of hours to make a decision may cost hundreds of pounds, far greater than the cost of one manager's time. The extra cost needs to be recouped through a better-quality decision and a smoother implementation as those who have to put it into effect have already taken part in the process.

In complex, non-programmed decisions, the group processes may appear to slow the rate of progress. This may arise if stages such as establishing criteria or even selecting the problem result in serious disagreement. Later, attempts to incorporate the knowledge and perspectives of a wide range of stakeholders may result in a serious information overload for participants. Frustration felt by members in such circumstances can be so demotivating that they allow unsatisfactory compromises and do not develop the necessary commitment to the outcomes. Paradoxically, it is in the most complex and uncertain cases that groups are most necessary and have the greatest potential. The difficult issues need to be sorted out.

Beyond these general points about disadvantages, there are particular difficulties that must be confronted, namely groupthink and polarisation.

Groupthink

Intrigued by the notorious venture of the Bay of Pigs, *see* Exhibit 9.7, Janis began to ask how a group of senior military personnel and civilian administrators could make

---

Exhibit 9.7 The Bay of Pigs

On 17 April 1961, a force of 1500 exiles attempted a covert invasion of Cuba at the Bay of Pigs. In spite of air and naval support from United States forces, it was a failure. The hoped-for popular uprising within the country did not materialise, and 1173 people were taken prisoner. The following year, President Kennedy agreed to ransom most of them for $53 million in food and medicine. The incident strengthened the ties between Cuba and the Soviet Union and harmed relationships between the United States and friendly Latin American and European nations.

The disaster occurred in spite of hundreds of hours of planning by a presidential special advisory committee and training of the forces by the CIA. Kennedy and his advisers had approved a plan based on wishful thinking. Expecting a quick overthrow of President Castro, they played down the risks and failed to consider the consequences of failure.

such a rash decision. Although selected for qualities of intelligence, motivation and abilities at decision making, it seemed that when people worked in a group, they abandoned their skills. This was *groupthink*.

Janis defined it as 'a mode of thinking that people engage in when they are deeply involved in a cohesive in-group, when the members' striving for unanimity overrides their motivation to realistically appraise alternative courses of action'.[23] He suggested it was a kind of disease that infected otherwise healthy groups. Members' desire to maintain consensus overrides the need to seriously explore alternatives. Why?

The eight main symptoms of groupthink, according to Janis, are:

- *An illusion of invulnerability* gives members a sense of power, reassures them about danger signals and encourages them to take excessive risks.

- *Rationalisation* enables the group to dismiss evidence that contradicts its emerging consensus.

- With an *illusion of superior morality*, the group does not question its own motives yet outsiders are considered evil, to be treated with suspicion.

- *Negative stereotypes* of leaders and powers outside the group mean that negotiating with them is regarded as futile. Since their opposition is expected, they are easier to cast aside in the decision making. Kennedy's group believed that Castro's air force was so weak that a few obsolete American bombers could easily eliminate it.

- *Pressure to conform* results in those who express momentary doubts being immediately brought into line or ostracised.

- Using *self-censorship*, victims of groupthink remain silent about any misgivings and convince themselves of the insignificance of their worries. Several of Kennedy's advisers later wrote of their regrets at not having objected more strongly.

- *An illusion of unanimity* follows from the previous symptom. The group assumes that silence means that members are willing to go along with the prevailing view.

- *Mindguards* sometimes take it upon themselves to interpret the leader's thoughts to the rest of the group and control the flow of information. Several members, including the President's brother, the attorney-general Robert Kennedy, took it upon themselves to restrict the flow of critical information into the Bay of Pigs group.

Behind the symptoms, researchers have identified four basic causes of groupthink. First, there is the existence of what may otherwise be considered a valuable trait, *group cohesion*. Strongly bonded groups can be either positive, if working well, or negative, if the symptoms begin to appear. Second, there is the danger of *group isolation*. Many of them work in secret. Unfortunately, this works both ways. Limiting the outward flow of information means that potential advisers and critics do not know enough to be able to offer sound advice. Third, a leader may unwittingly bias the course of events: expressions of authority will increase pressures to conform; procedures of meetings, such as agenda setting and style of discussion, can be manipulated; an early expression of preferences may dampen debate; and pleas for consensus building will restrict critical discussion. Fourth, all members are likely to feel the stress of an important decision. It is natural to look for ways, such as underlining the positive and rationalisation of action, to alleviate it. These causes are manifest as the groupthink symptoms.

Like any infection, remedies for groupthink are best directed at removing the cause, although dampening down the symptoms may also bring benefits. Since a working group would not wish to reduce its cohesion, efforts should be made to reduce isolation, for example by bringing in outsiders at every opportunity and allowing members to debate issues with trusted subordinates. Changing the structure of the group, for example by breaking into smaller units for a time, is recommended. Furthermore, leaders should learn to be impartial, let it be known that criticism and argument are expected, state their preferences only after they have participated in debates and give ample time to reflect on the final decision. They should encourage members to critically evaluate the process – and be prepared to listen to this criticism! For important decisions, it is worth having a final meeting at which everyone is again invited to express doubts before the choice is confirmed.

Polarisation

Most of us assume that work groups exert pressure to draw radical members towards more cautious views. In other circumstances, they persuade the excessively cautious to be more ambitious. In either case, we believe that groups have a moderating influence. Through a series of experiments in the 1960s, however, Stoner showed that this assumption was unsound.[24] *Risky shift* is the phenomenon in which groups subscribe to riskier positions than those taken by their individual members. Other experiments and observations confirmed Stoner's discovery and sought to explain it. They also found that some groups moved towards a more cautious position than the members would take on average if acting alone. This leaning was labelled the *cautious shift*. What was happening?

We have no space to cover the range of social and psychological explanations. It is, however, clear that many attitudes, beliefs, values, judgements and perceptions are intensified in group discussions. Groups, therefore, tend to move to extremes depending on the initial inclination of the members. Let us say that a group of managers is meeting to discuss whether to attack a rival's market. A predisposition to caution will lead to a very tentative policy, perhaps a request for further market research. On the other hand, a group that starts by thinking the proposal to be 'quite a good idea' may end up betting half the company's resources on its success.

Discussion, therefore, does not lead to moderation but to *polarisation*. Evidence suggests that, when individuals discuss ideas, they shift towards what they think matches the values of the group. Perceiving a culture of risk taking, cautious people will begin to advocate taking more chances. This shift will, in turn, encourage those who were originally risk takers to become more so, and so on. Discussions become biased, information is perceived selectively and rationales for one position or the other are reinforced.

The context of the decision is important. Vecchio points out that, in business and career planning, the dominant culture favours risk taking, almost seeing it as a prerequisite for success. Consequently, risky shift is a common occurrence. In the area of social and personal life, however, groups of families and friends will urge caution on individuals who face important decisions. Examples include assessing medical risks, which are weighed more cautiously by a group than by individuals,[25] and the cautious approach to arranged marriages.

■ Avoiding pitfalls

For a manager responsible for effective decision making by a group, a basic skill is to use awareness of the pros and cons to good effect. It is good practice, for example, to restrict cost by setting limits on meeting schedules. Having agreed membership and agendas, avoiding groupthink and polarisation is important. Again, recognising and responding to their symptoms is a mark of good group leadership. Changing the size and layout of group meetings enables reticent members to come forward and restricts the dominance of senior members. We shall return to this question in Chapters 11 and 12.

Creativity

Many opportunities or problems, especially those messy ones requiring non-programmed decisions, offer opportunities for creative solutions. Clearly, creativity is relevant to the generation of alternatives, for the more and better the potential choices, the better will be the outcome. Yet it is also relevant to other stages, for instance in the many ways to unravel the mess into problem definitions and in working out detailed routes to implement solutions. Its importance to organisations cannot be overstated because, in the end, competitive edge arises from doing things better than one's rivals. That often means thinking of these things first. Creativity is, therefore, important in product and process innovation, which are covered in Chapter 17. Here we shall look at its general relevance to decision making both by individuals and in group settings. 'Whatever creativity is, it is part of the solution to a problem.'[26]

▨ What is creativity?

It is very difficult to demonstrate creativity, for, as de Bono says, 'Any valuable creative idea is always logical in hindsight'.[27] When the Venetian traveller Marco Polo visited China in the thirteenth century, he was surprised to find that the Chinese had used single-gate *flash locks* on the 1600-kilometre Grand Canal for about a thousand years. These meant that every level change could only be small. Huge efforts were required to drag boats against the stream and water was wasted. The two-gate *pound lock* system was introduced in China about that time and, according to later travellers, was quickly perfected.[28] The idea reached The Netherlands in the fourteenth century. With hindsight, we recognise the pound lock as logical, just as the wheel before it and most other developments later. The danger is then to argue that, since the lock is so logical, not discovering it represents a failure of logic and has little to do with creativity!

Of course, this is a false argument, for de Bono goes on to show that hindsight colours our perception. Things that are obvious in hindsight are not necessarily so *in foresight*. Creativity is to do with seeing things ahead and not reasoning about them afterwards. Since post-event explanations will always suffer from this difficulty, it is best to recognise it as it happens. Whenever you might say to someone, 'That's a good idea!' you will have recognised creativity but you can't quite say what it is. 'True creativity often starts where language ends.'[29]

Observing friends playing a party game can reveal creative puzzle solving. Dingbats allows a team about thirty seconds to decode symbols printed on a small card. Exhibit 9.8 is a transcript. Of course, it's obvious with hindsight…?

▨ Creative individuals

Many people believe themselves to be uncreative and tend to point to famous artists, designers and so on as examples of highly creative individuals. Whether anyone

---

Exhibit 9.8 LOOK KOOL U^X

Various:	'Let me see … Turn it the right way up … This is hard … We get all the difficult ones … What's that – an X? … Squared? … Or a cross?'
Ben:	'Look back in anger'
Carole:	'How do you mean?'
Ben:	'Well, it's a cross … anger means you're cross.'
Andrea:	'… *you* cross. Look before you cross.'
Carole:	'Look back before you cross.'
Ben:	'But what about the first look?'
Andrea	'Look forward and back bef …'
Will:	'Look both ways before you cross.'
All	'Yeah!!!!!!!'

---

lacks creative ideas is controversial. Some argue that it is our habit not to recognise or apply the ideas that make the difference. Chopra argues that around 95 per cent of our 60 000 thoughts per day are the same as yesterday's: the challenge is to break out of automatic response mode and take up some of that 5 per cent.[30]

Vecchio summarises many research studies of personal differences.[31] United States research found that from 10 years old, females are more creative than males. This is the reverse of the case in India, underlining how culture plays its part in defining appropriate behaviour. Peak ages are the 30s, with scientists in the 30–34 range and artists 35–39. Afterwards, creativity does not vanish but output declines.

Looking at personal characteristics, studies bring out independence, breadth of interests and the search for fulfilment. Having studied creative managers, Raudsepp concluded that, compared with others, they:

- looked to the long term rather than immediate gain;
- had a great deal of energy;
- found the status quo irritating;
- persevered;
- followed hobbies and special interests;
- held that daydreaming was not a waste of time.[32]

These points raise questions for organisations that see the creativity of their employees as a critical resource. Recruiters need to understand how to assess individual creativity. One method is to observe responses to problem-solving tasks. Another is to create or apply standard tests. Recruitment is covered in Chapter 14.

■ Cultivating creativity

Extending the notion that creativity is dampened by habits and cultural constraints, methods for enhancing it stem from the idea of temporarily releasing individuals and groups from them. Perhaps the best-known technique is brainstorming. In a group session, members are asked to concentrate on a problem and come up with as many unusual solutions as they can, pushing these ideas as far as possible. To make the meeting work, certain 'rules' have become accepted, *see* Exhibit 9.9.

Exhibit 9.9 Good brainstorming practice

- A leader should set up the meeting, announce its fixed length, encourage participation by all and suggest new beginnings if one train of thought has been followed for too long.
- Group members should be drawn from a range of disciplines and experience.
- The atmosphere should be informal and participants should be encouraged to joke about crazy proposals. Conversation may match that in the dingbats game of Exhibit 9.8.
- There should be no evaluation of ideas during the session.
- A large board is helpful. In any case, a record of ideas, either tape or notes, should be studied afterwards for good ideas.

The most important rule in Exhibit 9.9 is the enjoinder not to evaluate ideas as they emerge (or half-emerge). It is common to hear creative suggestions put down with a 'That's no good because...' response before they have had time to grow.

Brainstorming has many variants. Seeds, such as randomly selected words, can be thrown into the meeting as starting points. In other cases the group may work on a list of *forced comparisons*, say between the question and a randomly selected problem or situation. These are helpful in individual brainstorming which, unexpectedly, is often reported as more productive than when done in a group.

A good personal skill is to 'listen for' ideas that might appear during times of relaxation and jot them in a special notebook at the first opportunity. The thoughts can then be sorted and grown using tools such as the mind map, Figure 9.1, or de Bono's *PMI*.[33] *Plus, Minus, Interesting* is a method of recording perceptions, assigning weights to different possibilities and, for some, an aid to decision making.

Whether for individuals or groups, fostering creative thinking in organisations requires that attention be given to:

- tolerance of risk taking and failure;
- tolerance of a range of personalities;
- autonomy;
- open communication;
- appropriate measures of output and related personal rewards.

At the organisational level, many firms have become concerned at the way cultures sustain conformity and complacency. How to break this down is a subject for Chapter 17.

Conclusion: the right alternatives and choices

Central to the managerial process, decisions range from the programmed routine to sorting out the non-programmed mess. Messes have uncertain boundaries, incomplete information and no consensus over objectives. Yet decisions about messes tend to be more significant in the long term and a good manager can display value through taking effective action in such circumstances. Uncertainty and ambiguity are compounded by risk. Different managers have varying propensities to take risks and will tend to evaluate situations in optimistic or pessimistic ways accordingly. It is up to organisations to ensure consistency in the management of risk.

Decision making involves making the right choices from among appropriate alternatives. Many authorities advocate the use of a formal decision process in which aims, alternatives and choices are developed rationally. The prescriptive classical, or rational, method represents something of an ideal. Yet it is weak in that it does not account either for the cost of obtaining the vast amount of information or for the time required to agree criteria in advance. In contrast, the administrative model comes closer to the way managers behave in practice. They recognise the impossibility of knowing all alternatives and of reaching consensus over problem definition and objectives and, instead, satisfice. With information becoming cheaper, we may see a shift towards incorporating more of it in decisions but there will always be a tension between the contrasting models.

Decision traps lurk, whether for the individual or the group. Training can help managers avoid the personal traps such as heuristics, framing, escalation of commitment or overconfidence. These can also affect groups, although they also have difficulties of groupthink and polarisation.

Valuable at all stages is creative skill. Studies show that creativity varies among cultures and according to a person's age, gender and other personal traits. On the other hand, a good manager should see that all staff are creative to some extent. The challenge is to release inventiveness from time to time. Organisations, in the end, depend on inventing the new at least as much as doing the old well.

QUICK CHECK

Can you ...

- Give eight reasons for complexity of decisions.
- Define risk, uncertainty and ambiguity.
- Summarise four common decision traps.
- Relate problem-solving styles to decision types.
- Contrast the classical and administrative decision models.

- Outline the purpose of a decision tree.
- Differentiate groupthink and polarisation.
- Define creativity.
- Separate hindsight and foresight in assessing creativity.
- Sketch a mind map.

QUESTIONS

Chapter review

9.1 List the causes of increasing complexity for decision makers, giving an example for the owner of an SME and the local manager of an ethnocentric MNE.

9.2 What are the conditions needed before an operations research model can be used in the rational decision process?

9.3 When would you expect individual decision making to be superior to group decision making and when inferior?

9.4 Do you agree with William Pollard's definition of a good decision? (See the quotation at the start of the chapter.)

Application

9.5 Would the air traffic controller in the BA5390 crisis have used elements of either decision model given in the chapter? Explain.

9.6 Examine the website of a leading pharmaceutical company to gather information on how it incorporates risk and uncertainty into its decision making.

Investigation

9.7 Study an important decision whose outcome has not turned out as expected. Use the ideas discussed in the chapter to identify possible causes. You could collect information on construction projects, new model launches or information system developments.

9.8 Construct a mind map of a case study you have worked on previously. Explain whether the process caused you to notice any new angles or avenues for further investigation.

OVERCONFIDENCE TEST

We noted that overconfidence exposes people to unnecessary risk. So recognising it in yourself is important. How can you tell? You can look at your past behaviour but people tend to remember successes and forget mistakes. Asking friends may be a guide, but they will be biased too. Try this quiz instead.

Rules

The idea here is not to get 'spot on' but to give a fairly good answer. The questions are tough and you are not an expert but you probably can guess. Each of the ten questions asks you for three numbers. In the first column put your best guess, which is the answer you would give if you were in a conventional quiz. In the other two columns, write the confidence range that you are very sure – 90 per cent sure – includes the correct answer. For the bottom of the range, give a number that you are quite sure is below the correct answer; for the top, a number that you are quite sure is higher. Remember you are trying to be about 90 per cent sure so do not give silly limits either way. Then the test would have no point.

In the example, the best guess is 3750 and the range 3000 to 4500.

	Best guess	Min	Max
What was the London FTSE-100 index on 5 March 2003?	3750	3000	4500
In what year did Lewis Carroll write *Alice in Wonderland*?			
For how many years is a French senator elected?			
How many bedrooms has the London Hilton hotel?			
What was the 2002 turnover of construction company Balfour Beatty?			
How long is the Panama Canal?			
When was the Superbowl inaugurated in American football?			
What is the height of Mont Blanc, the tallest mountain in the Alps?			
How many United States presidents preceded F.D. Roosevelt?			
How many pence was the US dollar worth on 1 January 2000?			
When was Ludwig von Beethoven born?			

Scoring

Check the answers on page 302. To score, ignore your best guesses. Gain one point if the correct answer falls within your range, otherwise zero.

Comparison

Since the standard was for 90 per cent sure, you should reach 9 points. Scoring 8 or less means you are overconfident; you have chosen ranges that are too narrow.

Lots of misses? You're in good company. Russo and Schoemaker,[34] who devised this form of quiz, tested more than 1000 managers from around the world. Fewer than 0.5 per cent scored one miss or none. Most had 6 or more!

You felt disadvantaged by lack of expertise? On their special subjects, experts were found to do slightly better; they missed 5 on average. Naturally, their answers tended to be close but they narrowed their confidence ranges too.

Personal message?

Think twice, be less sure and get some more information before making decisions.

CLOSING CASE

Risky decisions at Merck[35]

The leading pharmaceutical business, Merck and Co. Inc., invests annually about $2.4 billion in R&D and capital projects. Most of it goes into long-term high-risk projects for which conventional cash flow analyses are unsuitable. The breadth of uncertainty is so great that single estimates of, say, sales, exchange rates, market launch dates and so on would be worthless.

Merck has developed its own risk analysis models based on Monte Carlo simulation. They take probability estimates of input variables and produce a corresponding probability profile of the outputs. Two applications are in research planning and exchange rate hedging.

Research planning

The high risks inherent in research and development mean that Merck prefers to finance projects internally. Only 1 in 10 000 candidate chemicals makes it through to market. The company studies potential in income over the whole patent life of about twenty years. Risks include failure to pass safety trials of all kinds, difficulties in manufacture, the chance that a rival may reach the market first or enter later with a more effective formulation, market resistance and the appearance of side-effects after introduction. An emerging prob-lem is the cautious approach of the US Federal Drug Administration. Worries over side-effects have slowed approvals, meaning loss of revenues for the shorter patent period. Some risks can be assessed from experience (objective probability) while others are little more than informed guesses (subjective probabilities). The research planning model combines these with macroeconomic assumptions to provide probability profiles of cash flow and return on investment.

Revenue hedging

As a global business, Merck trades in many currencies. Hedging involves trading in actual currency or options to buy or sell in order to reduce the impact of unfavourable shifts in rates. Within its planning horizon of three years, Merck has options to sell foreign currencies at a fixed price. Were the dollar to weaken, the option would remain unexercised; were it to strengthen, the option would protect the dollar equivalent of overseas revenues. Again, all the data are expressed in terms of probability distributions. The model enables rapid comparisons of different hedging strategies and informs managers of the currency risks to which the company is exposed.

What do managers do with the models? Merck's chief financial officer, Judy Lewent, explains that the models do not make decisions. Instead, they give managers an assessment of risk and return that is drawn from their own judgements of the future environment. 'The models are not some black box that completely ignores the great wisdom of management and tries to mechanise the decision making of the business. They understand both the potential and their limitations.'

Questions

1 How well do the case examples match the risk, uncertainty and ambiguity categories of Figure 9.2?

2 Use the same categories to compare the decisions faced at LATCC and Merck.

3 Despite Lewent's denial, reliance on complex models at Merck has its dangers. Referring to the stages of the decision-making process, illustrate what these might be.

4 How might modelling support or hinder group decision making?

Bibliography

Mark Teale and colleagues (2002) *Management Decision Making: Towards an integrative approach* (Harlow: Financial Times Prentice Hall) discusses the subject from many points of view. For work on the intriguing idea of lateral thinking, try any of the 45 books by Edward de Bono. Thinking aids are presented by MindMapper, **www.mindmapper.com**, and Mind Tools, **www.mindtools.com/index.html**.

References

1 National Air Traffic Services (2003) *Services: The London Area Control Centre, Swanwick*, NATS, **www.nats.co.uk**, accessed 1 March 2003; Noxon, Julian (1996) 'Delays loom for advanced European ATC systems (air-traffic-control)', *Flight International*, 4537, 21 August, 11; 'AEA slams European ATC performance', *Flight International*, 4526, 5 June, 8; Learmount, David (1995) 'The future's controller: air traffic control in the foreseeable future will continue to depend heavily upon direct human input', *Flight International*, 4493, 11 October, 39–43; Harper, Keith (1997) 'The peril in Britain's skies', *Guardian*, 3 October, 17; Department of Transport (1992) *Report on the accident to BAC One-Eleven, G-BJRT over Didcot, Oxfordshire on 10 June, 1990 – Air Accident Report 1/92* London: HMSO.

2 Buzan, Tony (2002) *How to Mind-map: The Ultimate Thinking Tool That Will Change Your Life*, London: HarperCollins; *see also* SimTech (2003) *MindMapper*, **www.mindmapper.com**, and Mind Tools (2003) *Information and Study Skills*, **www.mindtools.com/index.html**, both accessed 3 March 2003.

3 *Financial Times* (2003), 'Worries grow over Ariane rockets', 16 January.

4 Clements, Alan (1995) 'Put in a spin by financial advice – amid a welter of conflicting opinions, the corporate point of view can be lost', *Financial Times*, 24 July, 8.

5 Waldmeir, Patti (2001) 'The guinea pigs demand justice: Those who claim to have suffered in medical trials are seeking redress the American way – through the courts', *Financial Times*, 18 October.

6 Holian, Rosalie (2002) 'Management decision making and ethics: practices, skills and preferences', *Management Decision*, 40(9), 862–70.

7 Buckingham, Lisa (1997) 'City told to curb bonuses', *Guardian*, 6 March, 17; Davies, Daniel (1997) 'Remuneration and risk', *Financial Stability Review*, quoted in 'A bit rich', *The Economist*, 8–14 March 1997, 103.

8 BMW (2002) *Group Management Report 2001*, BMW Group, 27; **www.bmw.com**, accessed 3 March 2003.

9 Henisz, Witold J. and Delios, Andrew (2001) 'Uncertainty, imitation, and plant location: Japanese multinational corporations, 1990–1996', *Administrative Science Quarterly*, 46(3), 443–75.

10 Ackoff, R.L. (1974) 'The systems revolution', *Long Range Planning*, 7(6), December, 2–5.

11 Vecchio, Robert (1995) *Organizational Behaviour*, 3rd edition, Fort Worth, Tex.: Dryden Press, 403–5.

12 Halifax Bank (2002) *Halifax Bank Accounts: Interest rates and account charges*, Halifax plc leaflet, December; also **www.halifax.co.uk**, accessed 6 March 2003.

13 Fraser, K. (2000) 'Ferry-tale alarms: report on Pacificat tells of higher costs and reduced service', *Vancouver Province*, 14 June; Willcocks, P. (2000) 'Fast ferries may sell for under $40 million each: BC Ferries' board was told that there is "an over-supply of existing vessels"', *Vancouver Sun*, 31 May.

14 Drummond, Helga and Kingstone Hodgson, Julia A. (1996) 'Between a rock and a hard place: a case study in escalation', *Management Decision*, **34(3)**, 29–34.

15 Simon, Herbert A. (1977) *The New Science of Managerial Decision Making*, Englewood Cliffs, NJ: Prentice-Hall.

16 Harrison, E. Frank and Pellitier, Monique A. (2000) 'The essence of management decision', *Management Decision*, **38(7)**, 462–9.

17 Barnard, Chester I. (1938) *The Functions of the Executive*, Cambridge, Mass.: Harvard University Press, 190.

18 *See* www.math.princoton.cdu/tsp/index.html for discussion of this problem; accessed 4 March 2003.

19 Adapted from Coles, Susan and Rowley, Jennifer (1995) 'Revisiting decision trees', *Management Decision*, **33(8)**, 46–50; *see also* Mind Tools at www.mindtools.com/pages/article/newTED_04.htm, accessed 6 March 2003.

20 March, James (1994) *A Primer on Decision Making*, New York: Free Press, 8.

21 Simon, H.A. (1976) *Administrative Behaviour*, 3rd edition, New York: Free Press, 68.

22 Wilkes, F.M., Samuels, J.M. and Greenfield, S.M. (1996) 'Investment decision making in UK manufacturing industry', *Management Decision*, **34(4)**, 62–71.

23 Janis, Irving L. (1982) *Groupthink*, 2nd edition, Boston, Mass.: Houghton Mifflin, 9.

24 Stoner, J.A.F. (1961) 'A comparison of individual and group decisions involving risk', Master's thesis, MIT Sloan School of Management, quoted in Vecchio, Robert (1995) *op. cit.*, 410.

25 Vecchio (1995) *op. cit.*, 412.

26 Aldiss, Brian W. (1990) *Bury My Heart at W. H. Smith's: A writing life*, London: Hodder & Stoughton.

27 de Bono, Edward (1988) *Letters to Thinkers: Further thoughts on lateral thinking*, Harmondsworth: Penguin, 188.

28 United East India Company (1655) *Beschrijving van't Gesandschap der Nederlandsche Oost-Indische Compagnie aan Den Grooten Tartarischen Cham, nu Keyzer van China*, Amsterdam.

29 Koestler, Arthur (1989) *The Act of Creation*, Harmondsworth: Penguin.

30 Success consultant Deepak Chopra quoted in Landale, Anthony (1997) 'Into the new year and daring to be different', *Guardian*, 4 January, 11.

31 Vecchio (1995) *op. cit.*, 418.

32 Raudsepp, E. (1978) 'Are you a creative manager?' *Management Review*, **58**, 15–16.

33 de Bono (1988) *op. cit.*, 79; *see also* www.mindtools.com/pmi.html.

34 Russo, J. Edward and Schoemaker, Paul J.H. (1990) 'The overconfidence quiz', *Harvard Business Review*, **68(5)** September–October, 236.

35 Grosvenor, Alex (2002) 'Testing times for pharmas – the future of world pharma companies' earnings is in the hands of US regulators, who are becoming ever-more strict about new drug approvals', *Investors Chronicle*, 8 March; Merck (2002) *Annual Report 2001: Financial Section*, Merck, 13–23; 'Mastering Management 5.6: Risk analysis at Merck', *Financial Times*, 24 November 1995.

Overconfidence test answers (questions on p. 299)

The FTSE was 3563.5 and the other answers are:

1865; 9; 450; £3.1 billion; 80 km (50 m); 1966; 4807 metres (15 772 feet); 31; 61.82; 1770.

PART 4

Organising, leading and communicating

Part 3 Planning and decision making

Chapter 8	Chapter 9
Planning and strategic management	**Decision making: choosing from alternatives**

Part 4 Organising, leading and communicating

Chapter 10	Chapter 11	Chapter 12	Chapter 13
Organising: principles and design	**Leadership and motivation**	**Groups and teams**	**Communication in management**

Part 5 Implementing policies and plans

Chapter 14	Chapter 15	Chapter 16	Chapter 17
Human resource management	**Operations management**	**Marketing: managing relations with customers**	**Innovation: from ideas to customer benefits**

Since management is concerned with 'getting things done through people', working with groups and individuals is a dominant feature of the role. Therefore, covering this large field, Part 4 is devoted to the social aspects of management – establishing and leading groups from small teams to large organisations. The study begins in Chapter 10, which contains definitions and studies ways to differentiate and integrate functions through different organisational forms. It relates these structures to situational factors such as uncertainty, globalisation and technology. The contingency approach reminds us that every situation is unique, yet we must generalise to understand and compare.

After structure, Chapter 11 takes us to leadership, considering what it is, where it comes from, and how it is put into effect. We also examine its mirror, motivation. Both areas have generated many theories concerning the nature of work rewards and their link to performance.

Management is a social activity, often conducted in work groups and teams. In Chapter 12, these terms are defined and compared to provide an understanding of their origins and how they function. Effective teams depend on how they are constituted and the processes they use to reach decisions and overcome conflict. In the global context, cultural diversity makes the operation of teams more complex.

Communication is often seen as the glue binding working relationships. Chapter 13 presents both a technical, process model of communication and broader perspectives on sense making and order building. We apply ideas to questions of enhancing skills, especially in listening and writing. In the organisational context, there are many means of making improvements, although those are hindered by problems of jargon and, especially, overload. Improved organisational communications may be the answer but the chapter sounds a note of caution. It may be that those in power do not wish to share accurate information. Instead, the intention of many messages may be to keep people in the dark.

CHAPTER 10

Organising: principles and design

Chapter objectives

When you have finished studying this chapter, you should be able to:

- explain and justify: hierarchy, specialisation, centralisation; co-ordination; line and staff;

- use organisation charts, process models and rich pictures to represent organisations;

- illustrate and compare functional, divisional, matrix and network forms;

- explain and illustrate contingency theory and relate it to universalist and particularist perspectives;

- demonstrate and criticise how structure and performance are related to situational factors;

- explain and illustrate three situational factors in the environment, namely uncertainty, globalisation and technology;

- untangle the ties between strategy, interdependence and culture, and organisational design;

- set out the limitations of the contingency approach to organising.

This island is almost made of coal and surrounded by fish. Only an organising genius could produce a shortage of coal and fish in Great Britain at the same time.

Aneurin Bevan, British politician

Siemens AG: integrating a worldwide portfolio of businesses[1]

Siemens is a decentralised global business with almost 60 per cent of its 426 000 staff employed outside Germany. Sales for 2002, of €84 billion, placed the company twentieth in the world. It sees itself as committed to 250 business fields within the electronic and electrical industries, having sustained growth through innovation and customer service.

In 2003, the company had its own organisations in 190 of the world's 200 countries. These ranged from small agency offices to giant manufacturing plants spread throughout the most important economies. In the United States, where sales were $20.3 billion, 70 000 staff worked in 780 locations; 5700 were in R&D. There were 20 000 in China. How does such a company organise its effort to innovate and focus operations while, simultaneously, presenting a local 'Siemens' face to each customer?

At the highest level, reporting to the managing board, responsibility for the worldwide business lies with 14 operating groups arranged in 7 areas, see Figure 10.1. At headquarters, there are corporate departments. Spread throughout the world, regional units are responsible for local sales and service on behalf of the whole organisation. Siemens also has interests in joint ventures, such as the 50–50 Fujitsu–Siemens Computers, Europe's leader. With 7500 staff, it achieves sales of €5.4 billion.

Siemens' main board is responsible for co-ordinating all the activities. For example, it has to decide where to focus R&D activity to provide the innovations on which future business depends. Almost €5.8 billion is spent on R&D. The 53 100 staff throughout the world registered 4600 patents in 2002. More than 40 per cent of the spending, and more than half of the staff, are in the Information and Communications area. This emphasis is based on the recognition that microelectronics is the key to the future and makes Siemens one of the world's largest software houses.

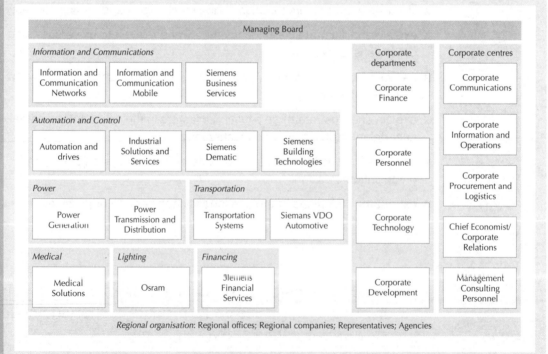

Figure 10.1 **Siemens AG – board and business groups**

Some critics argue that the business has become too difficult to manage and should be separated into high technology and low technology companies. The board sees advantage in covering fields with different market cycles, stressing the value of global integration. Beyond internal development and innovation, however, it continues to reshape the portfolio through acquisitions, disposals and joint ventures. For example: major acquisitions of the 1990s included Westinghouse, in power generation, and VDO in automotive; several component manufacturing units were sold; and the 1999 computing joint venture with Fujitsu took the Siemens–Nixdorf group out of direct ownership.

Beyond changing the portfolio, the board is improving all activities. In 1993, it started the top+ programme focused on: innovation management, asset management, project management and quality management. The board is also pressing for better exploitation of synergies. Key areas are: joint development and application of technologies; purchasing; process standardisation; in-house services; one face to a customer; and the optimal use of the Siemens brand.

Introduction

Commensurate with its global reach, Siemens faces the problem of structural design on a grand scale. Once challenged by analysts to split into separate electronic and electrical divisions, chairman Heinrich von Pierer points to the recognition of the value of the broad portfolio. Not only does it give balanced earnings but it also enables Siemens to win large infrastructure projects. For a new power station in a developing country, for example, there will be work for many of the groups shown in Figure 10.1. The company wants to present a single face to the customer yet divide its manufacturing and service operations into efficient, focused units each of which achieves the highest standards of quality and productivity. Bridging strategy and operations is the problem of organising. We can define this as follows:

> *Organising is the arrangement of all elements of an organisation to achieve its strategic objectives.*

We can see that the definition implies choice. Clearly, there are many possible configurations of Siemens' business units spread across 250 sectors and 190 countries. As in most organisations, there is a tension between the need to deploy resources into identifiable departments, the notion of *differentiation*, and the requirement to link them in patterns that match customers' needs, the idea of *integration*. The structure is important here. Close linkages allow the business to take advantage of synergies. As Siemens shows, however, they can be difficult to achieve in practice. It is only recently that Siemens has set up a headquarters unit for purchasing. Unless this activity is confined to the largest buying contracts, the benefits of centralisation can be lost in extra administration and slower service.

Organising is never a once and for all task. Just as we picture strategic management as a flow of decisions producing an emergent strategy, an organisation structure emerges as adaptation to change. History has a great effect. While most groups at Siemens are integrated into the single business, Osram was a major acquisition and remains legally separate. Through acquisition and disposal, the business form is continually being reshaped.

The points made here are among the fundamental ideas that apply to all organisations, whether businesses, government agencies or in the voluntary sector. We begin this chapter with a study of these principles and show how they work out in practice. Then we relate structures to wider questions such as environment and change. We also point to some new challenges to the conventional, hierarchical form.

Principles

In this section, we shall examine four key issues in organising, namely hierarchy, specialisation, centralisation and co-ordination. None of these is new. Writing a century ago, Fayol was concerned with much the same questions, *see* Chapter 1. To illustrate the general nature of the issues, we shall compare Siemens with a voluntary organisation. Measured by turnover or employment, The Network,[2] described in Exhibit 10.1, was only a few millionths of the size of the German MNE. Yet they shared the same sorts of questions.

Exhibit 10.1 The Network: the satisfaction of sharing

The Network was a skills exchange established in the premises of Merseyside Council for Voluntary Service (MCVS) in Liverpool. Facilities included a small office, a workshop and lounge. Any person, employed or unemployed, could become a member by signifying some 'offer' of skill or time and some 'want' to be satisfied. There was no cash payment, exchanges did not necessarily take place reciprocally and the basis of all transactions was reasonable give and take. The group behind The Network was searching for alternative ways to reward work. A resource exchange could offer many non-economic functions of employment – time structuring, widening experience, a sense of usefulness, personal status and enforcing activity. Further, a successful operation would change attitudes in the wider society, towards work, the unemployed and welfare benefits. The 12 founders hoped for a large-scale operation in an area where the number of registered unemployed was around 100 000. They foresaw problems of coping with a large membership. Instead of this extensive impact, however, an organisation with average membership of 130 emerged. Jobs done for others ranged from typing to transport and dog handling to dressmaking. Besides exchanges, members were involved in group projects, workshops and social events.

The weekly members' meeting, with rotating chairman and minutes secretary, was the decision-making body. Day-to-day running of the organisation began with a members' rota. After a year, however, the rota was supplemented by members becoming, for one month at a time, a full-time, paid co-ordinator. Financial support came from foundations via MCVS as guarantor. Concerned by his duty to ensure wise spending, the MCVS secretary exercised considerable influence over how The Network was run, insisting on detailed financial records. Given that this person's signature was required on all bank drawings, the members felt obliged to comply.

Hierarchy

In Exhibit 1.9, we noted Weber's studies of bureaucracy. He saw bureaucracy as emerging from the change from traditional authority to the rational and legal system of organisation and control. Bureaucracy established a relation between people at the top, such as directors or elected politicians, and their subordinates. The legitimacy of the top people arises from an external source, such as ownership, appointment or election, while the rights and duties of others in the organisation come from delegation. Weber preferred these rights to be prescribed in written rules. Many organisations, however, do not stick to this strict approach. While the rules are embodied in people's job descriptions, the pace of change is such that written documents cannot keep up. Members are expected to continually rethink and renegotiate their tasks. Nevertheless, the ideas of authority, its delegation, and corresponding responsibilities are important ones.

> *Authority is the formal right of a manager to act as a manager, that is to plan, decide, give instructions, allocate resources, and control, to achieve the aims of the organisation.*

Barnard was among the first to point out three features of organisational authority:[3]

- *It resides in the position and not the person.* As chief executive of Siemens, von Pierer must exercise authority related to his roles. His wide discretion exists within board policies and legal and ethical frameworks. Similarly, The Network chairman exercised that role according to the rules of the group guided by knowledge of good practice in the conduct of meetings.

- *It must be accepted by subordinates.* As Chapter 11 shows, the manager's authority vanishes if the subordinates refuse to follow. Politics shows us how power, positional or personal, can quickly evaporate when associates withdraw their support, *see* Exhibit 10.2.

- *It can be transferred from one level to another.* Delegation to the lowest feasible level maximises flexibility and responsiveness to customers, and can improve motivation. Siemens suggests that its 'decentralized structure gives the Groups the greatest possible degree of entrepreneurial responsibility and the ability to nurture close ties to their customers'.[4]

There are limits to what can be delegated. Only a company board can approve accounts and directors are responsible for safety. The Network struggled with a similar tension. Members wanted wide discretion to spend funds yet MCVS had promised donors that it would account for every penny.

Exhibit 10.2 Vanishing power

In a struggle after the death of Chairman Mao in 1976, the Gang of Four ousted the moderates led by vice-premier Deng Xiaoping, who went into hiding. Hua Guofeng was installed as party chairman and head of government yet soon he had the Gang arrested on treason charges. During Hua's stop-gap administration, Deng recovered his former influence and progressively challenged Hua. Deng installed his protégés in key politburo positions so that, in 1982, Hua's group was removed. They had lost the support of the party and the people. Although not holding the highest offices, and gradually retiring from those that he did fill, Deng remained highly influential until his death in 1997.

Closely tied to authority is responsibility. It mirrors authority in that *responsibility is the duty to act according to the authority that has been delegated*. Therefore, if managers have legitimate authority to act, then that is what they must do. Normally, managers are given responsibility that matches their authority. If responsibility is excessive, the manager's job becomes very difficult, relying on persuasion rather than giving orders. If the balance swings the other way, there is the possibility of a manager using power for personal, wasteful or, ultimately, tyrannical ends.

Line and staff

There are many cases of managers not having formal authority. As the range of special problems increases, dealing with them is taken over by separate individuals and departments. They are 'off-line', so to speak. The *line managers* concentrate on the main processes of the organisation. In manufacturing, these could be obtaining materials, production and distribution. In a hospital, line activities are medical and nursing. Support comes from *staff departments*, which cover functions from engineering to employment law and systems to personnel development.

There is much scope for interpretation. The link between the line and staff managers can range from superior–subordinate to an advisory link between colleagues in different departments or even from an outside consultant. Why establish such a complex arrangement?

The *line and staff* idea comes from military practice. A fighting (line) unit frequently has staff officers to provide specialist knowledge and skills. For example, they might gather and interpret intelligence using skills in data management or foreign languages. Scarce specialists can be deployed without having to clog the traditional command structure.

In the civilian sphere, staff departments operate at all levels, providing vertical channels of communication for specialist, technical information. The corporate functions at Siemens are staff advisers to the CEO, the senior line manager. In practice, they will not consult with the chief on every detail. Usually they exchange information and instructions directly. For example, the corporate information unit will issue guides to the businesses on website design. Exhibit 10.3 gives a further example, this time from the pharmaceutical industry. Here, technical complexity means that manufacturing line managers need support from staff teams. Rotation of scientists between line and staff functions helps build experience and teamwork.

Exhibit 10.3 Line and staff in manufacturing at Merck

'The Manufacturing scientist can rotate from staff process positions into technical manufacturing areas that provide participation in line management. These supervisory positions give the scientist a thorough understanding of process safety, quality, productivity, and employee issues that affect the daily production operation. The varied experiences that scientists bring to this role are invaluable for effective interaction with support departments that assist in meeting market demands.'[5]

The growth of staff roles presents dangers. Godfrey and others[6] warn against line managers delegating responsibility for a key activity to staff managers, whose role should be limited to advising on, and handling, its technical aspects. Their example, given in Exhibit 10.4, is taken from health care management yet could just as well apply anywhere. There are many instances of quality improvement programmes failing because they have been seen by senior line managers as essentially *technical* solutions to problems and therefore the province of specialists. Note how the director of quality management is made accountable for the programme yet has not the authority to carry it through.

The director was left without support. In another organisation, the staff department could win too much support and begin to act in an arrogant way, overestimating its own importance. Self-serving attitudes may grow as the staff managers forget that their primary task is to support the line.

Exhibit 10.4 Responsibility without authority

'In health care, executives initially intent on quality management as a strategy easily become distracted by new threats from purchasers, crises in physician relationships, restructuring, mergers, capital needs, and a thousand other short-term demands. ...[senior managers] easily yield to the temptation of delegating the quality management initiative to others.

'Over-delegation can occur in disguise. No executive who has read the quality literature ever says to the staff quality director, "I am expecting you to handle this change, so that I can attend to other matters." Instead, the language is of "full support," "generous budgets," and "regular reviews." But, by other salient tests, the work of leadership may not have changed at all. Has the Chief Executive's daily calendar really changed so as to make quality the strategy of the organization? Have behaviours among senior managers evolved so as to teach, support, and sustain the breaking down of barriers, the customer focus, the "process-mindedness," and the new use of statistical thinking without which quality management is only rhetoric? Do organization-wide quality strategies exist? Are they managed? Are they, in fact, the top priority, or not?

'Many executives who have over-delegated the change process do not appear to realize it. No wonder; no one tells them. It would be a rare, courageous, and perhaps short-lived "Director of Quality Management" who would make an appointment with the CEO to say, "I have been thinking, boss. The job you gave me, and are expecting me to carry out, I now realize, is, in fact, your job. You are holding me accountable for changes in culture, behaviour, strategic priority, and organizational methods that only you ... can really deliver. In the end, you may think that I let you down; but it's the other way around."'

■ Specialisation

Work can be more efficient when employees specialise. They focus on a limited number of activities and hone their skills accordingly. Organisations develop around this principle. The Network displayed the beginnings of specialisation. Not all members could take the chair, keep the minutes or conduct administrative tasks. These were shared among those who were willing and able to take on the burden. Siemens has problems of specialisation on a much larger scale. The company chose to build its business units around technological groupings such as power generation or automation. Yet there could be arguments for specialisation by region or by type of customer. Some firms resolve this tension with a matrix structure that we shall examine later.

Within business groups, each level is split further until, at the operating level, there are departments for supply, operations, sales, distribution and so on. Efficiency benefits seem to be available down to the single task. Yet, as explained in Chapter 11, there are limits. Ultimately, specialisation leads to low motivation as workers carry out a single repetitive and boring job. Therefore, many companies are rethinking their organisations along team lines. As with many other aspects, the problem concerns not whether specialisation is good or bad but finding its right pattern and degree.

■ Centralisation (and decentralisation)

Centralisation refers to the level in the hierarchy at which decisions are made. In a centralised organisation, they are made by those near the top, whereas decentralisation means authority passes to lower levels. The latter features less monitoring of employee decision making and performance.

Measuring centralisation of an organisation is difficult. This is influenced by the positive image of decentralisation in both managers' and commentators' minds. Many claim its existence while behaviour shows otherwise. Furthermore, the possibilities for decentralisation vary from firm to firm and from time to time. Crisis, for example, leads to centralisation. This is because crisis management procedures, *see* Chapter 8, require all aspects of the emergency to be handled through a single 'command and control' office.

Trends are also difficult to perceive. Many authorities espouse policies of decentralisation to match developments such as flatter organisation structures and the recruitment of better educated employees. Reality is, as usual, more complex. Opposite trends coexist within the same organisation. For example Siemens, with many global companies, has policies for centralised purchasing, technology application and brand development. Meanwhile, the geographic spread to 190 countries requires service organisations to move closer to customers than ever. Service operations cannot be controlled from an office in Germany, however efficient it may be.

Figure 10.2 summarises the advantages and disadvantages of centralisation. The benefits lie in: gains in economic performance through administrative cost savings; taking advantages of scale; avoiding wasteful conflict; and competition among units. Decentralisation, in contrast, offers: decisions closer to the point where they are needed; more flexibility; and benefits to employees such as higher motivation and chances to broaden experience. A wise organisation will consider these issues in relation to all its policies. For example, strong arguments can be advanced for centralising the following activities:

- allocation of capital investment and R&D expenditure;
- managing international cash flows;
- design of information systems;
- purchasing of major items;
- development of senior managers;
- setting conditions of employment.

Meanwhile, here are some tasks that may be better decentralised:

- management of day-to-day operations;
- links to national and regional industry organisations;
- small-scale purchasing;
- sales;

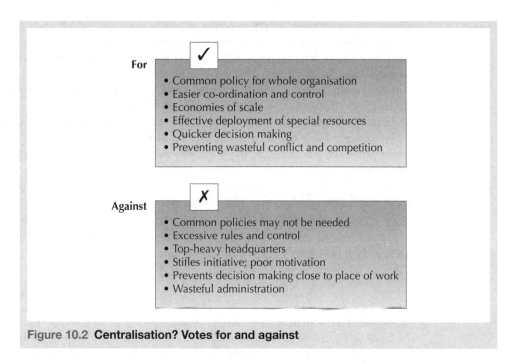

Figure 10.2 Centralisation? Votes for and against

■ recruitment;

■ training of locally recruited staff.

Since Siemens spends more than 7 per cent of turnover both on fixed investments and on R&D, allocating funds among groups must be a board-level decision. Yet the management of approved projects is carried out by teams within the businesses.

In human resource management, many companies set standard conditions of employment. This aids harmony and simplifies transfer of middle and senior managers among units. Such a policy begins to break down, however, when the group merges with new businesses. The costs of harmonisation outweigh the benefits and it may be better to maintain each person's original conditions of employment.

International differences in employment conditions raise problems. The aid agency Oxfam has a commendable policy of not paying the senior person in any country more than five times the salary of the most junior. This comes under strain where wages are very low; the centralised international scale used for expatriate managers makes the night watchperson's wage much higher than demanded in the local market. Polycentric MNEs avoid such problems by resolving all employment issues locally.

■ Co-ordination

Co-ordination refers to the *need for staff to act in unison*. This is not difficult in the small entrepreneurial set-up. Here, all but the most trivial decisions are made by the owner-manager who continually adapts the business to its changing environment. Unless the entrepreneur behaves haphazardly, co-ordination is implicit. When organisations grow, they spawn specialist roles. These carry out important internal functions, such as accounting, or deal with different aspects of the environment, such as through regional sales managers. Adding such positions makes organisations more complex. Further growth means that specialist roles become departments. Co-ordination requires collaboration both within and between them. The snag is that, as departments become stronger, their staff develop loyalties to their immediate managers and colleagues. Barriers between departments increase and hinder the management of work flow across them. Witness how professionals, such as teachers, doctors or engineers, often speak of their departments as though they were in competition with others with whom they are supposed to co-operate.

What means are available to achieve co-ordination? Figure 10.3 illustrates four basic methods: line management, liaison staff, information systems and cross-functional teams.

Line management

Line managers, working within an appropriate hierarchical structure, are fundamental in achieving order. Later on, we shall see how structure takes many forms. Design is based partly on seeing co-ordination as a critical responsibility of managers at each level.

Liaison staff

Co-ordination difficulties for line managers derive from complexity and the number of tasks to be linked. One solution is the appointment of liaison, or linking, staff who connect the work of several individuals or departments. A common sight in factories dedicated to batch production is the *progress chaser* who, clipboard in hand, follows orders between processes, ironing out snags in the flow. Managed from a centralised production control office, these staff are attached to none of the manu-

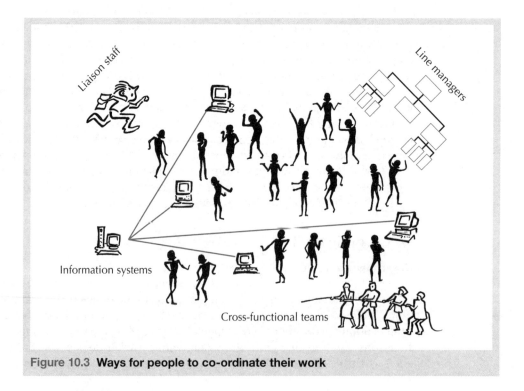

Figure 10.3 **Ways for people to co-ordinate their work**

facturing sections. They rely for their authority on personal drive, persuasive powers and detailed knowledge.

At The Network, it had been hoped to achieve co-ordination through volunteers taking on the task for a week at a time. The outcome was neither continuity nor consistency. Consequently, members took it on for longer periods, receiving small salaries for agreed weekly hours.

At a broader level, leading companies making ranges of consumer goods rely on product, or brand, managers to co-ordinate each line. Exhibit 10.5 illustrates typical tasks. Note the links both with other managers in the organisation and with outside agencies.

Exhibit 10.5 The category manager as link person

'This is a challenging mixture of both category and brand management, offering the autonomy to play a leading role in the development and growth of our quality portfolio. You'll also have the chance to mastermind the launch and commercialisation of both existing and new brands on the back of our phenomenal success. Your impact on the business will be immediate, encompassing a whole range of strategic initiatives in line with present and future customer-orientated objectives.

'Working within a multi-functional team, you'll define and evolve detailed category development programmes, carefully positioning and monitoring brands so that each is poised to make maximum impact in terms of distribution, market share, volume and profitability.

'Integrating your skills with customer managers, marketing/commercial management and external agencies, you'll oversee the development of marketing communications material and other below-the-line activities to fully support your planning and launch of new products.'[7]

Information systems

Information systems enable transmission of vast quantities of information through and between organisations irrespective of hierarchical, departmental or geographical separation. Both Dibrell and Miller[8] and Mukherji[9] trace the way computers first made bureaucracies more efficient through cutting clerical and supervisory work, speeding data flows and enabling greater centralisation of decision making and control. They did not, however, resolve the mismatch of the bureaucracy with uncertain environments. Improved information systems, however, supported horizontal co-ordination within new flexible structures, such as the matrix. Later in the chapter, we see how matrix structures support process management, in which co-ordination is vital. These are giving way to network forms through which co-ordination is extended into supply chains. Beyond such operational links, *knowledge management* has emerged with a much wider scope. Sharing information of all kinds is vital for efforts, such as at Siemens, to achieve synergies between units. Note that all these changes modify Mintzberg's roles of *nerve centre* and *disseminator* discussed in Chapter 1.

Cross-functional teams

Cross-functional teams, known sometimes as *task forces* or *working parties*, work on problems involving several departments. They gather different perspectives and expertise. For instance, at Swindon Body and Pressings, production managers were concerned about the best specification of glove to be worn for occasional handling of steel panels jammed in machines. Sharp corners risked cuts and abrasions. Line managers are responsible for safety and are expected to resolve such questions. A group assembled with advisers and potential suppliers to find a common solution. Incidentally, even this outcome was a stop-gap since the best way to approach risky tasks is to eliminate them. As they said at the plant, 'We should design them out'.

Task forces and working parties are often temporary. Permanent arrangements include standing committees that meet regularly to co-ordinate activities. As we shall see later, teams can become so important and numerous in some organisations that they are represented in their permanent structures – the so-called matrix organisations.

Co-ordination in voluntary organisations is both operational and motivational, as inclusion is an important part of retaining commitment. Typical of small groups, The Network used its weekly meetings to make decisions from spending several thousand pounds on a new project to choosing which colour to paint the snack bar ceiling. Large organisations would see this co-ordination as excessive.

Representing organisations

When asked to describe their organisations, many managers will reach for an organisation chart, such as in Figure 10.1. This picture tells something about the organisation, including our respondent's status within it! It is a representation, or *model*, of the structure, usually showing the relatively permanent links among businesses or officials. The model is useful if we are interested in these links. Like all good descriptive models, it tells us what we want to know and leaves out other details. Yet it does not reveal many things. We learn little of what happens, of how the system behaves. Important features not shown include: relationships that cut across the normal hierarchy; power distances between levels; information flows; committees and other group activities; and details of each manager's responsibilities.

Let us illustrate this difficulty by looking again at The Network. A useful skill for managers approaching a situation for the first time is to sketch something related to the mind map of Figure 9.1. In this context, such sketches are known as *rich pictures*. Figure 10.4 gives one for The Network. On a single sheet, it captures the main organisational elements and the processes that occur within them. We used this example both to record our first impressions and, in a tidier and enlarged layout, for communicating to the group, 'This is the way we see you'. The compressed form of the rich picture, however, means that it communicates little without verbal support. The notes in Exhibit 10.6 summarise the introductory points of a presentation made to a meeting of members and sponsors.

■ Representing structure and process

To capture multiple aspects of what happened at The Network, Figure 10.4 sacrifices detail. Like other models, it is a simplification, here designed to support and record an initial impression. It leads to further questions, about both relationships and how things work. To proceed, we tend to use two further models to represent structure and process.

■ *Structure* refers to those features of the organisation that are fixed. Besides the hierarchy, these include features, such as plant and buildings, systems from infor-

Figure 10.4 **The Network skills exchange**

Exhibit 10.6 Notes to support the rich picture of Figure 10.4

The Network sought to recruit new members through free promotion spots in local media (a). On arrival, prospective members were invited to declare 'offers and wants' (O and W) to be compared in a matching system (b). Decisions were taken at the weekly decision-making body (DMB), which included a rotating chairman, the co-ordinator, the MCVS secretary, and up to 12 volunteers. Volunteers, not always the same ones, covered administration with the co-ordinator. We noted conflicting attitudes between the two groups. The DMB dispensed funds and MCVS guarded them.

The Network knew little about members who left or those who did not join after visiting (c). They assumed people stayed as long as their needs were satisfied (d).

mation technology through to working rules, and the basic culture shared by members. Being unchanging, they share the property that they can be depicted with static models such as charts, sketches and manuals.

■ *Process* refers to those features of the organisation that are continually changing. They include flows of goods, cash and information.

Structural models have already been introduced and are used extensively in the rest of this chapter. Process models are common in management, for example planning in Chapter 8, decision making in Chapter 9 and control in Chapter 18.

Forms of organisation

Organisation charts describe structure. They are useful in studying formal relationships and staff deployment between departments. They use the two dimensions of the chart to depict:

- *Hierarchy* – the number of levels and the chain of command.
- *Specialisation* – the division of tasks between managers and deciding who is responsible for linking their work at each level.

Organisation structures try to balance the need to specialise with the need for co-ordination. Therefore, the organisational design both *differentiates* and *integrates*. Yet, many choices are available for splitting staff into departments. Within a department people have work that is more closely related than with that of members of other departments. The snag is that these links can be drawn in many ways, and change as new situations arise. Hence the variety of functional, divisional, matrix and network structures that we shall now examine.

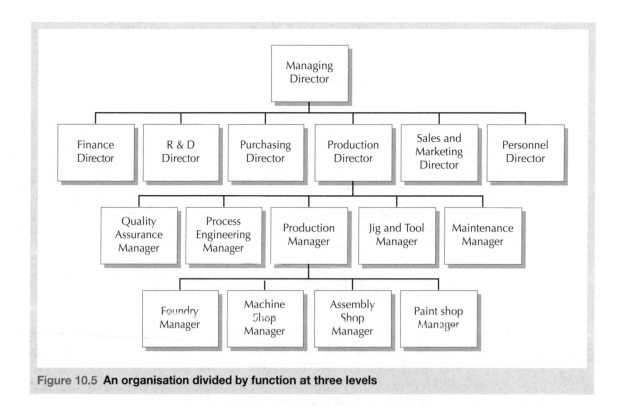

Figure 10.5 **An organisation divided by function at three levels**

◼ Functional form

Organisations planned along functional lines place together people using related technical skills in similar tasks. They are based on disciplines such as production, marketing, finance or personnel. Figure 10.5 shows a company creating functional departments at three levels of production. Structures within other departments would appear in a full chart, but there is no space here.

The advantage of functional departments is the enhanced co-ordination through having people with similar skills and outlook working together. Such departments grow in SMEs as each manager takes on assistants to cope with the increasing workload. Disadvantages arise from departmental members becoming more concerned with their specialism than with the whole company. Measuring the department's contribution is difficult as it is not responsible for the delivery of identifiable products. Especially in the case of large functional departments, the structure emphasises differentiation at the expense of integration.

Hospitals often have functional departments, based on clinical specialities. They enable the professional development of staff within each discipline and allow for departmental heads having specialised knowledge. Yet, hospitals experience interdepartmental rivalry. Figure 10.6 shows the functional structure within South Tees

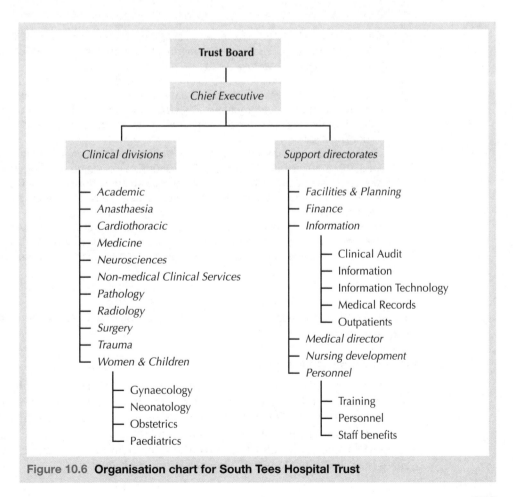

Figure 10.6 Organisation chart for South Tees Hospital Trust

NHS Trust. Heads of the units shown in italics form the management group that oversees operations. The Trust Board combines internal and external members to give strategic direction. The change to increased operational control of medical functions has created much tension in the health service.

■ Divisional form

The invention of the divisional, often called the *multi-divisional*, form is attributed to Sloan who reorganised General Motors this way, *see* Exhibit 10.7.[10] The unifying theme of the division is its output. Each division operates as if it is almost an autonomous business within the whole organisation. This type of organisation is valuable when:

■ the size of each division is sufficient for it to be able to provide its own specialists, such as accountants and engineers; and

■ the work of each division is relatively independent so that their operations do not need close co-ordination.

Exhibit 10.7 Alfred P. Sloan pioneers the divisional form

Alfred P. Sloan (1875–1966) became president of General Motors in 1923, chairman in 1946, and honorary chairman after retirement in 1956. He wrote the influential book, *My Years with General Motors* (1963).

Sloan took over a business struggling with competition from Ford's Model T. Sloan replaced the bureaucratic, centralised organisation with product divisions, the opposite of the way Ford was structured. Chevrolet and Cadillac, both GM cars, competed with each other. Internally, Sloan maintained a delicate balance between centralisation and decentralisation.

Divisionalisation was an outstanding success. GM's home market share, 12 per cent in 1923, exceeded 45 per cent by 1980. Executives could avoid the detail and focus on divisional performance targets and overall direction. General Motors became a model of management for the large corporation. Today, more than 85 per cent are organised this way.

Sloan's balance was lost in the 1960s, however. A web of committees and groups led to continual power struggles. The powerful finance function, with tight targets and narrow performance measures, stifled innovation. GM became paralysed by what had made it strong.

There are three themes found in the setting up of divisions – products, geography and customers.

Product-based divisions

Many large organisations are organised by product. The advantage of such organisation lies in the unification of effort towards the supply of a particular bundle of goods and services. Figure 10.1 shows Siemens' organisation structure based on product areas from Automation and Information to Power Generation and Transportation. Although they share the 'electrical and electronic' theme, differences between technologies justify splitting on a product basis.

Geographically based divisions

Geography is a common basis for structural design, especially in large companies whose operations are widely dispersed. Service companies, from transport to retailing, can offer the same group of products to customers in many locations. They may then be best organised by region. British Airways has geographic divisions, such as BA Manchester; the separate divisions of large bus operators such as Arriva run services in different towns, often keeping the brands of previous companies; electricity companies, such as ScottishPower, organise their maintenance operations by district. Among global corporations, the polycentric MNE splits geographically.

Customer-facing divisions

Here the organisation matches customer differences in its structure. This approach is useful when customer groups demand dissimilar products or require them to be supplied in distinct ways. Dell, for example, separates its sales and service organisations between businesses and consumers; Nokia, *see* Chapter 8, has a Business Communications SBU; ferry companies frequently separate passengers and freight.

▓ Hybrid forms

We have presented each basis of departmentalisation in its ideal form. In practice, however, organisations stray from the ideals, adapting them according to circumstances. This point is shown in the example of the Hospital Trust structure of Figure 10.6. It has a mixture of customer-facing and functional designs, for example gynaecology and paediatrics versus anaesthetics and radiology. Many organisations, moreover, split differently at each level. Figure 10.7 illustrates a supermarket firm with a functional structure at board level, two levels divided geographically and lastly product departments within each store. International retailers often have another geographic layer on top.

Organisation design is often a compromise. Whichever principle is used to group staff, it will create difficulties elsewhere. For example, BT moved in 1991 from a regional to a customer-facing structure. In urban areas where business and personal customers are abundant, having teams for both will be easy. A rural district, on the other hand, may have few domestic subscribers and even fewer businesses. Here, having separate installation teams would be foolish. Similarly, Siemens sales and service offices are divided by technology in large markets, whereas in small countries, one office acts as link for the whole company.

The multidivisional form, Sloan's legacy, is the commonest structure in today's large organisations. Yet, in our comments on General Motors in Exhibit 10.7, we saw how GM became bogged down in complex webs of power, rivalry and control. Its sluggish response to the rise of the compact car in the United States is but one symptom. More competitive and dynamic times require more entrepreneurial, flexible forms.

▓ Matrix form

The internationalisation of a business structure takes one of two broad paths. To start foreign sales, a first step is to establish an 'international sales' department, which may possibly grow into an *international division*. Then, according to how

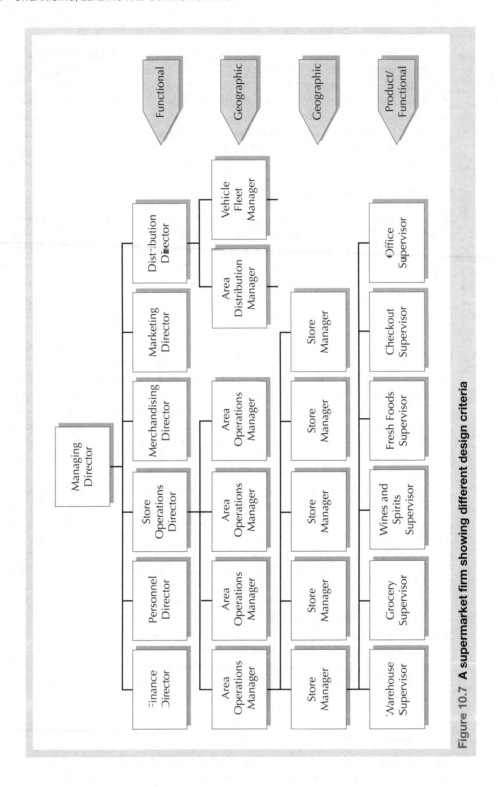

Figure 10.7 A supermarket firm showing different design criteria

foreign investment develops, the paths diverge, leading either to *international subsidiaries* based on customers' locations, or to *global product divisions* based on processes and technology. The former approach was followed by Electrolux, General Motors and Shell for many years. This polycentric form gave power to country managers but made difficult the co-ordination of manufacturing, technology, brands and so on. Product divisions were chosen by Matsushita and, as we have seen, Siemens.

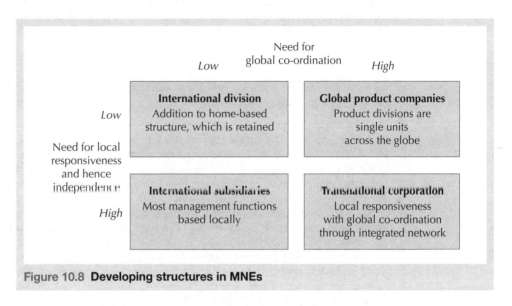

Figure 10.8 **Developing structures in MNEs**

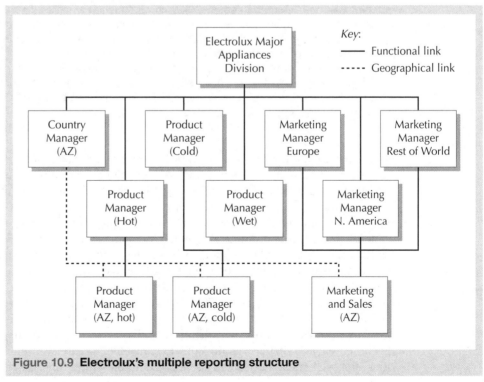

Figure 10.9 **Electrolux's multiple reporting structure**

They co-ordinate production but pay less attention to regional market variations. Finally, the company seeks to combine local responsiveness with global co-ordination. This is the *transnational corporation* of Bartlett and Ghoshal, who also summarised the links between these types and globalisation, as in Figure 10.8.[11]

Seeking the benefits of both paths, businesses turned, from about 1980, to the matrix form. Two dimensions of region and product were common, although others such as global customers or industry sector were also added. Electrolux adopted such a structure in the 1980s, *see* Exhibit 10.8. Following acquisitions and expansions into new countries, however, it found the matrix had become too complex, inflexible and demanding on key managers.

Exhibit 10.8 Complex co-ordination at Electrolux[12]

The Electrolux Group is the world leader in kitchen, cleaning and outdoor appliances. Its 'major appliances' product division, 80 per cent of sales, is widely dispersed into about 500 business units. Each is a nationally based company with its own accounts. In the late 1990s, there were some 43 factories in 15 countries grouped in three 'product areas', namely cold, hot and wet. Within the product areas, the national 'product divisions' had at most two factories each. Generally, the factories did not duplicate production so each was responsible for the supply to all markets. There were 135 marketing and sales companies in 40 countries, their work co-ordinated by three international marketing managers.

Electrolux operates in a polycentric way. Country managers monitor production and sales in their countries. They also deal with national issues, such as relations with large retail customers and trades unions, national salary structures, and ensuring that the company is seen as a 'good citizen'. Figure 10.9 outlines how complex the relationships can be. A European country, AZ, has production facilities for hot (cooking) and cold (refrigeration) appliances. Since goods are supplied to both the home market and overseas, the marketing and sales manager in country AZ could report to all international marketing managers as well as the national manager.

Faced with the need to move some production to low-cost countries, and curtail the excessive product range, Electrolux found its structure to be inflexible. From 1998, it began to manufacture in fewer master plants, supported by satellites and outsourcing. The matrix was being dismantled.

Others have matched the withdrawal of Electrolux. Texas Instruments gave up its matrix structure in the 1980s in favour of a simpler structure of loosely co-ordinated, independent business units. In 1995, Royal Dutch Shell gave up the multidimensional matrix structure it had used for 35 years. The complexity of defining units by geography, sector and line of business led to creeping bureaucracy with excessive co-ordination effort and powerful regional 'fiefdoms'.[13] In contrast, Ford introduced a matrix structure in 1993 to support its integrated global business strategy.[14]

The Electrolux example illustrates the advantages and disadvantages summarised in Exhibit 10.9. Problems arise because Fayol's basic axiom of each person having a single supervisor is breached. The change can lead at least to stressful ambiguity and, at worst, to destructive power struggles among managers. We should remember, however, that many such difficulties also arise in the simpler structures we discussed earlier. Structures do not of themselves create well-managed organisations, but well-chosen ones can create favourable conditions. More than anything, success depends on the skills and willingness of the managers to interact within them in a positive way.

Exhibit 10.9 Advantages and disadvantages of a matrix organisation structure

Advantages
- Integration of important functions such as sales and marketing, production and project management
- Improved information flow
- Flexibility in response to changing market and competitive environments
- Co-ordination at appropriate levels in the organisation
- Managers report directly to those who are responsible

Disadvantages
- Conflict between managers over range of responsibility
- Some doubt about whether more information is at the expense of its quality
- Possible loss of efficiency through extra managerial overhead
- Conflict that has to be referred to higher levels for resolution
- Stress caused by having several bosses with potentially conflicting interests

---

While these examples focus on MNEs, much smaller organisations adopt the form. Although sometimes not labelled a matrix, the general notion of a grid of authority is found in private and public sector organisations seeking to integrate along several dimensions. Schoolteachers, for instance, are usually organised into departments according to discipline – maths, humanities, sport, etc. Yet teamwork by level – lower school, upper school or in year groups – is also required. Then there are pastoral care teams, and so on. Describing the arrangement as a matrix organisation may over-complicate the patterns. In university business schools, however, managers see the co-ordination of subjects, courses and levels as problematic and often express the organisation as a matrix structure.

Supported by innovations from knowledge management systems to e-commerce, some organisations are trying other solutions to the problems of complex organisations. They look to market mechanisms, as opposed to hierarchical ones, to achieve co-ordination. Network organisations are one outcome.

■ Network organisations

Since the 1980s, new forms of organisation have emerged. The network form is founded on the idea of disaggregation – separating major functions into independent units linked through a small core. Rather than having design, manufacturing, distribution, sales and marketing and customer service under one roof, some of these functions are supplied by separate organisations. Support functions, from engineering maintenance to information systems, are also included in this trend towards slimmer, more flexible structures. Networks have advantages in: sharing resources and risk; matching complementary core competencies; increasing actual or perceived size; reaching new markets.

Using a marketing perspective, Achrol identifies four situations:[15]

- Internal market, such as the one introduced within the UK National Health Service during the 1990s and subsequently scaled back. ABB (Asea Brown Boveri) has independent SBUs.

- Vertical market, as when assembly companies, from cars to computers, subcontract component manufacture to specialists.

- Intermarket, for instance, alliances among Japanese (*keiretsu*) or Korean (*chaebol*) cutting across technologies and industries.

- Opportunity market, for example companies joining for a particular project and then dissolving. This is common in large civil engineering projects where consortia of engineering companies do the construction and consortia of banks provide the finance.

This list also suggests an evolution from the modular, through the virtual to the boundless network.[16] Unfortunately, all these terms tend to be used interchangeably.

Modular networks

The modular organisation maintains much of its previous identity but operates internally with a quasi-market. The internal market can be formed by decentralising existing structures; the vertical market can be approached in the same way or by forming long-term relationships with preferred suppliers or distributors. The firm separates as much as possible, keeping to itself the core competence that gives the whole network its strength. The decentralised company ABB has many semi-autonomous businesses. When the Norwegian government suddenly approved construction of the new Oslo airport, ABB's country manager appointed a project leader who persuaded 20 units to work under his leadership. With their external links, all the resources needed had been assembled.[17]

Ouchi's work, discussed in Chapter 19, shows that market mechanisms succeed when well-understood processes produce easily measured outputs so that 'contracts' are clearly understood. Further, the interaction costs using the market mechanism must be lower than those for the hierarchy.[18] It seems that the 'internal market' of the National Health Service foundered because these principles did not apply. Health processes and outputs are not clear-cut. Furthermore, the market was overlaid on a form of 'clan control' among clinicians used to sharing information efficiently with colleagues over a wide area. One doctor commented, 'We have various discussions with Hospital B … on how we may collaborate to provide better care for patients. This is absolutely frowned upon between the two [competing] Trusts.' Others point to benefits when building links with units either non-competing or outside the service. One consultant in geriatric medicine, referring to elderly people's care, said, 'We are striving for a seamless level of effective care'.[19]

Running a modular network demands new skills. Since control is exercised through market mechanisms, managers become brokers and network designers, initiators and builders.[20] Others argue that new organisational forms will not develop unless problems of leadership are recognised and overcome.[21]

Virtual networks

Overlapping the modular idea is the virtual network. Made possible by the emergence of high-quality communication systems, these assemble swiftly to take

Exhibit 10.10 Virtual organisations: advantages and disadvantages

Gains from ...	Yet problems with ...
▪ productivity	▪ relying on existing expertise
▪ lower direct costs and overheads	▪ training very difficult
▪ speed and responsiveness	▪ building and retaining knowledge
▪ higher levels of expertise	▪ costs rather than results orientation
▪ overcoming time-zone constraints	▪ not a preferred lifestyle for some staff
▪ organisational flexibility to match customer needs	
▪ preferred lifestyle for some staff	

advantage of opportunities. They combine the competences of companies and individuals, do tasks anywhere and then disband.[22] From the customer's point of view, the grouping is as real as if it were a single company. Advantages and disadvantages of virtual organisations are summarised in Exhibit 10.10.

Boundless networks

In many industries, companies yield specialist skills, leaving suppliers to contribute sub-systems and components. Privatisation of services in United Kingdom local governments began with basic tasks, such as street cleaning and park tending and extended into information processing. Links go further than these do, however. Car assemblers achieve broad product ranges through focus on integrating product ideas with consumer demand. To maintain the focus, it is common to delegate input technologies, such as braking systems, to suppliers. Ford uses specialist Chemfil for fluid management, from lubrication to cleaning operations. The contractor manages materials application and waste disposal and obtains supplies from other sources where necessary.

Such external networks, or *extraprises*, function well when benefits are clearly shared among members, standards are continually checked through customer evaluations and there are agreed protocols for information sharing and Internet trading. Networks also need what Häcki and Lighton call 'orchestrators', who:

▪ in *community networks* based on transactions among many parties, promote open exchange of products and information among all parties;

▪ in *value chain networks* focused on supplying the needs of particular end users, integrate and align processes to satisfy those needs;

▪ in *knowledge service networks* designed to exploit varied opportunities, assemble services and providers to give a complete customer package.[23]

For managers thinking in more conventional terms, the idea of a network stretching beyond their organisational boundary is difficult to comprehend. Yet many companies, such as Nike, Motorola and ABB, are gaining from network flexibility. They have found, however, management to be more challenging than in conventional, rule-bound bureaucracies.

Organisational design

As academics search for the general theory, managers search for the best design. Choosing a structure might involve understanding key factors, studying successful firms and copying their structures. We might conclude, 'SMEs should be organised along the lines of ...' or, 'International banks need global treasury operations because ...' 'Therefore, do this ...'

Practice suggests this approach is wrong. While some detect a drift towards, say, decentralisation, others point to movement in the opposite direction. We saw how some MNEs establish matrix structures while others abandon them. An organisation can learn from its own and others' experiences. Yet it faces its choice in its own way and it makes an individual response.

This is the *contingency approach* to organisational design. It recognises that the organisation is a complex, open system in an equally complex environment. There is no optimal design. Instead, managers' choices depend on unique perceptions and interpretations of the situation and historical constraints. The mix of hierarchy, flexibility, centralisation, working teams and so on will be unique, with every principle somewhere in the structure. In short, the contingency approach recognises common elements and themes but stresses the special nature of every situation.

Can the outsider say anything constructive? We can, if we study the contingencies. We are looking to say something along the lines of, 'If the company finds itself in these circumstances, then it would be better if the organisation structure had the following features'. An example might be, 'If a global, multi-product electrical and electronics company, such as Siemens, tried to operate with a single, functional hierarchy, it would not be successful'. While we could claim this example to be true, it is only a beginning. To improve, we must review studies of the relationships among many variables, organisational form and success. In the rest of this chapter, we examine some leading research linking structure to: environmental factors; strategy; departmental interdependence; and culture.

Environment and organisational design

■ The role of theory

Researchers studying links between environment and organisation design face a daunting task, *see* Figure 10.10. Not only must they decide which aspects they are comparing, but also they have to establish yardsticks for measurement, including outcomes. Then, having compared environment, organisational design and firm performance, they have to show that the design choice caused the performance result. Assuming this causal link can be established, they may halt with satisfaction, saying, 'Over the past ... years, it appears that those organisations that faced the following features in their environment would have been more successful if they had adopted the following structures'. The risks of converting their descriptive statement into a predictive theory are high. They should remember the fate of Russell's inductivist turkey of Chapter 1.

Managers are different, for they are concerned with the future. They seek prediction, such as, 'If we organise ourselves along these lines, the following will occur ...'

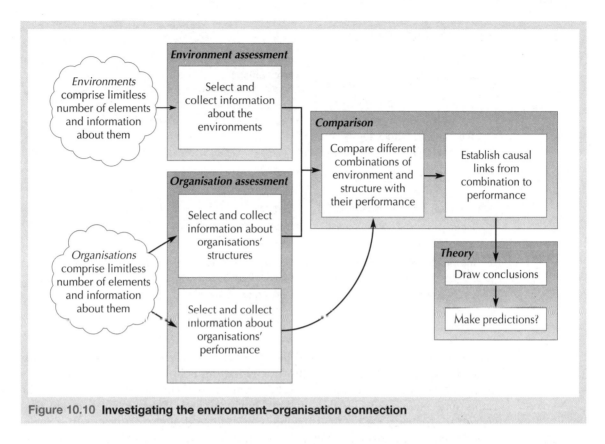

Figure 10.10 Investigating the environment–organisation connection

To make the inductive leap from past studies to the future requires experience and judgement as well as understanding of what the studies were about.

■ Environmental uncertainty and organisation

Two important studies that compared the effects on the organisation of uncertainty and change were those conducted by: Burns and Stalker, into diverse bases of internal structure; and Lawrence and Lorsch, who applied the more specific ideas of differentiation and integration.

Burns and Stalker

Burns and Stalker[24] examined how firms adjusted to the changing environment. From the late 1950s, they examined electronics manufacturing companies in Scotland, comparing them with other firms in Britain. Their key contribution is the typology for characterising organisations that has become embedded in management thinking. *Mechanistic organisations* have rigid structures in contrast to *organic organisations* that are flexible and adaptive to change. Exhibit 10.11[25] lists the clues for discerning them.

Matching the process of Figure 10.10, Burns and Stalker studied the business environments and assessed their success. They found that:

■ in stable environments, mechanistic organisations were more successful;

■ in unstable and uncertain environments, organic organisations did better.

329

Exhibit 10.11 Mechanistic and organic organisations

Characteristic	Mechanistic	Organic
Employees' task definitions	Precise, narrow	Imprecise, broad
Link from personal contribution to organisation's purpose	Obscure	Clear
Task flexibility	Limited	High
Rights and obligations	Explicitly set out	Vague
Locus of control	Hierarchical	Self-control
Channels of communications	Vertical	Lateral, as needed
Nature of vertical communications	Orders, instructions	Advice, information
Expected loyalty	To organisation	To project and work group
Knowledge required of employee	Narrow, related to specified job	Broad, professional
Personal prestige	Related to position in hierarchy	Built on personal contribution

The implications are important. We should not react to the descriptions of mechanistic and organic by saying that the first is bad and the second good. In today's changing environment, many successful organisations run on organic lines. At the same time, many environments change slowly. As with Weber's bureaucracy, they strive for efficiency rather than flexibility and, in so doing, relate to their environments successfully. From McDonald's restaurants to branches of the Inland Revenue, mechanistic structures serve customers' unchanging needs efficiently.

Real organisations vary from these ideal types. First, functions may be mixed – running operations in a mechanistic style and R&D organically. Second, they may face diverse parts of the environment in different ways – consumers against business customers. Third, they adapt their structures as the environment evolves and perhaps becomes more dynamic.

Lawrence and Lorsch

First published in the United States in 1967, the work of Lawrence and Lorsch[26] is better known than that of Burns and Stalker. It drew on the latter and to a lesser extent on the work of Woodward (see below under Technology and organisation) to pose the following questions:

1 *How are the environmental demands facing various organisations different, and how do [they] relate to the internal functioning of effective organisations?*

2 *Is it true that organisations in certain or stable environments make more exclusive use of the formal hierarchy to achieve integration, and, if so, why? ...*

3 *Is the same degree of differentiation in orientation and departmental structure found in organisations in different industrial environments?*

4 *... Does this influence the problems of integrating the organisations' parts? Does it influence the organisational means of achieving integration?*[27]

Lawrence and Lorsch looked at the structures of six companies in the dynamic plastics industry to assess their degrees of differentiation and integration. Differentiation was defined as '*the difference in cognitive and emotional orientation among managers in different functional departments*'. This means that dissimilar work required people with unlike backgrounds, levels of education, frames of reference and so on. The researchers saw that managers varied according to: attachment to goals (focused or broad); time orientation (long for research, short for sales); interpersonal relations (people oriented in sales, task oriented in production); and formality of structure (high in production and sales, low in research).

Integration was defined as '*the quality of the state of collaboration that exists among departments that are required to achieve unity of effort by the demands of the environment*'. Integration does not erase differences but involves methods of linking units to resolve conflict and achieve co-ordination.

Lawrence and Lorsch found:

■ The organisations that did best had internal structures that permitted high differentiation while promoting matching integration.

This point was reinforced when the researchers added four further firms. Two faced medium uncertainty in the food industry, while the two in the container industry enjoyed the most stable environment. The authors concluded:

■ Organisations needed to match their differentiation to their environment – more complexity meant higher differentiation; and

■ More differentiation required more attention to integration.

How was integration achieved? The best plastics firm had a special integrative department, had set up permanent cross-functional teams and encouraged direct managerial contact. This successful organisation was most differentiated and had the most elaborate set of integrating processes. The better food company had a less complex approach. Here, managers had integrating responsibilities and temporary teams were established when needed. Finally, the better container business relied on its hierarchy, supported by occasional direct contact and a paper system to resolve routine questions. With little differentiation, the formal hierarchy was adequate for most purposes. In the words of Burns and Stalker, its mechanistic organisation matched its stable environment.

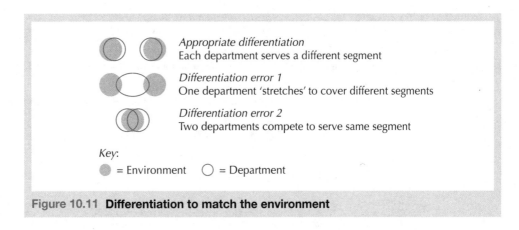

Appropriate differentiation
Each department serves a different segment

Differentiation error 1
One department 'stretches' to cover different segments

Differentiation error 2
Two departments compete to serve same segment

Key:
● = Environment   ○ = Department

Figure 10.11 Differentiation to match the environment

Lawrence and Lorsch drew lessons for organisational design. We can pick out two here. Figure 10.11 summarises differentiation. Faced with variety in the environment, two aspects of which appear as shaded circles, the best response allows separate departments to deal with each part. The first error occurs when one department stretches to cover too much variety, while the second follows two departments competing to do the work of one.

Figure 10.12 summarises integration. The top and bottom of the list show effective cases. With mild differentiation, normal supervision is a satisfactory integrator; if it is high, a special unit is needed. Failures occur if either the hierarchical or special unit approach is used inappropriately.

More on organisation and environment

Other studies of have underscored the view of a unique blend of factors in every situation. In *The Change Masters*,[28] Kanter compared firms more or less receptive to change. Her two organisational types were not unlike mechanistic and organic. The *segmental corporation* displayed a sense of control of internal boundaries. Pressure from other departments, and the environment, was perceived as a threat. *Integrative organisations*, in contrast, found success from flexibility. They had more 'surface' open to the environment, with which more people, with greater skills, interacted. Managers of these innovative organisations required three key skills:

- political – obtaining resources, information and support;
- team leading – encouraging participation in flexible teams;
- coping – welcoming change and being able to take its opportunities.

When Giants Learn to Dance[29] explored how large corporations nurtured innovation. Echoing Lawrence and Lorsch, Kanter found that success followed separating innovation areas from the mainstream of the business. Innovatory people and teams would not last long without such insulation. Effective means of integrating new ideas into the mainstream were also required. Similar ideas arose in our discussion of intrapreneurship in Chapter 7.

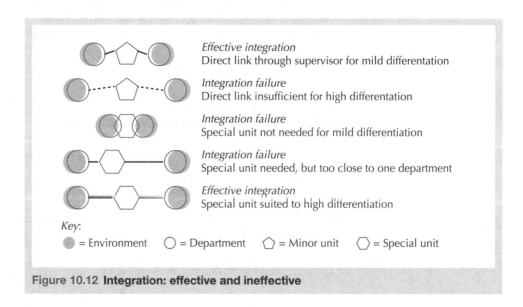

Key:
⬤ = Environment ◯ = Department ⬠ = Minor unit ⬡ = Special unit

Figure 10.12 Integration: effective and ineffective

■ Technology and organisation

Woodward also sought to develop a contingency model based on the links between process technology and organisation structure. Her classic study of 92 manufacturing firms in south Essex during the 1950s[30] stimulated new thinking about production organisation. *See* Exhibit 10.12 for a brief biography.[31]

Exhibit 10.12 Joan Woodward – practical academic

Woodward (1916–71) gained practical experience as operations and planning manager in a wartime munitions factory. In September 1953, a small Human Relations Research Unit was established at South East Essex College of Technology. Using both its own and United States aid funds, the British government sought to extend the application of social science to industry. Technical colleges were seen as ideal bases for some of this work. Woodward led the team during five years' fieldwork and then moved to the Department of Mechanical Engineering at Imperial College, London. Here she conducted detailed follow-up studies of control. She was appointed Professor of Industrial Sociology in 1969.

Woodward collected data on many aspects of operations, management and measures of success. She counted the percentage of costs allocated to wages, the number of levels in the hierarchy and the *span of control* of managers. The span of control is the number of subordinates who are directly responsible to a manager or supervisor. Firms try to even out responsibilities by taking it into account. Other factors, such as spatial dispersion or technical content, also come into play.

Woodward found that different systems of production fell into three clusters with similar characteristics – *unit and small batch, large batch and mass* and *process* systems. They are summarised in Table 10.1.

Table 10.1 Groupings of Woodward's 92 firms

	Unit and small batch production (jobbing)	Large batch and mass production (line)	Process production
Outputs	Single items or small batches to customers' orders; prototypes; large items built in stages	Large batches, possibly on assembly lines; mass production	Batches of chemicals in flexible plant; continuous flow of chemicals in dedicated plant
Critical function	Product development	Production	Marketing
Examples	Making cranes; small print jobs	Automobile parts; printing magazines	Paint making; oil refining

Table 10.2 summarises some observations. Differences among the systems are striking. For example, first-line supervisors in large batch and mass companies looked after many more staff than their counterparts elsewhere. Reasons lie in the different supervision. Dominated by routine jobs, this type of factory runs itself,

once supervisors and engineers have made the plans. Tasks in the jobbing shop, on the other hand, involve more variety and uncertainty. Work to be done and the way it was to be carried out is planned as it proceeds with more worker–supervisor interaction. At the other end of the scale, the few subordinates of process plant supervisors are accounted for by their work having been replaced by machines.

Table 10.2 **Selected data on firms with different production systems**

	Jobbing	Line	Process
Mean number of levels in hierarchy	3	4	6
Percentage of costs allocated to wages and salaries	40	35	15
Mean span of control of first-line supervisors	22	49	13
Mean ratio of managers and supervisors to all staff	35	17	7

Taken alone, these results would not have been regarded as significant. So far, Woodward had described the firms in one area and created clusters among them. She went further than this, however. In collecting data about *success*, Woodward investigated which features distinguished the better from the worse. In doing so, she sought statements about the ways firms *ought* to be organised, that is to develop a *normative theory* of production organisation.

Woodward presented the results as in Table 10.3. The first line shows the number of continuous process firms whose span of control fell into defined ranges. Then the table shows the data for the more and less successful ones. Clearly, the former had spans that were close to each other and to the median of the whole group. Less successful firms were scattered. Observations of other organisational factors showed similar patterns; successful firms were similar to each other and closer to the median values. This pointed the way to the normative theory.

Table 10.3 **Spans of control of first-line supervisors in continuous process firms**

	Number of people controlled				Median	Firms
	<10	11–20	21–30	31–40		
All firms	6	12	5	2	13	25
More successful	1	5	–	–	–	6
Less successful	1	–	1	2	–	4

> *The fact that organizational characteristics, technology, and success were linked together in this way suggested that not only was the system of production an important variable in the determination of organization structure, but also that one particular form of organization was most appropriate to each system of production.*[32]

Conclusions that jobbing shops need short pyramids while process plants need tall ones leave us far from a general theory of organisation. To achieve research rigour, Woodward chose a narrow approach, taking the systems in each company as given and not ignoring, for example, whether each matched its market. Furthermore, she disregarded the historical development of each company. Despite these comments, however, the study did reveal the implications of process technologies. Not only did it develop a taxonomy of technical characteristics but also it supported the argument that there is no best way to organise.

Following Figure 10.10, we have presented technology as an 'environmental influence' upon organisation design. This is reasonable only if we regard the technology as 'given'. Clearly, however, managers are responsible for both organisation and technology. Chapter 12 relates this *socio-technical systems* view to job design. Meanwhile, we see that technology lies somewhere between the external factors of Burns and Stalker and Lawrence and Lorsch, and the internal factors we shall now examine.

Internal factors in organisational design

The relationship between strategy and organisation design has been much debated during the past thirty years. We shall open this section with this topic and move on to two other important issues, interdependence and culture.

Strategy and organisation

The prescriptive view of the relationship between strategy and organisational design is that the former should come first. It is summed up by Lynch:

> *From a prescriptive strategy perspective, the purpose of an organisation structure is to allocate the work and administrative mechanisms that are necessary to control and integrate the strategies of an organisation. Thus work is allocated to functions, such as finance and marketing, and recombined in divisions or departments, with power being distributed accordingly. ... Importantly, in this definition the strategy is developed first and only then is the organisational structure defined. For the prescriptive strategist, organisational structure is a matter of how the strategy is implemented: it does not influence the strategy itself.*[33]

There is a problem with this view. The stage 'Determine structure' is a long way from the start of the strategy process of Figure 8.5. It contributes to rational implementation. Yet, a second look at Figure 8.5 shows structure also appearing in the analysis stage. Questions such as, 'How are resources organised?' and 'What is the fit between organisation and strategy?' come early. Furthermore, Figure 8.10 points to the *emergent* nature of strategy. Despite intentions, strategy is adapted according to events, people and other resources. Lynch explains the contrast:

> *From an emergent strategy perspective, ... the relationship between strategy and structure is more complex. The organisation itself may restrict or enhance the strategies that are proposed. The existing organisational structure may even make certain strategies highly unlikely. For example, an informal, free-flowing structure might be better able to generate new strategic initiatives than a bureaucratic structure.*[34]

Beyond merely seeing structure as a variable to be analysed, this view shows that the way managers are organised, linked with the perceived role of strategic management within the organisation, affects the way it emerges.

Figure 10.13 develops Figure 8.10 to capture the two explanations. The *prescriptive* explanation sees a causal link *from* strategy *to* structure. The *emergent* explanation shows how, as the intended strategy becomes the realised strategy, so the present structure is adapted. Changes to strategy and structure interact. What about the evidence?

Strategy precedes structure

The leading advocate of the prescriptive model, Chandler, studied change in United States businesses between 1850 and 1920.[35] As companies grew, they created a general office supported by specialised departments. The general office set the company strategy and then designed a suitable structure. Chandler was impressed by Sloan's work at General Motors and advocated the decentralised, divisional structure for the large, multi-product businesses that were emerging during his era.

Multidivisional corporations became more diversified and decentralised and some grew into the modern conglomerate companies. Williamson's theoretical work in economics concluded that *well-managed* diversified companies could work better than if each division was independently owned.[36] His reasons were based on frictions within capital markets such as the stock exchange. Further, he saw structure as the means to carry out the strategy of conglomerate diversification.

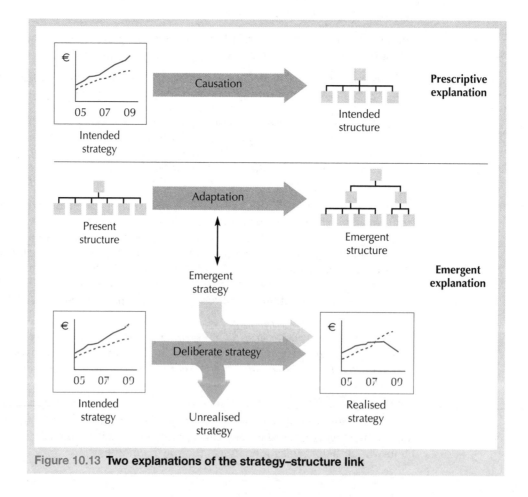

Figure 10.13 **Two explanations of the strategy–structure link**

In contrast to these studies of corporations, others have examined structures within functional departments. Differences in performance are explained in terms of how functions are organised. Bailetti and Callahan argue, 'To support a successful business strategy, the acquisition and development of technical and non-technical skills must be driven by the congruent assembly of organisational components rather than by the internal characteristics of individual components within the firm'.[37] They are saying two things relevant to our discussion. First, the way people are organised is at least as important as the skills of the people themselves. Second, the arrangement of people in the organisation follows the business strategy that has been chosen.

Interlinking strategy and structure

Contradicting these arguments, Mintzberg advocates the knitting of strategy and structure. To show how organisational elements fit together, he conceived of six components.[38] Different patterns among them correspond to organisational types met in practice:

- *Operating core* produces the goods or services.
- *Middle line* managers connect the operating core with the apex.
- *Strategic apex* runs the whole organisation
- *Technostructure* designs and controls the processes (e.g. engineers, accountants, information specialists).
- *Support staff* provide direct services to the operating core (e.g. office, transport, canteen, cleaning).
- *Ideology* binds all together.

According to Mintzberg, six fundamental organisational configurations are to be found. Each is dominated by one component part. For instance, the entrepreneurial organisation is dominated by the strategic apex, the owner-manager. Furthermore, the primary means of co-ordinating work within the organisations differ. The entrepreneur, for example, co-ordinates through direct supervision.

Table 10.4 Dominance and co-ordination in Mintzberg's configurations

Mintzberg's configuration	Dominant element	Main means of co-ordination	Examples
Entrepreneurial organisation	Strategic apex: the owner-entrepreneur	Direct supervision	SME
Machine organisation	Technostructure	Work standardisation	Assembly line; fast service restaurant
Professional organisation	Operating core	Skills standardisation	Auditing practice; school
Divisionalised structure	Middle line	Output standardisation	Hotel and catering group
Innovative organisation	Support staff	Mutual adjustment	Biotechnology company
Missionary organisation	Ideology	Norms standardisation	Charity; political party; pressure group

Table 10.4 summarises the characteristics. We shall elaborate just two of the examples. The machine organisation has routine basic work, usually dominated by a production line. The technostructure assures success in such situations. In contrast, the professional organisation has a highly skilled staff of doctors or lawyers working directly on its output. Since the organisation is only as good as its professionals, the operating core is critical. Since the key staff work with little supervision, co-ordination among them is based on professional standards and training. Practice and values are aligned.

The configuration model helps when studying organisational change. Whether part of strategy or the result of adaptation, change is needed whenever a mismatch between the configuration and the situation appears.

A firm of structural engineers and surveyors was a well-developed professional organisation. Each of the 19 partners 'looked after' a set of clients and led small teams. While each respected the others' competence, status among partners was based on seniority and client prestige. During a period of industry upheaval, traditional work was declining and competitors were merging. This firm found change difficult. Partners were unused to the processes of mutual adjustment common in innovative organisations. Tasks such as winning new clients, rather than waiting for references from other agencies, and forming joint ventures, which had become fashionable in the industry, threatened the traditional 'pecking order' and led to loss of trust.

This change, from professional to innovative organisation, is but one shift that might be needed if the fit between structure and strategy is lost. It exemplifies, however, how structural change may not follow a deliberate strategy, but is the result of complex factors to which the organisation tries to adapt.

■ Interdependence and organisation

The second internal contingency influencing structure is interdependence – how far departments depend on each other to achieve their ends. The more units have in common, the more they benefit from sharing resources, processes, information and so on. Achieving the links, however, is not so easy, requiring great effort to ensure that they happen.

Rather than consider divisions, we shall shift down the scale to relate interaction to the functional structure, which usually cuts across work flow. Three forms of interdependence appear in Figure 10.14 – pooled, sequential and reciprocal. They correspond to three process technologies proposed by Thompson. More general than those of Woodward, they apply to both manufacturing and service activities.[39]

- *Mediating technology*. Common processes of otherwise independent units serve different types of customer. Standardisation is the key. Designing each process once, and using it throughout, permits economies of scale. For instance, bank branches have standard procedures and equipment. The difficulty is restricted adaptation to special circumstances.

- *Long-linked or sequential technology*. Assembly lines and supply chains link stages that depend on previous and subsequent ones for their performance. Planning is the key, and modern scheduling methods allow for some flexibility.

- *Intensive technology*. Skills and experience are applied at each stage to achieve mutual adjustment. Rather than the work flow being predetermined, tasks have to

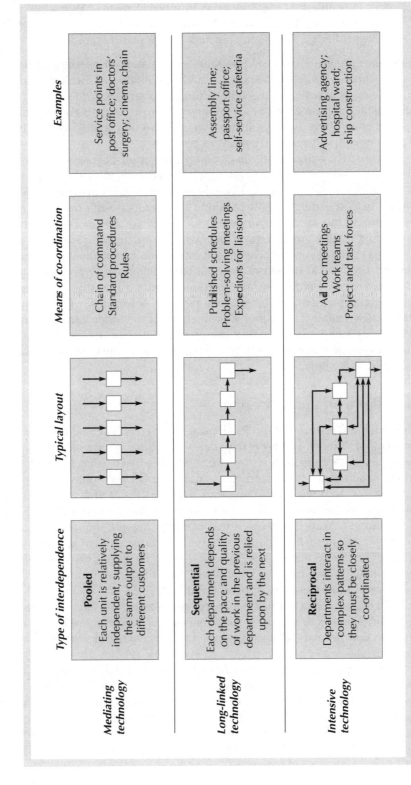

Type of interdependence	Typical layout	Means of co-ordination	Examples
Pooled *Mediating technology* Each unit is relatively independent, supplying the same output to different customers		Chain of command Standard procedures Rules	Service points in post office; doctors' surgery; cinema chain
Sequential *Long-linked technology* Each department depends on the pace and quality of work in the previous department and is relied upon by the next		Published schedules Problem-solving meetings Expeditors for liaison	Assembly line; passport office; self-service cafeteria
Reciprocal *Intensive technology* Departments interact in complex patterns so they must be closely co-ordinated		Ad hoc meetings Work teams Project and task forces	Advertising agency; hospital ward; ship construction

Figure 10.14 **Pooled, sequential and reciprocal technologies**

adapt, depending on what happens in other elements. An example is a hospital, where doctors continually revise treatment in the light of each patient's response. This level of adaptability requires high interpersonal co-ordination.

Different business areas need different co-ordination, depending on their processes. For example, Hennes and Mauritz (H&M), a chain of clothing retailers based in Stockholm, is expanding into other European markets. It faces stiff competition in its chosen 'fashion at value for money' niche.[40] As with rivals such as Marks & Spencer, functions such as design, buying and marketing are highly centralised. Such companies illustrate Thompson's typology.

Figure 10.15 shows patterns of co-ordination for processes 'flowing across' the organisation. For example, we can distinguish between the sequential interdependence of operations and the reciprocal interdependence of planning new fashion ranges. The former uses scheduling and expediting within a conventional hierarchy. The latter needs project managers supported by task forces, possibly in a matrix structure.

Leading retailers forge strong links with their suppliers, either for quick call-offs of goods or for deeper involvement in innovation. Co-ordination, therefore, extends beyond the formal organisation boundary. Thompson's work suggests that the method is again contingent on interdependency. Since supply chains are sequentially interdependent, they require contracted schedules, rules for calling-off and staff whose task it is to iron out problems. On the other hand, involving suppliers in designing new ranges means reciprocal interdependence. Retailers frequently include outside members on development teams. In these ways, the supply chain is managed as a whole.

◼ Culture and organisation

To begin our discussion of the relationship between culture and organisation we return to Hofstede. Exhibit 4.7 shows that, in some cultures, such as Malaysia, Venezuela and West Africa, there is high power distance. This means that hierarchies have many layers, subordinates heed instructions and there is close control. Low power distance cultures, on the other hand, value staff independence. Denmark, Ireland and Sweden have flatter organisational hierarchies with much consultation between levels.

A cultural perspective is also a way of comparing different organisations and even functions within them. This is suggested by the 'cognitive and emotional orientations' of Lawrence and Lorsch. In short, we would expect organisation structures to be contingent upon culture. What effect does this have in practice? Two examples, from Sweden and Germany, appear in Exhibits 10.13 and 10.14.

In Exhibit 10.13, Czarniawska-Joerges is pointing out that other aspects of management, apart from structural preferences, differentiate Sweden from elsewhere.[41] She also detects that management orientation is changing towards more formality in relationships.

Change that is more rapid was forced on many German organisations after reunification. Sweeney and Hardaker point to two levels of culture: national and organisational.[42] Differences in the former justified cross-cultural training to dampen down anxiety and frustration for new managers. Yet they argue that the main dissimilarities experienced were organisation specific. Managers from the West were posted to new jobs in the East and locals experienced huge changes. Exhibit 10.14 summarises what happened.

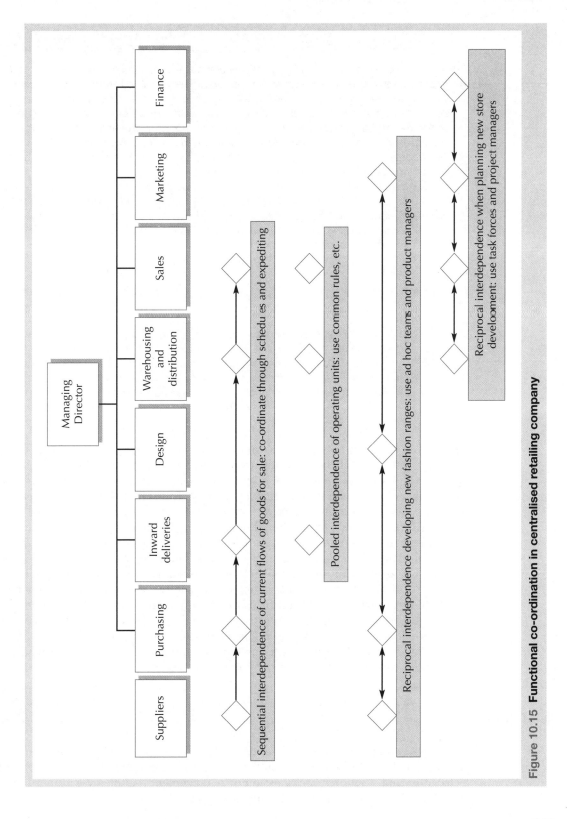

Figure 10.15 Functional co-ordination in centralised retailing company

Exhibit 10.13 Sweden's obscure structures

'As perceived by executives in multinational companies, the structure of Swedish corporations is ambiguous. This is sometimes interpreted as a preference for matrix structures, and it is sometimes simply perceived as being chaotic. Decision-making processes are slow. This, again, is interpreted by some authors as the result of a striving for technical perfection and by others as a routine aimed in effect at preventing action. Control processes are experienced, paradoxically enough, as informal but tight. Also, although the importance of consensus is obvious, this is variously interpreted as a cultural trait, or as a conscious choice of democratic procedures ...

' "No bureaucracy at all," sighs an Italian who has just made an important deal in a telephone conversation. "Why don't these people say what they mean?" wonders, in turn, an American who participated in a typical consensus-reaching meeting where everyone was speaking around the matter and the meeting ended at apparently the same point where it began.'

Exhibit 10.14 Rush to reunify

With no blueprint for success, German reunification turned out to be a wholesale and rapid takeover. Almost overnight, the West German system was applied to the East. Within the context of industrial transformation, three key elements – strategy, structure and individual behaviour – were not synchronised. The pace of change exceeded the ability of managers to keep up with them. Individuals had to operate within new frameworks without the necessary experience. Success was limited by cultures of the past.

Apart from showing how persons can be left out during upheaval, Sweeney and Hardaker remind us of the importance of individual behaviour within the structural framework. A structure may work not because it is perfect for the job but because the members have found ways of making it work. Transplanted into another cultural setting, a generation of managers with different experiences may not be able to 'fix it'. We will return to this point when discussing the informal organisation below.

Another test of the effect of culture is to compare matched organisations. Results are mixed. Mullins[43] summarises three studies; one compared Canada, the United Kingdom and the United States and two looked at Germany and the United Kingdom. The first found no cultural effect. Yet the two Germany and UK enquiries suggested otherwise. One found that British companies spawned more specialist functions than their German counterparts. This was explained by different specialisation in education and the strong influence of professions in the UK. The other did not discover specialisation as an issue but explained variations through managers seeing their roles and authority in contrasting ways.

Criticisms

Contingency theory has attracted several criticisms: on practical grounds, it may not be particularly useful; it is based on few studies; it plays down the impact of human behaviour; and it ignores the question of management legitimacy within a unitary model. Each is covered in the following discussion.

■ Limits of the contingency approach

In this chapter, we have followed studies that have seen organisational design as an important intermediary between situational factors and performance, *see* Figure 10.16. Managers could think, 'Pick the right structure and we'll cope'. Warnings, shown as 'Stop' symbols in the figure should, however, surround this argument. They are listed below:

A Causal relationships between structure and performance are difficult to tie down. Many other changes play their part. Effects in the opposite direction are possible, for firms may change structures in response to outcomes instead of to cause them.

B Since so many factors influence success, the effect of any particular combination will be unclear.

C Some situational factors have direct impact on performance, 'bypassing' the structural effect. For example, choice of process technology depends on the situation. We have seen how it relates to structure. Yet it also affects outcomes directly.

D Situational factors are assumed to be outside the control of the organisation. Chapter 3, however, showed how organisations shape them to suit themselves, rather than adapt internally

E All the studies reported here used performance as the dependent variable. They have assumed that the same measures, for example profit or growth, always apply. This is unlikely.

F Structural adaptation changes factors other than those in paragraph E. Unanticipated effects include shifts in attitudes among individuals and work groups. In turn, they may make a chosen structure succeed or fail.

G Reorganisation costs make change infrequent. Chapter 19 shows it is more likely at crises when mismatches become clear. Otherwise, change is gradual, happening when opportunities arise. Examples include the retirement of a key manager or the opening of a new department. The emergent structure will lag behind the ideal.

H Structure and performance will never wholly depend on contingencies stated so impersonally. People interpret any organisational design in many ways. Each case is unlike any other. We shall develop this point in the next section.

The contingency approach has shown managers that there is no one best design. Stressing the unique nature of each case, however, is to overreact and ignore similarities. The empirical work identifies both sides, the differences and the similarities. Understanding the latter enables a manager to generalise, learn and incorporate experience into structural design.

■ The informal organisation

A limitation of formal structures, as represented in charts, is that they tell only a partial story. Real managers learn how to make almost any structure work by building their own networks and cutting corners when it is advantageous to do so. This is the informal organisation. Personal links between machinist and manager, chauffeur and chairman, or secretary and superintendent, emerge as alliances to share information, exchange favours and get the work done. In times of little change, the informal network delivers and the basic hierarchical form is unchallenged. Later, as the pace picks up and organisations grow and diversify, the strains show and the

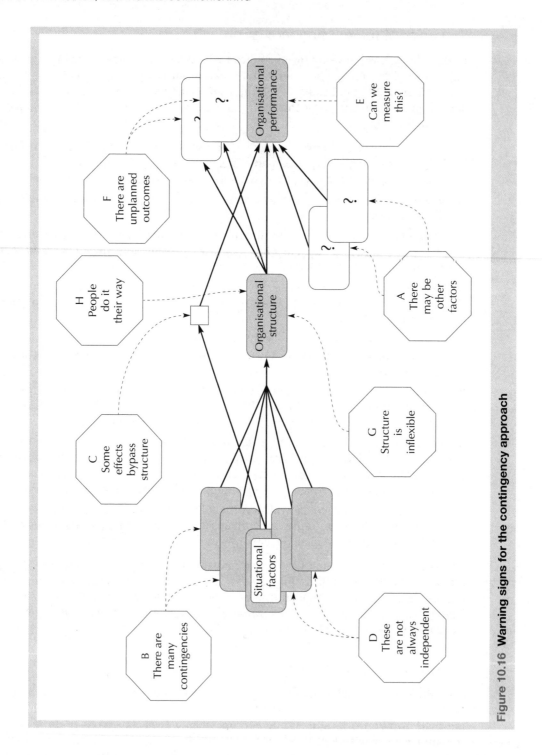

Figure 10.16 Warning signs for the contingency approach

informal organisation can compensate no longer. Barsoux' interpretation of what happens is shown in Exhibit 10.15.[44]

Exhibit 10.15 Making it work – informally

'It then dawned on managers and management thinkers that the informal organisation was quite good at capturing and channelling corporate energy. These looser configurations clearly made things happen, switched people on and sustained corporate competitiveness.

'If the informal organisation was where the company's real energy lay, why not redesign the formal organisation to look more like it? This realisation led to a host of new organisational forms ... Fluidity was the underlying theme. These organisations were characterised by the fact that they were adaptive, team-based, project-driven, with semi-permeable boundaries. ...

'We must beware of assuming that structure has a logic of its own, independent of the people who make up the organisation.'

Organisation structures are only means to ends. They are enabling mechanisms, allowing the energy and initiative of people to be channelled into co-operation. A badly designed organisation will hinder success. If it suits the situational factors, it will enable success. But enabling is different from guaranteeing. This comes from the efforts of the members. A problem with the argument of Barsoux is that imitating informal networks will not build a successful organisation. Not only would this merely replicate the needs of the past but mapping informal arrangements does not make them work.

One study of MNEs showed the effect of decentralisation with fewer hierarchical layers.[45] Such businesses come to rely on personal networks for informal horizontal communication. Further structural changes can interrupt these flows, which can then work against the formal system.

This leads us to another difficulty with Barsoux' view of the informal organisation. He assumes it to be benign, as it overcomes weaknesses in the formal structure. Why should we assume this? It could equally be malignant, slowly eroding the carefully built structure. Symptoms could be: resistance to change; nagging rivalry; permanent jockeying for position; unwillingness to do tasks that do not make a manager look good; lack of co-ordination in crisis situations; and lack of control. These are features of an organisation falling apart.

Responses to these fears should avoid attempts to stamp out either politics or informal networks. Both are facts of organisational life. They should make the formal structure work better.

Unitary and pluralist views

Sociologists have recognised two contrasting ways of perceiving an organisation – unitary and pluralist.

- The *unitary* perspective sees the organisation as an assembly of people acting with common purpose, and willing to share work and co-ordinate effort under an agreed leader. Accepting this viewpoint, managers stress communication, creating a team spirit, selecting staff who fit in and matching rewards to appropriate effort. In particular, senior managers see they must create an organisation for everyone to pull together.

■ From the *pluralist* perspective, an organisation comprises competing individuals and sub-groups. Each has its own sense of purpose, direction of effort and leader. Managers tolerate the existence of differences, of rivalrous groups, of distorted communications and of people limiting their commitment. Senior managers must acknowledge these issues and engage in bargaining. People may be unwilling to work, but will do so provided the deal is right.

Elements of both perspectives appear in real organisations. No one believes that a large corporation works solely on unitary principles, although the language of leaders suggests that they can! Similarly, a business run on pluralist lines with no appeal to shared purposes would hardly be a business. Reality lies somewhere between.

We have argued that there is no one best way to organise. Yet this contingency view still places managers at the centre of things since it is they who select the structure. Therefore, unitarist notions such as hierarchy, the 'manager's right to manage' and the legitimacy of common goals are not challenged.

■ Critical perspective

Critical theory takes a more radical and humanistic stance than the above debate. It disapproves of the emphasis on instrumental rationality. This means that ends (e.g. business success) are unquestioned and means (e.g. structure) are legitimated by the ends. While not inherently wrong, a concentration on means leads to acceptance of power, position and status. These in turn yield high incomes for those fortunate enough to do well out of the 'system'.

Alvesson and Willmott[46] urge a more critical and reflective perspective. They point to one effect of hierarchies. Managers expend much effort in constructing favourable images of themselves and what they do. One use of management 'language' is to *mystify the hierarchy* to suggest the absence of negative effects and that all members benefit. The talk is of 'flattening', 'empowerment' and 'flexible work teams' whereas things continue much as before. The authors quote the case of a Swedish computer company, *see* Exhibit 10.16.[47]

The contrast between the 'official' line of flatness and the acknowledgement of Sten's role suggests that this employee had not reflected on what was happening.

Exhibit 10.16 Believing in a flat hierarchy

'Employees were repeatedly told that the hierarchy was extremely flat, with only two grades – subsidiary managers and consultants – and no intermediate grades. ... Social relations within the firm were represented as non-hierarchical, close, friendly and family-like.

'One consultant ... was asked to compare it with his former workplace. [He acknowledged that] at his present workplace there was a flat structure. "My only boss is Alf (Subsidiary Manager)," he said. Later in the interview, he was asked about possibilities for exerting some influence in the allocation of assignments. It turned out that his last assignment had been given to him by Sten, without his being asked whether he was particularly interested in it. The researcher then asked if Sten, a consultant, had managerial responsibilities and received the answer, "Yes, he works directly under Alf." In practice, then, it seemed that Sten functioned as a middle manager with semi-formal status as second-in-command.'

The 'flat' talk was a subterfuge to ensure compliance. Nor is this an isolated instance. From 1990, the National & Provincial Building Society underwent a 'transformation into a process-driven organization'. In a report on the change process,[48] two of the consultants involved confidently noted that, by 1993, 'The hierarchical organisation had ceased to exist'. At the time, N&P employed some 4500 people! It became part of the Abbey National bank in 1996.

Conclusion: which structure?

All companies work out organisational designs blending their histories with notions of the ideal. What are these notions? In this chapter, we have identified principles, such as authority and responsibility, general concepts, such as centralisation, and desirable ends, such as vertical and horizontal co-ordination. We have also introduced means of representing, analysing and comparing different organisational forms.

Structure can be related to maturity. In the smallest organisation, it will revolve around the owner-manager. Growth leads to the functional form as the entrepreneur brings in specialists for tasks such as engineering or accounting. After further growth and diversification, such structures begin to creak when the firm suffers co-ordination failures. The divisional structure, with each unit a miniature business, comes into its own.

Further growth, change and globalisation have challenged the divisional form. The matrix tries to reconcile the pulls of several dimensions by placing hierarchies on a two- or three-dimensional grid. Some have found, however, further problems of co-ordination and conflict. The matrix is either a refreshing way of supporting initiatives or a creator of committees and politics.

Now firms are dismantling. Supported by information system developments, networks replace hierarchies with quasi-market relationships. They change the notion of manager from leader or administrator to innovator and broker.

Generalisation helps us to understand but not to find the 'one best way'. Contingency studies show how organisations succeed despite being different. Researchers searched for links between fundamentals and optimal structures. The environment dominates such studies. We focused on uncertainty, globalisation and technology. Inside, too, there are factors such as strategy, size, interdependence and culture. The cocktail has so many ingredients that we move to the opposite of the universalist view – the particularist. Each case is unique and cannot be compared with others.

Contingency theory also presents a paradox. Although the notion seems to be wisely flexible, it remains a search for *theory*; the 'one best way' becomes the 'five best ways'. Does putting these together turn the contingencies into a new universal theory? Certainly, Woodward thought she was moving in this direction.

Perhaps the best use of the contingency work is practical. It helps us identify both the special features and commonalities in every situation. It alerts managers to the factors that are likely to be important and shows why and how organisations must differ. Structures should be modified for different parts of the business and they certainly must change with time.

Criticisms of structural studies refer to the risk of ignoring the informal organisation. It may support the formal structure, lubricating seized joints. Yet, for lubricant read acid, eating away the structure, for the informal organisation can also hinder. Further, we should recognise that organisations do not merely support the interests of one group.

The pluralist perspective sees them as riddled with rivalry. Yet this work rarely challenges the legitimacy of the hierarchy and the powerful roles played by managers. Critical theory seeks to expose managers' espousal of flattened hierarchies and flexible work teams as empty words, used as weapons in their battle to maintain the status quo. Handy takes a moral stance. 'Managers', he argues, 'have been brought up on a diet of power, divide and rule … preoccupied with authority … Though the world is a good one for professional executives, they are a minority of the human race.'[49]

QUICK CHECK

Can you …

- Explain: hierarchy; specialisation; centralisation; vertical and horizontal co-ordination; contingency theory; structure and process; informal organisation.
- Define: authority; responsibility; delegation; differentiation; integration; line and staff role.
- List four main means of co-ordinating organisational work.
- Sketch a rich picture of functional, divisional and matrix structures.
- Name three bases of divisionalisation.
- Summarise the features of a network organisation and name three types.

- Outline the work of: Burns and Stalker; Lawrence and Lorsch; Woodward.
- Offer arguments in the strategy–structure debate.
- Name Thompson's three categories of interdependency.
- List eight warning signs for the contingency approach.
- Distinguish between unitary and pluralist views of organisations.
- Offer a critical perspective on organisational structure.

QUESTIONS

Chapter review

10.1 Use your own examples to illustrate the four key issues in organising.

10.2 Explain with examples the three main bases for organisational divisions.

10.3 Why are some MNEs changing to the matrix structure while others are shying away from it?

10.4 Relate the works of contingency theorists to the warnings given in Figure 10.16.

10.5 How can the functional, divisional, matrix and network structures be matched to situational factors?

10.6 Explain and illustrate Thompson's ideas on interdependence in an organisation with which you are familiar.

Application

10.7 Use the information on Siemens in the opening case to explain what sort of organisation this is and suggest why.

10.8 What structure is emerging at Nokia (Chapter 8, closing case) and why?

Investigation

10.9 Study an organisation that has recently announced a reorganisation. Comment on the reasons given for the change and the benefits you might expect.

10.10 Sketch a rich picture using the Siemens case and information from its website. In relation to organisation design, what issues does the picture raise?

ETHICS TEST: 'IT'S NOT YOUR DEPARTMENT'

Ben, a young graduate, was managing a department producing ceiling panels and door linings for the building industry. The raw material, now obsolete, was 2.4 × 1.2 metre boards of asbestos cement. This mixture gave strength and fire resistance, but dry fibres are dangerous when breathed in large quantities over a long period. They cause asbestosis, a disease leading to a lung cancer, mesothelioma. Stringent safety precautions apply in all plant using this material. Air quality is regularly checked for the presence of fibres.

The company's engineers prided themselves on the dust extraction equipment surrounding the saws and panel finishing equipment. It usually cost more than the basic machinery. Although managers felt the Asbestos Regulations were too strict, company policy was to keep the air cleaner than the lowest limit. Men could, therefore, work without having to wear masks. Yet the engineering department was also responsible for monitoring the air quality.

Ben often met the engineers as they visited on alternate days. They spent about fifteen minutes each time, collecting samples at regular spots. Ben would discuss how the test equipment worked and how results were recorded. Yet, he was puzzled that the readings were put down in a notebook and later transcribed to the official forms. One day, a pallet of scrap slipped from a fork lift truck during the tests. The engineer commented that this would put the result over the limit.

The following week, Ben stood in for his boss at a management meeting. As usual, the test records were among the agenda papers. He noticed that results for the day of the pallet incident were inside the safe limit, as were all readings throughout the site. He expressed his concerns to his boss the next day, but was told, 'Don't worry about it. It's not your department.'

Ben was unsure of what to do. He had suspicions, no evidence and a boss who didn't seem concerned.

- *Is safety not his department?*
- *What would you have advised?*

Abbott's structural dilemma[50]

Illinois-based Abbott Laboratories has operations in 40 countries and sells in 130. Half of its 2002 turnover of $17.7 billion was generated outside the United States. Abbott's strategy is to grow quickly while maintaining its reputation for consistent financial performance. Its has four elements – internal R&D, market expansion, external collaboration and acquisition. Commitment to the first two is shown by the spending of $1.6 billion on R&D, the primary driver of growth. Collaboration and acquisition cover the full range of market research, licensing, manufacturing and entry to new business areas. The purchase of Knoll in 2001, for example, added a range of drugs and increased by 4200 the number of sales representatives.

In the mid-1990s, senior managers were wrestling with the problem of how to reconcile two alternative organisational models that had grown up. It was in the late 1960s that Abbott first split itself into three product-based divisions – pharmaceuticals, hospital products and nutritional preparations. Each operated as a self-contained business including R&D, manufacturing and marketing. A fourth division, Abbott International, handled all operations outside the United States. It was organised on geographic, as opposed to product, lines.

Parallel to the four divisions, however, a new business emerged. Formed in 1973 by bringing together several disparate activities, the diagnostics division had become a world leader with sales

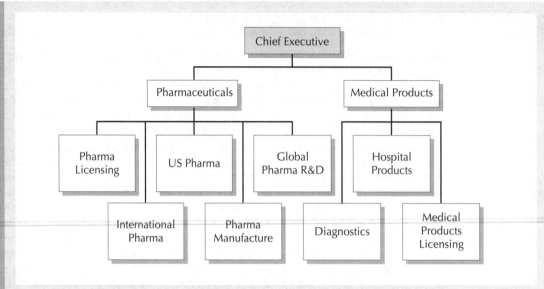

Figure 10.17 Abbott's structure in 2003

of $2.4 billion. Unlike the other businesses, it was managed globally, using its own personnel and not working through Abbott International. Therefore, two approaches to running international business appeared within the same company.

Abbott could have lived with this difference indefinitely were it not for long-term environmental changes. The first is towards global product development in the healthcare industry. Intent on cutting launch costs and speeding the rate of market entry, companies increasingly co-ordinate trials of new drug formulations in all major markets. The same goes for hospital products; launching in the United States and subsequent trials abroad mean delays and expensive modifications. This trend, then, pushes companies towards having global product divisions.

The second pulls companies in the opposite direction. Healthcare purchasers in the United States are consolidating their activities, either because of merger or through buying groups. Co-ordination is occurring across product ranges. This means that suppliers such as Abbott look towards building company-based relationships rather than selling each line independently. Abbott has to find a way of linking its divisions' marketing in its home market. One benefit is the possibility of synergy among products of different divisions. For instance, Abbott has an HIV diagnostic test, a nutritional product for AIDS sufferers and a drug, Norvir, which shows promise in reducing HIV to

undetectable levels. To achieve such linkages, Abbott created a separate marketing unit to build closer ties with key customers.

Should the home business have become more like the international? Or should the international have mirrored the home on a global scale? Some senior managers pointed to the costs of change and the risk of a new structure becoming obsolete, and the danger of meddling with a flourishing arrangement.

In 2001, Abbott had focused on three core areas and, by 2002, had reorganised into two divisions, each covering the globe, *see* Figure 10.17. Pharmaceuticals, the larger and faster growing, had separate sales units for home and international but was otherwise globally organised. Its R&D division was a single global operation based on seven centres of excellence.

As for serving buying groups, the future may lie in e-commerce. In one trial, Abbott joined several healthcare companies to create the Global Health Care Exchange for customers to buy a full range of products at one point.

Questions

1 Summarise the Abbott case using a rich picture. What issues does the picture reveal?

2 Describe the important situational factors relevant to Abbott's structure.

3 Comment on the new organisation using the concept of interdependency

Bibliography

Besides *The Empty Raincoat* (London: Hutchinson, 1994), Charles Handy has written many titles on organisations, including *The Elephant and the Flea* (London: Arrow, 2002), *Beyond Certainty* (London: Century, 1995) and *Gods of Management* (London: Pan, 1979). For strategy and structure, see Henry Mintzberg and Sumantra Ghoshal (2002) *Strategy Process: Global Edition* (Harlow: Financial Times Prentice Hall). Any of the studies described in the text provide insights into the work of contingency theorists and the difficulties that have to be surmounted. These include Burns and Stalker (1961), Chandler (1962), Kanter (1983), Lawrence and Lorsch (1986), Mintzberg (1979), Thompson (1967) and Woodward (1971). Laurie Mullins (2002) *Management and Organisational Behaviour* (6th edition, Harlow: Financial Times Prentice Hall) has good chapters on structure.

References

1 von Pierer, Heinrich (2003) *Chairman's address*, Siemens AG, Annual Shareholders' Meeting, Munich, 23 January; www.siemens.de, w4.siemens.com/annual report_2002/index.shtml, www.fuji-siemens.com, www.osram.com, www.usa.siemens.com, all accessed 6 March 2003.

2 Senior, Barbara and Naylor, John (1984) 'A skills exchange for unemployed people', in Koopman-Iwema, A.M. and Roe, R.A. (eds) *Work and Organisational Psychology*, Lisse: Swets and Zeitlinger, 98–116.

3 Barnard, Chester I. (1938) *The Functions of the Executive*, Cambridge, Mass.: Harvard University Press.

4 Siemens AG (2003) *Annual Report 2002: Our portfolio*, Siemens.

5 Merck & Co., Inc. (2003) *Career Choices in Manufacturing*, www.merck.com/careers/m-e/science.html; accessed 8 March 2003.

6 Taken from Godfrey, Blan, Berwick, Don and Roessner, Jane (1997) *How Quality Management Really Works in Health Care*, The Juran Institute, www.juran.com/research/articles/article001.html, accessed 21 June 2003.

7 United Distillers (1997) job advertisement, www.united.distillers.co.uk/udp2.htm, 2 March 1997.

8 Dibrell, C. Clay and Miller, Thomas R. (2002) 'Organization design: the continuing influence of information technology', *Management Decision*, **40(6)**, 620–7.

9 Mukherji, Ananda (2002) 'The evolution of information systems: their impact on organizations and structures', *Management Decision*, **40(5)**, 497–507.

10 Crainer, Stuart (1994) 'Management pioneers and prophets – Alfred P. Sloan', *Financial Times*, 14 November, 10.

11 Birkinshaw, Julian (2002) 'How long division can add up to bigger numbers', *Financial Times*, 7 August; Bartlett, C. and Ghoshal, S. (1989) *Managing across Borders: The transnational solution*, Boston, Mass.: Harvard Business School Press.

12 Treschow, Michael (2002) *Presentation at Annual General Meeting*, Stockholm; Electrolux (2002) 'Electrolux board authorises restructuring within major appliances and compressors', *Press Release*, 17 December; Lorenz, Christopher (1994) 'Management: How to bridge functional gaps', *Financial Times*, 25 November, 14.

13 Corzine, Robert (1995) 'Shell to shed 1200 jobs in shake-up: Anglo-Dutch group plans radical restructuring', *Financial Times*, 30 March, 1; Lascelles, David (1995) 'Barons swept out of fiefdoms; Shell's far-reaching shake-up is dramatic but necessary', *ibid.*, 19; Lex (1995) 'Reshaping Shell', *ibid.*, 20.

14 Lynch, Richard (1997) *Corporate Strategy*, London: Financial Times Pitman Publishing, 725–6.

15 Achrol, R.S. (1997) 'Changes in the theory of interorganizational relations in marketing: Towards a network paradigm', *Journal of the Academy of Marketing Science*, **25(1)**, 56–71.

16 Dess, G.G., Rasheed, A.M., McLaughlin, K.J. and Priem, R.L. (1995) 'The new corporate architecture', *Academy of Management Executive*, **9(3)**, 7–20.

17 Eisenstat, Russell, Foote, Nathaniel, Galbraith, Jay and Miller, Danny (2001) 'Beyond the business unit', *McKinsey Quarterly*, **1**.

18 Hagel III, John and Singer, Marc (2000) 'Unbundling the corporation', *McKinsey Quarterly*, **3**; Day, Jonathan D. and Wendler, James C. (1998) 'The new economics of organisation', *ibid.*, 1, 4–17.

19 Jones, C. Stuart (1999) 'Hierarchies, networks and management accounting in NHS hospitals', *Accounting, Auditing and Accountability Journal*, **12(2)**, 164–87.

20 Miles, Raymond E. and Snow, Charles (1992) 'Managing 21st century network organisations', *Organisational Dynamics*, Winter.

21 Willis, Gordon (1994) 'Networking and its leadership processes', *Leadership and Organization Development Journal*, **15(7)**, 19–27.

22 Kasper-Fuehrer, Eva C. and Ashkanasy, Neal M. (2001) 'Communicating trustworthiness and building trust in interorganizational virtual organizations', *Journal of Management*, **27(3)**, 235–54; Davidow, W. and Malone, M. (1993) *The Virtual Corporation*, New York: Harper Business.

23 Häcki, Remo and Lighton, Julian (2001) 'The future of the networked company', *McKinsey Quarterly*, **3**.

24 Burns, Tom and Stalker, G.M. (1961) *The Management of Innovation*, London: Tavistock.

25 Based on Burns and Stalker (1961) *op. cit.*, 5–6.

26 Lawrence, Paul R. and Lorsch, Jay W. (1986) *Organisation and Environment: Managing differentiation and integration*, Boston, Mass.: Harvard Business School Press.

27 Lawrence and Lorsch (1986) *op. cit.*, 16.

28 Kanter, Rosabeth Moss (1983) *The Change Masters*, New York: Simon & Schuster.

29 Kanter, Rosabeth Moss (1989) *When Giants Learn to Dance*, New York: Simon & Schuster.

30 Woodward, Joan (1971) *Industrial Organisation: Theory and practice*, Oxford: Oxford University Press.

31 Dickson, Tim (1994) 'Management: pioneers and prophets – Joan Woodward', *Financial Times*, 8.

32 Woodward (1971) *op. cit.*, 69–71.

33 Lynch, Richard (1997) *Corporate Strategy*, London: Financial Times Pitman Publishing, 624.

34 Lynch (1997) *loc. cit.*

35 Chandler, Alfred D. (1962) *Strategy and Structure*, Cambridge, Mass.: MIT Press.

36 Williamson, O. E. (1975) *Markets and Hierarchies: Analysis and Antitrust Implications: A study in the economics of internal organization*, New York: Free Press.

37 Bailetti, Antonio J. and Callahan, John R. (1995) 'Specifying the structure which integrates a firm's skills with market needs', *R&D Management*, **25(2)**, April, 227–40.

38 Mintzberg, Henry (1979) *The Structure of Organisations*, Englewood Cliffs, NJ: Prentice-Hall.

39 Thompson, J.D. (1967) *Organisations in Action: Social science bases of administrative theory*, New York: McGraw-Hill.

40 Carnegy, Hugh (1995) 'Swedish fashion retailer proves model performer', *Financial Times*, 23 February, 36.

41 Czarniawska-Joerges, Barbara (1993) 'Swedish management: modern project, postmodern implementation', *International Studies of Management and Organisation*, **23(1)**, Spring, 13–27.

42 Sweeney, Eamonn P. and Hardaker, Glenn (1994) 'The importance of organizational and national culture', *European Business Review*, **94(5)**, 3–14.

43 Mullins, Laurie J. (1996) *Management and Organisational Behaviour*, 4th edition, London: Financial Times Pitman Publishing, 386.

44 Barsoux, Jean-Louis (1995) 'Management: The importance of the creative spirit – The organisational structure is only a means to an end', *Financial Times*, 26 April, 19.

45 Marschan, R, Welch, D. and Welch L. (1996) 'Control in less-hierarchical multinationals: the role of personal networks and informal communication', *International Business Review*, **5(2)**, April, 137–44.

46 Alvesson, Mats and Willmott, Hugh (1996) *Making Sense of Management: A critical introduction*, London: Sage.

47 *Ibid.*, 101–2.

48 Hurcomb, John and Chapman, Paul (1997) 'Organizational learning at National & Provincial Building Society', *Knowledge and Process Management*, **4(1)**, March, 34–48.

49 Handy, Charles (1994) *The Empty Raincoat: Making sense of the future*, London: Hutchinson.

50 Leiden, Jeffrey (2003) 'Transforming Abbott's Global Pharma Business', *Merrill Lynch Health Care Conference*, 5 February; http://media.corporate-ir.net/media_files/NYS/ABT/presentations/abt_020503/tsld043.htm, accessed 10 March 2003; Abbott (2003) *2002 Annual Report to Shareholders*, Abbott Laboratories Inc.; Waters, Richard (1995) 'Two's company – Abbott Laboratories, debating the best way to run an international business', *Financial Times*, 7 July, 17.

CHAPTER 11

Leadership and motivation

Chapter objectives

When you have finished studying this chapter, you should be able to:

- differentiate leadership from management;

- outline five sources of power for leaders and managers; explain how power can be delegated through empowerment;

- compare four types of leadership theory – trait, behavioural, contingency and transformational – giving examples of each;

- demonstrate the importance of motivation in the generation of work performance;

- explain how rewards for effort may be intrinsic or extrinsic;

- compare three main classes of motivation theory, summarising them in the Porter–Lawler model;

- apply and illustrate theories in the context of job design and performance-related pay.

He was not a bad person at all and had very generous traits but, if footballers think they are above the manager's control, there is only one word to say to them – goodbye.

Sir Alex Ferguson, manager, Manchester United F.C.

Peace, joy and results for Juve[1]

Fans were sure that Marcello Lippi made a difference. Appointed manager of a football club frustrated by lack of success, he led Juventus to win the Italian league and cup in his first season, become European champions in his second and, in his third, reach a second European final and regain the Italian title.

After this run, Lippi broke with conventional wisdom and rebuilt his squad. His hand was forced by changes in the transfer market after the Bosman case and the huge fees offered by English clubs for Vialli and, especially, Ravanelli. Other members left too. How was the reshuffle accomplished so successfully? 'One of the characteristics of this squad is that no one feels unimportant. ... five or six players, because of their charisma, their personality, their class and experience will always play if fit. ... When a player signs for Juventus, he doesn't ask "But I will always play, won't I?"'

Lippi's approach to training showed in the way the team played possession soccer at high speed. Coaching focused on ball work, passing and moving quickly off the ball. While believing in the superiority of his methods, Lippi was tactful about other teams. Typically, he would admit that losers were 'a little unlucky'. This manner came easily to the 50-something-year-old whose good looks resembled Paul Newman's.

Although tactics were important, Lippi's strongest asset was his astute treatment of players. He was sensitive to their human qualities. Of Frenchmen Zidane and Deschamps, he said, 'They are very different types of player, but as people they are as similar as two drops of water, possessing a rare intelligence and a rare humility, a willingness to put themselves at the disposal of others.' On taking charge, he announced he would make his team *Baggioindipendente*. Some saw this as a snub for the star Roberto Baggio who, after a brilliant 1994 World Cup, was feeling the pressure of expectations. Yet the comment revealed Lippi's insight. His team would share responsibility. In another instance, Ravanelli was seen gesturing angrily towards the manager during a match. Afterwards, Lippi commented that the remorseful striker must have pointed at a spectator behind the dugout.

When Lippi was appointed, the club's president Umberto Agnelli had asked him to do nothing more than restore a sense of peace and joy and the results would follow.

(This case was written for the first edition. Lippi joined Internazionale in summer 1999, but was sacked after defeat on the opening day of his second season. Returning to Juventus for 2001–2, his team won Serie A in both 2002 and 2003.)

Introduction

What makes some athletes into good leaders? Some stars on the field fail in management while others who never win a medal become excellent, successful coaches. Those who succeed do so in many different ways, depending on their character, the organisation and its context. Both Lippi and Ferguson (quoted at the head of the chapter) had millions to spend. Yet, Lippi works through nurturing even the biggest egos while Ferguson appears as a footballing hard man who despises the star system. Lippi's success was instant but his tenure short; Ferguson's took many years of patient development.

Carl Lindström lifted the Finland ice hockey team from the doldrums to 1995 world champions. Of Swedish nationality, he spoke no Finnish. He was not a player, having qualified in special needs teaching and taken up coaching as a pastime. Following the final between Finland and Sweden in Stockholm, he received honorary Finnish citizenship and was asked to lecture widely. The win broke several cultural myths, for example: Finns could only succeed at individual sports such as running or skiing; fear of failure made players avoid risk; and Finland could never beat Sweden! Lindström's leadership philosophy had several elements – *acting as example* for the whole team; *doing things better little by little*; *a personal style* (for Lindström, caring for others); *taking risks* (making more shots on goal); *being honest*; and *knowing the team well*.[2]

Like many coaches, Lindström's leadership was charismatic; his behaviour was inspiring and he generated enthusiasm among those he led. This highly personal style of leadership can have extraordinary effects, yet may also be time dependent. Lindström's charisma grew with the team's success. Yet, after the famous win, the team began to lose. While remaining good, it could not recapture the 1995 momentum and the coach's charisma waned.

Lippi, Ferguson and Lindström displayed leadership. They made groups of people reach beyond their individual capacities. We will examine the nature of leaders and how they work with and motivate others, which are among the most talked-about topics in management.

Motivation mirrors leadership. Leaders motivate followers; followers are motivated by leaders. Yet, people are also motivated by other factors within themselves or their environment. Stars play for managers, teams, fans, their sports and themselves. The second part of the chapter explores this complexity.

Leadership and management

We start with a definition:

> *Leadership is the process of influencing people towards achievement of organisational goals.*

Here we see three key features about which authors agree – goals, people and influence. Surely, we might respond, this is the same as management? There are, nevertheless, differences. Management is concerned with goal setting, problem solving, controlling and studying the environment. Leadership provides inspiration, risk taking, creativity and change. The power available to managers arises from their position as managers while, for leaders, it often arises from within themselves. Good chief executives, such as Sir David Barnes at Zeneca, leave to others the 'hands-on' management. His role is 'providing the leadership, ensuring appropriate allocation of resources, giving a sense of direction and values; making the company live'. He also takes the lead in maintaining high ethical standards.[3]

For Senge, 'Leadership is a phenomenon, not a position. It's absolutely nothing to do with hierarchy. Leaders are people who move ahead and who have some influence over others. They are not necessarily in any position of authority.'[4] In Senge's ideal *learning organisation*,[5] leaders emerge from among empowered teams of middle managers, for if exercised from the top only, leadership can be fatal. Summarising, Capowski suggests that management and leadership differ in that one comes from the head and the other from the heart.[6] Figure 11.1 sets out the qualities of the two ideal-types.

Both management and leadership involve power – *the potential to influence the behaviour of others*. Note the word potential. This suggests a set of resources that

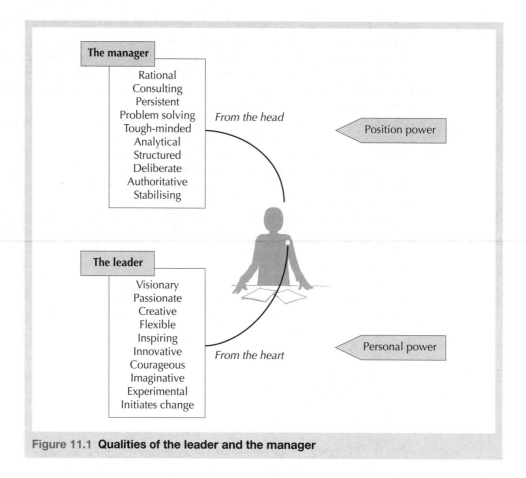

Figure 11.1 Qualities of the leader and the manager

a leader can deploy to influence others. Power is a resource; leadership is a process that involves exercising power. Power can be built and expanded until it is applied.

Apart from the definition used above, it is worth noting two other usages of the word power. First, it often carries connotations of independence: 'You are not my boss and therefore you cannot tell me what to do', asserts this feeling. Second, power is often so closely related to control that the two words are used interchangeably. In this book, however, control is used in a narrower way, as detailed in Chapters 18 and 19.

To analyse power in the organisation, French and Raven[7] proposed five categories. We shall group them in two sets, depending on their origins – formal position or personal characteristics.

■ Power from formal position

Here, the source of the manager's power is the organisation. Three forms – legitimate, reward and coercive – are used to influence others' behaviour in the direction of goals.

Legitimate power

Legitimate power arises from a person's role. Also known as *position power*, it is based on formal authority, linked to a position. Provided the hierarchy has been legitimately constituted, with rules governing the exercise of authority, occupants of each position have the right to exercise corresponding power. Although we normally look upwards in the hierarchy, power can arise anywhere. For instance, in railways, the rules place the signaller in charge of the line and the guard in command of the train. Not even a company director can overrule their legitimate decisions.

Reward power

Reward power relies on subordinates perceiving that the leader can reward those who comply with instructions. Benefits can range from immediate payments to bonuses and promotion in the future, to privileges, praise and factors such as allocation of more interesting and responsible work. The opportunity for managers to offer such incentives underpins practices related to work motivation discussed later in the chapter. Clearly, for managers who cannot offer rewards, or for subordinates uninterested in the ones on offer, reward power does not exist.

Coercive power

Mirroring reward power, coercive power arises from subordinates recognising that the leader can punish those who do not comply with instructions. Punishments may be financial, such as fines or restricting pay increases, allocation of unpopular tasks or work rotas, removal of support, reprimands or even dismissal. Fear of coercion may be as strong a driving force as the coercion itself. Whatever its type, the strength of coercive power depends on the willingness of managers to apply it and staff to accept its use. If used arbitrarily and excessively, the effect is to create an alienated and resentful workforce. Therefore, enlightened management will exercise sanctions only when it feels its hand is forced by indiscipline.

◼ Power from personal characteristics

In contrast to power drawn from external sources, personal power arises from the characteristics of the individual, especially knowledge and personal traits. Since we are now considering power that belongs to a person, rather than to an organisational position, we can see that personal power is the resource of the *leader*.

Expert power

Expert power arises from others' perceptions of a person's special knowledge. For it to be real, evidence of its existence must be accepted by others and it must be relevant to the circumstances. For instance, when facing a question of employment law, a manager turns to the human resource specialist. In contrast, one would not rely on an accountant to repair a puncture! Usually, expertise is confined to a narrow function or specialism and may be confirmed by qualifications.

Referent power

Personality characteristics, which engage in others a sense of identification, respect or admiration, are the source of referent power. To strangers, referent power can be based on reputation. It is possessed by charismatic leaders, discussed in our opening case, who often encourage emulation of their behaviour.

Whatever the type of power, and in many cases managers and leaders are able to exercise a combination, we have stressed that it depends on the *perceptions* of others. Therefore, a person may be able to bluff by creating the impression of power although it does not exist. Yet a different person may not be able to convince others that it is real. Then attempts to influence them will fail.

Abuse of power

Power is abused when the leader exercises it at the expense of others. For example, large pay rises given to senior managers, at the same time as shop floor wages are frozen, show the leader not taking responsibility to provide adequately for all. A departmental manager can look good by over-delegating, that is by overloading staff with work. The manager is rewarded by climbing the hierarchy while the rest suffer from burn-out.

Sankowsky showed how abuse is a particular danger with charismatic leaders.[8] Followers reinforce the leader's position through seeing the leader as being one or more of the following:

- *omnipotent* – nurturing and guiding;
- *mystic* – knowing the way and the answers;
- *heroic* – moving mountains for the good of all; and
- *pure* in spirit – driven by ethical values.

When such leaders, often with grandiose visions, are 'found out', not only may the business have failed but also followers suffer distress ranging from anger and anxiety to cynicism and self-blame.

■ Empowerment

Since the 1980s, the term 'empowerment' has entered the managerial vocabulary. It usually means that staff can act according to their own choice within a context of general direction. According to Waterman, 'People know what the boundaries are; they know where they should act on their own and where not. The boss knows that his or her job is to establish those boundaries, then truly get out of the way.'[9] Sir Ernest Harrison spent thirty years at the top of Racal (now part of Thales) making it into a leading supplier of defence products and, on the way, multiplying its value 411 times. He believed in leadership and empowerment. 'I love people who have intensity,' he said, 'who anticipate trouble and take action.' A former subordinate commented, 'Harrison is an excellent boss. He gave me my head in virtually everything. If he trusts you, he trusts you.'[10]

Carefully managed, empowerment can yield benefits at all levels of the organisation. We should note, however, that empowerment depends on people's perceptions of how much power they and others have. Therefore, a group of workers will not feel empowered unless they see their manager as both having power and being supportive. Knowing that the manager has resources and influence makes group decisions meaningful.[11]

The idea of a 'chain of empowerment' echoes the organic structure of Burns and Stalker, *see* Chapter 10, and expresses a democratic ideology. Difficulties arise in many public service organisations with many powerful stakeholders and a government fearful of failure. Kay prefers constructive to destructive accountability. The former gives people freedom to make decisions but holds them fully responsible for their consequences. The latter, in contrast, is a process of supervision that undermines the responsibility of operational managers without attaching it to someone else. In 1995, after several failures including escapes from Parkhurst high-security prison, the Home Secretary dismissed the head of the Prison Service, Derek Lewis. He had refused to resign, denying responsibility for events at Parkhurst because so many of his proposals had been overruled. An inquiry exonerated Lewis, citing excessive supervision and control.[12]

Theories of leadership

Alongside the study of management, leadership has been the subject of investigation almost from the time one person exercised influence over another. Using models, from Caesar to Castro and Mao Zedong to Mandela, one school of thought looks to innate abilities possessed by those who stand out from others. We shall start with this *trait* theory, now regarded as too simplistic, and compare it with others that have been developed in the past half century. Figure 11.2 sets them out on a rough time-line.

■ Trait theory

While it has been accepted that leadership traits both are inherited and can be acquired, there is little consensus on what these traits might be. Studies have covered physical attributes, social background, intelligence, personality, motivation, focus on tasks and social participation. In a typical study, Dulewicz and Herbert[13] tracked 72 managers from a 1988 course at Henley Management College. At the start, participants were split, according to rate of advancement, into 'high flyers' and 'low flyers'. Almost all the high flyers became directors of their organisations. They had had exceptional scores on eight characteristics: risk taking; assertiveness and decisiveness; achievement motivation and competitiveness; together with the conventional managerial skills of: planning and organising; controlling; managing staff and motivating others. These traits combine personal attributes with management skills.

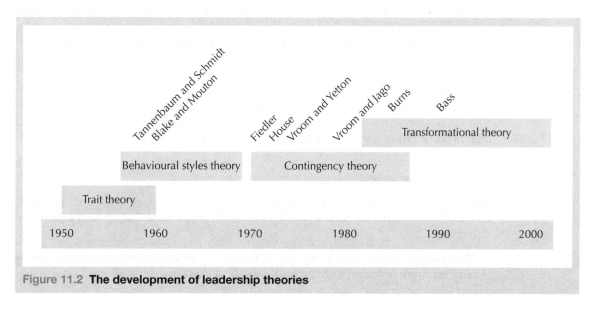

Figure 11.2 **The development of leadership theories**

National differences

The trait theory begins to break down in cross-national studies, showing context to be important. Bertin-Mourot and Mauer examined the career paths of the chief executives of 200 large companies in three European countries.[14] The results show many similarities: average age 57 with appointment at 50; male; and almost all from the home nation. Yet they picked out a sharp distinction between the French and the others. French leaders started their business careers later than their British or German counterparts, but spent less time rising to the top. More were appointed directly from outside (*parachutés*) than from within. After school, 40 per cent had been to the elite establishments, *la Polytechnique* or *l'École Nationale d'Administration*. Such paths imply that the heads of large French enterprises know their businesses the least.

Littrell, when studying China, examines the cultural limitations of leadership trait theory. Like Hofstede's studies, *see* Chapter 4, ideas are grounded in Western industrialised culture. The theories:

- suppose individualistic rather than collectivist behaviour;
- stress follower responsibilities rather than rights;
- assume that self-interest is the primary motivator;
- place work at the centre of life;
- assume democratic values; and
- stress rationality rather than asceticism, religion or superstition.

Littrell concludes that there may be some universal dimensions of leadership – such as task or person orientation, discussed below. Other traits possessed by the ideal leader, however, are highly culture specific.[15]

Gender

A frequent question is whether men and women possess different leadership traits. One United States study found that females were judged by subordinates to be slightly more effective leaders. It offered two possible explanations. First, Western women develop the values and skills that support an empowering, facilitating style. Although *preferred* by both men and women, it is not always the most effective. Second, since women face promotion barriers, those who do break through may be more competent than males at the same level.[16]

In another study, among mayors in New Zealand, Tremane found *transformational* leadership, *see* below, to be a more feminine style. Women mayors stressed communication and people skills, and perceived leadership as working with a web of relationships rather than from the top of a hierarchy.[17]

■ Behavioural theory

Interest in the *behaviour* of leaders was stimulated by the comparison of autocratic and democratic types by Lewin and colleagues.[18] They found that groups performed differently:

- Autocratically led groups worked well so long as the leader was present. Members, however, were unhappy with the leader's style and often expressed hostility.

■ Democratically led groups did nearly as well. Members had positive feelings with no hostility. Efforts continued even when the leader was absent.

The directive–participative continuum

This either/or dichotomy proved too inadequate in describing real managers. It was refined by Tannenbaum and Schmidt in their well-known continuum reflecting different degrees of subordinate participation.[19] This model, shown in Figure 11.3, shows different mixes of boss and employee participation. In suggesting that leaders adjust their styles according to the character of subordinates and the demands of the situation, Tannenbaum and Schmidt clearly saw leadership as something that could be learned.

We should avoid thinking of either directive (autocratic) or participative (democratic) leadership as superior. For example, under time shortage or difficult conditions, the directive leader will do better. On the other hand, subordinates trained in decision making and willing to take responsibility do better with a participative style. Information also presents a difficulty. If the manager has the relevant information, the time taken to brief the subordinates may exceed the advantages in morale and motivation that participation brings.

The Leadership Grid

Various studies confirmed the above dimensions and suggested others. Best known is the work of Blake and Mouton.[20] In 1961, they published a two-dimensional grid using axes for *concern with people* and *concern for production*. Later, they added another axis, motivation. The original grid presented five leadership styles. Since the two axes had notional scales from 1 to 9, these styles came to be known as 1,1; 1,9 and so on. They appear as the first layer of Figure 11.4.

Blake and Mouton wanted to encourage people who are not steeped in psychological theory to recognise their own styles. This would be a springboard to developing ones that are more effective. In their later work, the motivational dimension, sug-

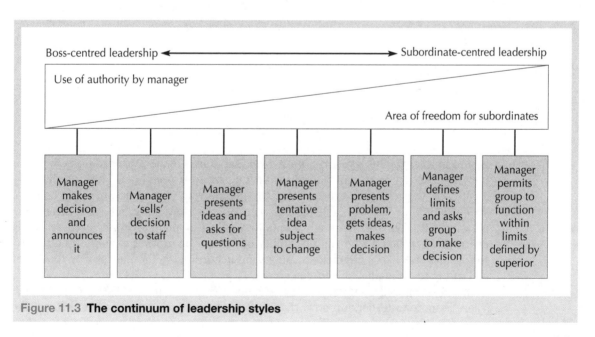

Figure 11.3 The continuum of leadership styles

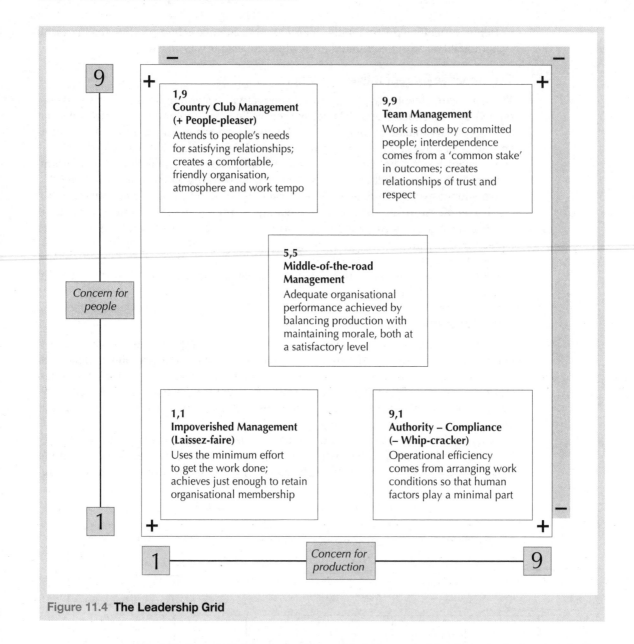

Figure 11.4 The Leadership Grid

gested by the second layer in Figure 11.4, separated leaders according to whether they were driven by fear of failure (–) or a desire to succeed (+). Through this they identified other common types, especially people who moved between two or more styles. The *paternalist* oscillates between the whip-cracking 9,1– and the people pleasing 1,9+. This person really wants to be liked by people yet needs to be highly coercive when faced with the possibility of failure. In another example, the *opportunist* changes like a chameleon, operating according to the needs of the moment and rarely revealing his or her true colours.

In the last paragraph, we pick up a theme first noted in the discussion of traits. There is more to leadership style than the character of the person. The needs of the situation, the influence of culture and the expectations of subordinates all seem to play a part. This takes us towards the notion of contingency.

Contingency theory

In developing a contingency model, the normal method is to compare leadership effectiveness across a wide range of work situations. We shall illustrate the approach by referring to the work of Fiedler, Vroom and Yetton, and House and Dessler.

> A **contingency factor** is any condition in any relevant environment to be considered when designing an organisation or one of its elements.

Fiedler's contingency theory

Having observed the different styles of leaders, Fiedler and colleagues sought to match them with favourable situations.[21] If the characteristics of the latter could be observed, then the ideal leader could be chosen. They looked at the effect of relations with subordinates, clarity of task structure and the amount of formal position power given to the leader's role. Through putting these possibilities together in different ways, they reached the following conclusions:

■ *When the situation is either*

very favourable (good interpersonal relations, clear task structure and strong position power), or

very unfavourable (poor interpersonal relations, unclear tasks and weak position power), then ...

a *task-orientated leader* will be more effective. This means applying clear direction and control.

■ *When the situation is*

intermediate (moderately favourable with mixed characteristics), then ...

a people-orientated leader with a participative approach will be more successful.

Although this result may be puzzling at first, it can be explained with a sailing analogy. In clear water, someone takes the helm to provide direction. Others know what to do and are willing to follow. In a heavy storm, a leader is needed to provide clarity and establish control in the crisis. Interpersonal relations disappear into the background. Finally, the intermediate position is represented by moderate weather, which is probably most common. The crew will gain from resolving differences, clarifying tasks and building commitment. There is the time to do so. The theory helps us understand why the hard captain sent in to improve a failing ship can be less valuable once things get better.

Vroom and Yetton contingency theory

Vroom and Yetton[22] focused on a narrow question of leadership – which style to adopt in decision making. They proposed that the decision and its setting are characterised by three aspects:

■ decision quality refers to its impact on performance;

■ decision acceptance refers to the willingness of the group to put it into effect; and

■ the time needed for the decision to be made.

The authors proposed five main decision styles for the leader, set out in Table 11.1.

Table 11.1 **The five decision-making styles of Vroom and Yetton**

Style	Process – what the leader does		Decision
Autocratic	A1	Uses available information	Makes decision
	A2	Seeks information from subordinates	
Consultative	C1	Shares problem with subordinates individually	Makes decision which may or may not reflect subordinates' views
	C2	Shares problem with subordinates as a group	
Group	G	Shares problem with subordinates as a group	Focuses discussion but does not impose will

The authors proposed a series of seven questions to select the best decision style. Figure 11.5 shows this rather complicated model for completeness. Although most readers will not want to investigate its detail, it is worth demonstrating the method of linking styles to contingencies through an example.

Suppose a manager of an order office realises that one clerk handles fewer orders than the rest. Observation reveals that the clerk lacks product knowledge and is unfamiliar with the stock control system. As traced in Figure 11.5, the answer to both questions 1 and 2 is yes. The manager knows enough to decide on a remedy – further training. Next come questions about subordinate acceptance. If training is to work, the clerk must accept it; yet the manager is certain of a favourable response to such a proposal. Therefore, the manager can adopt any non-participative style from categories A or C, depending on the details.

Since the model diagnoses decision situations, it is more practical than others put forward in this section. Other studies support it and it is used in the design of management training programmes.[23] The model has been modified by Vroom and Jago, whose method generates scores by adding further questions using five-point scales. These indicate the appropriate style.[24]

It is also important to note that Vroom and colleagues refer to alternative styles that might be chosen by one manager according to circumstances. This contrasts with the work of, say, Tannenbaum and Schmidt, who saw styles differing between managers, each of whom should follow one consistently.

Path-goal theory

The path-goal theory, developed by House and others,[25] applies the expectancy theory of motivation, which we meet later in the chapter. In essence, the approach reaches directly towards the motivation of individuals. It sees they are motivated by two beliefs: more effort will lead to improved performance; and such performance will generate positive rewards and avoid negative outcomes. Leaders can influence subordinates by recognising and satisfying their expectations. In particular, they should make it clear that:

■ subordinates' needs will be satisfied if they perform effectively; and

■ leaders can provide support in terms of direction, guidance, training and other assistance that might be lacking.

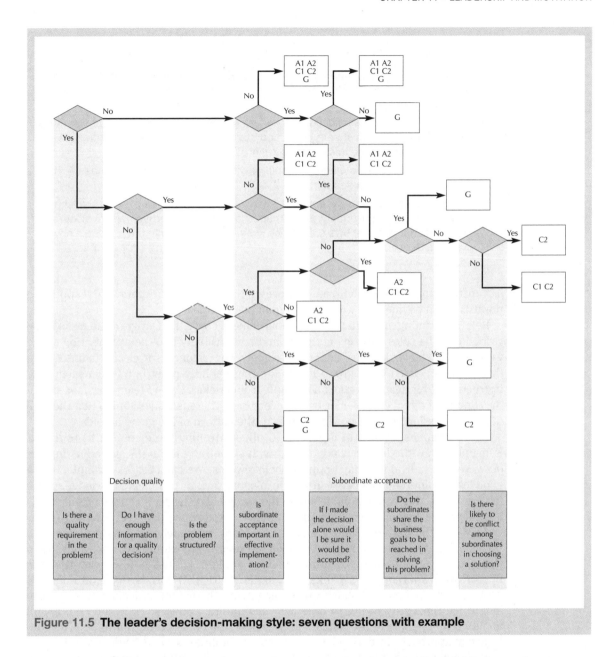

Figure 11.5 The leader's decision-making style: seven questions with example

The job of the leader, therefore, is to tailor the pay-off available for each person to his or her expectations and to make it easier for each to achieve the work objectives. While Fiedler argued that different leaders are needed in different circumstances, House's model sets out different leadership styles to match situational factors. Listed in Exhibit 11.1, they can be learned by the same person.

The two main situational factors included in the path-goal theory are the characteristics of the personnel and the work environment that they share. Personal characteristics include factors such as ability, skills, needs and motivation. For instance, one person may derive great satisfaction from teamwork on projects. In response, the leader may select and organise work to offer that satisfaction. Another,

> **Exhibit 11.1** Four styles among which a leader can switch
>
> - *Supportive leadership* implies an approachable, friendly manner and displaying concern for employees' needs and welfare. The leader creates a team, treating others as equals.
> - *Directive leadership* describes the boss telling subordinates exactly what they have to do. The leader plans, sets goals and standards of behaviour and stresses the importance of following rules and regulations.
> - *Participative leadership* means consulting with subordinates and considering their views before making a decision.
> - *Achievement-oriented leadership* is seen when the leader sets clear, challenging goals, stresses high-quality performance and seeks improvement over current levels. Such a leader shows confidence in staff and works with them to learn how to meet the targets

in contrast, may be self-centred and prefer to work alone. Again, corresponding rewards, from payment to work itself, could be arranged.

Relevant contingencies in the work environment cover the clarity of the tasks to be carried out, the rules covering authority and responsibility and the organisation of the work group. The leader must adapt accordingly. For instance, for clearly defined tasks that a well-practised work group has to do, there is little point in a leader giving the instructions over again. To take an example from cricket, a good team does not expect the captain to direct each fielder before every ball. There is a shared plan that the captain, in discussion with the bowler, adjusts as the pattern of the game unfolds.

Four examples, shown in Figure 11.6, illustrate how the elements fit together. Remember that the leader is concerned with smoothing the *path* and adjusting the *goals* so that individuals may optimise their rewards. We can see, for example, how a good leader differentiates between a subordinate's lack of technical knowledge, in the first example, and lack of confidence, in the second. The leader's actions mean clarifying the path or building the person's confidence to follow the path that is already clear.

Applying the path-goal and other contingency approaches seems practical and sensible. Yet, lest we accept these recipes too readily, we should note possible objections. The various theories, and we have looked at just a few, lead towards perceiving leadership as a package of skills. Critical theorists, for examples *see* Alvesson and Willmott,[26] show how management theory often deals with the problem of legitimacy by trying to hide it in metaphors. Leadership, in the end, is still about getting people to do things that they may otherwise prefer not to do. The contingency approach, in particular, is less about finding out what leaders are like and more concerned with getting those in charge to select appropriate behaviours. The brand labels, such as *supportive*, *participative* and *achievement*, offered by this supermarket of manipulative styles hide their true function. This is to apply technique to dehumanise human relations.

■ Transformational leadership

As an antidote to the calculative and tactical approach embodied in what he termed *transactional leadership*, Burns put forward the notion of *transformational leadership*.[27] This was to take the concept away from manipulation through an endless stream

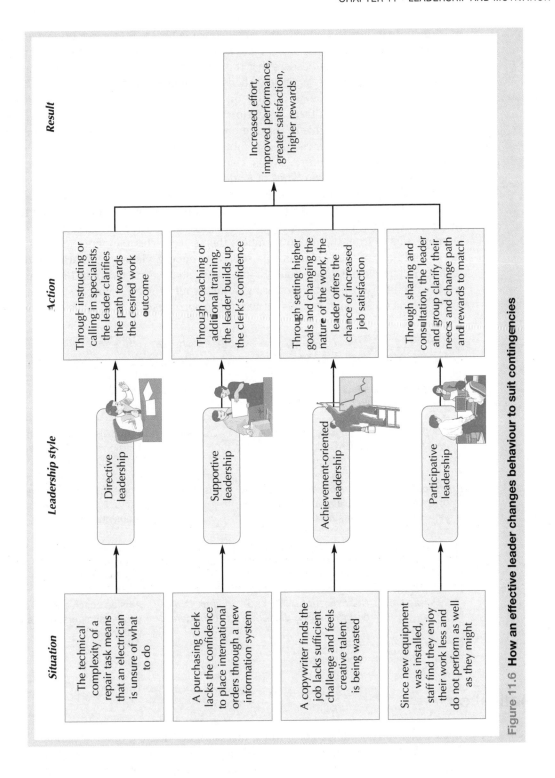

Figure 11.6 **How an effective leader changes behaviour to suit contingencies**

of bargains that, in effect, modify the employment contract. Burns saw leaders as visionaries who challenge people to accept and achieve high standards in everything they do. It is upon transformational leaders that the rest rely, to follow new directions and overcome resistance to change that is so embedded in modern organisations.

Having *charisma*, that is relying on personal power to encourage others to follow, is part of being a transformational leader. Within the modern corporation, however, the person capable of making change has to be able to do so within a functioning organisation. This requires a subtle combination of concern for the present as well as vision for the future. Burns's work was developed by Bass, who set out the differences between the two types of leader as in Exhibit 11.2.[28]

Others link the idea of transformational change with the learning organisation, as explained in Chapter 19.[29] Action learning involves group members explicitly questioning their own conduct. Advocates see transformation as emerging from this learning, that is from the group members themselves. This tempers the views of both Burns and Bass of the leader as sole source of energy, vision, inspiration, rationality, high expectations and intellectual stimuli. As we shall see in Chapter 12, groups often work with different members offering some or all of such resources. The effective leader becomes the one who can harness the group's resources to achieve change.

Exhibit 11.2 Transactional and transformational leaders compared

Transactional leader 'Do what is required'		Transformational leader 'Go the extra mile'	
Contingent rewards	Manages exchange of rewards for effective performance	Charisma	Offers vision and sense of mission; instils pride, trust and respect
Management by exception (active)	Seeks out deviations from rules and standards; takes corrective action	Inspiration	Spreads high expectations using clear messages to focus attention
Management by exception (passive)	Takes corrective action only when deviations brought to leader's attention	Intellectual stimulation	Advocates use of intelligence, rationality and problem-solving skills
Laissez-faire	Avoids responsibility and dodges making decisions	Individual consideration	Acts as coach and adviser; treats each person as an individual

Motivation

What makes us do things: go to work, take a higher degree, practise snooker, or support Juventus? The reasons are many and complicated. Sometimes we attempt to explain; other times we act with little thought of why. Motivation is a catch-all that draws together all these reasons:

> *Motivation is the set internal processes and external forces that direct behaviour.*

Studying motivation is important for managers. Yet it does not stand alone, since ability is also significant. Managers recognise that performance results from a combination of competence and motivation.

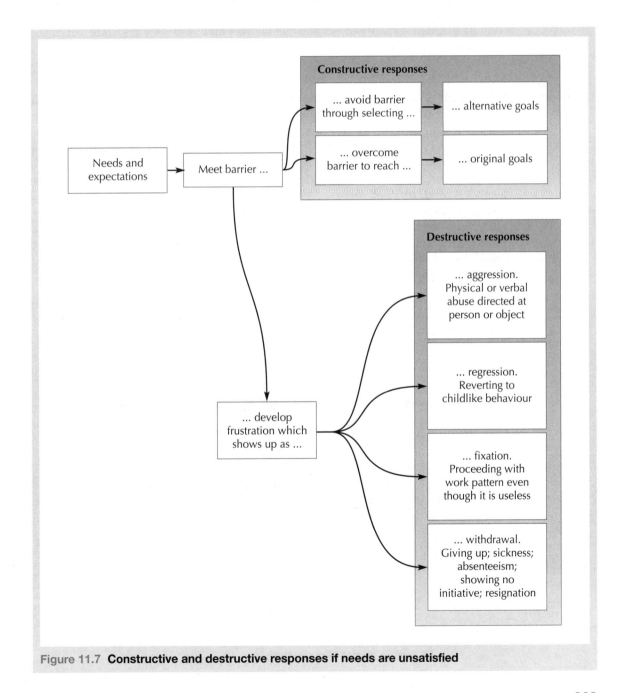

Figure 11.7 Constructive and destructive responses if needs are unsatisfied

Frustration

> *Frustration refers to negative feelings that result from unfulfilled needs or expectations, or failure to achieve a goal.*

At work, as in the rest of life, needs and expectations are often unfulfilled. A good leader helps people overcome barriers. Constructive responses are: to strive harder to resolve the problem; or to select alternative goals or tasks. Frequently, however, feelings of frustration break out and people respond as shown in Figure 11.7. The manager as leader must learn to recognise and redirect such destructive behaviour.

Motivational theories

Figure 11.8 provides a process model of motivation. People have basic *needs* or expectations which, when unsatisfied, stimulate *behaviour* directed towards their satisfaction. *Reward* is the satisfaction of the needs or expectations. The model also allows for *feedback*, that is the person learns about success and can follow the behaviour again. The model helps us picture three groups of theories about motivation. First, *content theories* consider how far employment satisfies people's innate needs. Second, *process theories* see employees as conscious individuals gauging how to maximise benefits through their jobs. This is the rational world of *homo economicus* – economic man. Third, *reinforcement theories* link desired behaviour to rewards, which encourage employees to continue acting to the benefit of the organisation. Figure 11.8 connects each with a particular stage of the motivation model.

Authorities distinguish between two types of reward:

■ *Intrinsic rewards* derive from the process of performing a particular function. Accomplishing a complex task, overcoming a serious problem or resolving a difficulty bring feelings of satisfaction. They arise from pleasing oneself.

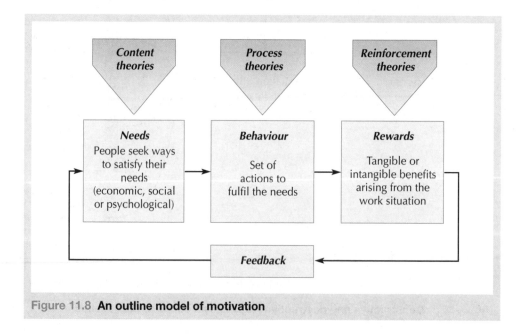

Figure 11.8 **An outline model of motivation**

■ *Extrinsic rewards* are provided by someone else. They include increases in pay and responsibility. They stem, therefore, from pleasing someone else. Although extrinsic rewards are frequently provided by a manager, colleagues can also offer them through their appreciation.

We can find the roots of motivational theory in the development of scientific management more than a century ago. Chapter 1 shows how Taylorism worked on the competence–motivation connection mentioned above. Competence was achieved through specific training. As for motivation, Taylor assumed that man was driven by economic needs. Payment per tonne drove the men to higher productivity. Hawthorne challenged that basic assumption, starting the search for more subtle factors that motivated work behaviour. The debate was influenced by developments in psychology. Some members of the behavioural school held that all human activity could be traced to conditioned reflexes and habits based upon them. Although the movement started in the United States, perhaps the best-known behaviourist was Pavlov, *see* Exhibit 11.3.

Exhibit 11.3 Pavlov – famous for his dogs

Ivan Petrovich Pavlov (1849–1936) became professor at the Imperial Medical Academy in St Petersburg in 1889. He is remembered for his studies of conditioned reflexes in animals, especially dogs. He studied the effect of repeatedly ringing a bell when food was given. Eventually, the bell triggered salivation even though the food was not present. For his work in many branches of psychology and physiology, Pavlov received the Nobel Prize in 1904.

His *classical conditioning* contrasts with *operant conditioning* identified by Thorndike and Skinner. In the latter, the likelihood of a voluntary response can be increased if it is followed by a reward.

An implication in the behaviourists' work is that how to gain rewards is learned from experience. The picture is further complicated, however, by work implying that motivation can be inherited. One study compared 34 pairs of identical twins who had been raised separately and had reached their forties.[30] The results showed a strong genetic component to intrinsic motivation. If true, they imply that the managerial task of influencing motivation is more difficult than previously thought.

Given the many strands in the development of studies of motivation, it is not surprising that multiple theories abound. None gives a full explanation so the manager does best by understanding the nature of each and judging its applicability accordingly. It is to these theories that we now turn.

■ Content theories

Content theories stress *what motivates*. This means they look for specific things that motivate. Central to the search are inner needs, their strength and the way these are expressed in the goals that people follow. The hope is that, if managers can understand these needs, they can design the reward system both to satisfy them and to meet the organisational goals. Four of the best-known content theories are summarised in Exhibit 11.4.[31]

Exhibit 11.4 Content theories of motivation

Theory	Summary	Comment
Maslow's Hierarchy of Needs (1943)	Five levels of needs arranged in a hierarchy. People not conscious of needs but normal people proceed to make predictable climb from bottom to top: physiological ⇨ safety ⇨ affection ⇨ esteem ⇨ self-actualisation.	Widely known and influential because simple and plausible. But note that Maslow made original proposal after studying mentally ill patients. There is little supporting evidence from studies of people at work.
Alderfer's Modified Hierarchy of Needs (1972)	Condensed Maslow's list into three levels – existence, relatedness and growth. Suggested a continuous rather than a strict step-by-step progress. Frustration at one level may lead to regression to the next one down.	An attempt to overcome some of the weaknesses of Maslow. Experiments showed that existence needs were more important if they were less fulfilled but did not support the notion of a rising hierarchy.
Herzberg's Two-Factor Theory (1950)	Two different factors affect motivation at work. *Hygiene* factors prevent dissatisfaction but do not promote more satisfaction even if provided in abundance. *Motivators*, or growth factors, push the individual to greater performance.	The contribution of Herzberg was to recognise that the opposite of *dissatisfaction* is not satisfaction but *no dissatisfaction*. Both hygiene factors and motivators are important but in different ways. His theory is based on field studies and has direct implications for job design.
McClelland's Acquired Needs Theory (1985)	McClelland proposed that some important needs are not inherited but are learned. Most frequently studied are the needs for achievement, affiliation and power. People with strong needs in these categories are often found in the roles of entrepreneur, team co-ordinators and top managers of large hierarchies.	Compared with other content theories, McClelland's work looks more towards senior managers' development. Rather than focus on management skill, he argues that attention should be given to developing the drive for achievement.

As noted in the Exhibit, Maslow's theory is widely known. Maslow is one of the few behavioural theorists to have an entry in encyclopaedias such as Britannica or Encarta, *see* Exhibit 11.5.[32] Contributing to his fame are the ease of explanation of his theory, its common-sense plausibility, its age and its American origins. The last points mean that it has been taught at business schools for several generations! Figure 11.9 shows the theory as a hierarchy, including some examples. Having satisfied their workers' basic physiological, safety and belongingness needs through work arrangements with satisfactory wages, job security and co-operative work groups, managers are attracted by the idea that motivation comes from responsibility, autonomy and the esteem of others. Not only may this be true, but also it matches what many want to believe. 'I am motivated by interesting and stimulating work,' a manager might say, 'therefore it is good that others are influenced likewise.'

Whether drawing upon Maslow or Alderfer, or common sense, many companies believe that work performance can be improved by better satisfying employees' needs. Although attractive, the simple hierarchical models have been largely superseded. Herzberg's original work was based on interviews with 203 accountants and engineers. Its outcome, dividing factors into two classes, was an important step. Managers learn to distinguish hygiene factors from motivators, *see* Figure 11.10.

Exhibit 11.5 Abraham Maslow: provided a language to describe motivation at work

Abraham Harold Maslow (1908–70) studied psychology at the universities of Wisconsin and New York before starting his teaching career at Brooklyn College in 1937. In 1951, he became head of the psychology department at Brandeis University, where he stayed until retiring in 1969. Finding current psychology to be too theoretical and concerned with illness, he developed his step-by-step theory in which, as each level is achieved, the motivation to reach the next is activated. Maslow sought to describe the progress of a healthy person. This idea of incremental personal growth forms the basis of humanistic psychotherapy, often manifested as group therapy. This supports individuals in their development from stage to stage.

Maslow believed that all could have 'peak experiences' that induce very positive and powerful feelings and may strongly influence future behaviour. Yet he believed there to be few self-actualised people, who have such experiences more often than other people. Using a set of 14 characteristics to distinguish self-actualised people, he cited presidents Lincoln and Jefferson as examples.

The hygiene factors must be up to expected levels: the pay should be adequate; the office comfortable; or the working conditions reasonably clean and quiet. There is no point in paying excessively, having luxurious offices or over-investing in clean and quiet workshops. According to Herzberg, what really draws staff along is the chance to achieve the motivators: achievement; advancement; responsibility; recognition; and work itself. B&Q uses these ideas in measuring and developing its employee-customer-profit chain.

Figure 11.9 **Maslow's hierarchy of needs**

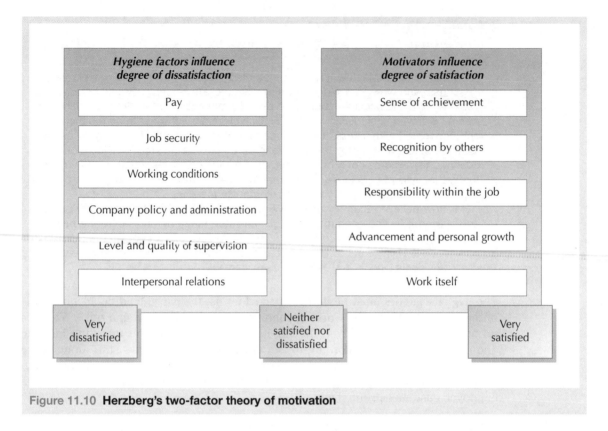

Figure 11.10 Herzberg's two-factor theory of motivation

Since 2000, B&Q has used Q12, a twelve-question survey designed by Gallup, to track changes in employees' emotional commitment to their jobs. Results have been related to scores for customer satisfaction and measures of staff turnover, absenteeism, stock shrinkage and sales. Stores with higher Q12 scores showed higher customer satisfaction, averaging £2.4 million greater annual sales. If all stores in the lowest quartile of Q12 results could be raised to the top quartile levels, B&Q estimated annual savings for shrinkage of £35 million and staff turnover of £23 million. In one store, Q12 revealed that some staff felt they lacked the materials to perform well. A team identified ways to overcome this frustrating problem. The next survey revealed an improved average score, although differences among workgroups remained.[33]

■ Process theories

Rather than examine innate traits, process theories aim to link several variables that make up motivation. They tend to be more complex than content theories because of the multiple perspectives used. Each school of thought is diffuse and is not identified with single authors in the same way as content theories. We shall look, however, at some important examples, mentioning leading authorities where appropriate. Four main approaches are based on the notions of equity, expectancy, job characteristics and goal setting, *see* Exhibit 11.6.

Equity Theory

Equity Theory matches the notions of 'a fair day's work for a fair day's pay'. It really focuses on perceptions of inequity in the output/input ratio whose effect may be

374

Exhibit 11.6 Process theories of motivation

Theory	Summary	Comment
Equity Theory (Adams 1960)	Recognises individuals' perceptions of how they are treated compared with others. They assess a ratio of inputs (e.g. education, experience, effort and competence) to outcomes (e.g. pay, prospects, benefits, recognition). People try to reduce inequity.	The theory links to the idea of group norms, found to be very important in the Hawthorne Studies. It also shows that motivational forces are contingent on the local situation. Apart from this, it gives little practical guidance.
Expectancy Theory (Vroom 1964, Lawler 1973)	Motivational strength depends on expectations of work outcomes and associated rewards. It increases if both increase. Incorporates different people's assessments of tasks and rewards and how they may change over time.	Focuses on the individual's perceptions of the situation. Explains changing motivation in the light of circumstances. The theory is supported by common sense and empirical results.
Job characteristics (Hackman and Oldham, 1980)	Job characteristics – skill variety, task identity, task significance, autonomy and feedback – are most important. They contribute to critical psychological states that in turn lead to outcomes.	Places job design at the centre. The interpretation of job characteristics is 'mediated' by each person, but Hackman and Oldham were looking for key factors independent of individual variations.
Goal-setting Theory (Locke 1984)	Focuses on participation as the route to achieving personal ownership of goals. Motivation follows from: *pointing* towards a target; *encouraging* effort in moving towards it; *promoting tenacity* in the effort in spite of problems; and *permitting the creation of strategies and plans.*	This is a broad theory that clearly applies to those motivated by goals (and perhaps not to others). Studies emphasise the importance of feedback of information on progress. Underpins formal systems such as Management by Objectives and employee participation generally.

similar to the hygiene factors of Herzberg. Inequity leads to tensions and motivations to restore the balance. There are several possible responses for the person affected by feelings of inequity:

- *Change outcomes*: ask for more pay, different working conditions, or formal recognition with office, job title and responsibilities to match.
- *Change inputs*: reduce (or increase) effort, attendance, commitment, training and so on.
- *Distort perceptions*: distort the perceived difficulty or importance of jobs, or the rewards that flow from them.
- *Quit*: find a new job with closer balance.

Shrewd leaders consider both the group norms of equity and individual deviations from them. As illustrated by the bank wiring room in the Hawthorne Studies, group norms can be difficult to change. Leaders often try, however. They may use role models such as the famous Stakhanov (*see* below). When problems arise among work group members, the leader has to work to reduce their scale or impact. Schemes such as job evaluation enable organisations to both maintain a balance and

375

demonstrate that they are intent on doing so. At senior levels, organisations report difficulties in maintaining equitable salaries when operating in the global labour market. Tomkins' pay agreement with Jim Nicol, recruited from Canada as chief executive, broke pay norms in London, justified by the company because three-quarters of sales were in North America.[34] Others claim the problems are exaggerated. Gloria Stuart resigned as company secretary of BOC without a pay-off, in protest at the size of salaries, bonuses and 'golden handshakes' awarded to some senior colleagues.[35] In the City of London, different bonuses for men and women, determined by opaque methods, are being challenged in the courts.[36]

Aleksei Stakhanov (1906–77) was a Soviet miner whose output continually overshot the norms. In the 1930s, Stakhanovites searched for means to simplify and improve work processes and were rewarded accordingly. Stakhanov was a hero of the Soviet Union, and many pictures and statues of him appeared during the Stalin years.

Expectancy Theory

Expectancy Theory follows from the view that people are influenced by the expected outcomes of their behaviour. One way of thinking of this echoes the discussion of decision trees in Chapter 9. Here, the results of each possible action enable the selection of the most favourable. In contrast to such formal models, individual choices based on expected outcomes will be intuitive, continuously adjusted, frequently based on false assumptions and often difficult for an outsider to understand.

Vroom led development with an expectancy model related to motivation in employment.[37] His ingredients were expectancy (the link between personal effort and outcomes) and valence (the anticipated satisfaction from outcomes). The model was later modified by Lawler, who divided expectancy into E–P and P–O stages, *see* Figure 11.11.[38]

We should note the link between this theory and the path-goal model of leadership earlier in this chapter. To sustain motivation, the manager's tasks are threefold. First, match the subordinate's competence to the demands of the job so that the E–P expec-

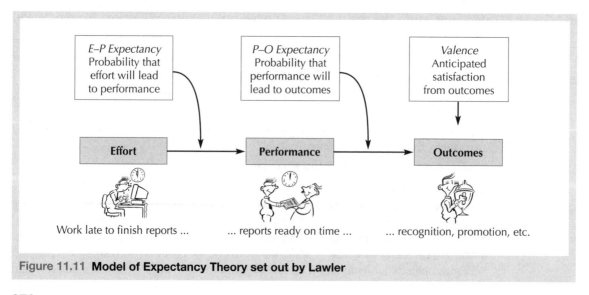

Figure 11.11 Model of Expectancy Theory set out by Lawler

tation is high. Second, design incentive schemes linking work performance to rewards. Third, ensure that these rewards are wanted by employees. A range of rewards, either short term or long term, could respond to different staff or the changing needs of each person. A fixed menu becomes boring. A successful colleague remarked, 'Being named Salesperson of the Year loses its gloss after the third time'.

Job characteristics

Hackman and Oldham searched for general factors within job tasks that would lead to high motivation.[39] Their model links core job characteristics through critical psychological states to results, as shown in Figure 11.12. Note that the focus is on features outside the individual. Furthermore, the model does not suggest that work satisfaction leads directly to high output. Instead, both arise from favourable psychological states. Differences among individuals are recognised in the 'mediating factors' that influence the links but are not central to the approach. The theory aims to offer practical guidance for managing all staff in one occupation, for example, assembly workers, supervisors, police and so on. For instance, it supports the policy of *job enrichment*, dealt with later in the chapter.

Goal-setting Theory

Goal theory starts from the premise that goals play a large part in determining behaviour. Some studies suggest that people who work to agreed output or time standards perform better than those who are exhorted with statements such as 'Do your best'. However, Yearta, Maitlis and Briner report that most research on goal

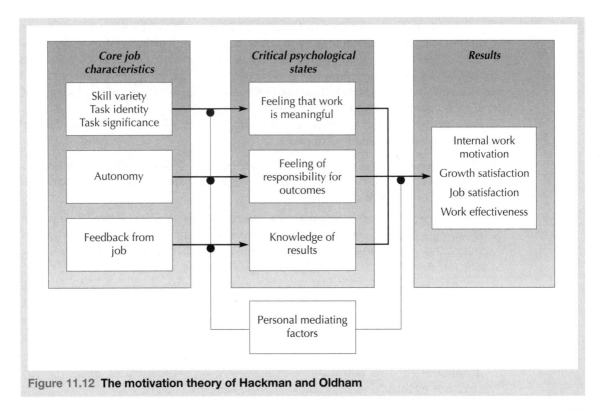

Figure 11.12 The motivation theory of Hackman and Oldham

PART 4 • ORGANISING, LEADING AND COMMUNICATING

setting concerns just one aspect. This is the link between goal difficulty and performance.[40] It is found that, given adequate levels of ability and commitment, difficult goals will produce better performance than easy goals. Yet, whether linking performance with goals or with participation, almost all research has taken place in laboratory conditions and has examined single-goal settings, something rarely met in practice. A further problem with the results is that experiments include clear measures of performance that often do not apply. Yearta and colleagues, in contrast, examined a real organisation, interviewing some 170 scientists and supervisors in a research centre. They found that performance declined when a goal became more difficult. It seemed that people simply switched to goals where they could make more progress and hence experience positive satisfaction. Further, in this complex setting, any link between participation and increased performance was weak.

The opening case of Chapter 1 includes a comment frequently made by school inspectors. Children's motivation falls when their learning goals are set too low. Such examples suggest the importance of selecting goals that are attainable but not too easy.

Therefore, plausible though it may be, the manager should apply the goal-setting model cautiously. Tough goals may not stretch employees. This weakness may explain the frequent disappointment with the effects of bonuses and other performance-related pay schemes. This is not to say that participation in goal setting is a bad thing. There are other reasons why managers and staff should get together to resolve plans, if only to avoid unrealistic expectations.

■ Reinforcement Theory

Reinforcement Theory relates to the idea of *operant conditioning* mentioned in Exhibit 11.3. Avoiding content or process explanations of motivation, it concentrates attention on the link between behaviour and consequences. Reinforcement is *any effect that causes behaviour to be repeated or inhibited*. Note how it can be positive or negative. Tasting champagne makes me sip some more; raw capsicums give me stomach ache and I avoid them.

Four types of reinforcement depend on the mix of desired and undesired employee behaviour and consequences:

■ *Positive reinforcement* – satisfying consequences following desired behaviour. From a simple 'Well done' to changes in pay and prospects, such actions increase the chance of repetition.

■ *Avoidance learning* – removal of unpleasant effects after desired behaviour. After some problems, an employee improves the standard of work and the supervisor stops criticising or watching closely. This is sometimes called *negative reinforcement*.

■ *Punishment* – negative consequences of undesired behaviour. Punishment may range from criticism over poor quality to formal sanctions for indiscipline. A common problem is punishment without guidance on how to achieve acceptable standards, so managers should strive to make it constructive.

■ *Extinction* – withdrawal of rewards in the light of undesired behaviour. Responses such as ostracism by colleagues, or withdrawal of praise or pay increases by managers, may counteract the undesired behaviour.

Many argue that the important lesson from Skinner's work is the manager's role in positive reinforcement. It not only shapes behaviour but also teaches norms and enhances the receiver's self-esteem. Managers should recognise that the way reinforcement is given is as important as the fact. Reinforcement should:

- contain as much information as feasible;
- happen as soon as possible;
- recognise achievability, responding to small gains as well as large;
- stem from the top;
- be unpredictable and irregular, maintaining the element of surprise.[41]

The last point shows up in Exhibit 11.7, relating alternative payment schemes to ideas of positive reinforcement. Daft notes that variable ratio and interval schedules can be the most effective because of infrequent reviews and the persistence of employee behaviour between them.[42]

Exhibit 11.7 Positive reinforcement through payment schemes

Reinforcement schedule	Effect on behaviour when used	Effect on behaviour when withdrawn	Example
Continuous: reward after each occurrence	Rapid learning of desired outcomes	Rapid decline	Sales commission
Fixed-interval: reward according to passage of time	Average results with irregularities	Rapid decline	Typical clerical worker: monthly payments
Fixed ratio: reward at given increments of output	High and stable performance	Rapid decline	Fruit picking (payment by weight); piece work
Variable interval: rewards based on assessments at unpredictable intervals	Moderately high and stable performance	Slow decline	Awards based on random inspections of employees' work
Variable ratio: rewards based on random work samples	Very high performance	Slow decline	Random checks on sales calls leading to sales bonuses

A comprehensive model

Starting from the model of Figure 11.8, we have studied a number of perspectives on motivation in employment. Clearly, each takes a different approach depending on its origin and which aspect of motivation is being investigated. The various theories, however, can be woven into a broad model, suggested by Porter and Lawler.[43] This combines aspects of content, process and reinforcement. Figure 11.13 shows the

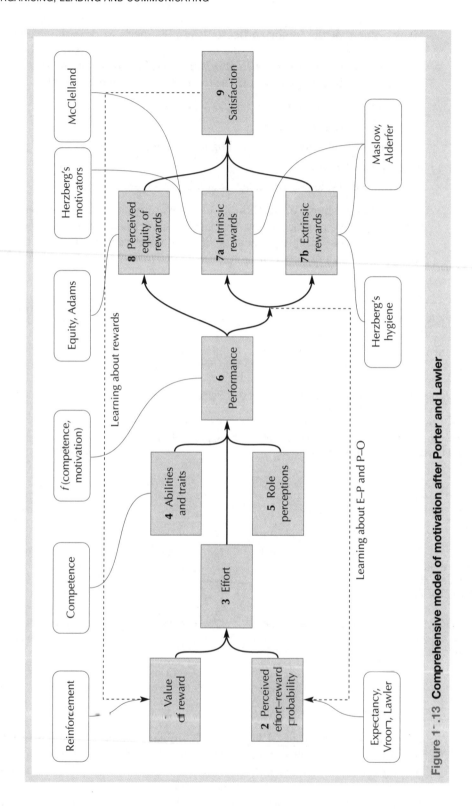

Figure 1⁷.13 **Comprehensive model of motivation after Porter and Lawler**

model with annotations giving links to some theories we have discussed in the chapter. Note how the model starts with process ideas of equity and expectancy. It links these to satisfaction through content ideas such as the nature of rewards. Two important feedback loops identified by Porter and Lawler are shown. First, there is the employee's assessment of the valence of rewards. This brings in Reinforcement Theory. If learning shows that satisfaction obtained is not high enough, subsequent effort will be diminished. Second, there is learning about how clearly the desired outcomes follow from performance. This is a combination of the E–P and P–O relationships of Lawler's model given in Figure 11.11. Other loops could be added.

We should not make too much of Porter–Lawler as a comprehensive model. Its core remains a process view that cuts across at least some of the other perspectives. For instance, Porter and Lawler adhere to the idea that satisfaction is a result of the chain leading from effort through performance to reward. Clearly, this conflicts with the views of Herzberg for whom job satisfaction is a motivator. The model, however, is valuable in summarising the various strands of theory. It shows that each theory differs not through contradiction but because they examine different parts of the jigsaw. Each cell of the model suggests a constructive point for the manager. Numbers correspond to the items in Exhibit 11.8.

Exhibit 11.8 Nine lessons on motivation for the manager

1 Ensure that rewards are valued by staff.
2 Find ways to encourage staff to perceive the links from effort to rewards.
3 Through job design, make it possible for high effort to lead to high performance.
4 Select and train people with appropriate competence.
5 Coach staff to understand what is expected of them in their roles.
6 Agree measures to assess performance.
7 Maintain reward systems that match the desired performance.
8 Ensure that rewards are seen as equitable.
9 Continuously study and monitor staff satisfaction.

Motivation in practice

Of the many possibilities for practical examples, we shall concentrate on two lessons from Exhibit 11.8. First, job design considers the relationship of individuals to their work. Clearly drawing on the human relations tradition, advocates of motivation through job design argue that performance and satisfaction are both available from good applications. Second, variable pay can be a motivator. This represents a return to notions of economic man.

▨ Job design

Job design is *the identification and arrangement of tasks, which together form a job*. It is clear that boring jobs carried out under harsh conditions are demotivating. At the other extreme, jobs that have too much variety, uncertainty and challenge can also demotivate if they make inequitable demands on the people who are expected to do them. Good job design seeks the happy medium. It searches for a balance between job demands and the capacity of staff to satisfy them. There are two basic approaches to achieving a balance – matching people to jobs and matching jobs to people.

Matching people to jobs

Industrialisation led to many jobs becoming dominated by technology. Assembly line jobs arose from the search for lower costs in the light of intense competition. Although the growth of automation meant that many of the most repetitive jobs have been mechanised, millions continue to work as automatons. The second industrial revolution creates similar dilemmas as information and communication technologies change jobs. Rubery and Grimshaw show the unclear effects. A pessimistic perspective has jobs being destroyed or becoming more intensive and closely controlled, with pressure to work non-stop. The optimist, however, points to potential up-skilling and reduced effort, with new opportunities and relationships.[44] In the former scenario, people continue to have to fit in.

Given that such unsatisfactory jobs exist, what can managers do to relieve some of their negative consequences? There are three possibilities:

■ *Establish clear expectations*
During recruitment, the nature of the job should be made clear to candidates. It is better to announce 'the most tedious job in the world' than to lie about enticing possibilities. Personnel managers in car plants find many new line workers leave within months. Those who stay, however, remain for many years. They are comfortable with a simple, predictable job. Unfortunately, knowing in advance whether someone will make the adjustment seems impossible.

■ *Job rotation*
Moving people among tasks at intervals may prevent mental stagnation. It may also bring physical relief if each involves different muscles or posture. Clearly, a balance is needed between the advantages of rotation and its costs. Change has to be organised, training provided and disturbance taken into account. Moreover, the benefits of job rotation are very limited. Surveillance staff at the Museum of Anatolian Cultures in Ankara change their position every break. One said, 'I'd rather stay in one place. In that way I would have one boring job instead of four.'

■ *Earning relief*
Some employers have experienced success through offering *contingent time off (CTO)*. In an eight-hour day one group was producing 160 units with a 10 per cent reject rate. Managers and staff agreed to a new daily target of 200 plus 3 for every rejected unit. Within a week, output exceeded 200 and defects fell to 1.5 per cent. Staff could leave after the daily quota. The average work time became $6\frac{1}{2}$ hours.[45] Although this example suggests a poor state of affairs before the change, it shows that the workers were enticed by earning time off. In their circumstances, it was an important motivator. In spite of such reports, however, CTO agreements are rare.

Matching jobs to people

The limitations of adapting people to jobs have led many to the reverse view. Jobs must match people's capabilities. Drawing on ideas of socio-technical systems, the nature and boundaries of the job are considered alongside the needs of the people. Productivity and needs satisfaction are dual aims of the two policies – enlargement and enrichment.

Job enlargement creates involvement and variety if several tasks that had been divided are combined into a single job. In a simple case, the work of four clerical staff, each handling a separate stage of order processing, may be reorganised so that each does all steps on one quarter of the orders. Other cases, however, may need new processes or extra equipment. For instance, instead of an electrical goods assembly line, each worker would require a complete set of tools and assembly jigs. As with job rotation, critics point out that combining a few boring jobs does not make a job interesting. Yet, if the cycle time is increased substantially by combining a dozen or more tasks, feelings of boredom and frustration may recede as a sense of achievement is reintroduced.

Job enrichment means redesigning the job with the express intention of increasing its motivational content. Hackman and Oldham placed job design at the core of motivation. As we saw in Figure 11.12, core job characteristics were key ingredients of those critical psychological states that influence performance and satisfaction. All job characteristics can be changed:

- *Skill variety*: the range of skills in use can be increased. For example, planning, leading, communicating, recording and monitoring can be developed within the context of manual jobs.

- *Task identity*: enabling a person to complete a whole task with a meaningful outcome. This could range from a complete assembly to looking after all the requirements of a customer instead of referring queries to specialists.

- *Task significance*: designing the job so that its outputs are important to the work of others. Encouraging staff to see colleagues as customers is an important message in quality management.

- *Autonomy*: allowing discretion over job pace, sequence, checking and so on. This is related to the notion of empowerment. There are operational limits to the possibilities for individual discretion. Many employers, however, have developed the idea of group autonomy where a few people share control over the work.

- *Feedback from job*: providing information on how well a person is doing.

■ Performance-related pay

Matching pay to performance has a long tradition, especially among workers whose output depends on their own efforts. Under simple systems such as piecework or commission rates, employees from carpenters to carpet sellers earn bonuses directly related to measured units. About 17 per cent (13 per cent in 1980) of United Kingdom employees are included in a great variety of schemes.[46] The percentage of variable earnings can range from 100 per cent for an outworker to between 10 and 20 per cent for a factory employee. One bank plans to pay clerical staff the same proportion, rising to 30 per cent for managers.

In many instances, however, the idea of an employee being personally responsible for output has declined. Work is increasingly carried out by machines, or at least paced by their rhythm. Moreover, work for many is a collective activity and the group is the unit that determines output.[47] For example, someone engaged in selling consumer goods may work hard to achieve personal targets while ignoring the rest of the selling team. Concentrating on sales may be at the expense of not building long-term relationships, picking up bad debts or pressing operations to make too many special deliveries. To counter this, Allied Carpets and Nationwide Building Society tie bonuses not only to sales or efficiency but also to customer satisfaction ratings.

As with all motivation, the essence here is threefold. First, rewards should be related to factors under a person's control. Second, they should be related to the authority delegated to the job. Third, relevant performance elements should serve as the basis of rewards. Therefore, if a salesperson has the authority to negotiate discounts, bonuses should conform not to sales volume but to gross profit achieved.

Incentive pay schemes are more than motivators. They double as communicators, suggesting to employees the things managers rate as important. More than any mission statement, telling staff that bonuses relate to turnover, profit margin or quality is a strong message. Oliver underscores this view when she points out that typical bonuses in the middle ranks of major organisations amount to between 1 and 4 per cent of salary.[48] Clearly, the bonus symbolises objectives rather than directly stimulating extra striving for a couple of per cent more salary.

Although many organisations have tried *performance-related pay* (PRP) schemes, results are mixed.[49] Oliver reported how managers do not place it high among motivators. It trails in ninth place behind challenge and interest (1), authority and freedom to get on with the job (2), high basic salary (3) and other rewards such as formal recognition, job security and the opportunity to learn. Notable, however, were the responses of the same managers about their employers' views. They felt that employers placed PRP as second, behind challenging and interesting work.

This represents a serious mismatch between employer and employee perceptions. From this and similar studies, many conclude that a link between incentive pay schemes and corporate performance is tenuous.[50] Apart from sales commission, for which there is a long tradition, extrinsic motivators such as pay have a short-term effect and schemes degenerate within a few years.

The evidence is controversial. There is little to support the alleged benefits of PRP. Yet there is little to deny them either. Clearly, some companies believe in the advantages and, if they are yet to materialise, continually refocus their schemes. Oliver notes that rewarding teamwork is an emerging trend. In 1990, BP Exploration, with 2500 staff on and around the North Sea fields, had introduced an annual bonus based on the results of the whole company. Recognising its feeble link with motivation, a new team-based plan was brought in from 1993. Bonuses, averaging 9 per cent with a maximum of 15, are paid to teams whose performance exceeds predefined standards. These are set higher than normal budget levels to encourage 'stretch'.

For others, the risk of demotivation from badly designed or implemented schemes looms large. Some plans have demotivated 10 people for each one they have motivated. The controversy over performance pay for teachers arises from loss of the traditional collective spirit and varying school environments. Tensions worsen when the bonus depends on measurements conducted by the teachers themselves.[51]

Conclusion: follow the leader ... partly

This chapter discussed the interlinked ideas of leadership and motivation. They are connected because part of the leader's intention is to motivate others while followers are partly motivated by the actions of the leader. The one reflects, but is not the reverse of, the other.

It is worth drawing the distinction between leader and manager, although both can be found in the same person. A valuable perspective is to compare their use of power. Both use it, although the leader can draw on more power sources, especially those not provided by formal position in a hierarchy. Empowerment is the process of delegating power to subordinate individuals or groups, but only some types of power can be passed down in this way.

Leadership research began with personal traits such as competence, appearance and drive. Later studies moved away from this 'Born not made' view to define it as behaviour. Several behavioural models explore different aspects but none conclusively. As with other management studies, the difficulty of capturing many variables in a single theory meant the emergence of contingency theory. Styles could be tailored to match circumstances. By implication, managers as leaders can be given skills to diagnose a situation and adopt the appropriate style. More recently, interest has swung away from building some skills in all managers to understanding the exceptional leader who possesses them in abundance. There has never been greater demand for the person who makes all the difference – the transformational leader.

In the employment context, motivation and competence deliver work performance. Many believe that people devote effort for a combination of intrinsic and extrinsic rewards and satisfactions. Yet the links are complex with many theories explaining the patterns. Content theories look to the satisfaction of needs as the starting point. People work better if the work is satisfying. Other theories see satisfaction as an outcome of work. Behavioural theories suggest that people are driven to achieve meaningful goals, seek equity or maximise their expected returns. People's perceptions are the keys to all of these; they give meaning to the results of their work and its link to motivation. Reinforcement Theory takes this a little further, adding in the notion of learning. People's perceptions, both of rewards and of expectations of their being gained, are learned from what happened last time round.

Ideas of leadership and motivation have many applications. The chapter closed with two examples: job design and performance-related pay. Both have shown mixed results. Job enrichment, for example, offers opportunities to many at the expense of unwelcome stress for the few. PRP works for a few but seems to have failed in many instances. Frustratingly for managers, the theories we have covered do not come down on one side or the other. Yet they provide the tools that can be used to analyse practical proposals and understand their likely consequences.

QUICK CHECK

Can you ...

- Define leadership.
- Identify the five kinds of power proposed by French and Raven.
- Name four broad classes of leadership theory.
- Lay out the continuum of Tannenbaum and Schmidt.
- Sketch the Leadership Grid.
- Summarise three contingency theories of leadership.
- Relate the essence of transformational leadership.

- Define motivation.
- Give three classes of motivation theory.
- Name four content theories.
- Name four process theories.
- Explain operant conditioning.
- Define job design, giving five examples of matching people and jobs.
- Outline the functions of performance-related pay.

QUESTIONS

Chapter review

11.1 Make lists of the main themes of each theory of leadership covered in the chapter. Use these to draw up a table showing the main similarities and differences among them.

11.2 Explain the types and sources of power available to the manager and leader.

11.3 Is it better for a leader to adopt a fixed or flexible style?

11.4 To what extent do you support the argument that motivation is a mirror of leadership?

Application

11.5 Assess the arguments for and against performance-related pay in the light of various theories of motivation.

11.6 Relate the B&Q–Gallup studies of the employee-customer-profit chain to the theories of motivation in the chapter.

Investigation

11.7 Compare the portrait of Marcello Lippi, given in the opening case, with other successful sports coaches you know about. What gives them their legendary leadership status?

11.8 Select a service industry for a study of job design. Assess the extent to which job rotation, enlargement or enrichment are, or could be, used to encourage motivation of employees.

11.9 Comparing world leaders, Freedland identified five characteristics, *see* Exhibit 11.9. Discuss the relevance of these ideas to organisations as well as nations.

Exhibit 11.9 Five facets of the foremost?[52]

Be physically strong	Mandela endured Robben Island; Thatcher slept little; Churchill kept going on champagne and cigars.
Have an unshakeable conviction	Mandela faced apartheid; Thatcher was notoriously obstinate about European integration.
Include one's enemies	Mandela involved apartheid ministers and became a Springbok fan; Churchill built a coalition; Thatcher drew in the 'wets' (at first).
Personify one's national struggle	Churchill and Mandela became national role models; so did de Gaulle for France.
Fight the current and next war, not the last	Churchill started to fight the Second World War from the mid-1930s; in 1939, the French generals fought the First again.

Messing about in lifeboats[53]

The Royal National Lifeboat Institution (RNLI) dates from 1854 when the National Institution for the Preservation of Life from Shipwreck changed its name and began to receive a subsidy from the Board of Trade. The subsidy brought with it government involvement in management. By 1869, however, voluntary funds had improved to such an extent that it was agreed that the government would withdraw both subsidy and representation from the Committee of Management. Since that time, the RNLI has been supported entirely by voluntary contributions. It spends £105 million annually on its fleet of 450 lifeboats stationed around the shores of the United Kingdom and Eire. In 2001, there were 6882 launches, rescuing 6918 people. Demand has grown at more than 5 per cent each year since 1980. By 2000, the RNLI could reach any point 50 miles offshore in $2\frac{1}{2}$ hours, and, in 2001, it began to cover risky beaches and inland waters.

About 80 per cent of revenue goes into operations, the rest into income generation and administration. Major costs are salaries for the 750 full-time staff and investment in new boats. The organisation, however, is heavily dependent on its volunteer crews. These 4250 men and 250 women are ready to leave home or work the moment their alarm sounds to spend an indefinite time on a rough sea. Furthermore, they give much of their spare time to training. Payments are limited to expenses and lost earnings while they are in action.

The RNLI is a charity. Tens of thousands of people are involved in revenue raising through 1800 financial branches throughout the United Kingdom and Ireland. They admire the crews' work, enjoy fund raising and believe that their efforts make the difference when it comes to saving lives. Some branches are small, for instance Chester has just ten permanent members.

Flag days and similar events gather money and keep the charity's name in the public eye. This is important since about 60 per cent of the RNLI money comes from legacies. In the United Kingdom, this income stream has declined each year by up to 5 per cent. The cost of sheltered accommodation for the ageing population means that, while the number of legacies has remained steady, the size of each gift has dwindled. Among United Kingdom charities, the RNLI's income ranks sixteenth.

The permanent staff have a crucial role in motivating crews, shore helpers and fund raisers. They offer a 24-hour back-up service to every station and meet other groups at times to suit them. They learn to treat volunteers as much as customers as a workforce. Yet, they must be firm in ensuring that procedures are followed, standards are maintained and the stations operate efficiently and effectively.

Competence-based training is a core activity for crews. Volunteers only form a high-performing team if they have the confidence and skill to handle a high-specification boat. With fewer people from these islands going to sea for a living, the RNLI has to build its own expertise rather than draw it from elsewhere. Training at the station during an inspector's visit used to be enough; now members volunteer to take time out for week-long courses. They must learn and practise navigation and boat handling, including capsizing, night rescue, helicopter winching and emergency beaching.

Achievement is recognised. Sometimes a crew member receives an award for bravery while all volunteers can receive official recognition for distinguished service. More important, though, is the spreading of news of collective achievement of either a lifeboat station or a fund-raising group.

The RNLI prides itself on high standards in every aspect of its activities. The lifeboats are built to stringent specifications and are fitted with the best equipment. Like similar societies in Germany, the Netherlands and Sweden, it prides itself on its voluntary status. Management stability and continuity 'could well be lost if it were subject to the whims of politicians and Government funding'.[54] Members set great store by this spirit and would resist any change. The RNLI gives its nations very good value for money.

Questions

1 From what you know of fund raising, discuss the extent to which the motives of RNLI volunteers differ from those who support other charities.

2 Using what you have learned about motivation, show how you would persuade someone to join a volunteer lifeboat crew.

3 Is voluntary work the same as employment, except for the pay?

4 What lessons would you recommend to business managers after studying the RNLI's motivational methods?

Bibliography

A wider treatment of theories of leadership and motivation can be found in Laurie Mullins's *Management and Organisational Behaviour* (6th edition, Harlow: Financial Times Prentice Hall, 2002) or Robert Vecchio's *Organizational Behaviour* (Mason, Ohio: Thompson/South Western, 2002). Derek Torrington, Laura Hall and Stephen Taylor discuss pay in *Human Resource Management* (Harlow: Financial Times Prentice Hall, 2002). Warren Bennis is a renowned authority, see *On Becoming a Leader* (Cambridge, Mass.: Perseus Books, 2003). *Gallup Management Journal*, online at **http://gmj.gallup.com**, publishes data on leadership and motivation.

References

1 Aspden, Peter (1997) 'Peace, joy and Marcello Lippi', *Financial Times Weekend Section*, 24/25 May, XI.

2 Aaltio-Marjosola, Iris and Takala, Tuomo (2000) 'Charismatic leadership, manipulation and the complexity of organisational life', *Journal of Workplace Learning: Employee Counselling Today*, **12(4)**, 146–58.

3 Brierley, David (1996) 'Business portrait of Sir David Barnes: Keeping Zeneca on the side of the gods', *The European*, 12 December.

4 Quoted in 'The poor suffering busters at the top', *Business Age*, 1 May 1996.

5 Kofman, Fred and Senge, Peter M. (1993) 'Communities of commitment: The heart of learning organizations', *Organizational Dynamics*, Autumn, 4–23; Senge, Peter M. (1990) *The Fifth Discipline: The art and practice of the learning organization*, New York: Doubleday.

6 Capowski, Genevieve (1994) 'Anatomy of the leader: Where are the leaders of tomorrow?' *Management Review*, March, 12.

7 French, J.R.P. and Raven, B. (1968) 'The bases of social power' in Cartwright, D. and Zanier, A.F. (eds) *Group Dynamics Research and Theory*, 3rd edition, New York: Harper & Row.

8 Sankowsky, Daniel (1995) 'The charismatic leader as narcissist: Understanding the abuse of power', *Organizational Dynamics*, Spring, 57–71.

9 Waterman, R.H. (1988) *The Renewal Factor*, New York: Bantam Books, 75.

10 Bevan, Judi (1996) 'Hard work, hard play Harrison', *Sunday Telegraph*, 8 December.

11 Parker, Louise E. and Price, Richard H. (1994) 'Empowered managers and empowered workers: the effects of managerial support and managerial perceived control on workers' sense of control over decision making', *Human Relations*, **47(8)**, August, 91–108.

12 Kay, John (1995) 'Sharing responsibility is to pass the buck', *Financial Times*, 17 November, 13.

13 Dulewicz, Victor and Herbert, Peter (1997) 'How to spot high-flyers: What makes a successful general manager?' Henley Management College.

14 Cohen, Emmanuelle (1996) 'Comment devient-on dirigeant', *Le Figaro économique*, 9 April, 21.

15 Littrell, Romie F. (2002) 'Desirable leadership behaviours of multi-cultural managers in China', *Journal of Management Development*, **21(1)**, 5–74.

16 Moss, J. Jr. and Jensrud, Q. (1995) 'Gender, leadership, and vocational education', *Journal of Industrial Teacher Education*, **33(1)**, 6–23.

17 Tremane, Marianne (2000) 'Women mayors say what it takes to lead: setting theory against lived experience', *Women in Management Review*, **15(5/6)**, 246–52.

18 White, R.K. and Lewin, R. (1960) *Autocracy and Democracy: An experimental inquiry*, New York: Harper.

19 Tannenbaum, Robert and Schmidt, Warren H. (1958) 'How to choose a leadership pattern', *Harvard Business Review*, **36**, May–June, 95–101.

20 Blake, Robert R. and Mouton, Jane S. (1985) *The Managerial Grid*, 3rd edition, Houston, Tex.: Gulf; Flower, Joe (1992) 'Human change by design: Interview with Robert Blake', *Healthcare Forum Journal*, **35(4)**.

21 Fiedler, Fred E. (1958) *Leader Attitudes and Group Effectiveness*, Urbana, Ill.: University of Illinois Press; Fiedler, Frederick E. and Chalmers, M. M. (1974) *Leadership and Effective Management*, Glenview, Ill.: Scott, Foresman & Co; Fiedler, Fred E. (1984) *Improving Leadership Effectiveness: The leader match concept*, New York: Wiley.

22 Vroom, Victor H. and Yetton, Philip W. (1973) *Leadership and Decision Making*, Pittsburgh, Penn.: University of Pittsburgh Press.

23 Field, R.H. and House, R.J. (1990) 'A test of the Vroom–Yetton model using manager and subordinate reports', *Journal of Applied Psychology*, **75**, 362–70.

24 Vroom, Victor H. and Jago, Arthur G. (1988) *The New Leadership: Managing participation in organisations*, Englewood Cliffs, NJ: Prentice-Hall.

25 House, Robert J. (1971) 'A path-goal theory of leadership effectiveness', *Administrative Science Quarterly*, **16**, September, 321–38; House, Robert J. and Dressler, G.

(1974) 'The path-goal theory of leadership' in Hunt, J.G. and Larsen, L.L. (eds) (1974) *Contingency Approaches to Leadership*, Urbana, Ill.: University of Southern Illinois Press.

26 Alvesson, Mats and Willmott, Hugh (1996) *Making Sense of Management*, London: Sage, 91–109.

27 Burns, James M. (1978) *Leadership*, New York: Harper & Row.

28 Bass, Bernard M. (1990) 'From transactional to transformational leadership: Learning to share the vision', *Organisational Dynamics*, **18(3)**, 19–31; Bass, Bernard M. (1985) *Leadership and Performance beyond Expectation*, New York: Free Press.

29 Limerick, David, Passfield, Ron and Cunnington, Bert (1995) 'Transformational change: Towards an action learning organization', *The Learning Organisation*, **1(2)**.

30 Furnham, Adrian (1995) 'Management: Shave off the beard and don a toupée', *Financial Times*, 20 February, 11.

31 Mullins, L. (2001) *Management and Organisational Behaviour*, 6th edition, Harlow: Financial Times Prentice Hall, 426–35.

32 'Maslow, Abraham Harold', *Encarta* (1993) Microsoft; *Encyclopaedia Britannica* (1996).

33 Tritch, Teresa (2003) 'B&Q boosts employee engagement – and profits', *Gallup Management Journal*, 8 May, **http://gmj.gallup.com**.

34 'Shopping across the Atlantic is so expensive: Tomkins' new chief has high pay deal', *Financial Times*, 12 February 2002, 25.

35 'Weekend Press Briefing', *Financial Times Companies & Finance*, 6 January 2003.

36 Saigol, Lina (2002) 'A lower return in the city: Investment banks and law firms are facing legal action from women who earn lower bonuses than men doing similar work', *Financial Times*, 22 June.

37 Vroom, Victor H. (1964) *Work and Motivation*, New York: Wiley.

38 Lawler, E.E. (1973) *Motivation in Work Organizations*, Monterey, Cal.: Brooks Cole.

39 Hackman, J.R. and Oldham, G.R. (1980) *Work Redesign*, New York: Addison-Wesley.

40 Yearta, Shawn K., Maitlis, Sally and Briner, Rob B. (1995) 'An exploratory study of goal setting in theory and practice: a motivational technique that works?' *Journal of Occupational and Organizational Psychology*, **68(3)**, September, 237–52.

41 Creech, Regina (1995) 'Employee motivation', *Management Quarterly*, **36(2)**, Summer, 33–9.

42 Daft, Richard L. (2000) *Management*, 5th edition, Fort Worth, Tex.: Dryden Press, 549.

43 Porter, L.W. and Lawler E. E. (1968) *Managerial Attributes and Performance*, Homewood, Ill.: Irwin.

44 Rubery, Jill and Grimshaw, Damian (2001) 'ICTs and employment: The problem of job quality', *International Labour Review*, **140(2)**, 165–82.

45 Kreitner, Robert (1992) *Management*, 5th edition, Boston, Mass.: Houghton-Mifflin, 324–5.

46 'Extra Rewards For Employees Play A Much Bigger Role In Performance Pay', *Financial Times*, 16 December 2000, 4.

47 'Mastering management: Why piece work went out of fashion', *Financial Times*, 19 July 1996.

48 Oliver, Judith (1996) 'Cash on delivery', *Management Today*, August, 52–5.

49 Carnell, Bob (1995) 'Panacea? Not even a placebo: performance related pay', *Management Accounting*, **73(1)**, January, 32–3; 'Management: Is performance-related pay worth it?' *Financial Times*, 22 July 1996.

50 Rines, Simon (1996) 'Trigger happy: The vast majority of employees feel insecure in their jobs and cite employer complacency as a real problem', *Marketing Week*, 5 July; Nelson, Bob (1996) 'Dump the cash, load on the praise', *Personnel Journal*, **75(7)**, July, 65–8.

51 Lester, Tom (2001) 'Number crunchers search for the right yardstick: Measuring performance is increasingly seen as a way to improve services, but the assessment criteria used can be highly contentious', *Financial Times*, 30 November, 16.

52 Freedland, Jonathan (2003) 'Want to be a world leader? Learn the vital five steps', *Guardian*, 15 March, 10.

53 Royal National Lifeboat Institution (2003) *The RNLI Strategic Plan 2003-2007*, RNLI, January; Royal National Lifeboat Institution (2002) *Annual Review 2001*, RNLI; Home page, **www.lifeboats.org.uk**, accessed 7 April 2003; Miles, Brian (1997) 'Where pay has no part to play...' *Management Today*, January, 5; Armstrong, Neil (1996) 'Legacy funding – Finding the will to stop the decline and fall', *Precision Marketing*, 16 December.

54 RNLI (2000) *Why a voluntary service? Fact Sheet 2*, RNLI, February, 2.

CHAPTER 12

Groups and teams

Chapter objectives

When you have finished studying this chapter, you should be able to:

- define the terms group and team and use examples to illustrate the types found in organisations;

- account for why people join groups, demonstrating the effect of motivation and notions of distance and social exchange;

- defend managers' reasons for setting up work groups and cross-functional teams and suggest ways they can do this well;

- outline some theories related to group formation, development and the roles people occupy within them; point out the limitations of these theories;

- explain important factors affecting group performance – composition and cohesiveness – and show how they can resist undermining and handle conflict;

- illustrate models and theories by reference to problems of cross-cultural teams and group rewards.

Talent wins games, but teamwork and intelligence win championships.

Michael Jordan, American basketball player

Work teams at Volvo[1]

Some European firms have consistently striven to create semi-autonomous work groups. They have been influenced by people-centred production traditions, markedly in Sweden and The Netherlands. Learning from unrest in the 1960s and 1970s, Volvo has been among the leaders. Although its pioneering car assembly plants at Kalmar and Uddevala have closed, the use of teams remains widespread, notably in the commercial vehicle company, Volvo Truck Corporation. VTC is a multinational enterprise manufacturing vehicles from 7.5 to 42 tonnes. The truck market has witnessed pressures to reduce costs paralleled by increasing demands for customised products. The response of VTC has been to remove hierarchical layers and cut the proportion of indirect staff while making production more flexible. Central to the policy are efforts to develop a different type of worker and work system. Unions are supportive. One official stated, 'You cannot work with a traditional work organisation on our line. You must have another type of person, another type of skilled worker than in traditional single machine systems. We cannot do exact work instructions for our type of machines, so you must work in another way, you must trust people, you must educate people, you must give them more responsibility to see over the whole system.'

In most of the Skövde plant, traditional output-based incentive schemes have been replaced by rewards based on competence ladders, such as in Table 12.1. This outlines how staff can progress from level to level as they learn roles that are more responsible. Within the plant, however, different sections have had to develop their own approaches. The foundry, among the largest in northern Europe, has a capital-intensive single flow process. Functions such as melting, core making and heat treatment have up to 50 men. Within sub-groups, they practise some limited job rotation but the scope for job enrichment is constrained by the technology.

After casting, items such as engine blocks and crankshafts pass to the machine shops. Here, the highly automated equipment needs to be kept running at optimal level. Teams of staff at different steps on the competence ladder work flexibly to achieve this aim. When things are running

Table 12.1 Competence ladder at VTC Skövde

Level	Status	Approximate time to reach
A/B	Induction, trainee	3 weeks
C	1 job	2–6 months
D	3–4 jobs	1 year
E	6–8 jobs and team leader	2 years
F	Inspector	3 years
G	Relief operator	3–5 years
H	Instructor	> 5 years

smoothly, they also carry out indirect tasks such as material supply, examining quality problems, housekeeping and work allocation.

In another plant at Köping, team working was brought in when new machines were installed. Teams of six have no formal leaders. Their responsibilities include controlling absenteeism, planning, material control and handling, overtime and task allocation. A production manager commented, 'Team working was not necessary before when there was one person to one machine. When you are working in a larger environment with several machines you have to work in a group and you need social skills.' Managers report that productivity has risen, with 40 to 90 per cent gains in machine efficiency. They admit that the new system places greater demands on staff and there is more stress. Yet absenteeism, traditionally a stress indicator, declined from 15 to 12 per cent in the two years after the change.

The assembly plant at Tuve has two production areas. High-volume vehicles are put together on standard assembly lines. Customised vehicles are assembled in one of six dock areas where work cycles last some four hours. In theory, dock team members can rotate their jobs every cycle, depending on their position on the competence ladder. Production leaders and some specialist roles, however, do not rotate. These leaders usually select operatives for their teams. Requirements are health, loyalty, 'a desire to be a good employee' and, above all, the ability to work with others. In turn, managers have selected the team leaders with the assistance of psychological profiling.

Shop floor attitudes at VTC have changed. A Skövde plant manager commented, 'Today, we have a very interested and a very skilled workforce in all systems ... we do not need tough guys here any more, it is OK to have a brain.' Change has paralleled a rise in the number of women blue-collar workers. Staff agreed that behaviour had improved. One manager saw the justice in not discriminating against half the population, adding, 'it gives you another climate. Suddenly the guys shave in the morning, they have taken down the pin-up pictures. Suddenly it is more friendly, it gives you another atmosphere.'

Notwithstanding their success in some sections of VTC, work teams have not spread through the whole production system. Barriers to change include: the conservative attitudes of some managers; the demands of technical efficiency, especially for high-volume standard products; and the cultural environments of each plant. Lacking the history of collaborative relations found in Sweden, foreign VTC plants, such as in Belgium and Scotland, do not have mechanisms to support the introduction of team working.

Introduction

News about the introduction or failure of work teams in manufacturing plants creates mixed reactions. Some see a heroic failure in the closure of Volvo's pioneering car plants at Kalmar and Uddevala.[2] Worker autonomy along Volvo lines is seen by Womack and others[3] as utopian and a nostalgic expression of craftsmanship values. They point to Toyota and other Japanese firms to demonstrate how teams should be used as part of the *lean production system*. For Womack, it is the one best way, as demonstrated by its successful export through Japanese transplants. Ellegard and colleagues, however, argue that Swedish team working, *reflective production*, 'is as efficient as lean production and in addition more socially efficient'.[4] If it does not squeeze out the last drop of efficiency that is because the firm has found the middle ground between efficiency and improvements in labour turnover, absenteeism and quality. The case of VTC parallels the experiences of DaimlerChrysler and BMW in North America, which also sought productive, yet flexible, manufacturing.[5] There is no panacea. Each plant or section must find its own solution related to the technology, the people and their traditions.

Not only do managers set up and work with groups, but they also spend much of their time working within them. Groups are important in every organisation. The effectiveness has a substantial effect on the total performance. As well as getting things done, groups offer social satisfaction to members. This dual function makes it essential for managers to understand how groups emerge, survive and succeed or fail. In this chapter, we examine how and why groups form, their processes, the main influences on their performance and typical issues to be found in modern organisations.

What are groups and teams?

Clearly, people are social animals. They have a long history of association to achieve their ends, whether it is to accomplish great results or simply to satisfy need for contact. We shall detail the reasons in a moment but first let us examine two definitions:

> *A group comprises at least two people, who continually interact with each other, have something in common and recognise that they are members of the group.*

Although cast broadly, this definition narrows the possibilities. The key ideas are interaction, sharing and perception of the group's existence. It does not include, therefore, examples such as: people travelling on a bus (something in common but no interaction); a customer and shop assistant (interaction but no continuing commitment); or an unsuccessful get-together (people with little in common).

The term *team* presents more of a problem. As implied in the opening case, it is widely used to refer to a work group although with overtones of coherence, harmony, practice and training. Mullins identifies a spirit of unity and co-operation, adding rather oddly, 'Members of a group must work well together as a team'.[6] For shopfloor work, Osborne and colleagues defined the *self-directed work team* as a highly trained group jointly responsible for one stage of the production process.[7] At other levels, managers find themselves part of cross-functional teams to resolve inter-group difficulties. These ideas make us see a team as a special kind of group:

> *A team is a group chosen from members with complementary capabilities so that together they can achieve a planned purpose.*

Note the ideas of choosing, complementary capabilities and goal seeking. A successful student quiz team does not contain the four brainiest class members. It balances one who can quote Shakespeare, another with knowledge of hydrogen peroxide, yet another familiar with the hits of an obscure band, and so on. Among companies, Kodak uses cross-functional teams to work on problems stuck in the conventional organisational structure, *see* Exhibit 12.1.

As Michael Jordan said, teamwork matters in sport. Here, ideas of coaching, communication and personal strengths such as vision and self-belief have long been recognised. Such ideas have grown in management as the autocrat makes way for the

---

Exhibit 12.1 Kodak's commitment to teamwork

A film product development team included not only Kodak's research and manufacturing engineers and marketing specialists, but it also invited in customers such as top cinematographers and film makers. The resulting EXR colour film won an Academy Award and gained the lion's share of its market.

To streamline its annual report, the company built a team from three of the units involved in its production as well as printers, graphic designers and postal staff. More than $100 000 was saved in the exercise.

Beyond such task-oriented cross-functional teams for problem solving or one-off projects, Kodak is also looking to teams as the unit for organisational learning. This needs training, sharing of goals and a change of attitudes towards improvement. Kodak's black and white film manufacturing unit was transformed by these methods. From a number of rivalrous groups blaming each other for misfortune, it has returned to profit.

George Fisher, chief executive officer, has led the change with a more participative management style. Information on progress is shared widely.

team leader. Will Carling, who captained the English rugby union team, set up the WCM hospitality business. He saw the role of captain as 'maximising potential: communication, strategy, getting the mind-set right. Both rugby and business are about teamwork.'[8] Then came rugby's turn to learn from business, shown in Exhibit 12.2.[9]

Exhibit 12.2 Pride of Lions

The British Lions team, made up of players from the United Kingdom and Ireland, normally assembles every four years. Its 1997 tour was the first visit to South Africa since the end of apartheid. Management had just one week to prepare the squad before it left. Tactical discussions were interspersed with leadership and team development training normally taught to executives. One reason was the risk of unfavourable comments about off-the-field behaviour, similar to those made about touring soccer and cricket teams. Players who were not chosen for the star games had to hide any dissatisfaction from the press and behave themselves.

The last meeting of the course was the most significant. Here, all players, managers and assistants formed small groups to work out a code of conduct and means of sustaining spirit over two months. All undertook to share rooms with others they had never met before or knew little. Players who were not selected for any game agreed to join the pre-match alcohol ban. A disciplinary procedure was established. All 21 points of the code were given to the 47 squad members when they left London. Unexpectedly, the Lions won the international matches 2–1.

▓ Formal and informal groups

In organisations, people are often assigned to groups or teams. These are set up to achieve ends giving their activities purpose and focus. Examples are maintenance units, customer service teams, research groups or aircraft crews. An effective work group will build shared values and ways of working so that both the organisation's ends and members' needs are satisfied. In contrast, an ineffective work group can be agony for its members and useless for the organisation.

Within the organisation, all are part of at least one formal group. In a widely quoted model, Likert replaced the idea of hierarchy as a set of relationships between individuals with the notion of a set of groups.[10] Managers act as link pins binding them together, *see* Figure 12.1. Its simplistic nature, however, means the model has not been taken further. Although a valuable reminder that managers participate in at least two groups, it misses their complexity. Departmental sub-groups, cross-functional teams, working parties and project units are just some of the arrangements met in practice. Likert would labour to represent these.

Informal groups

Informal groups arise from the natural social intercourse within all organisations. We count among these all groups not deliberately set up to further the organisation's aims. Membership is voluntary and based on people finding common ground. Some engage in specific activities, such as an office hiking club, while others comprise looser clusters meeting occasionally to share grumbles or rumours over a drink. We should not assume that informal groups work either for or against the interests of the organisation. Frequently, their function is beneficial, such as creating

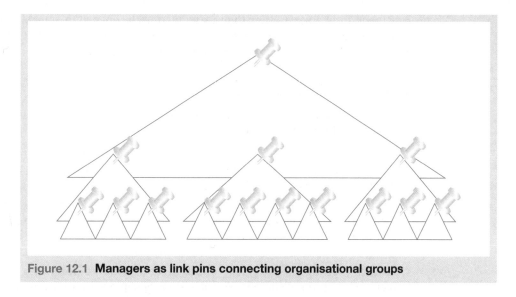

Figure 12.1 **Managers as link pins connecting organisational groups**

bcttcr working rclations or allowing the release of tension. They can, however, be centres of resistance to change. The output restriction among some groups in the Hawthorne Studies is a famous example of an all too common experience.

◼ Open and closed groups

Open groups frequently change their membership as people move in and out. Their internal structures fluctuate as members take up various roles including that of leader. Closed groups, on the other hand, have a defined membership and often have a well-established internal structure. Many formal groups in the organisation are closed.

The work teams at VTC are good examples. Most had defined membership and some fixed structure, although efforts were made to rotate roles for flexibility and motivation. Being closed risks stagnation. Echoing Janis's groupthink, *see* Chapter 9, Manz and Neck coined the word *teamthink* to refer to its incidence within self-managed teams.[11] The risk is that preference for cohesion and conformity replaces creative difference and effectiveness.

Among professional and technical staff, closed groups are best for tasks such as long-term planning. Once the group is some way into the project, it is difficult to bring in newcomers. Again, many groups benefit from the infusion of new ideas brought by a new entrant. An open arrangement for creative groups may, therefore, be advantageous.

Group formation

The varied nature of groups means that there are numerous explanations for why people join them. Voluntarily joining an informal group, for example, will be a different process to being placed in a formal team by a manager. Many groups develop spontaneously when patterns of work bring people into frequent contact. For the manager, these gain from helping to smooth the work flow but lose if they focus on resistance to change. Rather than leave matters to chance, a sensible manager may allocate staff, wisely assigning people to those teams that they would join voluntarily. To do this, a manager must understand group formation.

■ People joining groups

For a clue about why people join groups, we can start with motivation. Alderfer offers a useful start. His list of motivators has three items:

■ *Existence* – people join organisations for income to cover their basic needs. When at work, they form support groups or join trade unions to defend their employment rights.

■ *Relatedness* – affiliation and emotional support needs are satisfied through group membership. Often people notice these benefits only when they are removed. One unemployed person remarked, 'When I was at work, I hated the sniping, nagging and gossip that went on. Yet when I lost my job I found I missed it terribly.'[12]

■ *Growth* – groups help to carry out difficult tasks. Therefore, they offer enhanced feelings of accomplishment. For new staff, acceptance into a group enables learning from others and building self-esteem.

Beyond the idea of joining groups in general, however, is the question of why people join particular groups. In other words, why are certain clusters of people drawn together? Two important ideas involve distance and similarity.

Distance

Group formation is influenced by opportunities to interact, which depends on proximity. This can be represented by physical distance, as in groups of workers in a

Figure 12.2 **Mental map of physical and psychological links and barriers**

section or people who travel together, or psychological distance. The latter can be pictured as a mental map of the organisation, sketched in Figure 12.2. The map represents: links among colleagues; distances among them; and all kinds of barriers. An example of a link is found among staff who regularly contact others across the world. They report feelings of closeness although they never meet. Barriers can separate staff on the same site or even in the same room. Differences in status, backed up by formal status symbols, are often important here.

Although proximity often depends on chance arrangements, managers can make interpersonal links one factor in layout design. Consider a short assembly line, say 25 metres long, with seven staff each engaged in one step of a process. This could be assembling kitchen equipment or packing toys. Such lines are often set out in straight lines, seen in A of Figure 12.3. This is ideal with a balanced line, where all workers need the same time for each cycle. Unfortunately, in the common case of imbalance, communication restrictions hinder work sharing. A coherent work group may not coalesce. Curved layouts may improve matters. Under arrangement B, people can see each other but are separated by the equipment. Layout C, on the other hand, places the workers closer and avoids the barrier. However, each now faces away from colleagues.

Similarity

The sayings 'opposites attract' and 'birds of a feather flock together' seem to contradict. Yet, as Vecchio shows, these may be describing different aspects of group formation. It is widely accepted that people will be drawn together if they:

- share similar *attitudes*;
- have different *needs* that complement each other; and
- possess matched *abilities*.[13]

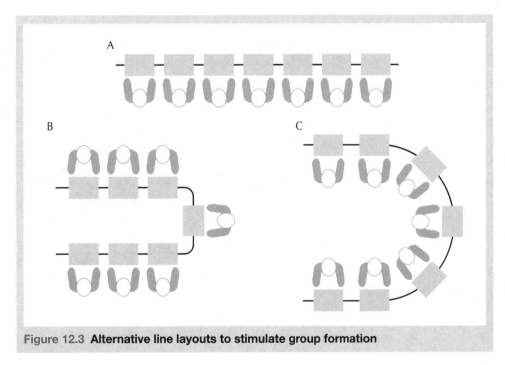

Figure 12.3 **Alternative line layouts to stimulate group formation**

Jack Sprat could eat no fat.
His wife could eat no lean.
And so between the two of them,
They licked the platter clean.

Mr and Mrs Sprat illustrate complementary needs with a shared attitude of parsimony. In many successful partnerships, we find people who share the same goals and values. Yet one, say, is an expert at administration, while the other excels at innovation and marketing.

An alternative to the theory of interpersonal attraction considers the individual's attachment to the group. In *social exchange theory*, Thibaut and Kelley argued that people assess the rewards and costs resulting from being a member.[14] They compare the outcomes, taken as reward minus cost, with both their expectations and what is available elsewhere. If the answers to both questions are unsatisfactory, they quit. Other answers indicate continuing membership at varying levels of commitment, *see* Figure 12.4. Opposite the quitter, the *full member* is satisfied and committed to remaining. The *hanger-on* waits for a chance or excuse to move on. The *grumbler* stays, dissatisfied with the group but knowing there is nothing better.

In many voluntary organisations, people join for practical reasons. They need help or an outlet for their energies. Yet their involvement may outlast their reasons for joining. Exhibit 12.3 gives an example of the Stroke Association.[15]

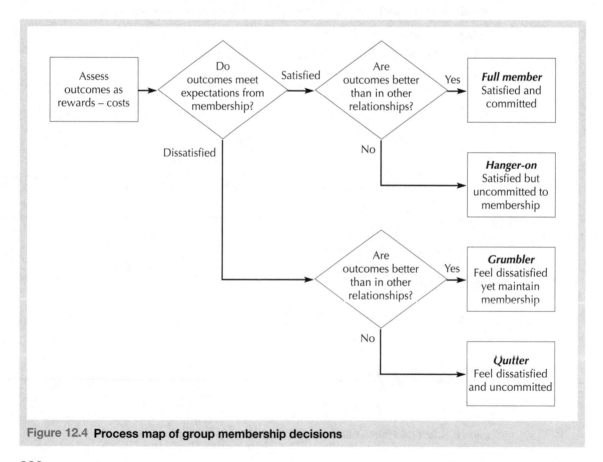

Figure 12.4 Process map of group membership decisions

Exhibit 12.3 Multiple functions of patient support groups

The Stroke Association is a charity that both offers support for patients and carers and sponsors research into the disease. Most members of the local branch join for instrumental reasons. Often referred to the group by doctors, they look for help when a family member becomes a victim. Yet many stay on well after the patient has recovered or died. In finding themselves able to understand, they reap the rewards of being able to share their experiences with new members and give assistance. The group also offers a sense of belonging at a time of loneliness. For some, these benefits are not available elsewhere.

Managers setting up groups

For managers, despite expressed concerns for the humanisation of work, choice is instrumental. In other words, work groups are set up to optimise output, not as ends in themselves. We should expect considerable variation in their design, depending on what is to be achieved. The opening case showed how, even within one plant of VTC, teams of manual workers were established differently according to various technologies. Other contingencies range from national culture to the impact of individual personalities. Thompson and Wallace distinguished three dimensions – technical, governance and normative – that help to explain why managers establish work groups on the shop floor.[16]

Technical
Team working changes the Taylorist division of labour. Labour flexibility allows scheduling problems to be smoothed out and enables delegation of responsibility for process control, stocks and housekeeping. Teamwork also enables learning to improve quality and productivity together. Its introduction may be supported by new technology, as in the VTC Köping machine shop of the opening case. Yet the Skövde foundry showed the limits of this approach when applied to automated production lines.

Governance
In current management rhetoric, team working represents a shift away from hierarchy towards empowerment of employees. Often, however, the degree of control ceded is small. Delegated functions arise from the technical requirements of new processes rather than the goal of participation itself. Three issues arise: how much power is delegated; the process of team leader selection; and how the team fits into the wider management of the plant. Although Volvo is regarded as a pioneer, studies suggest that its 'semi-autonomous' teams have little impact beyond their immediate work area.

Normative
Groups have often been seen as means of deepening employees' identification with the goals of the enterprise. Rather than let informal groups resist change, goes the argument, it is better to establish and train formal ones. Team working is a modern expression of such a policy. Through careful selection of teams and their leaders, management hope to quieten problems of motivation, conflict and diversity present in any workplace. Developing team players is a central theme of much management development. In its various centres, VTC intended the work groups, alongside new pay structures, to build employees' support for enhanced quality and productivity.

Although these examples relate to the shop floor, groups are found at all levels. Studies have covered all layers from board meetings and consultative councils downwards. Needing to make organisations work as well as possible, managers must understand group processes as a prerequisite to improving them.

Group processes

Groups are dynamic. Not only does the group as a whole change, but also individuals perform different functions at different times. Sometimes they lead, sometimes they follow the rest, and so on. We shall start by describing two well-known perspectives on group development and roles. Then we shall comment on their limitations and look at a more recent alternative view.

Group development

Of many studies of phases that groups pass through, Tuckman's is the best known.[17] Choosing rhyming labels for his four steps doubtless helped to popularise the model:

- *Forming*
A new group of people comes together. Caution is the watchword. People behave according to their anticipation of acceptable behaviour and attempt to focus on the task. For a formal group, this may be given by management; for an informal group the task may be 'protest' or 'have a party'.

- *Storming*
Members come out of their shells enough to express and appreciate their conflicts and the difficulties of their task. Hostility and confusion frequently appear.

- *Norming*
The group works out how to come together as an effective unit. Members begin to match their capabilities with aspects of the task in hand.

- *Performing*
Group roles are defined and shared. The group begins to work co-operatively on its task. This is when the group becomes a team.

The time taken for the stages could vary from a few hours to many weeks. We should also note that groups need not always follow the sequence strictly. A formal management group, with people who have worked together previously, may start at the norming stage and only revert to forming and storming if new members come in or a new leader emerges.

We can use a party to illustrate Tuckman's model. With few people knowing each other, the first hour could be spent forming. Unsure of themselves and their surroundings, guests stand around nervously, discussing 'the weather'. Later, as things warm up, some begin to talk more animatedly, joking with some and arguing with others. Groups form and, as they norm, they begin to perform. They relax, dance, joke and discuss politics. The host's role is critical, both in the design of the party and in managing the process. Is there music? Are there separate rooms for dancers and non-dancers? Are there to be charades and, if so, must one take part? Are there icebreakers to shorten the forming and dampen the storming? If such points are unclear, and the storming becomes uncomfortable, some guests leave early.

■ Group roles

The role perspective relates members' behaviour to their positions within the group and the wider organisation from which they are drawn. Personal factors also come into play. Therefore, a person with the most experience within a cross-disciplinary team may be given the role of leader. Another person, anxious to get on with the job, may begin by trying to set an agenda and find out facts about the problem.

A role is behaviour in a social context.

Belbin's work on group roles is well known.[18] He observed how group members in simulations made different contributions according to their personalities and abilities. The team's success depends on how they fit together. The range of roles is shown in Table 12.2. According to Belbin, the list gives us insight into the sort of people needed for a successful team. Those who cannot fill the roles, although offering personal qualities such as expertise or humour, will not aid the team building.

Table 12.2 **Valuable team members**

Role	Features	Positive qualities	Negative qualities
Implementor	Conservative, dutiful, methodical	Organising, common sense, hard work, self-discipline	Inflexible, deaf to untested ideas
Co-ordinator	Calm, self-confident, controlled	Treating all contributions fairly; sense of objectives	No more than average intellect or creativity
Shaper	Excitable, outgoing, dynamic	Drive; opposes inertia, complacency, self-deception	Provocative, impatient
Plant	Individualistic, serious, unorthodox	Genius, imagination, intellect, knowledge	Impractical, dreamy, ignores protocols
Resource investigator	Extroverted, enthusiastic, curious, communicative	Makes contacts, checks out new ideas, responds to challenges	Loses interest after initial obsession
Monitor-evaluator	Sober, unemotional, prudent	Judgement, discretion, hard-headedness	Lacks inspiration, cannot motivate
Team worker	Social, mild, sensitive	Responsive to people and settings; promotes team spirit	Indecisive in crisis
Completer-finisher	Painstaking, orderly, conscientious, anxious	Follows through; perfectionist	Worries about small matters; reluctant to let go

Belbin weakens his argument by admitting that not all roles are needed in all groups. Furthermore, some people can offer more than one role. For example, a combined monitor-evaluator and completer-finisher, *see* Table 12.2, could be a sober, hard-headed person who is also capable of tying up loose ends.

■ Limitations

The work of Tuckman, Belbin and others has been criticised by Herriot and Pemberton.[19] They identify two persistent myths that hinder our understanding of teams:

■ The *All Friends Together* myth, derived from the human relations tradition, proposes that people work better once they know and accept each other well. This implies that once the team processes have been sorted out, effective performance on the task will follow.

■ The *Stages of Team Development* myth implies that teams must pass through various initiation steps before work can start.

Evidence supports neither. In organisations, teams rarely spend time on process before plunging into the task. Then they alternate between making progress and considering better ways of going about it. There is no fixed pattern since tasks vary so much in familiarity, complexity, time pressure and information requirements. Herriot and Pemberton also note the drawbacks in Belbin's work we mentioned above. In particular, the categories were developed not in work but from observing managers involved in business simulation exercises at a training centre. Their alternative model, shown in Figure 12.5, offers a more comprehensive summary of the relationships among context, processes, tasks, roles and outcomes.

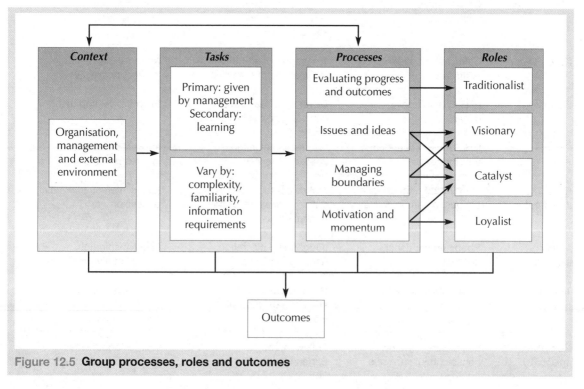

Figure 12.5 **Group processes, roles and outcomes**

Links among these four main elements show how *tasks* are determined by the *context* in which the group works. Tasks are fulfilled by group *processes* which determine the *roles* that are needed. Furthermore, the processes interact continually with the context. Interactions include support from the rest of the organisation, time pressures and the degree of autonomy permitted. In return, the team attempts to influence the context, buffer itself against external fluctuations, promote its cause and make alliances with other groups.

Among team processes, Herriot and Pemberton identify four that enable both task achievement and team learning. Shown within the *processes* box of Figure 12.5, they are always needed but in different proportions according to the task. They correspond to four roles, more broadly defined than by Belbin:

- *Traditionalists* prefer facts and logical decisions. They avoid situations requiring subjective judgements and involving personal factors. Good at running existing systems, they respond reluctantly to change.
  - Traditionalists are important when it comes to *evaluating progress and outcomes.*

- *Visionaries* like to be analytical but are comfortable with less information. They see the big picture, devising new systems and projects. Detail does not interest them and they avoid personal feelings and emotions.
  - Visionaries spot *issues* in the broad picture and generate *ideas* for *managing boundaries.* They can fit in with the whole organisation, scan the environment, draw in extra resources and so on.

- *Catalysts* develop their own and others' skills and talents. Disliking routine and conflict, they persuade people to co-operate and resolve interpersonal problems.
  - Catalysts are good at bringing *ideas* to completion and are vital in *managing boundaries.*

- *Loyalists* act pragmatically to help colleagues and clients. They look to the common good, seeking efficiency and harmony. Avoiding conflict, they may not notice change.
  - Loyalists keep up *motivation and momentum* to ensure the task is completed.

The final part of the model relates to outcomes. The primary function of the group is to accomplish its task. An important secondary outcome is learning. All elements of the model contribute to the group's outcomes. The authors argue that context is the strongest factor in success with the group's capability at managing its boundary the most underrated.

Factors influencing group performance

In the previous section, we began to discuss the composition and cohesiveness of groups. The work of Tuckman described how a group might develop; Belbin examined roles. Yet neither approach considered performance. Herriot and Pemberton is a partial response, showing how different roles fit circumstances. We shall now look in more detail at performance. Issues are: the influence of composition and cohesiveness; how they face up to efforts to undermine them; how they handle conflict; and how to assure success.

■ Composition

Size

What is the optimal size of a group? In his whimsical essay on the life cycle of councils and committees, Parkinson noted that they have a tendency to grow, and as they grow, they divide into sub-groups where the real decision making power lies. What is now known as the Cabinet, the central organ of government in the United Kingdom, has moved through this cycle five times in history, *see* Exhibit 12.4.[20]

Exhibit 12.4 A 'history' of the Cabinet

In mediaeval England, the Council of the Crown began with five members but its hereditary membership soon reached a level of between 30 and 50. By the mid-17th century, it had grown to 140. Then, in century steps, it grew to 220 and 400. By 1950, when granting hereditary peerages had almost ceased, the House of Lords numbered 850.

By 1300, an inner group had formed. The Lords of the King's Council were fewer than ten and remained so until Tudor times. In 1504, there were 41, rising to 172 for its last meeting.

The Privy Council developed from the King's Council. Starting with nine members, it reached 20 in 1540 and 44 by 1558. 1723 saw 67 members and the 20th century saw its numbers grow from 200 to 300.

By 1615, the Cabinet Council had taken over the reins. Starting with eight members, it reached 12 by 1700 and 20 a quarter century later.

In 1740, yet another inner group emerged – a Cabinet of five members. The nineteenth century saw its numbers steadily rise from 12 to 20. Since then, membership has been held in the range 18 to 23. Naturally, throughout this period many have complained of Prime Ministers running an Inner Cabinet of trusty confidants...

Although written with tongue in cheek, Parkinson's tale brings out two points. First, as groups grow, problems arise. They become more difficult to handle, require more supervision and meetings suffer from lower attendance and lack of attention. They often break up into sub-meetings at each end of the table so that factional rivalry becomes more noticeable. The group closest to the centre assumes more power. The second point is that there is no optimal size. Our earlier discussion suggests that the number needed depends on the group's task and its constituent processes. Parkinson concluded that the optimal size of a national cabinet should be eight. This was the only number between six and 22 that had *not* been chosen by any nation!

Vecchio makes the following serious points about group size:[21]

■ Organisations settle on between five and seven as an ideal number for full participation by each member. For simple, formal tasks, larger numbers can be chosen. (Another study put the average in North America at 10.)[22]

■ In larger groups, members become more tolerant of authoritarian and directive leadership. Participation is inhibited.

■ Larger groups need formal rules and procedures. Even with such rules, they take longer to reach decisions than small groups.

■ Job satisfaction declines with group size.

- Productivity declines with group size. Increased co-ordination difficulties and falling member involvement mean that work groups of 12 typically produce less than two groups of six.

- Social loafing, or free-riding, becomes a problem with larger groups. Recognising the inefficiency of the group and the infeasibility of sanctions, some individuals feel that their slack can easily be taken up by others.

Composition

For a group to function effectively, its members must have enough relevant resources. Discussing Cabinets, Parkinson argued for members with resources of specialised knowledge. 'Four may well be versed, respectively, in finance, foreign policy, defence and the law. The fifth, who has failed to master any of these subjects, usually becomes the chairman or prime minister.'[23]

When discussing decision making in Chapter 9, we noted the importance of diversity of membership in ensuring creativity in problem solving and avoiding groupthink. Yet, when the group faces a clearly defined task, similarity of outlook may be better. That is why self-managed work teams are often permitted to select newcomers when replacements are needed.

Diversity, therefore, must be treated cautiously. The mix of group members must relate to the task in hand. Variety is not of itself advantageous if the extra dimensions brought by additional members are irrelevant. Moreover, leadership roles must be held by those who are the most competent.

■ Cohesiveness

We can define cohesiveness as a measure of how much members are attracted to, and wish to remain with, a group. Here we can add to our previous discussion of why people join and remain. Six means of sustaining cohesiveness are given in Exhibit 12.5.

Strong work groups have drawbacks. In general, groups that are more cohesive perform better and provide more satisfaction to their members. Yet their perceptions of the benefits of group membership may make them more resistant to change.

Exhibit 12.5 Sustaining group cohesiveness

- *Social attraction* – people take pleasure in each other's company or are attracted to the values and goals of the others in the group.

- *External threats* – sharing a mutual enemy or competitor can be an important source of cohesion. Members see sticking together as the best way to succeed.

- *Isolation* – being cut off from others enhances the sense of interdependence in facing external forces.

- *Size* – small groups tend to be more cohesive. Yet they may not encompass all shades of opinion or areas of expertise.

- *Complementary skills* – groups whose members offer a range of skills will succeed, provided that the balance of skills is relevant.

- *Rewards* – as noted in Chapter 11, reward systems both directly motivate and specify the behaviour management wishes to see. Incentive schemes based on group results, rather than individual performance, will be important.

■ Preventing undermining

All work groups, intentionally or accidentally, may be undermined. Depending strongly on building up an atmosphere of trust among people from disparate backgrounds, they risk being hit by negative behaviour patterns and attitudes. Slobodnik and Slobodnik identified eight 'team killers' that can erode the work of a group.[24] Table 12.3 shows them alongside a list of potential remedies.

Table 12.3 **Team killers and associated remedies**

Team killer	Remedy
False consensus – mistaking silence or vague assent for consensus	Questioning to ensure that all accept the outcomes
Unresolved overt conflict – a few members persist with rowdy arguments; others may make allowances just to avoid the war	Encourage recognition of the problem; agree rules of conduct to which all must subscribe
Underground conflict – disputes played out covertly damage group health by creating a climate of distrust	Making disagreements overt; appointing a neutral arbitrator
Not reaching closure – long discussions without results give a team a bad reputation	Agree how decisions are to be made; break into sub-groups to make progress
Calcification – a rigid pattern means each member plays the same role in every meeting	Rotate roles such as leader and record keeper; form different sub-groups
Uneven participation – dominance by a few and passivity by the rest means waste of the team's resources	Devise means of 'gatekeeping' to give each a say; ensure all are invited to contribute
Unaccountable to others – empowerment can create feelings of the group being answerable to no one	Clarify the line of accountability from the start
Customer forgotten – satisfying members' wishes may mean that unrepresented stakeholders are forgotten	Appoint further representatives or assign extra perspectives to current members

Many symptoms from the team killer list were evident in a case reported by Chaudron, *see* Exhibit 12.6.[25] This article is unusual in detailing a failure. Only the company name is not revealed. The team had been set up without clear guidance or enough power to carry out its brief. As circumstances unfolded, these points should have been clarified. Yet the five middle managers found this difficult once things had begun to go wrong.

■ Conflict

Table 12.3 shows that two of the team killers are conflict, covert and overt. Not only does this directly hinder progress but also it increases anxiety for members and dilutes their commitment. Yet conflict is not something to be avoided. Clearly, some

Exhibit 12.6 How not to set up an effective quality team

The profitable company, of 150 staff, supplied items to customers such as Motorola and Texas Instruments. Quality audits had been favourable. One line, however, had some problems, causing despatch delays, so a problem-solving team was set up.

The team's five middle managers came from manufacturing, engineering, sales, service and accounts. Meetings, averaging three hours per week for a year, were well attended. They occurred during the lengthy, 60–80 hour weeks of these busy people. After the period, their superiors realised the team had failed to reach its target and called in consultants for advice.

The consultants studied the team at work and interviewed each member. They also applied a standard survey of team effectiveness. They found members frustrated, angry and tired out. Once interested in the quality problem, they were now 'stuck in the mud'. Senior managers had attended meetings but had been rebuffed.

What had gone wrong?

The consultants identified the following external causes:

- no quality measurement therefore only anecdotal evidence of the problem;
- no direction or purpose;
- little senior management involvement from the beginning;
- lack of management support;
- organisation structure working against the team;
- poor production scheduling;
- no improvement incentives.

There were also internal group problems:

- no measurement of progress;
- no early team building;
- poor interpersonal relations with frequent rows;
- wrong team membership – too many engineers and an inexperienced accountant;
- haphazard training – some attended seminars, others did not;
- mismatch between heavy responsibility and little authority.

The consultants proposed three choices: disband the team because the members had no energy to restart; cut the project's scope and team membership; or reorganise the company around its three product lines. The last would make a cross-functional team unnecessary. None was chosen. Chaudron reported, 'this company suffered from a common malady called consultant d'jour'. A new expert was brought in. A new scheduling system was installed and the quality team disbanded with no thanks for its efforts.

interpersonal conflict is always present and, through the definitions of their roles, some members will find themselves opposed to others. They may represent, for example, different projects among which the group has to decide.

So, two types of conflict, based on personal factors and stakeholder interests, are to be expected. The third type concerns the structure and processes of the group itself. Especially in a group whose members are just finding their feet, disagreement over the way things should be done can have damaging effects. Such a group may be unable to make progress to resolve or accommodate the normal personal and stakeholder differences.

Inter-group conflict

Conflict also appears between one group and another. Generally, managers want to avoid this. They prefer co-operation in achieving the goals of the organisation. This is especially true if the work of the groups is interdependent; the output of one is received by the second as a 'customer'. Yet conflict among groups arises for as many reasons as conflict among individuals. This gives us a warning about all groups, whether they are boards of senior managers or self-managed work teams. They can avoid or absorb inter-personal conflict, but at the expense of introducing something more severe.

Inter-group conflict results from practical and perceptual difficulties as follows:

- *Scarce resources.* When several groups compete for the same inputs, for instance people's time, equipment, investment funds or space, fighting can become fierce. In a cramped office complex, two project teams both spotted an unused room as a temporary base to store and use working documents. Senior managers were faced with favouring one or the other. This choice would signal which they thought was more important.

- *Lack of clarity.* Unclear working assumptions in an atmosphere of poor communication create problems for any group. Its needs for internal effectiveness may cause it to determine its own terms of reference, including responsibilities that other groups also claim.

- *Perceptions and attitudes.* A problem-solving group may perceive its work to be more important than any other. Consequently, it expects senior managers to pay great attention to its recommendations. Furthermore, it may claim first call on the time of any of its members. Yet, other groups may adopt the same attitudes. If managers intervene to clarify these differences, they may make them worse.

- *Goals.* If the goals of group members differ from those of others in the organisation, conflict results. For instance, when asked to report on security arrangements in a rambling office building, a staff group focused its attention on the concerns of employees, especially when working late. They sought to prevent access by intruders and provide safe exits to the car park. Management, on the other hand, had perceived theft of office equipment as a more serious problem.

■ Successful groups

There is a rising interest in group performance at all organisational levels. Pressures to reduce costs and increase flexibility have combined with a keenness to improve job satisfaction. Self-managed work teams are the result. But how can success be assured?

High-performance work teams

Although we have studied some descriptive models of group formation and development, they give little of the prescription so sought by managers. One response is to gather clues from the differences in team performance in the same organisation. This can be as great as 100 per cent.[26] Some organisations study these so-called *high-performance work teams* and use members as pioneers to spread learning to others. This practice, however, may not develop the deep understanding from which generalisations can be drawn. To move research beyond description, Sheard and Kakabadse used interviews and observations to study differences between loose groups and effective teams.[27] They identified nine key factors, set out in the left-hand column of Table 12.4. They differed between the two types of group.

Table 12.4 Key factors in effective team performance

Key factor	Loose group	Effective team	Forming	Storming	Norming	Performing
Clear goals	Individuals ignore unclear goals	Understood and shared	FF		N	
Priorities	Some have split loyalties to other groups	Cohesive	FF			PP
Roles and responsibilities	Unclear	Understood and shared	F			P
Self-awareness	Do not foresee effect of own behaviour on team	Behaviour matches team needs			N	
Leadership	Directive	Catalytic	F		NNN	P
Group dynamics	Guarded commitment	Social processes accepted		SS	NN	P
Communication	Formal	Open	FF		NN	PP
Context	Focused on task	Influenced by organisation			N	
Infrastructure	Focused on task	Stable support from organisation				PP

The "Link to Tuckman's group processes" header spans the four columns: Forming, Storming, Norming, Performing.

Not only were the authors interested in comparison, with results summarised in the second and third columns of the table, they wanted to understand the process by which an effective team was formed. Using Tuckman's model, they found the key factors to have varying importance at different stages. When *forming*, for example, the key factors are clear goals, priorities and communication. On the other hand, *storming* requires good group dynamics as it involves creating the social system within the team. The right-hand columns of Table 12.4 summarise the factors important at each stage; the number of characters in each cell represent the significance of the links found.

Sheard and Kakabadse suggest how managers can learn from these results. When a group is forming, for example, the sponsoring organisation should start with a formal goal planning and prioritising session, enabling understanding and sharing of purposes and the setting of review milestones. Such a key agenda is also an excellent way to build communication patterns. The significance and type of leadership for each stage should also be recognised and acted upon.

Avoiding pitfalls

Another approach is to avoid pitfalls. Bergmann and de Meuse suggest that many plants may not be ready for teamwork. Unless all staff are able to adapt to a new relationship, the venture is doomed.[28] Tudor and others, estimating a 50 per cent failure rate, propose basic means of securing co-operation. Unless they take place, the change will meet resistance and probable failure. Preparation should be along the following lines:

- good initial presentation by committed senior managers;
- consultation with unions or other representatives;
- gradual team building with new rules, communication channels and other procedures;
- attention to employee motivation;
- guarantees over job security;
- training.[29]

Horses for courses

One problem with all types of teams is that they have become fashionable. The temptation is to establish them when they are not needed. On the shop floor, for example, the team may be little more than a unit of job rotation, as in the foundry at VTC Skövde. There is a danger of pseudo-empowerment, where the job enrichment on offer is confined to deciding upon who does which boring task. This is hardly better than allocation by a supervisor.

Among professional and technical staff, cross-functional teams have recently gained prominence. Offering open communication and autonomy, they contribute to higher creativity, better decisions and job satisfaction. Using the example of product development, however, Andrews argues that these teams are not suited to all decision situations. Although they may be ideal for 'blue sky' thinking about completely new products, developments of current ranges may best be handled through traditional structures.[30]

Groups in practice

The point that groups pervade organisations has been made several times in this chapter. While there is much in common among them, the differences are also significant. A permanent self-directed work team on the shop floor will differ from a temporary project team and the senior management board. The organisational and national settings add further variation. To demonstrate issues concerning groups in practice, therefore, we will focus on two examples. These are how groups can be set up within multinational companies and the link between reward systems and team performance.

Culture and teamwork

International teams are common throughout MNEs. As Govindarajan and Gupta argue, diversity can be a source of strength. But it brings with it some problems, as indicated by their survey that ranked cultivating trust among members, overcoming communication barriers and aligning goals as both the most important and the most difficult issues.[31]

Myers and colleagues studied the impact of different management styles on the effectiveness of cross-national teams.[32] Building on the work of pioneers such as Hofstede, they chose to focus on European countries. First, they showed that thinking of a single European style was unrealistic. Using questionnaire data from 2500 respondents, they identified four contrasting styles:

■ *Consensus*

Found mainly in Finland and Sweden, this style stresses team spirit, effective communication and attention to detailed organisation. Consensus, generated at open meetings, leads to job satisfaction.

■ *Common goal*

Typified by managers in Austria and Germany. These people favour technical expertise applied in harmony to achieve a clear goal. It is acceptable to have an authoritative leader to achieve this. Controls are advantageous.

■ *Managing from a distance*

Confined to French participants in the survey. These managers like to be left alone to do their work as they see fit. Consensus is seen as unimportant. There is little attention to consistency of action, with middle managers experiencing high levels of uncertainty. Resentment builds up among subordinates.

■ *Leading from the front*

Common among managers from Ireland, Spain and the United Kingdom. Leadership is seen as an individual performance. Both Latin and Anglo-Saxon cultures adhered to the belief that charisma and skills of individuals make a great deal of difference to corporate success. Explanations, however, differ. Spanish top managers may resent any restriction on their status, while the British and Irish are pragmatic and results orientated.

Myers and colleagues illustrated situations where different styles lead to problems in cross-national teams. To illustrate, we shall focus on one – promoting discipline at meetings. In a meeting run under the *consensus* style, it will be important for all to show that they are moving in the same direction. There will be detailed discussion of the agenda points and deviation into wider issues will not be tolerated. If a group is operating under the *working towards a common goal* style, the agenda will have been set with the sole intention of reaching decisions. Again, deviations are unlikely to be condoned. If the style is *managing from a distance*, debate will cover many issues. Each person will pursue a personal agenda. Even if decisions are made, implementation is unlikely without further contact after the meeting. Finally, a *leading from the front* meeting will also allow discussion beyond the agenda, particularly if led by a Spaniard. The British and Irish would tolerate this provided there is a prospect of a conclusion. In conclusion, Myers and colleagues recommend a return to basics, such as the establishment of ground rules for commonality while allowing for national variations.

Although we could argue that the ethnocentric multinational could merely spread its own style, the problem would be shifted, not solved. The company still has to engage with suppliers, agencies, trade unions and so on. Each of these will expect interaction along national lines. A German expects a two-hour meeting to cover up to three important agenda items. A group from southern Italy would take all day. These and other problems of different expectations are illustrated in the example of Exhibit 12.7.

Exhibit 12.7 Clashing cross-national cross-functional teams

A French multinational organisation sought to implement its mission of customer care and service quality through a matrix structure. Its effectiveness depended heavily on the links between the line of business managers and the country managers.

Conflict became the norm. A typical case was the running argument between business managers who wanted standard pricing throughout Europe and country managers who preferred a differential policy, depending on local conditions. Everyone saw the issues and the strength of the arguments. The problem was the way such debates were conducted.

Meetings were a problem. French senior managers would invite the regional and business managers to address particular problems. Germans expected to reach a decision. The French saw meetings as talking shops, appearing to reach agreements but sometimes announcing a different line later. The British, often in frustration, would concentrate only on their responsibilities, following courses of action that suited them. These opposed, at times, directions from above. The Scandinavians expressed disquiet. They felt that, without meaningful discussion, real commitment to resolving the team issue could not emerge.

Several authors have studied leadership of cross-cultural teams. For global teams, Odenwald argued that the leader must: tolerate ambiguity; be flexible, persuasive and patient; build consensus; coach; and expect change.[33] There are other cultural differences too. In a study of airline crews, Liao and Tsai related performance both to members' civilian or military backgrounds and to the purpose of group selection. If *minimising team conflict*, personnel from a similar background worked better together. Yet, when *dealing with crises*, crews with military experience were superior. A wholly military crew did best on both counts. Civilian-only teams improved their crisis handling if they contained at least one ex-military person; but then their conflict levels rose. The solution to this trade-off was to use mixed crews while managing the conflict. Constructive criticism could be used to enhance decision quality while communication training helped to cope with attitude differences.[34]

■ Rewarding team performance

We briefly noted the emergence of team performance rewards near the end of Chapter 11. Individual performance-related pay has failed to provide hoped-for results in many cases, so attention has turned to pay and other rewards for the whole team. Armstrong notes how innovative United Kingdom companies are increasingly adopting the idea.[35] Yet results seem mixed. In a survey conducted by the Institute of Personnel Development, over half of those respondents that had adopted team pay were confident that performance had improved as a result. Unfortunately, only 22 per cent could quantify the gain.

Shop-floor group incentive schemes follow a general pattern. Bonuses are linked to output or time saved on team tasks. In contrast, for managerial, technical and office staff, there was little in common save some means of distributing sums among members. Sometimes there are fixed criteria. For instance, Pearl Assurance relates bonuses to speed, accuracy and customer service and satisfaction. The last criterion is commonly used in financial service firms. Other organisations use criteria that are more open. The Benefits Agency has its local managers assess teams' contribution to overall performance. It is normal to pay bonuses as a percentage of basic salary.

Armstrong notes that team-based pay works best where a team:

■ works to its own targets;

■ has a high degree of autonomy;

■ comprises staff whose work is interdependent (otherwise the team would have no point);

■ has stable membership so that each knows what to expect from the rest;

■ is well established, used to working flexibly to meet targets;

■ is made up of multi-skilled team players.

There is anecdotal evidence of employee preference for team reward schemes, especially where they have replaced discredited individual performance-related pay. Like so many innovations, they should not be introduced in isolation. Pearl Assurance combined its scheme with empowerment, upward appraisal of managers, regular feedback and non-financial rewards.

Clearly, team rewards are given to all members according to an agreed formula. Indeed, we should add the criteria and methods of measurement to Armstrong's list. Yet the group formula may not match any individual's needs. Matching is one of the points made in the previous chapter. Subsuming of the individual's interests into those of the group is a disadvantage of the reward system and raises further questions on what some would see as a rush to set up work teams everywhere.

Disadvantages

The complex relationship between people and their work groups is disturbed by moves towards shared rewards. From the individual's point of view, there may be several drawbacks:

■ Teams can enter a downward spiral. Falling expectations mean the best staff will not join.

■ More effective employees migrate towards the strongest teams, especially if they can choose. (*See* the assembly plant at VTC Tuve in the opening case.) Reassigning work among teams, or even breaking them up, will be resisted.

■ Team pay, according to the above list, works best in mature teams. Yet can it be assumed that staff in such teams will be motivated in this way?

■ Some staff find team pay illogical and damaging to self-worth.

■ There will be pressure to conform and accept the speed of the slowest. People will not be able to gain more than what is acceptable to the average.

■ Since individual performance is no longer measured, those who are willing to extend themselves in return for recognition may be demotivated.

Finally, we should note that schemes have been brought in to reinforce commitment to group working. On the shop floor, to establish costs and output is usually straightforward. Among professional staff, however, how are the gains from 'greater co-operation' to be quantified? If the bonuses do make such a difference, one could ask why staff were not co-operating previously.

Conclusion: getting the most out of an old idea

Semi-autonomous, self-directed, high-performance, cross-functional and cross-national work teams are recent terms in the managerial language. All can contribute to the organisation's goals and enhance the individual's working life through learning and enhanced satisfaction. We should not, however, see groups and teams as new. What is new is the increased interest in getting the most out of them.

It is useful to differentiate between group and team. The former refers to any collection of people with something in common. The latter, by analogy with sport, implies selection, matched capabilities, cohesiveness, practice, coaching and leadership. Moreover, a team is goal seeking. In the new shop-floor operating systems, self-managed work teams are introduced for their potential gains in output, productivity and quality.

Mankind's social nature means that groups form, as it were, on their own. They can be seen to satisfy motivational needs and are more likely to emerge among people who come into close contact. In employment, therefore, there will be many criss-crossing informal groups. Although they do not necessarily work against the organisation's interests, managers often seek to strengthen formal structures to counter or limit their influence. If managers set up the teams, they feel they can affect their norms in relation to output, quality, ethical standards and so on.

When it comes to group processes, applicable theory is weak. Not only is it undeveloped but also the complexities of any work situation are huge. Although there are several models of the stages of group formation and others of the roles that members take up, few attempt to prescribe what a group should do. Managers should be aware that context, task, team processes and roles all have their impact on outcomes.

Groups and teams have limitations. Set up for inappropriate purposes, they can waste resources. They can also present difficulties in becoming powerful resistors of change. Furthermore, some individuals may become demotivated. As they see it, discussion may waste time and the group norms may be set too low. For them, coping with the conflict within and between groups may not be worthwhile.

QUICK CHECK

Can you …

- Distinguish groups and teams.
- Explain two further dimensions used to broadly classify groups.
- Apply Alderfer's list to suggest why people join.
- Give two reasons why particular clusters form.
- Outline Thompson and Wallace's three reasons for setting up shop-floor work groups.
- Name Tuckman's labels for group development.
- Summarise Belbin's model of group roles.
- Sketch the group process model of Herriot and Pemberton.
- List six ways of sustaining group cohesiveness.
- Explain what is a 'team killer'.
- Suggest four reasons for inter-group conflict.
- Link the key factors of Sheard and Kakabadse with Tuckman's stages.
- Summarise the effect of four management styles on cross-national teams.
- Outline reasons for and against work group performance-related pay.

QUESTIONS

Chapter review

12.1 Using your own examples, distinguish between: group and team; open and closed; formal and informal.

12.2 Why do managers set up temporary or permanent cross-functional teams? Relate your ideas to the matrix organisation.

12.3 What is a high-performance work team? What lessons can we learn about how they should be established? What difficulties might arise?

12.4 From the management point of view, is it better to encourage strongly cohesive working groups?

Application

12.5 Critically assess the value of performance-related pay in group situations.

12.6 The chapter draws on Alderfer's theory from Chapter 11 to explain an individual's motivation for joining a group. Examine a range of other theories from that chapter to see whether they offer alternative explanations.

Investigation

12.7 Through interviewing people on their membership of voluntary or informal groups, illustrate the notions of distance and social exchange. Establish how and why they joined and why they maintain their attachment.

Tax office groups and teams[36]

In the 1990s, the Board of the Inland Revenue began a change programme to cut costs, improve compliance and provide better service. Taxpayers, other government agencies and agents such as accountants and solicitors were redefined as customers. Many experienced the switch to self-assessment (SA) from 1996. As part of this change, the two functions of assessment and collection were combined in newly arranged offices. Each major town now has a single point of contact. Staff numbers fell by about 20 per cent during the 1990s. They were 66 000 by 2003 and offices were down from 768 to 350. These figures were planned to fall further as procedures were simplified. Reductions have been mainly natural or voluntary. Total costs now amount to 1.2 per cent of tax collected.

Following the merger of six units, Portsmouth now has one of the largest revenue offices in the United Kingdom. An early move by manager Chris Chant was to set up a task group to consider whether and where team working was appropriate and how it should be approached. Advice from above was that team working was needed to cope

with change; advice was disseminated through a 1996 booklet *Developing Successful Teams* followed up with self-learning packs. Mistakes in other public sector organisations, however, had soured industrial relations. More than 94 per cent of staff at Portsmouth were members of the PTC – the Public Services, Tax, and Commerce Union.

The group proposed that, with managers and staff having little experience of the issues, teamwork should be piloted in a few areas using volunteers. Gradualism means that, 18 months after the merger, about 75 of the 600 employees were working in self-managed work teams. Teamwork, however, meant little change in tasks, skills or responsibilities although there were decisions on work allocation using team targets. An important problem was the inconsistency of the personal appraisal process, based on individual targets, with this limited team approach.

With the number of management layers between chairman and staff reduced to four, decentralisation was the order of the day. The five managers reporting to Chant formed a self-managed team, referring much less frequently to head office than in the traditional Revenue style. They made decisions on re-organisation within agreed guidelines such as, 'Staff must be involved'. Other task groups looked at: merging the six former offices; convincing taxpayers that the Revenue does not see everyone as a potential scoundrel; and changing the process to the SA principle of assess first and check later. Throughout its first years, all offices faced uncertainty over the public response to the SA system.

The task groups comprised staff from all grades. Chant wanted to offer people the chance to work to their full potential. In such a big office, there would be people who could do more senior jobs than his own. He added, 'Giving them these chances ... is about using their potential for the benefit of the business – and also giving them the opportunity to enjoy what they are doing.'

In spite of the optimism over change reported from Portsmouth, others pointed to low morale in the Inland Revenue. The London School of Economics investigated the effects of perform-ance-related pay schemes, finding that two-thirds of staff were less willing to co-operate with colleagues than before. Perhaps this explained the slow progress at Portsmouth?

Questions

1 Compare Chant's method of introducing self-managed work teams and task groups with the ideas discussed in the chapter.

2 Some staff suggested that co-operation within work teams had risen, but at the expense of reduced support among them. Since a large tax office has many people engaged in parallel work, what should a manager do about this problem?

3 Given that most Inland Revenue offices carry out the same functions in different areas, what are the limitations on the effectiveness of local task groups and how might these be overcome?

4 Having agreed with the PTC branch that team working should be 'purely voluntary', how could Chant and the other managers step up its rate of introduction?

Bibliography

Beyond the sources listed in the references, with Mullins especially thorough, *see* Charles Margerison, *Team Leadership: A Guide to Success with Team Management Systems* (London: Thomson Learning, 2002).

References

1 Thompson, Paul and Wallace, Terry (1996) 'Redesigning pro-duction through team working: case studies from the Volvo Truck Corporation', *International Journal of Operations and Production Management*, **16(2)**, February, 103–20.

2 Sandberg, A. (1995) 'The Uddevala experience in per-spective' in Sandberg, A. (ed.) *Enriching Production*, Aldershot: Avebury. Uddevala has since reopened.

3 Womack, J.P., Roos, D. and Jones, D.T. (1990) *The Machine that Changed the World*, New York: Rawson Associates. Lean production is a logical extension of mass production in which all costs, stocks and waste are minimised.

4 Ellegard, Kajsa, Engstrom, Tomas, Johansson, Bertil, Johansson, Mats I., Jonsson, Dan and Medbo, Lars (1994) 'Reflective Production in the Final Assembly of Motor Vehicles: An emerging Swedish challenge', *Actes du GERPISA, Université d'Evry*, **9**, 109–25.

5 Pries, Ludger (2001) 'Emerging New Production Systems in the Transnationalisation of German Carmakers: The case of BMW/Spartanburg and DaimlerChrysler/Tuscaloosa', *Actes du GERPISA, Université d'Evry*, **11**, 11–24.

6 Mullins, Laurie J. (1996) *Management and Organisational Behaviour*, 6th edition: Financial Times Prentice Hall, 495.

7 Osborne, J.D., Moran, I., Musslewhite, E., Zegger, J.H. and Perrin, C. (2001) *Self-directed Work Teams*, Homewood, Ill.: Irwin.

8 Sims, Josh (2002) 'Carling's New Pitch', *Financial Times*, 21 September.

9 Merrick, Neil (1997) 'The Lions share', *People Management*, 12 June, 34–7.

10 Likert, Rensis (1961) *New Patterns of Management*, New York: McGraw-Hill.

11 Manz, Charles C. and Neck, Christopher P. (1995) 'Teamthink: beyond the groupthink syndrome in self-man-aged teams', *Journal of Managerial Psychology*, **10(1)**, January, 7–15.

12 Naylor, John and Senior, Barbara (1988) *Incompressible Unemployment*, Aldershot: Avebury, 26.

13 Vecchio, Robert P. (1995) *Organization Behaviour*, 3rd edition, Fort Worth Tex.: The Dryden Press, 443.

14 Thibaut, J.W. and Kelley, H.H. (1959) *The Social Psychology of Groups*, New York: Wiley.

15 Further information on this charity is at **www.stroke.org.uk/index.htm**, accessed 10 April 2003.

16 Thompson and Wallace (1996) *op. cit.*

17 Tuckman, R.W. (1965) 'Developmental sequence in small groups', *Psychological Bulletin*, **58(6)**, 384–99.

18 Belbin, R.M. (1981) *Management Teams: Why they succeed or fail*, Oxford: Butterworth–Heinemann, 76.

19 Herriot, Peter and Pemberton, Carole (1995) *Competitive Advantage through Diversity*, London: Sage.

20 Parkinson, C. Northcote (1957) *Parkinson's Law or The Pursuit of Progress*, London: John Murray, 31–43.

21 Vecchio (1995) *op. cit.*, 446–7.

22 'Noted', *Industry Week*, **244(12)**, 19 June 1995, 11.

23 Parkinson (1957) *op. cit.*, 32.

24 Slobodnik, Deborah and Slobodnik, Alan (1996) 'The "team killers": behaviours, attitudes and patterns of inter-action that undermine effectiveness of work teams,' *HR Focus*, **73(6)**, June, 22–3.

25 Chaudron, David (1995) 'An effective quality team. Not!' *HR Focus*, **72(8)**, August, 6–7.

26 Scott, K.D. and Townsend, A. (1994) 'Teams: why some succeed and others fail', *HR Magazine*, **39(8)**, August, 62–7.

27 Sheard, A.G. and Kakabadse, A.P. (2002) 'From loose groups to effective teams', *Journal of Management Development*, **21(2)**, 133–51.

28 Bergmann, Thomas J. and de Meuse, Kenneth P. (1996) 'Diagnosing whether an organization is ready to empower work teams: a case study', *Human Resource Planning*, **19(1)**, March, 38–47.

29 Tudor, Thomas R., Trumble, Robert R. and Diaz, Joanna J. (1996) 'Work teams – why do they often fail?' *SAM Advanced Management Journal*, **61(4)**, Autumn, 31–9.

30 Andrews, Katherine Zoe (1995) 'Cross-functional teams: are they always the right answer?' *Harvard Business Review*, **73(6)**, November–December, 12–13.

31 Govindarajan, Vijay and Gupta, Anil K. (2001), 'Building an Effective Global Business Team', *Sloan Management Review*, **42(4)**, 63–71.

32 Myers, Andrew, Kakabadse, Andrew, McMahon, Tim and Spony, Gilles (1995) 'Top management styles in Europe: implications for business and cross-national teams', *European Business Journal*, **7(1)**, Winter, 17–27.

33 Odenwald, Sylvia (1996) 'Global work teams', *Training and Development*, **50(2)**, February, 54–7.

34 Liao, Wen-Chih and Tsai, Chen Chang (2001) 'A study of cockpit crew team behaviours', *Team Performance Management*, **7(1/2)**, 21–6.

35 Armstrong, Michael (1990) 'How group efforts can pay dividends', *People Management*, 25 January, 22–7.

36 Arkin, Anat (1997) 'Tax incentives', *People Management*, 20 February, 36–8; Kellaway, Lucy (1997) 'Why bad management is all in the genes', *Financial Times*, 16 June; Procter, Stephen and Currie, Graeme (2002) 'How team-working works in the Inland Revenue: meaning, operation and impact', *Personnel Review*, **31(3)**, 304–19; Inland Revenue (2002) *Annual Report for Year Ending 31 March 2002*, The Stationery Office.

CHAPTER 13

Communication in management

Chapter objectives

When you have finished studying this chapter, you should be able to:

- define communication and show its importance in every manager's job;

- compare three perspectives used in understanding communication processes;

- set out the psychological model of communication, showing the effect of noise and the purpose of feedback;

- demonstrate ways of becoming a better communicator, especially in listening and writing;

- clarify the purpose of communication in organisations, highlighting practical ways of improvement;

- show how communication can be hindered by jargon, sexist language and overload; outline how a manager can respond;

- comment critically on the notion that organisational communication is about sharing accurate information.

'Whom are you?' said he, for he had been to night school.

George Ade, American writer

Fossilised communications[1]

The roots of the Natural History Museum lie in Sir Hans Sloane's 1753 bequest to the British Museum, from which it became independent in 1963. Now it occupies some 60 000 square metres of splendid but sprawling buildings in central London. Most of the £39 million revenue, including £32 million from the government, is spent on staff and buildings. The 863 NHM staff are organised into three management groups: Communications and Development; Visitor and Operational Services; and Science, with its five departments of palaeontology, mineralogy, botany, entomology and zoology.

The impressive scope of the exhibitions ranges from cases of bones to interactive displays of earthquakes, robotic dinosaurs and the ascent of humankind. Staff range from internationally renowned scientists to those catering for the annual two million visitors. The NHM is among the most visited attractions in the country.

Yet, in 1990, the picture was less rosy. Money was tight. Admission charges, introduced in 1987 (and removed in 2001), brought fears of a declining spiral of rising costs and falling revenues. Appointed director two years previously, Neil Chalmers began a major restructuring programme. This was intended to modernise, improve and refocus on core themes of the museum's work. Job cuts, although achieved voluntarily, had a massive emotional effect. Many employees felt betrayed and insecure.

To develop external publicity, Jane Bevan was brought in to a new post of public relations manager. She soon found that much work was needed on internal communications. The embedded tradition of semi-autonomous, hierarchical departments discouraged communications between, and even within, groups of staff. Isolation spread cynicism and distrust, especially during a time of change. Snobbery based on grade or intellectual arrogance was common. Junior staff often felt cut off.

Bevan started with an employee attitude survey, having agreed the principle with both Chalmers and the staff unions. To underline the openness of the process, results were supplied to all staff. Concerns were divided into those related to particular departments and those covering the organisation as a whole. Since work on the latter category would have greater impact and be less personal, it was given priority.

By 1995, a steering group had been set up to oversee change. Membership cut across departments. Included were junior managers from key business areas, union representatives, health and safety officials and administrators. The group chose to work on four problem areas revealed by the survey:

Newsletter

There was a strong demand for a new internal newsletter to improve upon the current *Museum News*, a weekly summary gathered and circulated by the personnel department. It was not an effective means of two-way communication. Change was not easy. Managers were afraid of a more popular version becoming scurrilous, while staff distrusted management propaganda. The outcome was a new bimonthly 12-page magazine with news, features and information. It worked. Readers pressed to increase its frequency and change to full colour.

Team briefing

Team briefings had been introduced in 1990. Designed to cascade management information throughout departments, they were not working well. While 30 per cent found the system very useful, 14 per cent had had no briefings at all. The initial training had not been followed up and many who had been trained had left or lost interest. Bevan ran new workshops for 95 managers to share good practice. Since most staff now had a computer, email was used to support briefings.

Staff suggestions

The suggestions scheme had run for many years, but staff remained unsure about its procedures. Suspecting this to be mainly a publicity problem, Bevan explained the scheme in the new magazine. Her view was confirmed when the article triggered as many suggestions as in the previous year. The magazine publicised successful proposals.

Information 'hot spots'

Although departments had local notice boards, Bevan introduced several sites where broad information would be available. At these points, staff could pick up the newsletter and see advertisements for new ventures such as staff forums.

Beyond the work of the steering group, there were other innovations. The bimonthly staff forum encouraged two-way communications. For instance, Chalmers had an open question time addressing employees' concerns. These hour-long meetings attracted audiences of 75 to 120. In another development, the museum's intranet began to be used to share information widely. In its first few months of operation, an internal news system was tried and all employees given immediate access to the minutes of meetings between union and management. An improved internal directory of staff responsibility and expertise was created.

Introduction

So there it is. You've had your 'sneak preview' of Figure 13.1 even before it's come up in the text. So you know it captures the essence of the problems in the case study. It shows the fossilised old hierarchy, the snobbery of the seniors, the juniors cut off and the spiralling finances. Or perhaps you'd decided not to read the case yet? No matter, it's only a little story of how an organisation can ossify. And how new energy can rejuvenate it. A newsletter (initially opposed), team briefings, suggestions scheme and hot spot information points were none of them new. What was new was the commitment by a team to show they could work.

Don't worry if you started in the middle. You are among friends. Newspaper people have known for years that readers don't start at page 1, line 1. You know your paper. You flip to the sport, the lottery numbers, the television listings, the flats, the stock market or even the crossword. Entry points get you into the paper. Then you read the rest. Editors make you turn every page. *Readers* look at advertisements. Advertisers provide half the revenue. That's why even the free sheets jamming your door when you have been away carry news material. Funny how we browse the snooker results or note how it rained in Alice Springs. With a book like this, we know you are unlikely to read it from begining to end. So the chapters, pictures, headlines and index offer you entry points. They steer you once you are in.

The story of the Natural History Museum case flows roughly from top to bottom in Figure 13.1. Its problems are common. Many organisations, facing similar problems, set up communications programmes. To support strategic change and become ever more efficient, businesses such as Safeway and British Nuclear Fuels work on ways to sustain cross-functional links, two-way vertical flows and intra-team communication. WPP Group, well known in the advertising world, helps clients with internal communications.[2]

The footer of Figure 13.1 picks out the general points to form the headlines for the chapter. What is communication? A sort of process where some people tell things to others? Well, maybe. We need to look at the process in depth. Then we can think about how to become better. This means both becoming better personally and learning how to spot and fix problems in the organisation. Lastly, we must look again at what communication is. What is this about integrating communications strategy? Do managers really want to share, or are improved methods of communication really improved methods of conning people? Well, the Jurassic jury is still out on that one.

Managers are not brilliant communicators. After all, most of them are human. They may even be getting worse. Stimulated by easy email, 'vanity publishing' is the

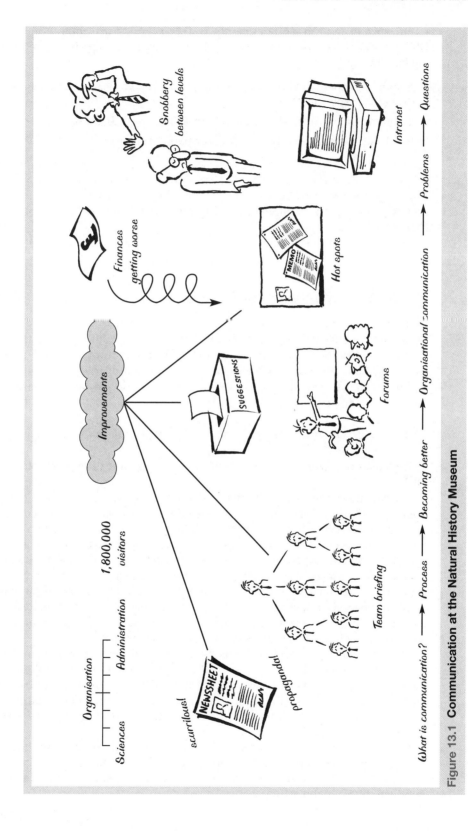

Figure 13.1 Communication at the Natural History Museum

circulation of ever more documents in the interests of 'open' communications. Office workers feel stressed. A survey by consultants Synopsis showed some growing bad habits:

- issuing information without signalling purpose, significance, intended audience or expected response;
- assuming that, if once sent, information is read and absorbed; and
- requiring immediate responses to information requests.[3]

Exaggeration? Possibly. Some take pride in receiving most email. We will return to this flood before the chapter end. This is to grab your attention. Communication problems everywhere. Pressure. Fragments. Like this. Discourse gone. Errors bigtime. Opening quote – Whom? Ha ha! Dumb. capitals uncool. txt rls ok. qwik speak future? Hip? Hope not.

Now let us quit this style, with its one word sentences. Let us consider the issues more soberly.

What is communication?

Definitions of communication can be broad – capturing a wide range of behaviours – or narrow – concentrating on a specific process. For some, it includes any understanding transmitted from one to another. For others, only intended meanings are treated as communication. We also have the question of roles. For some, communication is what the sender does; for others, the dialogue between originator and audience has to be considered.

> *A perspective is a coherent picture drawn from a single point of view.*

We shall open with three *perspectives* on communication, summarised in Table 13.1.[4]

If asked, most managers will refer to the psychological perspective. Communication training – 'getting the message across' – is based on this view. Hackley contrasts it with the social-constructionist when he writes, 'Meaning is a social construction as opposed to a purely private cognitive construction'.[5] The problem of relative reality is answered by noting that we are not constructing worlds of arbitrary make-believe. Although people see the world through 'personal lenses' that present them with images to be interpreted, communication is about sharing these interpretations. This becomes more difficult in global business. Considering cultural barriers between regions and nations, Perlmutter advocates the development of *deep dialogue*, 'the exchange of information as well as constructive feelings and attitudes to reach shared objectives'.[6]

The pragmatic perspective helps us understand change. For example, seeking explanations of how intellectual capital develops rapidly in new industries such as information systems, O'Donnell and colleagues describe 'the creative transformation and recombination of data, information, knowledge, relationships, learning processes and ideas by innovative people within particular entities, networks or communities of practice'.[7]

Switching among these perspectives gives us insight into communication in organisations. The next section on process, however, is based mainly on the psychological model. We consider the question of how we transmit our ideas to others and, in return, find out about theirs.

Table 13.1 **Perspectives on communication**

Perspective	Definition of communication	Focus	Difficulties
Psychological	A process in which people exchange information through the transmission of messages as coded stimuli.	How closely the ideas produced in the receiver's mind match those intended by the sender. Good communication is about accuracy.	The stress on mechanistic accuracy ignores the benefits of creativity or discovery. Further, it pays little attention to the social and cultural context.
Social-constructionist	A group's process of making sense of the world.	How elements of culture – symbols, habits, traditions and rules – form a symbolic, constructed and shared reality. Good communication achieves shared views.	If everything becomes relative to a person's interpretation, what is left of 'reality'?
Pragmatic	A set of interlocking interactions that develop patterns over time.	How action and interdependence lead to outcomes with benefits to those involved. Good communication is represented in action.	Understanding such patterns is difficult, especially as processes neither begin nor end. A systems perspective can assist in drawing boundaries. Personality is ignored.

The communication process

From the psychological perspective, communication is the *exchange of information through swapping coded messages*. Contained in the definition are the ideas of: exchange, that is a two-way process; swapping, suggesting both parties have active roles; and coded messages, implying conversion from one code to another and transmission through media.

The process can be modelled using the stages set out in Figure 13.2. Here we see a telephone interaction between two people, the sender and receiver. The sender has an idea and intends to transmit it to the receiver. To do this, the sender translates the idea into a form that is both meaningful and can be transmitted as a message along a channel. The receiver then interprets the message into a meaningful form. The active receiver may acknowledge the message, for example through an 'Aha', to confirm receipt and suggest common understanding. This is feedback.

Unfortunately, possibilities of distortion appear at all stages. Translation and interpretation, normally called *coding* and *decoding*, are points where things go wrong. Furthermore, as the star bursts show, interference from *noise* may disrupt the message at any point. Let us look at these steps in more detail.

■ Encoding

Let us say that the sender, Angela, has an idea that she wants Bertie to know about. This idea might arise in Angela's mind or result from an external stimulus. In either case, Angela begins with the process of encoding. This means translating the idea into a set of symbols that can be transmitted. The set is usually a natural language

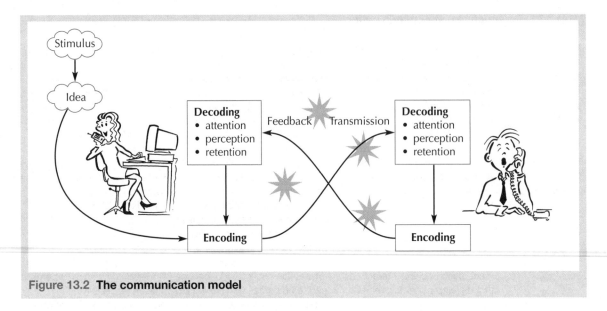

Figure 13.2 **The communication model**

common to Angela and Bertie. It has specific symbols learned by Angela, Bertie and others in their group. The size of this group can range from a few persons to billions. There are about 10 000 languages in the world, *see* Exhibit 13.1.[8]

Language is a powerful communication tool. It works through rules, summarised in Exhibit 13.2, that enable the user to pass on routine information or say things

Exhibit 13.1 The world's biggest and smallest languages

Many languages have no written form and have few speakers. Bikya, from Cameroon, is spoken by one person; in a nearby village, Bishuo is spoken by a father and son. The chart shows the numbers who speak the Top 10 as first or second languages. Counting countries whose official language is English, it leaps to first place with 1730 million.

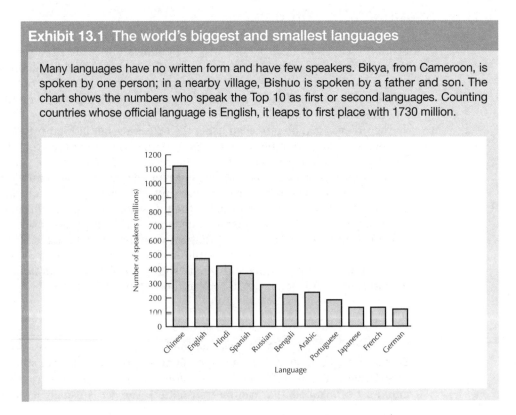

never said before. A good communicator is aware of the rules, applying them intuitively. Communication is based on shared knowledge of these rules. It is also set in the shared context of the relationship between sender and receiver. In the encoding process, the sender makes assumptions about the receiver's capacity and willingness to receive the message. For instance, although both parties have the same language, such as English, the parties will probably converse in a special subset using dialect, jargon, family words and so on. Easily noticed in speech, such variations convey with the message notions of social status and group membership, friendship or formality, sincerity or cynicism and so on. 'Shet thi 'ed, an' mind thi own business, else I'll fetch the gaffer to thee! Pull up ther', an' le's 'ev un out on't. We be all Wind agyen! Everybody else ull a done afore we begins! Hang on to that chayn, Fodgy! Now, then! ALL together! Ugh!' In this version of English, a century ago, the drop stampers at Swindon Railway Works drew a white-hot ingot from the furnace.[9]

Exhibit 13.2 Language's rules

- *Phonological* – sounds and their combinations.
- *Semantic* – links between sounds and meanings.
- *Syntactic* – construction of phrases and sentences.
- *Pragmatic* – relating words, phrases and sentences to context, for example culture, behaviour, history and relationships.

Although offering great potential to the good communicator, the flexibility of natural languages also creates problems. This is especially true for those, like the March Hare, who say, 'Then you should say what you mean'.[10] There is rarely a one-to-one link between a word or phrase and a meaning. In fact, for many words, the opposite is true. *Like*, for example, can take up eight parts of speech from noun and verb to preposition and interjection. It appears in the famous sentence, 'Time flies like an arrow', illustrated in Exhibit 13.3. Groucho Marx grasped the difficulty: 'Time flies like an arrow. Fruit flies like a banana.'

Exhibit 13.3 Saying exactly what you mean

Time flies like an arrow
The intended sense compares time passing quickly (flight is a metaphor) with the speed of an arrow (a simile). Confusion begins when we realise that arrows fly towards targets. The statement now suggests time to be a countdown to our destiny. Further, we could take the statement literally – time actually flies.

Other meanings following syntactic rules, but nonsense in practice, are:

- Measure the speed of flying insects as you would that of a missile; measure the speed in the same way that an arrow would; measure only those flies that are like arrows.
- A certain species of flying insect prefers a well-known brand of chewing gum; or they like a piece occasionally.
- An American weekly journal moves through the air in a straight line; it rests in an aircraft like a piece of gum.

Encoding has to take into account the risks of misunderstanding from ambiguities like the ones illustrated here. In informal conversations, there are many opportunities to check and repeat messages. In formal reports and presentations, on the other hand, greater care is needed in their preparation. A recipient will not tolerate badly constructed, repetitive material.

■ Media

Media, or channels, carry the message. The term *media* is often used to refer to the mass media designed to carry messages from the few to the many. Yet media include all methods from face-to-face meetings to letters and memoranda and from newsletters to electronic bulletin boards. We saw how staff at the Natural History Museum learned to use media to convey messages in different ways to different sets of receivers. Simple messages, such as notices of meetings, could be posted on the hot spot bulletin boards. More difficult and subtle questions had to be mulled over in team briefings or debated at the management forum.

These ideas have been formalised by Lengel and Daft. They found that, like a pipeline, media channels differ in their capacity to convey information. They can be classified according to the richness of the information they can cope with. *Channel richness* is the measure of information that can be transmitted during a communication event. Figure 13.3 shows the hierarchy of channel richness.[11]

The richness measure is not a technical figure to be measured in bytes per second. It is a combination of three important characteristics:

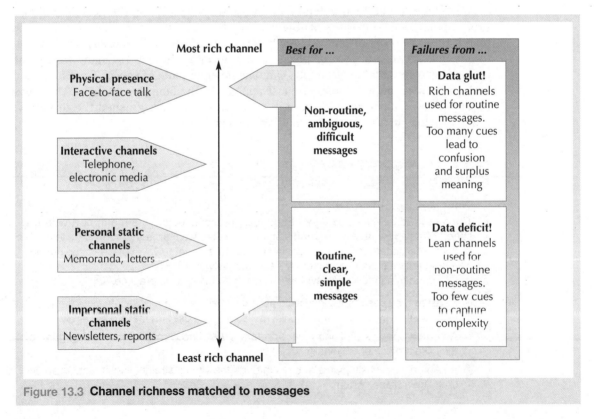

Figure 13.3 **Channel richness matched to messages**

- the number of cues handled simultaneously;
- the availability of rapid, two-way feedback; and
- the possibility of creating a personal focus for the communication.

As Figure 13.3 shows, the richest channel involves physical presence. This is because: many cues, from voice to body expressions, can be handled simultaneously; two-way feedback is spontaneous; and the focus is personal. Therefore, it is best used for sharing deep understanding of problems and situations. At the other end of the scale, impersonal static channels offer few cues, slow feedback and no personal relationship. Printed media work best if confined to straightforward messages that can be assimilated quickly.

The model of Lengel and Daft also brings out two causes of communications failure. These result from using unmatched channels for messages. A *data glut* arises from a deluge of cues whereas a *data deficit* comes from a dearth of them. Looking back at the communication methods introduced at the Natural History Museum enables us to gauge their effectiveness in these terms.

- *Data deficit*

Museum News was an impersonal, one-way channel to distribute approved information. The breadth of the staff audience limited the content to general and simple messages. In its replacement, the complexity of some messages was increased. Having more pages allowed coverage of sectional interests and inclusion of more detail. Further, soliciting responses stimulated some two-way communication, resisted by those managers who feared the introduction of scurrilous reporting.

Suggestions schemes also suffer from data deficit. Given the complexity of problems on the shop floor, the best improvement suggestions may be untapped. Staff may be unable to condense ideas into simple messages ready to go in the box. Compare such methods with quality circles. In the latter, a group may spend many hours discussing complexity.

- *Data glut*

Regular team briefings are face-to-face sessions with groups arranged as in Likert's link-pin hierarchy of Figure 12.1. At the museum, they were to keep all staff informed of changes. Yet, use for downward communication only may be a waste of such a rich channel. Other organisations use briefings to gather the responses of staff to management's policies. Data glut is common in meetings. Many managers use group sessions to make routine announcements. These could use less rich channels. The museum's management forums succeeded when they included debate; were managers to cover little more than newsletter content, they would fail.

Decoding

Decoding refers to *the process of giving meaning to the received message*. It is an active process set in the context of the link between sender and receiver. We can look at decoding in three steps – giving attention, perception and retention.

Attention

Attention is important because, without it, no communication can occur. Several tactics can be used to enhance it. The receiver will attend if the message is important. Therefore, relating it to personal goals or needs is advantageous. For instance: receivers focus on those parts of a report that affect them; or we concentrate on the weather forecast for our area. Another approach is for the sender to engage the receiver spontaneously. This is done by including novel, vivid or surprising stimuli. Examples range from public speakers' changes in tone of voice to sensational headlines in the tabloids.

Perception

Perception is at the heart of giving meaning. Like the other steps in communication, this is a learned process. The way we perceive data is given to us by our culture. It is also an active process in which we impose meaning on the signals we pick up. Through selection among the data and relating them to each other, we construct an internal representation of the world.

Graesser and colleagues present perception in stages.[12] The raw material of the message, its *surface code*, is held by the receiver for only a short time, perhaps a few seconds. It is stripped down into a storable form, the *text base*, which is then converted into the *mental model*. Take, for example, these pages on communication. The surface code is the stream of data organised into words and pictures. The text base is the selection you make depending on your purpose. You may be a general reader, someone searching for a particular example, or a student making revision notes. The mental model connects the text base to knowledge you already have, such as systems, group dynamics or linguistics.

Creating shared perceptions is, according to the social constructionist perspective, a key function of communication. Otherwise, difficulties arise when people perceive things in different ways. Optical illusions illustrate the point. Figure 13.4 is based on a set of illusions by Botwinick, published a century ago. Here you may see

Figure 13.4 **Son or husband?**

a young or old man. (The former's chin is the latter's nose.) Illusions are not always intended to confuse. Artists have long used 'tricks' such as perspective and colour to overcome the two-dimensional limitations of their media. As Figure 13.5 shows, the *trompe-l'oeil* lines on web pages bring this application right up to date.

Managers should recognise that perceptual differences are natural. People will interpret message stimuli in their own ways. Expecting and allowing for these differences, especially how they vary among individuals, groups, organisations and cultures, helps to make a good communicator. Good practice includes:

- adapting the message and channel to the receiver's needs and capacity, supporting processing of the surface code;
- organising the message well, enabling conversion to the text base;
- relating new information to old, facilitating extension of the mental model.

Retention

Recognising that the receiver retains the surface code for only a few seconds, the sender can support retention. Methods include pointing out the need for retention, summarising, repetition of key message points and suggesting skills that the receiver might use. Good teachers use these methods. Generations of students have learnt mnemonics such as 'Face', 'Never eat Shredded Wheat' or 'Richard of York gave battle in vain'.

■ Feedback

One-way channels have a serious disadvantage. The sender does not receive any indication of the receiver's response to the process. Two-way channels allow for *feedback*, giving the sender at least some knowledge of how effective the communication has been. As we saw in the Lengel–Daft model, richer channels offer plenty of feedback cues while the less rich ones do not.

We could think of the conversation in Figure 13.2 as having been initiated by Angela to send Bertie a message. Yet the roles of sender and receiver very quickly

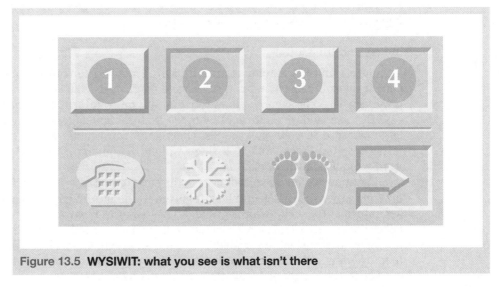

Figure 13.5 **WYSIWIT: what you see is what isn't there**

reverse. Unsure of a point, Bertie formulates a question. In asking it, he becomes the sender and Angela the receiver. We can thus think of a good conversation as a dance, *see* Exhibit 13.4.[13] Angela and Bertie work together to make a good conversation. And, again like dancing, they improve through practice.

Exhibit 13.4 Conversation as dancing

'To understand how to make a conversation a genuine two-way experience, think of it as dancing.

'When you dance ... you work as a partnership, responding to each other's movements and trying not to tread on each other's toes ... The idea is to co-operate rather than compete so you feel satisfied by the experience.

'It's about each person having the opportunity to express their point of view, explain their needs, and make their thoughts and feelings clear.

'An unsatisfactory conversation feels more like a game of table tennis, where the aim is to score points and for one person to win at the other's expenses. Conversations like this are about competing rather than co-operating.

'An open conversation is ... a duet rather than two solos.'

Noise

Noise is any interruption of the normal flow of understanding between the parties. This broad definition covers more than sound noise. In a telephone conversation, for example, we may point to faults in the equipment: crossed lines, interference and poor sound quality are sometimes the cause for complaint. Distractions in the offices at either end also add data for one party to filter out. There is, moreover, noise in each person's head. This ranges from sudden recall of the work one has to do later to physical barriers caused by overload or tiredness. In all, noise can interfere with any part of the cycle.

How can noise be overcome? Experts often think of the quality of a transmission in terms of the signal to noise ratio. The higher this ratio, the easier it is for the receiver to pick out the message data from the background. Clearly, the ratio is improved by increasing the signal or cutting the noise.

Increasing the signal

Computers and fax machines are often programmed to transmit messages twice. Only if the two correspond is the message confirmed. This is an example of *redundancy*, where messages deliberately contain more information than is needed in case *glitches* add or remove a few bytes. Natural languages display redundancy in large measure. The surplus sounds, characters, words and phrases overcome transmission errors. For instance, if there was no redundancy, we could never tell if a word was mispelt (misspelt).

Sometimes we increase redundancy in messages. Experiences of noise interference in early wireless telegraph systems led to the introduction of codes to spell out key information such as aircraft call signs. 'Charlie Foxtrot Victor' is an example. Other codes cut redundancy to use limited channel capacity fully. Hand signals grew up where the normal aural medium was overwhelmed by noise. In the late nineteenth century the American Stock Exchange operated as an informal outdoor market in the centre of Manhattan. Brokers congregated on the street while their

y
Can you read this?

Figure 13.6 **Seeing shadows**

clerks, with telephones, sat above on window sills. Although the market moved indoors in 1921, the hand signals persisted until a wireless computer network was introduced in 1996.[14]

Figure 13.6 demonstrates the effect of character redundancy. You cannot be sure about the symbol at the top of the picture until you see it repeated below. This illustrates our capacity to reconstruct messages if much of the signal is missing.

Unfortunately, we sometimes make the wrong reconstruction, such as the two faces of Figure 13.7. (Sorry! It's a vase.) This well-known example has been used in many experiments. For instance, picking out faces or vase is influenced by the colour of the two areas. Yet we cannot say for sure until some more data are added.

Clearly, the redundancy in a two-way informal conversation is higher than that accepted in a formal report. This again illustrates the need for careful preparation before communication occurs.

Reducing the noise

As a first step, one can consider cutting distracting external noise. For sound, sources are obvious and can be worked on. Visual noise includes all sorts of external distractions plus stimuli within the medium. In print, we often see inappropriate use of symbols, fonts, colours and so on. These need to match the message. Noise can arise within messages. Rich channels carrying parallel messages can be confusing if the messages contradict. Posture and face may not match the content. Witness the shy vicar who smiles during the funeral oration.

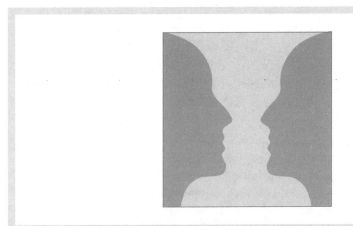

Figure 13.7 **Seeing the wrong picture**

◼ Non-verbal communication

Contradiction between intended and unintended messages is a problem of non-verbal communication. This is the exchange of messages through actions and behaviour rather than through words. Although most attention is focused on formal, verbal interaction, non-verbal communication is important when using rich media.

Non-verbal communication differs from verbal in several important ways. First, it is often unintentional, such as 'preening' when males meet attractive females. Men are often seen straightening the tie or cuffs, touching the hair or even retying shoelaces! Second, the 'languages' of non-verbal communication do not correspond to verbal languages. The sign in Figure 13.8 means 'OK' in the United States and 'Excellent, really excellent' in The Netherlands. In France, it means something worse than 'You are worthless', while it puzzles many Britons. Third, non-verbal communication is especially powerful for conveying some emotions such as grief. The eyes are strong indicators of emotion. Fourth, non-verbal communication contains several dimensions that may, or may not, work in harmony. These are:

◼ *Body language*
Including facial expression, gestures and posture, body language conveys messages from sender to receiver often without either thinking about them. For example, attentiveness is confirmed by gaze, upright posture and hand signals. The latter are *kinesics*, among several categories of body language:

kinesics – minor movements that many call body language;

proximics – ownership and occupation of interpersonal space;

chronemics – time that lapses between verbal exchanges;

oculesics – eye contact; and

haptics – body contact.

To illustrate some cultural differences in these forms of communication, Exhibit 13.5 looks at the proximic and haptic behaviour around the 'space bubble'.[15]

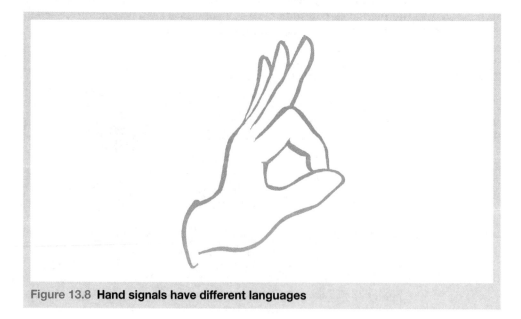

Figure 13.8 **Hand signals have different languages**

Exhibit 13.5 Space invaders

Spaniards like back slapping, Argentineans grip your arm and Americans delight in bone-crushing hand shakes. People from many Asian and northern cultures find such effusive gestures uncomfortable.

The 'space-bubble' of Oriental, Nordic, Anglo-Saxon and Germanic people extends to about a metre. This zone is barred to strangers, although half the radius applies to close friends and relatives.

Mexicans happily come within half a metre of strangers during meetings. When at this distance, they are ready to discuss business. Faced by such a space invader, however, British managers tend to back off beyond the metre line. Finding themselves back in the 'public zone', the Mexicans think the British do not like them or do not want to do business. They find discussing confidential matters over such a gap akin to using megaphones.

The Japanese are particularly sensitive about personal space. Anglo-Saxons, Nordics and Germans tolerate closeness uneasily. In East Asia, apart from Indonesia, distance is a sign of respect. Latins, Arabs and Americans interpret closeness as evidence of confidence while distance infers loss of approval.

■ *Paralanguage*

Paralanguage is the way we speak, as opposed to the words we use. Variations include: changes in the speed, tone and other voice qualities; special sounds from groans to rapid catching of breath; and hesitations or silences to gather thoughts or impose dramatic effect.

■ *Physical appearances*

Appearances, both personal and of one's surroundings, convey messages. A manager can use the office arrangements to convey signals ranging from power to informality. Do you sit face-to-face, separated by a desk? Alternatively, are you invited to share a corner with easy chairs? To many, the first suggests that the manager is conscious of position and intends to discuss a serious matter. The latter, in contrast, implies an intention to 'have a chat'.

Suspicions

Some people are suspicious and critical of making non-verbal communication the subject of analysis and managerial training. Learning to interpret unintended messages will only increase the dominance of some artful people over those who are not in the know. Yet, sales training includes interpreting gestures. If a customer leans forward on the edge of the chair, interest has been aroused. Sitting back suggests boredom. An open posture shows willingness to talk while crossed arms or legs reveal defensiveness. In the last case, experienced sales people would not try to close a sale.

Another criticism is that sending out false cues to support untrue messages increases the possibility for manipulation. Political leaders are trained in techniques to improve their appearance of sincerity. The exceptional Margaret Thatcher was coached to lower her tone of voice as she grew from the shrill education secretary of the 1970s to the Prime Minister of the 1980s. Otherwise, politicians are usually such bad performers. Comparing the skill of actors with the clumsiness of ministers on the stump or at the dispatch box, Ratcliffe differentiates between gesture and body language. Gesture is deliberate. Body language is the involuntary give-away.[16] Hence our leaders stress points with rehearsed table-thumping gestures. The Soviet leader Khrushchev famously used his shoe to do this at the United Nations. Other politicians try to make points with their arms folded. This defensive, self-defeating male kinesic gives away the emptiness of their case.

One counter to suspicions of error, power and manipulation is that we send and receive non-verbal signals anyway. Studies suggest that people respond to body language 55 per cent of the time and to tone of voice 38 per cent. The actual words are worth a mere 7 per cent.[17] Should not the argument be to rely more on body language? This seems too extreme. Perhaps a good approach would be to reinforce what we do intuitively. Look for consistency between verbal and non-verbal communication. If the latter suggests that something is amiss, probe a little further. Being attentive in this way is a skill we should know. Trenholm[18] recommends that we should:

- pay attention to non-verbal cues;
- decode non-verbal messages cautiously;
- review our own non-verbal messages to see where they are inappropriate;
- remember the invasive and threatening potential of non-verbal messages.

Becoming a better communicator

Communication skills are important for any manager today. Many studies show that managers spend up to 80 per cent of their working days in this activity. Although the accent in the psychological model is on the efficiency of transfer of information *from* the sender *to* the receiver, we could look at it the other way round. How successful is the receiver at gathering information from the sender? As with the illustration of a conversation as a dance, both roles are vital. This section, therefore, starts with listening before looking at an aspect of sending so far glossed over – writing.

Listening

Clearly, averaged across all oral communication settings, there are more listeners than senders. That means we spend more of our time listening than speaking. Yet formal training is given mostly for the latter activity. Three reasons suggest themselves. First, communication is thought of as presentation. This is a one-way process, as in public speaking. Second, audiences think it easy to make an immediate evaluation of the speaker while the reverse is rarely possible. Lastly, we assign responsibility for the effectiveness of the transaction to the presenter. Failure is the speaker's fault.

There are many business situations where good listening skills make all the difference. Diplomacy is said to be about achieving one's aims while letting the other party do all the talking. From encouraging staff to overcome a personal setback, to selling the latest design of widget to a busy customer, diplomatic listening pays dividends.

Take the listening test in Exhibit 13.6. (This is designed as a quick diagnosis so don't worry if you find some questions ambiguous. The aim is to gather a general impression.)

If you gave positive answers to half or more of the list, you are normal. That means, like the rest of us, you have some poor listening habits. A complimentary phrase used to be, 'A great talker who could sell anyone anything'. The modern sales

Exhibit 13.6 Listening test: tick each box that applies to you

When engaged in a serious conversation with a colleague, customer or friend, do you ever:

- Glance at the time while the other is speaking?
- Complete the other person's sentences?
- Think, 'I want to say something but I'll wait until it's my turn'?
- Find eye contact difficult?
- Interrupt when the other is struggling to make a point?
- Think, 'I've heard this all before'?
- Anticipate what the other is about to say?
- Find your thoughts frequently distracted?
- Wonder what the other has just said?
- Work out your response while the other is talking?
- Feel you know the issue before the conversation has started?
- Find it difficult to get the other to speak?

Exhibit 13.7 Listening skills

1 *Block out distractions*. Arrange meetings to avoid interruptions. Surroundings familiar to you may distract a stranger. Do you need that James Dean poster or Venus flytrap?

2 *Tune in.* Clear your own mind; if you cannot, delaying the event may be better. Face the other person square on if possible. Show you are interested in both the subject and the person.

3 *Encourage the other to talk*. Say, 'Go on', 'Tell me more', or even 'And?' Summarise the other's contribution: 'So it wasn't a problem with the paint ...'

4 *Pick out highlights as you proceed*. Sometimes jotting a note may be best, especially if details are important.

5 *Learn to use open-ended questions*. They elicit other than one-word responses. Compare the closed 'Did you finish the job?' with 'How do you feel now that your first project is over?'

6 *Try to reach feelings and facts*. Discussing responses to the facts gives us an idea of why the speaker thinks these facts important. Compare the following responses to, 'I could really do with a day off'. Either the generous, 'Yes, go on, I'll cover for you', or the probing, 'You could do with a day off ...' (Note that 'Why?' would be intrusive.)

7 *Watch the body language.* Observe whether the other feels comfortable with the conversation and its setting. Check your own body language, too, but do not manipulate.

8 *Give feedback*. Feedback, focusing on the highlights, helps the conversation along. The other's confidence is raised if you show understanding. Attentiveness confirms that you find the subject matter important. Summarise what has happened, not what you anticipate.

9 *Ask for feedback*. Summarise what you have gained from the conversation. Ask for clarification of key points or matters you may have misunderstood.

person, however, uses less 'gift of the gab' and spends less time trying to build a personal relationship with the client through irrelevant chat. Buyers are more cautious, better informed and more closely controlled than ever before. The seller must now learn the buyer's needs quickly and this can hardly be done while talking. Listening habits that improve selling, *see* Exhibit 13.7, apply equally well to other business or social conversations.[19]

Writing

Generations of employers and managers have complained about the poor writing skills possessed by young people. Now companies recognise that the problem occurs at all levels. A Royal Mail survey showed how business relationships were threatened by over-familiarity in written or oral communication, addressing customers by the wrong sex and grammar and spelling errors.[20] One explanation lies in firms expecting senior staff to do tasks hitherto done by secretaries. Computers offer the chance to improve some aspects of writing. Not only do they make it easier to rewrite poor work at little cost but also they offer support through spelling, grammar and style checkers. They miss, however, many errors, as seen in Exhibit 13.8.

Exhibit 13.8 McDisaster averted

A colleague asked me to look over the proofs of his book chapter. At this late stage, only the smallest corrections were possible. The work assessed 'MacDonald's' policies in relation to the natural environment. Although the company's name occurred almost a hundred times, editors and typesetters had not noticed the error.

Written media lack channel richness on the Lengel–Daft scale. The capacity of the channel is low and there is no chance of immediate feedback. Encoding, therefore, concentrates on incorporating far less redundancy in the message compared with oral media. Furthermore, the encoding anticipates the reader's decoding skills. In the publishing world, many firms issue style guides. These are less concerned with the rules of syntax than with setting style and clarifying alternatives, *see* Exhibit 13.9.[21] At journals such as *The Economist*, guides help contributors and editors to achieve a consistent, authoritative approach to the magazine's well-educated, international readers.

Exhibit 13.9 Pearson's preferences

- -ise not -ize spellings;
- dates in the form 15 November 1993;
- spell out numbers under 10;
- single quotes (double within single);
- use 1 not (i) for numbered lists;
- use (a) or a, not a) or A for lettered lists, etc.

Accuracy is both important and demanded in formal business communications. Yet Ober and colleagues found differences between public oral and written communications of senior managers. Compared with the written form, 'business managers in the United States use overstatement in oral communication to show their confidence and assertiveness, whereas in other countries such as China and Japan ... [they] use understatement to show their modesty'.[22]

Whatever the medium, stakeholders require managers to write and speak in clear, definite, and forward-looking language. Even when problems abound, clarity helps direct employees to the problems and how to resolve them, while investors can have the correct expectations. It is better to 'tell it as it is'.

Communication and organisation

Communication and organisation are closely connected. In Chapter 10, we saw how one principle of organisational design was to place closer together those staff whose work interlocked. This was to reduce the length of the communication chain. Design will, however, only resolve communication issues to a limited extent. Whatever the structure, the organisation has to ensure that information can flow in all directions. We shall study the downward, upward and horizontal directions. Then we look at another type of flow, which follows its own path – the grapevine. Lastly, we shall look at the role of meetings in organisations.

Downward communication

Managers often feel aggrieved when they hear reports such as, 'No one ever tells you anything', or, 'I don't know what is going on'. Although some may mean, 'I never listen to anything', or, 'I don't agree with what is going on', managers will often respond with a review of the communication system. In larger firms, the desire to exercise more control over how downward communication works leads to the establishment of centralised communication functions. Often these are adjuncts of the public relations or personnel sections. At the Natural History Museum, inadequate downward flows were overcome by improvements to moribund existing systems, such as the newsletter, notice boards and team briefings. A new centralised function, staffed with new people, can revitalise structures that have fallen into disrepair.

Another approach is to add a channel. Although the United Kingdom opted out of the European Union's Social Chapter, many firms decided to adopt its principles in all countries. Unilever was criticised by some shareholders for being too eager to comply. Defending the action, chairman Niall Fitzgerald argued that acceptance meant two minor policy changes. First, 'Works councils provide helpful additional channels of communication with employees'. (The second policy covered uniform parental leave.)[23] Other examples are electronic media. We have already commented that these might add noise and redundancy instead of offering a new, rich channel.

Upward communication

Successful organisations need good upward and downward communication. This is difficult to achieve especially in large firms. Yet it is vital if only because sound decisions often depend on gathering sound information from the grass-roots level. There are several methods of stimulating upward communication: intelligence gathering units; attitude surveys; suggestion schemes; and informal meetings.

Intelligence gathering

Structures of the armed services, designed to pass instructions downwards, are poor at collecting and interpreting information picked up by the troops. Debriefing prisoners, for example, can often yield valuable information provided it is pieced with other snippets. Recognising this problem, armies have long-established intelligence branches where special skills in languages, technology and analysis are applied to data. One of the best-known British intelligence officers was T.E. Lawrence (1888–1935). His leadership ability, linguistic skills and knowledge of the region helped him, in 1916, to unite the Arabs against the Ottoman Turks. He led the Arab army into Damascus two years later. Today, other branches of military intelligence, such as MI5 and MI6, gather and interpret data from all around the world.

Attitude surveys

Companies often replicate the military experience. For instance, personnel specialists will interview leavers to assess their attitudes. From these *exit interviews*, they assess factors from pay and conditions to attitudes within particular work groups. The same department is often responsible for broad attitude surveys. Conducted at regular intervals, these are means for senior managers to gauge how shop-floor attitudes are changing. The directness of the survey eliminates distortion by the middle ranks.

Suggestion schemes

Suggestion schemes are means for managers to gather ideas. Some yield large flows from which occasional inspirations yield valuable benefits. BMW used a suggestion scheme as part of culture change process at its Mini plant. The turnaround from a rundown, under-invested works has been supported by staff co-operation in incremental change. BMW was the first in the United Kingdom to link suggestions award and pay bargaining, *see* Exhibit 13.10.[24]

Exhibit 13.10 Sustaining suggestions

The BMW Oxford plant made more than 160 000 Minis in 2002, 30 per cent more than planned. The voluntary suggestion scheme saved more than £6 million from 10 339 ideas – more than two per worker. Four pence per car was saved by changing details of cross-braces; £4500 came from shrinking progress report cards from A3 to A4; the best suggestion, saving £115 000, was that of a group who showed how to safely halve the number of roof soundproofing blocks. Their cash reward was supplemented by a big night out.

After the rapid growth, managers sought stability and cost reduction. For 2003, under an innovative deal, workers were to receive a £260 annual bonus if, in addition to quality and output targets, they came up with an average of three ideas yielding £800 savings.

Informal meetings

Many advocate that there is no better means for gathering information than by looking around. *Management by Wandering Around* (MBWA) was made famous by the founders of Hewlett Packard. It has had many imitators. The forums at the Natural History Museum are another form of meeting, although the numbers attending probably restrict the chances of debate. The difficulty with such methods is that they do not guarantee to reveal important information. In addition, they tend to sideline middle managers who may not feel part of the process.

■ Horizontal communication

A quarter-century ago, Drucker placed knowledge alongside other critical elements – capital, physical resources and employees' time – as a crucial resource to be managed.[25] He later revised his view to place knowledge as *the key resource.* Senge's *learning organisations* [26] absorb and apply new ideas and practices at all levels. At their heart is the need for shared mental models and team learning. This is the field of knowledge management.

At the team level, sharing arises from daily activities. At a larger scale, despite their reliance on knowledge, many organisations do not know what they know. Valuable information is dispersed in computer databases, file drawers and even employees' heads. Work is repeated, and mistakes replicated, because of the difficulties of accessing knowledge kept elsewhere. Now leading firms have a senior post, the knowledge manager. Exhibit 13.11 has some examples.[27]

Exhibit 13.11 Nurturing, sharing and valuing knowledge

Dow Chemical has a director responsible for global intellectual assets. Through improved management of its 29 000 patents, it found savings of some £25 million and made plans to increase its licensing income substantially. The starting point was to create a database from patent records, describing each according to 100 possible points. The work was extended through trademarks and copyrights to cover all of Dow's intellectual assets.

Some companies use knowledge management to help in assessing their true worth instead of relying on intuition. Celemi, a Swedish consulting firm, has developed software to assist this. It values its own knowledge assets at £5.2 million, more than twice the figure shown on the conventional balance sheet.

A knowledge management system has four key elements:

- ■ a *database* to allow information sharing quickly and efficiently;
- ■ a *common language* to allow users to easily code and decode usable data and reinforce the constructionist and pragmatic purpose of shared knowledge;
- ■ a *network* to send and retrieve information;
- ■ an *intelligent processing system* allowing direct transfer or the creation of new knowledge through the combination of database information with users' experience.[28]

There are drawbacks. Computer-based knowledge management systems are limited by the complex nature of the knowledge itself. Explicit knowledge comes as words and numbers and can be readily stored and transmitted. The so-called 'tacit', or deep, knowledge, on the other hand, relates to anything from the subtle aspects of running a tricky process to a deep understanding of cultural values. Capturing that on databases remains a challenge.

The grapevine

The *grapevine* is the informal information channel found in all organisations. It often bypasses formal systems, compared with which it is faster and sometimes more accurate. After all, if it did not satisfy some needs it would not exist! Because so many of its messages are passed face to face, it is a rich medium with strong influence on users. Therefore, especially from the social constructionist or pragmatic perspectives, the grapevine is very important.

Grapevines prosper in work places that facilitate contact both physically and through email lists. Ideas proliferate among densely packed staff seeking entertaining diversions from boredom or insecurity. So-called 'viral issues', such as pensions, mergers, repetitive strain injury, bullying, rage and burn-out, become hot topics of the day. For a virus to spread, a message must have a special property – novelty, fear, scandal or shock. Then it must be pushed by pundits (people who are thought to know) and networkers (people who trade in gossip).[29] Receivers do the rest. For many, work is the principal social activity; no one wants to be on the outside

The richness and immediacy of the grapevine might tempt managers to use it, or at least try to manage it. They can, for instance, cultivate recognised networkers as personal 'listening posts'. Alternatively, they may spread rumour or news to achieve their own ends. These approaches suffer if the grapevine is unreliable. Although, typically, three-quarters of information may be true, the problem is to know which three-quarters! To limit such undesirable effects, managers should improve other forms of communication. When key decisions are made, for example, they should be shared, using formal channels, immediately.

Running meetings

Running a meeting is an important skill. Among many purposes, meetings form a vital link between staff and the organisation. This is especially true for those who work off-site, such as sales and services crews, outreach workers, home workers and managers of store chains. Yet, in spite of their frequency, many do not seem to work. Common complaints are that meetings are boring, are a waste of time, lack direction, never achieve anything, go over old issues, are incoherent, do not focus on the individual's problems or offer an opportunity for the boss to give a lecture.

In Chapter 12 we studied how, as the attendance at meetings grew beyond 10 or more, there was increasing tolerance of directive leadership and a need for formal rules. Therefore, the communications aspects of a meeting should support this approach. Valuable elements are as follows:

■ *Have a real meeting.* Ensure that the same results, such as giving instructions, could not be achieved elsewhere.

■ *Issue an agenda in advance.* Beyond giving information on time and place, the agenda allows people to prepare themselves.

- *Invite only those who are needed.* Others become frustrated and may be disruptive.
- *Give undivided attention.* Prevent interruptions and distractions.
- *Prepare.* Make information available. Know your target. Brief key members in advance.
- *Encourage contributions from all delegates.* Use questioning skills to build participation.
- *Keep to the agenda.* Especially important when people from different cultures attend, keeping to the agenda is a way of maintaining momentum.
- *Conclude and summarise.*

Overcoming problems

Our review of communication and organisation outlined the links between these two elements. Although easing the flow of communication seems to help to make organisations work better, many are increasingly worried about the rapidly increasing volume. As with new six lane motorways, the traffic soon grows to fill the space. Besides this management issue, other problems arise in developing personal communication skills. We shall start with two of these, jargon and gender.

Jargon

Semantics, the study of the meaning of words, throws up many stories of the causes and consequences of misunderstanding. Difficulties are to be expected in international business but jargon is perhaps a subtler problem. This language of a class, profession, sect or organisation has a constructionist function. It provides opportunities for ready communication among members of the group, thus reinforcing feelings of membership. Problems arise when the parties think they share this special language, *see* Exhibit 13.12.

Exhibit 13.12 Separated by a common language

Surrounded and outnumbered eight to one by enemy infantry, Brigadier Tom Brodie of the Gloucester Regiment reported to General Robert H. Soule, 'Things are a bit sticky, sir'. Brodie's British understatement meant that the 'Glorious Gloucesters' were in severe difficulty. This, however, was 1951 and the Korean War, and General Soule was American. He understood there was some fighting but the British were holding. Neither reinforcement nor withdrawal was needed.

Within four days, the British were overrun. They lost 400 dead and 500 prisoners; only 39 escaped. An American officer would have used the expression, 'Sir, there is all hell breaking loose here'. The General would have understood.

Jargon is everywhere. Information specialists, in their *virtual reality*, *surf web pages* using *hyperlinks*; they know their wares – *soft*, *hard*, *course*, *people*, *free*, *share*, *pay* and *net*; and, for them, *PostScript* is a page design language. In business, instead of making a plan, some *dimension a management initiative*.

Political correctness in education requires *disadvantaged learners* not to fail. Instead, they *achieve a deficit*. Having *gained insufficient credits*, they may still receive an award provided they *achieve the necessary exit velocity*. Some such words and phrases spread and enrich general usage. Others wither. In business communications, avoiding jargon is impossible. The skill is to tailor its use to the awareness of the audience.

■ Gender

There are differences between sex and gender. The former is a biological definition based on physical attributes. Gender, on the other hand, is not strictly biological. Socialisation usually encourages people to learn the values and behaviour of the gender role corresponding to their sex. Critics argue, however, that sharp dichotomies have grown up in both sex and gender definitions. Men should occupy male gender roles and display masculinity; women should occupy female gender roles and display femininity.[30]

Sexist communication has been criticised for contributing to the glass ceilings and walls in organisations. Among occupations, *chairman, statesman, businessman* and *foreman* have implied various degrees of power, while *cameraman, airman, fireman, middleman* and even *highwayman* have suggested some reserved occupations. While many say that such words are understood to refer to both genders, critics argue that they have a subtle effect on role images. Women are not seen to be chairmen, statesmen or highwaymen. The problem spreads beyond individual words into the imagery and metaphor used throughout the organisation. Alvesson and Willmott argue that the language used in jokes or for discourses about corporate strategy contains 'strong elements of masculinity that act to strengthen male identities and thereby reproduce asymmetrical gender relations in organisational life'.[31]

The authors point out, however, that, since both men and women vary so much, both sexes experience advantages and disadvantages from the present situation. In the main, however, women come off worse. Sexist vocabulary often overlaps with speech habits that reinforce notions of (male) power, *see* Exhibit 13.13.[32]

Exhibit 13.13 You may call me 'Sir'

The modes of address that differentiate managers from workers were the subject of a survey by the Manufacturing, Science and Finance Union. Responses were received from 557 workplaces that together employ more than a quarter of a million people.

On average, 33 per cent of managers expect to be addressed as 'Sir' or by their title. Regional differences were marked. In the north and in Wales the proportion was 45 per cent, falling to 15 per cent in the south west.

Many found managers' interpersonal skills inadequate. Sixteen per cent of respondents had been shouted at in public and 23 per cent openly criticised. Moreover, 39 per cent had never been thanked by the senior people in their organisation.

Women may learn to compensate for such difficulties in subtle ways. Lind found that, although there was no difference between the sexes in the amount of communication within small groups, women use email much more than male counterparts.

She suggested they prefer this lean communication channel because its facelessness equalises power and avoids conflict.[33]

Exhibit 13.14 Communication: more is not better

A 2000 study by Pitney Bowes found that a typical British employee received 191 messages daily, of which 39 were emails. People are checking their in-boxes more frequently, both at the office and at home. Almost three-quarters of staff feel overwhelmed by the number of messages; 84 per cent are distracted three or more times per hour. Secretaries face more than 190 letters, email, faxes, telephone calls, voice messages, sticky notes, pager messages, courier deliveries and internal mail.

Teamwork is another reason for increased information loads. Sixty per cent of office workers were on a team, with 51 per cent on more than one. An assistant is often assigned to keep all members up to date; this means many messages, often in different formats.

Rather than replace existing tools, new communications technologies are added on. Yet, the preferred method of external communication remains the telephone, at 79 per cent. For internal communication, however, email, at 66 per cent, has come to dominate.

■ Overload

In the introduction, we briefly noted a survey showing some bad communication habits of managers. Other surveys bring out the daily deluge of messages and consequent feelings of overload, *see* Exhibit 13.14.[34] Meredith Fischer of Pitney Bowes, said, 'It is as if the communication demands are driving the work and the conduct of business, and not the other way round'. He suggested that 'traffic police' might be used to sort and filter information for colleagues and guide them through the jams.

Computer Associates, one of the world's largest software companies, acted to stop employees constantly checking their email. Logging on was restricted to three times each day. Other approaches include limiting all messages to one screen or imposing a notional charge on departments to cover the computing costs.

The rapid growth of electronic mail is expected to swamp all other media within a few years. Companies must clearly develop policies to manage. Not only must these stem the flood but also they must cover three further issues:

■ *Privacy* – are employers at liberty to read employees' email?

■ *Legal liability* – it is known that people are less cautious and diplomatic in email than in paper letters or memoranda. Storing such messages may lead to legal problems.

■ *Security* – sharing information means more leakage of confidential data.[35]

The limits to truth

Much discussion of communication in organisations treats information unquestioningly. In particular, the psychological perspective concentrates on transferring understanding from one person to another *with the minimum of distortion*. Consequently we look to match messages and media with training in sending and receiving for those involved. But what if the messengers were setting out to avoid the truth or, at least, paint a one-sided picture?

When discussing upward communication, managers reveal fears that they may not be told all they should. *Forbes* magazine interviewed eight senior executives in the United States to find out how they coped with the problem. Exhibit 13.15 notes some of their comments.[36] The responses show the managers to be aware of the problem. Yet they feel that the extra provision they make more than counters it. According to Larson and King, however, much of this is unrealistic. Many managers advocate open communication while rewarding knee bending and punishing dissent. Studies show how individuals are motivated to create favourable impressions; therefore, they hide weaknesses and emphasise strengths. Recipients have a natural tendency to accept information that supports their beliefs and reject the negative or critical. So good news travels quickly while bad news is distorted or blocked.[37]

Exhibit 13.15 Eight managers' routes to the truth

- *'The women are the catalysts for telling the truth round here. Men are brought up to be discreet. Otherwise, they get into fights.'* (Female chief executive.)
- *'Alarm bells ring when someone says it's so complicated I can't explain it to you. I just don't believe them.'*
- *'I have a phone that is not screened by anyone.'*
- *'People tend to tell you the good news and not speak honestly about problems. I don't let them off the hook. I've got to make it wrong not to talk about problems.'*
- *'A staff complaint that I parked my car in a disabled spot reassured me that people who work for me aren't afraid of me.'*
- *'Suggestion boxes all over our offices do bring about a level of truth.'*
- *'Don't rely on intuition. There's nothing like the facts.'*
- *'To get to the truth, go to its source.'*

Beyond personal reasons for misinformation, Alvesson and Willmott argue it arises from the nature of organisations themselves. They present organisations as sites of psychological imprisonment and question whether structures of communication reinforce oppression.[38] In other words, does communication serve to present power difference, such as capitalism, hierarchy and management itself, as natural and beneficial rather than arbitrary and harmful?

Drawing on the work of Forester, two dimensions are identified. First, there is the question of whether distortion is inevitable or unnecessary. Second, there is its origin. Does it stem from the choices of individuals or is it embedded in the social order of the organisation? Combining these dimensions gives us the 2×2 matrix of Figure 13.9. The matrix brings out four sources of communication distortion:

- Cell 1 refers to the psychological communication model. Any distortion is noise, arising inevitably as individuals and channels reach the limits of their processing capacities.
- Cell 2 refers to distortion arising from specialisation. We have shown how managers work hard, at least officially, to overcome this problem through trying to

improve the upward, downward (and sideward) flows. These efforts can be seen to be futile, however. The problem arises not from poor connections but from the nature of the organisation itself.

■ Cell 3 shows distortion as action chosen by the individual. Here the limits to 'open' communication are tested when a manager justifies deception because it will achieve the required ends. Depending on the direction down or up, the subordinate is persuaded or the wrath of the boss avoided. In societal terms, this is propaganda.

■ Cell 4 covers cases where information is distorted for reasons justified by the social order, which is the hierarchy. 'We cannot reveal costs because we need to bargain' or 'The basis of overhead allocation is confidential' are typical statements of the genre.

From their critical theory standpoint, Alvesson and Willmott argue that Cell 1, the domain of the psychological perspective, is the least interesting. To understand the function of communication means taking a broader, pragmatic approach. This means looking critically at why communication takes place and expecting that there will be a degree of distortion in many of its practices. Cell 4 ought to be the place where work starts.

Many managers ignore pleas to 'tell it as it is'. Prasad and Mir suggest that 'reference to the negative' is used frequently to deflect attention from pressing issues.[39] In detail, Crombie and Samujh show distortion at work in the case of a chairman's letter to members of a farmers' co-operative.[40] Its focus on problems serves three purposes: to divert attention from questions that are more serious; to present senior managers as

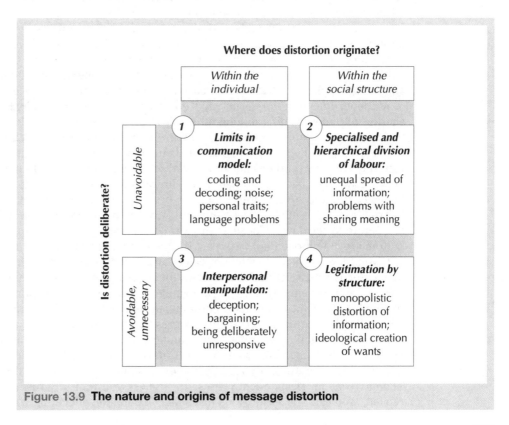

Figure 13.9 **The nature and origins of message distortion**

capable problem solvers; and to undermine potential challengers. The last point is illustrated by a paragraph on the problems of producing a new constitution:

Thankfully, we do not need to write a new constitution every year because I firmly believe that no matter how much time is spent on it, it is impossible to produce a perfect document. If it was possible to do so you would not need solicitors. However, we are fortunate in having . . . as our legal advisor and I thank him for steering us through a difficult period.

This suggests that those who had objected were wasting the time of the Board, its solicitors and other stockholders.

Conclusion: responsible communication

We began the chapter with a common enough illustration. A survey shows that employees complain of being poorly informed. This triggers a review in which channels are revitalised, replaced or reinforced. Meanwhile key agents, especially line managers, are trained to be better communicators. They learn about verbal and non-verbal communication, selection of media whose richness matches the message and how to tailor their presentation to suit the needs of the audience, avoiding jargon and sexist language. Above all, they are trained to listen. As a result, more information flows more smoothly between people and through the organisation.

There are dangers at every turn. The fearsome one is overload. Channels do not replace, they add. Traffic becomes heavier with each technical innovation. Communication resigns as servant to reign as master. Resisting the flood is difficult. Imposing limits seems fraught with danger. If an efficiency doctor prescribes 'email access three times a day after meals' the purpose of the service is lost. Rather than waste time on screen, staff will return to the telephone or fax for urgent business. Other problems cover staff suspicions over detailed supervision of correspondence and the possibilities of legal action based on evidence from careless e-chat.

A deeper question concerns what communication is. Is the ideal to be seen as sharing of understanding among all parties? Critics say this is both impossible and undesirable. It ignores both human nature and the oppressive reality of organisations. Both provide ready reasons for distortion in communication. Only if people can fully trust each other can they afford to tell all. Since they do not, we find that good news flows faster than bad and subordinates plot to keep the boss out of the know. Furthermore, the interests of the organisation are served by maintaining an information differential between those in power and those who have to be persuaded to operate lower down. Those at the top do not want to reveal all and those at the bottom are conditioned not to expect it. Open communication has its limits.

Given these suspicions, why not call a halt, asserting that becoming a better communicator is wasted effort? The reason for pressing on is that organisations do not have to fail their employees. Ethical managers, believing in a responsible, participative style, will want to be good communicators. Leading, directing, coaching and controlling all require the capacity to present ideas clearly. They also require the corresponding skill of listening. Trust can be built. Staff will tell the boss more if bad news is received as openly as good. According to IBM folklore, after losing $10 million in a risky venture, a young manager was summoned to the office of founder Thomas Watson. Despondently, he said, 'I guess you want my resignation'. Watson replied, 'You can't be serious. We just spent $10 million educating you.'[41]

QUICK CHECK

Can you ...

- Name three perspectives on what communication is.
- Define communication from one of these perspectives.
- Sketch the communication model.
- Define channel richness.
- State the steps of decoding.
- Distinguish body language from paralanguage.
- Suggest ways of handling non-verbal communication.

- Give five of the nine listening skills.
- State four means of encouraging upward communication.
- Explain the term grapevine.
- Outline the problems of jargon and gender in language.
- Suggest two approaches to coping with noise.
- Summarise the criticism by Alvesson and Willmott of the communication model.

QUESTIONS

Chapter review

13.1 Explain and illustrate the three perspectives on communication.

13.2 Describe the communication model for interpersonal communication, explaining how it can be used for diagnosing problems.

13.3 List the difficulties with upward communication in organisations. How effective do you think the solutions proposed in the chapter are likely to be?

Application

13.4 Review the attempts to improve links at the Natural History Museum in the light of the psychological perspective on communication. What extra light do the other perspectives throw on the picture?

13.5 We have seen some firms establish controls over communication channels because of message overload. Examine the ethical issues arising from such action.

13.6 Use the communication perspectives to explain Ober's finding of differences between oral and written communications.

Investigation

13.7 Examine any publication designed for people within an organisation, professional group or common interest group. Identify any jargon. What are the advantages and disadvantages of using language in this way?

13.8 Study the Chairman's letter from the annual report of an organisation found later to be in difficulties. Examine how the letter refers to these problems, using Figure 13.9.

Selling products or solutions[42]

Act 1: Selling a product

Representative: That's a fancy looking cup. What's it for?

Customer: Thank you. Our team won the quiz league this season.

Representative: Ah. Well, you'll know the 5 Premier and football league clubs with an X in their name?

Customer: No. I'm in for history, geography and that sort of thing.

Representative: Well, ask the lads on your staff if they know ... But I see you're busy so we mustn't waste your time ...

Customer: (*You* are doing so very effectively)

Representative: ... so I will come to the point. As you know, we have a proud tradition stretching back to before yours and my time of offering top rate service to our clients. I am sure you'd be interested in our latest all-in-one shampoo. It's just designed for cleaning businesses like your own. You have to do lots of square footage in a very short time. The shampoo is more concentrated than all the others so it dries more quickly and the customer can use the room pretty well straight away. We've even designed a special adaptor that will suit most cleaners so I'm sure it will suit yours ... Trials in Spain show that the time spent scrubbing can easily be cut by 10 per cent ... The packaging is particularly secure and attractive ... The bottle can be recycled ... (ten minutes in all).

Customer: Well, it's delightful to hear everyone's improving. I would like to read about the details. Would you leave the literature with the receptionist on your way out? I'll phone you when I've had a chance to think about it.

Representative: You'll be better if you call by next Friday. That's the last day of the introductory offer I was talking about. (And it's the last day for working out this month's bonus.)

Customer: OK, I'll let you know.

Act 2: Selling a solution

Representative: What would it mean if you had a shampoo you could use almost up to the minute that customers wanted their offices?

Customer: We could get more done in the early mornings. (The staff could each do an extra half-hour. Part-timers could do with the extra money.)

Representative: And what about a shampoo that's so effective you can cut the scrubbing time by nearly 10 per cent?

Customer: Well, we'd have to see. It might help a little. Ten per cent isn't much. (But possibly a great deal in those large government offices. I could afford to pay a little bonus.)

Representative: Do your machines leave the occasional damp patches on the floor for an hour or so? Would you like to avoid that?

Customer: Yes. We must always strive to look professional. (Customers complain about this.)

Representative: And you are now committed to environmental purchasing? (I checked on the way in.)

Customer: We prefer all our materials to pass the standard, and packaging should recycle.

Representative: We don't launch a product unless it can pass. Tell me, do you use the Emca ZA machine? (I checked that on the way in too.)

Customer: Yes. Why?

Representative: Well, we've designed a small adaptor to measure the shampoo more carefully. It will regulate the flow and avoid those damp patches. They're easy to fit. But if you would like to place a trial order, I'll call next week and fix up half a dozen machines free of charge.

Customer: What's the price of the shampoo?

Questions

1 What sales tactics are the salespeople using in Acts 1 and 2? Which seller is likely to be successful?

2 Compare the two conversations in terms of the communication perspectives.

3 How do the conversations compare with any recent experiences you have had as a customer?

Bibliography

Among the books you find under 'communications' in the library, many are devoted to the sender's skills of clear writing, speaking, presenting and so on. Setting communication in context, however, are Nicky Stanton *Mastering Communication* (Basingstoke: Macmillan, 1996) and Frances Cairncross *The Company of the Future: Shaping Up to the Management Challenges of the Communications Revolution* (London: Profile Books, 2002). For more on body language, look for neuro-linguistic programming, such as Ursula Lyon 'Influence, communication and neuro-linguistic programming in practice' in Jim Stewart and Jim McGoldrick (eds) *Human Resource Development* (1996, Hemel Hempstead: Prentice Hall).

References

1 Prickett, Ruth (1997) 'Alive and kicking', *People Management*, 15 May, 28–31; Natural History Museum (2002) *Annual Report 2001–2*, NHM; **www.nhm.ac.uk/info/report/report2002/**, accessed 3 April 2003.

2 Killgren, Lucy (1997) 'Internal affairs', *Marketing Week*, 3 April.

3 *Financial Times*, 10 July 1997.

4 Trenholm, Sarah (2001) *Thinking through Communication: An introduction to the study of human communication*, 3rd edition, London: Allyn and Bacon.

5 Hackley, Christopher E. (1998) 'Social constructionism and research in marketing and advertising', *Qualitative Market Research*, **1(3)**, 125–31.

6 Perlmutter, Howard V. (2000) 'On deep dialog', Wharton School, University of Pennsylvania; **http://knowledge.wharton.upenn.edu/PDFs/629.pdf**, accessed 2 April 2003.

7 O'Donnell, David, O'Regan, Philip, Coates, Brian, Kennedy, Tom, Keary, Brian and Berkery, Gerry (2003) 'Human interaction: the critical source of intangible value', *Journal of Intellectual Capital*, **4(1)**, 82–99.

8 Carvel, John (1997) 'Global study finds the world speaking in 10 000 tongues', *Guardian*, 22 July, 5.

9 Williams, Alfred (1969) *Life in a Railway Factory*, reprint of 1915 edn, Newton Abbot: David & Charles, 213.

10 Carroll, Lewis (1865) *Alice's Adventures in Wonderland*, London: Ward Lock, Chapter 7, A Mad Tea-party.

11 Daft, Richard L. (2000) *Management*, 5th edition, Fort Worth, Tex.: The Dryden Press, 569–70.

12 Graesser, Arthur C., Millis, Keith K. and Zwaan, Rolf A. (1997) 'Discourse Comprehension', *Annual Review of Psychology*, **48**, 163–89; Graesser, Arthur C., Gernsbacher, Morton A. and Goldman, Susan B. (2002) *Handbook of Discourse Processes*, Mahwah, NJ: Erlbaum.

13 BT (1997) *Let's Dance: How to get more out of life through better conversations*, British Telecommunications, 7–8.

14 Davies, Erin (1996) 'The Amex's old hand signals give way to computers', *Fortune*, **134(8)**, 28 October, 52.

15 Lewis, Richard D. (1996) 'Space at a premium', *Management Today*, September, 105–6.

16 Ratcliffe, Michael (1996) 'Gesture, posture and pose: everybody's acting nowadays', *New Statesman*, **126(4322)**, February, 41.

17 Arthur, Diane (1995) 'The importance of body language', *HR Focus*, **72(6)**, June, 22–3.

18 Trenholm (2001) *op. cit.*

19 Based on: British Telecommunications (1997) *op. cit.*; Phillips, Rick (1996) 'Listening your way to more sales', *Sales Doctors Magazine*, 15 July; **www.salesdoctors.com**, accessed 22 July 1997.

20 Tobin, Anna (2003) 'Intensive case for English patients', *Guardian: Jobs and Money*, 12 April, 20–1.

21 Pearson Education (2001) *Author guide: Guidelines for writing textbooks and their lecturer support supplements*, Harlow: Pearson Education.

22 Ober, Scott, Zhao, Jensen J., Davis, Rod and Alexander, Melody W. (1999) 'Telling it like it is: the use of certainty in public business discourse', *Journal of Business Communication*, **36(3)**, 280–1.

23 August, Oliver and Bassett, Philip (1997) 'Unilever defends its social chapter stance', *The Times*, 7 May.

24 Mackintosh, James (2003) 'How BMW put the Mini back on track: a pioneering bonus scheme has given fresh impetus to workers at a once run-down car factory', *Financial Times*, 19 March.

25 Drucker, Peter (1980) *Managing in Turbulent Times*, London: Pan, 31.

26 Senge, Peter M. (1993) *The Fifth Discipline: The art and practice of the learning organisation*, London: Century.

27 Mullin, Rick (1996) 'Knowledge management: a cultural evolution', *Journal of Business Strategy*, **17(5)**, September–October, 56–9; Houlder, Vanessa (1997) 'Knowledge management: the high price of know-how', *Financial Times*, 14 July.

28 Based on: Soo, Christine, Devinney, Timothy, Midgley, David and Deering, Anne (2002) 'Knowledge management: philosophy, processes and pitfalls', *California Management Review*, **44(4)**, 129–49.

29 Overell, Stephen (2002) 'Crazes that capture the office: Social epidemics: the workplace is an ideal environment for "viral" ideas', *Financial Times*, 13 March, 15.

449

30 Giesen, Erika (1996) 'Communication and gender lessons', **cyberschool.4j.lane.edu/People/Faculty/Duke/ CoMMG/lessons/Lessons.htm**, accessed 2 August 1997.

31 Alvesson, Mats and Willmott, Hugh (1996) *Making Sense of Management: A critical introduction*, London: Sage, 113.

32 Smith, David and Higgins, Sarah (1997) 'Call me "Sir", demand British bosses', *Sunday Times: Section 3 Business*, 13 July, 1.

33 Lind, Mary R. (2001) 'An exploration of communication channel usage by gender', *Work Study*, **50(6)**, 234–40.

34 Uhlig, Roger (1997) 'Office workers sinking under tide of technology', *Daily Telegraph*, 24 June; McGookin, Stephen (1997) 'Better communication: managing information flow', *Financial Times*, 7 July; Pitney Bowes (2000) *Messaging practices in the knowledge economy*; Gallup (2001) 'Almost all e-mail users say internet and e-mail have made lives better', *Gallup Organisation*, 23 July.

35 Houlder, Vanessa (1997) 'Failing to get the message. E-mail's advantages could be lost by staff misusing it', *Financial Times*, 17 March.

36 Conlin, Michelle (1997) ' The truth', *Forbes*, **159(3)**, 10 February, 20–1.

37 Larson, Erik W. and King, Jonathan B. (1996) 'The systematic distortion of information: an ongoing challenge to management', *Organisational Dynamics*, **24(3)**, Winter, 49–61.

38 Alvesson and Wilmott (1996) *op. cit.*, 116–17.

39 Prasad, Anshuman and Mir, Raza (2002) 'Digging deep for meaning: A critical hermeneutic analysis of CEO letters to shareholders in the oil industry', *Journal of Business Communication*, **39(1)**, 92–116.

40 Crombie, Winifred and Samujh, Helen (1999) 'Negative messages as strategic communication: a case study of a New Zealand company's annual executive letter', *Journal of Business Communication*, **36(3)**, 229–40.

41 Larson and King (1996) *op. cit.*

42 In this fictitious case, you will probably recognise real behaviour. It was suggested by Phillips, Rick (1996) 'All I want is an unfair advantage', *Sales Doctors Magazine*, 25 November; **www.salesdoctors.com**, accessed 22 July 1997.

Implementing policies and plans

Part 5 is about doing. Converting words into action is the job of the functional manager, be it in human resources, operations, marketing or design and development. Chapter 14 applies many ideas from Part 4 to the practice of building and sustaining the organisation with people, either individually or in groups. It covers human resource planning and policies for appraisal, welfare, pay and industrial relations.

Chapter 15 explains the importance of operations in any organisation. Often known as the 'technical core', operations usually accounts for most of its employment and cost. The chapter picks out common themes, such as the effect of volume on processes. It sets these ideas in the context of manufacturing and service provision, pointing to similarities and differences.

Many believe that business begins and ends with marketing. Chapter 16 explains the trend towards forming closer relationships with customers. This growing contact, combined with the alleged power of brands and advertising, makes marketing the most visible and criticised of functions. The chapter closes with an evaluation from the perspective of ethics and social responsibility.

Chapter 17 continues the theme of action by studying how organisations can convert their wish to innovate into a flow of new products and processes to keep ahead of competitors. The process of converting ideas into marketable products is as much about management skill as about the original inspirations.

CHAPTER 14

Human resource management

Chapter objectives

When you have finished studying this chapter, you should be able to:

- define, and describe the role of, human resource management and explain how it fits into the whole organisation;

- distinguish between hard and soft approaches to HRM, outlining the ideologies on which they are based;

- outline the nature and purpose of HR planning, showing its links with recruitment and selection to satisfy the organisation's staff needs;

- explain the purpose of performance appraisal and its underpinning of training and development;

- compare the training and development approaches to the extension of people's talents;

- summarise the design and purpose of different pay schemes, suggesting circumstances where they may be applied;

- demonstrate changing attitudes towards involvement in employee welfare;

- review how employee relations policy has changed in recent years;

- clarify four critical questions facing managers with HR responsibilities: cultural differences; ethics of HRM practice; special issues within SMEs and equal opportunities.

Hire the best. Pay them fairly. Communicate frequently. Provide challenges and rewards. Believe in them. Get out of their way – they'll knock your socks off.

Mary Ann Allison, American banker

Skills at the Skipton[1]

Founded in 1854, the Skipton Building Society was, by 2003, the seventh largest in the United Kingdom. It faces increasing competition and more stringent control by national bodies set up to oversee financial institutions. To prosper while maintaining continuity, the society decided, from the mid-1990s, upon a concentric diversification strategy. By 2003, the Skipton had become a 16-strong group of companies, built mainly through acquisition. Examples include the purchase of Britannic Assurance's mortgage portfolio and the Direct Life and Pensions company, and taking a controlling stake in estate agency Connells to extend geographic cover. The 2003 purchases of Private Health Partnership and Medical Insurance Association further extended the customer base. The branch network had expanded to 80.

Such growth meant that all staff needed greater knowledge of financial products combined with enhanced selling and administrative skills. Growth exacerbated both succession difficulties in some key managerial roles and the problems of skill shortage in the Skipton area. The unemployment rate was 1.9 per cent in 1999.

To support change, the Skipton decided to augment the development of its people. Aided by consultants, the society selected the key management characteristics critical to achieving business goals. These were placed in three categories: interpersonal skills; thinking skills; and energies, including adaptability and personal effectiveness. Focusing at first on 40 head office managers, the human resources team, again advised by consultants, devised a development centre programme to measure managers' skills. Tests and exercises included: occupational personality questionnaires, to assess each individual's self-perception; group discussions; presentations; in-tray studies; ability tests; and structured interviews. The process was so thorough that only six managers could work through the development centre at once. Since four were run each year, the flow was constrained.

From the outset, it was stressed that attendance was voluntary. Although some successful managers did not take part, many found that the process enhanced performance and promotion chances. A human resources team member gave feedback to each participant. Then, in co-operation with the line manager, a personal development plan was agreed. This comprised actions addressing the areas chosen for development. Examples have included: formal courses; one-week job swaps; longer secondments to other parts of the organisation; and project work. Group workshops enabled participants to share experiences, build relationships and motivate those falling behind. A resource centre holds management development material. Formal courses featured in many plans. Beyond the immediate management group, many staff studied for professional qualifications.

A danger in small, stable organisations is limited opportunity. Advancement is only to fill 'dead men's shoes'. In spite of its moderate size, the society encourages career mobility by advertising all vacancies internally. Sickness and maternity leave present opportunities for secondments, letting staff take on senior roles outside their normal discipline. In this way, the flatter organisation structure has offered enhanced career mobility, in contrast to the experience of many organisations. Job grading structures have been simplified to four broad bands. This again aids switching among roles.

Practical ways to improve the business have been sought through the 'Eureka' suggestions scheme, which rewards good ideas. Business process reengineering examines traditional tasks and managers are expected to join teams working on such projects.

Senior management support the staff development programme. They look to sustain commitment and opportunity through a policy of internal appointments. This will reinforce the friendly and informal culture that prevails. Of the 50 headquarters managers passing through the development centre, only one has resigned. Individuals recognise the advantages of a personal development plan. Liz Stephens had been working on hers for two years before being promoted to manager level. She cited the extra confidence and recognition gained in the process as contributors to her advancement. In a survey, 84 per cent of staff agreed that the Skipton Building Society cared about their development. For its commitment, the society has twice won the prestigious Investor in People award.

Training extends to all levels of the society. For example, it has 15 modern apprenticeships at headquarters on a scheme commended for its effectiveness and prospects, although lacking in overall structure.

Introduction

The Skipton Building Society believes that success depends mostly on its people. 'Our aim is to offer customers the very highest standards of service. One vital ingredient is the professionalism of our staff.'[2] No longer able to offer people 'jobs for life', it recognises that preparing them for the future is critical in terms of recruitment and retention of the best. Meanwhile, it provides a pool of talent and experience from which the next generation of senior managers can be drawn.

Managing the development of people, commonly known as *human resource management*, involves many practices sketched by Mary Allison in our opening quotation. The core activities of most HRM functions will be described in the first part of this chapter. Then we shall consider issues about which there are questions and doubts. Four follow the main themes of this book: ethics, quality, international contexts and practice within SMEs. HR managers are also taxed by questions of equal opportunities and we shall illustrate these by looking at the role and rights of women in employment and management. First, however, we shall consider what HRM is.

What is human resource management?

At a deeper level than issues of practice in HRM lies the question of what it is. As we see later in the chapter, there are considerable variations in the way the function is seen in different parts of the world. Even within nations, however, opinions vary. Truss and colleagues[3] note two distinct descriptions of HRM, soft and hard. The difference arises from whether the emphasis in the HRM label is placed on the *human* or the *resource*. Broadly, the former, soft HRM, is related to the human relations movement, the growth of individual talent and McGregor's Theory Y, *see* Exhibit 1.14. Hard HRM, on the other hand, is based on planning the resource in the same way as any other, fitting it in with the needs of the environment incorporated in the business plan, and McGregor's Theory X. A mind map of these points and their consequences appears in Figure 14.1.

As with many management models, the hard and soft approaches can be seen as the ends of a scale. Much practice displays a mix. In a study of eight leading British companies, Truss and colleagues looked to see whether one approach predominated. They found that many managers expressed the dual aims of the soft model, which are business development with personal growth. Yet this was mostly management rhetoric. Training is a good example. '[It] was taking place in the organizations, [yet] the *aim* of much of this training was not the development of the individual as an end in itself, but ensuring that individuals had the skills necessary to carry out their jobs in such a way as to improve organizational performance. One side-effect of this training could be individual development, but it was not an explicit aim.'[4] Other managers seem to reject the soft model altogether. Siebert and colleagues refer to 'toadyish professionals ... too ready to make a distinction between developing individuals and conducting business'.[5]

The soft approach is exemplified by the so-called Harvard framework[6] in which the outcomes of HRM are:

- *In the short term* – commitment, competence, congruence and cost effectiveness.

- *In the long term* – individual well-being, organisational effectiveness and societal well-being.

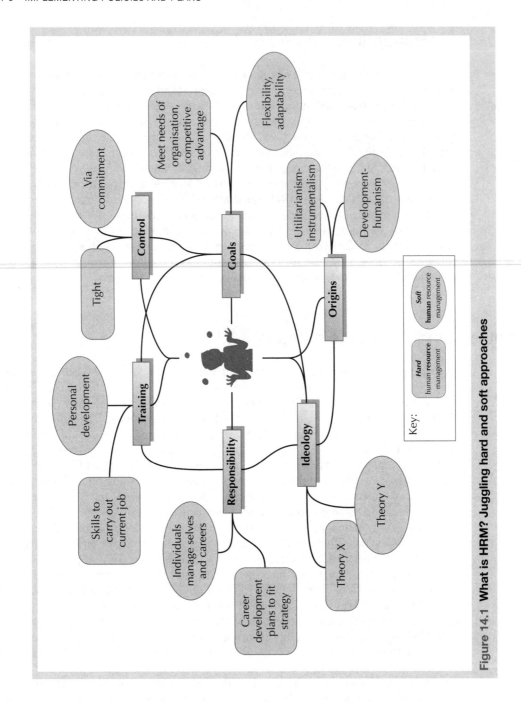

Figure 14.1 What is HRM? Juggling hard and soft approaches

Note how this approach envisages a positive-sum game. All stakeholders gain if they take part. In contrast, the hard approach sees HRM as processes that link business strategy to human behaviour at work.[7] The aim is to carry out business policies in an optimal way from the organisation's point of view. It means managing:

■ personnel flows – that is recruitment, development and leaving;

■ work systems – job design as part of process design;

■ reward systems – formalising notions of fairness and motivation;

■ employee relations – links between the organisation and groups of staff.

The Skipton case illustrates these points. An expressed aim was to have career development guided by each individual. In this ideal, senior managers create opportunities both for development and for a choice of promotions. Staff choose the direction and extent of their participation. Meanwhile, the society has to press on with strategic change. It wants its HR strategy to deliver a flow of new managers who can operate in the new, competitive market environment. Practice combines self-control with harder aspects such as team bonuses matched to sales targets and performance appraisal by managers and peers. The tension is clear.

It is not easy to translate 'motherhood' statements about building 'the professionalism of our staff' into actions for staff in the personnel department. HR managers have to convert such aims into practice while recognising many constraints. In doing so, they move from the rhetoric of the soft model to the practices presented more clearly in the hard version. HRM is pushed towards personnel management, a term that has gone out of fashion. While HRM incorporates notions of both strategy and practice, personnel management has connotations of putting business policies into effect. Studies show that most organisations eschew a strategic approach, concentrating more on conventional personnel practice.[8] Here, the function supports line managers with specialist advice and skills.

Activities of the HRM function

Taking the hard, practice-oriented view of HRM, we can use the following definition:

> *Human resource management is the creation, development and maintenance of an effective workforce, matching the requirements of the organisation and responding to the environment.*

The definition, seeing the people subsystem in the context of the whole organisation and external influences, covers the processes laid out in Figure 14.2. The diagram shows how the three broad HRM activities occur in a continuous cycle. Within each of the creation, development and maintenance categories there are process elements as shown. We shall begin with creating the workforce and its first element, planning.

■ Human resource planning

Planning focuses on the complete approach to satisfying needs for human resources. Processes such as recruitment and promotion are expensive investments,

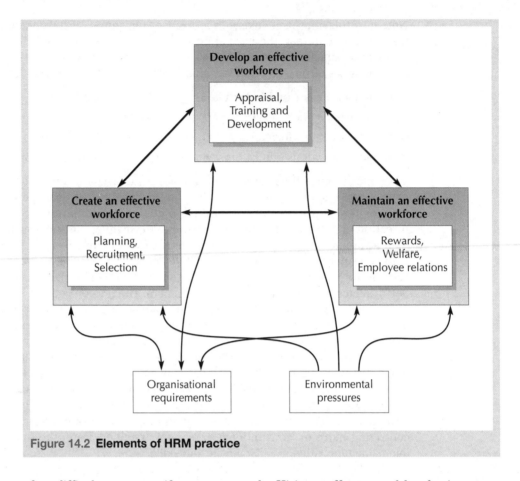

Figure 14.2 **Elements of HRM practice**

often difficult to reverse if errors are made. Hiring staff on an *ad hoc* basis puts at risk continuity and development of the whole team. A planning approach counters these difficulties through both analysing current needs and anticipating future changes. Environmental or business changes can quickly lead to a mismatch between ideal and actual staffing levels. Exhibit 14.1 shows how environmental change, here in the political policy arena, can create new issues for the human resource manager.

In another example, we can note how the strategy of creating external alliances demands new staff expertise. While there is no one way to form and maintain these alliances, clearly they involve closer and deeper relations between partners. Activities include vendor rating, technical co-operation, and auditing of processes, quality and costs. One report noted, 'Working with suppliers is becoming more important ... supply of materials, products, and expertise ... represents a relatively greater proportion of the cost and lead time which are key elements in competitiveness.'[9] Yet management performance is often poor.

Collaborative relations have implications for HRM. Not only do the skills of current 'boundary-spanning' staff have to be enhanced, but many more become involved in new 'brokerage' roles, *see* Chapter 10. For some, this will be the first time they have engaged in such activity and it has implications for training and

> **Exhibit 14.1** Nuclear Electric: manpower planning under uncertain political conditions
>
> Nuclear Electric (now British Energy Generation) was responsible for the construction and operation of nuclear power stations in the United Kingdom. Although construction was the responsibility of civil engineering contractors, Nuclear Electric required, during construction, its own mix of design, supervisory and commissioning specialists. When each station was complete, needs changed to operating engineers with yet different skills.
>
> To maintain continuity of employment among skill groups, the company relied on a steady construction programme. Indeed, a programme constraint was the supply of staff to put it into effect. In the late 1980s, however, it became clear that the government would not place any new orders. Nuclear Electric had to decide what to do with its staff once the construction programme was complete. In its analysis, the company examined the skills, age and other details of all its engineers. It offered severance terms to those it could no longer employ and retraining opportunities to others who could eventually become operators. Since Nuclear Electric was the main employer of such experts in the country, it was not feasible to obtain new people through the labour market.

development. Moreover, there are cases where the HR policies themselves begin to be transferred from one company to another. Marks & Spencer, for instance, has a strong HR culture and has for many years been prepared to advise its suppliers on practice.[10]

Whatever its context, the outcome of the human resource planning process is a detailed analysis of the staffing requirements for the organisation. Included in the plan will be a statement of how the gaps are to be filled. As shown by the scheme drawn up by the Skipton Building Society, the gaps may be filled by a mixture of recruitment and development of suitable personnel. Recruitment may be internal or external and will, in any case, be followed by appropriate training.

■ Recruitment

The second element of creating a workforce, recruitment, means finding staff whose attributes match available jobs. Figure 14.3 sketches a simplified flow model of the recruitment and selection procedure. The first steps are to decide whether a new person is required. This means defining the requirements of the job and clarifying that it cannot be done by current employees, or removed altogether. Then efforts are made to ensure that sufficient candidates of appropriate calibre come forward for selection. Meanwhile, the firm considers how the choice is to be made. For all but casual appointments, there is a series of filters to remove less suitable prospects until a shortlist is presented for the final choice. Filters may include checks on qualifications, skills and experience, physical and psychological tests and so on.

The aim of recruitment is to encourage suitable applicants to apply but the process should not look to maximise their number. Filters screen out unsuitable people even at the initial stage of advertising. Gone are the days when 'Boy wanted. Apply within' would be regarded as adequate. Not only is there no information as to the nature of the job but also the notice is clearly unfair. Recruitment, therefore, needs to be realistic and fair.

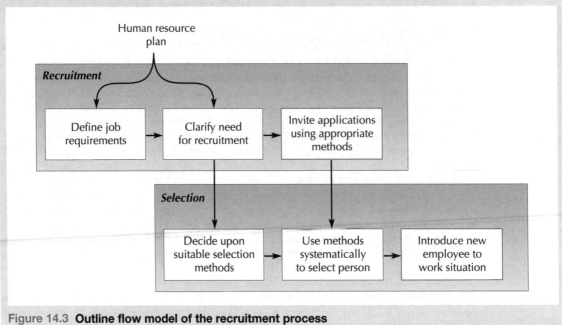

Figure 14.3 Outline flow model of the recruitment process

Exhibit 14.2 Job advertisement

Project Officer

£17 055–£18 180 (3 Year Contract)
The Council's Regeneration Plan provides a framework for addressing the economic and community needs of the Borough. An officer is required to help develop and implement a range of regeneration projects, working with community organisations, agencies and funding partners. You will have particular responsibility for projects in and around Okehampton and you will be responsible for the Council's efforts to promote the development and use of public transport.

You will have four years relevant experience, a good understanding of rural development issues and a proven ability to work independently in conjunction with local communities.

For an application form and job description, please contact ...

Realism

For the first point, an organisation can help itself by publishing exact information about the job. For instance, if there are attributes or qualifications that are definitely required of applicants, they should be stated. The example shown in Exhibit 14.2 illustrates good practice.[11] Within a small 6 × 10 cm space, the council outlines the post and specifies both the attributes it is seeking and key terms of the contract. It is normal to expand on these in the mailing prepared for enquirers.

Fairness

Recruiting procedures must be fair. Not only are there legal requirements in many countries but many managers and organisations recognise ethical considerations too. We have insufficient space to explore the range of issues such as positive discrimination (or affirmative action) and how they appear in different nations. We shall confine ourselves to two common pitfalls in the United Kingdom setting. First, *direct discrimination* occurs when an organisation unlawfully selects on the grounds of sex, race and disability.[12] There are two exceptions: *authenticity*, for example, in acting or clothes modelling gender can be specified; and in some kinds of personal *service*, such as childcare or home nursing. The second pitfall is more subtle. *Indirect discrimination* occurs when an organisation's behaviour has unintended consequences that restrict the rights of groups of people. In recruitment, bias can be introduced innocently, for example, through choice of language or advertising media.

At the board mill in Queensferry in the 1980s it was normal to 'ask around the shop floor' when recruiting for unskilled vacancies. This gained by producing applicants known to current staff. They would, therefore, be appraised of what the work was like. Managers' tasks were made easier by this informal process; there was little paperwork and expense, and jobs could be filled within days. The problem was that the method discriminated indirectly. The net was trawled among people whom current workers already knew. Therefore, the racial mix within the plant reproduced itself. It did not match changes in the town.

■ Selection

Selection completes the stage of creation of the workforce. It involves choosing employees from among the pool recruited. Since the validity of any selection method is, at best, moderate, good practice means using a combination to improve the chances of success.

A well-designed application form presents candidate information so that unsuitable applicants can be eliminated. For instance, people can be rejected because they are unqualified, cannot start immediately or simply do not complete the form. A clear form also helps where applicants have to be ranked. In times of high unemployment, it is common to hear from many people who satisfy the basic criteria. Ranking should be done with care to avoid indirect discrimination. If, for example, closeness to the place of work is used, racial bias may be introduced.

> ***Validity*** *refers to how closely the results of a selection test match a person's later job performance.*

Interview

The interview is the most widely used technique and sometimes the only one. The *unstructured* interview, with neither a prepared schedule nor systematic scoring, should be avoided. Its flexibility can be an advantage but also a weakness. Many managers believe they are good interviewers but do not recognise that the validity of unstructured interviews is low. Discussions stray into irrelevant or personal issues that, interacting with the prejudices of the interviewer, lead to poor decisions. In legal challenges to bias, it has been difficult to defend the unstructured interview.

Exhibit 14.3 Structured interview schedule

Question category	Information sought	Example from machine shop supervisor
Situational	The applicant's ability to handle the range of challenges met on the job.	What would you do if you saw an employee wrongly removing a machine guard?
Job knowledge	The applicant's knowledge of practical, technical, legal, etc. aspects of the job.	Can you explain to me the various grades of tungsten carbide?
Job simulation	The applicant's ability to carry out critical aspects of the job.	What instructions would you give if you were asked to arrange for ... to be done?
Personal requirements	The applicant's ability to fit the job needs such as hours, travel, location and so on.	Are you willing to work nights if asked to do so?

Effectiveness follows planning. In the *structured* interview, all are asked a series of job-related questions. Exhibit 14.3 shows four categories of information with examples from a supervisory job. While some of these data could be elicited before the interview, it may be useful to check or ask for clarification. The four categories of Exhibit 14.3 are not definitive. In selecting apprentices or young graduates, an organisation may be as concerned with potential as with current abilities. Therefore, qualifications and references will be important and the interviewer may probe attitudes to learning.

Although the structured interview may seem to have advantages, its rigidity restricts contact among participants. As Chapter 13 showed, conversation involves parties in two-way flows, alternately speaking and listening as the interaction unfolds. This is effective use of the face-to-face channel. A good interviewer, therefore, uses some structure, but must allow flexibility for fruitful communication.

Having a panel of interviewers, although expensive, helps in removing personal bias. In any case, the structured interview provides a formal basis for recording results that can be referred to if its outcomes are challenged later.

Selection tests

While structuring improves the interview validity, it remains imperfect. This has stimulated the search for other forms of selection. Tests include written assignments and simulation exercises. The former can be used to assess intelligence, aptitude, attitudes and personality. Cooper, Baker and Maddocks note marked increase in the use of psychological tests in the United Kingdom.[13] This has arisen from their apparent reliability and ease of use. Further questions concern the obligation of testers to the test takers, for many subjects have been unhappy with the experience. In the United States, legal challenges have been brought over the intrusiveness and relevance of some tests. Ethical standards should ensure that: candidates are treated fairly and with dignity; staff are competent to apply the tests and give feedback on results; and the tests are valid for selection. The British Psychological Society advises that tests should be used alongside other methods and only when their application can be validated.

McHenry takes up the validity point.[14] Noting the rise in use over twenty years from 10 to 75 per cent of companies in the United Kingdom, he fears that many tests are ineffective and biased on cultural and gender grounds. Those imported from the

United States have been calibrated using alien and out-of-date norms. For instance, one test has the statement, 'I very much like hunting'. About 70 per cent of American men agree with this statement, but only 10 per cent of British. Gender biases are shown by statements such as, 'I think I would make a good leader of people'. Men agree with this twice as often as women do. Are they twice as likely to be good leaders, or are women more modest about their abilities? We cannot answer these questions here but can conclude that tests need to be used with great care by competent people.

Furnham notes widespread scepticism among managers. He notes that professionalisation of HRM has stimulated the growth of psychometric testing and questions the validity of links between results and job performance. Long-term links are especially unclear, as when a firm recruits people for managerial careers. What is the best predictor of potential? Furnham quotes one study of middle-aged, middle ranking managers:

> The list of factors thought to be relevant was long: which school they went to; position in the family; age of first mortgage; sport preferences, etc. In fact, this study found that for those middle-aged Britons the best predictor of managerial success was at what age they first travelled abroad: the younger the better.[15]

Furnham relates this odd result to the observation that, in the days when travel was more expensive and difficult, only adventurous and curious parents took their children overseas. Did these parental characteristics result in their children's later success? We cannot tell, but the story illustrates the difficulty of validation. The correlation emerged only in retrospect and could hardly have been predicted. Moreover, it is a statement about the past; easier travel and lower xenophobia mean the result cannot apply in the future.

Notwithstanding the difficulties, the hope of finding a few carefully researched questions that will predict good job performance is not as far-fetched as it may sound. Telephone interviewing is usual in the catering and leisure industries where large numbers of seasonal workers have to be recruited quickly. Exhibit 14.4

Exhibit 14.4 DIY recruitment

Staff turnover at B&Q has fallen from 35 to 29 per cent since its automated selection system was introduced in 1999. The DIY chain has also been praised for recruiting older workers. Each of the annual 200 000 job applicants contacts a call centre. After a person collects details, a machine conducts the interview. Responses to a personality questionnaire cover values, outlook, conscientiousness, aspirations, integrity and cleanliness. They assess whether a candidate's personality fits the company's values: customer focus, 'can do', striving, down to earth and respect for people.

A five-point scale is used for statements such as 'I believe most people will steal if they can get away with it' or 'Nothing gives me a buzz like dealing with a customer.' Afterwards, the system sends a letter telling candidates whether they are suitable. Results are supplied to store managers without names or indicators of age, gender or ethnicity. Only after this first stage are previous skills and experience examined. Final selection is done locally by interview.

In 2003 different tests for roles such as customer service, logistics or night crews have been introduced. Sets of 80 questions are based on measures of the performance and personality of 1000 current employees. As well as being used for selection, these should reveal likely team leaders, or people with leadership potential. After the test, each applicant receives a personality report, with data set against population norms and supported by explanations.

explains how the how DIY chain B&Q uses automated psychometric testing at one stage of selection.[16]

Assessment centres

Assessment centres are commonly used for selecting managers and higher-grade technical personnel. The curious name refers to the place where candidates are assembled, sometimes for several days. They are tested and engage in social exchanges with potential colleagues and superiors. The tests involve a series of managerial simulations, such as in-basket exercises, role playing and group tasks, as well as psychometric tests and interviews. A panel of trained assessors observes how each candidate makes decisions as well as their interpersonal and communication skills. Beyond selection, variants on assessment centres can be used for appraisal and promotion. In the opening case, Skipton Building Society used a centre to identify managers' development needs.

Clearly, as with all HRM practices, recruitment and selection must be done with care. Not only are failure costs high but also the process builds an implicit contract between organisation and candidate. In return for undergoing selection procedures, people expect them to be valid and fair. It is good practice to explain the procedure before it starts.

Nowhere are the high costs of recruitment and selection seen more clearly than among military pilots. Success cannot be forecast before training begins. The Royal Air Force seeks minimum wastage while maintaining an adequate supply of pilots. Since training also involves considerable personal commitment, the RAF ensures that those who do not make the grade switch to other roles. Exhibit 14.5 traces the process.[17]

Exhibit 14.5 Integrated selection and training in the RAF

The Royal Air Force needs to maintain a planned ratio of pilots to aircraft. Pilots both fly and act as officers; they must have appropriate skills and be leaders of others. Initial selection for this demanding role is based on tests and interviews. All who pass move on to courses of initial officer training and basic flying. Then there are three streams: Fast Jet; Multi-Engine; or Helicopter. The Fast Jet role is the most demanding. These trainees move on to Advanced Training and then Operations Conversion. Each stage builds up the accumulated investment in the pilot, who can fail at any point. The cost of training one Fast Jet pilot is estimated at £1.5 million.

■ Performance appraisal

We now move on to consider staff development. As shown in Figure 14.2, this has two elements, appraisal and training and development. Performance appraisal means evaluating people in their jobs to make relevant decisions. These cover pay, promotion, training and development, counselling and human resource planning. Although formal systems are being extended to cover more managers and supervisors, they are rarely used for junior staff. In these cases, any assessment is based on direct measures such as output and quality, often as part of a bonus scheme.

Appraisal interviews form the core of many formal systems. They incur the same problems of fairness and consistency explained above. Interviews need, therefore, to be set in a framework of planning, training and control. Planning an effective and equitable system means answering the following questions:

■ *What is the purpose of the appraisal scheme?*

Appraisal is more than a manager's assessment of a person's progress. From the exchange arise opportunities to improve relationships, share problems and enhance team performance. Sometimes, results are used for assessing bonuses, although such practice can restrict frank discussion.

■ *Who should be appraised?*

While extending appraisal to all staff helps to break down barriers, it is often seen as impractical to cover more than managers and supervisors.

■ *Who should appraise?*

Immediate managers are usually involved although the inclusion of more senior people could improve communications and spread a sense of fairness. Also advocated is all-round appraisal, known as '360-degree feedback', under which responses are gathered from those who depend on a person's performance. These include colleagues, subordinates and even suppliers and customers. One sample showed the use of 360-degree appraisal in fewer than half of large United Kingdom companies, although the number was growing.[18] Supporters of 360-degree feedback recognise the differences between perceptions by others and how we perceive ourselves. Men overrate themselves in self-appraisal whereas women do the opposite. Since successful people tend to have a self-image close to how they are seen by others, closing the gap should be beneficial. Critics, however, point to process cost and the stress caused in a few companies when results are linked to pay.

■ *What training and preparation do appraisers need?*

Training and plans support consistency among all appraisers. For example, three general orientations towards assessment have been identified. First, *trait-oriented appraisal* is the weakest and most susceptible to prejudice. Concentrating on personality traits, such as charm, stated ambition or initiative, is hardly connected with job outcomes. Second, *outcome-oriented appraisal* refers to how objectives are set and achieved. While having the appearance of rationality, it has the disadvantage of referring to individual goals, thus making comparison among staff difficult. Using this approach for pay review is especially problematic. Third, *behaviour-oriented appraisal* concentrates on behaviour relevant to the job. It is usually the most effective. Establishing reliable dimensions is time consuming, however, and is only likely to be worthwhile in large organisations with many similar jobs.[19]

■ *When should appraisals be conducted?*

Although, as we noted in Chapter 11, speedy feedback is an important element of motivation, annual appraisals are the most common. This pattern encourages managers to conduct the process thoroughly. Intervals, however, should match the nature of the organisation, the scheme and the people involved. There may be more than one session per year in dynamic situations, for inexperienced staff or for those with problems.

■ *Who sees the results?*

Open reporting, that is sharing results openly, may inhibit open discussion between boss and subordinate. On the other hand, too closed a system may reduce confidence of participants in its fairness. It is normal, therefore, to share reports among appraisee, appraiser, appraiser's manager and an independent monitor whose role is to assess how the scheme is working. Appraisees often read the report before completion; they add comments before signing.

■ *What about monitoring?*

Monitoring occurs at both the detailed and broad levels. Agreements for change made between boss and subordinate are recorded and followed up in 'action plans' before the next round. Examples include training opportunities or changes to the way work is carried out. More broadly, the independent monitor has to check that practice is consistent, fair and lawful.

■ Training and development

Training and development needs are often identified in the appraisal process. Indeed, for the soft HRM organisation, they will be its most important outcome. Training is *the provision of guided experience to change employee behaviour, attitudes or opinions*. According to Mullins, its benefits are as follows:

- greater confidence, commitment and motivation of staff;
- recognition and greater responsibility matched by improvements in pay;
- feelings of personal satisfaction and achievement with enhanced career prospects; and
- improved availability and quality of staff.[20]

To this list we can add, from the trainee's point of view, enhanced job mobility.

Implied within the definition of training is the notion that change is to be related to the job. Planning a training programme, therefore, starts with a comparison between the attributes needed to do the job effectively and those already possessed by the employee. This *training needs analysis* identifies specific gaps. In turn, the training plan is designed to fill them.

In principle, therefore, each trainee is different. Each needs a tailored plan. Managers then face the costs of a bespoke service. In practice, employees undertake standardised training packages despite their not needing every element of them. While wasting some resources, this may be the most efficient supply method. Worse waste occurs when training is given as a sort of reward in spite of subjects not needing it. Lloyds Bank wasted 40 per cent of its effort largely because individuals received it when it was 'their turn'.[21] Experienced trainers find that up to a tenth of participants on external courses attend few sessions after registration. They regard such events as informal holidays in pleasant locations.

Training takes place either at the workplace or away from it. The advantages and disadvantages are summarised in Exhibit 14.6. Off-the-job methods are often criticised for the difficulty of incorporating learning directly into the workplace. Unless the training aligns with other changes, the subject may unlearn immediately the new ideas and skills. A combination of on- and off-the-job modes should ensure retention and optimise the application of new skills. For this to happen, the training should:

- occur in settings similar to the job;
- enlarge the trainee's experience;
- offer challenges not normally encountered by the trainee;
- enable learning of underlying concepts rather than 'recipe following';
- occur when the employee can best appreciate the programme's benefits;
- use a tempo suiting the employee's capacities for learning and reflection.

Exhibit 14.6 Comparison between on-the-job and off-the-job training

	Advantages	Disadvantages
On-the-job training	Learning directly applicable.	May offer only narrow experience.
	May not need specialised trainers.	Bad habits passed to the trainee.
	Trainee contributes to output.	Trainee may inhibit productivity.
	Cheap.	
Off-the-job training	Suitable for tasks not currently practised.	Difficult to match to individual's needs in the job setting.
	Vital when trainees' errors may risk disaster or be expensive.	May need expensive development and testing if to be effective.
	Offers wider experience and practice in unusual situations.	Expensive to operate.
	Training experience may be more readily planned and directed.	Attendance at special training centres used to reward performance, not to meet need.

For example, in training a clerk in the use of new software, off-the-job training means experts can deliver it without interruption. Modules can teach procedures, explain the reasons for them and allow practice. Later, the programme may switch to the work situation, giving the trainee access to the software for live use. Other examples of off-the-job training are simulators for airline pilots. Compare these with on-the-job practice for car drivers. In the former, much has to be done before pilots can take over a real aircraft. In the latter, most people come to the driving school knowing much of the task context. The learner driver has to rehearse skills that have to be combined and made intuitive before passing the test.

Cultural differences in training

Designing training programmes from job-based analysis can lead to narrow prescriptions if the short-term behavioural approach is overemphasised. For example, bank trainees are taught all the processes that working in a branch entails. Yet the service function must go further than simply counting cash or checking customers' accounts. It involves relating to customers at the personal level. Generally, Western employers try to achieve this through influencing employees' *attitudes*. For example, they stress that 'the customer is always right' and that being pleasant is always the best way. Training programmes include elements on how to handle awkward situations. Within this general framework, however, staff are encouraged to express their own personality when they give service. Along with other leading retail organisations, banks rely on selection and guided development to produce staff with good interpersonal skills Development both improves skills and motivates staff towards delivering high-quality service.[22]

Contrast this with the way service training is traditionally given in Japan. Figure 14.4 is based on one of many sketches in the training manual of the Hiroshima Sogo Bank.[23] The book features dozens of instructions on how to behave in service settings. Greetings, addressing clients, colleagues and superiors, and many other

Figure 14.4 **To pour tea, half fill each cup. Then top up in reverse order**

aspects of social behaviour are set out in detail. Formal social processes are, of course, much more important in Japan than in most Western countries. Therefore, employers stress *behaviour* in their training.

Limitations of training needs analysis – the development perspective

The above remarks mention that training based simply on needs analysis sets arbitrary limits on the scope and time scale of expected benefits. The wider perspective, usually called development, looks to enhance competences beyond those presented by the immediate job. Bergenhenegouwen and colleagues identify four levels of competence that are relevant to how people carry out their work:[24]

■ *First level*
Knowledge and skills that enable the occupation, job or task to be done properly.

■ *Second level*
Intermediate skills applicable in a wide range of job settings: social and communicative abilities, general technical and vocational insights, organisational qualities and basic approaches to work situations.

■ *Third level*
Values, standards, ethics and morals of the person, the organisation and any professional group to which the person belongs. These are learned by the person through insights, experiences and education and are expressed through a special mentality, a specific view of the world, and distinctive opinions about culture, worth and traditions. This is the personal and professional frame of reference.

■ *Fourth level*
Deeper-lying personal characteristics, such as groundedness, image of self, motives and the source of the enthusiasm and effort that goes into work. Hardly visible to others, these factors nevertheless strongly influence how a person acts in work situations.

The first level corresponds to the behavioural training mentioned in the Hiroshima Sogo bank example. The second is closer to the development of attitudes favoured in Western banks. The third is exemplified by professional development programmes that are less directly related to the immediate task. Much of the Skipton programme is concerned with developing managers who have a 'personal and professional service' frame of reference. The fourth, deepest level can only incidentally be affected by training programmes so Bergenhenegouwen and colleagues recommend that such traits be looked for at the selection stage. The authors go on to question how a competence-oriented development programme may be steered. In response, they refer to the notion of organisational core competences and suggest that the challenge for HRM professionals is to link these to individual development.

Motorola requires all employees to complete at least 40 hours' training each year. For managers, the emphasis is on doing international business. Motorola recognises that competitive advantage, even for a high-technology firm, will flow from being able to deal in different cultures. Sales in India are expected to overtake those in the United States by 2005. The company has several new learning programmes such as an MBA spread between five business schools. Since the future is uncertain, the key is to develop managers who can cope with whatever it brings. Flexibility is more important than developing skills related to a defined job.[25]

■ Rewards

The third block of Figure 14.2 covers the means of maintaining an effective workforce. The first feature we shall examine is the reward system. HRM staff are involved in setting up a system of payment and other benefits, which combine general design principles and relate to factors within and without the organisation, *see* Figure 14.5.[26] Relevant issues arise both in all organisational subsystems – goals, structure, technology and people – and in key environments – the business and labour markets, the legal framework and stakeholders such as trade unions. Finally, a pay and benefits system should be designed so that it works well. Through efficiency and consistency it will avoid disputes and problems while contributing to achievement of organisational objectives.

Limited space means that, in the rest of this section, we shall concentrate on payment systems. This does not mean that other benefits do not matter. In some settings, they are more important than the term 'fringe benefits' would suggest. Depending on the country, up to 30 per cent of labour costs cover medical insurance, pensions and help with housing, schooling, childcare, further education and transport.

Lockyer also notes a shift in emphasis away from negotiated collective agreements. This follows pressures to integrate HRM into business strategy:

■ *the reduction of labour costs through more-efficient and flexible patterns of work organisation and division;*

■ *the introduction of more-flexible and efficient technologies;*

■ *increased control over the employee, to reduce the gap between potential and actual performance, to generate employee commitment rather than compliance;*

■ *a move towards the individualisation of employment relations.*[27]

While these items can all be found in Figure 14.5, the emphasis is changing. An inconsistent pattern of flexibility, individuality and expectations of commitment, combined with teamwork, cultural change and close control, is replacing the traditional collective agreements of the past. Pay schemes are increasingly seen as a tool of management rather than a bargain between management and employees.

Fixed and variable payment schemes

The complex demands placed on a payment system, including efficiency, fairness, motivation, flexibility and so on, mean that every organisation comes up with its

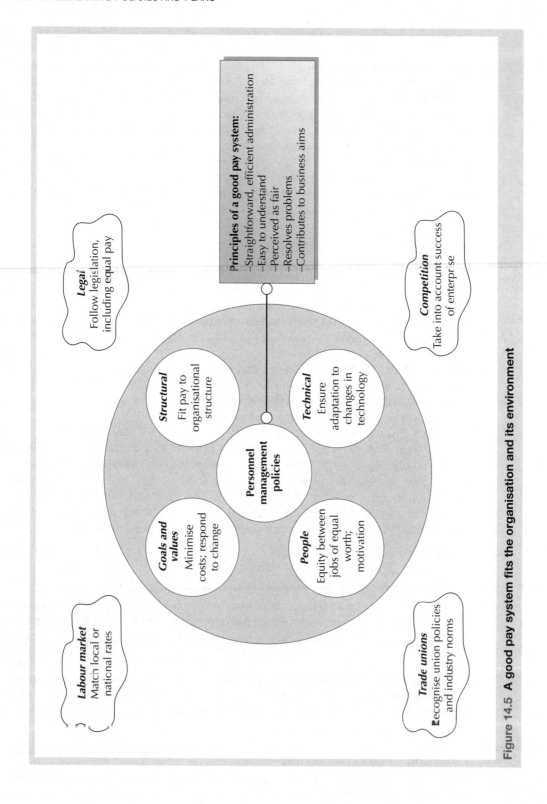

Figure 14.5 A good pay system fits the organisation and its environment

own formula. Conventionally, schemes have been compared according to whether pay is fixed or variable. As noted in Chapter 11, fixed pay methods are the dominant form; about 83 per cent of United Kingdom employees are paid this way. Most are based on time; payment is by the hour, week or month and does not vary according to effort. In quota-based schemes, sometimes called in factories *measured day-work*, staff are paid a fixed rate when they have achieved an agreed work quota irrespective of the time taken. They operate as if they were subcontractors.

Variable pay has two broad types according to whether alterations relate to characteristics of the person, or to his or her effort. In the former, which we can call *input-based* schemes, variations are based on length of service, skills or other factors that the company regards as important. *Output-based* schemes match pay to achievement of work targets. The oldest and simplest of these is piecework. Employees are paid for each item produced at a rate traditionally set by negotiation with the supervisor or, more recently, by work-study. Piecework survives among outworkers, who again act as if they were subcontractors, and among many sales people, who call it commission. In each case, success can be directly related to the person's efforts. It is unsuited, therefore, to work paced by machines, such as production lines, or where there is a high degree of interdependence among members of a team.

Levels of aggregation

Another consideration is whether each person should be treated separately or rewards should be shared among teams or, possibly, across the whole organisation. This problem arises from one of the tensions mentioned above – the desire to stimulate personal effort and commitment compared with group co-operation or loyalty to the whole business. We often find a bit of both. Sometimes, weekly or monthly individual incentives are combined with annual bonuses shared by all. The annual bonus is sometimes the only variable element. Following a 5 per cent increase in sales to 2003, not-for-profit retailer John Lewis increased its salary bonus from 9 to 10 per cent for all its 58 800 partners.[28] Benefits of such an arrangement, such as long-term loyalty, have to be balanced against the loss of a link to effort and demotivation if bonuses fall.

Exhibit 14.7 Pay for individuals, groups and the organisation

	Individual	Work group	Whole organisation
Fixed rate by time or for a work quota	Hourly rate; measured day-work; job rate; annualised hours; annual salary.	Quota-based payments to work teams.	Standard rates across the whole organisation.
Input-based variable	Seniority or merit pay; skill-based pay; qualification-based pay; suggestions and other reward schemes.	Skill, contribution to the group; peer assessment based.	Discretionary profit-sharing and share bonuses to individuals based on competence, potential contribution or scarcity.
Output-based variable	Piecework; payment by results; performance-based pay.	Team bonuses.	Share options, joint ownership and profit-related pay available to all.

Comparing fixed and variable pay with three levels of hierarchy produces a typology of pay schemes illustrated in Exhibit 14.7.[29] Many variations and hybrid schemes mean that the table is just an outline of what is found in practice. The complexity of many arrangements, some of which have grown up over decades, is illustrated by the pay of train drivers, *see* Exhibit 14.8.[30]

Exhibit 14.8 Driving a bargain

Until the privatisation of British Rail, drivers were paid according to nationally agreed scales. A basic, pensionable salary of about £12 000 per year could be topped up by six or more allowances to £15 000. A further £6000 to £7000 overtime pay meant that the average package came to a little over £21 000. The extras included merit pay, flexibility allowances, mileage bonuses, bonuses for 'knowing the road' (that is learning more routes), driving fast trains, walking time and so on.

After passenger services were taken over by 25 operators, HR managers sought new schemes aimed at: simplification of job grades and pay components; versatility through flexible hours and benefits; incentives to take on more training, development and education; and participation in business success. For example, Midland Main Line agreed to cut the average working week and pay a basic £20 850. In return, drivers gave up most enhancements and agreed to work more flexibly.

Pay structure

Whatever the principles of the pay scheme, the question of deciding how much to pay each person remains. This means finding a balance among the HRM objectives discussed above. Negotiation, either with each employee or through trade unions, is one approach. Yet it creates tensions as rates are set according to bargaining power as opposed to shared understandings of job factors. The result is an *ad hoc* series of agreements with many inconsistencies. The next section deals with a formal approach that is widely accepted as fair.

Job evaluation

Job evaluation is a process of comparing all the jobs in the organisation both with each other and with benchmarks outside. It can be used to set both fixed and variable rates. The starting point is often a collective agreement on the nature of the process and how it will be carried out. Investigations are conducted either by small panels drawn from among managers and staff representatives or by outside consultants. Panels arbitrate in reviews, such as at Sainsbury, which used them in a project to develop a more consultative management style.[31]

The most straightforward method of evaluation is *job ranking*. Using the general criterion of benefit to the organisation, the panel lists all jobs in rank order. Then, key jobs spread throughout the list are chosen for rating. Pay rates are decided either by negotiation or by surveying the labour market. This task is not for the job evaluation committee, which remains neutral. Using the benchmark rates, however, the rest of the jobs are filled in by extrapolation.

In large, dispersed organisations, the committee would not be familiar with all jobs. Here, *job classification* improves upon ranking by setting out a list of bands or classes into which all jobs have to be fitted. Each band is given a description with examples. The pay review sets the rate for each band, with the possibility of variations for merit or long service. Job classification is common in government and large commercial organisations. One snag is that fitting the bands involves comparing dissimilar jobs and leads to many appeals for regrading.

Answering some of these difficulties, a *point plan* assigns points to predetermined attributes, for example, skill requirement, responsibility, effort and working conditions. These may be subdivided. Scoring takes place on agreed scales and the totals become the points values to be used in ranking.

Job evaluation gains by bringing methods of pay determination out into the open. Some managers may rue the loss of flexibility offered by more *ad hoc* arrangements. For instance, lack of flexibility may make it difficult to keep a valued employee who receives a better offer from elsewhere.

Welfare

The second element of maintaining an efficient workforce is welfare. Practices in this area have often grown out of the philanthropic or human relations approaches to HRM. In a mid-twentieth century factory, for example, the staff welfare unit would: supply work clothes at low prices; offer loans to families in difficulties; provide counselling and health advice; act *in loco parentis* for apprentices; and maintain links with sick or retired staff. Nowadays, especially in smaller or less traditional organisations, many of these functions are left to others. Line managers, colleagues and friends may or may not find the time.

The question for the HR manager is how far an employer should be responsible for the welfare of employees and their families. Let us take the example of stress. Many applaud the introduction of high-performance manufacturing systems based on the ideas of lean production, teamwork and quality circles. Cappelli and Rogovsky show how these changes demand better decisions, a higher pace of working and more commitment from employees.[32] About a quarter of employees find their work 'very stressful'.[33] Should the employer be concerned with avoiding excess stress or mitigating its effects?

Among organisations learning how to help their staff cope with stress are the non-government organisations (NGOs) engaged in overseas aid. It was estimated that some 200 NGOs were involved in relief during the 1994 Rwandan civil war. Some of these were small and ineffective. They sent inexperienced workers out to central Africa for two or three weeks at a time. Yet many agencies throughout the world had problems in finding staff who could go at short notice and speak French. Stress can hardly be avoided. One study showed, unsurprisingly, that witnessing suffering is the major cause. Yet other factors, such as poor communications and rivalry with expatriate colleagues, also play their part. Moreover, staff complain about bad field management, poor selection practices, lack of career development, poor appraisal and inadequate training. Clearly, these can be influenced by the employer, who should also provide debriefing and counselling for workers on their return.[34]

Employee relations

It is easy to imagine that management relations with employees as a group have declined in the face of the individualisation of HRM practices. The term *Industrial Relations* refers to patterns of bargaining and consultation between collectives – employers, or groups of employers, on the one hand and trade unions on the other.

Ideological reservations among the latter meant that their initial response to the 'new' HRM was confusion and resistance. More recently, the change has been accepted in spite of reservations. Maintaining their role of defending members' interests, unions in many countries have adjusted their stance towards the new styles of management. Unions have recognised that strategies for improving quality and encouraging innovation do bring long-term benefits to members. They increasingly advocate action to improve training and career opportunities. Thus, in the United Kingdom unions support members in new-style plants such as at Toyota, Nissan and Sony. In Germany, the large union IG Metall has taken a lead in responding to the development of teamwork and other new practices.[35]

Perhaps the most notable feature of unions in Western countries over recent decades has been the fall in membership. This has been greatest in countries where adversarial national collective bargaining had been the unions' main function, see Table 14.1.[36] Changes are in different directions, with most European countries, save the Nordic ones, in sharp decline. In many countries, co-operation and engagement have replaced conflict. To what extent this represents a change of philosophy or a tactical retreat in the light of declining membership remains to be seen. In some sectors of some economies, unions remain strong and militant. In France, for example, the low density in the whole workforce disguises the strength in nationalised industries and government service.

Table 14.1 **Union membership 1995**

	% of workforce	% change in 10 years
Australia	35	−30
Canada	37	2
China	92	0 (1997)
Denmark	89	2 (1998)
Finland	79	16
France	9	−37
Germany	27	−18 (1997)
Greece	24	−34
Italy	44	−7
Japan	22	−17 (1998)
Korea, Republic of	12	2 (1997)
Netherlands	30	−11 (1997)
Norway	72	4 (1997)
Sweden	91	9
Switzerland	25	−22 (1998)
United Kingdom	33	−28
United States	14	−21 (1998)

How does this look to the HR manager? Traditionally, industrial relations has fallen into two parallel functions – negotiation and consultation. Negotiation, or collective bargaining, covered wages and conditions and was depicted as a zero-sum game where the issue was how to 'share the cake'. Joint consultation, on the other hand, was based on a unitary model where both sides worked together to discover ways to 'bake a bigger cake'. Structures for both could run from the department up to national level, since disputes could be referred upwards in the hope that they might be resolved. The sluggishness of these systems, however, coupled with the rise of plant-level bargaining, meant a decline in use.

Ramsay notes that, nowadays, consultation commonly coexists with bargaining at plant level. It often spawns committees focusing on specific remits. The HR manager may, therefore, be part of health and safety committees, productivity and quality groups and so on. In most European countries, works councils are established either by statute or, in Sweden, by national agreements. The Social Chapter may eventually spread the practice through the whole European Union. Objectives for joint consultation, as seen by management, may include one or more of the following:

- strengthening of communication channels;
- co-operation in facing competitive or other environmental threats;
- restricting the scope of union activities to the point of exclusion;
- enlisting the co-operation of local union officials against the national union's wishes;
- offering (token) participation in decision making.[37]

In some of these aims, there lie the seeds of failure. Ramsay notes three that are commonly found:

- the committee deals only with trivial issues – tea, towels and toilets;
- a powerless committee attracts little interest;
- the process breaks down because problems are too severe or the parties' expectations differ too much.

The problem of marginality is seen by some authors as widespread among works councils throughout Europe. Others find that beneficial outcomes are possible provided the approach is genuine and not simply a gesture. Ramsay's summary of good consultation appears in Exhibit 14.9.

Exhibit 14.9 Features of good consultation practice

- Consultation occurs before change – otherwise it becomes manipulation.
- Committee momentum requires an ambitious agenda.
- All members require research and secretarial support.
- Representatives should report back fully to avoid isolation of the process.
- Training of managers and staff is necessary.
- Management members must be sufficiently senior to demonstrate serious commitment.
- Agreed actions should be swiftly put into effect; reasons for rejection should be given clearly and promptly.
- Unions should be kept informed even if they are not directly involved; trying to bypass them is risky.

Questions for the human resources manager

We shall now turn to a brief review of some critical questions facing HR managers, linking them to the themes of this book. They relate to national differences, ethics, SMEs and equal opportunities.

■ Are national differences important?

Clark and Mallory are among many who show that HRM varies between nations, with many differences in the meaning of the term.[38] Its growth from personnel management began in the United States of the 1980s as that country sought to overcome perceived failures in its industries. The 'new HRM' was integrated into strategic management and reflected the 'American Dream' business-centred culture. Many MNEs followed the lead. This is instanced by the assertion of a senior HR manager of Hilton Group, 'we believe strategic HRM is absolutely fundamental to guest satisfaction'.[39] Hughes takes the argument further, supporting the emergence of a 'Universal HRM' that focuses on competitive advantage through the adoption of best practices.[40]

National differences persist. Although Child notes some convergence of HR practices adopted by foreign companies that have acquired United Kingdom subsidiaries, distinct differences arise depending on the countries of origin.[41] Hofstede's work, *see* Chapter 4, invites us to see countries in cultural clusters. On this basis, we would expect the American model to transfer most readily to other countries in the Anglo cluster, notably the United Kingdom. Models of HRM processes and practice do not fit so well in mainland Europe. Each nation 'understands' HRM in different ways. For example, the French state still plays a major role in shaping the framework, through both the legal context and its involvement in many large organisations where unions are also very influential. Liberalisation is led from the centre. Outside big business, however, HRM as a movement seems to have had little impact.[42]

In contrast to this 'stumbling' model of development, frequently influenced by the experiences of foreign firms, German HRM is home grown from a long tradition of practical application, research and teaching. HRM stresses the value of human resources in gaining competitive advantage and integrates HR and corporate strategies so they reinforce each other. Ideas of partnership and strong representation by employees at all levels remain central to the way things work.[43] In Sweden, the collective tradition counters moves to individualisation found in other countries, especially the Anglo group. Expressed through the strength of trade unions, this feeling is even stronger in Denmark, which, like Finland, is a country where union membership has not been declining.[44] These examples suggest that, while there are pressures towards convergence of policy and practice in HRM, important differences between nations and cultures will remain. Beyond the European shores, we expect the gaps to be greater.

■ Is HRM ethical?

Obviously, the answer to this question is yes – HRM is here to help people. Or is it? One problem with the question is the lack of agreement over what HRM is. We have just looked at international differences and there is the contrast between soft (human) and hard (resource) approaches explained earlier. To make progress, Legge suggests we evaluate HRM according to how it approaches three features: flexibility; team building, empowerment and involvement; and cultural management.[45]

Under each feature we can spot winners and losers. Flexible working may suit very well the people close to the core of an organisation but at the expense of those at the fringe, on casual contracts. Empowerment has worked well in many firms but in others it merely increases stress and blame if things go awry. Changing cultures may be done with the best intentions. Yet we must ask whether culture change programmes secure real commitment or mere compliance. Is soft HRM real? Furthermore, is it really about developing people as people?

What do ethical ideas have to contribute to this debate? In Chapter 5, we looked at the Kantian, Utilitarian and Aristotelian schools.

■ Kant's categorical imperative requires any principle to be capable of generalisation. Further, actions must respect the dignity of individuals and be acceptable to them. Self-interest is immoral. To Kant, hard HRM, however well intentioned, would be immoral. It uses people for an end, such as the success of the organisation. Soft HRM, based on mutuality and the development of all employees as an end in itself, passes the test. But this would be true only if all employees were treated alike. Core and periphery models of employment are ruled out. Culture change programmes that involve the manipulation of one group by another are also off limits.

One difficulty for Kant's laws is the potential clash between two rules. What about 'I must look after the interests of owners' against 'I must look after the interests of employees'? It is difficult to construct a more general rule to choose between the two so we may fall back on looking at consequences. This means the utilitarian approach.

■ Utilitarians judge the morality of actions according to their outcomes. Choices look for the greatest good for the greatest number. To this aim, some *distributive* ethicists would add that nobody must be worse off.

This gives hard HRM some hope. In spite of the stress and loss that HRM policies bring to individuals, managers have the duty to satisfy stakeholders as a whole. Competitive advantage ensures business survival, stimulates innovation and doubles the average standard of living every 10, 20 or 30 years depending on which country you live in. Further, questions of distributive ethics can be handled if steps are taken to correct the disadvantages for the losers through counselling, retraining, switching jobs or redundancy payments.

■ An Aristotelian stresses goodness or virtue. This means offering everyone the possibility of realising his or her moral, social and mental potential within the broader community. Clearly, employment cannot do this on its own but it must follow practices that help growth on its way.

Genuine soft HRM, full of ideas about learning and development may qualify. But what of staff employed in unskilled jobs with little training? How much more is there than the exchange of labour for payment? Even for professionals there are great difficulties for this virtue ethics. Systems of reward encourage interpersonal competition. Promotion is at someone else's expense. Moreover, stimulating commitment from ambitious people leads to workaholic behaviour, burn-out and negative consequences for employees' development in their family and community roles. Many modern HRM practices, therefore, would not figure well on the Aristotelian scoreboard.

We can see that genuine soft HRM may be seen as ethical from several points of view. On the other hand, it is difficult to justify hard HRM unless you are an out-and-out utilitarian. Yet, maybe the world is going that way.

■ Are SMEs a special case?

Hendry and colleagues show that SMEs face problems due to their small size or narrow focus in terms of processes, products or markets.[46] Many well-run SMEs follow up-to-date HRM practice with mixtures of soft and hard approaches. One critical problem is excessive reliance on key personnel, with skills in short supply. Fear of losing them is real. Of these, reliance on the leader is usually the most serious. The entrepreneur has to consider succession, which is how the business is to survive his or her departure.

There are several problems for entrepreneurs planning for succession. The first lies in understanding management development. Since many have learned by doing, they assume that others do the same. This is, however, rarely feasible. Followers cannot follow the same path as an enterprise's founder, so preparing people to take over must involve another sort of training and experience. The second problem is the close personal identification between the entrepreneur and the enterprise. So many find devolving key tasks such as marketing or technology very difficult. Hendry and colleagues found little evidence of succession planning among SMEs. Then, if this issue is blocked, managers cannot create any coherent HR policies for the wider group of staff.

■ How does HRM respond to equal opportunities issues?

Most Western countries have legislation against employment discrimination on grounds of gender, race, religion, nationality or age. Many organisations have policies beyond these minimum rights, *see* Exhibit 14.10.

Exhibit 14.10 Equal opportunities at the Inland Revenue

'The Department wants to get the best from everyone. Our policy is to include everyone, to value differences in people and harness those differences to improve our work for the benefit of all our different customers. We will not unlawfully or unjustifiably discriminate against anyone on any grounds, including their race, colour, nationality, ethnic or national origin, sex or sexual orientation, working pattern, marital status, religion, gender reassignment, disability or age. We will act positively to address under-representation particularly of women, people from ethnic minorities and people with disabilities. In Northern Ireland, we will also eliminate unfair discrimination because of political opinion and act positively to address under-representation of people due to their religious beliefs or political opinions.'[47]

To illustrate ethical and practical problems for HRM, we shall focus on gender. Two decades ago, there were few women in influential positions in government, business or most other areas of organisational life. In the 1990s, things seemed to change. The United Kingdom Labour government, elected in 1997, had 18 women ministers. Now, many large corporations, university departments, charities, newspapers and SMEs are run by women. While there are still fewer than there ought to be, many commentators feel that at last the glass ceiling has been smashed. There are enough women in senior positions to act as role models. Equality of the sexes is only a matter of time. It is as though the system is waiting for the flow of graduates from business and professional education to move into the ranks. The Inland Revenue, *see* Table 14.2, illustrates the progress.[48]

Table 14.2 **Employment of women in the Inland Revenue (%)**

Band	1998	2000	2002
Senior Civil Service	8.9	15.4	20.3
B	22.6	23.6	25.6
C1	21.8	26.5	31.0
C2	36.6	39.0	41.6

Women figure increasingly in business start-ups not only in Britain but also in China, Germany, Singapore and the United States. Nearly all Japanese currency traders are women. Worrying, though, is the proportion of company directors, which, in the United Kingdom, has crept up to just 3.3 per cent. This last figure makes others argue that the glass ceiling has not so much been smashed as raised.

> The **glass ceiling** is the invisible barrier that prevents women from rising to the top of organisations. The term is also used to cover minority groups.

There is a difference between female managers and feminine management. The few exceptional figures of the 1970s and 1980s, for instance Prime Minister Margaret Thatcher and a scattering of senior judges, were said to behave as 'men in disguise'. That is they practised 'masculine' management. Nowadays, successful women still show many attributes of successful men: good with people; taking well-judged risks; self-reliance; energy; and the need to prove oneself. Differences are subtle: women are better time-managers, better able to accomplish several tasks at once and are more flexible. They are often less interested in the trappings of power such as size of office, chauffeur-driven car or class of air travel. Other concerns often attributed to women, such as openness, integrity, equal rights and representation are really feminine traits that are often also displayed by men.[49]

What does this mean for HRM? Monitoring the representation of women in management positions would identify defects in recruitment and development procedures. Provided equal opportunity is sincerely offered, achieving equality among the management cadre is only a matter of time. Unfortunately, such a rosy picture cannot be painted lower in the hierarchies of many industries. Glass ceilings combine with glass walls, which are barriers between professions and even roles in the same organisation. Some 80 per cent of hairdressers, cleaners, caterers and clerical workers are women compared with 0.8 per cent of surgeons. The reality is frequently at odds with the claims of equal opportunities employers. Biswas and Cassell investigated the state of HRM in a hotel in northern England, *see* Exhibit 14.11.[50]

From the business point of view, there is considerable pressure to follow the status quo. The good hotel wins through reproducing a sense of homeliness. This is partly conveyed by modelling the traditional domestic division of labour, placing women in caring roles with men to do the heavy jobs. At the same time, a hotel needs to sell its services to, predominantly, business*men*. Receptionists and sales

> **Exhibit 14.11 Sex stereotypes in an English hotel**
>
> With 100 beds, the city centre hotel was part of an international chain. Despite its size it had no equal opportunities policy, either explicit or implied in the HRM policy. Typical of the industry, the business employed a core of 50 full-timers supported by part-timers and casual workers.
>
> There was evidence of sexual discrimination: women, usually older, were preferred for breakfast service to promote the image of comfort and homeliness; at reception, the stress was on appearance; and only one porter was female, the token woman finding it difficult to be taken seriously and often being given the light jobs. Perhaps more problematic was the way in which women co-operated in reinforcing sex stereotypes. Chambermaids, for instance, saw housekeeping as a female reserve, and all accepted that the night receptionist should be male. Both women and men seemed content with the gendered notions surrounding their roles. Exceptions had to develop personal survival strategies. Women in the 'macho' environment of the kitchen or men in the domestic department adopted behaviours more commonly found in the opposite sex.

staff succeed through fulfilling glamour roles. Hence the culture of the industry includes having women matching both caring and selling stereotypes.

The dilemma for HRM is clear. Fitting HR with corporate strategy means matching the expectations of the market. This means both men and women occupying gendered roles to meet customers' expectations. This is incompatible with any equal opportunities policy. The notion of recruiting the right person for the job is undermined if the 'rightness' is seen mainly in terms of a person's sex. In defence, the business may say that it is merely responding to the social environment and to behave otherwise would be futile. Yet, in law, a defence based on such role definitions would fail.

Conclusion: the paradox of HRM

At one level, HRM can be perceived as a set of techniques for creating, developing and maintaining an effective workforce. It can be seen to have grown out of conventional personnel management functions that were responsible for recruitment and selection, training, setting up reward systems, industrial relations and staff welfare. The accent changed with the move towards planning and the integration of these tasks into the organisation's strategy. Then, HRM changed its stance from caring and development to optimising and integrating human resources. This position is stressed in the so-called *hard* HRM where the accent is on the *R*. Planned reduction in staff and how it can be achieved, a topic for which we have had no space, is clearly related to the way HR and business strategies are intertwined.

In this chapter, we have mainly used an Anglo-American perspective although enough has been said to show that HRM is strongly influenced by national systems and socio-cultural environments. Variations between nations mean that there is no universal understanding and MNEs need to tailor their policies to meet local needs. Coping with differences also raises ethical questions such as how far one should go along with local conventions in such areas as employment. Looking more broadly, far from appearing to be free of ethical difficulty, HRM is full of questions. Beyond national contrasts, we have referred to the contrast between hard and soft approaches to show

how the former hardly stands up to ethical analysis. In detail, too, there are questions of selection testing and policies towards equal opportunities. The role of HR managers in promoting equal opportunities is, perhaps, obvious. Yet, as the paradoxical strategy at the hotel in Exhibit 14.11 showed, policy is never so clear-cut. Strategic goals, which either have been, or ought to have been, clarified do not bridge the chasm between attitudes of staff and customers and legislation. In this and other difficult areas, HR managers often prefer to leave matters in an ambiguous, messy state. In becoming an instrument of business policy, HRM now shares the complex, incoherent questions faced by the rest of the management team.

QUICK CHECK

Can you ...

- Define HRM.
- Name the three elements of HRM practice.
- List four features of the hard and soft approaches.
- Sketch a model of the recruitment process.
- Outline the issue of validity in selection.
- Give examples of indirect discrimination.
- Identify the four elements of a structured interview schedule.
- Summarise the activities in an assessment centre.
- Define training.
- List four benefits of training.
- Tabulate the benefits of on-the-job and off-the-job training.
- State what is meant by levels of aggregation in pay schemes.
- Name two methods of job evaluation.
- Explain the term *glass ceiling*.

QUESTIONS

Chapter review

14.1 Draw and annotate a diagram showing the main HRM processes of an organisation within the business environment.

14.2 Relate training and development as approaches to the growth of people's capabilities.

14.3 Compare on- and off-the-job training, using your own examples to illustrate circumstances where each may best be used.

Application

14.4 Analyse in ethical terms the position of managers at the hotel of Exhibit 14.11. Whose interests should HRM serve?

14.5 To what extent do you think soft or hard HRM was practised at the Skipton Building Society? What effects do you think increasing competition may have on this position?

14.6 Assess how far B&Q's recruitment process, *see* Exhibit 14.4, represents good HRM practice.

14.7 In what way does the equal opportunity policy of the Inland Revenue, Exhibit 14.10 and Table 14.2, go beyond minimum legal requirements?

Investigation

14.8 Find out how a small business recruits staff and why it chooses its methods. Assess the impact of equal opportunities legislation.

14.9 Through interviewing a sample of employed people, discover the principles upon which their pay and other benefits are worked out. Compare the design of the schemes to assess how far they are likely to be effective.

CLOSING CASE

Do we expect too much of aid workers?[51]

Nurse Ann Smith was in charge of a Red Cross feeding centre in Huambo, Angola, when, with 53 other aid workers, she was robbed and taken captive by rebel forces. Released after several days, she was sent by lorry and cargo aircraft to Luanda. There, the Red Cross ensured that the staff, 30 of whom were its employees, stayed in the same hotel and had plenty of time to discuss events before being flown to Europe. For Ann Smith, 'This was terribly important. The only people I have spoken to properly about this are those who were out there with me.' Like many in her position, she finds it difficult to tell others who 'can't possibly understand'.

Formal debriefing took place at Red Cross headquarters in Geneva before Smith's return to the United Kingdom. She was offered counselling and had a few weeks' leave before undergoing a physical and psychological check-up.

Experiences such as these are becoming more commonplace. Personnel managers meeting workers returning from Somalia found themselves listening to responses they felt inadequate to handle. As the list of disasters, and the number of agencies, has lengthened, so has the number of problems grown.

While the Red Cross has sent people to stressful and dangerous areas for many years, only recently has it started to consider systems for care and support. Influential have been the growing body of research into stress management and the ways the armed forces and emergency services help their people cope with trauma.

To ensure that field workers are better prepared for their assignments, the British Red Cross has strengthened its personnel practices. One-hour selection interviews have been replaced by one-day assessment centres. The aim is to find better communicators and team-workers. Pre-departure briefing has been extended to seven days and includes stress management and cross-cultural training. A specialist agency, InterHealth, has been brought in to provide medical checks and counselling both before and after assignments.

Paul Eames, overseas personnel manager for the British Red Cross, has more plans. He wants to see a career structure and job security replacing the short-term contract system. This has grown in response to uncertain funding but makes it difficult to build up experienced teams. Eames also wants to improve management training and clarify the roles of field managers.

Field managers' first responsibility is to look after staff health and security. Otherwise, their work would be useless. Yet one remarked, 'It is quite common to work all hours God gives in reaction to the crisis, and because you are going into areas where the infrastructure has collapsed, there are few distractions'. It is not surprising that many return drained. Expatriates come home yet often feel guilty about the local people they must leave behind. One Oxfam manager explained, 'When we pulled out of Kigali, all we could do was share the office money among the Rwandan staff and say we hoped to employ them again some day'.

Questions

1 What factors in the environment contribute to the personnel practices that have developed among NGOs working in overseas aid?

2 Suggest a design for a one-day assessment centre for a charity recruiting staff for central Asian emergency relief.

3 The effects of trauma have been vividly illustrated by cases in recent years. To what extent should organisations be responsible for its effects on employees?

Bibliography

For a round-up of trends, developments and details of HRM, see Derek Torrington, Laura Hall and Stephen Taylor, *Human Resource Management* (Harlow: Financial Times Prentice Hall, 2002). Jim Stewart and Jim McGoldrick (eds) *Human Resource Development* (Hemel Hempstead: Financial Times Prentice Hall, 1996) gives a more advanced discussion of issues; it may be in the library.

References

1 Worts, Chris (1996) 'Building a society with special skills', *People Management*, **2(2)**, 25 January, 36–8; 'Skipton teams up with GA Life to launch instant-access portfolio', *Money Marketing*, 31 October 1996; 'Skipton buys mortgages', *Northern Echo*, 3 October 1996; Training Standards Council (1999) *Skipton Building Society: Inspection Report*, January; *Annual Results for 2002*, Skipton Building Society.

2 Skipton Building Society (2003) Home page; **www.skipton. co.uk/about_us/index.asp**, accessed 12 April 2003.

3 Truss, Catherine, Gratton, Lynda, Hope-Hailey, Veronica, McGovern, Patrick and Stiles, Philip (1997) 'Soft and hard models of human resource management: A reappraisal', *Journal of Management Studies*, **34(1)**, January, 54–73.

4 *Ibid.*, 69.

5 Siebert, Kent W., Hall, Douglas T. and. Kram, Kathy E. (1995) 'Strengthening the weak link in strategic executive development: Integrating individual development and global business strategy', *Human Resource Management*, **34(4)**, 549–67; summarised in (1996) 'A centre-stage role for executive development', *Management Decision*, **34(5)**, September, 51–2.

6 Beer, M., Spector, B., Lawrence, P., Mills, D. and Walton, R. (1985) *Human Resource Management: A general manager's perspective*, New York: Free Press.

7 Hendry, C. and Pettigrew, A. (1990) 'Human Resource Management: an agenda for the 1990s' *International Journal of Human Resource Management*, **1(1)**, 17–44.

8 Kane, Bob and Palmer, Ian (1995) 'Strategic HRM or managing the employment relationship?' *International Journal of Manpower*, **15(5)**, May, 6–21.

9 Marsh, Peter (1996) 'Companies fall down on "people issues"', *Financial Times*, 18 November, 11.

10 Hunter, Laurie, Beaumont, Phil and Sinclair, Diane (1996) 'A "partnership" route to Human Resource Management', *Journal of Management Studies*, **33(2)**, March, 235–57.

11 West Devon Borough Council (1997) Advertisement, *Guardian*, G2, 21 May, 29.

12 To be extended to age, religion and sexual orientation; *see* the Equality Direct website – **www.equalitydirect. org.uk**, accessed 12 April 2003.

13 Cooper, John N., Baker, Barry R. and Maddocks, Jolyon S. (1996) 'Occupational testing practice: sustaining testing processes through CPD: a case study', *Journal of European Industrial Training*, **20(7)**, July, 3–9.

14 McHenry, Robert (1997) 'Tried and tested', *People Management*, 23 January, 35–7.

15 Furnham, Adrian (1995) 'A performance that can tip the balance', *Financial Times*, 18 December, 10.

16 Overell, Stephen (2002) 'The right personalities in store: DIY retailer B&Q is using automated psychological tests to help recruit people who can fit into its culture', *Financial Times*, 5 December.

17 Moffat, J. (1992) 'Three case studies of operational research for the Royal Air Force', *Journal of the Operational Research Society*, **43(10)**, 955–60.

18 Donkin, Richard (1996) 'Jury out on all-round appraisal', *Financial Times*, 9 October.

19 Mullins, Laurie J. (2001) *Management and Organisational Behaviour*, 6th edition, Financial Times Prentice Hall, 706.

20 *Ibid.*, 694.

21 Tragg, Roger (1995) 'New culture, new ideas: Consultants apply commercial thinking to the public sector', *Independent on Sunday*, 24 September.

22 Saigol, Lina (1997) 'On with the counter revolution', *Guardian: Jobs and Money*, 15 March, 2–3; Papasolomou-Doukakis, Ioanna (2002) 'The role of employee development in customer relations: the case of UK retail banks', *Corporate Communications*, **7(1)**, 62–76.

23 Hiroshima Sogo Bank (1994) *Watashitati no tekisuto [Our textbook]*, 32nd edition, Hiroshima Sogo Bank, Personnel Training Section, 114.

24 Bergenhenegouwen, G.J., ten Horn, H.F.K. and Mooljman, E.A.M. (1996) 'Competence development – a challenge for HRM professionals: core competences of organizations as guidelines for the development of employees', *Journal of European Industrial Training*, **20(9)**, 29–35.

25 Bradshaw, Della (1995) 'Chips off the old block', *Financial Times*, 13 November, 15.

26 Lockyer, Keith (1996) 'Human resource management and flexibility in pay: new solutions to old problems?' in Towers, Brian (ed.) *The Handbook of Human Resource Management*, 2nd edition, Oxford: Blackwell, 298.

27 *Ibid.*, 299.

28 Hampson, Stuart (2003) 'Chairman's statement: Preliminary results for the year to 25 January 2003, John Lewis Partnership', UK *Regulatory News*, 10 April.

29 Lockyer, (1996) *op. cit.*, 286.

30 Greenhill, Richard (1997) 'All change', *People Management*, 1 May, 22–5; Brown, Barry (1997) 'Getting there', *People Management*, 1 May, 25–6.

31 Williams, Alan and Dobson, Paul (1996) 'Culture change through training: the case of Sainsbury' in Towers, *op. cit.*, 416–31.

32 Cappelli, Peter and Rogovsky, Nikolai (1995) 'What do new systems demand of employees?' *Financial Times: Mastering Management*, 24 November, II.

33 Guest, David and Conway, Neil (2002) *Pressure at Work and the Psychological Contract*, London: Chartered Institute of Personnel Development.

34 Pickard, Jane (1996) 'Stopping disaster from ruining lives', *People Management*, 25 July, 32–4.

35 Based on Beaumont, P.B. (1996) 'Trade unions and human resource management' in Towers, *op. cit.* 115–30.

36 International Labour Organisation (1999) 'Changes in Trade Union Membership Numbers Worldwide', *ILO World Labour Report 1997–1998*, Geneva: ILO.

37 Ramsay, Harvie (1996) 'Involvement, empowerment and commitment' in Towers, *op. cit.*, 223–58.

38 Clark, Timothy and Mallory, Geoff (1996) 'The cultural relativity of human resource management: Is there a universal model?' in Clark (ed.) *European Human Resource Management*, Oxford: Blackwell, 28.

39 Maxwell, Gillian and Lyle, Gordon (2002) 'Strategic HRM and business performance in the Hilton Group', *International Journal of Contemporary Hospitality Management*, **14(5)**, 251–2.

40 Christensen Hughes, Julia M. (2002) 'HRM and universalism: is there one best way?' *International Journal of Contemporary Hospitality Management*, **14(5)**, 221–8.

41 Child, John (2002) 'International mergers and acquisitions in the UK 1985–94: a comparison of national HRM practices', *International Journal of Human Resource Management*, **13(1)**, 106–22.

42 Jenkins, Alan and van Wijk, Gilles (1996) 'Hesitant innovation: the recent evolution of human resources management in France' in Clark, *op. cit.*, 65–92.

43 Scholz, Christian (1996) 'Human resource management in Germany' in Clark, *op. cit.*, 118–51.

44 Schuer, Steen (1996) 'Denmark: Human resource management under collective bargaining: The sociological perspective' in Clark, *op. cit.*, 185–214.

45 Legge, Karen (1996) 'Morality bound', *People Management*, 19 December, 34–6.

46 Hendry, C., Jones, A., Arthur, M. and Pettigrew, A. (1991) *Human Resource Development in Small to Medium Sized Enterprises*, Research Paper No. 88, University of Warwick Business School.

47 Inland Revenue (2002) *Annual Report for Year Ending 31 March 2002*, London: The Stationery Office, 57.

48 *Ibid.*, 128.

49 Porter, Henry (1997) 'Smashing the glass ceiling', *Guardian*, *G2*, 26 May, 2–4; Wilkinson, Helen (1996) 'Cracks in the glass ceiling – a new generation of women believe they will win equality in the boardroom, not the common room', *Observer*, 2 June.

50 Biswas, Rashmi and Cassell Catherine (1996) 'Strategic HRM and the gendered division of labour in the hotel industry: a case study', *Personnel Review*, **25(2)**, February, 19–34.

51 Pickard (1996) *op. cit.*

CHAPTER 15

Operations management

Chapter objectives

When you have finished studying this chapter, you should be able to:

- define operations management and explain its scope;

- distinguish between manufacture and isolated service and other types of service;

- explain how volume is the key influence on process design and layout decisions;

- show how scale and customer involvement relate to service process design;

- identify the factors in location selection and show how they influence different types of enterprise;

- explain the way capacity planning establishes a framework for scheduling decisions and outline three approaches to production scheduling;

- give reasons for the existence of inventories and queues and show how good operations management can turn them to advantage.

How do I drive productivity? How do I get my supply chain to be more efficient? How do we link our customers? Just fundamental, blocking-and-tackling, roll-up-your-sleeves kind of work that has very clear and tangible benefits ...

Michael Dell, founder of Dell Computers

Flawless flooring from Amtico[1]

Maker of high-quality vinyl floorings, Amtico became an independent company in 1995 when its managers bought the business from Courtaulds for £49 million. Today its products lead the United Kingdom market, command 30 per cent price premium and are in demand throughout the world. The 350 staff work on applications in both the luxury domestic sector and commercial sites where style must be combined with durability.

Having built its reputation over some forty years, the company aims to be the most exciting flooring company in the world. Its extensive range, including vinyls that closely mimic natural materials, can be supplied in whatever combination a customer chooses. Patterns of sweeping curves or detailed mosaics are designed and cut using computer-aided design and manufacturing (CAD/CAM) technologies. Customers visit the company's design studios across the world where, assisted by Amtico personnel, they create individual floors. The studios, which double as regional headquarters, use CAD to finalise ideas and channel orders to the sales office.

Amtico's policy of making to individual orders could only succeed if its manufacturing system coped with the variety of demand. It makes its range of standard 300mm square tiles in batches according to forecasts. Then each order has to be cut precisely from these blanks, depending on the design. Service is very important in winning orders. Through reorganisation of production into cells, the lead time for these orders has fallen from three weeks to three days. Cells are groups of workers and machines that focus on a particular type of order. For instance, the 'Galaxy' cell offers quick turnaround for small floors for the residential market. It stands next to, and is controlled by, the sales office so that designers and producers work hand in hand.

Introduction

Amtico is among many companies that have learned how to fulfil demand for individual products using combinations of standard components. This *customisation* is delayed as long as possible in the supply chain, allowing most processes to work efficiently on batches. In this twenty-first century shift away from mass production, fitting goods or services to customers' needs occurs either at the output stage of the factory or in the distribution chain. For example, customisation of computers at Dell, with combinations of motherboard, monitor and mouse, occurs at the last stage of production; while most kitchen furniture is assembled by installers from mass-produced, standard elements. At Amtico, we see a combination of both. A special finishing unit cuts special items from standard tiles, and floors are customised from a mix of these specials and standards. The plant has a highly automated main production line making quality tiles at low cost. Then, the finishing stages handle unique customer orders, each being sorted and checked manually.

Customisation arises because the basis of much competition has shifted from minimum price based on large volumes to a mix of the six PQRRSS factors – price, quality, reliability, responsiveness, service and speed. These are the concerns of operations managers who, through both their strategic and day-to-day decisions, offer an optimal mix of goods and service to their customers. It is, as Michael Dell says in our opening quotation, 'fundamental, blocking-and-tackling, roll-up-your-sleeves kind of work'[2] but its benefits for competitiveness are clear.

The *value chain* of an organisation refers to the series of processes through which it transforms a range of inputs into outputs for the customer. Operations managers integrate the elements of this chain. In manufacturing, it connects inbound logistics (supplies, transport, stockholding), the transformation processes, outbound logistics and any after-sales service needed by the customer. Service companies have much in common, but the resources are transformed into intangible service outputs instead of tangible goods. As we shall see, however, most firms offer a blend of the two.

Outline of operations management

Operations is essentially a transformation process. Its role can be defined as:

> to plan, organise, operate and control a transformation system that takes inputs from a variety of sources and produces outputs of goods and services at times and places defined by internal or external customers.

The issues faced by operations managers involved in this process extend to both the strategic and operating levels. At the former, they work on product design, facility location and process design. Then, within this strategic framework, they cover medium and short-term capacity management and scheduling to the control of inventories and queues. Figure 15.1 sketches how the operating system converts resources into products, using capacity and resources that it has set up. The strategy level is about 'doing the right thing'; the operating level 'does things right'.

■ Manufacture and service distinctions

Figure 15.1 also notes that the operations output is a mix of goods and services. There is a long tradition of distinguishing between the two types of products, setting

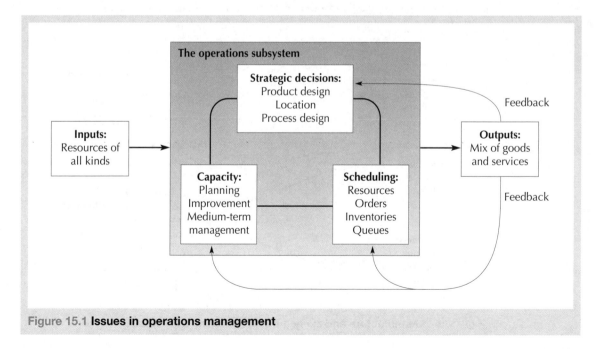

Figure 15.1 **Issues in operations management**

apart the physical from the ephemeral and denigrating the latter.[3] Many now focus on processes rather than products. Peters, for example, says, 'Would you believe that 96 per cent of us ply service trades? ... 79 per cent of us work in the service sector ... and of the 19 per cent still employed in so-called manufacturing, 90 per cent do service work (design, engineering, finance, marketing, distribution and so on)'.[4] From the process point of view, organisational life is dominated by service.

Peters is arguing that there is such an overlap between manufacturing and service business that to classify operations this way is not fruitful. Most so-called manufacturers include customer service functions, for example, despatch, promotion and after-sales service. Furthermore, many service functions are organised along similar lines to manufacture. Examples range from pension management to equipment repairs. Aircraft engine maintenance illustrates:

Aircraft maintenance is carried out by specialists. Not only is it important for the airline to have a short downtime, it must also be predictable. Major components such as engines are not maintained in situ but are exchanged for replacements already serviced. The engines are then taken apart and rebuilt under factory conditions after the aircraft has resumed flying.

Despite these overlaps, one distinction is very useful in our discussion of operations – whether the customer is present. If not, operations take place under so-called 'factory conditions' where manufacture and service have much in common. We can call this *manufacture and isolated service*. When the customer is present, we have *personal service*. Some authors call them 'back office' and 'front office' respectively.

Figure 15.2 compares the flows of resources through the two arrangements. In both, the process is separated from environmental uncertainty by buffers to absorb fluctuations in demand. In *manufacture and isolated service*, stocks (also called inventories) frequently separate the core process from the supply and customer environments. Typically, stock is present both before and after the transformation, although some techniques, such as OPT and JIT (discussed later), smooth processes and reduce inventory. *Personal service* is different. Stocks are not possible so the buffers are surplus capacity or queues. Extra resources like these are known as slack.

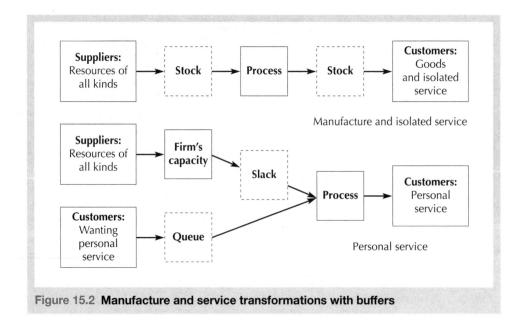

Figure 15.2 Manufacture and service transformations with buffers

Both manufacture and service organisations are strongly influenced by scale. Large scale enables producers to use facilities that have been especially designed for their function and tuned to achieve optimal efficiency. Economies of scale are evident in manufacturing and isolated service operations such as paper making, chemical plant, sewing machine assembly, blood testing and film processing. Among personal services, the effect is seen in telephone banking, supermarket retailing and some forms of higher education.

Small-scale operations, often called *jobbing shops*, gain their advantage from offering variety and flexibility. In manufacturing and isolated service, such firms print invitations, make dresses, bind theses and convert specialised vehicles. Jobbing personal service businesses offer medical care, exclusive dining or hair cutting.

Exhibit 15.1 classifies operations according to both the degree of customer involvement and scale. Key operational tasks differ. Personal service requires both interpersonal skills, understanding of the needs of the customer in relation to the way the service is provided, and some technical skills. Manufacturing and isolated service, in contrast, are not concerned with personal interaction and depend heavily on technical skills.

Exhibit 15.1 Service and manufacturing operations affected by scale		
	Services supplied in the customer's presence stressing interpersonal skills	Manufacturing or isolated service stressing technical skills
Small scale	Personal service: medical advice, manicure, child minding.	Jobbing: building, *haute couture*, computer repairs.
Large scale	Mass service: banking, trains, supermarkets.	Mass production: vehicle assembly, newspapers, pension management.

Despite these contrasts, operations systems share many features. As illustrated in Figure 15.1, they are broadly concerned with:

- At the strategic level:

    Product and process design; facility location;

- At the intermediate level:

    Capacity planning;

- At the day-to-day level:

    Scheduling orders and resources; inventories or queues.

We shall examine these topics throughout this chapter.

489

Planning the operations process

Whether in a newspaper shop or a brewery, operations occur within a planned facility. The starting point could be seen as product design, for unless a product decision has been made, there can be no progress on establishing how to supply it. Yet the link should not be seen as merely sequential, as *process capability* is an important design constraint. Product decisions, arising from interactions of the design function with marketing and production, are covered in Chapter 17. Here we shall concentrate on layout.

Layout of manufacturing and isolated service systems

Layout design depends on many factors including the range and scale of the operations, and the way they link with complementary processes within the value chain. The prime difference is between:

- *manufacture and isolated service*, where the concern is with the way goods flow through the production process; and
- *personal service* in which the customer enters the facility area and attention switches to questions such as queues, convenience, comfort and the way the work environment contributes to sales.

Within manufacturing and isolated service, there are five basic processes – fixed position or project, jobbing, batch, line and continuous, *see* Figure 15.3. There are many combinations or *hybrid* systems.

Fixed-position, or project layout

The fixed-position layout is required when the item being made, or serviced, remains stationary. The staff, materials and other resources are brought to the work area when needed. Industries from civil and marine engineering to film making and research centres use such layouts. This is because of the uniqueness, complexity or weight and volume of the items they produce.
Fixed-position layouts face difficulties with:

- limited space for safe working and storage;
- irregular flows of materials;
- variable numbers of staff and rate of use of materials; related services from accommodation to transport;
- isolating hazardous processes;
- working out of doors or at remote sites; uncertainty imposes extra costs;
- supervision and inspection.

These problems can be alleviated by carrying out as much work as possible away from the assembly position or site. In heavy engineering such as the manufacture of oil rigs, the policy is to make sub-assemblies indoors and bring them to the site only when needed. In the public sector, recent developments in planning and partnership, *see* Exhibit 15.2, have replaced the traditional conflict relationships leading to delays and budget over-runs. In all cases, *project management* involves a special set of techniques for scheduling and control.

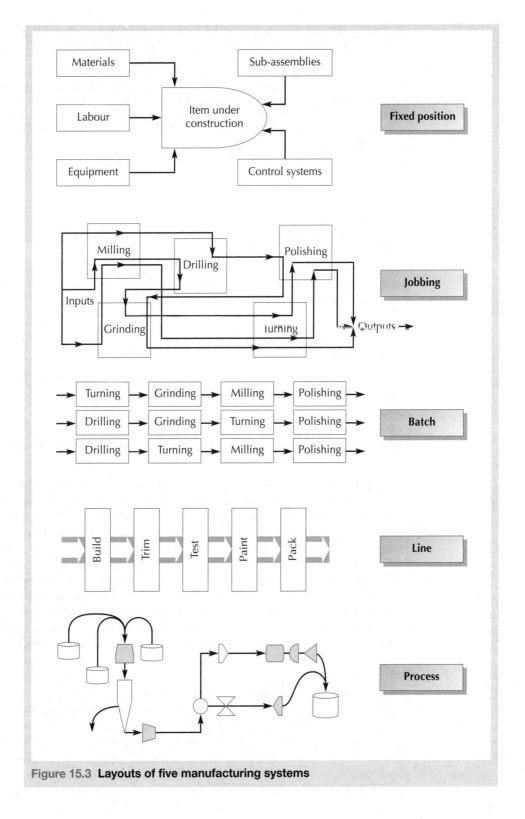

Figure 15.3 **Layouts of five manufacturing systems**

491

Exhibit 15.2 Blackpool rock[5]

A £3 million project to rebuild a 400-metre sea wall at Blackpool demonstrates the benefits of a new approach to public construction projects. Features included: choosing a contractor based on the quality of its bid, and not the lowest cost; establishing construction teams at the planning stage; improving communications among all parties; and recognising from the outset all aspects of quality, health and safety, 'buildability' and risk.

The 52-week project was completed 10 weeks early and came in £75 000 under budget.

Jobbing-shop layout

In the jobbing factory, work is carried out on many single items or small batches, each under a different contract. In principle, the type and sequence of tasks are unlimited but the sensible jobbing company will specialise in some way. It will either restrict the acceptance of orders or put out work it cannot handle to subcontractors. Specialisation may be:

■ By facilities. The jobber may have facilities such as printing machinery, lathes or saws so that certain classes of work can be taken on. Competitive advantage flows from expertise.

■ By knowledge of customers or markets. The jobber seeks work connected with a particular product area or customer. Advantage is built around this customer focus.

Motor car repairs display each type of specialisation. Tyres are changed at depots that stock a range of sizes and have invested in efficient changing and balancing equipment. Many repair shops, on the other hand, offer comprehensive service focused on a named range of models. There are specialists for Toyota, Jaguar, VW, old MGs and so on.

For layout decisions, jobbing shops have little obvious work sequence. Since orders are unpredictable and the corresponding sequence of operations equally so, there is no linkage of machinery into a production line. We would find a range of general purpose equipment surrounded by space for storage of partly finished work. The example in Figure 15.3 shows the flow routes of three different contracts passing through up to five machining departments.

This grouping of families of machines and tasks into departments is called a *process-based* or *functional* layout. The flow is flexible, but it needs close supervision. Production controllers ensure orders pass among the groups, or departments, as required. Because of uncertain work loads, jobbing shops tend to fill with part-finished orders. The piles of work in progress make them seem cluttered.

Batch production

Scale in batch processing is a step up from jobbing. Batch firms concentrate on larger quantities of a narrower product range. The process-based layout is still common. With increasing scale, however, it becomes more efficient to dedicate a family of machines and a team of specialists to each product or product range. As shown in Figure 15.3, this product-based layout represents the beginnings of the production line. Batch firms are often torn between the flexibility offered by the process-based system and the efficiency that comes from specialised lines. Cell-based manufacturing, using dedicated yet flexible equipment and skilled teams, seeks the best of both approaches, *see* Exhibit 15.3.

Exhibit 15.3 Sony's homecoming[6]

Sony earns more than 60 per cent of its revenues from hardware. Commoditisation has challenged many Japanese companies in sectors with tiny margins. To survive, Sony had shifted off-shore, especially to China. In 2002, however, production of camcorders for the United States was returned to Japan. Mass production of a wide range of products with short life cycles meant too much inventory and risk. The aim was to improve service speed and flexibility, so that a customer could order online and have the product air freighted within 48 hours. This is the basis of customisation.

Assembly time for a camcorder is 240 minutes. The facilities use cell-based manufacturing; products are made in batches by small groups. It is easy to switch between the 250 models that Sony offers. Supply management has been integrated into the Engineering, Manufacturing and Customer Service, which includes Sony's 12 previously independent manufacturing companies divided along product lines. Now television factories also make video cameras, whose demand peaks at different seasons. Responsibility for inventory has been switched from marketing to EMCS. The former stockpiled to avoid missing sales; the latter uses EPOS and other data to minimise holdings. Electronics inventory fell from ¥923 billion in 2000 to ¥507 billion (£2.6 billion) in 2002.

Line production

Mass production owes its efficiency to a combination of mechanisation and specialisation. The assembly line is both the symbol and the outstanding achievement of industrial engineering. Its purpose is to produce standard designs in large volumes, which are sufficiently high and stable to justify the huge investment. The ultimate line produces just one item. In practice, however, many are designed to cope with a small family of products. Lines, created around conveyors, use purpose-built equipment and specialised staff. Each stage operates at the same rate so that buffer stocks are not required between them. Line speeds can be changed according to market demands. When this happens, the challenge for operations managers is to ensure adequate equipment capacity and efficient personnel assignment. This is *line balancing*.

Ford's first moving assembly lines, for the Model T, had work carried out while the product was fixed to the line and moving with it, *see* Exhibit 15.4.[7] Compared with previous methods, it was successful for the following reasons:

- The skill required was reduced. Jobs were divided into elements of short cycle time, sometimes as low as 30 seconds. This reduced the training time for workers.

- It enabled optimisation of work methods, integrating them with the line design and efficient equipment. For example, the four or five nuts on a car wheel are tightened to the correct torque simultaneously using one pneumatic spanner.

- It reduced the stock of work in progress. Feeder lines, acting as tributaries to the main line, could be balanced to deliver at the rate required and therefore avoid excessive stocks.

Process production

Process, or continuous process, manufacturing is carried out for products such as chemicals, oils, polymers, paper, glass, beer, cement and some foods. These differ

---

Exhibit 15.4 Henry Ford: the inventor of the line

Henry Ford (1863–1947) is usually acknowledged as having led the introduction of the modern line. He did not invent it, however. For example, Ford knew of its use at Chicago abattoirs and the Whitney factory where ideas of standardisation and volume production were applied to the production of muskets. Ford's contribution was to recognise the opportunity presented by the line to create a mass market in affordable cars.

In 1896, Ford was in business with an old friend, Frederick Strauss. They produced petrol engines but, at the same time, Ford secretly built his first car. He began his own company in 1903 and launched into the process of building a standardised product. Between 1908 and 1927, 15 million Model Ts rolled off the lines. At its peak, in 1920, the rate was one a minute. Efficiency through specialisation was everything. For instance, in 1913, Ford's magneto assembly line reduced the labour content per item from 20 minutes to 5. By 1914, a vehicle line had reduced assembly time from 12.5 to 1.5 man-hours.

Ford lost his touch in the 1920s. As other makers, such as General Motors, began to compete through refinement, model variations, service and credit, Ford strove more intensely than ever to reduce costs through specialisation and standardisation. To him is attributed the statement, 'They can have any colour they like as long as it's black'. It was the fastest drying colour.

---

from line products in that they are measured by *dimensions*, such as mass or volume, rather than by counting units. Plant is characterised by large scale and high capital costs. Changes to capacity are often only available in large increments so that close attention needs to be paid to market demands before investments are made. For instance, in brewing for the mass market, increments of about 90 million litres per year are required if the plant is to maintain economies of scale.

Plant layout is determined by the nature of the product. Special machines have balanced capacity to allow the product to flow through the plant without delay. Such would be the case in an oil refinery where there is little room to store intermediate products. Balance enables operations managers to achieve optimal efficiency and match customer demands. Attention must also be paid to reliability and safety.

The transmission networks of utility companies, such as gas, water, electricity and telephone, can be thought of as very large, and widely distributed, process plants. Their purpose is to maintain interconnection, either from sources to consumers or, in telephones, between any pair of users. High reliability and safety are achieved both by component design and by *redundancy*. This means there are many duplicated routes and items of equipment as illustrated by the National Gas Transmission System in Figure 15.4.

■ Service process design

Not only are service operations influenced by scale, but they are also strongly affected by the degree of involvement of the customer. Compared with personal service, we have noted the possibility of *isolation*, carrying out much of the work in 'factory' environments. Another trend is *detachment*, shifting towards self-service. Figure 15.5 sets these changes on a model showing three patterns of service delivery at small or large scale.[8] Also shown are the effects of volume; *standardisation* or *customisation* occurs when the service is either growing or shrinking. We can see six types of service process:

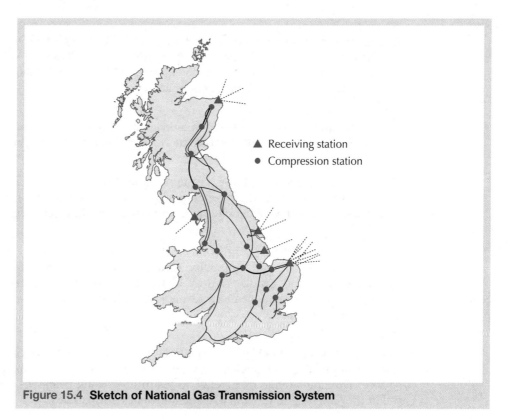

Figure 15.4 Sketch of National Gas Transmission System

■ *Service shop*

Each customer's needs are treated individually but the service takes place without the customer being present. This enables the back room to be organised as a jobbing shop.

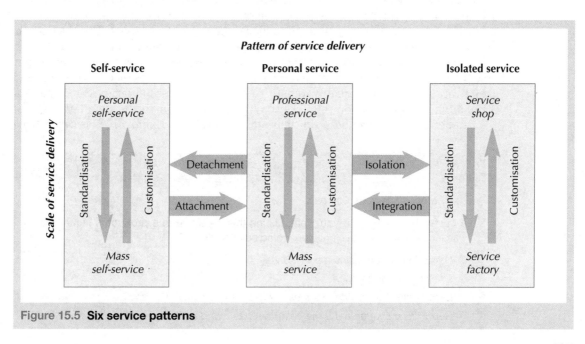

Figure 15.5 Six service patterns

■ *Service factory*

This is the service shop operating at large scale. The range of services available is standardised and they are offered through *gatekeepers*. These are staff whose role is to bridge the gap between the customer and the 'back room'. The service factory may be organised as a batch production plant.

■ *Professional service*

Service is supplied in the presence of individual customers by professionally trained personnel. Examples include doctors, counsellors, beauticians and music teachers.

■ *Mass service*

Mass service operations replicate the supply of professional services on a large scale. They are carried out in the presence of groups, or even crowds, of customers. Examples include some higher education, large-scale retailing, television and concerts.

■ *Personal self-service*

These systems are developing from the desire to combine the needs for personal service with the cost and availability advantages of self-service. The sector is not well developed and awaits growth in the application of expert systems and person–computer communications technologies. 'Intelligent' ticket machines are an example of the trend.

■ *Mass self-service*

Detachment has been achieved through the removal of human servers and the lowering of physical, psychological and technical barriers between customers and the service. Examples range from retail stores to dispensing machines. These all work well if they are easy to use and present sufficient information.

The two dimensions of scale and customer involvement have strong influence on service system design. The labour intensity of small-scale operations means that managers are continually pressed by labour cost increases while seeking to maintain quality. Because of the unpredictable nature of the tasks to be carried out, staff must be flexible and offer a variety of service on request. Large-scale operations, on the other hand, seek efficiency through reducing the reliance on labour. The challenge is to establish and maintain the feeling of good-quality service under such conditions. Physical surroundings are important and there must be sufficient staff to offer personal contact when needed. Where personal contact does occur, training and motivation aim at high-quality, repetitive delivery. Successful large-scale organisations, such as the major retailers, pay great attention to the detailed steps of customer transactions and train their staff accordingly. Exhibit 15.5 is taken from

Exhibit 15.5 Detailed attention to service

'The price has gone up again.'

A customer walks up to you, complaining that the price of a product is higher than it was last week. List the things you would say and do

■ *Listen to the complaint in a polite way.*
■ *Offer to check the price.*
■ *Explain the increase and suggest a cheaper alternative, if possible.*
■ *Report to management if the customer has found an item cheaper elsewhere.*

the staff training manual of Superdrug, the major retailer of household and personal care products.[9]

The focus on the customer must be maintained at the contact point of the isolated service operation. Effective and efficient running of this 'front office' requires personal service skills.

Layout of personal and self-service systems

The fact that personal services cannot be stocked has important consequences for system design. The organisation can only cope with maximum demand at the expense of spare capacity at other times. Examples are the rush-hour train or the crush at the theatre bar. Queues are common. Therefore, the way in which a service provider manages queues offers it an opportunity to display to customers positive aspects of its attitudes towards them. A clear, active and fair approach to queue management is a key element of good service.

The involvement of the customer in service has other implications for layout design. Especially in self-service, a layout must be attractive and convenient for customers. Good layout is an important element of sales promotion.

We shall now examine some issues of queues and service layout.

Balancing demand and capacity

The personal service system rarely balances demand and capacity. Before examining queues, we can consider why this is and how imbalances can be improved. Demand can be influenced by restricting access at peak times to customers who have reserved, paid a premium or fall into a special category. Capacity changes come from:

- flexibility: employ multi-skilled staff with extras at peak periods;
- adapting the service, switching from *customised* to *standardised* service;
- switching to self-service from personal service, the processes of *attachment* and *detachment* of Figure 15.5;
- sharing capacity with other organisations;
- automation of some operations to reduce service times.

A service organisation will follow several of these policies. For instance, restaurants use differential pricing between lunch and evening and weekday and weekend; promotional offers may run from Mondays to Thursdays; they may offer a fixed-price, quick-service lunch menu and a fuller one at dinner; reservations may be advised on weekend evenings; some events may be for 'privileged diners only'; staff are employed according to anticipated demand.

In carrying out the balancing policies, managers must also recognise constraints. These include:

- negative responses to complex pricing structures;
- the danger of cheapening the service in the eyes of full-price customers;
- perceptions of unfairness by some customers;
- quality;
- limits to flexibility in service design.

The extent to which the balancing policies work is influenced by the traditions of each industry. Many customers expect restaurants to vary their policy at different times, although perhaps not at the Ritz. The convention of higher fares on commuter trains is well established. Yet, higher prices for some long-distance train tickets on 'Fridays, certain Saturdays in July and August, and 23 December' are less understood and anger some travellers. Many customers respond little to period-based charging for telephone calls and electricity.

The queuing problem

While some balancing can be achieved, imbalances are common. Unless capacity is very high, variability results in queues. Given this difficulty, the management challenge is to reconcile:

- providing enough capacity to keep waiting lines down to a tolerable length while avoiding excessive costs, and
- avoiding excessive waiting times leading to dissatisfaction among customers.

Performance against these objectives can be assessed as follows. First, operations managers accept that there needs to be some spare capacity at the service points. In other words, the ratio:

$$Service\ capacity\ utilisation = \frac{Service\ time\ demanded}{Service\ time\ made\ available}$$

is less than 100 per cent. Second, the effectiveness of managing queues can be judged from their average length, measured either by number or by waiting time. This is a less than perfect means of assessing customer responses because, as we shall see, different individuals experience queuing in different ways.

Figure 15.6 sketches a typical relationship between waiting time and capacity utilisation. An attempt to increase service capacity utilisation, mainly by reducing the number of service points in use, inevitably leads to longer queues. This effect becomes more acute as utilisation approaches 100 per cent. One approach is to keep waiting below a threshold, as shown in Figure 15.6, by adjusting the service capacity.

Managing queues

Queues occur in many service situations. Beyond standing in a line, they include waiting:

- for service to arrive: in a restaurant, after a breakdown or in a sick bed;
- for an item to be serviced;
- in an electronic queue: terminals or telephones;
- over a long period: to enter a hospital, join a golf club or obtain a visa.

In industries where queues are commonplace, the successful organisation will be one that demonstrates awareness and response to queues. Four questions arise: the acceptable length; avoidance; differentiation; and changing the waiting experience.

Acceptable queue lengths

Factors affecting acceptability vary from case to case:

- *The significance of the wait.* Some people have more time than others; they are prepared to wait for some services more than for others; some services are more

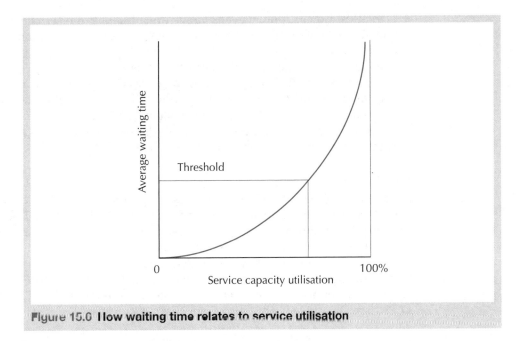

Figure 15.6 How waiting time relates to service utilisation

important or lack alternatives. For instance, non-urgent patients accept waiting lines for a hospital bed; yet they do not agree how long they should wait!

■ *Perception of queue length.* Customers perceive line length differently. For instance, some prefer a short, slow-moving line to a longer one moving faster. Therefore, queue structures affect customer feelings. A further variable is the customer's sense of urgency. Lining up for a railway ticket well ahead of time is more comfortable than when the train is about to leave.

■ *Information.* Uncertainty fuels customer anxiety. Some organisations offer information on waiting times. For this policy to succeed, customers need confidence that the estimates are accurate and the organisation will keep to them. Theme parks such as Disneyland place signs in queuing areas.

■ *Competition.* Competition influences expected service quality, including the time spent waiting. In the important business market, many airlines offer fast or automated check-ins to premium-price passengers. In supermarkets, checkout delays explain Tesco's competitive policy shown in Exhibit 15.6.

Exhibit 15.6 Every little helps at Tesco

'If there's ever more than one other customer in front of you at the checkout we'll aim to open another until all our tills are open.'

Tesco launched its 'one-in-front' policy in 1995. It was a potent weapon, for Tesco customers already experienced waiting much less often than at rivals Sainsbury. After the change, the gap increased. Sainsbury had to introduce its own queuing promise.[10]

■ *Priorities.* Competition may encourage organisations to discriminate among customers and replace the common first-come-first-served rule. Alternative priority criteria include:

– *urgency*, for some medical cases while others wait;
– *consequences*, fire and other emergency services answer any call but, in case of overload, they are allocated according to the potential consequences of the crisis – for instance to large public buildings;
– *special customers*, for instance those who place large orders or buy premium services, such as first class tickets.

Queue avoidance

A sensible alternative to the problems resulting from queuing is avoidance through regulation. This will limit demand, either to cut it altogether or to shift it to times that are more favourable. One policy uses peak pricing but, as we have noted, this is a blunt weapon. Reservations are used in various industries; in some, they are commonplace while in others they are not expected. Declining demand for cinema seats in the United Kingdom meant that few customers thought of booking. The recovery of the 1990s, however, meant that reservation systems were reintroduced. Chains such as UCI showed how to gain advantage from offering a good service, *see* Exhibit 15.7.[11]

Exhibit 15.7 UCI's growing reservation system

United Cinemas International operates 28 cinemas. Its Manchester computer-answering system was designed to answer 95 per cent of calls within 20 seconds. Customers make up to 23 000 calls daily using a range of Freephone numbers, each of which enables the computer to recognise from which cinema area the call originates. The system replaced cinema offices, where up to four operators would lose enquiries at busy times through engaged tones or long waits. More than 60 per cent of sales at some cinemas were by telephone.

When answering, the operator's screen shows the programme of the caller's local UCI with prices and availability. After booking, all details are transmitted to the customer's cinema where tickets and receipts are prepared for collection. The facility is staffed for almost 100 hours per week. At other times, a touch-tone telephone can be used.

Sales rose about 6 per cent in the year after the system was installed. Since the cinemas were connected to the network in stages, it was possible to separate the effects of the better service from the impact of the films being shown.

A difficulty for some customers is that reservations increase the delay in receiving urgent service. A person may prefer to queue straight away rather than make a later appointment.

The policies for queue avoidance laid out in this section imply the need to keep demand below capacity. While many businesses view excess capacity as wasteful, others will compete through promising that it will always be available. McDonald's and other quick-service restaurants, for instance, have high capacity, simple technology and flexible staffing that enable them to offer fast service effectively under a wide range of demand conditions.

Queue differentiation

The most common form of queue operates as first-come-first-served, for instance in small shops, banks and so on. When there are several servers, complications arise, particularly where the layout and atmosphere of the serving area conflict with the need for orderly lines to form. Competition at a crowded theatre bar is an extreme example. Several arrangements are possible for more than one channel:

■ *Multiple lines to full-range servers*
This is the typical supermarket checkout arrangement. All servers offer full service and customers join any queue. With high variability among service times, however, queues move at different speeds and frustration can become acute. The problem is worse for those with few purchases. Customers may switch lines.

■ *Multiple lines to specialised servers*
A common way to split lines is to have some servers for particular transactions such as selling stamps in the post office or dealing with those with few purchases in the supermarket. There may be some efficiency gains but most benefit arises from reduced customer anxiety. Sometimes customers see special lines empty while they are standing, but local management should cope with this. Further, if servers are too specialised, some customers have to queue twice to satisfy all their needs. Hospital patients often have this experience, a problem being addressed by the introduction of 'patient-centred care'.

■ *Single line to multiple servers*
Perceived by many to be the fairest method, this arrangement ensures that customers are served in order of arrival. This arrangement occurs in many offices and banks and applies in telephone systems. When demand is high, the queue appears long, yet moves quickly. The arrangement requires a waiting area set out to maintain the queue organisation and servers able to provide the full range.

There are several hybrid arrangements. For instance, banks combine a single line to multiple servers with a specialist counter for foreign exchange.

Changing the queuing experience

In service businesses, excellence will only be achieved if the perspective of the customer is fully considered during planning. This clearly includes the customers' perceptions of waiting. Both Maister[12] and Davies and Heineke[13] identify factors influencing waiting perceptions, *see* Exhibit 15.8. Items towards the top of the list can be more influenced by the manager. At its foot, items such as customers' attitudes and value systems cannot easily be affected. Using these ideas, managers should consider:

■ Reducing the anxiety from uncertainty. Informing customers of the likely length of the wait both enables them to plan what to do and shows that the business cares about them.

■ Influence time perception by distracting customers. Distractions include drinks in a restaurant, chats with Mickey at Disneyland, videos in the post office, coffee at the garage and ensuring that complementary parts of the service are not too fast, *see* Exhibit 15.9.[14]

Exhibit 15.8 Factors that make waiting seem longer

Queuing seems longer if it:

- occurs before the process rather than during it   ↑↑↑↑↑
- has an uncertain duration   Under
- is unexplained   firm's
- seems unfair   control
- feels uncomfortable
- involves idleness   Shared
- concerns anxious people
- is for a service of low value   Under
- is done alone   customers'
- comprises people whose current attitudes are unfavourable   control
- incorporates customers who always perceive waiting negatively   ↓↓↓↓↓

Exhibit 15.9 Walking as a distraction

The baggage reclaim hall at Dallas–Fort Worth airport is close to the gate area. Passengers have a short walk to collect their luggage but usually arrive first. At Los Angeles they have to walk much further and arrive after the luggage. Dallas passengers grumble more about luggage delays.

There is also the well-known story of the up-market New York hotel where customers complained of having to wait for the lifts. Grumbles became fewer when full-length mirrors were installed on each landing.

- Relieve stressful elements of the environment. Problems include room temperature and noise. Of course, the latter may come from the queue itself!

- Include the queuing time in the service by taking orders, handing out registration forms or briefing customers about what to expect.

- Use numbered tickets to maintain the sequence while allowing people to leave the queue. For instance, this happens at the supermarket delicatessen counter.

Whatever the queue structure and management policies chosen by an enterprise, showing clients that the operation is *under control* is essential. There is nothing more disheartening for the anxious customer than the feeling that no one is in charge.

■ Service facility layouts

So far, we have focused on the waiting line. Although this is a critical issue in layout design, we must also consider other aspects of customer interaction. Retail stores raise typical questions of the links between operations and other functions, especially design and marketing.

Store layout

Retail stores use many ploys to promote sales. For example, goods presented at eye-level are more likely to sell, as are goods displayed towards the ends of rows of shelves. The row end is a particularly strong promotional position. Less well known are the following: customers tend to turn right when entering a shop; they take 20 paces to slow to browsing speed; in supermarket aisles they push trolleys towards the right and scan shelves from left to right. These rules of thumb are backed by direct observation of customer behaviour and the analysis of sales mixes.

Using such data, leading grocery chains plan layouts centrally. They allocate some 50 per cent of shelf space to own-label goods, perhaps 40 per cent to the leading proprietary brand and 10 per cent to other brands that might have some local following. The last can be important in some categories or when makers of new lines are trying to build support. Fair trade products, such as Café Direct, do well in cities with well-educated populations. Sainsbury found particularly strong performance for this coffee in its Edinburgh Morningside store.

Store design is a component of company image and influences shoppers' perceptions of value. Compare the small cramped aisles of the discounter with the spacious layouts of the leading, quality-oriented superstores. Dividing a large store into sections, each with its own ambience created by scale, colour and, perhaps, smell is an extension of the overall design philosophy. Safeway believes that, with rising expectations for service, hygiene, quality and choice, an excellent bakery department creates a difference.[15]

Facility location: push and pull

The location decision combines cost and service factors. It is useful to distinguish between *push* and *pull* factors in the decision. Push factors, arising from dissatisfaction with a current location, trigger the organisation to consider alternatives. They include:

■ poor service from current site;

■ labour problems;

■ competitors with better locations;

■ site costs such as rents and property taxes;

■ shortage, or surplus, of space;

■ regulatory actions related to safety, effluent, noise or planning issues;

■ a wish to release capital;

■ unusual events or risks such as flood and fire.

Kirkham, Richbell and Watts confirm these items in a discussion of selecting plant for closure. Managers gave their reasons as small size, limited range of on-site activities, difficulties of access or expansion, labour problems, old capital equipment and remoteness from head office.[16]

The push factors stimulate the decision process, and then the pull factors come into play. They represent a set of forces that draw the organisation to a place. The choice may involve several overlapping stages. At a very broad level, an MNE looks for a trading bloc, nation or region to set up a new facility. Then, within this broad area, it considers detailed issues of site selection. In practice, these steps are often combined because available choices are restricted. Pull factors include:

- economic policies of governments and blocs such as the European Union;
- different risks associated with one country as opposed to another;
- raw materials and energy sources;
- location of markets;
- transport links and communications infrastructure;
- climate and quality of life;
- labour costs, supply and training opportunities;
- competitors and allies;
- availability of sites, including local subsidies and inducements.

No dominant location factor applies to business overall. Factors vary according to industry and through time. Karakaya and Canel studied choices in New York and New England made by firms in five industries. The list was headed by the availability of skilled labour, transport facilities and government regulation and taxation. Business consultants were strongly influenced by airport access, while retailers were concerned with land prices, construction costs and *low-cost* labour.[17] Examples of recent investment into the United Kingdom also illustrate the range of reasons given by companies, *see* Exhibit 15.10. All had received government assistance.

Exhibit 15.10 Examples of UK inward investment[18]

- Alveo, a subsidiary of Sekisui Chemical Co. of Osaka, is among Europe's leading suppliers of polymer foams. More than half of the output from its Merthyr Tydfil plant is exported, mostly to the rest of Europe. Reasons for choice of location were: English language; community of Japanese companies; and positive attitudes towards industry.

- United States-based Bibby Sterilin is one of the world's leading manufacturers of glassware for laboratories. It has 65 per cent of the United Kingdom market and supplies products across the world. Good communications and the country's location within the global service network are very important.

- Call centre management company TeleTech, based in Denver, Colorado, built its main European base in Glasgow to house more than 500 staff. The UK has the largest demand for call centres in Europe. Glasgow is one of Europe's major service centres.

- Sony's first British plant was built in Bridgend, South Wales in 1973. Now it employs 4500 people in the region to make 10 000 television sets daily as well as other devices. Over 85 per cent of its output is exported. There is also one of the most active research and development groups within the Sony Corporation at Bridgend. Further investment is justified by access to European markets, a supply of educated staff and a hospitable climate.

- Oregon-based integrated circuit specialist Lattice Semiconductor chose the United Kingdom for its first European research and development facility. It favoured the centrally located M4 corridor, which has many highly qualified engineers and excellent business and education support.

Retail location

Since retailers require visits from customers, the weighting of considerations changes. More emphasis is placed on many *micro* issues in site selection that are not of interest to the factory or warehouse operator. The sales performance of sites even a few metres apart can differ substantially. Many analytical models have been put forward, including those using data from Geographic Information Systems. These are being used more widely as the cost of computing falls, although many retailers do not fully integrate them into their decisions, as political and cultural factors remain important.[19] Bowlby and others describe the decision sequence as narrowing the search from geographical area, through site shortlisting to investigation of micro issues such as access, costs and planning controls.[20]

Capacity management

Capacity management is about matching the size of a facility with demand. This is a two-way process of ensuring capacity to meet demand while influencing demand to go with whatever capacity is available. We can take the short-, medium- and long-term points of view. In the short term, balancing is tactical. Routine adjustments are made by winning individual orders and adjusting output from planned resources. In the medium term, the firm can make limited changes to capacity and try to change demand, again within the fixed facilities. In the long term, all aspects are variable. The capacity of the facility can be altered and the organisation makes choices about market and product policy. We shall look at these three aspects, starting with the long term.

Capacity in the long term

Choosing long-term capacity is among the most uncertain decisions an organisation has to face. Not only is the business relying on its ability to develop over several years but also it knows that competitors have similar information and are making parallel responses. If all make the same decisions during a boom, they end up facing overcapacity during decline, *see* Exhibit 15.11.

Figure 15.7 summarises the capacity-planning decision. Within the framework of the organisation's strategic plan, capacity requirements are influenced by three choices. First, the marketing policy estimates sales volume and whether it is smooth

---

Exhibit 15.11 Bridalwear – boom and bust?[21]

With about 72 small, private manufacturers and about 1000 outlets, the UK bridalwear industry is highly fragmented. Demand is thought to be stable, and prospects are uncertain. With few published data, designers and retailers base short-term forecasts on their order books and experience. Lengthy delivery times enable fair accuracy. Yet the millennium year showed how difficult medium-term forecasting can be. Many expected a surge in weddings, but it did not happen.

In the long term, the market has been supported by the trend to marry later; older brides buy gowns that are more expensive. High costs, however, are pressing many to produce in the Far East. This may reduce the number of designer-manufacturers while all continue competing for market share.

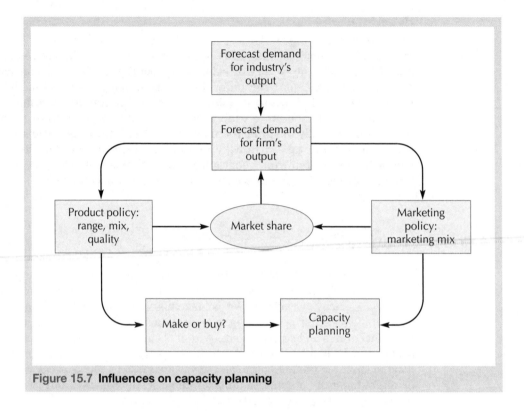

Figure 15.7 **Influences on capacity planning**

or seasonal. It is also concerned with how and where the customers are to be supplied. Second, the product policy is linked to marketing and concerns range, mix, quality, batch sizes, speed of response and so on. Third, the make or buy decision addresses how much capacity will be provided by subcontractors.

Forecasting demand over a long period is subject to the sources of uncertainty identified in Chapter 9. In the case of air travel, for example, planners have identified an underlying annual growth of about 7 per cent. Manchester Airport used it in justifying its investments in a second runway, ground links and infrastructure, *see* Exhibit 15.12.[22]

Learning

Forecasts of trends in capacity also apply to the supply side of the balance. While some facilities have a capacity that, without major change, is fixed, others are susceptible to steady improvement. This is usually called *learning* as managers and employees gradually discover how to make their facility work effectively. Improvements of between 15 per cent and 30 per cent have been reported for each doubling of cumulative output, at least in the short term. This means that the hundredth item requires only between 70 and 85 per cent of the time taken for the fiftieth. The two-hundredth item is reduced by the same ratio again.[23] Although its size and existence is controversial, learning has implications for capacity planning.[24] It may result in:

■ better use of capacity;

■ lower cost budgets;

■ more responsive schedules as some tasks are speeded up;

■ demand increases and further market opportunities.

Exhibit 15.12 Forecasting demand for runway capacity at Manchester Airport

Manchester Airport is the third busiest in the United Kingdom after Heathrow and Gatwick. In 2000, it handled 18.6 million passengers (mppa). Some 100 airlines offer 170 charter and scheduled services. The airport's second runway opened in 2001. Forecasts for the 1990s were for 8 per cent compound demand growth but the out-turn was 6 per cent. This meant that this runway was ready about a year early.

Demand is forecast to rise to 30 mppa by 2005. Based on 100 passengers per air transport movement (ATM), this means 300 000 ATMs. This implies a peak capacity of 60 ATMs per hour. This output is achieved neither at all times of the day nor all year, so annual capacity utilisation would be about 57 per cent. Peak daily demand occurs from 0700 to 1000 and 1600 to 1930. Summer demand, especially for charter movements, is higher than in the winter. Furthermore, runways are closed from time to time for maintenance and occasional emergencies.

The 2005 demand was expected to generate 124 000 road vehicle movements daily. The 80 per cent on the M56 would account for 13 per cent of this road's traffic. This motorway and connecting roads were widened during the 1990s in anticipation. A quarter of ground journeys were planned to be by public transport, leading to railway improvements and construction of a new tramway into Manchester. Since the transport interchange links all ground modes, a regional hub may develop, generating traffic from people not taking flights.

■ Capacity in the medium term

In the medium term, we are looking to make some changes to flexible parameters within the built plant capacity over periods of weeks or months. In a factory, it may mean the recruitment of a second shift; a retailer may extend the hours of opening or increase the number of tills to augment throughput. As shown in Figure 15.8, this

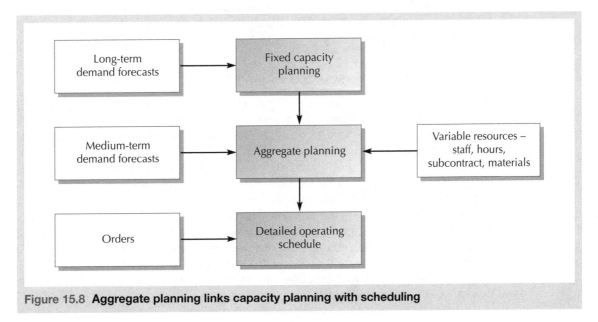

Figure 15.8 Aggregate planning links capacity planning with scheduling

process is *aggregate planning*. It forms a bridge between the long-term capacity plan and detailed schedules. It combines medium-term sales forecasts, which can be established with more confidence than the long-term ones with knowledge of current capacity. Arrangements can then be made for the processing of anticipated orders.

Scheduling: short-term operations management

The scheduling task follows the aggregate plan to ensure that customers' orders are delivered according to promises. We shall briefly compare the apparent chaos of the jobbing shop with modern approaches to scheduling batch and line production. In two of these, OPT and JIT, efforts are made to cut inventory levels to save costs and space, and shorten the system response time. Inventory is the bugbear of many manufacturing systems and we will conclude our discussion with its purposes and disadvantages.

Scheduling the job shop

In jobbing shops, with layout designed for flexibility, the scheduling task is most difficult. In practice, jobbers get the work done using a mixture of: rough planning based on priority rules such as 'first come first served' or 'longest processing time first'; having surplus capacity; expecting individual employees to use their initiative to progress orders; and the employment of progress chasers. The last, as their name suggests, intervene to keep things moving. While many jobbing shops seem chaotic as a result, we should remember that they win their business through offering flexibility. They can change both their rate and type of output, often at short notice.

Scheduling batch production

Batch production units could work in similar ways. Indeed, as many have grown from jobbing shops, they have a history of doing so! Yet, the increase in order size and the more limited product range enable the use of formal scheduling systems. Among the best known are Manufacturing Requirements Planning and Optimised Production Technology.

■ Manufacturing Resources Planning

MRPII is the name for this group of approaches linked by common principles. They are used to plan all manufacturing resources, cascading down from the aggregate plans to giving detailed instructions to every function, including raw materials supply, staff allocation and machine scheduling. Extensions allowing for tool preparation, maintenance planning and financial analysis are possible. Work of this complexity lends itself to information system applications and many software specialists have produced MRPII programs.

The core of an MRPII system is the Master Production Schedule. Continually updated, it links the aggregate plans and customer orders to plans for materials and shop-floor capacity. This enables the purchasing function to obtain materials and components matched to each order. At the same time, capacity requirements planning makes detailed plans for known orders and somewhat more flexible plans for those that are anticipated a little later.

Although MRPII programs use sophisticated information technology, they are not automatic. The software contains algorithms to resolve local sequencing problems and will warn managers of, say, overloads at key points. Yet the basic decisions are made by managers. A scheduling office will contain a few experienced staff who know the production process well and have diplomatic skills needed to cope with friction when plans are changed. Considerable benefits have been reported, although only the minority of projects are wholly successful. In these cases, Spreadbury[25] notes how manufacturing efficiency and on-time delivery can rise to above an excellent 95 per cent.

Problems with MRPII

In contrast to this optimism, several surveys describe failure.[26] This may arise from poor performance of the production system or non-achievement of high expectations of MRPII projects. Failures arise in both the technology and the way it is managed:

- Computing power can encourage excessive rescheduling. Many small changes reduce efficiency and create stress among users.
- Changing culture is part of successful implementation. Luscombe gives two examples.[27] First, the sales department is unwilling to make forecasts for which it is accountable. Second, even if forecasts are made, sales continues to accept rush orders to be 'slipped in' to the schedule with the effect of delaying the rest.
- MRPII is complex. It attempts to manage the whole production system in detail. The more complex the system, the more difficult this task becomes, *see* Exhibit 15.13.[28]

Exhibit 15.13 MRPII failure. Or was the problem deeper?

There is widespread recognition that the factory is not performing effectively. High inventory levels, poor due date performance and manufacturing times all appear to be excessive.

The product-led expediting practice appears to set expediter against expediter in a battle to establish order priority within the manufacturing areas. As a result, a disproportionate number of manufacturing shop orders are on the highest priority, due dates are changed to effect queue jumping and real priorities, i.e. customer delivery dates, are masked.

The real culprit is the [name] MRPII system as there are clear and obvious planning and control difficulties...

One possible explanation for this lies in the nature of the three product lines manufactured at the site. One application of [name] MRPII is used to control all of them yet factors in one may be different from [those in] the other two.

Optimised production technology

Responding to the question of complexity, Goldratt and Cox challenged three key assumptions about the way plants are planned and organised:

- capacity to be balanced with demand, followed by attempts to maximise the use of the capacity;

- incentives to be based on the utilisation of workers in the tasks they have been set;
- activation and utilisation of resources amount to the same thing.

These assumptions mean that, under a MRPII system, shop-floor managers try to keep as much running for as much of the time as possible. Yet this effort does not always mean progress. Why? In most manufacturing, a few bottlenecks limit the throughput. Otherwise, there is slack. Hence, only a few key points need management attention. There is no point in maximising the use of all resources, including paying incentive bonuses to non-bottleneck workers. All that happens is a build-up of parts queuing at the bottlenecks.

From this realisation, Goldratt created the breakthrough *Theory of Constraints* and developed the software system known as *Optimised Production Technology*.[29] Depending on the business, different constraints dominate, as shown in Exhibit 15.14. Using these ideas, Goldratt shows how to simplify the scheduling of complex systems.

Inventory reduction is an important benefit. It comes from both recognising bottlenecks and batch size reduction, *see* Exhibit 15.15.

Gardiner *et al.*[30] summarise the impact of OPT:

- complexities better understood;
- fewer resources scheduled;
- early warnings of problems given;
- lead time reduced;
- areas for improvement identified;
- advances over other systems are gained;
- measures of performance aligned.

OPT does not eliminate scheduling; it focuses it. Companies have used OPT with modified MRPII so that only bottlenecks are scheduled in detail.[31]

Just-in-time

Originating in the renowned Toyota Company, *see* Exhibit 15.16, just-in-time systems are ideal for high-volume repetitive operations although they have been adapted for batch and even jobbing shops.[32] JIT minimises stocks of work in

Exhibit 15.14 Bottlenecks and constraints

Operation	Constraint (in environment)	Bottleneck (in operations system)
Brass ware manufacturer	Supply of castings from foundry	Any process, e.g. turning, milling, plating
Retail shop	Access; parking; deliveries	Number of checkouts
Open-air pop festival	Roads near site	Food and water supplies; toilets; number of sets
Chocolate factory	Raw materials supplies	Any processing plant; distribution system
Hospital specialising in transplants	Donors	Operating theatres and equipment; recovery beds; trained teams

Exhibit 15.15 Focusing on the bottleneck

Work upstream of a bottleneck, if done too early, contributes little to performance. Whereas an hour lost at the bottleneck is an hour lost from the whole system, an hour saved at a non-bottleneck saves no time. Mounting stocks of partly finished goods are the only outcome.

Batch size reduction can reduce inventories and improve deliveries. Imagine 1000 items passing through two bottlenecks A and B. If A takes 4 hours then B can start 4 hours after A. But what if the batch size is cut to 250? B can follow A by an hour if four smaller deliveries are made from A to B. Distance may mean this simple change raises some costs. Yet, it will take 3 hours out of the lead time and will cut stocks as the product goes through more quickly.

progress and keeps all materials in motion. Besides cutting the cost of stockholding, work simplification and the reduction of throughput times are elements of the Toyota system, often referred to as *lean production*. It requires firms to:

- create sub-assemblies just as they are needed in the final assembly shop;
- make components just in time for fitting to sub assemblies;
- receive bought-in items at the time they are needed.

JIT differs from conventional production planning. Instead of *pushing* materials through the process, it *pulls* work through the system. The rules prevent any stage from working before its output is needed. Having deliveries at least once a day implies small batches and little stock.

Lean production goes beyond stock minimisation, however, to continuous improvement and incorporation into other business functions. It has been extended

Exhibit 15.16 The origins of *kanban*

JIT grew in Japan by linking many series of small factories, each with hundreds, rather than thousands, of employees. Each plant made daily deliveries to its successor, the quantity being the exact amounts required for the following day. For this to be stable and efficient, all the suppliers knew the monthly production schedule of the final assembler. This last company became the 'drummer' setting the rhythm for the flow of supplies.

Kanban is a term used for the way the information is recorded and process rates regulated. It refers to the card attached to each component bin in the original system. Development of the *kanban* system was helped by the proximity of the factories. For example, until Toyota began to develop overseas plants in the 1980s, all its plants were located in the Aichi prefecture, a district close to Tokyo.

Toyota, led by Taiichi Ohno as Manufacturing Director, was a pioneer of *kanban*. Its success after the sudden oil price rises of 1973–4 stimulated the interest of rivals both in Japan and elsewhere. Another company, Toyo-Kogyo, whose brand is Mazda, was almost bankrupted by the same oil shock. Its recovery had much to do with its introduction of the Toyota production system, already regarded as good practice throughout the country. Ford's close connection with Toyo-Kogyo began when it bought a 25 per cent stake in 1976. Then followed an intensive programme of training of Ford managers in Japanese techniques.

into batch technology through cell-based manufacture, as at Sony in Exhibit 15.3. To operate flow systems with little stock combines a family of approaches including Total Quality Management, *see* Chapter 6. Disruption arising from poor quality work is felt more acutely if there is little spare stock. Therefore, quality standards at all stages must be raised.

JIT works both within and between manufacturing organisations. For example, in 2002, Faurecia opened its Deeside factory to supply 700 seat sets daily to General Motors. Under JIT scheduling, all seats are built to order and delivered within a few hours. Problems sometime arise in the planned 20-minute journey to Ellesmere Port. Drivers know alternative routes to avoid blockages that would otherwise cost an hour. Faurecia, global leader in seat production, would have preferred to be on the Ellesmere Port supplier park, but there was no room. Building over the border in Wales attracted a development grant, although it was not a key factor in the location decision.[33]

Inventory management

Inventories, or stocks, are the goods that the organisation transforms in the production process. Usually there are three types:

- *Raw materials*: the physical resources that are inputs to the transformation process. Examples include the metal, timber, stone and paint of the construction firm or the meat, bread and drink of the bistro.

- *Work in progress*: the items moving through the production process; they are sometimes being worked upon but commonly idle. Partly constructed buildings and half-cooked meals are the WIP of the civil engineer and the restaurant.

- *Finished goods*: the completed products which are yet unsold. For instance, builders hate to have a stock of unsold houses and, for the bistro *patron*, the display of quick snacks becomes a headache if it remains unsold.

Inventory management is a tricky task. On the plus side, inventories are important to the functioning of many organisations. Shops need stock to sell; jobbers hold materials to satisfy that rush order. Inventory is one of the assets of a firm – the more stock, the greater the firm's worth. On the downside, many see stock as dead weight. It ties up capital that could be more usefully put to work elsewhere. The balance means carrying enough stock to satisfy most users, such as 99 per cent service levels, but to carry no more.

High inventory levels hide many scheduling problems. The Japanese *kaizen*, continuous improvement, is applicable here. The approach is to make small reductions in stock levels and solve the problems that emerge. These could range from poor forecasting to poor quality and maintenance at a bottleneck stage. This incremental approach must take place within an inventory management strategy that sets out the way levels are to be maintained and regulated. We have already looked at three of these; MRPII, JIT and OPT systems include stocks that are allocated to known customer orders. In principle, there is no stock that is not needed for orders.

Many businesses do not know orders in advance and carry stocks 'just in case'. They include the retailer, the service centre and the jobbing manufacturer. Each responds to random customer demands more quickly than it takes to obtain raw materials. To operate, they need an inventory control system. Among many types is the fixed quantity procedure, illustrated in Figure 15.9.[34] This graph is a time plot covering one item. The downward-sloping lines record items leaving the inventory

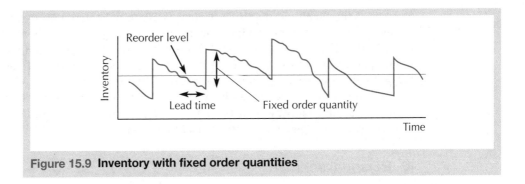

Figure 15.9 Inventory with fixed order quantities

while the vertical steps show deliveries of replenishments. For the latter, fixed quantities are favoured when it is economic to buy by the carton, container, train or ship load. The procedure works as follows:

- the inventory is replenished from time to time with the fixed order quantity;
- replenishment occurs at irregular intervals;
- new orders are placed when inventory falls to the reorder level;
- delivery of the orders follows a delay called the lead time.

The reorder level is high enough to limit the risk of there being a stock-out before delivery but not so high as to make stock levels excessive. Several formulae are available to calculate order quantities and reorder points within the different control procedures. These are based on cost data whose accuracy is difficult to justify and should only be used as starting points. Improvements are made in the light of experience under the *kaizen* philosophy.

Scheduling services

For a framework to discuss service scheduling, we can return to the classification of Figure 15.5 with its three patterns – isolated, self- and personal service.

■ Isolated services

Verma[35] found that the scheduling challenge varied according to both the isolation/integration and standardisation/customisation dimensions. Delivery sequencing was a greater problem in the isolated and customised *service shop* than in the other patterns. On the other hand, the isolated and standardised *service factory* focused more on process efficiency. Since, however, isolated services are similar to manufacturing, we have covered these cases earlier in the chapter. The service shop is akin to jobbing and the service factory parallels batch and mass production.

■ Self-service

Self-service rarely needs scheduling. The provider offers capacity that the customer uses when required. There is no personal interaction; the user consumes any amount of the facility at any time. Unless fees are collected automatically, however, payment needs personal service. For instance, the supermarket is not a pure form but mixed self- and personal service. Pure self-service includes free facilities such as municipal parks, items requiring a fixed payment, such as cable television or toll bridges and cases such as telephones where billing is automatic.

Some telephone services with limited capacity have to be booked, as do keyboards in a busy learning centre or Internet café. In these cases, the self-service requires some personal service to regulate the flow.

◼ Personal service

Personal or *direct* service, poses special problems for the operations manager. Why is this?

- Demand is variable and cannot be levelled as with a master production schedule. Queues form unless the operator has high, or rapidly adjustable, service capacity.

- Customisation is expected in many service activities. This ensures high job variety.

- The presence of the customer impedes adherence to any planned schedule. For example, the customer may ask for a change of service halfway through.

Having laid out the facilities and designed the service process, the service manager can attempt to influence demand or fine tune capacity and service levels. Reservation or appointment systems work in some circumstances. Otherwise, where demand is variable and unregulated, how can a business adjust to maintain a high standard of customer service? It uses a combination of anticipation and changes in staff and service levels.

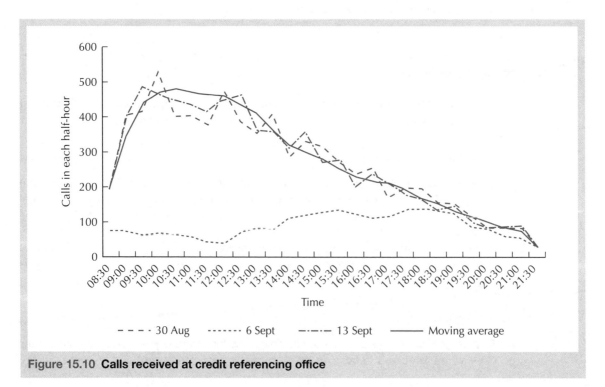

Figure 15.10 Calls received at credit referencing office

Telephone home shopping is an example of mass personal service. In bureaux handling such transactions, the capacity is established to cope with anticipated demand but local, short-term adjustments are always necessary. Figure 15.10 shows the pattern of calls received at a large credit referencing bureau for three consecutive Saturdays in 1997. Two Saturdays, 30 August and 13 September, are typical of a consistent pattern, with small variations around the quarterly moving average. Whatever the day of the week, the staff roster is planned to cover the average call rate plus about 10 per cent. This is adjusted for known events such as public holidays. On each day, random peaks are handled by delaying breaks and cutting the times spent with each customer.

Scheduling is more difficult under effect uncertainty, *see* Chapter 8. Managers knew of the funeral of Diana, Princess of Wales, but could hardly predict its effect. So many people participated at the event, or watched it on television, that business was quiet, as shown in Figure 15.10. Retail sales for the month fell by about 1 per cent due to the 'Diana effect'.[36]

Conclusion: managing primary functions

Operations management is the primary function of the organisation, the transformation of inputs into products. While there are some differences between goods and services, we find many features in common. Tough competition among manufacturers means they increasingly look to customer service for competitive advantage. Examples lie in despatch, promotion and after-sales service. In service provision, many organisations find benefits in arranging back office operations along similar lines to manufacture. We saw, therefore, that rather than use the goods–services distinction, it is more useful to distinguish between operations according to whether the customer is present. Back office services have much in common with manufacturing while front office services have special problems of capacity and queues.

In the competitive environment, organisations gain through offering the right mix of price, quality, reliability, responsiveness, service and speed. We reviewed processes involved in achieving these to conclude:

- The strongest influence on process design is volume. The larger the planned output, the more the organisation will dedicate special-purpose facilities to its delivery.

- Facility location depends on how close the organisation needs to be to its market. Both push and pull factors influence location decisions, the former stemming from dissatisfaction with existing sites, the latter accounting for the new locality.

- Capacity planning is carried out in stages from the long term to the short term, depending on the factors that can be adjusted.

- Scheduling involves short-term capacity management. Inventories and queues uncouple the technical core of the operations system from the changing environment. They enable the core to limit the cost of flexibility but imply that both elements, inventories and queues, must be well managed in the successful enterprise.

QUICK CHECK

Can you ...

- Define operations management.
- Explain the difference between front and back office.
- List five manufacturing systems layouts.
- Identify six patterns of service provision.
- Give three arrangements of queues with more than one service channel.
- Suggest five ways to change the experience of queuing.

- Provide four examples of each of push and pull location factors.
- Outline MRPII and JIT.
- Name the assumptions challenged by OPT; give four examples of constraints.
- Summarise why inventory management is required.
- Suggest three reasons why it is difficult to schedule personal service.

QUESTIONS

Chapter review

15.1 What are the main types of production plant layout and how do they relate to the goods that are made?

15.2 Explain the impact of scale on manufacturing and service process layouts.

15.3 Discuss the advantages and disadvantages of queues from the viewpoints of various stakeholders.

Application

15.4 Consider how the PQRRSS factors apply in the case of Amtico and Sony. What are their implications for production in countries with high labour costs?

15.5 Compare the reasons given for location in Exhibit 15.10 with the pull factors given earlier.

15.6 Investigate the effects on capacity at Manchester Airport if any of the planning assumptions explained in Exhibit 15.12 turned out to be false.

Investigation

15.7 Observe and compare the formation and management of queues at service facilities known to you. How could the facilities be improved?

15.8 Report on the reasons for the siting of any one manufacturing or service facility in your area.

ETHICS TEST: LOCATION

Should a plant, such as the MHO refinery, be forced to move if it cannot cut emissions to near to zero? If so, where should it go?

Metallurgie Hoboken-Overpelt[37]

MHO (now part of Union Minière) was known globally for refining metals from gold to lead. Its plant at Hoboken, Belgium, employs 2500 staff to process 125 000 tonnes of lead each year. In 1973, ten cows and horses died of lead poisoning after grazing near the plant. Soil analyses found lead concentrations of 800 to 9000 parts per million (ppm), while dust on the factory roof measured 72 500. Accepted safe levels are 40 ppm. Forty years of production, with each year sending around 30 tonnes up the chimney, had caused dangerous accumulations of toxic metals.

Government blood tests found that people living locally had high lead concentrations. Children are particularly sensitive. Some had more than three times the recommended safe maximum. Workers' health data were not revealed by a reluctant MHO management. By 1978, protesters were active and the scale of the problem was well known.

The government considered moving all the population at a cost of 2.5 billion francs. Moving the plant would cost four times as much. A compromise was reached; a green belt was established and all contaminated soil was removed. Furthermore, emission and cleanliness standards were tightened. Little changed. Restrictions were stiffened yet, in 1991, lead and cadmium emissions exceeded World Health Organization standards. Fear for the loss of 2500 jobs weighed more heavily than risk to health.

IKEA furnishes the world[38]

In fifty years, Ingvar Kamprad has built Ikea into the world's leading furniture retailer. It operates 150 stores in 29 countries. The average size is 17 250 sq.m. Each, when fully stocked, carries 10 000 separate lines. Allowing for colour and size variations, inventory can exceed 80 000 items. With 100 million copies, the catalogue is among the world's biggest print runs.

Kamprad's breakthrough was to encourage suppliers to use line production for flat-packed furniture coupled with self-service in huge stores. When the first IKEA store opened in Imhult in 1958, furnishing a flat could cost five times a new graduate's annual salary. From IKEA nowadays, the same furniture and fittings would cost less than half a year's pay.

International operations started with stores in Norway and Denmark (1963). IKEA's largest current market is Germany (from 1974), followed by the United Kingdom (1987) and the United States (1985).

Although 10 per cent of items come from the Swedwood subsidiary, IKEA has around 1700 closely monitored suppliers in 53 countries. Sweden (17 per cent), China (9 per cent), Poland (9 per cent), Germany (7 per cent), and Italy (7 per cent) are the most important.

Expansion continues. In 2000, IKEA opened 25 000 sq.m. stores San Francisco, Beijing, Shanghai and Moscow. Thirty-five thousand Muscovites turned up at the Moscow opening to hear Kamprad, who had chosen the city 'on a hunch' greet them in elementary Russian. The aim is to double worldwide sales in five years, with up to 70 new stores. In the United Kingdom, plans are to spend almost £800 million over 10 years to expand from 10 to 30 outlets. Glasgow will be followed by Cardiff, Sheffield and Southampton in 2003. There will be a new £40 million distribution centre in Peterborough.

Despite the popularity of the brand, development often meets opposition. United States applications met resistance from local retailers. Now local authorities are concerned with congestion and the environment. Yet they welcome the stores for their several hundred jobs and up to $1 million of local sales taxes. Furthermore, as 'magnet' stores, they enhance the prestige of shopping developments and contribute to urban renewal. In the United States, agents find potential sites and conduct the statutory environmental impact reports. In the San Francisco area, they found three 8-hectare sites close to major traffic flows, each capable of holding a 25 000 sq.m. building with 1500 parking spaces. Further, they identified a 180 000 sq.m. warehouse to serve the west coast. Meanwhile, Chicago rejected, on traffic grounds, an application for a site near a busy intersection. In Boston, IKEA has searched for 15 years for the right combination of space and location. Boston is attractive for its numbers of college graduates aged 20 to 50.

Questions

1 List and rank the factors in Ikea's location strategy. Explain your ranking.

2 How does IKEA offer a wide range of products at low prices? What are the implications of scale for retail service?

3 What risks and uncertainties are faced by IKEA in globalising its particular business?

Bibliography

Many points covered in this chapter are covered in more detail in John Naylor (2002) *Introduction to Operations Management* (Harlow: Financial Times Prentice Hall). Recommended for further reading are: Nigel Slack *et al.* (2001) *Operations Management* (3rd edition, Harlow: Financial Times Prentice Hall) and E.M. Goldratt and J. Cox (1989) *The Goal* (Aldershot: Gower). The latter has stimulated much original thought in the operations area.

References

1 New, C. and Wheatley, M. (1996) 'The Amtico Company', *Management Today*, November, 84–7; **www.amtico.com**, accessed 23 June 2003.

2 Shepard, Stephen B. (2001) 'The tech slump doesn't scare Michael Dell', *Business Week*, 16 April.

3 In *The Wealth of Nations* (Methuen edn., 1981) Adam Smith classed the work of servants as 'barren and unproductive'.

4 Peters, Tom (1984) 'Hit and run strategy for hypercompetition', *Independent on Sunday, Business News*, 9 October, 22.

5 M2 Communications (2002) *Blackpool coastal protection project is a beacon for modern construction*, M2 Press release, 2 October.

6 Nakamoto, Michiyo (2003) 'A speedier route from order to camcorder: once mass production and high inventories were the order of the day', *Financial Times*, 12 February.

7 Crainer, Stuart (1994) 'Management: pioneers and prophets – Henry Ford', *Financial Times*, 7 November, 12.

8 Developed from a four-element model given by Schmenner, R.W. (1993) *Production/Operations Management*, Macmillan, 18–22.

9 Superdrug (1993) *Success: Customer Care and Service Skills Programme*, Unpublished company materials.

10 East, Robert (1997) 'The anatomy of conquest: Tesco versus Sainsbury', *Kingston University Occasional Paper Series*, **29**, July.

11 Morton, Nuala (1994) 'Cinemas dial box-office hit', *Independent on Sunday, Business News*, 17 July, 8.

12 Maister, D.H. (1985) 'The psychology of waiting lines' in Czeipel, J.H., Solomon, M.R. and Surprenant, C.F. (eds) *The Service Encounter*, Lexington, Mass.: Lexington Books.

13 Davies, Mark M. and Heineke, J. (1994) 'Understanding the roles of the customer and the operation for better queue management', *International Journal of Operations and Production Management*, **14(5)**, 24–31.

14 Render, Barry and Heizer, Jay (1994) *Principles of Operations Management*, London: Allyn and Bacon, 356.

15 Jenkins, Ray (1993) 'The evolution process of the in-store bakery', *Paper No.379, Proceedings of British Society of Baking*, 76th Conference, October.

16 Kirkham, J.D., Richbell, S.M. and Watts, H.D. (1998) 'Downsizing and facility location: plant closures in multi-plant manufacturing firms', *Management Decision*, **36(3)**, 189–97.

17 Karakaya, Fahri and Canel, Cem (1998) 'Underlying dimensions of business location decisions', *Industrial Management and Data Systems*, **98(7)**, 321–9.

18 Invest UK (2003) *Inward investment: case studies*, **www.invest.uk.com/investing/case_Studies.cfm**, accessed 16 April 2003.

19 Hernández, Tony and Bennison, David (2000) 'The art and science of retail location decisions', *International Journal of Retail and Distribution Management*, **28(8)**, 357–67.

20 Bowlby, S., Breheny, M. and Foot, D. (1984) 'Store location: problems and methods 1', *Retail and Distribution Management*, **12(5)**, 31–3; Governments throughout Europe are restricting the growth of out-of-town shopping. *See* Lawson, David (1995) 'Resistance grows in Europe', *Financial Times*, 29 September, 15.

21 Key Note Report (2002) *Bridalwear*, London: Key Note, June.

22 Manchester Airport plc (1993) *Runway 2: Planning application supporting statement*, July, mimeo.; Cobham Resource Consultants and Consultants in Environmental Sciences Ltd (1993) *Runway 2: Environmental statement – non-technical summary*, Manchester: Manchester Airport plc, July, mimeo; Manchester Airport plc (2001) *Exciting new public transport developments at Manchester Airport*, press release; **www.manairport.co.uk**, accessed 20 July 2001.

23 Henderson, B. (1984) *The Logic of Business Strategy*, Cambridge, Mass.: Ballinger, 49–50.

24 Naylor, John (2002) *Operations Management*, 2nd edition, Harlow: Financial Times Prentice Hall, 349–50.

25 Spreadbury, A. (1994) 'Manufacturing resources planning' in Storey, J. (ed.) *New Wave Manufacturing Strategies*, London: Paul Chapman Publishing, 154.

26 For example: Waterlow, G. and Monniot, J. (1986) *A Study of the State of the Art in CAPM in UK Industry*, SERC/ACME, 1986; Whiteside, D. and Ambrose, J. (1984) 'Unsnarling industrial production: Why top management is starting to care', *Industrial Management*, March, 20–6.

27 Luscombe, M. (1994) 'Of course I'm committed to MRPII but...', *Management Services*, March, 12–13.

28 Notes made by a student at John Moores University, 1994. This was a factory with sales of £50 million. Its first MRP system was installed in 1977 and been added to in many steps. Managers reported that they had never been happy with it.

29 Goldratt, E.M. and Cox, J. (1989*) The Goal*, Aldershot: Gower.

30 Gardiner, Stanley C., Blackstone, John,H. and Gardiner, Lorraine R. (1993) 'Drum-Buffer-Rope and buffer management: impact on production management study and practices', *International Journal of Operations and Production Management*, **13(6)**, 68–78.

31 Spencer, M.S. (1991) 'Using *The Goal* in an MRP system', *Production and Inventory Management Journal*, **32(4)**, 22–8.

32 Harrison, A. (1994) 'Just-in-time Manufacturing' in Storey, J. *op. cit.*, 181.

33 Jones, David (2003) 'Careful timing at the heart of a one-to-one relationship', *Liverpool Daily Post*, 26 February.

34 For more on inventory control, *see* Naylor *op. cit.*, 462–81.

35 Verma, Rohit (2000) 'An empirical analysis of management challenges in service factories, service shops, mass services and professional services', *International Journal of Service Industry Management*, **11(1)**, 8–25.

36 Segall, Anne (1997) 'Spending recovers as Diana effect wears off', *Electronic Telegraph*, **901**, 11 November; Segall, Anne (1997) 'High street sales hit by mourning for Diana', *Electronic Telegraph*, **873**, 14 October: **www.telegraph.co.uk:80/et**, accessed 15 October 1997.

37 Schokkaert, Erik and Eyckmans, Johan (1994) 'Environment' in Harvey, Brian (ed.) *Business Ethics*, Hemel Hempstead: Prentice Hall, 195–7; Parti de Travail Belgique (2003) '28 ans de lutte contre le plomb', PTB, **www.ptb.be/solidaire/f1299/um129904.htm**, accessed 16 April 2003.

38 Heller, Robert (2000) 'The Billionaire Next Door', *Forbes*, 8 July; George, Nicholas (2001) 'One furniture store fits all', *Financial Times*, 8 February; Voyle, Susannah (2001) 'Ikea stores for two more cities', *Financial Times*, 4 May; Materna, Jessica (2000) 'Ikea shops for third Bay Area location', *San Francisco Business Times*, 15 December; Goodison, Donna L. (1999) 'Ikea group homes in on Somerville location', *Boston Business Journal*, 30 June.

CHAPTER 16

Marketing: managing relations with customers

Chapter objectives

When you have finished studying this chapter, you should be able to:

- outline the functions of marketing within the organisation;

- evaluate the product life cycle as a model of market behaviour;

- compare different market orientations;

- define marketing research; describe the key activities of understanding customers and segmenting markets;

- show how businesses build relationships with customers;

- define the term *brand*; show where brands have become a battlefield and decide who gains or loses from them; assess the advantages of brand development;

- weigh up ethics and social responsibility issues in marketing.

In business, it is useless to be a creative original thinker unless you can also sell what you create.

David Ogilvy, founder, Ogilvy & Mather advertising

Focus on cameras[1]

Facing a 30 million unit world market that has been, at best, static, leading camera makers followed two strategies. First, they co-operated in the launch in 1995 of the Advanced Photo System, which uses film in self-loading cassettes. Smaller than conventional 35 mm packs, they allowed further miniaturisation of the camera. APS film never leaves the cassette; each shot is addressed so that it can be found for reprints without being marred by dust or sticky fingers. It offers varied picture formats and quicker processing. The price of Kodak's 'Plus Digital' single-use camera, launched in 2003, included a Picture CD made during processing. Presented as the best way to make digital pictures without a digital camera, the system appealed to many wanting to email images without the trouble of editing them. In 2002, APS reached about 8 per cent of the 78 billion exposure film market but was expected to decline slowly. The second strategy saw manufacturers cut dependency on camera sales by diversifying into printers, photocopiers and related optical equipment. Canon, Minolta and others now rely on cameras for less than a quarter of turnover.

Many see the market for the camera-film system as dying, despite APS. As in other fields, the future is digital, which took 30 per cent of camera sales in 2001 and 40 per cent in 2002. It was expected to reach par in 2003 and 63 per cent in 2006. Inclusion in the figures of the cheap single-use film cameras masks the strong switch to digital in the expensive compact zoom sector. For instance, United Kingdom sales in 2002 were 1.5 million for digital and 1.7 million for conventional, yet their average prices were £261 against £73.

Consumers spend almost equally on cameras and film. With a billion cameras in circulation, demand for film and processing is rising slowly. Fuji and Kodak, both of which make both cameras and film, stand to lose most by a switch to digital.

Both have developed mass-market digital cameras. Three barriers constrained the switch, although they have begun to fall. The first is resolution. Casio's QV10, launched in 1995, offered 350 000 pixels for each shot, compared with the equivalent of 20 million using 35 mm film. The smallest capacity of 15 mid-range models announced in March 2003 was 3.1 mega pixels. While most PC screens could not beat even Casio's standard, the difference shows in grainy printing. The second factor is price, with digital units matching compact zoom cameras and not competing at the very cheap end.

The third constraint is computing. Many households have PCs but users do not care to master software such as PhotoSuite and related printing techniques. According to Mr Kobayashi, owner of Japan's leading consumer electronics stores, those that buy seek to make more use of their PCs or become involved in desk top publishing. The 'I want' customers, buying for fun, attach pictures to email, or make greetings cards. The 'I need' customers make images for their small businesses to be used in products or advertising on the Internet. Neither group represents the consumer market.

This market will be put off if the system is too complex or expensive. Most people do not want to send pictures over the Web. Benefits such as instant results seem attractive, but these are available from £20 Polaroid cameras. Yet, alongside other goods with electronic data capture and storage, performance is increasing and prices are falling.

Oddly, the digital revolution may have stimulated interest in 'back to basics' cameras, especially at the top end. Users can control all features, with separate range finders and light meters. At the top end, following a major investment by Hermès, Leica relaunched itself as a luxury brand. Its MP model sells at £1850. Lenses and range finder are extra.

Introduction

Of all the functions, marketing is the one that does most to connect the organisation with the environment. True, others also span boundaries. For example, finance maintains links with banks and money markets, purchasing relates to suppliers, and HRM engages in industrial relations and follows the labour market. The primary role of marketing, however, is boundary spanning. It maintains relations with customers.

Our opening case study, summarised in the rich picture of Figure 16.1, illustrates the scope of the issues in which marketers become involved. The camera makers knew that sales were sluggish. Some had been applying their *brand images* to new product ranges such as photocopiers and medical equipment. Meanwhile, within the camera market, they needed something to stimulate sales. Each company had spent years of development on increasing the flexibility and convenience of cameras while reducing their size and weight. This had become a battleground in the competitive war in which they were engaged. Yet the results were not all advantageous. As sales slowly recovered from the 26 million trough in the mid-1990s, many consumers were buying the cheap, throwaway models that meant less profit from equipment yet more from film and processing.

In the drive to add more convenience, the 35 mm format had itself become the constraint. The APS, requiring wide agreement among the rivalrous camera and film makers if it were to be accepted by a cautious public, offered further enhancement in reliability and convenience. Yet critics saw the changes as offering little more than an extension of the *product life cycle*, discussed in Exhibit 16.1. APS sales replaced 35 mm in a market sustained by rising leisure spending and use of photographs as communication, but hit by falls in tourism.

> A ***brand image*** *represents the set of beliefs that people hold about a brand.*

Possibly distracted by their commitment to APS, leaders were surprised by the speed of growth of digital photography. Casio was the first to step in. There seemed to be a new market, for temporary imaging, that the industry was not aware of. Photography had long since seen itself as producing a permanent record of authentic or artistic images. Yet, as Figure 16.2 suggests, challenging the permanent assumption opens new possibilities.[2] Business people were the first to reach for digital. Entrepreneurs from website creators to estate agents found uses for the new technology. Early sales were not at the expense of film cameras. The potential was uncertain but some, including Fuji, thought it to be huge. As people learned to play with light and shade, focus and framing, the new technology could reawaken an interest in photography generally. Furthermore, the opportunities for add-on products seemed unlimited. The scope and scale of the new opportunity presented new uncertainties for marketing managers. Who would buy? What did they want? Where would they buy? How much were they prepared to pay? Such are typical questions for all products. Yet, in cameras, few had any idea of the answers.

After outlining and defining marketing, this chapter examines the key issues brought out in the case study. These are knowing the market environment, building relationships with customers and creating brands. Finally, since marketing is the most visible of functions, it attracts the most questioning and disapproval. We must discuss, therefore, whether ethical marketing is both possible and desirable.

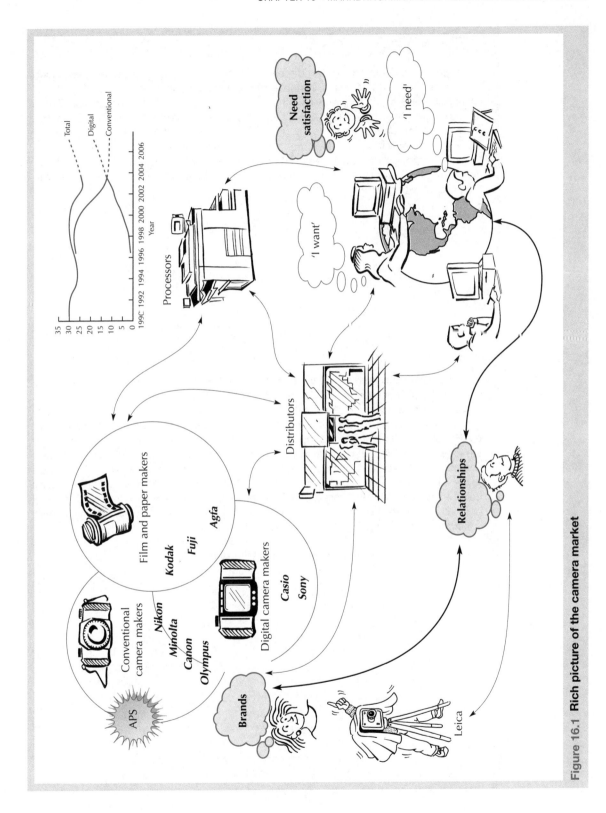

Figure 16.1 Rich picture of the camera market

Exhibit 16.1 Strengths and limitations of the product life cycle

The product life cycle (PLC) is a time series model describing changes in sales. Used in the right way, the PLC gives valuable insight into how markets develop. The model is usually presented in four phases – introduction, growth, maturity and decline. There are corresponding marketing tactics. Advertising is needed during introduction and early growth to gain acceptance and build market share. As sales mature, there is increasing competition and the emphasis changes to pricing policy. Finally, as sales tail off, promotion through special offers and discounts takes over. One means to extend the PLC, shown by the dashed curve in the diagram below, is by relaunching the product with new features.

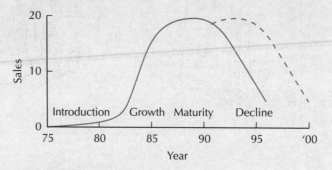

The PLC has its weaknesses. First, it does not apply in all cases. The demand for some products hardly changes at all. Others, such as Beecham's Powders, have been around for so long that it would be a rash person who forecast when decline is to set in. Second, the patterns of the past may not give a guide to the future. The car industry was used to the PLC of models that needed replacing every few years. As development costs rose, the time between model changes was increased. Recently, however, intensive competition and new design approaches have tended to cut the cycle time again. This leads on to the third difficulty, unpredictability. The PLC suggests how sales of a new product may behave; yet, it is useless if we are looking for forecasts for any time in the future. The graph in the diagram below shows the fraction of American firms' equipment investment spent on IT. Who can guess the future shape of this curve?

IT spend as % of total investment, US

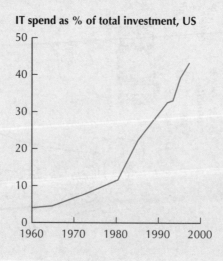

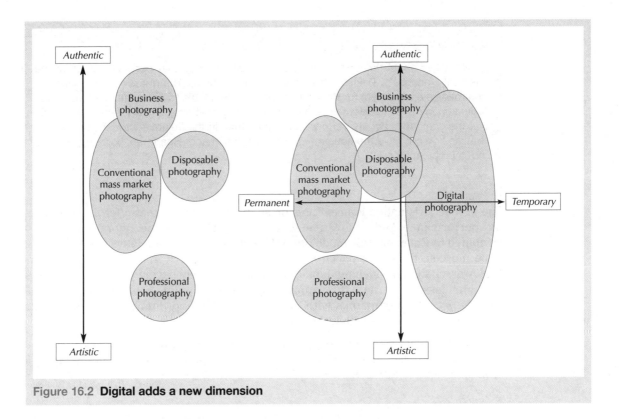

Figure 16.2 **Digital adds a new dimension**

What is marketing?

Many think of marketing as a clever form of selling. The marketing approach in business involves a commitment to satisfying the needs of customers. It incorporates both a set of values, concerning market orientation, about the way business should be conducted, and a set of processes that put them into practice.

■ Market orientation

Several authors investigate the orientation shown by marketing managers as they consider stakeholder interests, especially those of customers, the organisation and society. Kotler and colleagues identify five alternative approaches.[3]

■ *Production*

Stressing production arises from the view that customers prefer products that are both widely available and affordable. Management's focus is on efficiency. *See* the example in Exhibit 16.2.[4]

Note how the manager uses the first person to present himself as the embodiment of the railway company. He reveals his production orientation both by denying the significance of competition and in the choice of words he uses to describe his problems.

Exhibit 16.2 The dilemma of excess demand

When asked about the competition between rail and road transport in his country, the General Manager of Pakistan National Railways replied, 'The question is not whether the roads are a problem for Pakistan railways. I am unable to cope with the load which is laid upon me. In the passenger sector, I am responsible for fifty per cent of the traffic yet the demand is twenty per cent more than that. In the freight sector, the figures are similar. I do not have the equipment to carry the demand. Road transport, therefore, is not a problem for me.'

■ *Product*

The product orientation concentrates on supplying products that offer the best quality, performance and innovative features. Captured in the quotation (below) attributed to Emerson, this mode of thinking continues to dominate some industries, none more so than pharmaceuticals, where most believe that science counts. As Ogilvy asserts in our opening quotation, however, merely having brilliant products is bad business. Why has this apparently obvious point been neglected? *The Economist* cites companies with cultures founded and dominated by scientists working within markets with little price competition.[5]

> *'If a man write a better book, preach a better sermon, or make a better mouse-trap than his neighbour, though he build his house in the woods, the world will make a beaten path to his door.'*
>
> *Source*: Ralph Waldo Emerson

■ *Selling*

Here the assumption is that customers will not buy unless the organisation devotes substantial effort to selling and promotion. Perceiving the limitations of using inefficient distributors to sell goods in growing markets, some manufacturers were attracted by vertical integration into retailing. One example is Bata, described in Exhibit 16.3.[6]

Exhibit 16.3 Bata's empire under threat

Traditionally, the key to success in the shoe business had been a highly efficient manufacturing system coupled to an extensive distribution network. Tomáš Baťa (1876–1932) was a self-made man who built his shoe business to become one of Czechoslovakia's largest enterprises. He pioneered the application of modern work methods and the provision of decent working and living conditions for employees. The tradition was continued by his son, Tom, after the family, fearing Nazi occupation, moved the business to Canada in the 1930s. In 2003, the company employed 55 000 staff in 46 factories and 4700 shops, supported by over 100 000 independent retailers and franchisees. They made and sold 140 million pairs of shoes each year. The business had returned to the Czech Republic, operating 76 shops selling 3 million pairs.

The previous quarter-century, however, had seen rapid change. The key factor in the industry was no longer selling from a low-cost manufacturing base. Marketing came to the fore. Strong, distinctive and innovative brands, such as Nike and Reebok, were sold through large retailers in shopping centres or on the edge of town. Tom Bata admitted, 'Whereas at one time our retail operation was primarily a means of distributing the products of our manufacturers, in these more sophisticated types of outlets, no manufacturer could possibly produce the variety of products which the consumer would like.' In spite of opposition from strong-willed family members, trustees and managers, the company was being forced to respond to the new situation.

The selling approach is also used with *unsought items.* These are items that the customer does not think of buying but becomes interested in once the benefits have been pointed out. A good example is the *clockwork radio*, whose development and selling are described in Chapter 17.

■ *Marketing*

Nike and Reebok, mentioned in Exhibit 16.3, made the breakthrough in marketing. This means that they found out the needs and wants of target customers and satisfied them better than competitors did. In contrast to selling, which starts with the product and the system to supply it, marketing 'puts customer needs and preferences at the centre of all decision making'.[7] It is critical in consumer markets. A survey by McKinsey in the United Kingdom found that managers from companies dealing with consumers placed marketing as the most important factor in achieving business objectives, followed by sales and operations. Those whose goods go to other companies, however, saw it as less important than sales.[8]

■ *Socially responsible marketing*

Growing out of the marketing concept, socially responsible marketing responds to the ethical issues raised by marketing practice. These range from the way information about customers is collected and used to the need to be truthful in the way products are promoted. We shall return to these questions later in the chapter.

Drawing these points together, we reach a definition:

> *Marketing is the process that identifies and anticipates customer requirements and satisfies them responsibly, in the face of competitive pressure, to meet organisational objectives.*

This definition means that the marketing manager focuses on exchange with that important element of the environment – customers. There are wider interactions, too, shown in Figure 16.3. The organisation supplies its products to customers, either directly or through distributors. Mirroring the sales and supply chain is the

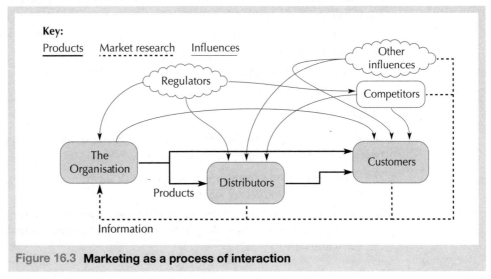

Figure 16.3 Marketing as a process of interaction

process of *market research*. This gathers information on relevant aspects of the environment, from the needs of customers to the behaviour of distributors, competitors and other actors and stakeholders. The diagram also shows influence links. The organisation promotes its sales, through advertising and other means, while competitors do likewise. Many markets are influenced by regulators, such as price controls by governments to voluntary codes of conduct in advertising. Other stakeholders, such as consumer groups and those concerned with the natural environment, exercise pressure in the marketplace.

Marketing research

The first part of the marketing definition refers to identifying and anticipating customer requirements. Together with studying the competitive environment, this is marketing research. We can define it as *the collection and analysis of data about any problem in the field of marketing*. It has four aspects:

- to identify opportunities and problems in the marketplace;
- to help in planning marketing activities;
- to monitor marketing performance; and
- to learn, that is to improve understanding of the marketing process.[9]

The scope can be wide. Some groups or agencies specialise in one aspect, such as measuring advertising effectiveness or retail spending, while others cover most aspects of the discipline. The scope of such studies can be summarised as follows:

- *Market research*: demand for new and current products; local and international markets. (Note that *market* research refers to finding out about markets. The more general term, *marketing* research, is concerned with the marketing process.)
- *Product research*: comparison among rivals; testing demand; analysing problems; packaging.
- *Promotion research*: effectiveness of selling methods; motivation; sales force management.
- *Distribution channel research*: selecting channels; locating distribution centres, dealers and agents.
- *Pricing research*: elasticities; attitudes; forecasting.

▓ Data

Central to any study is the collection of data. Researchers commonly distinguish between two types, according to their sources:

- *Primary data* come from direct contact with customers, buyers, users or other actors within the marketing system.
- *Secondary data* are not drawn directly by their user, nor are they specific to the user. They may have been collected for reasons and by means that the user would not have chosen.

Secondary data, although easy and cheap to obtain, have limited value, *see* Exhibit 16.4.[10] Marketing studies often start with a review of secondary data that can form a context for the design and carrying out of the more difficult and expensive primary data collection.

Exhibit 16.4 Secondary data on security systems

Abundance is an advantage of secondary data. Any information from any source – inside the firm, official agencies, commercial providers or casual origin – can be fruitful. It is often cheap and quickly obtained. Despite these advantages, secondary sources are poor substitutes for direct involvement with the customer.

The table compares the rate of car theft in various countries. A car is broken into every 20 seconds in Britain and insurers settle some £500 million of claims. There is no convincing explanation of why this happens more than elsewhere.

Such data are readily available to makers of cars, car radios, alarm and tracker systems, immobilisers and so on. But what do the data tell them about the market for new security devices? On its own, the information says very little.

	Cars (millions)	Thefts per 1000 cars
UK – England and Wales	22.4	22.7
UK – Scotland	1.9	15.5
UK – Northern Ireland	0.5	14.6
United States	133.9	11.5
France	25.1	11.4
Italy	30.0	10.2
Norway	1.7	10.0
Spain	16.2	7.0
Netherlands	5.6	6.1
Germany	40.5	3.2
Austria	3.6	1.4

The collection of primary data starts not from a scan of what is available but from asking managers what they want to know. All aspects of marketing can be studied, for example distributors, advertisers and especially customers. We can use the last to illustrate some problems of primary data collection.

■ Understanding customers

Like opening a Russian doll, understanding of customer behaviour is multi-layered. We shall refer to three layers here. First, many organisations collect data on who customers are, what they buy and when they buy. While detailed analysis was once only possible with a few customers, databases support studies when there are many more. Leading retailers have, through loyalty schemes, built up huge resources recording the habits of their customers. Even small and medium enterprises have found that sales analysis gives them a better appreciation of which customers are important to them, *see* Exhibit 16.5.[11]

Exhibit 16.5 Using an information system to know about customers

Mersey Equipment distributes equipment for welding and related trades. It has 16 staff. When it bought a small computer system, the firm expected benefits from faster invoicing and cash flow. Yet it was the spreadsheet facility that brought pay-offs. Using it for sales analysis, the managers studied trends for each product line and customer, leading them to change their stock range and pricing structure.

The second layer of understanding starts to unravel *why* customers make purchases. Exhibit 2.5 gave an instance of DIY sales.[12] Relating sales to factors such as house prices, a marketing manager can be more confident about planning. Yet the data give no more than behavioural observations, suggesting what responses may be expected to policies such as increasing floor space. It does not, so to speak, get under the skin of the customer to find out why these responses occur.

The third layer, therefore, is concerned with customers' attitudes. The conventional view in marketing is that changes in attitudes lead to changes in purchasing behaviour. To see the implications of this, we can again refer to DIY. Increased car ownership has changed consumers' attitudes to store size and location. They are now happy to buy bulky items from stores especially designed to stock them.

Difficulties with attitudes

Examining changes in attitudes is more difficult than observing changes in behaviour. Sales data give a simple measure of the latter. Yet if focusing on attitudes, the marketing researcher has to study shifts in both attitudes and behaviour to understand the connections. The plausibility of the link from attitudes to behaviour hides a serious flaw, however. Favourable attitudes towards products may not affect buying behaviour. You may be impressed by the humour of Guinness commercials, the green credentials of Body Shop or the strength of the Volvo safety cage. Indeed, you may concede that these companies provide good value *for those who deal with them*. Yet you may never buy. Excellent promotion may increase your intention to buy, but this is only one factor in the purchase decision.

A further difficulty arises from looking for the source of attitudes. We can assert that attitudes are the result of beliefs. In turn, beliefs are affected by experiences ranging from advertising to previous encounters with the brand or product. For instance, you may acknowledge that Guinness is a good product cleverly advertised. Yet you may not like the taste. While marketers may be tempted, therefore, to investigate beliefs and how they are formed, they then face even greater difficulties in linking them through to sales and profits.

Many companies have given up theorising about behaviour and using broad survey techniques to uncover its causes. Instead, they are taking a more holistic perspective, emphasising qualitative research. *Focus groups* assemble invited consumers to discuss all aspects of marketing. *Storytelling, see* Exhibit 16.6, is a relatively new approach to probing behaviour and discovering feelings.[13] In each case, broad surveys give way to in-depth studies of a few customers. The purpose is to gain flashes of insight rather than measure marginal shifts in response levels.

Exhibit 16.6 Following customers home

Known for the *Quicken* range, software company Intuit built its business through offering simple software to individuals or small businesses. Customers are less interested in technology than convenience. Intuit tests new products on small groups of people, four-fifths of whom are non-users. Employees visit people's homes to find out how people organise their finances when left to themselves. In *Follow Me Home*, company staff watch over customers' shoulders as they try to install and use Intuit software. They leave behind cassette machines for users to record comments or complaints.

Market segmentation

A key use of customer data is in matching customers to products. For instance, restaurants offer American, Chinese, Greek, Indian, Italian, Mexican and Turkish cuisine. Each specialises, appealing to the segment interested in its style. In other industries, firms offer a product range, each part of which aims at a different customer group. News International segments its newspaper market by country and readers' needs. The *Sun* and *The Times* are just two of many titles it produces throughout the world.

Segmentation has three elements:

- to define and understand the market in terms of realistic segments to which products can be offered;
- through product differentiation, to create a range of offerings to suit the segments;
- to promote the products using appropriate selling methods.

The ultimate expression of this process is *customisation*, which is offering a unique product to each customer. As we saw in Chapter 15, many businesses, from architects to fashion houses, already achieve this. Most customers, however, cannot afford such luxuries. To supply them, the key is to find ways of creating differentiation while maintaining low supply costs. The product range is limited not only by the production system but also by the extra cost of making choice available to consumers. Exhibit 16.7 gives an example of how differentiation may be getting out of hand.[14]

Exhibit 16.7 Product clutter

Boot's stocks 75 kinds of toothbrush, not counting colour variations, and 240 kinds of shampoo. John Lewis carries 12 kinds of kitchen scissors. Philips produces 13 kettles and 24 irons. Nike offers 347 separate varieties of training shoe. There are least 110 different types of personal stereo on sale in the United Kingdom.

Segmentation in practice

Segmentation has become standard practice for companies that market to large numbers. There were two conventional ways:

- Location segmentation works when consumption patterns depend on where customers live, work or otherwise spend their time. Locally, the position of many shops near passing trade influences their success. Tobacconists, sandwich shops and newsagents are examples. On a broader scale, customers for utilities have tradition-ally been segmented geographically. Technological and regulatory changes, however, have recently broken down such barriers. Separating product and trans-mission charges enables gas and electricity consumers to buy from anyone.

■ Socio-economic segmentation is based on the notion that consumption patterns relate to differences in basic personal variables such as age, gender and income. Government income statistics are published using groupings such as A, B, C_1, C_2, D and E. Since so many secondary data are published on such groups, many marketers build their own analyses around the same classifications. They help understand demand for some products, such as the press; broadsheets are spoken of as 'ABC$_1$ newspapers'. Yet, they say little of the consumption of roller skates or rock music. This emphasises the difficulty of using secondary data in marketing research.

Segmentation by lifestyle

Rather than start from classes based on secondary data, research and media agen-cies now choose clusters according to observed consumption patterns. For instance, young people living in cheap rented accommodation around universities have more in common with each other than do their parents. Whether they are offspring of pro-fessional or manual workers, or come from the town or the countryside, their spending habits will be similar. They drink much wine, but buy little life insurance.

Identifying sets by behaviour is known as segmentation by *lifestyle*. Groups are discovered from marketing data using statistical measures of similarity. Details of the technique, cluster analysis, are beyond our scope; it is enough to say it associ-ates individuals according to their patterns of survey responses or actual consumption. Different agencies come up with their own patterns to which they often attach labels evoking the essence of each cluster. Figure 16.4 is based on the Claritas approach, *Lifestyle View*. United Kingdom households are divided into four main 'life stage' groups, 16 sub-groups and 60 clusters, each averaging about $1\frac{1}{2}$ per cent of the population; only a few of the latter are shown in the figure.[15]

Armed with lifestyle data, the marketing manager focuses on potential customers more closely than ever. Claritas deals in marketing information originated from Littlewoods' long involvement with the consumer market through mail order and football pools. Its market targeting system combines census and electoral lists with mail order and credit data to build understanding of people, households and neigh-bourhoods. For example: Bromley has three times the national average of 'City Slickers' – the most affluent Empty Nesters – but only a third of the national average in the 'Hand to Mouth' cluster; 41 per cent of its households shop at Sainsbury (compared with 17 per cent for the nation); 49 per cent (24) carry a Sainsbury loy-alty card; and 5 per cent (3.7) have three or more cars. The implications for holidays, health clubs, hearing aids, hairdressing or horticulture are clear.

Limitations of lifestyle

As if improving the sharpness of photograph prints, analysts attempt to identify clusters ever more finely. Yet their groupings remain aggregates of people with broadly similar habits. Clearly, the selection of the groups depends on the criteria being used to separate them and these in turn are related to both the quality and quantity of the original survey data. There may be differences, however, among members of a cluster that are not picked up yet are critical to a potential user.

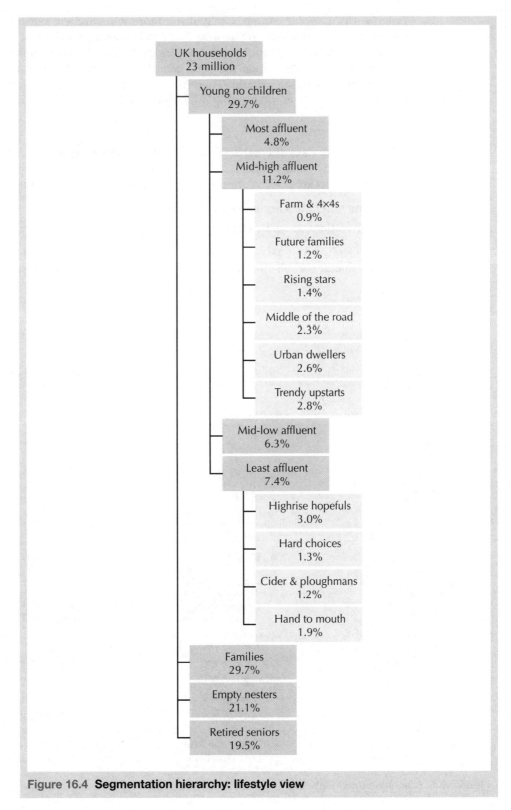

Figure 16.4 Segmentation hierarchy: lifestyle view

Trendy upstarts, for example, may drink more wine and eat out more often than the population as a whole. Yet, among them will be asthma sufferers, guitarists, football players, primary school teachers, foreign nationals, philosophers and so on. Users of the profiling system will only gain if their particular requirements can be linked to the clustering criteria. Therefore, a vegetarian products company will not gain if questions about meat eating are never asked.

Freakish patterns

Refining clusters risks discovering freakish patterns. One study compared answers from 30 000 respondents to the British General Household Survey with their birth dates.[16] Two explanations are possible for the unexpected results shown in Figure 16.5:

- consumption habits are influenced by the stars; or
- the correlations arose by chance.

Before rejecting the astrological link, we should recognise that half of United Kingdom adults consult their horoscopes at least once a week. Most may reject the

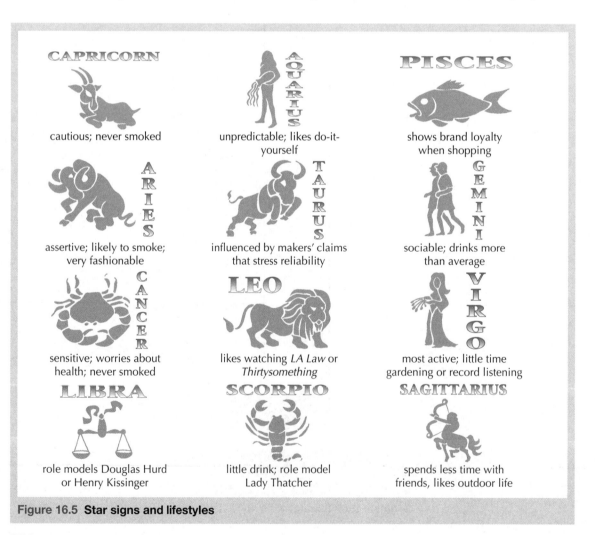

CAPRICORN
cautious; never smoked

AQUARIUS
unpredictable; likes do-it-yourself

PISCES
shows brand loyalty when shopping

ARIES
assertive; likely to smoke; very fashionable

TAURUS
influenced by makers' claims that stress reliability

GEMINI
sociable; drinks more than average

CANCER
sensitive; worries about health; never smoked

LEO
likes watching *LA Law* or *Thirtysomething*

VIRGO
most active; little time gardening or record listening

LIBRA
role models Douglas Hurd or Henry Kissinger

SCORPIO
little drink; role model Lady Thatcher

SAGITTARIUS
spends less time with friends, likes outdoor life

Figure 16.5 Star signs and lifestyles

birth-sign to behaviour link, although some will believe in it.[17] But we could think of the correlation in reverse. Through studying horoscopes, people learn about the way people with their signs are supposed to behave. Tell Scorpios that they 'are loyal and deep yet vindictive, ruthless and jealous', and they might turn out that way. In other words, they are influenced not by the stars but by astrologers! Is this the subtlest form of marketing?

Segment size one

The variation of questions that could be asked of databases is endless, especially as they gather and store more data. Cluster sizes are becoming smaller so that firms looking, say, for 'childless people who like to holiday abroad and list walking and theatre among their leisure interests' obtain short, yet high-quality mailing lists. Eventually, the cluster size comes down to one. With powerful information systems, it becomes unnecessary to aggregate data at all. In principle, each research question can be answered by scanning personal profiles according to relevant criteria. Marketers seek to cater for the needs of each individual by gathering data on, and responding to, their unique preferences.[18] This takes us on to the notion of relationship marketing, RM.

Building relationships with customers

Partly from having only a vague understanding of who customers were, much effort in mass marketing had been focused on winning customers with less attention being paid to keeping them. Competitiveness was based on getting the market to respond to clever manipulation of the 4Ps. These are the four competitive strategies conventionally seen as available to the marketing manager, as shown in Exhibit 16.8.

Exhibit 16.8 The 4Ps of marketing

- *Product* – design of new products, extending the life of current ones; brands, packaging and associated services.
- *Price* – pricing policies and their links to costs and competition.
- *Promotion* – communication – advertising, sales promotion, public relations; personal selling.
- *Place* – distribution channels; logistics, including stockholding; location of outlets.

Despite careful segmentation, these strategies are crude instruments: products only approximate to customer needs; pricing effects are difficult to track; much promotional effort is wasted; and stocks and outlets do not satisfy everyone. Top marketers see them as outdated. Emphasis has shifted to *adding value through the quality of the relationship between firm and customer*. Loyal customers come back many times and, when they do, they spend more.

For marketers, the shift incorporates a new emphasis on matching. They have learned from both conventional service industries and industrial marketing. In the latter, with few buyers and sellers for many products, understanding and solving a customer's problems has long been a key strategy. Now, many more businesses see that they must get closer to their customers. At the heart of the paradigm is the notion of partnership with customers, and rapid response. Can this be achieved in the consumer market? Certainly, advances in information systems suggest such a goal is attainable. As Crainer points out, 'When it comes to creating loyal customers, the database is king'.[19] Exhibit 16.9 shows how it works.[20]

Exhibit 16.9 Driving the database

A bank wants to test the effectiveness of three types of incentive, communicated by telephone or mail, to customers with a current account living in a certain region. This means six combinations, $I_{1\text{-phone}}$, $I_{1\text{-mail}}$, $I_{2\text{-phone}}$, etc. It tests these variations against separate groups from its database; then, in the light of results, it modifies the offers and tests them again. Results show which customers prefer which offers. Having found these customers in the database, it launches the full programme.

■ Relationships and episodes

RM, or 'one-to-one' marketing, treats each customer as an individual. Products are matched to a customer's needs, thereby building a permanent relationship. Ravald and Gronroos distinguish between a relationship and the episodes from which it is built: 'An episode can be defined as an event or interaction that has a clear starting point and an ending point and represents a complete exchange. In an episode there can exist several interactions, such as check-in, room and breakfast during a stay at a hotel, where the stay represents the actual episode.'[21] Then, like the pragmatic communication model of Chapter 13, the relationship between customer and hotel develops from the series of episodes.

To understand what happens during an interaction, therefore, we must look into both the episode itself and its contribution to the relationship. The value of the episode to the customer depends on its benefits compared with its costs, as follows:

$$Total\ episode\ value = (Episode\ and\ Relationship\ benefits) - (Episode\ and\ Relationship\ costs)$$

This equation has two important implications. First, managers should increase the benefits of episodes and the relationship while reducing the costs that the customer has to face. The latter fall into three categories:

- direct costs are money payments to maintain the relationship, including subscription fees, insurance premiums and bank account charges;
- indirect costs are incurred by the customer because of failure. These include costs of a breakdown, delays in delivery or correcting errors;
- psychological costs are mental burdens such as uncertainty over the supplier's performance, the need to solve problems in the relationship, or worry over whether the relationship is the best one.

The second implication comes from the interaction between episode costs and relationship costs. A poor episode within a positive relationship may be ignored. For instance, poor service may be tolerated once if a complaint is well handled and the overall relationship is satisfactory. On the other hand, a positive relationship can only be built from a series of positive episodes. Therefore, relationships and episodes are closely interdependent.

The emergence of RM highlights the cost side of the value equation. Customer-perceived value rises if any cost is reduced. To achieve this, the supplier must understand each customer's needs. A first step is to cut direct costs, such as the price, and increase purchase convenience. Improvements can also be made to the indirect and psychological costs. For instance, when a retailer is out of stock, or a washing machine repair is delayed, the customer experiences indirect and psychological costs that could be avoided.

■ Building relationships

The idea of episodes building into a relationship is useful for understanding RM. It implies involvement over a period. Time is only one element, however. Kotler and colleagues see RM as 'creating, maintaining and enhancing *strong* relationships with customers'.[22] Maintenance and enhancement are achieved through multiple episodes, but what does it mean to develop strong relationships? Three approaches are proposed:

■ Offering financial benefits – such as vouchers or discounts for regular purchasers. Examples include frequent filer and shopping reward programmes.

■ Adding social benefits – increasing social bonds through learning about customers and their needs. Staff think of customers as *clients*, treating them less as ciphers and more as individuals. For example, rather than a customer dealing with many departments, banks now assign one person to look after all aspects of their accounts. Individuals become 'personal banking advisers'.

■ Creating structural ties – furnishing customers with equipment or technical support to ease regular use of the supplier's products. This is the effect of BSkyB's provision of aerials and decoder boxes as part of television service contracts.

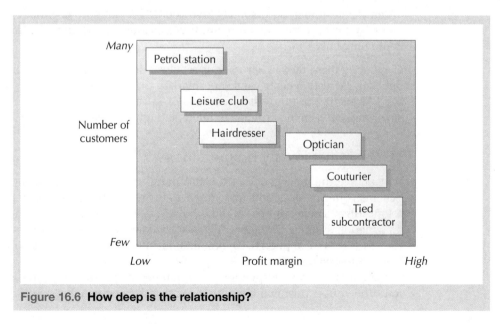

Figure 16.6 **How deep is the relationship?**

In practice, what organisations can do, and what customers will accept, depend on the business environment. As mentioned above, close relationships are common in many industries. Kotler and colleagues show how profit margins and number of customers influence how deep the relationship can be. Figure 16.6 uses these scales to show some examples. The deepest relationships occur in the area of darkest shading. A specialist, such as an engineering consultancy, has few customers and seeks a high profit margin. To maintain its position, the specialist works with the customer to improve service value. In contrast, the petrol station has the shallowest interaction. Selling is by self-service without after-sales follow-up.

Not all companies follow the same strategy. Some opticians, for example, develop traditional relationships with regular customers, charging high prices for personal service with 'extras' included. Others operate more like supermarkets, stressing value from low basic prices with a tariff of extras.

In a study of consumer relationships, Pressey and Matthews identified four factors that influence their depth.

■ *Contact*

Personal contact facilitates RM. This suggests that the approach will work best where contact is frequent and the customer continues to require the service.

■ *Power*

Links with balanced power support RM. The experience of industrial marketing shows that the most stable relationships occur when the parties share power as opposed to one coercing the other. Power is equal when each party selects the other and is able to choose an alternative.

■ *Professionalism*

Encounters requiring or involving professional behaviour assist RM. A seller shows professionalism in offering expert advice and engendering trust. Further, where transactions share much technical information, a common outlook will be valuable.

■ *Involvement*

When the customer is personally involved, RM is supported. A high level of involvement by both parties leads to high commitment, sharing of information and a continuing link.[23]

Comparing these factors across four retail service sectors, namely hairdresser/ barber, optician, recreation centre and supermarket, the authors found that conditions favouring RM existed in the first three but not in the fourth. Yet, as we shall see below, supermarkets seem determined to build marketing strategies using RM principles.

■ Customer loyalty programmes

We can see the emergence of the RM paradigm in customer loyalty programmes. Schemes offering discounts and vouchers for repeat purchases have been around for a long time. Their application has, however, been stimulated by the availability of information systems. Frequent flier programmes offer extra rewards to regular customers. Yet, as Exhibit 16.10 explains, airlines gain as much from information as from increased turnover.

We can see how well-planned programmes meet Kotler's criteria for successful RM. They offer: financial benefits through prizes or vouchers; social benefits if the

Exhibit 16.10 The loyal air force

Frequent flier programmes, such as Lufthansa's *Miles and More* or BMI's *Diamond Club*, have become important factors in building customer loyalty. They have spread rapidly from their 1980s origins in the United States. Members earn points or *air miles* to be exchanged for flight tickets or other incentives, such as stays at partner hotels.

One reason for success is the limited price competition on tickets. About a quarter of European business travellers decide on their carrier because of loyalty points.

Although schemes may cancel each other out in their immediate impact, the real benefit to airlines lies in the information they deliver. Since more than 85 per cent of travellers used to book through agents, airlines have known little about their customers, not even their addresses. Now, airlines gather details on the travel patterns of frequent fliers. A firm that can make good use of these data stands to gain.

airline routinely responds to passengers' special needs, such as for meals or seating position; and structural links through simplified booking procedures and priority access to busy flights. Clearly, the *depth* of the relationship will depend on how episodes develop. At a basic level, more episodes yield more rewards. Trust will grow, however, if it is clear to the customer that shared information is handled professionally and the travel service is correspondingly enhanced.

■ Relationship marketing in retailing

Supermarkets are among many retail chains to develop loyalty cards as competitive weapons.[24] In return for about 1 per cent discount on purchases, shoppers reveal details of their shopping habits and, by implication, aspects of their lives. This information forms a platform for further relationship building:

■ The accent is on *customer share* and not on market share. If a firm satisfies all the needs of 10 per cent of the population, it will do better than satisfying 10 per cent of the needs of the whole population. It will be more efficient and resistant to competition. For instance, knowing the buying patterns of its key customers tells the retailer how to shape its stockholding policy to best suit them.

■ Promotional efforts can be tested and then targeted, as in Exhibit 16.9. A mailshot announcing a new flavour of *Whiskas* can be sent only to those with cats.

■ The database supports product diversification. Recognising customers' frustration with the location and opening hours of banks, Tesco used its *Clubcard* to found a new financial service. This is but one of many possibilities opened by access to detailed customer data.

■ Database skills can be transferred to new markets, enabling a brand to be adapted to each local culture. If price is more important to customers than number of lines carried, managers do better if they concentrate on volume sales of a narrow range.

Exhibit 16.11 summarises how letters to customers are generated. Loyalty cards have been introduced, with variations, throughout the world. Firms co-operate in schemes such as 'co-branded' Visa cards. In The Netherlands, traditional resistance to credit means that fewer people hold them. However, if a group offers affinity cards with both loyalty privileges and credit, the package is more acceptable. Tesco saw the potential of its database methods when entering new markets, such as South

Korea. Despite being an outsider, within two years it felt it knew more about local shopping habits than most rivals did.[25]

> ### Exhibit 16.11 Tesco writes to you, and you, and you ...[26]
>
> The first Clubcard mailshot, in 1995, contained an A4 letter with coupons. Now, contractor Polestar Direct sends more than 10 million statements every quarter. About two million pack variations have specific letters and flash messages linking locality and spending levels with new store openings and targeted offers. Some contain CDs. Polestar prints the stationery on 10-colour presses before personalisation using 12 laser printers.

Do loyalty cards work?

Will the adoption of RM principles bring long-term success? Notwithstanding their apparent advantages, retailers' benefits may be illusory when margins are slim. Some chains have withdrawn to refocus on 'low prices'. On the other hand, Tesco, first in the United Kingdom market, covered its start-up costs with increased sales. Rivals Sainsbury, having initially derided Tesco's 'electronic trading stamps', entered 15 months behind. On the day of Sainsbury's launch, Tesco announced the addition of a bank account. Few commentators believed Sainsbury's claim that the card would add 3 per cent to sales.[27]

Loyalty programmes yield temporary advantages to innovators who reach the market first. Later, as others copy, the gains may be cancelled. In the supermarket industry, customer ties remain weak. The financial benefits of membership are small. Further, social and structural ties are, at best, peripheral. A third of United Kingdom shoppers visit several stores to obtain the best prices.[28] Top reasons for choice of store are convenience, prices, distance, quality, range and parking. Therefore, the marginal benefit of loyalty cards is unlikely to tie down the so-called 'promiscuous shopper'.

The growth of loyalty programmes adds fuel to criticisms of marketing. These include sustaining high prices, adding to the costs of promotion and distribution, acting deceptively and disadvantaging some customers to benefit others. As we shall see, these points are not always supported by evidence. Yet they do concern those firms that seek to act responsibly. So why are cards so important to those issuing them? The answer lies in the value of the information on customers and consequently helping to build the retailers' brands.

Building brands

A brand is an ownership mark. In the marketplace, the term describes the names or symbols that identify and differentiate some products from others. Labels from Beecham's to BP and Saab to Sony conjure up brand images in consumers' minds. Their importance arises from people's preferences, which assign such value to the names that they represent a significant proportion of the assets of a business. One consultancy assessed the name Marlboro to be worth more than £27 billion.[29] When Ford bought Jaguar, an estimate placed physical assets at just one-sixth of the price.[30] The rest covered knowledge, systems and especially the brand.

The value of names is partly the result of the cumulative investment made in them. Owners constantly nurture, control and defend their meaning. In many countries, they are recognised as intellectual property to be protected both by the common law and by rules on trademarks and copyright, *see* Chapter 17. An entrepreneur can neither make Levi's jeans nor use an imitative name, font or logo. This does not normally prevent a Mr Levi from making photocopiers carrying his name, as long as he does not suggest an association with Levi Strauss Co.

> ***Brand image*** *refers to the set of beliefs that people hold about a brand.*

To avoid problems of imitation and to prevent the slide of a word into common use, brand owners continually support their names with advertising, promotion and packaging, and an occasional legal action. While still registered as trademarks, Biro, Fibreglass, Hoover, JCB, Jeep and Thermos have lost some of their worth through fame and common use. Among the world's big advertising spenders, Unilever invested €6.6 billion in 2002 across its wide product range.

Kellogg's European outlay has been some €300 million each year to defend and differentiate its products from the twin threats of own-label and world leader General Mills. Some countries are experiencing growth, but the main breakfast cereal markets, the UK and USA, have matured. Here, consumption has peaked at 250 bowls per person and competition keeps margins tight. Interest in muffins and bagels is rising.[31]

■ Manufacturers versus retailers

While we often think of brands as covering manufactured goods, other types of business have long recognised the potential of names and trademarks. Banks from Rothschild's to HSBC or media businesses from Bertelsmann to the BBC all have names with sterling reputations. Even nations, from Belgium to Thailand, are developing their names as brands, not only to support tourism but also to convey a range of values related to other national activities.[32] No brand builder, however, has bettered the great retailers. Bloomingdale, Boot, Fortnum and Mason, Gucci, Macy, Marks and Spencer were nothing if not great developers of brands. Another great name was F.W. Woolworth, *see* Exhibit 16.12.

Exhibit 16.12 Woolworth's life cycle

Frank Winfield Woolworth (1852–1919) opened his first 'five and ten cent' shop in Pennsylvania in 1879. With his brother, he built a chain of hundreds of similar stores in North America and Europe. After 1950, rising prices, changing habits, loss of focus and competition from specialists put the trading formula out of date. Overseas chains were sold and the last United States store closed in 1997.

In the consumer market, many predict the death of manufacturers' brands in favour of the retailers'. Some grocers, listed in Exhibit 16.13, already sell much of their packaged goods in this form.[33] Interpreting such data is crucial to manufacturers

Exhibit 16.13 Proportion of own-label goods sold by Europe's top dozen grocers

Carrefour	France	15%
Metro	Germany	18%
Rewe	Germany	24%
Tesco	UK	24%
Intermarché	France	12%
Auchan	France	12%
Edeka	Germany	10%
Aldi	Germany	95%
Ahold	Netherlands	25%
Leclerc	France	17%
Sainsbury	UK	44%
Casino	France	30%

and retailers alike. Manufacturers can choose between refusing to manufacture retailers' private labels and looking to such business for a steady flow of large orders. For retailers, a decline in manufacturers' brands could leave them stranded. Yet will they decline further and, if so, how far?

In United Kingdom groceries, the 2003 private label market was 38 per cent; other EU countries included Belgium (27 per cent), Germany (25 per cent), France (21 per cent) and Spain (19 per cent). Euromonitor, a market research firm, identified several factors supporting the United Kingdom market's notable switch to own-label until 1998. They appear as the dark cells of Figure 16.7. This *causal model* shows how changes in a dynamic situation lead on, one from another as shown. The links until 1998 were all positive, each factor sustaining the other, leading to a steady rise in private-label sales.

The United Kingdom has a highly concentrated supermarket industry, whose six leaders account for almost 80 per cent of turnover. Long-term promotion strategies had created positive attitudes to retailers' brands, contrasting with a cheap image in other nations. Own-label share peaked at 42 per cent in 1998. What then caused it to fall? It seems that three extra factors emerged, shown in the lightly shaded boxes of Figure 16.7. First, as smaller manufacturers changed to private-label production, their second-tier brands were withdrawn. Meanwhile, the remaining leaders spent heavily to resist further own-label development. Second, intense competition meant that several chains turned their attention towards store upgrading and diversification. They were happy to retain the leaders on the shelves. Each factor created a loop with a negative link, as shown in the diagram. Own-label penetration was held back. Further, competition and attempts by all to increase margins led to the third factor, the growth of premium sub-brands with names like *Finest*, *So Good* and *Extra Special*. Their effect on attitudes was mixed, depending on whether the innovation was by manufacturer or retailer.

■ Who benefits from brands?

Is the struggle between manufacturers and retailers a war with the consumer caught in the crossfire? Put more broadly, are brands generally in the public interest? Whom do brands benefit? Evidently, they benefit their owners. Otherwise, they

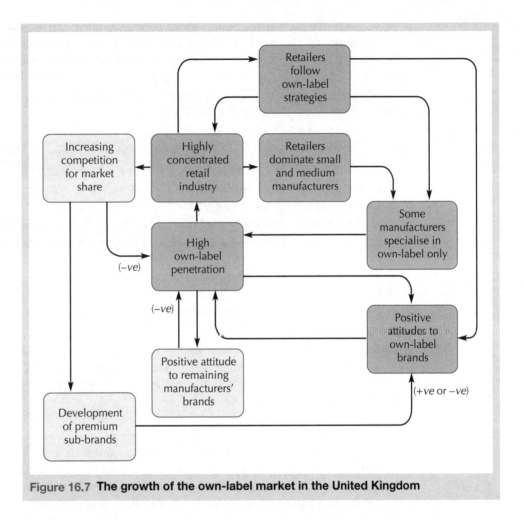

Figure 16.7 The growth of the own-label market in the United Kingdom

would not exist. Furthermore, the owners claim that they only exist to satisfy consumers. Or is it that marketers use brands to exploit consumers and manipulate markets to their own advantage?

Drawing on many sources, Ambler concluded that the evidence is in favour of brands. They serve consumers in three main ways: they bring value for money; they are the means through which quality is improved; and they offer psychological satisfaction.[34] Since these arguments tell us much about the nature of marketing, we shall look at them more closely.

Economic benefits

The economic benefits of brands arise from their importance in the sales transaction. In particular, brands:

- *Support competition.* Without brands, how would one choose between products with similar descriptions and, for goods, packaging?
- *Provide choice.* Surveys show that shoppers like variety. New products, and therefore greater choice, usually come from the leading brand manufacturers such as Unilever.

■ *Reduce risk in the transaction.* Names offer assurance. When assessing quality, for example, the buyer relies on the methods and cues listed in Exhibit 16.14. Brands are more important when the consumer has to rely on credence.

■ *Improve consumer value.* Overall, brands offer a wide range of products that satisfy buyers' needs in different ways. Although this argument is often advanced, whether value is better overall is unclear.

Exhibit 16.14 How consumers appraise quality

■ Search – ascertained by inspection, e.g. fruit, cloth, timber.

■ Low experience – quickly discovered from limited use, e.g. beer.

■ High experience – only established after prolonged use, e.g. domestic appliance.

■ Credence – not apparent in use but depends on belief, e.g. pain killers, engine oil.

Functional benefits

Functional benefits describe innovation and improvements in quality that may be stimulated by brands. In this respect, brands offer:

■ *Different value to different customers.* Rising incomes mean customers search for products that closely fit their needs. This has stimulated new product development, such as customisation in many markets. Cars, personal computers, kitchens and holidays are examples.

■ *Differences in quality.* Quality differences arise both through improvement of existing products and new product innovation. Brands must improve to match consumers' rising expectations and defend sales against own-label.

■ *Reliability.* Branding is part of relationship marketing. It is in the supplier's interests to ensure the customer is satisfied with every transaction. Reliability factors range from safety in use to full measures in packaged goods.

■ *Subsidise arts, sports and the media.* Advertisers pay at least half the cost of newspapers and magazines and for all of the 'free' media such as commercial television. Brands also directly sponsor the arts, civic programmes and sport. To the extent that consumers participate, the subsidies benefit them.

■ *Ensure fitness for use.* A key idea in marketing is that customers buy to satisfy a need. Successful brands survive through providing satisfaction in the long term.

■ *Wide availability.* Convenience is crucial if demand is to be created and met. Strong brands are the most widely distributed. For instance, being 'within an arm's reach of everyone' makes Coca-Cola the world's most valuable brand.

Psychological benefits

Psychological benefits arise in the mind of the consumer rather than in the product itself. Marketers are sometimes accused of creating brand images to represent 'quasi-persons' and so provide a false satisfaction from their use. Yet many consumers clearly care less about function than they do about style. Some (rational?) consumers buy every available product report before making a choice. Others do not. Whether this is natural behaviour, or weakness in the face of the barrage of advertising, is an issue we shall deal with later. Psychological satisfaction from purchases is, clearly, important. Brands contribute because they:

- *Simplify consumer choices.* A recognised brand enables a consumer to select from product clutter. For complex products, such as cameras or computers, the name replaces the need for extensive product knowledge. Brand building also provides the customer with a new vocabulary to use when choosing. The 'Intel inside' stickers on PCs encouraged them to think of the power and quality of the chip as the most important product feature. For new buyers especially, Intel's brand meant a safe choice.

- *Bring social benefits.* Many brands help to satisfy needs for social approval, personal expression or self-esteem. This is especially true for so-called 'badge' products that signal rank, self-image and social attachment. Nike's logo suggests membership of an identifiable group; Guinness means another.

- *Help consumers feel good.* In the end, customer satisfaction depends on how they feel about their purchases. A 'brand personality' helps a consumer to realise a sense of self. 'The Pepsi generation' was a value proposition to younger people who sought different lifestyles. The emotional support from friendly brands, such as the Mr Muscle and Mr Sheen cleaning products, often lies at the heart of building loyalty through trust.

How broad can a brand be?

Positive attitudes towards manufacturers' brands are often based on perceptions of expertise not possessed by retailers. After all, how can the latter know about goods ranging from textiles to tomatoes? The answer of some retailers is that they do have the expertise, although it is hidden from the customer. Leaders in own-label, such as Aldi, IKEA and Marks & Spencer, apply their buying skills on behalf of the consumer to offer a competitive, trustworthy range. Yet the broad question remains: how far can a brand be 'stretched' across a range of products?

Brand extension, the process of launching new products using the reputation of existing ones, is widely practised. Although about 3000 new products are launched in the United Kingdom grocery market each year, only about seven of the leading 100 brands are less than 10 years old. Most new products appear under existing names, as shown in Table 16.1. This lists a selection from announcements made in

Table 16.1 **Some new brands and extensions**

New brand or extension	Company	
MusicNet	EMI, Real Networks, AOL Time Warner and others	New online download platform
Fragrance for you	Fragrance for you	New corporate perfumes
Wafer thin meats	Bernard Matthews	Extension of Bernard Matthews
Foamburst scent-sations	Cussons	Extension of Imperial Leather
fcuk spirit	French Connection	Extension of fcuk to alcohol
Hartley's Luxury Conserve	Hartley's	Extension of Hartley's jam
Milkybar, Tigger and Smarties eggs	Nestlé Rowntree	Extension of confectionery brands
Bertolli Tuscan Lunch Café	Unilever	Extension of Bertolli olive oil brand to light meal and snack restaurants

January 2002.[35] With rapid innovation rates in some product lines, the brand establishes continuity. It frequently allows stretching of the product life cycle.

Although an often attractive strategy, brand extension has drawbacks:

- Some names are both brands and product descriptions. If they are closely associated with the latter, the range of brand extension is limited. This is a reason that Coca-Cola refers only to a narrow range of flavoured drinks.

- Brand extensions may be restricted. With clothing and boots, managers of Marlboro and Camel tried to stretch their images away from the cigarette market which, in the West at least, was declining. A European Union directive bans this form of indirect advertising.

- The risk of a favourable image being tarnished increases if it is applied to many disparate products. Among brands that have recently emerged on the global stage, contrast the sharp focus of rebellious Benetton and emotional IKEA with the breadth of Virgin. Its international recognition is remarkable. Apart from the airline, however, the rest of the business is tiny by world standards. One survey ranked the group's trustworthiness as high, although another placed its financial services arm among the least trusted.[36]

Marketing, ethics and social responsibility

Marketing is often the most visible and controversial among the functions of management. Critics point to cases of half-true advertising being used to promote unwanted or unnecessary goods. For the defence, however, these problems are presented as the excesses of the few. Most marketers, it is argued, act in the public interest. After all, one cannot charge bankers with antisocial behaviour simply because of a few loan sharks.

Part of the problem lies in different perceptions of what marketing is for. If we rely on the definition of Kotler and colleagues discussed earlier, which asserts that marketing is simply the science of transactions, then a utilitarian approach will suggest that marketing is ethical. Since capitalism and markets are beneficial, improving their performance will be in the common interest. Therefore, probing and interpreting customers' motives is a legitimate activity. The difficulty arises from the application of this principle. Definitions of responsible behaviour have gradually been extended. For example, marketing research has justified deeper prying into peoples' lives, especially the underlying thoughts and feelings that motivate their consumption. Advertising has become more subtle, invasive and, sometimes, subliminal. It has created demand for products in the interests of satisfying needs. Yet, without advertising, these needs might never have existed. Such actions, it is asserted, are all in the interests of improving marketing.

Therefore, while the marketing manager may seek to behave ethically within the business definition of what the marketing function is for, it is left to others to ask the uneasy questions concerning its legitimacy. Exclusive reliance on the principle of consumer satisfaction creates problems both for consumers and for the rest of society. Selling tobacco satisfies a need. Yet this is obtained at the expense of smokers' future health and taxpayers. Countering the approach based on utility, Nantel and Weeks are among those who call for the use of deontology, that is starting with principles.[37]

■ Fair exchange

The notion of fair exchange underpins the ethics of transactions. There has been a gradual change in societal attitudes from *caveat emptor* (let the buyer beware) towards *caveat venditor* (let the seller beware). In other words, there has been a shift in favour of consumers' interests over the suppliers'. Consumer sovereignty is the basis of the modem capitalist system. Through exercising informed choice, the consumer both expresses the principle and makes markets work.

Some firms have responded to consumerism and its consequences by perceiving markets as battlegrounds. They will behave to the minimum standards required by law and try to maximise their power over the buyer. Yet, following Kant's universal principle, we can see that marketers should exercise more responsibility than this. Since sellers in one context are buyers in another, Kant would point out that sellers must not treat customers in ways in which they would not wish to be treated themselves. A firm should not despatch poor quality or unsafe goods unless it tolerated its own suppliers doing the same.

In this view, ethics obliges vendors to make transactions as fair as possible. But how to put this notion into practice? Smith proposes a three-part consumer sovereignty test:[38]

■ *Consumer capability*

To what extent is the consumer vulnerable and how does this affect decision making? It is accepted, for example, that children are more so than adults and many countries restrict marketing activities focused upon them. Parents are too familiar with 'pester power', where children harass them into buying branded sports kit or merchandise from the latest Disney film. The difficulties surrounding this question were highlighted by the judge of the long-running 'McLibel' action mentioned in the closing case of this chapter. In his summing up, Mr Justice Bell accused McDonald's of exploiting children through its advertising. Yet, where do parents' and advertisers' responsibilities meet? A famous line from British advertising – 'Don't forget the Fruit Gums, mum' – would not be allowed under current anti-pestering rules. In Sweden, the government barred television advertising to the under-twelves.[39]

The vulnerability of adults is more controversial. The United States and other countries have rules and codes to protect the recently bereaved from predatory funeral directors. In the United Kingdom, daytime television has become dominated by advertisements for financial services. Although a few lenders with high reputations participate, O'Hara notes how the scene is dominated by sub-prime lenders whose high interest rates offer poor value. The loans are targeted at the most vulnerable groups with offers such as, 'If you're in financial trouble, we'll take over all your debts'.[40]

■ *Information*

The fairness of transactions is underpinned by both parties having adequate information for their decisions. This does not mean that both should have the *same* information. That would imply the seller revealing secrets about, say, costs that would yield advantages to competitors. Such facts are relevant to the seller's willingness to sell but not normally to the buyer's willingness to buy. The seller's duty, therefore, is not to offer misleading information and, further, to reveal information that could influence the purchaser's decision. The sweeping changes to United Kingdom rules governing the sale of investment products were brought about because many were not conforming to this standard. Although acting as 'financial advisers' some agents were selling savings and insurance contracts according to the commission they could obtain. Few advised clients either to refrain from buying or to invest in commission-free products such as National Savings.[41]

■ *Choice*

It may seem odd that market leaders should not reap the rewards of their efforts from rising market share. Yet dominance and monopoly have been shown to have economic disadvantages, underlined from the ethical point of view. Fairness requires that both parties enter the transaction willingly. This condition is less likely to hold under monopoly conditions. A customer should be able to switch to another supplier if others are more reliable, fair or honest. Therefore, despite of the pressure to push up sales, marketers should not seek to monopolise markets; nor should they unreasonably force up switching costs for customers who need repeat purchases; nor ought they to restrict channels of distribution in order to maintain high prices.

> *Perfume houses had for many years defended their practice of refusing to supply unauthorised 'grey' distributors because their products needed to be displayed and sold by experts. In fact, they were exploiting strong brand loyalty among the heaviest users, middle-aged women, and the system held prices high. Now new brands, aimed at younger women and men, have shaken up these cosy relationships. Examples include Tommy Hilfiger, Ralph Lauren and, above all, Calvin Klein. In the United Kingdom, wider distribution and discounting meant that sales value in real terms fell by 4 per cent in the five years to 1997. Since then, the market has grown steadily and is expected to continue at about 4 per cent.[42]*

Although tests like the sovereignty test could cover all transactions, its focus is on consumer relationships where there is likely to be a power imbalance between buyer and seller. In this field, it can be used to evaluate marketing practices.

■ Fundamentally flawed?

Some are less optimistic. Reviewing both the general impact and specific practices of marketing, Alvesson and Willmott[43] took a much more critical stand than those who look to codes of ethics to improve matters. To them, marketing is fundamentally flawed. A negative consequence of viewing relationships as transactions is to depersonalise them. The effect is to convert the seller into an instrument of distribution and the buyer into an instrument of consumption. A danger emerges of portraying all social interactions as 'marketised' transactions. One outcome is that the valuing of people is substituted by the valuing of objects; people's identities become increasingly linked to their status as consumers.

The notion of lifestyle, supported by the development of relationship marketing described above, implies self-expression and self-conscious individuality. People are encouraged to dress, speak, eat, drink and otherwise behave according to models implanted, and not 'discovered', by marketers. We can use the example of bars. On the one hand, an Irish pub in Italy is a bit of fun. On the other, it encourages Italians, particularly younger ones, to participate in a 'reality' of whose existence there is no guarantee. Meanwhile, they reject equally valuable norms and habits. Just as the smart places to be seen in Dublin are espresso houses, the place to be in Rome is Paddy's Bar.

■ Advertising and consumption

Alvesson and Willmott are further concerned about the support given by marketing to mass consumption. The outpouring of advertising reinforces the impression of consumption as an end in itself. While one can support the function of advertising in encouraging a person to select one product as opposed to another, a side-effect is to legitimate consumption as a whole. The authors, rather, place this as the most important effect. Advertising makes consumption itself normal and desirable. It becomes the *raison d'être* – I shop, therefore I am.

Through mass media, and more recently through closely targeted mailshots, advertising serves to institutionalise envy and build anxieties. A simple example from relationship marketing will suffice. To gain discounts on most frequently dialled telephone calls, customers (who used to be called subscribers) are invited to join BT's Friends and Family scheme. The intention behind lowering prices for frequent users may be admirable. Yet, the company presents confusing price comparisons that stress minor differences. To be morally defensible, RM should build a balanced relationship.[44] In other words, the information should facilitate fair comparison.

■ Deception

Deception is a common accusation levelled at marketers. Indeed, many methods are taught and used which are aimed at undermining consumers' will by inducing them to act habitually (brand loyalty), impulsively ('Go on, spoil yourself') or distractedly (*see* Exhibit 16.15). Kotler and colleagues classify deception into three categories, pricing, promotion and packaging:[45]

■ Deceptive pricing includes the widespread practice of advertising 'factory' or 'wholesale' prices or discounting from a notional 'recommended retail' or list price. Discounts may be offered subject to unstated conditions. The true cost of loans, or the start-up costs of savings schemes, may be disguised amid a mass of small print and 'technobabble'.

■ Deceptive promotion covers: overstating of a product's features, performance or benefits; luring a customer to a shop or sale by advertising bargains that are out of stock; or running rigged competitions. In selling insurance, many representatives have been accused of overestimating the risk and exploiting unstated fears. Advertisers have long seen themselves as having a limited licence to exaggerate. This so-called 'puffery' is seen in the not so subtle Heineken's 'refreshing the parts other beers can't reach' or the more explicit 'Guinness gives you power' used in Anglophone Africa.

Exhibit 16.15 Tricks of the traders[46]

■ Tinted, convex mirrors make customers look slim and tanned.

■ Chairs in women's clothes shops let men sit while partners buy.

■ Cool air at the door calms customers.

■ Shoppers fill bigger baskets and trolleys.

■ Ethical and health campaigns legitimate purchases.

■ Sales staff who greet customers increase sales.

■ Relaxing areas with sofas and coffee more than cover their costs.

■ Red, purple, blue, yellow, orange and green increase customers' confidence.

■ Coffee, citrus and bread scents, and coconut oil in a travel agent, make us spend more.

■ Folding clothes untidily encourages people to pick them up.

■ Deceptive packaging includes exaggerating the contents through package design or misleading labelling and size information. Reducing the coating thickness or size of a chocolate wafer is a common response to increased manufacturing costs.

Sensible marketers avoid deception since it destroys relationships in the long term. Furthermore, they recognise that most customers treat product claims sceptically, even when they are true. Levitt made the case for a little deception, for 'without distortion, embellishment and elaboration, life would be drab, dull, anguished and at its existential worst'.[47] The snag is when does distortion become dishonesty, or embellishment and elaboration turn into eluding and evasion?

Conclusion: responsible marketing

Our opening case outlined typical features of marketing in the global consumer environment. To succeed, companies must learn about the markets they both operate in and seek to enter. Meanwhile, they track rivals' actions and innovation. From the marketing perspective, an organisation best fits its environment if it satisfies its customers' needs in the long term. Marketing maintains links between the 'inside' functions such as operations and the outside world.

This idea, at least in its formal expression, has been current for barely half a century. Levitt's notion of marketing myopia was published in 1960. It presaged a surge of interest in markets and customers, aided by the growth of information systems and driven by the desire to be 'customer led'. Manufacturers were the first to build global brands, using them alongside technological prowess to expand. Globalisation of service companies followed. In each case, winners combine technology, brand management and organisation skills.

Marketing research illustrates the development of customer orientation. Early notions of market segments were crude, often using government classifications. Now, supported by huge database programs, the possibilities appear endless. Indeed, handling information in such detail challenges the concept of segmentation itself. The trend is towards treating each customer individually, even in the mass market. Despite all the numbers, however, the question of why customers behave in the ways they do remains unanswered. Observing behaviour is easy; understanding motivation is not.

The growth of marketing offers the organisation great power in its relations with consumers. Using relationship marketing and brands to keep customers loyal sounds innocent enough. Yet the possibilities of manipulation and exploitation are ever present. Even common practices such as test marketing, where a sample of consumers is offered new products to see whether they will take to them, can be criticised because they are unknowing participants in an experiment. The marketer must make sure that transactions are fair.

The visibility of marketing has placed it among the most criticised of business functions. At one level, we saw how brands work in the common interest. Probing further, however, we uncover many ethical questions. Optimists suggest that codes of ethics can support responsible marketing. Pessimists, on the other hand, see our current conceptions of consumers and consumption as flawed. Since its effect is to encourage excess, a fundamental rethink of the role of marketing may be needed.

QUICK CHECK

Can you …

- Sketch the product life cycle and assess its usefulness.
- Set out five alternative market orientations.
- Define marketing.
- Define and list four aspects of marketing research.
- Distinguish between primary and secondary data.
- Connect segmentation with relationship marketing.

- Name the four Ps of marketing and outline why they are being superseded.
- Link relationships with episodes.
- Define brand and name eight benefits of brands.
- Give examples of brand extension.
- Summarise Smith's consumer sovereignty test.

QUESTIONS

Chapter review

16.1 Outline the main purposes of marketing research, illustrating your answer with a flow diagram.

16.2 What are the arguments in favour of brands? Give your own examples.

16.3 Discuss the advantages and disadvantages of applying the same brand to a range of products.

16.4 Prepare and illustrate arguments against the consumer sovereignty test for responsible marketing practice.

Application

16.5 Direct marketing, by post, telephone and electronic mail, is becoming more common as organisations recognise its potential. What issues should be included in a code of ethics drawn up to guide such activity?

16.6 We said on page 532 that the implications of Bromley's profile for 'holidays, health clubs, hearing aids, hairdressing or horticulture are clear'. What are they?

16.7 The EU may investigate the concentration of grocery retailers and the power they have over manufacturers. How would this change Figure 16.7?

Investigation

16.8 Identify five organisations that, in your view, match the orientations described early in the chapter. Suggest why each takes its particular stance.

16.9 Investigate how firms in a consumer market not discussed in the chapter are developing the notions of relationship marketing. Examine why they are doing this and comment on whether they are likely to succeed.

16.10 Use a magazine such as *What camera?* to investigate how consumer goods suppliers segment the market and then advertise to segments.

Joburgers?[48]

With 31 000 outlets around the world, are there too many McDonald's? Not until recently. Although franchisees worry about rivals in their vicinity, putting more stores into a market increases share, sometimes spectacularly. Peoria, Illinois, has a population of 113 000. In 1981, McDonald's, with 10 stores, had 40 per cent of the market, double that of nearest rival Hardees, which had five. By 1991, however, Hardees had grown to 40 per cent from 18 outlets, while McDonald's, with 11, fell to 28 per cent. Big Mac decided to build. By 1995, it had boosted its count to 29, while Hardees cut to 17. Market share topped 50 per cent while sales volume, cash flow and profit per restaurant also grew. Having learned the lesson of market penetration, as opposed to optimising the position of each store separately, McDonald's began buying and refurbishing the properties of weak competitors everywhere.

McDonald's is really two businesses – limited service restaurant and real estate. Some 85 per cent of outlets are franchises, from which it takes a 4 per cent sales royalty. But it often owns the land and buildings too, charging about 10 per cent rent. Total 2002 consumer sales were $41 billion; company revenues, made up of franchisee payments plus sales from directly owned sites, were $15 billion. This ownership structure, supported by special skills in location selection and development, accounts for the company's drive for expansion. Rising home competition, where it has about 45 per cent share and 7 per cent of the population visits every day, meant the expansion has been overseas. Foreign operating profits overtook domestic in 1995.

In 1996, Inter-brand, a consultancy, placed McDonald's ahead of Coca-Cola as a global brand. Yet standards on the restaurant side had been slipping. Its last winning product innovation was Chicken McNuggets in 1983. It no longer rates highly on service quality measures. A respected United States index has placed it below other outlets since 1994, and even, by 2003, every airline and the Inland Revenue Service. Every American brand is affected by international conflict and the golden arches are the bombers' most obvious targets. One consultant noted, 'Brands play a political role ... they are in many ways our country and what we stand for'.

The company's ethnocentric culture and management practices support brand attributes recognised wherever the company operates. Common values and ground rules built strength and minimised costs. The formula worked, but no longer so well. There are some small signs of flexibility, with more localised images and products such as the McArabia chicken sandwich. In January 2003, however, McDonald's announced its first quarterly loss of $344 million. Some 500 store closures were announced.

The company is prepared to use its muscle to develop its business and protect its image. When local communities complain about too many takeaways, McDonald's promises to generate up to a hundred jobs with training for school leavers and special attention to the needs of disadvantaged groups. When two environmental activists distributed leaflets complaining about its farming, packaging and employment practices, McDonald's got stuck in the longest libel action in British legal history. After 313 days in court, it won £60 000 damages. In South Africa, where its trademark registration had expired during its absence for the sanction years, a local trader applied to use the name, while others were already using 'MacDonalds'. It won on appeal in 1997. Legal challenges continue, although a suit for causing obesity brought by two large New York teenagers was dismissed in 2003.

The South African market, however, was not easy to crack. After the 1995 return, McDonald's had set records in opening 30 restaurants in just 23 months, including 10 in one 78-day period. Nevertheless, its fame proved to be only among the minority white population. Bomb attacks occurred in 2000 and 2002. About 15 outlets of 80 were to close in 2003. During the apartheid years, strong local brands and two other foreign brands, KFC and Wimpy, had grown. While McDonald's quick service and attention to the needs of children were appreciated, its standard menu was seen as small and synthetic tasting with plastic bread.

It had judged the market as not different enough to need offerings, such as India's Maharaja Mac, made with mutton. The South African market splits on racial lines. Most blacks favour chicken, which accounts for two-thirds of fast food; McDonald's chicken burgers were too pricey and plain. Nando's specialised in 'real chicken' with a uniquely South African brand image. Whites like beef, but lots of it; McDonald's quarterpounder (120 grams) is puny beside Steer's 200 gram 'Big Steer'.

Questions

1 How, in marketing terms, does McDonald's differ from most other 'hamburger joints'?

2 Why is the company reluctant to vary its menu for local markets?

3 Several attempts to extend the McDonald's brand have failed. Is the company stuck with its formula?

4 Should McDonald's marketing become more glocal? How?

Bibliography

For a thorough coverage of marketing, see Phillip Kotler *et al.* (2001) *Principles of Marketing: The European edition* (Harlow: Financial Times Prentice Hall). *Marketing Week* is good for news and summaries of issues. For detailed studies, use your library for *Keynote* or *Mintel*. *Gallup Management Journal*, online at http://gmj.gallup.com, publishes regular studies on brands.

References

1 Chapman, Ian (2003) 'A camera focused on luxury: marketing: Leica may be bucking the mass digital trend but discerning photographers are snapping up its upmarket analogue equipment', *Financial Times*, 31 March; Lacey, Joël (2003) 'The state of the photo nation', *Amateur Photographer*, 26 April, 4–5; Eastman Kodak Co. (2003) *Interview*, *Photo Marketing*, 1 March; Digital Photography Review (2003) *Digital Cameras Timeline*, www.dpreview.com/reviews/timeline.asp?start=2003, accessed 6 April 2003; Infotrends Research Group Inc. (2002) 'Revenue from Worldwide Digital Camera Sales to Reach $11.8 Billion in 2007', Press release, 5 November, www.infotrends-rgi.com/press/2002110544374.html, accessed 8 April 2003.

2 'Digital snap', *The Economist*, 30 August 1997, 63–4.

3 Kotler, Philip, Armstrong, Gary, Saunders, John and Wong, Veronica (1996) *Principles of Marketing: The European Edition*, Hemel Hempstead: Prentice Hall, 14.

4 Tully, Mark (1994) 'Great Railway Journeys of the World', *BBC2 television*, 17 February.

5 'Too clever by half', *The Economist*, 20 September 1997, 99.

6 Simon, Bernard (1995) 'Quiet revolution at Bata Shoe – The paternalistic mould is being broken', *Financial Times*, 28 March; Lednicky, Václav and Matusikovà, Lucja (1996) 'A contribution for the Bata's management system recognition', *Selected Research Papers*, Faculty of Economics, Technical University of Ostrava, 89–92; 'Bata expects its turnover to increase', *Access Czech Republic Business Bulletin*, 24 March 2003; Bata (2003) *Bata today*, www.bata.com /about_bata/bata_today.htm, accessed 12 April 2003.

7 Meehan, Sean and Barwise, Patrick (1996) *Do market-oriented businesses perform better?* Working Paper 96–103, Centre for Marketing, London Business School.

8 Brady, John, Hunter, Carline and Santiapillai, Nirmila (2000) 'Marketing in the UK', *McKinsey Quarterly*, **2**.

9 Kotler *et al.* (1996) *op. cit.*, 214.

10 'World champion', *The Economist*, 13 September 1997, 36.

11 Naylor, J.B. and Williams, J. (1994) 'The successful use of IT in SMEs on Merseyside', *European Journal of Information Systems*, **3(1)**, 48–56.

12 Leaver, David and Al-Zubaidi H. (1996) 'Challenging conventional wisdom: a reappraisal of the UK DIY market', *International Journal of Retail & Distribution Management*, **24(11)**, 39–45.

13 Lieber, Ronald B. (1997) 'Storytelling: a new way to get close to your customer', *Fortune*, 3 February, 102–6.

14 Fielding, Helen (1994) 'Spoilt for choice in all the clutter', *Independent on Sunday*, 6 March, 23.

15 Claritas (2003) *What is lifestyle view?* and *Summary Prizm Report*, www.lifestyleview.com/LifestyleView/mmg/Description.htm, accessed 18 April 2003.

16 Chaudhary, Vivek (1997) 'Market researchers look to stars', *Guardian*, 16 September, 8.

17 A Harris poll found that 31 per cent of Americans believe in astrology: Harris Interactive (2003) 'The religious and other beliefs of Americans 2003', PR Newswire, 26 February.

18 'Relationship marketing: reaping the benefits of IT', *International Journal of Retail and Distribution Management*, **23(11)**, Winter 1995, xii–xiii.

19 Crainer, Stuart (1996) *Key Management Ideas*, London: Financial Times Pitman Publishing, 167–8.

20 Ching, Sungmi and Sherman, Mike (2002) 'Emerging marketing', *McKinsey Quarterly*, **2**.

21 Ravald, Annika and Gronroos, Christian (1996) 'The value concept and relationship marketing', *European Journal of Marketing*, **30(2)**, February, 19–30.

22 Kotler *et al.* (1996) *op. cit.*, 450.

23 Pressey, Andrew D. and Mathews, Brian P. (1997) 'Facilitators to relationship marketing in the retail context', *Marketing without borders: Proceedings of the Academy of Marketing Conference*, Manchester, 8–10 July, 757–68.

24 Miles, Richard (1997) 'Boots takes the loyalty pledge', *Guardian*, 7 August, 18.

25 Child, Peter N. (2002) 'Taking Tesco global', *McKinsey Quarterly*, **3**

26 'Polestar direct renews Tesco Clubcard contract', *Printweek*, 14 February.

27 Cowe, Roger (1996) 'Supermarket plays trump card', *Guardian*, 18 June, 18; Matthews, Virginia (1996) 'Loyal to what end?' *Marketing*, 29 August, 34–6.

28 Nielsen, A.C. (1996) 'Customer loyalty – The issue for the 90s', *The Researcher*, A.C. Nielsen.

29 Fletcher, Winston (1997) 'Ad lib: Words designed to bring added value', *Financial Times*, 11 August.

30 Bunting, Madeleine (2001) 'The new gods', *Guardian: Branding – a special supplement*, 9 July, 4.

31 Stuart, Liz (1997) 'Troubled Kellogg pressurises JWT', *Marketing Week*, 3 April; Willman, John (1998) 'Fast food spreads amid changing lifestyles', *Financial Times*, 27 March; Bowe, Christopher (2000) 'Kellogg seeking snap, crackle, pop: cereal pioneer hopes Keebler will wake up performance', *Financial Times*, 28 October.

32 'Trade-marking Thailand: Rebranding for an entire country', *Nation* (Thailand), 18 March 2002; Shannon, John (2001) 'Bolstering the Belgium brand', *Marketing Week*, **24(30)**, 9 June, 35–6.

33 Wiggin, Emma (ed.) (2003) *Supermarket own labels: Market assessment report*, 2nd edition, London: Key Note, April, 56–7.

34 Ambler, Tim (1997) 'Do brands benefit consumers?' *Pan'Agra Working Paper*, 97–901, London Business School.

35 'Database: New brands and brand extensions', *Brand strategy*, January 2002, 30.

36 'What's in a name?' *The Economist*, 11 January 1997.

37 Nantel, Jacques and Weeks, William A. (1996) 'Marketing ethics: is there more to it than the utilitarian approach?' *European Journal of Marketing*, **30(5)**, May, 9–19.

38 Smith, N. Craig (1995) 'Marketing strategies for the ethics era', *Sloan Management Review*, **36(4)**, Summer, 85–97.

39 Tylee, John (1997) 'Should advertisers take 'pester power' seriously?', *Campaign*, 18 July, 11.

40 O'Hara, Mary (2003) 'Ever been had?' *The Guardian: Jobs and Money*, 29 March, 2–3.

41 Diacon, Stephen R. and Ennew, Christine T. (1996) 'Ethical issues in insurance marketing in the UK', *European Journal of Marketing*, **30(5)**, May, 67–80.

42 Fenn, Dominic (ed.) (2003) *Cosmetics and fragrances: Market report plus 2003*, 16th edition, London: Key Note, March, 78–9.

43 Alvesson, Mats and Willmott, Hugh (1996) *Making Sense of Management*, London: Sage, 119–28.

44 Kavali, Stella G., Tzokas, Nikolaos X. and Saren, Michael J. (1999) 'Relationship marketing as an ethical approach: philosophical and managerial considerations', *Management Decision*, **37(7)**, 573–81.

45 Kotler *et al.* (1996) *op. cit.*, 38.

46 Fracassini, Camillo (2000) 'Psychological tricks of the traders', *Scotland on Sunday*, 27 August, 4.

47 Levitt, Theodore (1970) 'The morality(?) of advertising', *Harvard Business Review*, **48(3)**, July–August, 84–92.

48 Pike, Matthew, Sheath, Ray and Carey, Jim (1996) 'Developing a truly international brand and company', *International Journal of Physical Distribution and Logistics*, **26(7)**, July, 19–21; Samuels, Gary (1996) 'Golden arches galore', *Forbes*, **158(11)**, November, 46–48; Branch, Shelley (1996) 'McDonald's strikes out with grownups', *Fortune*, **134(9)**, 11 November, 157–60; Willman, John (1998) 'Fast food spreads amid changing lifestyles', *Financial Times*, 27 March, 7; 'McDonald's shrinks, but SA burger bosses say demand is not waning', *Africa News Service*, 3 December 2002; Hein, Kenneth (2003) 'All-American brands take hits overseas', *Brandweek*, **44(12)**, 6; David, Grainger (2003) 'Can McDonald's cook again?' *Fortune*, **147(7)**, 14 April, 120–6; Barker, Robert (2003) 'Are the golden arches that tarnished?' *Business Week*, **3828**, 14 April, 91; 'Fast food in the slow lane', *Sunday Times* (South Africa), 29 September 2002; McDonald's (2003) 'About McDonald's SA', **www.mcdonalds.co.za /mcdsa.htm**, accessed 16 April 2003.

CHAPTER 17

Innovation: from ideas to customer benefits

Chapter objectives

When you have finished studying this chapter, you should be able to:

- explain and illustrate the differences between invention and innovation;

- recognise the risks involved in innovation and discuss how they can be coped with;

- show where the benefits of innovation arise and how they increase a firm's value;

- demonstrate how innovation applies to all aspects of a product;

- outline the innovation process; summarise the difficulties in managing it in the organisational context and suggest how they can be overcome;

- assess the origins of innovation, whether it rests in the individual, the organisation or the environment.

Here's a human way to end scary spider misery, with the BugBuster motorised spider trap … £9.99 (batteries not supplied).

Innovations catalogue

Clockwork radio[1]

Trevor Baylis had had a career ranging from a film stuntman and circus escapologist to installer of swimming pools. The idea for a clockwork radio came to him in 1991 while watching a programme on the spread of AIDS in Africa. The cost of batteries often prevented radio being used for community health education. After three months in his workshop, Baylis had a radio driven by a dynamo. Knowing that the idea would work, he built a prototype. Primary energy was stored in a steel spring, just as in wind-up toys. The spring drove a generator via a gearbox. Its voltage was controlled by a diode.

Baylis was surprised that the system had not been invented before. Realising it might be used for all sorts of electrical devices, he registered a patent, not for the radio, but for 'electrical generators'. With his idea protected, Baylis looked for commercial partners. Rejection followed rejection. He recalls three visits to Marconi, where each time he was 'treated like a jackass'. Another company suggested that a 75 kilogram mechanism would be needed for four minutes running! His break came after the idea featured on BBC television's *Tomorrow's World*. One viewer that Friday was Christopher Staines, an accountant with experience in acquisitions and mergers. He faxed a business plan to Baylis the following day and by Monday had the worldwide development rights.

Baylis, inventor not businessman, realised he had taken his idea as far as he could. Staines, with his acumen and South African connections, brought in Rory Stear to undertake commercialisation. Another interview, this time on a Johannesburg radio station, was heard by Hylton Appelbaum, of Liberty Life Group. This fund invests in worthy projects, especially if they involve disadvantaged groups. After several meetings among Appelbaum, Baylis, Staines and William Rowland, the president of Disabled People of South Africa, Liberty agreed to put up £750 000 for development. The United Kingdom Overseas Development Administration also provided £143 000 support. DPSA became a partner in the embryonic company.

Developing the prototype into a production model was not easy. It seemed the components could not be made small enough. Then market research revealed that the radio must be big, heavy and loud! This realisation allowed the tensator (constant force) spring to be enlarged and the gearbox simplified to achieve a reasonable playing time.

Highlights of Baylis's first visit to South Africa were an emotional welcome at the new Baygen plant and a meeting with President Mandela. Despite having invented other devices for disabled people, this was his first commercial success, enriched by the employment of both able and disabled people in manufacture.

The launch was in November 1995. Of robust construction, the Freeplay radio offered 40 minutes of listening for 20 seconds of winding. It won design awards and was endorsed by more than 20 humanitarian aid organisations. Several bought it at the wholesale price of £19. The factory output, some 20 000 each month, was insufficient to meet demand. Ironically, the widespread publicity in the developed world made the radio an object of desire. It went on sale at Harrod's in London at £80.

After Baylis had sold his interest, the renamed FreePlay Energy Group focused its development effort on improving efficiency. The Mark III model incorporated a rechargeable battery, collecting the spring energy and extending playing time. By Mark V, the spring had gone and the winding action charged the battery directly. Three million radios and torches were sold in five years. The Mark V, however, opened the way to another important application, mobile telephones. Launched in 2002 in collaboration with Motorola, the FreeCharge offers a six-minute call for each 30 seconds winding.

Meanwhile, Stear had been restructuring the business. In two years, the 450 employees were cut to 50, mostly experts in the patented core technology work on development. Manufacturing and distribution were subcontracted, mainly to countries in Asia. Now, the little-known brand is being developed in partnership with household names. As with Intel, *see* Chapter 16, products are to be co-branded with the slogan 'Freeplay driven'.

Introduction

Trevor Baylis's story relates experiences undergone by many inventors. He had an appealing idea that, as he admits, may have been had by many people before him. In his case, however, he had the determination and skill to make a prototype that worked. Then came the difficulty – commercialisation. Sceptical engineers and companies turned him down and it was only through perseverance and good fortune that the product came to market. Although it was immediately successful, we can see the challenge posed by production and distribution costs. Sales to collectors in the first world subsidised distribution to the originally planned market. For the FreePlay Energy Group, small by industry standards, this was unsustainable. Stear changed direction to concentrate on enhancing the special knowledge while subcontracting almost everything else. To cushion the blow at the first South African plant, the group set up a subsidiary, FreeCom, to repair PCs.

For two other inventions that have been clear commercial successes, we can turn to floor cleaning. The first is lost in myth. In 1907, James Spangler, an Ohio janitor, built a 'suction sweeper' from a fan, pillow case and broom. He showed it to a friend, Susan Hoover, who showed it to her husband … And there the paradigm of filtering dusty air stuck until 1993 when James Dyson did away with the bag. Within a year, the DC-01 was the United Kingdom market leader by revenue; a year later, it was on top by numbers sold. By 2003, Dyson held half the United Kingdom market and a quarter of the European Union market. Total sales had exceeded £2 billion.

Best known for his Ballbarrow, James Dyson was already an inventor and industrial engineer when, in 1978, he opened up his Hoover upright to fix it. He had thought that suction loss occurred when the bag filled but found that was not the case. Dust clogged a new bag's pores and reduced suction almost as soon as it was fitted. Then followed many years of experimentation and rebuttals from manufacturers before Dyson set up on his own. Hoover, having rejected Dyson's licence offer, and having tried to scupper his product launch with its 'Free flights to New York' blunder, brought out its own cyclone model. Dyson sued for patent infringement and was awarded £4 million. Now with 20 models, the 'Dyson' was launched in 2002 in the United States. Hoover had retained a 28 per cent share of that $2 billion market. Dyson prices are high, so concern over manufacturing costs meant that production was moved to Malaysia in 2002.[2]

While Baylis and Dyson each epitomise the lone inventor seeing something that others could not, their stories illustrate many issues surrounding innovation in organisations. Someone has a good idea. By this we do not mean the clutter of odd inventions that used to populate the *Innovations* catalogue mentioned in our opening quotation. We mean an idea that may yield commercial benefits. Having one is often 'the easy bit'. From then on, gaining acceptance while working out ways of converting prototypes into production versions can be a battle. Some companies do this much better than most. Others barely try, preferring to buy inventions either from individuals or by acquisition of innovative companies. We shall be assessing different approaches to the management of innovation throughout this chapter.

Our examples also give us clues about the sources of new ideas. Those for both the Freeplay and DC cleaners came from unexpected quarters. Baylis had no experience and Dyson knew little of marketing. (Oddly, the DC-01 appeared in *Innovations* when the latter was trying every channel to reach customers.) Both sensed that what they had created would sell. It was a producer orientation. Companies that invest heavily in innovation, however, do not work this way. They start with the market. Their approach is to spot opportunities and direct their efforts towards exploiting them continuously. This is where we will launch our investigation.

Innovation in context

We have argued that rapid changes in the environment demand internal changes. These include varying the products offered to customers and the processes by which they supply them. For most, standing still is not viable. They must innovate, that is bring new offerings to the market. Innovation is not the same as invention, which refers to the creation of an original idea.

- Inventions are ideas that may or may not develop into new products or processes.

- Innovations are ideas that are developed into new products or processes. They result in improvements recognised by customers.

The relationship between the two is shown in Figure 17.1. Inventions, the fruit of creativity, frequently trigger the innovation process, although not necessarily. Innovation activity may originate in other ways. For example, managers could spot a market opportunity that they do not have the capacity to fulfil. This begins a focused search for new products or processes. Alternatively, managers might identify a problem requiring a product redesign or process enhancement. Clearly, fresh ideas are

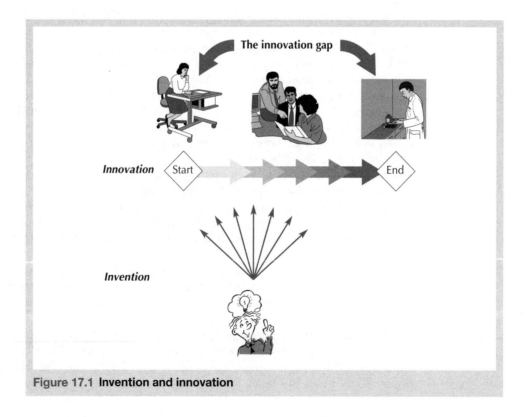

Figure 17.1 Invention and innovation

needed not only at the start but also at all phases of innovation. Therefore, we can see creative thinking, or inventiveness, as illuminating the whole cycle.

The transformation of ideas into new products is uncertain. Two problems arise for the manager, risk and lag. The risk refers to the possibility of failure along the way. While estimates vary, perhaps only one in five product ideas becomes technically viable. Of these, fewer than one in 20 become market successes. Hence the odds against winning are worse than 100 : 1!

In pharmaceuticals, the odds against are said to be higher and developments can fail at any stage. AstraZeneca, number two in Europe, lost a predicted 'megabrand', Viozan, at late development stage. Clinical trials of the treatment for smoker's cough did not show the expected long-term benefits compared with existing therapies. Estimated investment had been £300 million while peak annual sales might have exceeded £700 million.[3] In contrast, annual sales of AstraZeneca's heartburn drug Prilosec peaked at £4 billion before generic competitors entered the market.

The second problem is the lag between invention and innovation. This is known as the *innovation gap*. The television, zip fastener and heart pacemaker all took more than 20 years before commercial exploitation; the ballpoint pen and videocassette recorder came out in a sprightly six. Not only does the business have to wait for a return on its investment, but also lag represents an opportunity for a competitor to reap the advantages of being first to market. Managers need to understand the innovation process to both shorten the innovation gap and reduce the risks of failure. Hasselblad might have avoided an expensive failure through a more cautious appreciation of these questions, as explained in Exhibit 17.1.[4]

Exhibit 17.1 Hasselblad: tiny snapper in the digital pond

Hasselblad is a name respected by both photography professionals and astronauts for its medium-format, 6 × 6 cm, cameras. With sales of €200 million, it has about a fifth of the world market. The company spends 10 per cent of turnover on research and development. In the 1990s, Hasselblad was devoting most of this effort to digital technology. Early work was encouraging. An image management system found application in transmitting and storing images for the world's press. Then, in 1993, company president Stefan Junel decided to create digital versions of its cameras. By 1996, however, the company had given up. The image management system was sold. Technologist Junel was replaced by marketing expert Goran Bernhoff brought in from OKB, a Swedish glass company. Finally, Hasselblad's owners, part of the Wallenberg family empire, sold the business to a buyout consortium of banks and company managers.

Why the withdrawal? The new owners wanted more profit at lower risk. They were looking towards a flotation on the Stockholm stock exchange. Advisers warned that good, cheap, digital photography was further away than Hasselblad had imagined. Major players, such as Kodak, were spending heavily on research. Hasselblad's own R&D budget was miniscule in comparison. The company's declared intention was to watch developments closely and only return when the technological direction was clear.

The new H1 was launched with manual and digital backs. While Hasselblad does not manufacture the latter, more are available for Hasselblad than for any other make. The 16 megapixel Kodak DCS Pro is among the 70 per cent of all backs that will fit. Owners can update the digital elements while keeping the rest of the camera, designed to last a lifetime.

Products and processes

It is worth noting that innovation occurs in both products and processes. Although the test of innovativeness must ultimately lie in the number and value of new products brought to market, organisations must back them up with new ways of supplying them. Further, innovativeness is not confined to operations management. It can be applied throughout all aspects of the value chain. For instance, many product ideas fail because it proves impossible to supply them with consistent quality. It was only when the Baygen team realised that the market preferred big radios that it abandoned the frustrating search for ways of making an efficient miniature clockwork generator.

Inventors and innovators

The examples of Baylis and Dyson also illustrate that the roles of inventor and innovator are different. They require different skills. For an inventor, the key aptitude is creativity. This means recognising and applying some of the 5000 original thoughts each of us has every day. The innovator possesses a wider range of entrepreneurial and managerial skills. These include planning, persuading investors and others, leading a team and pressing on despite opposition.

Within organisations, this is the intrapreneur described in Chapter 7. As we saw, Baylis lacked some important skills needed to bring his radio to market. These were provided by Staines and others. Dyson, on the other hand, decided to undertake the whole innovation process because no current manufacturer believed in his invention.

Innovative cultures

The risks intrinsic to innovations mean that successful firms engage in a range of them. They spread the risk across diverse products and processes each of which involves a different degree of change. Continuous improvement means a series of incremental steps; in contrast, radical change requires the adoption of new product or process technologies. Although we might imagine that organisations choose between one and the other, studies have found that firms undertake both or neither. Change-oriented firms tend to have more programmes, from training and team working to quality circles and brainstorming, designed to encourage and back their staff in innovation. Innovation is not a process undertaken intermittently or in one or two areas of the organisation. If the culture is supportive, it is likely to be widespread.[5]

◼ Societal benefits

Innovation in products and the processes that supply them is a large element of our rising standard of living. It may seem odd, but official indicators do not show this. The modern television is barely comparable with one of a generation ago; clothes are more resistant to losing their colour and need less ironing; telephones are clearer, faster and carry more services. All these, and many more, make us better off. Yet by how much? To calculate this effect, Hausman proposed the idea of a 'virtual price'. This is what the customer would have been prepared to pay had the innovation occurred earlier. Take mobile telephones, for example. Since they are so different from conventional telephones, comparing their prices with those of their predecessors gives a false picture of changes over, say, 20 years. And since their use is widespread, the effect is significant. To estimate it, one should compare current prices with the virtual price that people would have paid had they been available 20 years ago. On this basis, the mobile telephone alone had improved Americans' welfare by an unmeasured 0.3 to 0.6 per cent.[6]

Although broad estimates, such figures support what we already know. If our incomes were to stabilise so that we could only buy the same quantity of goods each year, we would steadily become better off. This is because products are more reliable, are of better quality and include features that previous products did not. This change is a representation of the real value of innovation and is one indication of why people will pay more for it. Improvements even happen to traditional products such as corned beef, *see* Exhibit 17.2.[7]

Exhibit 17.2 Innovation for a corny product

Corned beef accounted for about a quarter of canned meat sold in the United Kingdom in 2002. Sales of this traditional product, worth about £60 million, had been declining for many years. Consumers were dominated by sandwich eaters, mostly men between 45 and 65.

Market leader Princes Foods, a subsidiary of Mitsubishi, planned to arrest the fall, whose annual rate had reached 6 per cent. In its first market research for years, the company found enthusiasm for new flavours. In 1997, to appeal to the sandwich group, it launched 200g cans with onion, mustard and sweet pickle. Other line extensions were 'finest corned beef' and a low-fat, low-salt version. Finally, a larger 340g spicy variety was for hot dishes. The increased range was expected to correct the 'underfacing' (lack of allocated shelf length in supermarkets) compared with other canned meats. By 2002, Princes had increased its penetration among younger, more affluent consumers.

■ What is a product?

New varieties of corned beef will bring extra profits only if they are accepted in the marketplace. This should make us question what Princes Foods is selling and how the new flavours and packs improve the offer to customers. What is innovation in marketing terms? To answer this question, we must look more closely at the nature of a product. Kotler and colleagues explain that designers and planners think of products on three levels, shown in Figure 17.2:[8]

■ The *core product* refers to the fundamental benefits expected by the customer. Note that benefits are what count. A person buys cleaner clothes, labour saving and convenience, not a washing machine.

■ The *actual product* is the set of features that, in rival products, are combined to provide the core benefit in different ways. Possibilities include quality, features, styling, packaging and branding, although their importance will differ according to the application. A washing machine may feature programme flexibility, drum capacity, easy loading and energy saving; its styling may suggest convenience, safety and reliability while fitting into the modern kitchen; and different brands have varying quality reputations.

■ The *augmented product* comprises the set of extra benefits and services that give a product an edge in the marketplace. These may include delivery, installation and set-up, warranties and after-sales support. Sales of leading washing machines are supported by national networks for maintenance and repair.

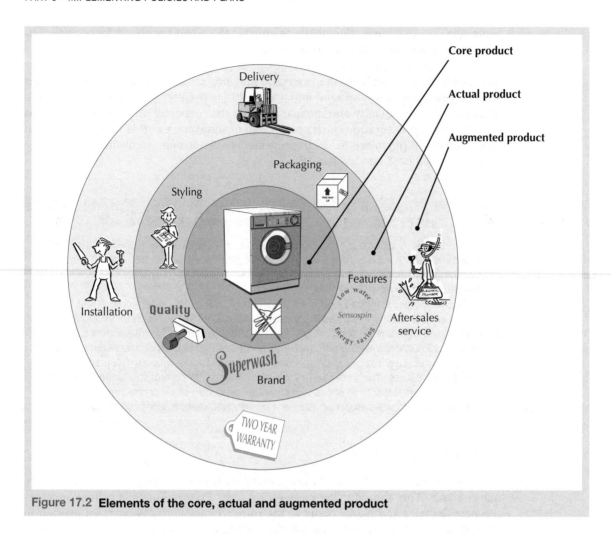

Figure 17.2 Elements of the core, actual and augmented product

A product, therefore, is more than the set of features described in its physical form, or, for a service, an outline of the process. From a free installation kit and box of *Superwash* to a friendly follow-up call from the distributor, the augmentation can be as important as the basic good or service. In marketing terms, innovation can refer to the improvement or complete redesign of any aspect. Examples in the augmented product zone range from extended warranties to a free maintenance visit after 12 months.

■ The market for invention and innovation

We have seen how innovation benefits society in general and customers in particular. Through the latter, who are prepared to pay more for new and improved products, innovative firms can become more profitable. Here we should note that all firms innovate to some extent, for if they do not change at all they are doomed. Those we call innovative, however, change more than most and change in the right direction. If innovation does create real value for society, customers and firms, we would expect this benefit to be evaluated in some way. There are two approaches, to value the firm and to value the innovations themselves. First, when businesses are bought and sold on the market, those with a good innovation record command higher prices. These represent how much the knowledge embedded in the business is worth. Being able to innovate is a competence that some firms, such as AstraZeneca and Hasselblad, are known for. Second, included in the worth of the business are its assets of intellectual property. These assets are represented by the registration of inventions, designs and names. Firms are granted exclusive rights to use or dispose of the assets, including the possibility of granting licences to others in return for payment.

Given that rights to ideas are available in the market, why should a firm undertake research and development itself? Frequently, acquisition may be cheaper, quicker, more certain and more profitable than internal innovation. Yet, as Hitt and colleagues[9] have shown, acquisition slows down the rate of innovation in both firms. The absorption process occupies much time and effort. During the change, long-term projects are often frozen, pending the outcome of negotiations. After the change, managers concentrate on integrating the businesses, again ignoring innovation. A supportive culture is difficult to sustain. The normal concentration on short-term results means that firms have little time to achieve adequate returns. Hence innovation programmes are cut further and the policy to acquire externally becomes the only option.

Given this argument, it is not surprising that firms that commit themselves to internal innovation do better in the long term. An alternative that has emerged in recent decades is to form alliances specifically to share knowledge. Innovation becomes external. We shall return to this point later.

■ Intellectual property

While the value of a firm is often enhanced by the embedded skills and knowledge of its people and teams, cumulative innovation is also encapsulated in the products and designs that it sells or uses. These assets, known as intellectual property, comprise patents, registered designs, trademarks and copyright. While differing in detail, all are rights granted by the state to exploit ideas for defined periods. Their value lies in the business advantages which flow from them. Prudent owners announce their rights using agreed symbols, such as ®, ©, ™ and ℠. Notices are not strictly needed in the United Kingdom but other countries require them to be placed on products or packages. Breaches of protection are usually civil wrongs for which the owner must seek remedy.

Leading companies defend their rights vigorously. For example, Intel has spent over $100 million on defending its rights. These support its earnings of about 20 per cent of the price of every personal computer.[10] Smaller companies, facing risky and expensive court proceedings, are often advised to grant licences in exchange for royalties. Some details of the types of protection are given in Exhibit 17.3, while Exhibit 17.4 shows some examples.[11] International treaties mean that United Kingdom practice broadly matches that of other countries.

Not only must firms create intellectual property (IP), they must maximise the gains from it. KPMG argues for managing IP as a portfolio of assets matched to the business strategy. There are three ways to increase value through good management:

■ Protect valuable IP for internal use. This builds strength to resist the effects of competition; it enables premium pricing and supports brand identity. Innovative banking operation Intelligent Finance has copyrighted its branding and applied for patents on elements of its processes. This protects it while it builds its customer base and experience.

Exhibit 17.3 Ways to protect intellectual property

Patents

A successful patent application must satisfy three conditions: it must be new, that is its details must not have appeared in public anywhere in the world; it must not be obvious in the light of previous inventions; and it must have a practical application. If approved, the state grants the right to prevent anyone using the idea for up to 20 years. In return, the Patent Office publishes details, usually 18 months after the application. Costs for the United Kingdom are about £200 for the first five years, rising to £3510 for the full 20-year period. Corresponding charges at the European Patent Office are £2715 and £11 952.

The Patent Office runs a search service to see whether an application is really new. It estimates that £22.5 billion is wasted annually by duplicate research in Europe alone. Eighty per cent of the world's technical information is to be found in patents.

Designs

Any product with an original shape or configuration gets the automatic protection of design right. Design rights come into existence at the moment of creation and are useful in that they do not have to be registered. Better protection is afforded by formal listing through the Patent Office. In registered designs, surface patterns and decoration can be included, besides shape and configuration. To qualify, the design must be new and have significant eye appeal. Registration applies in five-year blocks up to 25 years.

Copyright

Copyright applies to materials such as books, plays, music, dance, works of art, photographs, diagrams and computer programs. The right usually extends to 70 years after the author's death. An agreement between the Society of Authors and the Publishers Association allows short extracts to be quoted, with acknowledgement, from books or articles under the principle of 'fair dealing'. Music, songs and pictures are not covered by this dispensation.

Trademarks

A trademark is any sign that can identify the products of one business from those of another. The 1994 Trade Mark Act extended the scope of a mark from words and devices to three-dimensional shapes, sounds and smells. Advertising jingles and theme tunes could be covered, for example. The world's oldest trademark, number 1, has been held by Bass the brewers since 1876. Misuse of trademarks can be a criminal offence.

International protection

Globalisation of trade increases the importance of protecting intellectual property in many countries. A United Kingdom patent applies only within the UK. The European Patent Convention covers all EU countries and several others. The Community Trade Mark, CTM, was started in 1996 to cover the whole European Union with one registration. From 2003, the EU registered design offers 25-year protection. The World Intellectual Property Organisation oversees global co-operation and is especially involved with web issues such as domain names. The Patent Co-operation Treaty has more than 100 signatories. Using these international systems, although expensive, is cheaper than making separate applications in each country.

> ### Exhibit 17.4 Protecting rights
>
> In 2001, the leading companies to be granted UK patents were NEC (197), Motorola (167), Samsung (163) and Bosch (84). Telecommunications was the busiest sector with 12 per cent of the 12 000 applications.
>
> Avon Cosmetics, with 125, was the company registering most trademarks, followed by Pfizer (87) and Unilever (84). Since 1996, the Patent Office has permitted individuals to register their own names as trademarks, provided they are distinctive enough. England coach Sven-Goran Eriksson registered the name 'Sven' as a trademark for products including soaps, hair lotions, non-alcoholic drinks, sporting articles, medical services and rubber goods. In 2002 there were disputes between Victoria Beckham and Peterborough United Football Club over the use of 'Posh' and New Zealand and Neath rugby teams over 'All Blacks'.
>
> Trademarks have been given to colours connected with uses. The Automobile Association has registered its distinctive yellow so that similar organisations cannot use it.
>
> Sony, Ty Inc and Procter & Gamble led the list of design registrations.

■ Sell or license IP. Such action creates extra cash flow through exploiting underutilised assets. The licensee can open new markets for existing products and processes that the innovator could not reach on its own. For instance, Synaptic Pharmaceuticals sold a licence to GSK for $2 million.

■ Apply existing IP to new internal use or in another part of the company. This approach enhances the value of existing assets and enables quicker and cheaper expansion or diversification. General Motors has applied military night vision technologies to enhance the safety of cars.[12]

The innovation process

To examine the innovation process we shall take a narrower definition than one that covers all changes that might improve customer satisfaction. Some process improvements have only an indirect effect on customers such as reducing costs of computing through better maintenance practices or finding new suppliers for general materials. Here, however, we shall concentrate on one aspect aimed directly at customer satisfaction, product development.

In service industries, product and process are often indistinguishable. In many cases of personal service, the product is the process. What is often not appreciated is the closeness of the two in manufacturing. Not so long ago, it was typical for product designers to work out their ideas and then pass the results 'over the wall' to the process engineers in the factory. The latter would have to work out ways to make the designs. Modern ideas of parallel engineering and manufacturability recognised the waste that this behaviour causes. Furthermore, with rising concern for the environment, the question of disassembly and recycling has also emerged as an issue.

The product development process for a manufactured item is outlined in Figure 17.3. We can see that it is related to the rational decision-making process of Figure 9.4 in three ways. First, the developers need an aim. This is expressed in an agreed working brief. In a commercial relationship, the brief forms the contract with the designer or architect, etc. Second, the innovation proceeds by a mixture of creating alternative ideas and evaluating them against the brief. In the end, several 'good ideas' are taken forward for selection and testing. Third, selection is made from these alternatives. This is where differences between the innovation process and the decision process arise. Selection and testing face more uncertainty in development. Sometimes selection from a shortlist may be carried out by the client. For example, an architect would present several alternatives, each of which satisfies the original brief, and ask the client to make a judgement. On the other hand, for goods to be manufactured in large volumes over a long period, a series of prototypes will be made. They will be used to assess manufacturability and may help with test marketing.

Companies adhere to a formal development process to different degrees. Bass, striving to keep its lead, has a new product development department and uses a structured process for every innovation. The four stages, separated by 'gates' at which progress is appraised, are:

- Ideas generation and concept development. Ideas are taken from many sources: consumer panels, rivals' innovations and internal bright ideas.
- Feasibility study. Manufacture and packaging; market appraisal.
- Development. Naming the brand, packaging design, communications plan, and process trials.
- Final product.

Comparing the Bass process, which led to Caffrey's Ale and Hooper's Hooch, with the less formal approach of Carlsberg-Tetley, Nwabueze and Law suggest that the difference explains the former's relative success. Carlsberg-Tetley has recently launched several new products that have since been deleted.[13]

With consumer goods, test marketing usually requires full-scale operations in a controlled market for several months, if not years. Although expensive, test marketing yields benefits if mistakes are avoided. Yet there are two further drawbacks in addition to cost. The first is that they do not show up well in hindsight. If the product is eventually successful, the time devoted to the test represents loss of revenues that could have been earned with an earlier full-scale launch. On the other hand, if the test points to failure, the development money appears to have been wasted. Worst of all are erroneous test results. Positive test results may not be borne out by eventual performance. Then the marketing manager will be looking for a new job. False negative results, on the other hand, would mean cancellation of what would have been a viable product. Then, no one will know.

The second drawback is the way tests reveal information to rivals. Kotler and colleagues note the case of Carnation Coffee-Mate, which was test marketed over a period of six years before its United Kingdom launch. This gave ample time to Cadbury to develop and launch its own product, Marvel.[14] To counter such difficulties, firms may test products in remote markets, or only try out some aspects of them such as tastes or other ingredients. They try to disguise their intentions.

> *Manufacturability refers to a design's ability consistently and profitably to meet specifications. These include performance, reliability, availability and quality.*

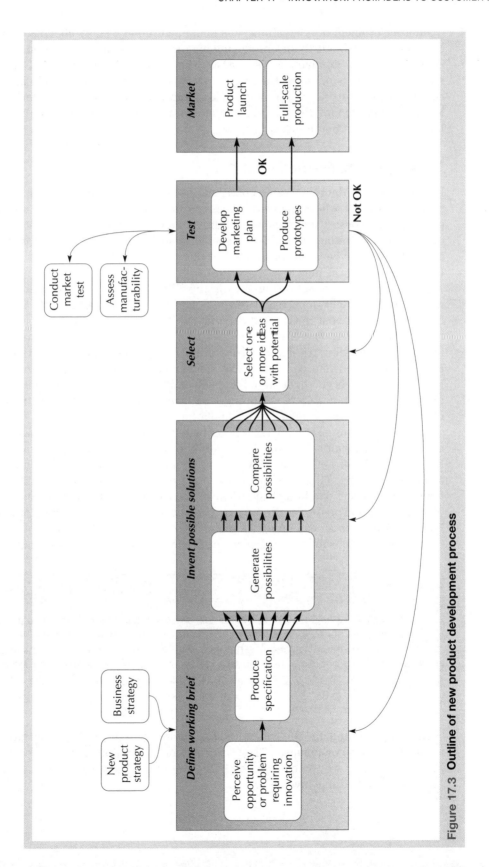

Figure 17.3 Outline of new product development process

Another problem in confectionery is manufacturability. Many chocolate bars can be made in the laboratory but producing and distributing them to consistent quality is more difficult. Supplying a test market, therefore, also confirms that industrial-scale production is possible. Cadbury's Astros were launched in Europe in 1997 to compete with Smarties (Nestlé) and M&Ms (Mars). The product was to be for 'mind-less munching' among the teenage market. Under the name Asteroids, the product had been tested in South Africa.[15]

■ Is inventiveness necessary?

History has seen the remarkable contributions of many inventors. It may, therefore, seem odd to ask whether inventiveness is needed to kick-start the innovation process. Some assert that it is not. Creative solutions can be found systematically rather than by waiting around for flashes of inspiration. Going further, they would argue that inventiveness is constrained by our paradigms which act as psychological barriers to seeing the new.

A remarkable contribution came from the USSR. From 1946, Genrich Altshuller worked in the patent department of the Soviet navy. He considered that, although little was known about the innovation *process*, its *results* could readily be observed in any patent office. Therefore, they must be susceptible to analysis from a techno-logical point of view. Altshuller discovered that 90 per cent of patents were for solutions within current paradigms. Put another way, more than 90 per cent of prob-lems had already been encountered and solved in analogous form. For instance, the problems of cleaning filters, stripping sunflower seeds and splitting diamonds are related and can be approached using similar methods.

Altshuller's team examined 1.2 million patents, 40 000 in detail. This work led to the method of Inventive Problem Solving, known by its Russian acronym, TRIZ. It has been applied to problems as varied as product development, service provision and manufacturing. TRIZ provides a systematic way of finding already available solu-tions. For instance, one branch shows how to cope with contradictions, the problem of making one aspect of a product or process better at the expense of another. Exhibit 17.5 gives an example of a razor. TRIZ generalises from this to show how conflicting functions in many areas can be separated spatially or sequentially.[16]

Exhibit 17.5 Cutting the compromise

To be as effective as possible at cutting hair, a razor needs to be as sharp as possible. The more finely honed it is, however, the greater the risk of cutting skin. In the days of unguarded 'cut-throat' razors, this problem was resolved by compromise, making the blade sharp but not too sharp. Modern razors spatially separate the two functions – cutting and guarding so that each can be done as well as possible.

Although tainted by the unsuccessful Soviet system, TRIZ ideas have been adopted by many companies.[17] They scour patent applications for evidence of rivals' intentions. This is why some avoid early registration unless they fear that a competi-tor is close to the same invention.

Managing innovation

We must avoid interpreting Figure 17.3 as a set of regular steps from an initial idea to a saleable product. In practice, innovation proceeds neither in a straight line nor so smoothly. Stages run into each other with much iteration as choices founder when tested against the criteria of market acceptance or manufacturability. A further problem appears because development work usually involves teams composed of specialists drawn from different departments. Some form of matrix structure is common, *see* Chapter 10. Not only must teams be formed, but also their composition varies as the process moves through its various phases. The interaction between the innovation process and the organisation structure is, therefore, dynamic. Figure 17.4 suggests what might happen throughout a project. The darker shaded elements involve the team. The project flows between departments, often with several working on it simultaneously. Clearly, the innovation needs to be integrated. The person responsible is often called a product or project manager.

Despite the apparent gains to be had from closer integration, especially of development with both marketing and production, many organisations face problems with achieving it. Aaby and Discenza point to two fundamental reasons behind this:[18]

- Many managers have little understanding of technology. This means they do not know how to fit it into the organisation, how technologies fit together and, therefore, how they relate to marketing.

- Many barriers stand between marketing and technology management. For example, managers will have different educational backgrounds and the functions will be organised in different and exclusive ways.

Therefore, finding organisations where the production and development functions are close is common, as in chart 1 of Figure 17.5. Separated by an organisational barrier, the contribution of the marketing department is limited to supplying market research data and information on test market results. Shifting design and development closer to marketing, *see* chart 2, runs the risk of their creating designs without full consideration of manufacturability. Matters can be worse. In chart 3, fears of leakage of plans to rivals mean that development is carried on in secret. Chart 4 suggests a balance with interactive work teams.

This example of the marketing–production–development triangle is but one of many instances of blockages to innovation in organisations. How is it that some firms are more successful than others? Many studies have looked for factors to explain this question. Drawing on the work of Slappendel,[19] we can classify these into three levels:

- The *individualist* perspective sees people as the main source of change in organisations.

- The *organisational* perspective assumes that innovation is largely determined by the characteristics of the organisation itself. Explanations cover the influences of structure and rules to the shared values and attitudes of members.

- The *environmental* perspective suggests that innovation arises in, or is stimulated by, the environment.

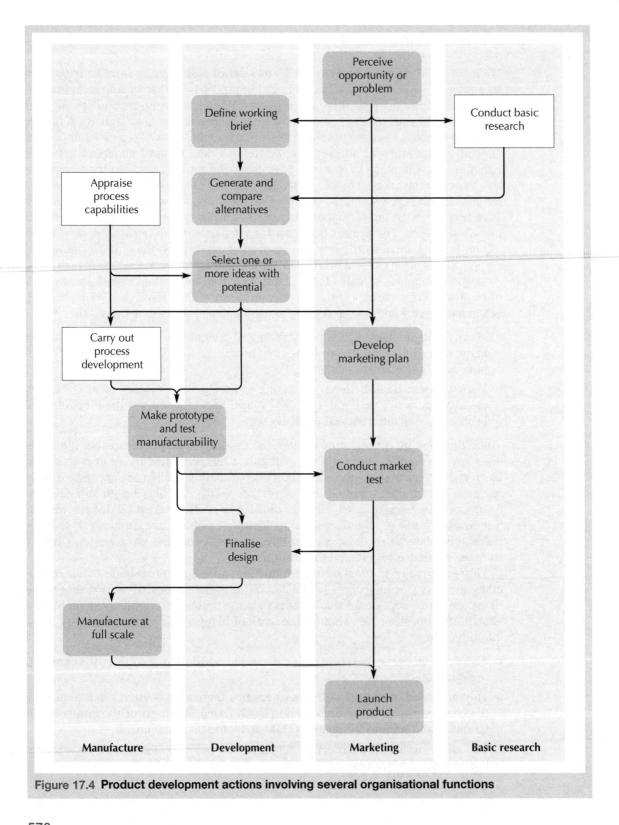

Figure 17.4 **Product development actions involving several organisational functions**

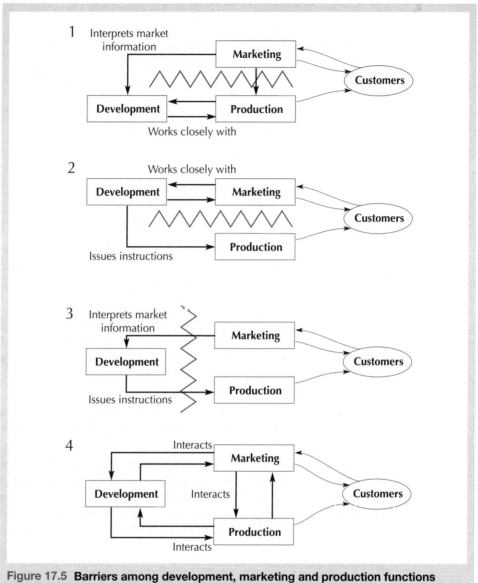

Figure 17.5 **Barriers among development, marketing and production functions**

▧ Individuals as sources of change

Work on the individualist perspective was exemplified by the 'What makes an entrepreneur?' question of Chapter 7. This approach looks for traits, which are personal qualities that predispose someone to certain behaviour. Here it is innovation. Slappendel shows how traits have some validity with respect to an individual acting alone. Yet weaknesses show up when individuals within organisations are considered. Then, success comes from both inventors and those who can push change past organisational barriers. Chapter 7 noted Pinchot's study suggesting that developments follow from having innovators, product champions and sponsors.

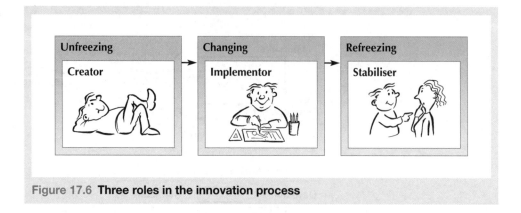

Figure 17.6 **Three roles in the innovation process**

Instead of this hierarchical approach, Chaharbaghi and Newman[20] present three roles needed at different phases of the innovation process, *see* Figure 17.6. (These match the unfreezing–changing–refreezing phases of Lewin's change model given in Figure 19.12.)

- *Creators* are involved with invention. They envisage what could be; they make new connections and see new patterns; they test and develop the new logic of what they invent. Only a few of these important people are found in most organisations.

- *Implementors* manage the change. They apply creativity to making the invention work in the organisational context. There are usually more implementors than creators but they are still in the minority.

- *Stabilisers* refreeze the organisation into a stable system after the change has been brought in. These people produce the new product, introduce the new personnel policy or consolidate the presence in a new market. Stabilisers account for most of the people in the organisation.

As usual with behavioural models, Chaharbaghi and Newman point out that the roles are stereotypes; people display mixed characteristics. The advantage of the model is in recognising that balance is needed to bring about innovation. Lacking an appropriate blend, innovations may never be sparked, may be snuffed out or may simply fade away. We should note also that innovation involves every person in the organisation.

Selecting individuals

With organisations giving priority to innovation, they must consider how they can achieve a balance among the three roles identified above. They might look to selection. Fletcher evaluates how the methods normally used in personnel selection may be applied to the search for innovating creators.[21] These are shown in Exhibit 17.6.

All four methods have weaknesses. First, using biographical data, whether collected in advance or elicited at an interview, assumes that the past is a guide to the future and that people cannot develop. Second, having shown innovative capability does not solely depend on personal traits, for people may have been in restricting roles. The third approach has come into vogue in recent years. Yet it may be as much a test of lucidity, leadership or gamesmanship as of innovativeness. 'Not building Lego towers again!' some candidates may groan. The fourth method, psychometric testing, is attractive in principle. Yet, to be dependable, tests must be

> ### Exhibit 17.6 Searching for innovating creators
>
> ■ Study biographical data, from application forms and references.
> ■ Ask interviewees to describe whether and how they have changed things, or produced new ideas, in the past.
> ■ Present candidates with unusual situations and ask them to respond.
> ■ Apply psychometric tests, such as *KAI*. This one separates adaptors, who work within a current paradigm, from innovators, who try to break out of it.

extensively tested to check whether their predictions are accurate. With innovativeness, it is doubtful whether such calibration is possible. Selecting for innovation, therefore, is very difficult and, in any case, is merely one step in development. Innovativeness must be nurtured and encouraged and the organisation must take risks for it to flourish.

■ Organisations as the incubators of change

The organisational perspective looks to characteristics such as size, strategy, structure, systems and technology as determinants of innovation. We must not fall, however, into the trap of treating the organisation as if it were independent of the people within it. This makes it unwise to argue that such-and-such a characteristic is the cause of low or high innovation. On the other hand, some studies have found links. We shall pick out two areas.

Size and structure

It is often assumed that large organisations find it difficult to sustain innovation. This is not always the case, as some have recently become large because of their innovative success. These will still carry the memory of how to innovate and retain managers who are prepared to take risks. Dougherty and Hardy, however, argue that the large, mature organisations have difficulty.[22]

A history of mergers slows innovation for reasons given earlier. In 2002, the newly formed GSK found this a problem among its 15 000 scientists who had already experienced upheaval. The constituent companies, GlaxoWellcome and SmithKline Beecham, were themselves the results of mergers. A flow of one new 'blockbuster' drug each year was too slow for a company of this scale. Trying to replicate the innovative spirit found in smaller companies, GSK split its main development function into six autonomous units. But some top scientists left and morale remained a problem.[23]

Complexity

Although complexity can be defined in many ways, we shall use the term to refer to the degree of structural differentiation that arises from the number and variety of tasks to be carried out. This is in line with the approach of Lawrence and Lorsch discussed in Chapter 10.[24] An organisation facing such complexity will need a corresponding range of specialists. External contacts mean that these people bring in new ideas while their experience and attitudes foster the take-up of innovation. Therefore, more complexity stimulates more innovation.

A counter-argument arises from the way complexity can lead to conflict. Altogether there may be many new ideas, an atmosphere of conflict will make their adoption unlikely. In addition, the organisation may have missed the second part of the Lawrence and Lorsch study – more differentiation needs more integration. The number of functions involved in the process places a premium on effective co-ordination.

Best practice

Differences among firms in the same industry suggest that organisational factors play a strong part in effective innovation. Krause and Liu conducted a detailed benchmarking study among 15 large international companies in the chemical, pharmaceutical and telecommunications industries. They pinpointed 13 best practices, summarised in Exhibit 17.7.[25]

Exhibit 17.7 Best practices in R&D innovation

- Strategy formulation and communication
  - Clear strategies well communicated to R&D organisation
  - Formal techniques used to identify core technologies
- Funding and investments
  - R&D investments made from multinational perspective
  - Basic research funded from corporate level; development funded by business units
- Organisational and cultural issues
  - Basic research at small number of centralised, specialised facilities; development activity decentralised, close to business units
  - Cross-functional teams for both basic and applied research projects
  - Formal mechanisms for interaction both among R&D staff and between them and others
- Performance evaluation
  - Analytical tools used for project selection and monitoring
  - Most important measure is the rate of transfer of technology from R&D to business units
- Personnel development
  - All levels in the R&D organisation have effective career development
  - Graduate recruits come from diverse universities and from other companies when needed
- Co-operative links
  - Some basic research is carried out internally but there are many outside links
  - External links are formally monitored.

It is worth expanding on some details of this study, not just for what they show about innovation, but also because they confirm important points about all work teams. Teamwork styles differentiated the most successful companies from the rest. They recognised the need for business unit participation in development. Whereas basic research teams had technical leaders, development teams were jointly managed by technical and business leaders. Teams were selected formally to achieve a balance of members' technical and group skills. This contrasts with the less successful companies where co-operation was informal. Scientists tended to do most research alone, supported by technicians. People from marketing or manufacturing were only involved late in the process.

Personnel policies varied. Best practice paid attention to career development and recruitment from a variety of sources. Relying on recruitment from a few favoured university departments was a habit among several less effective companies. Exceptional candidates from elsewhere were not interviewed and the method limited the diversity of candidates and restricted the vital global perspective.

The way funding is managed gives important signals to staff about the way they should act. The fourth point shows that long-term R&D is best funded from the centre while resources for development come from business units. The highly performing companies recognise the tensions between risky, long-term investments in basic science and short-term returns from development. The burden of the former, seeking to develop core technologies, should not fall on individual divisions. Development, on the other hand, needs to be tied in closely to the programme of the division that benefits from it. Resolution of this tension is also seen in the fifth point, where the physical location of the research facility matches its basic or applied purpose.

Chandler and colleagues took a culture perspective on some of these issues. They stressed the importance of consistency between employee perceptions of management support, the reward system and commitment to innovation. Formal HR processes were thought to work against an innovation culture. Firms with supportive cultures tended to perform better.[26]

Nokia uses a wide range of methods to manage current business performance and nurture innovation. It relies on differentiation to separate initiatives that either span, or fall outside, the existing unit structure. The new ventures organisation (NVO) looks after initiatives that are beyond the remits of the existing units but are still within Nokia's strategic vision. Groups with ideas that extend current technologies and may create new markets move into NVO, which accelerates their development. Later, they are reintegrated into the units, form a new unit, or are divested. The last is illustrated by a group working on means of treating diabetes using telecommunications technologies. The business was sold because the new owners could add more value. Nokia uses team-based and company-wide incentives, although their proportion of salary is small. This is to guard against rivalry. The internal mobility rules facilitate staff movement among units, further promoting the exchange of ideas.[27]

■ The environment as the source of change

The third of our perspectives examines the extent to which innovation arises in the environment. The origins of this point of view lie in ideas either that some nations or cultures are more creative than others, or that other environmental factors are at work. Let us look at some examples.

East versus West

It is often argued that competition in the future will be based on the ability to create and use knowledge. In the conventional sense of assembling large quantities of data, however, the 'knowledge-processing' style of Western business may not be optimal. Intuitive, or tacit, knowledge, nurtured in Japanese companies, may be more important. Tacit knowledge refers to the learning embedded in teams. These are the collective rules-of-thumb, hunches and skills passed on from trainer to apprentice, team leader to new starter, or middle manager to graduate trainee. Japanese firms, with national traditions of lifelong employment, respect for seniority and collective ideals, may be much better at creating, sharing and maintaining such knowledge than Western organisations are.

Does reliance on tacit knowledge make organisations more creative? Nonaka and Takeuchi argue that this is the case and propose that all firms can learn from the Japanese experience. Yet relying on intuition may not serve Japanese firms well as they move outside their national base. The Honda City, a car regarded as a major innovation for the 1980s and 1990s, incorporated much intuition but insufficient market research. Global sales averaged 40 000 each year and the model was withdrawn in 1994 after they had fallen to just 3800.[28]

Japan's loss of international competitiveness through the 1990s seems to have brought a change in attitudes. Rather than secretly nurturing ideas within large corporations, new venturers are anxious to use and deal in intellectual property. Major companies are working as much on new products as on honing the first-rate manufacturing processes that sustained the nation's growth for forty years. A surge in the number of patent applications occurred after legislative reform in 1998 and is rising at about 6 per cent each year.

Variations among nations

Arguing that competitive advantage ultimately depends on innovation, Porter identified four factors that appeared to account for different rates in different countries.[29] As shown in Figure 2.6, these are:

■ *Factor availability*

Shortages stimulate innovation. In the United States, high labour costs mean more automation; in Japan, space shortage means ingenious housing and miniaturisation of consumer electronics.

■ *Home market*

Pressure from knowledgeable customers is an important force in a virtuous circle. Restaurants in Belgium and France are good because customers know what a good restaurant is. Innovation raises the standard, and expectations rise too.

■ *Support industries*

Clusters of support industries stimulate innovation because of the flows of information and people among the firms. Best known in modern times is Silicon Valley where many famous innovating companies stand within walking distance of each other. Industrial districts in Italy, specialising in areas such as fashion, furniture and machine tools, grew because of the advantages of close proximity of designers and small, family-run manufacturers. No longer protected by repeated devaluations of the lira, however, these industries are consolidating and leading names are expanding throughout the world.[30]

■ *Rivalry*

Rivalry stimulates investment, cost reduction and all-round improvement.

When experienced in combination, these features make for a very competitive environment. Management skills within the firms are sharpened so they gain advantage over rivals from less stimulating circumstances. Note that this framework contrasts with Porter's earlier work on competitive advantage, which suggested firms were better off isolating themselves from the rigours of competition. Building barriers to industry entry or retreating into niches were favoured recommendations. The later argument represents a switch from products and locations to knowledge and innovation as key factors.

Germany illustrates both the stimulating effect of rivalry and the difficulty of creating an innovative culture. Bertschek examined the effect of greater competition from imports and inward direct investment on the innovation of firms in Germany in the 1980s. Domestic firms had to become more efficient, using both product and process innovation.[31] Despite such evidence, the innovation gap in Germany remains. In Silicon Valley, 73 per cent of firms with sales exceeding $50 million were founded after 1985. In the Stuttgart and Munich regions, the percentages are 20 and 17. Apart from the software giant SAP, no German company founded since the early 1970s has become a global leader in new technology. Kluge and colleagues suggest that the problem lies not in capital shortage but in the lack of knowledge of entrepreneurship itself, including the absence of role models. Within large companies, innovation focuses on current technologies and is kept within existing structures. Firms are not used to alliances and acquisitions.[32]

Conclusion: the vital process of innovation

Throughout this chapter, we have demonstrated the importance of innovation. It has been presented as a complex and subtle process requiring the contribution of teams rather than solely relying on the pioneering spirit of one person. The inventor may kick the process into life but it requires other skills to carry it forward, especially in large organisations.

Clearly, sound investment in innovation brings its rewards. We have seen how society as a whole is usually better off when products and associated processes are improved or new technologies are brought into play. Benefits flow to individuals and firms from the way they increase intellectual capital, protected by patents and other forms of registration.

Difficult questions for managers are whether innovation can be delivered to order and, in any case, where it originates. The TRIZ process was backed for many years by a Soviet government concerned that its economic system was not keeping up with developments in the West. None the less, systematic learning from others offers ways for organisations to avoid reinventing the wheel.

As for the sources of innovation, studies point in different directions. For some, freeing the individual spirit is an important element. This stems from concerns to increase the rate of invention. Methods to stimulate ideas were discussed in Chapter 9. Yet here we have shown that these will not succeed within an organisation whose structure and culture are unfavourable. Finally, firms must not underestimate the environment both as the cause of healthy competitive pressure and as offering possibilities for exploitation of new ideas.

QUICK CHECK

Can you ...

- Give examples of invention and innovation.
- Define innovation gap.
- Name the three product levels identified by Kotler.
- Outline four types of intellectual property.
- State the three conditions for a successful patent application.
- Summarise the rules of copyright.
- Define manufacturability.
- Give the five main stages of the product development process.
- List the three roles, according to Chaharbaghi and Newman, needed at stages of the innovation process.
- State the four factors that Porter uses to account for variations in innovation among nations.

QUESTIONS

Chapter review

17.1 Why are some firms more innovative than others?

17.2 Explain why and how the market values intellectual property such as patents and trademarks.

17.3 Is the innovation process a means of overcoming the lack of inventiveness in an organisation?

17.4 The United States licensing of AstraZeneca's cancer drug Iressa was delayed six months by the cautious Food and Drug Administration. How would this affect the company?[33]

Application

17.5 Using a consumer magazine such as *Which?* or *What Camera?* investigate the relevance of the product definition of Figure 17.2.

Investigation

17.6 Use the Design Council website to compare several innovations, using ideas from the chapter.[34]

17.7 Explore the lists of intellectual property registrations published by the Patent Office to discuss differences by region, industrial sector and firm.[35]

'Inspire the Next'[36]

The company motto, given in the headline, symbolises Hitachi's commitment to breathe new life into development for the long term. Number two electronics and electrical group in Japan and 171st in the *Business Week Global 1000*, it had seen its ranking fall through a combination of the week yen and its own struggling profitability. Yet it remains a truly global company. There were some 321 000 employees in a network of about 70 companies worldwide. In the tough market conditions of 2002, revenues were ¥7993 billion (down ¥500 billion in five years), yielding a loss of ¥586 billion, about 7 per cent. Hitachi had struggled to make small profits of 1 per cent, for most of the previous 10 years, but 1999 was also a loss maker, at 5 per cent of sales. Figure 17.7 gives other selected data.

Hitachi's medium-term plan, to 2007, is based on recovery. It sets targets for its promising busi-nesses while exiting those with a lack of synergy or whose prospects are poor. These amount to roughly 20 per cent of sales. Globalisation will be accelerated through channelling resources into units that have the potential to be among the top three in the world. These include data storage and biomedical applications such as advanced diagnosis and home medical equipment.

Hitachi Plan II extends the previous plan in looking to innovation to make Hitachi the best global supplier of total solutions. Now, core fields of information systems and social infrastructure systems are combined in the domain of 'New era lifeline support systems'. It joins information technology and systems such as electricity, gas and water. The second domain is 'Global products incorporating advanced technology'. It aims for

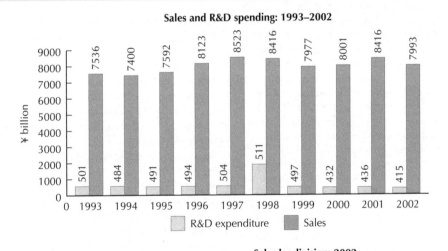

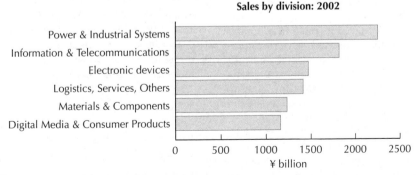

Figure 17.7 Some financial data from Hitachi

global growth by blending Hitachi's advanced technologies and knowledge. Further themes include:

- Lifestyle: building the information society.
- Healthcare: including biotechnology.
- Environment: safety based on energy and environmental technologies.
- Intelligent management: contribution to corporate innovation.

Research programmes cover these areas, ranging from new materials to home appliances and from knowledge-based management to nanotechnology.

The company has a bank of intellectual property in high technology areas. Since 1963, for example, it ranks fourth after IBM, General Electric and AT&T in the number of registered United States patents. From 1985, Hitachi's earnings from licences have exceeded the fees it has paid to others.

The business employs 20 patent lawyers, kept busy by the 15 000 applications made annually. This represents a fall of 30 per cent from the 1980s. Patenting policy has changed to focus on fewer registrations, concentrating on ideas with potential for cross-licensing deals. These are areas where Hitachi may be pushed out by competitors' registrations. If it perceives no external threat, however, the company avoids the disclosure required when filing applications and prefers to keep its technology secret for as long as possible.

In 2002, Hitachi employed almost 9100 staff in research facilities worldwide. About one in twelve of these had doctorates. There were six corporate research laboratories, listed in Table 17.1. These accounted for a quarter of R&D expenditure. Funds come in three categories: corporate headquarters pays for studies that are more than five years from the market; business divisions commission research with a horizon of three to five years; and work that is expected to be marketed within two years is conducted in the divisions' product development facilities.

Of the laboratories listed in Table 17.1, Central Research and Advanced Research have the largest proportions of their funds provided centrally. They work on generating fundamental breakthroughs as important as the transistor. Staff are encouraged to present papers at symposia and mix with the world's leading scientists.

R&D spending of all kinds is seen as essential to the company's future. Throughout the 1990s, efforts had been made to focus spending more closely on market-driven projects. *Tokken*, or special research teams, had created supercomputers, semiconductors,

Table 17.1 Hitachi's corporate research laboratories

Laboratory	Fields
Central Research, Tokyo	Information & communications, Life sciences
Hitachi Research, Hitachi	Public systems, Devices, Components, Materials
Mechanical Engineering, Tsuchinza	Mechatronics applications systems
Production Engineering, Yokohama	Production systems & processes
Systems Development, Kawasaki	Service solutions, Information networks, Software
Advanced Research, Hatoyama	Advanced measurement, Mind-brain sciences, Materials

disks, displays, power plants and intelligent robots. *Tokken* supported Hitachi's reputation for technological excellence through a bottom-up approach; the proposals of junior scientists were evaluated by those higher up. Yet this had resulted in an egalitarian and individualistic style. Concerns were expressed over researchers' orientation to market development. Rivals such as Matsushita, Sharp and Sony have done better at commercialisation.

In a switch of emphasis, selecting corporate projects has been made the responsibility of the business planning division and not the laboratories. A new system of committees under Hitachi Plan II will oversee commercialisation and promote innovation. Projects with time horizons beyond five years, however, will still follow the *tokken* philosophy.

Hitachi views the world as a single market, selecting optimal locations for facilities, including R&D. It believes its strength can only be sustained by investing in high-growth regions and forming alliances with first-rate partners.

Questions

1 How does the structure of Hitachi's R&D effort compare with the ideas explained in the chapter?

2 Why not patent basic research?

3 What are the advantages and disadvantages of bottom-up R&D?

Bibliography

The United Kingdom Patent Office is an excellent source on intellectual property, **www.patent.gov.uk/**; *see also* the World Intellectual Property Organisation, **www.wpo.int**. Accessible reports on innovation in several countries are available from the World Technology Evaluation Centre, **www.wtec.org/reports.htm**. Many companies provide details of their innovations, including 3M, **www.3m.com**, Siemens, **www.siemens.com/index.jsp** and Dyson, **www.dyson.co.uk/tech/dysoncyclone/default.asp**, while the Design Council offers interesting case histories, **www.design-council.org.uk/design/**.

References

1 Gourlay, Richard (1995) 'Working like clockwork', *Financial Times*, 8 August, 13; Arthur, Charles (1995) 'Wind-up radio is a hit', *Independent on Sunday*, 13 August; 'Wheel of fortune', *Times: City Diary*, 29 August 2002; 'Turn the handle and talk', *The Economist: Technology Quarterly*, **361**, 12 August 2001, 10–12; O'Sullivan, Kate (2002) 'The don't-take-it-to-market alternative', *Inc.*, **24(13)**, December, 128–30.

2 Levine, Joshua (2002) 'Carpet diem', *Forbes*, **170(8)**, 14 October, 206–8; Design Council (2002) *Innovation stories*, **www.designcouncil.org.uk/innovationstories/**, accessed 13 April 2003; 'Dyson's DC07, the high-tech tool that's a global phenomenon', *PR Newswire*, 2 October 2002; '£4 million award for Dyson in UK', *Managing Intellectual Property*, **124**, November 2002, 12.

3 Pilling, David (2001) 'AstraZeneca to cease development of Viozan', *Financial Times*, 28 June, 25.

4 'New technology is no snap', *The Economist*, 11 October, 1997, 125; Hasselblad (2003) *Digital photography*, **www.hasselblad.com**, accessed 23 April 2003.

5 Kanter, Rosabeth Moss (1983) *The Change Masters*, New York: Touchstone.

6 Hausman, Jerry (1997) 'Cellular telephones: new products and the CPI', *NBER Working Paper 5982*, March, quoted in 'And now prices can be virtual too', *The Economist*, 14 June 1997, 122.

7 Cawley, Richard (1997) 'Princes brings fresh interest to corned beef', *The Grocer*, 19 July; Tambe, Rozmeen (ed.) (2003) *Canned foods: Market Report Plus:* 13th edition, London: Key Note, February.

8 Kotler, Philip, Armstrong, Gary, Saunders, John and Wong, Veronica (1996) *Principles of Marketing: The European edition*, Hemel Hempstead: Prentice Hall, 546.

9 Hitt, Michael A., Hoskisson, Robert E., Johnson, Richard A. and Moesel, Douglas D. (1996) 'The market for corporate control and firm innovation', *Academy of Management Journal*, **39(5)**, October, 1084–1119.

10 Jackson, Tim (1997) *Inside Intel: How Andy Grove built the world's most successful chip company*, London: HarperCollins, quoted in Jackson, Tim (1997) 'Paranoia pays off', *Guardian: Online*, 30 October, 1.

11 Trapp, Roger (1994) 'Trademarks shape up: protection for a product's form, sound or smell opens new areas of dispute', *Financial Times*, 2 November, 35; 'Sven takes protective measure in battle for rubber-goods market', *Guardian*, 19 April 2003; Fry, Robin (2002) 'The money of colour', *The Times*, 17 September; *see also* the Patent Office site at **www.patent.gov.uk** and the World Intellectual Property Organisation at **www.wpo.int**, both accessed 16 April 2003.

12 KPMG (2000) *Strategic Management of Intellectual Property: Enhancing organisational success by unlocking the value of ideas*, London: KPMG.

13 Nwabueze, Uche and Law, Zoe Clair (2001) 'The journey for survival: the case of new product development in the brewery industry', *Journal of Product and Brand Management*, **10(6)**, 382–97.

14 Kotler *et al.* (1996) *op cit.*, 525.

15 Stuart, Liz (1997) 'New Cadbury brand to challenge Smarties', *Marketing Week*, 26 June.

16 Domb, Ellen, King, Bob and Tate, Karen (1995) 'Systemic innovation: inventing on purpose instead of waiting for the lightning to strike', *Journal of Innovative Management*, Winter, 65–70.

17 See *Triz Journal*, **www.triz-journal.com** and **www.mazur. net/triz/**, accessed 20 April 2003.

18 Aaby, Nils-Erik and Discenza, Richard (1995) 'Strategic marketing and new product development: an integrated approach', *Marketing Intelligence and Planning*, **13(9)**, September, 30–5.

19 Slappendel, Carol (1996) 'Perspectives on innovation in organisations', *Organization Studies*, **17(1)**, Winter, 107–29.

20 Chaharbaghi, Kazem and Newman, Victor (1996) 'Innovating: towards an integrated learning model', *Management Decision*, **34 (4)**, July, 5–13.

21 Fletcher, Clive (1997) 'Keep an open mind on selecting for innovation', *People Management*, **3(5)**, 6 March, 55.

22 Dougherty, Deborah and Hardy, Cynthia (1996) 'Sustained product innovation in large, mature organizations: overcoming innovation-to-organization problems', *Academy of Management Journal*, **39(5)**, October, 1120–53.

23 Dyer, Geoff (2002) 'GlaxoSmithKline's radical programme to increase the productivity of its 15,000

scientists is a test case for the entire drugs industry', *Financial Times*, 24 October.

24 Lawrence, Paul R. and Lorsch, Jay W. (1986) *Organisation and Environment: Managing differentiation and integration*, Boston, Mass.: Harvard Business School Press.

25 Krause, Irv and Liu, John (1993) 'Benchmarking R&D productivity', *Planning Review*, **21(1)**, January–February, 16–23.

26 Chandler, Gaylen N., Keller, Chalon and Lyon, Douglas W, (2000) 'Unravelling the determinants of an innovation-supportive organisational culture', *Entrepreneurship: Theory and Practice*, **25(1)**, 59–79.

27 Day, Jonathan D., Mang, Paul Y., Richter, Ansgar and Roberts, John (2001) 'The innovative organisation', *McKinsey Quarterly*, **2**.

28 'Now you know', *The Economist*, 27 May 1995, 58.

29 Porter, Michael E. (1990) *The Competitive Advantage of Nations*, New York; The Free Press.

30 Betts, Paul (2000) 'Survey Milan; Fashion and design', *Financial Times*, 16 November.

31 Bertschek, Irene (1995) 'Product and process innovation as a response to increasing imports and foreign direct investment', *Journal of Industrial Economics*, **43(4)**, December, 341–57.

32 Kluge, Jürgen, Meffert, Jürgen and Stein, Lothar (2000) 'The German road to innovation', *McKinsey Quarterly*, **2**, 98–105.

33 'Cancer drug wins limited US approval', *Financial Times: Companies & Markets*, 6 May 2003, 1.

34 *See* Reference 2.

35 *See* Reference 11.

36 Based on Hitachi Ltd., *About us*, **http://global.hitachi.com/index.html**, accessed 24 April 2003.

Control and change

Part 6 completes the cycle of planning, organising, implementing and controlling. As Chapter 18 shows, however, control is more varied than making corrections after deviations from plans have appeared. Better understanding of processes, supplemented by timely control data, enables managers to anticipate difficulties and take action to prevent them. The chapter also points out that control activity is effected through people. Without their co-operation, the cybernetic model of automatic control is worthless.

Expansion of information systems means ready access to more data. Although this might support the technocratic approach to management, excessive attention to numbers, especially accounting data, may lead to unbalanced development.

Chapter 19 discusses further problems of control, relating it to power and the behaviour of people and groups. The control dilemma concerns the balance between failure and the need to empower employees to make changes they think are necessary. Tightening of controls only makes things worse. Somehow, organisations must learn to change. The emerging theory of chaos, suggesting that the future is unknowable, challenges the single-loop model and further underscores the need. We use Organisation Development (OD) and Business Process Reengineering (BPR) to compare hard and soft approaches.

CHAPTER 18

Control of management processes

Chapter objectives

When you have finished studying this chapter, you should be able to:

- explain the nature of control in organisations;

- match contrasting views of control with the various schools of management thought;

- set out the purposes of control within the organisational context;

- identify three basic types of control system, explaining the steps that each involves; identify their differences and give examples of suitable applications;

- apply these models to illustrate circumstances when control systems can fail;

- show how control systems can be linked to cover a whole organisation, suggesting some weaknesses with this approach;

- describe and illustrate reasons for effective control;

- compare conventional performance measures with new ideas of balance;

- outline the limitations of the cybernetic approach in the human context.

Who controls the past controls the future. Who controls the present controls the past.

George Orwell, British writer

Home shopping services[1]

Home shopping grew out of mail order. The United Kingdom market, of about £15 billion, accounts for about 8 per cent of retail sales. In 2002, the catalogue division of Great Universal Stores, number four in the world, generated revenue of £1.5 billion. Second was Littlewoods with about half that amount. The market is growing at about 20 per cent each year, mainly through the development of new channels, such as the Internet, where food sales are expanding quickly. Among catalogues, focused, direct mailings are the growth area. Many small companies have entered the market, often appealing to younger customers in the ABC_1 categories. With conventional catalogues in decline, the major companies have responded by launching their own direct catalogue, television or Internet operations. A more fragmented market has emerged.

Leading companies take about three-quarters of all their orders by telephone. Connections are free or at local rates. Compared with mail, telephone ordering is easier, delivery is faster, and, when stock-outs occur, alternatives are offered. Operators check customers' credit records online so that satisfactory orders are immediately placed in the despatch schedule and picking instructions sent to automated warehouses.

Better service raises expectations. Mail order customers had been unaware of how quickly their orders were handled. Telephone users, however, want instant attention so the sellers set themselves response targets. In home shopping, GUS, Littlewoods and the others need telephone bureaux whose capacity balances their response targets against the cost of having staff idle for much of the time. At peak times, Littlewoods has more than 100 operators at work.

Callers join a single queue and are answered in sequence. The equipment connects them to desks in rotation. The call queue length is displayed prominently to warn staff and supervisors of excess demand.

Demand varies hourly and daily. Experience enables a forecast to be made for each half-hour interval. Companies recruit and train enough staff to cover the forecast pattern. Yet, as shown in Figure 15.10, changes occur by the minute. To cope with these short-term surges, the supervisors can:

- Reduce the time spent with each caller. When time permits, staff remind customers of special offers and pass on other information about the company. When they are busy, they cut this activity.
- Ask staff to delay their breaks.
- Call to the manager to divert staff from other activities, although this usually takes several minutes to arrange.

Performance is reviewed at three levels. First, each week, the supervisors receive information on operators' performance levels including the times that each individual takes to handle calls. They are expected to check on operators whose performance appears to be out of line. The accent is on coaching, through listening to an operator's work and discussing how to improve. Not overemphasising speed at the expense of quality is important. For the customer, each service episode is significant. The art, at peak times, is to give good quality while maintaining an efficient tempo.

At the second level, the departmental manager is responsible for achieving service standards within cost constraints. Significant staff must be allocated to the operation to have more than 99 per cent of calls answered within 30 seconds. The average wait should be much lower – about three seconds. Such performance has to be achieved within operating cost budgets.

The manager plans the allocation of staff according to latest demand forecasts. Hourly, daily and seasonal fluctuations are estimated from patterns identified in the management information system. The trend is also worked out from these data, modified by the effect of, say, short-run promotions. Forecasts are updated weekly. In addition, the management information system makes available the following summaries: costs; staff performance compared with standards; average times to answer calls; average length of call; and the number of enquirers who hung up before their calls were answered. Using this information, the manager discusses and adjusts the coming weekly programme with the supervisors.

The third level of control is with the divisional manager who receives summarised performance information each week on all channels and departments. Problems and possible changes are discussed with the departmental managers. Additionally, the divisional manager works with the other departments to improve the ordering activity in the longer term. These include: changes to the information system; new order processing methods; improved query handling; clarifying instructions and information given to customers; and the timing of special offers and other promotions.

The divisional manager must consider the switch to newer technologies. For the telephone, automated call handling (ACH) offers consistent call duration, greater line capacity and 24-hour availability. It also promises to relieve employee stress by eliminating tedious work. On the other hand, customers often rely on the knowledge and helpfulness of staff, who can deal with unexpected queries. Furthermore, introducing new items to the range, such as insurance and other financial services, is supported by selling and specialist advice at the point of contact.

The Internet beats ACH in several ways, mainly because it is a richer channel. More information can travel in both directions. Little growth has been seen, however, among traditional catalogue clients although the web has developed rapidly among those sectors with access to it.

Introduction

The case study illustrates many aspects of control in organisations. We see managers monitoring performance and, if it deviates from targets, acting to bring it back into line. This process view of control, based on correction of errors or *variances*, starts this chapter. Furthermore, beyond the simple loop of monitoring, comparison with target and corrective action, we can see a hierarchy of control. Each layer monitors the performance of the one below. Higher up the hierarchy, monitoring information is more aggregated and provided less frequently. In the same way, corrective action, immediate and detailed at low levels, is delayed and general at higher ones. This arrangement is typical of formal control systems.

*To accountants, the term **variance** refers to the difference between budgeted and actual spending or receipts.*

Within the case, we also find a hint of problems. Being controlled is stressful. In the United Kingdom, call centres have been among the fastest growing employment sectors. With more than 250 000 people at work, especially in cities in the north where costs are low, it is said that many centres echo the 'dark satanic mills'[2] of mass production. Closely supervised staff sit in lines or booths, with the performance of each monitored remotely. Assertions of high stress levels caused the Trades Union Congress to establish an advisory service, through yet another call centre. Complaints included tiny breaks between calls, and having to ask permission before leaving the desk. In India, the problem is worsened by the predominance of night shifts, upsetting circadian rhythms.[3] On treadmills, control generates a climate of fear.

Leading companies try to avoid stress and demotivation by varying routines and introducing longer rest breaks. Standard Life went further by: giving up the collection of individual statistics; abandoning detailed quality control; dropping the 270 standardised scripts to be used by operators; and cutting the link from monitoring to management pay. Customer response, staff morale and the proportion of queries answered first time all rose.[4]

In this chapter and the next, we examine both the process and motivational aspects of control. On the one hand, as we have argued at various points in the book, it is a poor manager who fails to monitor the outcomes of plans and instructions. Yet control must be exercised humanely and constructively if it is not to be seen as coercive. We shall start by studying control as an application of a rational model, closing the chapter by outlining some difficulties from the behavioural perspective. Chapter 19 explores its limits.

What is control?

The term control has many uses. From a narrow point of view, we have control meaning coercion or close direction. It is a feature of both 'hard' human resource management, *see* Chapter 14, and the autocratic or directive style of leadership discussed in Chapter 11. Through dominance and close supervision, organisations are 'under control' when they operate as extensions of managers' decision processes. They expect them to respond like the scalpels of telesurgery. This is the information age method of operating remotely, possibly on the other side of the world. Surgeons' tools include joysticks, robotic arms, cameras and a high bandwidth information link.[5]

In contrast to this close-up perspective, control is also used to describe the broad idea of being 'in charge'. It is represented in the oft-discussed question of the separation of ownership from control. O'Sullivan presents this in terms of: who controls the allocation of corporate resources; what decisions they make; and how they distribute the benefits among stakeholders.[6] These are questions of power, covered in the next chapter.

Anthony presents control as a management process, although a broad one. For him, planning and control are inseparable aspects of the same activity. Splitting them is too artificial for understanding what happens. 'Management control is the process by which managers influence other members of the organisation to implement the organisation's strategies.'[7] In other words, the steps set out in Figure 8.1 are combined into one. This is justified because, 'Although planning and control are definable abstractions and are easily understood as calling for different types of mental activity, they do not relate to major categories of activities actually carried on in an organisation, either at different times or by different people, or for different situations'.[8]

For his analysis, Anthony identifies three layers of control, each of which contains the planning and control loop. Shown in Figure 18.1, they are: *strategic, management* and *task*. The first, strategic planning, was covered in Chapter 8. Below in the hierarchy come management control and task control. The former covers interpretation of strategy into action while the latter concentrates on transactions. 'Task control is the process of assuring that specific tasks are carried out effectively and efficiently.'[9]

Unfortunately, although Anthony's three-level model provides a general framework, it suffers from the very difficulties it was meant to overcome. While searching for a holistic view of control, the three-tier approach runs the risk of missing it. As Berry and colleagues point out, 'interlinkages between levels, which are interdependent, are not shown'.[10] They are severed once we make the horizontal slices shown in Figure 18.1.

What does this mean in practice? How should we look at control? We could rely on the process model alone. Yet the home shopping case that opened this chapter tells us about how control is exercised at three managerial levels and about how these levels are linked. Both angles tell us something about control in this organisa-

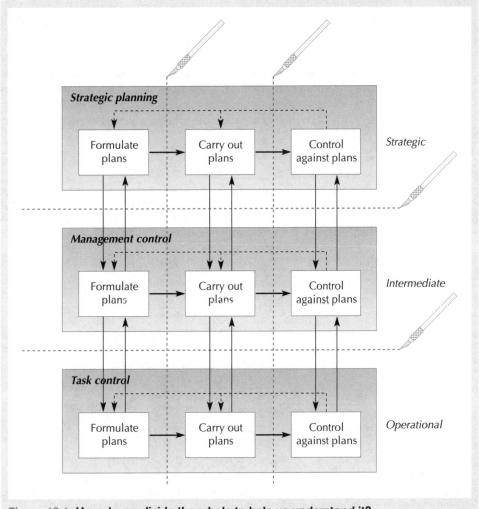

Figure 18.1 **How do we divide the whole to help us understand it?**

tion. But neither tells us everything. Neither is complete. We must switch between the two, and add in broader views such as the organisation–environment relationships drawn from Chapter 2.

There is a further problem with merging planning and control into a single idea. What about leading, communicating and other managerial roles and functions identified by authors from Fayol to Mintzberg? An objection to using any of these categories, demanding that management be viewed only as a whole, would make discussion and research impossible. Categories are useful for making sense of the world. Therefore, we shall distinguish control from planning although the same person is often responsible for both. Management is multifaceted. Stacey points out, 'Management is about more than making a decision and taking action – it is also about evaluating the outcome of the decision and its consequent action. In other words, it is also about control and about learning from the consequences of behaviour.'[11]

Origins of control ideas

Mullins[12] suggested how the emerging schools of management thought held different views of the nature of control, summarised in Exhibit 18.1. It is worth noting the modern view, that the choice of control methods is contingent on circumstances. For example, we would expect there to be much coercion, that is external control, in corrective institutions. Exhibit 18.2 describes one of many checks on prisoners returning from work assignments outside a camp in Stalin's Russia.[13] The 'zeks' were afraid to do anything that might displease the arbitrary, personal wishes of the guards.

Exhibit 18.1 Approaches to organisational control

School	Perceived nature of control	Main source of control
Scientific management – Taylor	Stress on detailed control of every aspect of a job	External
Bureaucracy – Weber	Predominance of rules and procedures	External
Administrative principles – Fayol	Management includes control as generic process	External
Human relations – Follett, Mayo	Control should not mean close direction	Internal
Theory Y – McGregor	Self-control is possible if a person is committed to the task	Internal
Management science – Urwick	Accent on inputs and outputs – control stresses linkages	Process
Socio-technical systems – Tavistock	Role of technology in the control of work	Process
Systems and cybernetics – Weiner	Learning from engineering control systems	Process
Systems and chaos – Gleick, Stacey	Limits of formal control – instability	Mixed – limited
Contingency	No single best way to control	As required

Exhibit 18.2 Taking risks for something to trade

'Meanwhile Shukhov had removed both mittens, the empty one and the one with the hacksaw, and held them in one hand (the empty one in front) together with the untied rope-belt. He fully unbuttoned his jacket, lifted high the edges of his coat and jacket ... and at the word of command stepped forward.

'The guard slapped Shukhov's sides and back, and the outside of his knee-pocket. Nothing there. He kneaded the edges of coat and jacket. Nothing there either. He was about to pass him through when, for safety's sake, he crushed the mitten that Shukhov held out to him – the empty one.'

Sources of control

Commenting on the variety of control observed in organisations, Mullins adds, 'It may even be that control systems provide a better means of predicting certain facets of organisational behaviour than the classification of technology.'[14] The schools in Exhibit 18.1 illustrate three assumptions about where control should originate. Classical theorists had no doubt; control is exercised by management and is largely external. Those in the human relations movement saw the opposite. They discovered that, despite managers' motivational efforts, from incentives to coercion, individuals and groups exercised great power in setting their own work targets. In this perspective, therefore, control is largely internal. Finally, the systems-cybernetics school saw control as essentially a process. Decision making, supported by a flow of relevant information, makes a complex process work. Literature on quality management, for instance, pays the greatest attention to this aspect. Oakland defines control as 'the process by which information or feedback is provided so as to keep all functions on track'.[15]

All three views of control are useful to understanding the issues. This chapter concentrates on the process view, giving a close-up of the stages of information processing, decision making and action needed to keep processes on track. Questions of internal and external control, and their relationship to organisation and motivation, covered in Chapters 14 and 11 respectively, are brought together in Chapter 19.

■ The purpose of control

Having effective control systems offers four advantages to the organisation:

■ *Achieving objectives*

As we shall see, formal control systems require managers to state their objectives clearly and consistently. The case of home shopping showed how managers at different levels aimed at customer service targets measured by call duration, waiting times and dropouts, and costs.

We should also remember the uncertainty surrounding all plans. As Burns wrote, 'The best laid schemes o' mice and men gang aft a-gley'.[16] Deviations from expectations may arise from unexpected variations in inputs, hidden process deficiencies, changes in the environment or imperfections in the plan itself. We should not set plans in motion and expect desired results to emerge on their own; managers must intervene.

■ *Limiting drift*

While acting upon every minor deviation from a plan is foolish for managers, there is a risk of small errors slowly accumulating and leading to serious problems. For instance, minor cuts in service quality flowing from the desire to reduce costs may have little apparent effect in the short term. Yet their long-term effect may be disastrous. This is a reason for the United Kingdom rail regulator to press for improvement to the enquiry service quality. If effective, rail becomes more accessible; if ineffective, passengers are turned away. National Rail Enquiries is the country's most called number, with 60 million calls each year. It employs 1700 staff at four call centres. There are 293 million route and fare combinations. More than 12 per cent of Intercity tickets were sold on the Internet in 2002.

■ *Managing complexity*

While all organisations need control, in the simple ones it can be basic and informal. When large, however, there will be complex structures, often with project teams or matrices imposed on divisions. At this stage, careful attention to control is important if the whole is not to get out of hand. Besides its home shopping business, Great Universal Stores has interests in Argos retail shops, the Burberry luxury brand and Experian information services. Each needs control appropriate to its setting, while linked so that the whole business is manageable.

■ *Environmental response*
We argued in Chapter 2 that irreversible environmental changes pose problems for the organisation. In the time between goal setting and achievement, turbulent environments can cause disruption, making assumptions inappropriate. While the home shopping bureau was practised at coping with random and seasonal fluctuations in demand, managers also knew they had to adapt to trends. Their control system, gathering information about environmental changes as well as cumulative data on customer demand, warned them of areas where they needed new responses.

Types of control system

Whatever the practical nature of control, or its position in the hierarchy, an organisation needs a process that will ensure that objectives are met, drift avoided, complexity coped with and environmental uncertainty responded to. Taking the open-systems view of an organisation and its processes, we think of a process system with inputs and outputs. Since the system does not automatically respond to change, it requires continual monitoring and adjustment to keep it on course. This is the function of control, which we can define as follows:

> *Control ensures*
> *that the plan is achieved*
> *in spite of obstacles, variations and uncertainties*
> *in both the organisation and its environment.*

This means that a control system must know the plans, be able to assess performance compared with the plans, and act to correct differences between the two. This control loop is seen in many systems whose survival depends on finding stability. For instance, living systems have many mechanisms conserving the delicate balance needed for life. Of the thousands in the human body, one keeps the brain temperature to within 0.1°C for healthy functioning.

Many natural systems rely on control action following change. They respond to past events instead of anticipating future ones. If our body temperature rises, we pump blood to the skin surface to increase the rate of cooling. We correct our overheating in arrears. On the other hand, intelligent behaviour involves built-in forecasting. To catch a bus, we arrive at the stop ahead of the scheduled time. If we anticipate being late, we correct by walking more quickly. The relationship between anticipation and correction distinguishes three types of control system: feedback, concurrent and feedforward.

Feedback control

Feedback control uses past information to correct performance. Cybernetics experts refer to the control activity as based on *negative feedback*. Its elements are shown in Figure 18.2. The process, often referred to as the *transformation process*, converts inputs into outputs. It could be a single process, for example a paint line converting unpainted into painted products. On the other hand, it could be a whole business, converting inputs of economic resources into products and, it is hoped, profits. The model has four key features:

Goals

A precondition of any control is a set of standards for the controller to make decisions. For instance, the home shopping bureau had to answer 99 per cent of calls within 30 seconds. Yet this performance should not be achieved at any cost. The managers had to plan staff deployment to achieve the standard within budget.

> ***Negative feedback*** *does not refer to an unfavourable response. It means that the control unit responds to errors so as to reverse them.*

Monitor performance

Monitoring means measuring process outputs. For many activities, monitoring operates routinely. The divisional manager received weekly reports on performance and could discuss the reallocation of resources to make improvements.

Comparison

The third feature of our model brings in the controller. This could be a person or an automatic device. It compares the monitored results with the goals. If the results are favourable, or close enough to target, then the controller takes no action. Otherwise, the controller acts to counter deficits in the process outputs.

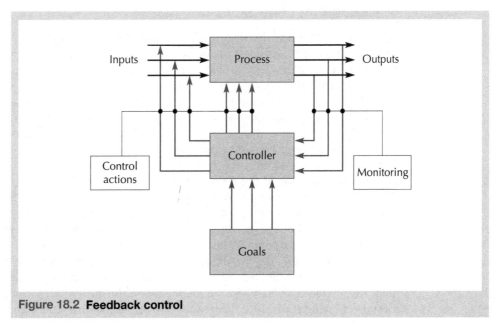

Figure 18.2 Feedback control

The comparison stage underlines the need for a plan backed up with contingencies. In the home shopping bureau, supervisors would know what to do if several staff called in sick. At Amtico, in Chapter 15, staff at the finishing stage would need sufficient blank tiles in stock for the order to be satisfied.

Intelligent controllers do not respond to every deviation; they know when they are significant. In quality control, for instance, small variations within *process tolerances* are permitted. Deming told of a printer at Nashua Corporation who adjusted his machine after each impression. The tiny variations from what he saw as ideal were caused not by systematic defects but by randomness. Instead of ignoring them, he was fruitlessly trying to adjust them out.

■ *Control action*

The corrective action to be taken depends on the details of the control system. With an automatic controller, the predetermined response is incorporated into the design of the device. A well-known example is a thermostat turning on a heater when the temperature falls.

Note how Figure 18.3 shows control actions directed at either the process inputs or the system itself. With many machines, such as the heater, the controller is designed only to regulate inputs, here to switch the energy supply. In contrast, a process involving people can be controlled either by regulating inputs or by adjusting the process itself. We could see both types at the call centre. In response to rising demand, supervisors would ask for more inputs, that is more staff resources. Alternatively, they would adapt the process by asking operators to spend less time with each client.

Figure 18.2 shows several inputs, outputs, goals and control actions. Although drawing three lines instead of one complicates the diagram, remember that multiples typify most processes. Unlike the simple thermostat, most process controllers monitor several outputs, aim at several goals simultaneously and have options when it comes to taking action.

■ Concurrent control

Feedback control has the drawback of controlling after the event. It responds to defects: the bottle of whisky is underfilled, the cakes are burnt, the seeds have not germinated or the budget is overspent. A manager paraphrasing Orwell, *see* the opening quote, might say that controlling the present lets us control the past – but we want to control the future. Interventions are 'just too late'. In response, concurrent, or real-time, control works on monitoring the present; it works as closely as possible to the action. Reflecting Anthony's view of the inseparability of process elements, monitoring and adjusting are seen as part of the whole. For instance, much of the call centre operator's work involves real-time control. The advantage of the human operator is continuous adaptation of the service to the customer's wishes. If the customer is worried, maybe there is a way of offering reassurance; if the company is interested in a new line, there is an opportunity to sell; if the customer wants to chat a little, perhaps the operator could oblige. So long as the warning is not showing a lengthening queue (a form of concurrent control for the team), this flexibility is valuable.

Some experts deny the possibility of concurrent control, arguing that it is merely feedback control carried out more rapidly. Yet, the distinction is valuable in management. In feedback control, we might monitor intermittently by sampling and have formal reporting links. In concurrent control, monitoring and control are continuous. With a trustworthy employee, the manager sets the goals and expects the person to act without further intervention. In contrast to other forms, whose loops run outside the system, concurrent control uses internal monitoring and action. The loops are all within a 'black box', as shown in Figure 18.3.

> **Black box** *refers to a system whose relationship between inputs and outputs is known, although we are not interested in the details of how it works.*

■ Feedforward control

We noted the 'just too late' criticism of feedback control. It is akin to driving a car whose windscreen is replaced by a monitor showing the road with a three-second delay. To counter the difficulty of such arrangements, many systems incorporate an element of anticipation, to deal with problems *before* they arise.

One way to picture feedforward, or *anticipatory*, control is shown in Figure 18.4. It differs from feedback in one critical aspect. The controller receives forecasts based on the monitored data showing what will happen to the process in the next period. Control actions use these forecasts.

Under a preventive maintenance policy, devices monitor the state of all critical machines including bearings, valves, motors and so on. For instance, electric motors produce unique current profiles and aero engines vibrate in special ways. By monitoring small changes in these 'signatures', engineers obtain early warnings of failure and can arrange repairs before breakdown. More approximately, car service requires oil changes every 12 000 km, well short of the oil's expected life. To change it then is more effective than waiting for an expensive bearing failure.

In the telephone bureau, it would be a poor supervisor who allowed waiting time to worsen before responding to increased queue length. Continuous monitoring and

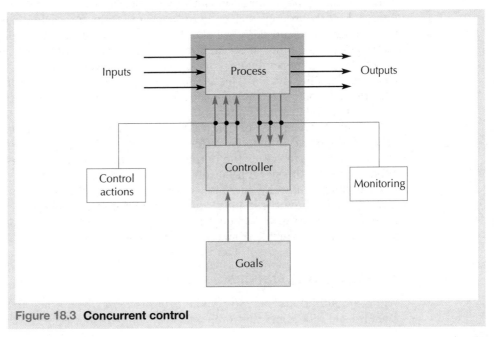

Figure 18.3 **Concurrent control**

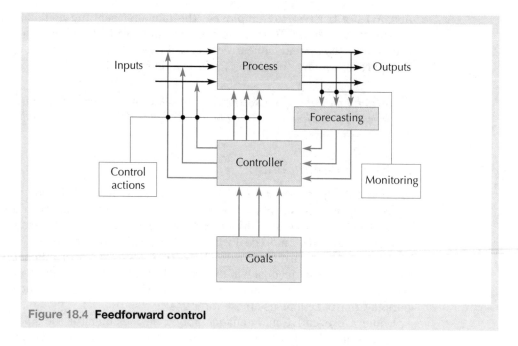

Figure 18.4 **Feedforward control**

forecasting enables preventive action to be taken in advance. In air transport, if there is a delay at a busy destination, flights are often delayed at take-off until their landing slot is confirmed. For aircraft already in the air, the crew adapts flight speed so as not to arrive ahead of time.

Although feedforward control takes place ahead of changes being required, it is different from planning. The latter considers the question: 'Which direction should we be taking and how can we ensure that we take it?' Compare this with feedforward control: 'What adaptations must we make in order to achieve our goal in the future?' Lest the examples given here suggest that the forecasting part of the model works only on output data, we should also recognise that anticipation also uses information from other sources. For instance, at the call centre, the management information system combines process data with extrapolations of demand from previous weeks and seasons. This is modified by trend lines based on the effects of advertising by both the company and its rivals. In addition, awareness of exceptional environmental changes is important.

Although three modes of control are shown here, many variations are possible. Within the general principles, differences of detail include: monitoring the inputs and the process as well as the outputs; forecasting all these elements; controlling either inputs or the system, but not both; and being controlled by other systems. When adding complexity, there is a chance of missing the point. Later, however, we must consider how these basic control loops link into chains and hierarchies. Meanwhile, before giving examples from operations management, it is worth summarising with an example from nature, *see* Exhibit 18.3.

Control of operations

Within organisations, none of the control processes beats the others all the time. Each is used widely and they often occur in combination. Feedforward control helps

Exhibit 18.3 Run, rabbit, run

There are only three breeds of dog – Feedback, Concurrent and Feedforward – and they only differ in one aspect, how they catch rabbits.

Feedback alternates observing and chasing. If a rabbit crosses its field of view, Feedback checks its position and runs towards it. After an interval, it checks again, finds the rabbit has moved and runs towards the new coordinates. Its path is 'dog legged' as shown in Figure 18.5.

Concurrent observes and chases simultaneously. This means it processes more data but it still runs straight at the rabbit. The path is smoother and shorter than Feedback's so we can say Concurrent does better.

Feedforward is more thoughtful. It checks the rabbit's position and velocity and runs straight to the point of intersection.

So, Feedforward is best? Well, its forecasting is enough for dim rabbits. However, if a bright one spots Feedforward on the way, it merely turns round and escapes. Of course, a really intelligent dog would know all about that …

If you think all this is a fable, try watching some dogs.

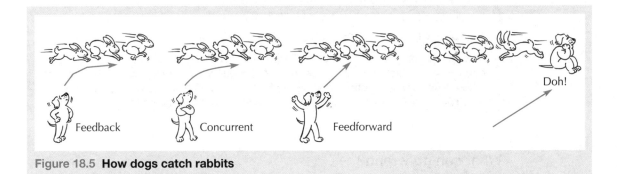

Figure 18.5 **How dogs catch rabbits**

to avoid hazards and errors; concurrent control refers to empowered staff overcoming difficulties as they occur; and feedback control allows post-event correction and prevents mistakes passing along to the next stages. Exhibit 18.4 illustrates the application of mixed control systems in quality and inventory management.

Exhibit 18.4 Examples of control found in operations

	Feedback control	Concurrent control	Feedforward control
Quality management	Finished goods inspection; customer complaints; supply of spares and after-sales service.	Limiting work in progress; preventive maintenance; empowerment.	Assuring quality of incoming supplies; obtaining new equipment; design for manufacturability.
Inventory management	Regular stock checks; audits of records.	Continuous monitoring.	Using sales forecasts to plan purchasing and production.

We should not see operations control as solely a mechanistic activity working towards clear goals. The examples of Exhibit 18.4 involve routine data collection followed by process adjustment. Here, monitoring of quality or stocks warns managers when things are going wrong. Success depends on having clear goals and deciding what is measured. Problems arise when gaps appear. For example, Roper and colleagues found that, among small firms, there were difficulties in deciding appropriate quality standards.[17] Exhibit 18.5 outlines the study.

Exhibit 18.5 SMEs and customers: not seeing the same quality attributes

SMEs may have gained some advantages from registering their procedures under assurance schemes such as ISO 9000. Yet, for the most part, sales are influenced by the way customers perceive their product quality compared with alternatives. Evaluation may include knowing about registration but will also depend on many other factors. There is 'a major disparity between the relative quality perceptions of ... suppliers and their customers'. Roper found that the SMEs gave themselves a higher rating because:

- they did not identify their true competitors;
- suppliers and customers stressed different product attributes in their assessments;
- suppliers made higher estimates of relative quality even on agreed attributes.

Through avoiding expensive outlay, SMEs often lack good market research data. This gap allows the first two disparities to arise, accounting for about half of the observed differences. Consequently, many firms strive towards the wrong quality goals and, in so doing, measure output parameters unimportant to their customers.

What can go wrong?

When studying processes in practice, the control models give us a set of paradigms against which we can assess the situation. They enable us to pick out faults, for example by checking to see whether all the elements are in place or if they are linked appropriately. Figure 18.6 presents some common examples, which arise in four areas: monitoring, goals, control action and forecasting.

■ *Myopic monitoring*

Being unable or unwilling to measure all process outputs risks ignoring important factors influencing performance. Hudson, Lean and Smart found this defect among many SMEs. They use financial measures, especially ones that are scrutinised by external stakeholders such as banks, but do not systematically collect control data on other aspects of the business. Checking warranty service, machine downtime, missed deliveries and productivity was often done *ad hoc*, if at all.[18]

Organisations of all sizes produce 'soft' outputs, such as changes in employee or customer attitudes. For the latter, it is easy to count sales but not so easy to assess satisfaction. Some firms monitor the proportion of repeat business, when control is almost too late, while others try to measure it directly using customer surveys. Leading hospitality businesses continuously monitor guests' satisfaction in this way. An extract from a Marriott Corporation questionnaire is shown in Exhibit 18.6.

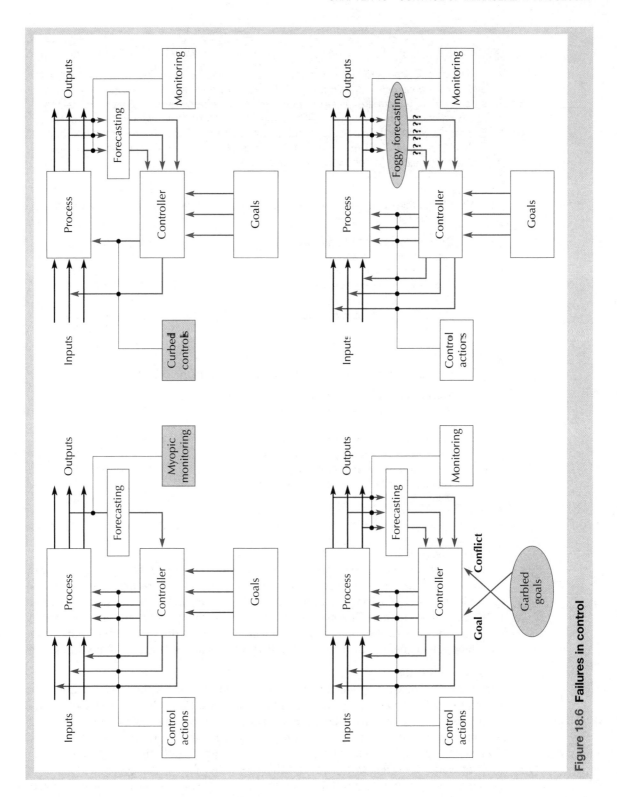

Figure 18.6 Failures in control

> ## Exhibit 18.6 Marriott's customer survey
>
> The Marriott Corporation is one of the world's leading hotel chains. It stresses service quality as a basic tenet of its strategy. Whether they have stayed overnight or attended a conference, guests are invited to complete a questionnaire to evaluate the hospitality. In an accompanying letter, the chairman, J.W. Marriott Jr., promises to share the comments with the hotel manager and follow up all comments and recommendations.
>
> The four-page computer-marked form has 36 questions and a space for open-ended comments. The following questions are typical:
>
> 12   Please think about the bathroom and bedroom areas of your hotel room and rate the following items:
>
> | | |
> |---|---|
> | Overall cleanliness of bathroom | 10 9 8 7 6 5 4 3 2 1 |
> | Cleanliness of tub and tile | 10 9 8 7 6 5 4 3 2 1 |
> | Cleanliness of vanity area | 10 9 8 7 6 5 4 3 2 1 |
> | Supply of bath towels and wash cloths | 10 9 8 7 6 5 4 3 2 1 |
> | Overall cleanliness of bathroom | 10 9 8 7 6 5 4 3 2 1 |
> | Condition of carpet in bedroom | 10 9 8 7 6 5 4 3 2 1 |
> | Condition of bedspread | 10 9 8 7 6 5 4 3 2 1 |
> | Condition of furniture in bedroom | 10 9 8 7 6 5 4 3 2 1 |
>
> 14   Please rate the following items if you ordered from the breakfast menu:
>
> | | |
> |---|---|
> | Server's knowledge of menu | 10 9 8 7 6 5 4 3 2 1 |
> | Server's familiarity with items on menu | 10 9 8 7 6 5 4 3 2 1 |
> | Friendliness of server | 10 9 8 7 6 5 4 3 2 1 |
> | Timeliness with which you received your beverages | 10 9 8 7 6 5 4 3 2 1 |
> | Food prepared the way you wanted it | 10 9 8 7 6 5 4 3 2 1 |
> | Timeliness of beverage refills during meal | 10 9 8 7 6 5 4 3 2 1 |
> | Timeliness with which you received check | 10 9 8 7 6 5 4 3 2 1 |
> | Value for price paid | 10 9 8 7 6 5 4 3 2 1 |

■ *Garbled goals*

Arbitrary and conflicting goals reduce control system effectiveness. For the controller, the goals serve as a yardstick for assessing performance. Therefore, they should be unambiguous and consistent. Multiple goals that cannot all be achieved are a weakness. Yet, as we saw in Chapters 5 and 8, this is typical of situations with many stakeholders. One solution lies in the Balanced Scorecard, discussed later in the chapter, which establishes in advance achievable standards across a range of measures.

■ *Curbed controls*

Failure of control systems can also arise in the 'action' side of the model. Inability to make the necessary changes comes from two sources. First, the controller may have insufficient understanding of how the system works. This may sometimes arise from incompetence or inexperience. Yet complex systems tax even the most experienced controller, especially when unusual circumstances arise. Exhibit 18.7 gives two contrasting examples where competent controllers either failed or succeeded.[19]

The second reason for not taking action is powerlessness. Little or large, control action means change, and change means resistance. Although the control model

Exhibit 18.7 Out of and in control

28 March 1979: Three Mile Island, Harrisburg, Pennsylvania

Following a misunderstanding over whether a valve was open or shut, the nuclear reactor ran out of control for several hours. Fearing radioactive emissions, the authorities evacuated thousands from the locality. Although by all accounts competent, the plant operators were unable to cope with the sequence of events. The control systems continued to function yet presented the staff with too much information too quickly. The design of gauges and dials did not help easy assimilation. No sooner had the crew appreciated one alarm than another went off. At one point more than fifty were sounding.

5 November 1997: Heathrow Airport, London

The crash landing of a Virgin Atlantic A340-300 Airbus with 114 passengers and crew led to no serious injuries. Approaching Heathrow, the crew learned that the left-hand undercarriage had failed. Captain Barnby, the pilot, following standard procedure, rolled the aircraft from side to side to try to dislodge it. Then he flew low over the control tower for a visual check that the wheels were stuck. Finally, with ground services prepared to douse the airliner in foam, the pilot landed and kept the aircraft upright almost until it stopped. The passengers escaped within one minute.

Although he had won aerobatic championships, Barnby had never crash landed. His ability to manage the emergency arose from long practice in flight simulators. To him, 'It was all in a day's work'.

suggests an active controller making process adjustment in the light of every variance from planned outputs, organisational reality is very different. Perhaps the effort required to overcome resistance is not justified by the expected improvements. On the other hand, there may have been too many changes already. One of the 'secrets' of the Toyota production system is its preference for stability. The whole supply chain, including many subcontractors, or 'partners', works to a consistent pace. *Kanbans* link stages with just-in-time deliveries. Toyota, the final assembler, sees itself as both the 'drummer' beating out the rhythm, and the 'buffer' between the production system and the market. Seeking to optimise efficiency through the chain, it is very reluctant to alter the tempo.

■ *Foggy forecasting*

Anticipatory control depends heavily on the quality of integrated forecasting. In operations, routine procedures control many processes. For instance, measurements of samples taken from a wood-sanding machine are shown in Figure 18.7. Clearly, the thickness will soon exceed the upper control limit and the machine needs adjustment.

Unfortunately, forecasting is often not so easy, especially when it comes to strategy. Organisations put much effort into implementing plans but omit to check whether the basis of the plans remains valid. Picken and Dess build on Mintzberg's arguments that strategies need to change frequently. 'An inflexible commitment to predetermined goals and strategy can prevent the very adaptability that is often the essence of a good strategy. Because goals and objectives are considered fixed and inflexible until the next planning cycle, the organisation typically does not alter either its strategies or its objectives to deal with the realities of a changed environment.'[20] Evidently, a control system must allow for changes in goals, as we shall see in the next section.

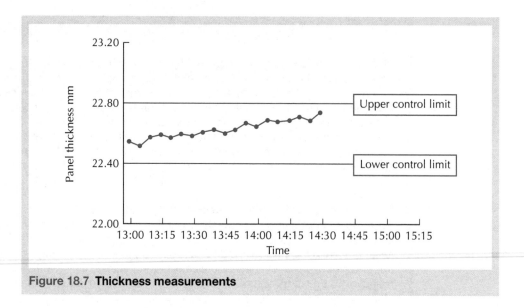

Figure 18.7 Thickness measurements

Building the control system

Just as there are many configurations of the basic control loop, there are many ways of fitting them together to build the total system. General models of organisations based on layers of nested loops have been put forward. Starting from an analogy with the human brain and nervous system, Beer proposed five levels of control, each connected to the ones above, below and alongside. Before looking at this work, we shall briefly consider vertical and horizontal connections.

Levels of control

Levels of control mirror levels of planning in the organisation. Exhibit 8.1 and Figure 8.2 show how managers at each level establish guidelines for their subordinates. In terms of the control model, the controller is given goals by some 'higher' authority. Yet, what if the goals turn out to be unachievable? Then change must be considered. Figure 18.8 shows how feedback from the control function can be incorporated into the goal-setting process. Fixed goals are best when the process and its environment are stable. If this is not so, there is more likelihood that the goals should be changed. It is as though we have a thermostat with the intelligence to decide what the temperature should be.

Being able to influence goals, known as *second-order control*, is common in successful organisations. Such organisations learn through practice, adjusting goals and control systems to become more efficient. We develop the idea of learning in Chapter 19. Meanwhile we should note that feedback to higher-level goals reinforces the means–end chain explained in Chapter 8.

Links along the value chain

Processes within, or spanning, organisations form chains. There are corresponding connections among control systems. The top row of Figure 18.9 shows three

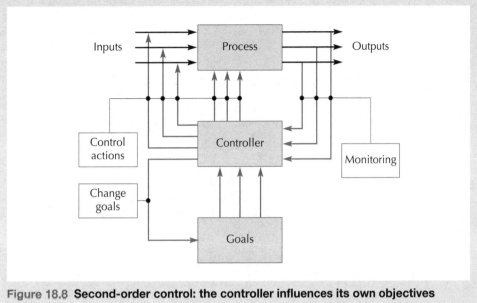

Figure 18.8 Second-order control: the controller influences its own objectives

processes, each with its loop. If no attention were paid to co-ordination, as if the three were independent organisations, instability would arise as small disturbances pass along the chain – the 'bullwhip' effect.[21] The hierarchy of control, indicated by the overall controller at the foot of the diagram, enables the chain to be stabilised.

We can think of Figure 18.9 as an outline for a supply chain control. Many chains have been established and improved recently through the application of information and communications technologies. Agfa Healthcare used e-business software to set up a direct link from its independent dealers to headquarters. This enabled it to 'see' customer transactions for the first time. In response, it could support its dealers with more reliable deliveries. Looking up the supply chain, DaimlerChrysler developed a control system through to Tier 8 contractors to give it early warnings of shortages.[22]

■ An integrated whole

Drawing on research and practice, Beer extended the basic model to create one of the whole organisation.[23] Eschewing organisation charts, he argued the importance of following the dynamics of instructions, decisions, monitoring and information flows. He divided the whole organisation into five sub-systems as follows:

■ *System 1* is the basic unit of control.

■ *System 2* connects the operational level to a stabilising centre.

■ *System 3* is this centre, akin to the overall controller of Figure 18.9. Together, Systems 1, 2 and 3 seek an internal balance enabling maximum efficiency.

■ *System 4* connects the internal activities to the top of the organisation, passing down instructions and channelling feedback. Additionally, it interacts with the environment, collecting information for planning and decision making.

■ *System 5* is top management, the ultimate thinking and directing centre.

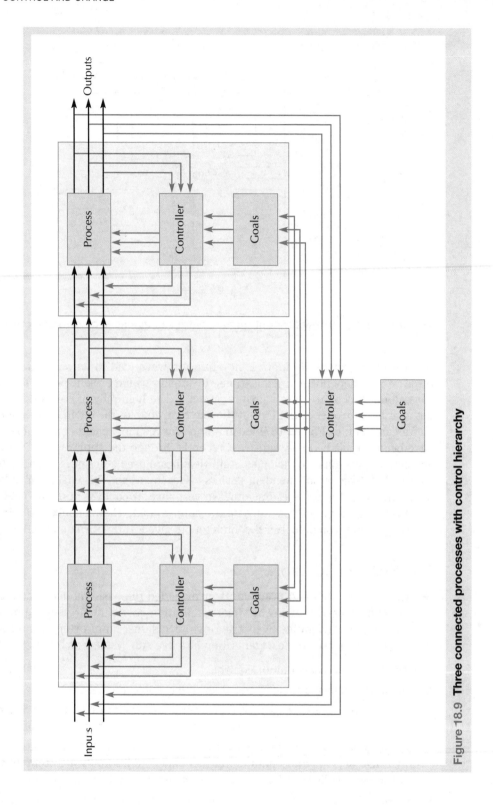

Figure 18.9 **Three connected processes with control hierarchy**

The example of Figure 18.10[24] shows a corporate model of a company with subsidiaries, A, B and C. This is the 'Viable Systems Model', one of a family of conceptual models describing the way an efficient corporation ought to be. Practitioners use them as templates in investigating and recording business processes with a view to improving them. Their comprehensive approach, connecting individual operations to top-level decisions and links with the environment, are particularly appealing.[25]

To illuminate his ideas, Beer frequently referred to the control systems within the human body. In Chapter 3, we noted problems with using weak analogies between organisms and organisations. Although they share some features, we should beware of thinking that all aspects are similar. Beer, however, defends the use of analogies for their insights and the transfer of learning from one to another.

Others remain unsure of the application of cybernetics to general management. Control theory has been successfully applied at the operational level. Moving it higher, however, has yielded few fruitful applications. Berry and colleagues are

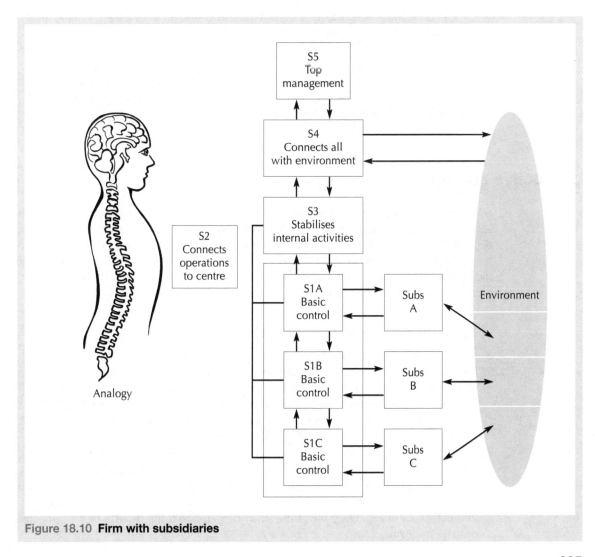

Figure 18.10 Firm with subsidiaries

doubtful whether Beer's modelling follows the notions of Exhibit 18.8. They comment, 'The presentation of Beer's work is intuitive rather than carefully argued, but, while it contains much stimulating material, it is difficult to assess how much derives from the models propounded and therefore its validity is not demonstrable.'[26]

Exhibit 18.8 Models that work

Four key notions of models:

- *Scaling down* in size and complexity. For instance, Legoland at Billund incorporates a model of a 'typical' English town.
- *Transfer across* – real parts of real things are represented as parts of the model in the appropriate positions.
- *Depiction* – the model behaves in some way like the thing it represents. This may be a model railway set or a flight simulator.
- *Appropriateness* – the model is good if it represents in a relevant way. A model train is made so well that it can represent a real one in a film. Yet it only represents it in scale appearance. Real trains do not run on 12 volts.

We use models to learn something about the thing we are modelling, but not everything. Cybernetics compares complex systems and looks for general laws that can apply to all. From this point of view, the many similarities between the organism and the organisation justify using the one as a model of the other.

Effective control

So far, we have examined the nature of control, various system designs and the problems that can arise. Another point of view is to consider effective control. Effectiveness depends both on features of the system itself and on how well it fits organisational structure and processes. Figure 18.11 shows these two domains. To the left we have four factors that all useful control systems should have, while, to the right, we see three factors that cover the fit. We can expand on the points in the diagram as follows:

■ Good design of all control systems

- A *comprehensible* control system produces meaningful data. From the simple knobs and scales on a domestic cooker to the many gauges and dials on the bridge of a modern supertanker, the data must help people understand what is happening. The power station and airliner described in Exhibit 18.7 had control systems of such complexity that their operators required many hours of training. Even so, staff at Three Mile Island could not cope with signals that were out of the ordinary.
- *Timeliness* does not necessarily mean speed. A healthy control system produces information as often as needed. A good example can be found in quality control. In the example shown in Figure 6.9, experience may suggest measuring a parameter every ten minutes. If staff spot unusual results, they can reduce the inspection interval. They continue until they make adjustments or the process returns to normal.

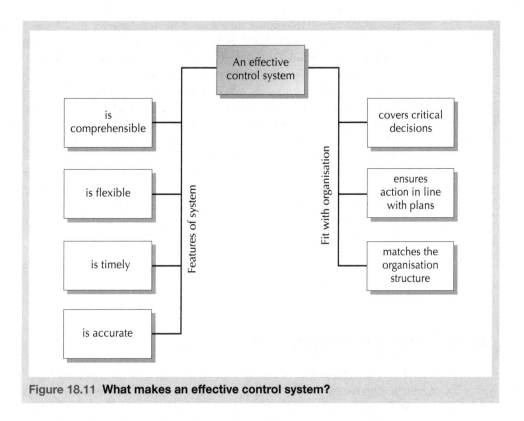

Figure 18.11 What makes an effective control system?

- *Flexibility* is also illustrated by the above example, for the intervals are changed in light of experience. Flexibility, moreover, has another aspect. Changes in the organisation's policies or environment must be accommodated. For instance, a state corporation could have a control system designed to track expenditure under yearly spending budgets. This might not be appropriate if the organisation is transferred to the private sector and has to focus more on margins.

- *Accuracy* sounds like a statement of the obvious. Cases arise, however, in which these are incentives to produce inaccurate control information. In a factory at Derby, job tickets were returned to the office when tasks were complete. These served to both monitor output and enable bonus calculations. However, prudent team leaders would delay submitting some Friday tickets if the group had had a good week. This served two purposes: the spares provided a buffer against a low output during the following week; and levelling peak bonus claims reduced the risk of management investigation. A series of good weeks led to the accumulation of tickets 'in the back of the book'. The practice destroyed the value of tickets for job control so supervisors had to create alternative methods of monitoring.

Fitting the control system to the organisation

- *Critical decisions* focus on both control system and information system design. A well-known comment is, 'If it isn't measured, it isn't managed'. Turning this round, managers will pay attention to any variable that is measured. Providing managers with unnecessary control information is not only uneconomic; it tempts them to become involved in matters they should have delegated. In a divisional company, for example, there is little point if headquarters, having agreed strategies and annual budgets, become involved in the day-to-day operations of each unit.

■ *Ensuring that action is in line with plans* is the purpose of any control system. Monitoring will warn a controller of things going wrong. It can be improved by suggesting ways to resolve the problem. One method involves careful structuring of information. For example, an executive information system may warn of deviations from budget. It could also offer the manager the chance to interrogate the database for more detail. This 'drilling down' enables the manager to separate causes more finely.

■ In *matching the organisational structure*, the system informs those responsible for control. This point extends the previous one concerning budgets. If a transport company finds its fuel costs are rising, drilling down into the records reveals causes. Propitious reasons include gaining more business through carrying heavier loads over longer distances. On the other hand, unfavourable ones arise from higher fuel prices, poor vehicle maintenance and unsound driving practices. Drilling down into more detailed records will identify the cause. Details should be reported to the relevant manager.

What to measure: broadening criteria

Many managers think of controls as built around the organisation's accounting system. True, the management of costs, cash and margins is essential in most cases. Yet, as we shall see, the pursuit of such ends to the exclusion of others leads to problems.

Mullins summarises the reasons why finance and accounting systems dominate:[27]

■ Stewardship of financial resources is vital. Managers are under pressure to show that their departments provide value for money. This is as true in the public sector as in the private. Many public authority departments have to bid every five years for their own work under the procedures known as Compulsory Competitive Tendering.

■ Aims, objectives and targets are frequently expressed in financial terms.

■ Money is readily measured and accounts can be precise. Statements of budgets and performance are easily understood. This commonality allows comparison across a diversified organisation.

■ Financial limits and controls are easy to identify with and readily accepted. Rules of authority can be specified without difficulty. For example, a manager may be allowed to spend £10 000 on equipment without reference to seniors.

Clearly, accounting systems appear to satisfy the criteria for effective control set out in Figure 18.11. They satisfy the general criteria of comprehension, timeliness, flexibility and accuracy. Further, they can be designed to support each manager's critical decisions, providing them with sufficient information, and allowing further investigation to establish causes and solutions. Yet the style of accounting in most organisations is narrowly focused. Driven by the need to maintain professional standards and pass formal audits, there can be too much accuracy at the expense of usefulness.

All statements in accounts are both backward and inward looking. Management control should be broader than this. Therefore, it should be concerned with wider aims, especially strategic ones. Examples include: enhancing product and process knowledge; broadening the customer base; developing quality; encouraging enterprise; and operating with social responsibility. The Balanced Scorecard was designed to respond to such questions.

The Balanced Scorecard

The Balanced Scorecard (BSC) presents a broader view than conventional accounts. The idea is to provide a quick yet comprehensive assessment of a wide range of activities. Kaplan and Norton explain that it 'includes the use of financial measures that tell the results of actions already taken. And it complements financial measures with operational measures on customer satisfaction, internal processes, and the organisation's innovation and improvement activities. These are the drivers of future financial performance.'[28] Current results are no more important than building the business for the future. Figure 18.12 suggests a typical presentation. The four cards shown correspond to four perspectives:

- *Customers* – how well do we serve them?
- *Internal business* – what are we good at and how good are we?

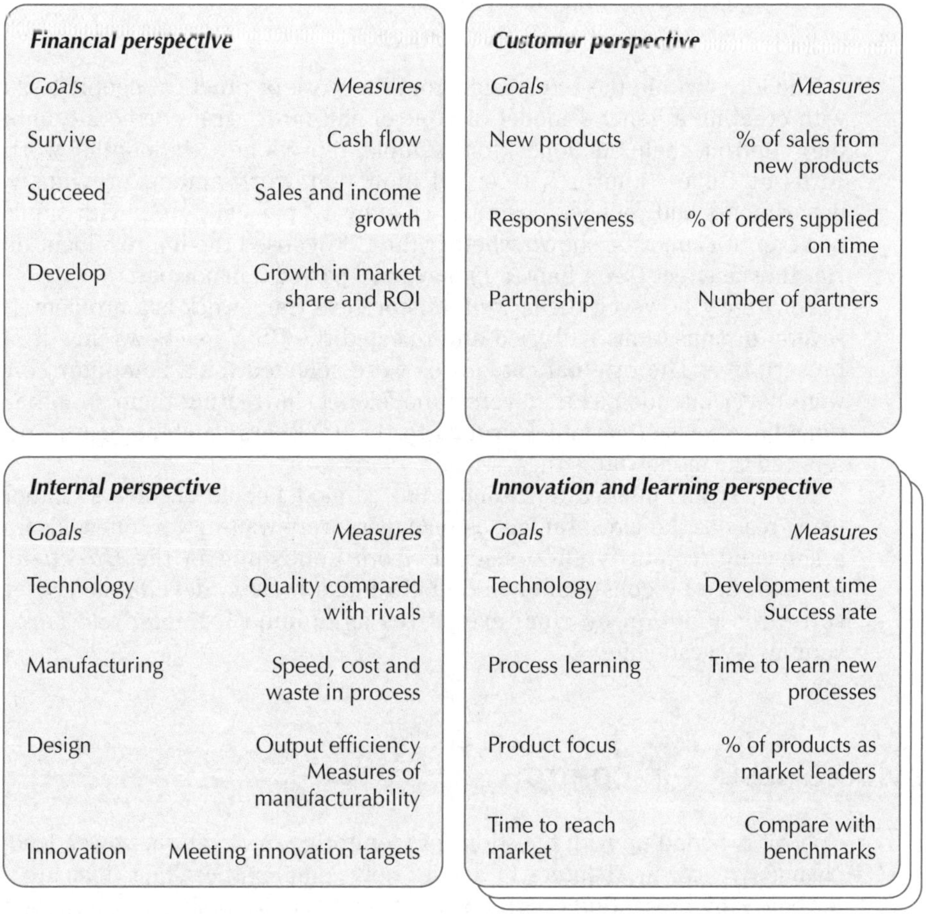

Financial perspective		Customer perspective	
Goals	*Measures*	*Goals*	*Measures*
Survive	Cash flow	New products	% of sales from new products
Succeed	Sales and income growth	Responsiveness	% of orders supplied on time
Develop	Growth in market share and ROI	Partnership	Number of partners

Internal perspective		Innovation and learning perspective	
Goals	*Measures*	*Goals*	*Measures*
Technology	Quality compared with rivals	Technology	Development time Success rate
Manufacturing	Speed, cost and waste in process	Process learning	Time to learn new processes
Design	Output efficiency Measures of manufacturability	Product focus	% of products as market leaders
Innovation	Meeting innovation targets	Time to reach market	Compare with benchmarks

Figure 18.12 The Balanced Scorecard

- *Innovation and learning* – how are we improving to create better value?
- *Financial* – how well are we satisfying those who put up the money?

Many variants of the basic idea of scorecards have been proposed. The essence is practical application in each firm. 'The objectives and the measures of the Score Card are derived from an organisation's vision and strategy.' There have been many applications in the public and not-for-profit sectors.[29] For instance, Teach for America, a voluntary organisation encouraging graduates to commit themselves to two years of teaching in disadvantaged schools, introduced five perspectives: social impact; constituents; internal operations; learning and growth; and finance. Their effect was to redefine success more broadly than measuring the immediate impact of each two-year placement.[30]

Users have extended the scorecard idea to propose an enhanced strategic management system. They report that only after this evolution does it bring significant benefits. This is because:

- it creates a more market and customer oriented strategy;
- it helps to monitor and assess implementation;
- it assigns accountability at all levels;
- it provides continual strategic feedback.[31]

The ideas within the BSC result from the work of practical people less concerned with creating a general model of control and more with correcting imbalances as they confront them. Meliones, for example, reports how six months' work on scorecards at Duke Children's Hospital built teamwork among previously rivalrous departments and reduced costs per case by 12 per cent.[32] As with similar reports, however, it cannot be shown whether the BSC caused the improvement directly. The Hawthorne effect (*see* Chapter 1) may have played a major part.

For Kenny, however, the lack of a theoretical framework is a problem. Noting that several organisations had tried and rejected the BSC, he shows how it became too prescriptive. The original categories were selected for a computer company and were never intended as a universal model. Yet, in treating them so, other organisations have missed variables crucial to them. Others, such as Sears Roebuck, just rejected the model altogether.

Kenny is also puzzled how such a flawed model could become so famous. Among many reasons, he cites: timing, as managers were waiting for a new idea; wide readership and 'celebrity endorsement' from publishing in the *Harvard Business Review*; use by consultants anxious to make money; development of supporting software; adoption by chief executives as opinion formers; and lack of critical scrutiny by academics.[33]

Behavioural issues in control

Control is bound up with questions of monitoring, motivation, power, leadership and change. We saw in Chapters 11 and 12 how complex these questions are. This chapter began by presenting control as a rational activity built on cybernetic principles. The presence of people, however, means that emotion, perception, attitudes and other factors influence their effectiveness. The manner with which control is carried out will be at least as important as the detailed design of monitoring and feedback loops. To close this chapter, therefore, we shall briefly note some behavioural issues. They are selected because we have not detailed them earlier in the book.

Limits to control

Whether organisations aim for centralised or decentralised arrangements, managers must exercise some degree of control. If carefully developed with people's needs in mind, control systems can be constructive and welcomed by members of staff. On the other hand, when perceived as coercive, control will be resisted. Although our rational approach suggests that the effects of negative reactions might be overcome with even more detailed monitoring, there are limits to what can be supervised. Further, there is no limit to employees' ingenuity in bypassing the best laid plans.

Close supervision echoes the patriarchal attitudes of many followers of Taylor. It both results from, and reinforces, a lack of trust between managers and workers. Beynon quotes a senior shop steward at Ford's Halewood plant shortly after production had started in the 1960s. Referring to supervisors who had been transferred from the main plant at Dagenham in Essex, the steward said, 'They thought they could treat us like dirt, them. We were just dirty scousers [natives of Liverpool] who'd crawled in off the docks out of the cold. We'd never even seen a car plant before and these sods had been inside one since they were knee high.'[34] Yet, the workers could always gain revenge. Exhibit 18.9 quotes one of the many acts of sabotage.[35] In more extreme circumstances, Solzhenitsyn recognised how prisoners spent so much effort trying to outwit the efforts of camp guards to apply arbitrary rules, *see* Exhibit 18.2.

Exhibit 18.9 The wet deck at Halewood, Merseyside, in 1970

'In the Paint Shop the car, after an early coat of paint, passes through the Wet Deck where a team of men armed with electric sanders – 'whirlies' – sand the body while it is being heavily sprayed with water. ...

'If there was a problem on the Wet Deck, a manning problem, speed-up, if the foreman had stepped out of line, they always had a comeback. They could sand the paint off the style lines – the fine edges of the body that gave it its distinctive shape. And nobody could know. The water streaming down, the whirlies flailing about, the lads on either side of the car, some of them moving off to change their soaking clothes. The foreman could stand over them and he couldn't spot it happening. Three hours later, the body shell would emerge with bare metal along the style lines. They **knew** it was happening.'

[This plant now produces Jaguar cars; *see* the opening case of Chapter 8.]

Resistance to control

The extent of resistance depends on the balance among the control system design, the people and the circumstances. Mullins, drawing on the work of Lawler, proposes that resistance will be greatest when the control system:

- measures performance in a new area;
- replaces a system that people have an interest in retaining;

- uses standards set without participation;
- does not provide results to those whose performance is measured;
- provides results to higher levels in the organisation;
- uses results in the reward system;
- affects people who are satisfied with the way things are and regard themselves as committed to the organisation's aims;
- affects people who are low in self-esteem.[36]

Control, therefore, is not a dry, technical process that occupies the time of 'bean counters' from quality inspectors to cost accountants. It is controversial. The benefits of control systems are not always self-evident to workers. If, for example, staff are paid bonuses according to output, the inspector at the end of the line becomes the enemy. Each time this person rejects an item, the team's pay is cut. Again, staff may greet programmes such as empowerment or shifts to 'self-control' with mixed feelings. This is especially true if schemes are backed up with job titles and related status symbols for those 'in control'. They may, as Alvesson and Willmott argue, 'simultaneously and inadvertently draw attention to the arbitrary and political nature of corporate arrangements, thus nurturing scepticism rather than tighter discipline'.[37]

Conclusion: control has its limits

Control has a range of meanings from close supervision to a broad activity encompassing planning, monitoring and adjusting performance. Different interpretations of its sources further complicate matters. For example: classical theorists see it done by managers; human relations proponents point to its origins within each person; systems-cyberneticists consider control to be a process.

In this chapter, we have taken the last view. Control is the management of activities to achieve a plan. This process is needed if objectives are to be achieved and drift avoided. Many managerial settings are so complex and variable that, without control, little of value would be done.

The control process has four steps: setting standards; monitoring performance; comparing performance with standards; and taking action on variances. Three variants exist – feedback, concurrent and feedforward control. Each has appropriate applications, frequently in combination with the others.

Corresponding to the steps of the control process are reasons for failure, labelled myopic monitoring, garbled goals, curbed controls and foggy forecasting. At first, we could argue that these failures should be countered by trying harder. There should be more effort in monitoring; goals should be clearer, and so on. Yet they indicate the limits of the approach. For instance, resources limit monitoring, goals can rarely be unambiguous and managers have neither the time nor the power to change continuously every aspect of the systems for which they are responsible.

Another limitation arises when we examine proposals for integrated control systems. Linking a hierarchy both horizontally and vertically, as exemplified by the work of Beer, has great appeal to the cyberneticist but has not been introduced widely. In contrast, horizontal linkages along internal and external supply chains have been successful. Just-in-time production, often involving several companies, has been aided by computer-based communication and control systems.

We commonly see process control in operating units. Examples of the monitoring-comparison-action cycle include quality, inventory and waste. At higher levels such as strategic management, the rigid approach breaks down. The search for unambiguous performance measures leads to over-emphasis of short-term financial controls at the expense of softer and longer-term issues. These suffer from the problem: 'If it isn't measured, it isn't managed'.

Through taking a broader perspective, the Balanced Scorecard counters the narrowness difficulty. We can compare it with the work of Beer. Both approaches are grounded in practical experience, yet the attitudes to measurement and control differ. Beer was interested in detail, seeking a comprehensive framework for all organisational processes to match the hierarchy. The BSC steers managers away from modelling and narrow short-term computation. It looks forward through bringing in flexible measures in areas such as innovation, learning and customer relationships.

Whatever system is chosen, it must be flexible. The ability of control systems to change in response to experience is crucial to long-term success. We shall return to this second-order change in the next chapter.

QUICK CHECK

Can you ...

- Define control.
- List four purposes of control.
- Draw models of feedback, concurrent and feedforward.
- Show on your models what can go awry.
- Give seven fundamentals of effective control systems.
- Justify the Balanced Scorecard.
- List eight reasons why people resist control.

QUESTIONS

Chapter review

18.1 Explain the purpose of control in organisations, showing why it is important.

18.2 Compare the three basic forms of control system. Illustrate their application using your own examples.

18.3 What is meant by effective control? Clarify the conditions when this is likely to occur.

18.4 Why do people resist the introduction or change of control systems?

Application

18.5 Produce an annotated diagram showing the control systems in the home shopping bureau. Identify areas where you think difficulties may arise and suggest ways of overcoming them.

18.6 How do the different perspectives at Teach for America (*see* page 610) relate to ideas of feedback, concurrent and feedforward control?

18.7 Use the control models to compare control in Air Traffic Control and at Merck (opening and closing cases in Chapter 9). In these cases, to what difficulties do the models alert us?

Investigation

18.8 Interview a few managers to identify examples of feedback, concurrent and feedforward control. For each example, ask about difficulties in control. Account for any differences you find.

Skandia's scorecard[38]

Skandia is among the world's largest providers of unit-linked insurance. It was among the first members of the Stockholm stock exchange and, in 1995, was the first European financial company to launch a website. It is also among several Swedish companies that have developed and published non-financial performance assessments. As well as making the annual accounting returns, it also reports on environmental performance and intellectual capital. Skandia recognises the importance of the latter, seen as the difference between the financial measure of book value and the company's real market value. Figure 18.13 indicates how Skandia perceives its intellectual capital as a combination of customer, human and organisational capital.

The company's vision is simply stated: 'Skandia enables people to provide themselves with a lifetime of prosperity.' Detailing this in its mission statement, the company says: 'Skandia creates unique skills around the world that allow us to provide the best financial solutions for our customers and enduring value for our shareholders. We build special relationships, engage the energy of our employees and transfer knowledge with pride.' To achieve the mission, the company is targeting the long-term savings markets of about twenty countries. In insurance, it has gradually reduced its risk, especially in two activities, exposure to catastrophes and to 'long-tailed' liabilities that are difficult to assess. Examples include, for the former, buildings in San Francisco, and, for the latter, pharmaceutical products given to patients who may develop adverse reactions symptoms after a long time.

The company takes appraisal further than annual financial reports. From time to time, the company supplements its statements with an assessment of one aspect of its intellectual capital. For example, an important task for group management is to seek out the next generation of leaders. There are some 7000 employees, of whom 2000 work in each of Sweden and the United Kingdom. Some 300 young staff were evaluated for leadership potential, and a third were added to a list of possible future leaders. Attitude surveys measure indices for leadership, human capital and empowerment.

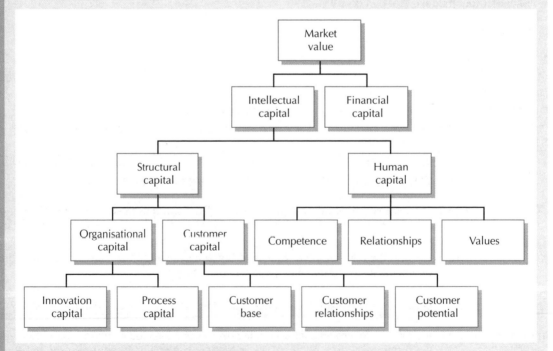

Figure 18.13 **Skandia's intellectual capital**

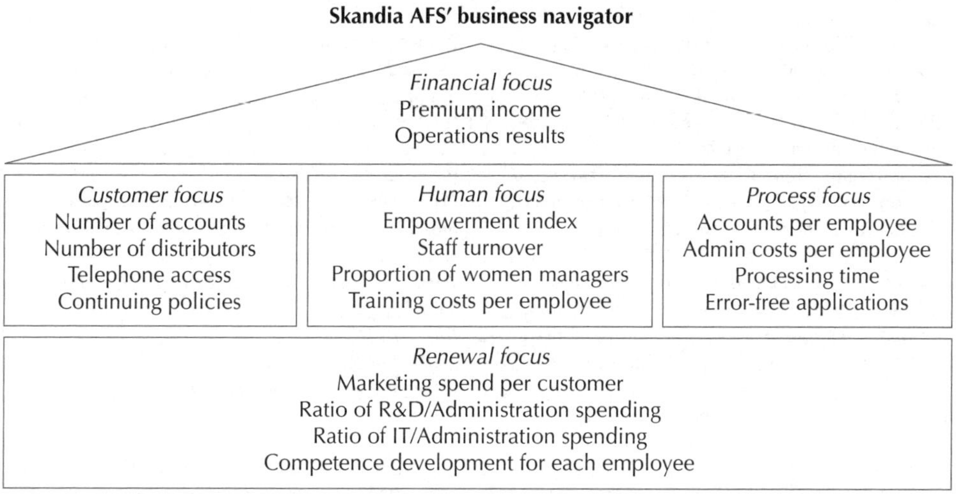

Skandia AFS' business navigator

Financial focus
Premium income
Operations results

Customer focus	*Human focus*	*Process focus*
Number of accounts	Empowerment index	Accounts per employee
Number of distributors	Staff turnover	Admin costs per employee
Telephone access	Proportion of women managers	Processing time
Continuing policies	Training costs per employee	Error-free applications

Renewal focus
Marketing spend per customer
Ratio of R&D/Administration spending
Ratio of IT/Administration spending
Competence development for each employee

Figure 18.14 Skandia's Business Navigator

Companies within the group have also used a Business Navigator with some 30 key indicators, outlined in Figure 18.14. The five foci chosen – financial, customer, process, human and renewal – show the influence of the ideas of Kaplan and Norton. Each has accompanying measurements as shown.

Following the downturn in financial markets at the turn of the century, Skandia has reduced the scale of its business and refocused on key markets and products.

Questions

Although the information in the case study is, as always, incomplete, you should be able to outline answers to the following questions:

1 How well are the measures used by Skandia Group related to its stated mission? Are there any gaps?

2 Draw a diagram to set out the group's strategy as a Balanced Scorecard.

3 Do you foresee any difficulties with Skandia's approach to planning, controlling and reporting?

Bibliography

Among Robert Anthony's many contributions to management control are: *Management Control Systems* (McGraw-Hill, 2001) and *The Management Control Function* (Boston, Mass.: Harvard Business School Press, 1988). Critical discussions of theories and issues, with descriptions of applications in many types of organisation, are to be found in Anthony Berry, Jane Broadbent and David Otley (1995) *Management Control: Theories, issues and practices* (Basingstoke: Macmillan).

References

1 Smith, Phillippa (2001) *Home Shopping: Market Report*: 9th edition, London: Key Note, May; GUS plc, Home page, **www.gusplc.com/index.asp**, accessed 23 April 2003.

2 Blake, William (1804) 'Milton: a Poem in Two Books', better known as the anthem 'Jerusalem'.

3 'Call centre staff jam complaints hotline', *Financial Times*, 20 February 2001, 2; 'Call centres ring in health hazards', *Hindustan Times*, 19 April 2003.

4 'Time to reroute call centres: allowing staff to use their own words and deal directly with customers could be the secret of success', *Observer: Business & Media*, 2 March 2003.

5 Houlder, Vanessa (1996) 'Scalpel by remote control: Routine long-distance surgery is increasingly possible', *Financial Times*, 28 April.

6 O'Sullivan, Mary (2000) 'The innovative enterprise and corporate governance', *Cambridge Journal of Economics*, **24(4)**, 393–416.

7 Anthony, Robert N. (1988) *The Management Control Function*, Boston, Mass.: Harvard Business School Press, 10.

8 *Ibid.*, 27.

9 *Ibid.*, 37.

10 Berry, Anthony J., Broadbent, Jane and Otley, David (1995) 'Approaches to control in the organisational literature', Chapter 2 in same authors (ed.) *Management Control: Theories, issues and practices*, Basingstoke: Macmillan, 19.

11 Stacey, Ralph D. (1996) *Strategic Management and Organisational Dynamics*, 2nd edition, London: Financial Times Pitman Publishing, 43.

12 Mullins, Laurie J. (2002) *Management and Organisational Behaviour*, 6th edition, Harlow: Financial Times Prentice Hall, 768–9.

13 Solzhenitsyn, Alexander (1963) *One Day in the Life of Ivan Denisovich*, Hamondsworth: Penguin, 107.

14 Mullins (1996) *op. cit.*, 595.

15 Oakland, J.S. (1993) *Total Quality Management*, 2nd edition, Oxford: Butterworth–Heinemann, 29.

16 Burns, Robert (1785) [... often go wrong] 'To a mouse'.

17 Roper, Stephen, Hewitt-Douglas, Nola and McFerran, Brendan (1997) 'Disparities in quality perceptions between small firms and their customers', *International Small Business Journal*, **15(4)**, July–September, 64–79.

18 Hudson, Mel, Lean, Jon and Smart, Andi (2001) 'Improving control through effective performance measurement in SMEs', *Production Planning & Control*, **12(8)**, 804–13.

19 Bignell, Victor and Fortune, Joyce (1984) *Understanding Systems Failures*, Manchester: Manchester University Press, 9–39; Butcher, Tim (1997) 'Pilot averts disaster as Airbus crash-lands', *Daily Telegraph*, 6 November, 1.

20 Picken, Joseph C. and Dess, Gregory G. (1997) 'Out of (strategic) control', *Organizational Dynamics*, **25(1)**, Summer, 35–48.

21 Naylor, John (2002) *Introduction to Operations Management*, 2nd edition, Harlow: Financial Times Prentice Hall, 409–10.

22 Robb, Drew (2003) 'The virtual enterprise: How companies use technology to stay in control of a virtual supply chain', *Information Strategy*, Summer, 6–11.

23 Beer, Stafford (1994) *Brain of the Firm*, Chichester: John Wiley.

24 *Ibid.*, 130.

25 Assimakopoulos, Nikitas A. (2000) 'Structured total systems intervention', *Human Systems Management*, **19**, 61–9.

26 Berry *et al.* (1995) *op. cit.*, 12.

27 Mullins (2002) *op. cit.*, 787–8.

28 Kaplan, Robert S. and Norton, David P. (1992) 'The balanced scorecard – measures that drive performance', *Harvard Business Review*, **70(1)**, January–February, 71–9.

29 Kaplan, Robert S. (2001) 'Strategic performance measurement and management in nonprofit organizations', *Nonprofit Management & Leadership*, **11(3)**, 354–71.

30 Kaplan, Robert S. (2002) 'The Balanced Scorecard and nonprofit organizations', *Balanced Scorecard Report*, November–December, Harvard Business School.

31 Kaplan, Robert S. and Norton, David P. (2001) 'Transforming the Balanced Scorecard from performance measurement to strategic management: Part II', *Accounting Horizons*, **15(2)**, 147–60; Inamdar, Noorein and Kaplan, Robert S. (2002) 'Applying the Balanced Scorecard in healthcare provider organizations', *Journal of Healthcare Management*, **47(3)**, 179–95.

32 Meliones, Jon (2000) 'Saving money, saving lives', *Harvard Business Review*, **78(6)**, November–December, 57–65.

33 Kenny, Graham (2003) 'Balanced Scorecard', *New Zealand Management*, **50(2)**, 32–4.

34 Beynon, H. (1973) *Working for Ford*, Harmondsworth: Penguin, 77.

35 *Ibid.*, 140–1.

36 Mullins (2002) *op. cit.*, 784.

37 Alvesson, Mats and Willmott, Hugh (1996) *Making Sense of Management*, London: Sage, 172.

38 Skandia Insurance Company (1995) *1994 Annual Report*; (1997) 'Customer Relationships and growth in value', *Intellectual Capital: Supplement to 1996 Annual Report*, Skandia Insurance; (1998) 'Human capital in transformation', *Intellectual capital prototype report*, Skandia; (2003) *About Skandia*, **www.skandia.co.uk/about/parent_company/index.htm**; (2003) *Our processes*, **www.skandia.com/en/about/processes.shtml#**, both accessed 28 April 2003.

CHAPTER 19

Control, learning and change

Chapter objectives

When you have finished studying this chapter, you should be able to:

- explain and illustrate the control dilemma;
- identify four alternative control levers, showing the purpose of each;
- apply Etzioni's ideas about power and involvement to control;
- distinguish among bureaucratic, market and clan control;
- differentiate single- and double-loop learning for individuals and organisations;
- recognise why and how people resist learning and change, and suggest how to overcome these problems;
- review learning organisations, pointing out the difficulties encountered in putting them into practice;
- evaluate Greiner's theory of stability and change;
- demonstrate the origins of change and attitudes towards it;
- apply force field analysis to change, suggesting why managers do not change when they should;
- summarise and evaluate organisation development;
- describe and assess process reengineering;
- outline chaos theory applied to organisations, drawing out its implications.

People don't resist change. They resist being changed.

Peter M. Senge, management scholar

All eyes on Bausch & Lomb[1]

German immigrants John Jacob Bausch, owner of a tiny optical goods shop in Rochester, New York, and Henry Lomb formed a partnership in the late 1850s. Soon, Bausch discovered by chance that vulcanite, a hard rubber material, was suitable for spectacle frames. Blockades during the 1861–5 Civil War restricted imports of traditional materials, gold and horn. Vulcanite, however, was so successful that Bausch & Lomb Inc. sold its retail operations to concentrate on manufacturing. The new factory began with eyeglasses and developed into precision equipment – microscopes (1876), camera lenses (1873) and searchlight mirrors (1890). By 1889, the company had enough capacity to stop importing spectacle lenses. In 1915, it opened an optical glass plant, to eliminate its dependence on European raw materials.

Optical equipment has many military applications. Sales of binoculars, periscopes and gun sights soared during the First World War, exceeding $14 million by 1918. The 1920s saw a contract from the Army Air Corps to develop a glass to reduce the glare encountered by pilots. Bausch & Lomb responded with its first Ray-Ban sunglasses. Introduced to the public in 1937, the original 'Aviator' style remains a leading line.

Innovation and expansion continued. In 1965 sales reached $100 million. The first approved soft contact lenses appeared in 1971. Business was going well. Through acquisition and divestment, sales in 1989 passed $1000 million with half from overseas. Diversification into hearing and pharmaceuticals further expanded sales but not profits. A refocused strategy meant cutbacks. Partnerships were used to enter new markets, for instance the 1992 agreement for a Levi's range. In the same year, Bausch & Lomb was a leading Olympic Games sponsor.

In 1996, however, the annual report admitted, 'Our 1996 financial results were as disappointing to us as, we're sure, they were for you'. Static sales and declining margins suggested a company in difficulties. The stock price had fallen from a 1994 peak of $53 to $32. The company noted 'continuing challenges in our US sunglass business' and admitted distribution difficulties. Traditional lines had declined, while replacements had been so successful that manufacturing could

not cope. Managers struggled with product supply processes and relationships with key vendors.

What had gone wrong with the business whose mission was to be 'Number One in the Eyes of the World'? Chief executive Dan Gill had led it to success between 1981 and 1991. Rapid growth in profitable products led to a five-fold increase in the share price. Gill promised annual growth exceeding 10 per cent. The demanding culture focused on numbers. Shortfalls received little tolerance, for goals had to be achieved. By 1991, however, market growth had slowed and competition was increasing. Gill's strategy of acquiring businesses beyond the optical arena was not paying off. Yet the rigid targets remained. How did managers respond?

■ Units in the Ray-Ban division frantically launched promotion after promotion to shift stock before quarterly reporting. In a typical 1993 deal, one Chilean distributor was persuaded to receive six months' stock. Another was carrying nine months' inventory.

■ In 1993, the head of the contact lens division instructed 30 distributors to take up to two years' stock of the older Optima lenses, with payment only required after sales. Otherwise, they risked their agreements. Two refused and were dropped. Shipments worth $23 million were booked in the last days of the financial year. Later, most were returned. Bausch & Lomb gained no revenue.

■ The contact lens division joined optometrists and other manufacturers in restricting distribution to hold up prices. It was estimated that users had been overcharged $600 million in five years.

■ International operations faced few constraints. Although sales through Hong Kong had been growing at 25 per cent, many dispatches were not to Asian distributors. Goods were moved to another warehouse, whence many leaked into the grey market. Dealers in Europe and the Middle East profited from lower Asian wholesale prices.

Unbalanced controls and arbitrary goals

Picken and Dess sum up the failure at Bausch & Lomb: 'There's nothing wrong with stretch targets, management incentives, or an aggressive culture, but organisations must also maintain standards of ethical behaviour and a sense of 'fair play'.' Managers adversely affected by the grey market became acutely aware of this. Culture, rewards and boundaries of responsibility were ill defined and lacked alignment. Goals and objectives, cast in stone, could not be adapted.

After the Security and Exchange Commission began an investigation, Gill changed tack. He told managers to follow more conservative practices and eliminate wheeling and dealing at each quarter-end; he cut incentives to distributors; and he changed bonus rules to focus on longer-term goals. Yet, the SEC found that 1993 sales had been overstated and instructed Bausch & Lomb to desist. Gill was forced to resign, to be replaced by William Carpenter.

Carpenter's honeymoon lasted two years. He sold slow-growing businesses such as sunglasses and relied on new areas like lasers, unfortunately very sensitive to recession. Meanwhile, contact lenses and lens-care products, roughly 60 per cent of sales, struggled. Bausch & Lomb had lost its lead in contact lenses to Johnson & Johnson, whose new disposable lenses were also cutting demand for lens solutions. Investors were disappointed when the year 2000 growth targets were missed. Ron Zarrella, who had left for General Motors in 1994, returned to take over in 2001. After he was appointed, someone noticed he did not have his claimed MBA. He forfeited his bonus but kept his job.

Recovering credibility is a slow process. The 2002 report noted 'sales levels that mirrored consumption' and the introduction of 'more disciplined business processes to yield better operating plans, better business reviews ... [and] a common method of assessing performance'. The common approach was supported by a new matrix structure and 'an integrated global information technology platform'.

Introduction

The downfall of Gill illustrates a problem facing all managers in the modern age. How can they enable the flexibility and creativity required by the dynamic environment while maintaining sufficient control? At Bausch & Lomb, Gill used the control system to press for ever-increasing performance. Yet, the measures used were unnecessarily strict and narrow.

In other celebrated cases, controls have been too slack. Exhibit 19.1 reminds us of how the deals of Nick Leeson brought down Baring Brothers, the oldest merchant bank in the United Kingdom.[2]

Simons addresses the dilemma: 'How do senior managers protect their companies from control failures when empowered employees are encouraged to redefine how they go about doing their jobs?'[3] He dismisses a solution based on the machine bureaucracy. Certainly, when standardisation is important, such as in large-scale administration or on the mass production line, rigid controls and close surveillance are feasible. Yet, if staff face coercive, unrealistic or continually raised targets that threaten their incomes or positions, they will resist. Managers at Bausch & Lomb or Baring Brothers, and saboteurs at Halewood (mentioned in Chapter 18), showed how to undermine controls. Other managers work in changing, competitive markets where they cannot spend all their time ensuring others are doing as they tell them. This does not mean no control, for it is unrealistic merely to hire well-qualified staff, design an incentive programme and expect them to deliver.

The snag for many managers, according to Simons, is defining control too narrowly. Reliance on the cybernetic model is both too restricting and incomplete. Consideration of beliefs, boundaries and interactive controls should supplement it. Summarised in Exhibit 19.2, each 'control lever' has a distinct function:

Exhibit 19.1 Weak safeguards topple Baring's

The immediate cause of Baring Brothers' collapse in February 1995 was the uncovering of unexpected losses. Nick Leeson had staked some £17 billion of clients' money on huge futures contracts, betting that the Japanese stock market would rise. Although Leeson was convicted, the case also exposed weak control both within Baring Brothers and throughout the external supervisory system.

Leeson was general manager and head trader of Baring's Singapore office from 1992 until the collapse. His authorised dealing was reported as profitable, although some queried how apparently 'risk-free' business could create such margins. In fact, he used secret account 88888 to 'park' trading losses, for example about £23 million for 1993. In that year, the bank reported profits of some £100 million with another £100 million used for staff bonuses. Similar profits were announced for 1994 but, by this time, the balance in 88888 had reached £208 million. January 1995 saw the Kobe earthquake further upsetting the Japanese markets. Losses soared to £337 million.

Here are some examples of failures in financial and management controls at all levels:

- Leeson traded both for the bank and for clients. Yet reporting lines had never been clarified. Ron Baker, head of equity business, assumed that he was responsible for the former while Mike Killian, head of global futures and options, covered the latter. But Killian thought that Leeson did not report to him.

- Auditors had questioned the front (trading) and back (accounting) offices at Singapore being run by one person, the general manager. Their recommendations were not acted upon. Leeson's wife worked in the back office. Here all trades should have been reconciled and reports sent to London. A 1994 audit missed account 88888 but advised more regular, weekly, reconciliation. Leeson had this guidance deleted from the auditors' report, complaining it would cause extra work.

- Baring Brothers did not report its heavy exposure in Japan and Singapore to the Bank of England. Yet the latter should have heeded other warnings. It knew of: the high funding supporting Far East operations; the exceptional Singapore profits; and large risks on the Singapore and Osaka futures exchanges.

In March 1995, the Dutch financial group ING bought Baring's for £1. Many managers implicated in the failure resigned or were sacked. Leeson received a six-and-a-half-year prison sentence. In his autobiography, he condemned the way he was allowed to gamble unchecked. Lisa Leeson remarried.

■ *Cybernetic systems*

As explained in Chapter 18, these systems work on correcting deviations from planned outputs. Bausch & Lomb, however, illustrates what can go wrong if employees are made accountable for rigid performance goals and are allowed to decide how to achieve them.

■ *Belief systems*

Incorporated into declarations such as mission statements, belief systems govern ethical behaviour and good management practice. For example, they encourage notions such as 'placing the customer first', 'pursuit of excellence through innovation' or 'respect for the less fortunate in society'. Such statements may not appear within the narrow cybernetic model, yet they can inspire employees. Better-educated employees have higher expectations from both the organisations they work for and their own careers. They want to increase their contributions but the policies of senior management must enable this.

■ *Boundary systems*

According to Simons, boundary systems apply the sometimes valuable power of negative thinking. Clarifying what *not* to do is sometimes better than explaining what to do. Operating procedures and rule books ensure that staff carry out routine tasks yet restrict creativity. In contrast, boundary systems identify minimum standards and those activities that are not permitted. They appear in codes of conduct or standards of ethical behaviour. Such codes are especially important in businesses whose reputation takes years to build and can be destroyed by recalcitrant employees. Major consulting firms, for example, prevent members from revealing any information about clients, even their names, to anyone. At Bausch & Lomb, the grey market should have been prevented. In normal circumstances, managers in the Far East would not have undermined the efforts of colleagues in other regions. Yet, the pressures to 'make the numbers' were so strong that unspoken codes broke down.

We can view the interaction between belief and boundary systems as a healthy tension. Together, the inspiration of the belief system, surrounded by the constraints of the boundary system, select from the limitless range a clear picture of the opportunities that an organisation is prepared to exploit. In the decision-making process, they help to define both alternatives and constraints.

We should not regard the boundary system as solely related to ethics. It may express, for example, the strategic directions that the organisation is unwilling to explore, or the type of employer it wishes to be seen to be. Of the many examples throughout the book, we can mention two here. First, as we saw in Exhibit 17.1, Hasselblad suspended research into digital technology until richer rivals had laid out the ground. Second, in the opening case of Chapter 14, the Skipton's personnel policies avoided any suggestion of 'hard' HRM.

■ *Interactive systems*

Because of the uncertainty surrounding many situations, managers must be involved with their staff. Through this, they can keep the focus on key issues and ensure that organisational learning takes place. Simons identifies four characteristics that set interactive control systems apart from the cybernetic ones:

- constantly changing information;
- information of sufficient potential to demand regular attention from managers at all levels;
- advantages of interpreting complex data in face-to-face discussions among many staff;
- stimulation of debate about the nature of the data, its assumptions and the actions that result from it.

In short, interactive control systems do not concern themselves solely with correcting deviations from a chosen plan. They are more engaged with asking whether the correct course of action has been chosen. A further question is whether circumstances have changed sufficiently to put prior choices out of date.

Therefore, there is more to control than spreading the plan–act–monitor cycle throughout every organisation. Although suited to routine tasks in a stable bureaucracy, the cycle breaks down in a changing environment. In this chapter, we shall be considering these issues, notably responses to control, learning and change.

Exhibit 19.2 Each control lever has a purpose

Control lever	Purpose	Responds to ...	Stimulates ...
Cybernetic systems	To identify and underpin clearly stated targets	Lack of clarity or shortage of resources	Achievement
Beliefs systems	To share the organisation's core values and mission	Uncertainty about overall purpose	Contribution
Boundary systems	To establish and sustain rules of managerial behaviour	Lack of clarity; unforeseen temptations or pressures	Doing things right
Interactive systems	To stimulate dialogue, learning and change	Absence of opportunities and unwillingness to take risks	Innovation and change

People and control

The dilemma of increasingly empowered employees in the flexible organisation is summarised by Leifer and Mills: 'Reliance on traditional, objective controls reduces the flexibility and adaptability necessary to cope with uncertain and equivocal information'.[4] Yet, they point out, coping with this uncertainty through flexibility and discretion increases the probability of control being lost. To overcome this negative consequence, 'it is in the organisation's best interest to develop mechanisms for enhancing commitment, trust and bonding'. This leads us to the work of Etzioni and Ouchi.

Power and involvement

In Chapter 11, we noted three types of power arising from a manager's position within the organisation – coercive, reward and legitimate. Etzioni used a similar classification to match power to involvement of participants, *see* Figure 19.1.[5] First, in coercive organisations, members resist following instructions and only do so under threat of punishment. A prison is an example; inmates display *alienative* involvement. Second, an organisation founded on utilitarian lines applies economic power; participants act instrumentally. Despite an individual's personal objectives, which are deemed irrelevant, managers achieve compliance through contracts or bargains. The link between employee and organisation is that of 'a day's work for a day's pay'; it means *calculative* involvement. The third dimension of power is normative. Here personal goals are sufficiently closely aligned to add up to a common set to which all adhere. Compliance is voluntary and people show a *moral* commitment. Members of voluntary organisations and movements, including religious orders, behave in this way.

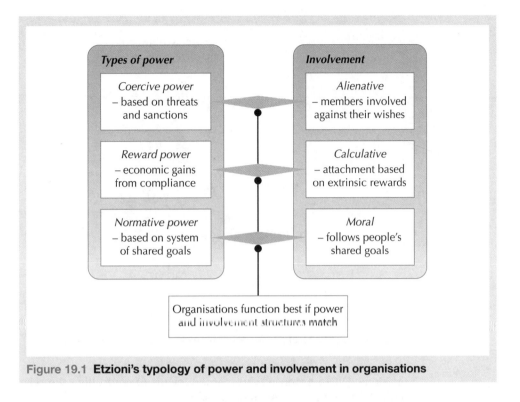

Figure 19.1 Etzioni's typology of power and involvement in organisations

Two further points must be made about Etzioni's views. First, the three categories are ideal-types. Some suggest that coercive control is typical of prisons, normative control of monasteries and reward control of wage labour in business organisations. It is likely, however, that most real settings will display a mixture. Figure 19.2 sets out some possibilities. Three organisations approaching the ideal-types are shown close to the points of the triangle. Others illustrate the mixed approach. For instance, the employment contract is often not an agreement between equals. Managers use both reward power (bonuses for achieving work standards) and coercive power (through threats of suspension or dismissal). Other mixtures shown are: a coercive sect, retaining members through a mixture of promises and sanctions; and caring professionals such as nurses, who may forgo some financial reward in exchange for being able to do a satisfying job.

Our second point is that involvement and control methods must match. For example, to expect voluntary commitment from an alienated prison inmate would be fruitless. In contrast, coercive control of volunteer charity collectors would not work. In choosing a balance for the organisation represented by the question mark in Figure 19.2, management must recognise that control is pluralistic. Different people will respond differently according to time, place and other factors.

■ Bureaucracies, markets and clans

Although Etzioni's work stresses the behavioural issues of control, its practical implications are unclear. This is especially true for large organisations. Control problems range from affecting individual performance to achieving targets for entire

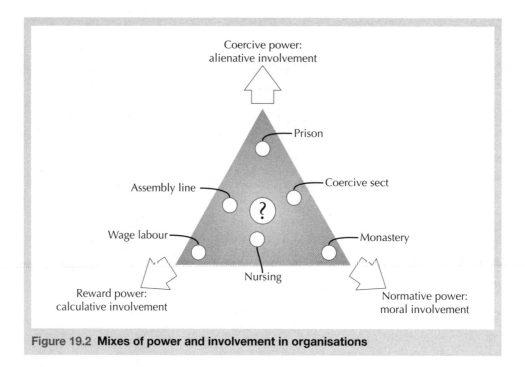

Coercive power:
alienative involvement

Prison

Assembly line

Coercive sect

?

Wage labour

Monastery

Nursing

Reward power:
calculative involvement

Normative power:
moral involvement

Figure 19.2 Mixes of power and involvement in organisations

divisions. Ouchi proposed three broad means of controlling the relationships among individuals and groups in all organisations:[6]

- *Bureaucracy*, which we investigated in Chapters 1 and 10, means that control is built into structure and processes. Each person's role is specified and monitoring systems are predetermined. It is the setting for the formal control models of Chapter 18.

- *Markets* have been rediscovered by large organisations meeting the limits of bureaucratic control. Weighed down by rules, they display *diseconomies of scale*. This means that the difficulties of co-ordination exceed the benefits gained from bringing units together. We saw in Chapter 10, how network, virtual and spherical organisations respond to this problem. They comprise units linked by market, or contractual, relationships. Examples are the 'internal market' of the National Health Service and planning at multinational ABB, based on a network of financial and psychological contracts between divisional managers and headquarters.

- *Clan control* fills a gap when bureaucracy or markets do not work. Ouchi saw that many managers occupy roles entailing high discretion. In carrying out their complex and uncertain tasks, managers must ensure that they maintain trust with other managers; this will be as important as skill at making 'rational' decisions. Clans rely on shared language, symbols, myths and stories to develop shared values. In other words, there is a common culture, issuing from and influencing the stream of actions taken by organisation members.

Figure 19.3 summarises these points.[7] Each approach has a corresponding control mechanism that focuses on a different aspect of the work: hierarchical control on tasks and processes; market control on resources and outcomes (with price the key factor); and trust (or clan) control on underlying attitudes. There are echoes of

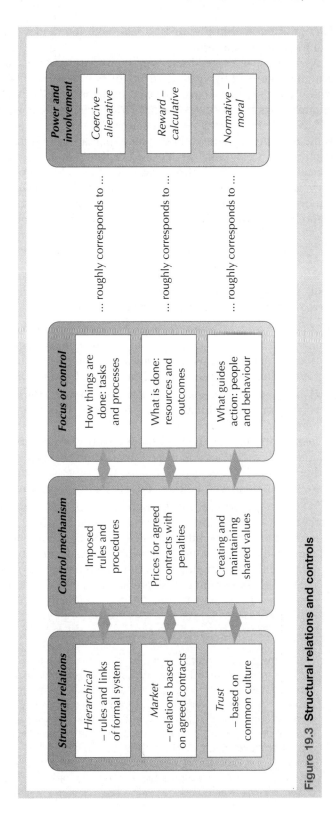

Figure 19.3 Structural relations and controls

Etzioni, suggested in Figure 19.3, although the model covers a wider range of sizes and forms of organisation.

As with our previous discussion, the three categories are ideal-types. 'Enterprises are characterised by various forms of hierarchical, market or trust relationships which coexist'.[8] Here are three examples. First, as Weber argued, bureaucratic organisations rely on everyone accepting the legitimacy of the framework. In a study of MNEs, Ferner saw how their bureaucratic control systems depended on shared value systems, understandings and expectations about the rules.[9] Second, market relationships rely on hierarchies of position that empower managers, for example to conclude agreements. Third, trust cannot be relied upon as the sole approach since variations occur within a common culture. Different levels, groups and people within the organisation have diverging interests. Therefore, some elements of hierarchy or markets are always required. Even monasteries have abbots.

■ Control when knowledge is incomplete

Ouchi argues that, when easily measured outputs emerge from well-understood processes, hierarchies or markets are equally valuable control mechanisms.[10] But what happens when these conditions do not apply?

■ *When outputs are easily measured but processes are not well understood*, market relationships do better. For instance, many managers employ subcontractors to carry out specialised functions. Since the organisation is inexpert in these fields, yet their outcomes can be readily assessed, it pays to use the market mechanism.

■ *When processes are well understood but outputs are not easily measured*, relying on hierarchical control is better. This follows from the importance of employee behaviour in these circumstances. The focus is on *how* they carry out tasks. Although challenged by advocates of privatisation, many argue that the complex core functions in health and social services should not be marketised. Despite the failings of hierarchies, well-practised staff learn to make them work. Replacing them with markets merely increases the costs of control.

■ *When the process is poorly understood and outputs not easily measured*, neither markets nor hierarchies have much to offer. Here, Ouchi argues for the importance of self-control implicit in the common culture of the clan. The norms and values of the group play leading roles in monitoring performance. Failures, delays and overspending in large-scale information system projects illustrate the weaknesses of both markets and hierarchies, *see* Exhibit 19.3.[11]

Exhibit 19.3 Better control of information investment

Government departments, recognising their lack of knowledge and capacity to do the work themselves, turned to the market for project management. Yet, they used conventional competitive tendering, dominated by price, to award very complex contracts with uncertain outcomes. Many failed. Recently, the government has sought a new direction, learning from supplier partnering in the private sector. For the next £1 billion phase of Internet development, the Office of Government Commerce chose six preferred suppliers, after assessment of 'their ability to provide quality, value-for-money broadband services'. This allowed any government department to appoint a supplier on agreed terms without going through a further tendering process. The uncertainty of the detailed project specification is replaced with a broad statement of the business problem.

The two dimensions of process knowledge and output assessment suggest the grid of Figure 19.4. It positions Ouchi's three control mechanisms, with shading representing information processing requirements. With well-known tasks and straightforward output measures, information needs are low. Managers and employees use formal control processes with little discretion. Under greater uncertainty, self-management, backed by more information, will become important.

The control dilemma

Control and flexibility present fundamental difficulties for all organisations. Some form of structure is needed to unify disparate elements. Managers have also to exercise some degree of coercion. The co-operative activity required in even the minimal organisation is achieved, therefore, under conflict-laden circumstances. Those responsible for the organisation, owners in the case of private enterprise, can never fully count on those to whom they entrust their resources. Stricter control, for example through the introduction of more rules or the replacement of informal agreements by tightly drawn contracts, may cause increased resistance among staff. Control that is even more stringent is then required.

On the other hand, many organisations have realised the advantage of flexibility and adaptability, although it leads to some loss of formal control. To overcome this loss, organisations work to increase commitment and bonding. We have seen throughout the book many examples of policies, from recruitment and training to participation, intended to build loyalties and underpin a common way of doing things.

Managers face a choice between the vicious circle of fear and tightening controls and the virtuous one of trust breeding trust, *see* Figure 19.5.[12] We look at the virtuous circle in more detail below, so let us examine the vicious one. Managers may opt for it when squeezed between owners and the increasingly detailed contract specifications demanded by clients. In Exhibit 19.4, Cohen describes her experiences when asked to produce a procedures manual.[13] In the short run, it seemed to yield benefits. Nevertheless, Cohen concludes that manuals 'send out a powerful message of compliance to employees; they are neither expected, nor invited, to offer new or

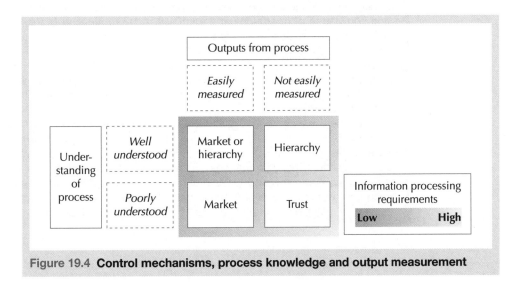

Figure 19.4 Control mechanisms, process knowledge and output measurement

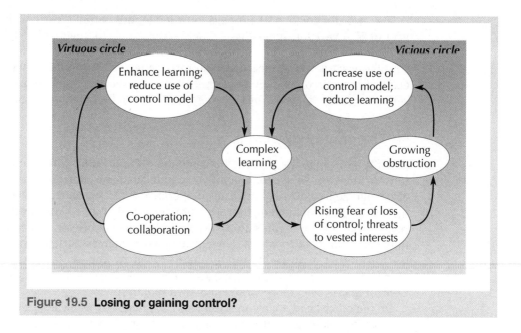

Figure 19.5 Losing or gaining control?

individual ways of doing things'. They cut across schemes for releasing creativity and making flexible responses to new circumstances.

Exhibit 19.4 Closer control of contract cleaning

A well-established contract cleaning company, with branches in most large United Kingdom towns, employed several thousand part-time staff. Each unit reported directly to head office. A new senior management team was struck by its distance from the operations level. Not only were the branches dispersed but also the team had no experience of cleaning. Members had, however, experience of other contracted services.

This sense of isolation, and pressure from the parent company to raise profits quickly, led managers to commission a procedures manual. They hoped it would provide knowledge of operations and administration practices at branch level. Beyond letting employees know precisely what was expected of them, the manual would support managers' decisions on rationalisation.

Cleaning service contracts are becoming more detailed. Contractors have to specify every task undertaken. For their employees, they lay out procedures that are correspondingly precise. Such statements of 'the one best way' signal a return to scientific management.

To the new managers, this goal was both desirable and achievable. They saw great merit in the manual as a new and refreshing idea. To them, the current procedures were unclear. Inefficiency and corruption were likely. Flexibility had to be replaced by standardisation. The manual was not merely a description. It was to be a set of instructions about the way tasks must be carried out. The managers justified this because the best procedures were included. This gave them an additional moral imperative, beyond responding to market needs, for coercive control.

Control, learning and change

There has to be a better way. How can the virtuous circle be entered and its effect sustained? To achieve this, organisations look to *learning*, applicable to both the individual and the organisation.

Individual learning

So far, much of our discussion on control has been based on the notion of *simple learning*, how to achieve a match between intention and outcome. Several authors present this as the first of a set of learning cycles. For instance, Stacey sets out the two loops as in Figure 19.6.[14] To the left, his acting–discovering–choosing loop corresponds to the steps of our feedback control models set out in Chapter 18. People learn from observing how their actions, combined with factors outside their control, influenced outcomes. This is simple, or single-loop, learning:

> *Single-loop learning means learning from previous actions to amend the next. The feedback process from action through consequence to subsequent action is done without questioning the underpinning mental model.*

On its own, single-loop learning would keep an individual working effectively so long as the plans remained appropriate. Learning does take place, yet consists of finding better ways of achieving the present goal. Kim called this building *know-how*.[15] Complex, or double-loop, learning involves further questioning, working on the *know-why*:

> *Double-loop learning occurs when the consequences of actions lead to the mental model behind them being challenged. The results of this may be shifts in the mental model or redefinition of the problem. In so doing, people destroy the old ways of doing things and create new ones.*

Complex learning combines the goal seeking of the left-hand cycle and the goal challenging of the right. As Argyris and Schon explain, 'Single-loop learning is concerned primarily with effectiveness, this is with how best to achieve existing goals ... In some cases, however, error correction requires a learning cycle in which organisation norms themselves are modified ... [There is] a double feedback loop which connects the detection of error not only to strategies and assumptions for effective performance but to the very norms which define effective performance.'[16]

Double-loop learning means both using and breaking the mould, and then creating a new one. It appears destabilising and revolutionary yet is necessary for innovation and change. It can be uncomfortable. Many organisations encourage stability rather than learning. Tucker and colleagues found that, among front-line staff, a strong motivation to solving current problems holds back double-loop learning. In a typical case, hospital nurses focus on continuity of patient care. Two newborn babies in sequence were missing their security tags on discharge. The nurse searched for the tags, but did not investigate why the tags had fallen off. In another

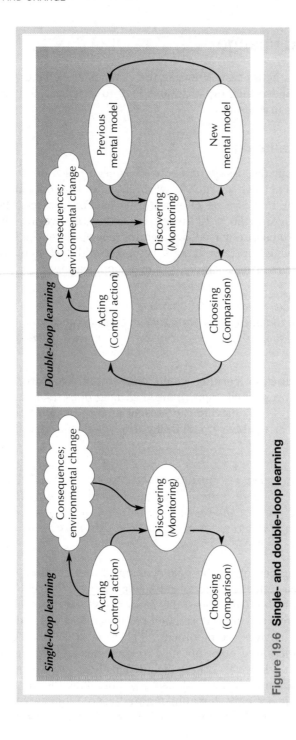

Figure 19.6 Single- and double-loop learning

case, a nurse observed a problem but limited her responsibility by passing the information to the leader.[17]

■ Organisational learning

Argyris and Schon distinguish between individual and organisational learning.[18] Employees follow established rules and routines, acting as automatons, but may also go further. Using intelligence, they look for better ways of working. Such individual learning may help the organisation. Yet, we also know that people seek ways to benefit themselves that have negative effects for the organisation. The Hawthorne Studies, *see* Chapter 1, are among many to have revealed such behaviour.

So, what is organisational learning? We can imagine the employee sharing the change with colleagues or even, if there is a climate of trust, with supervisors. If it is agreed and incorporated into normal practice, we can say organisational learning has occurred. The problem is that organisational learning faces resistance. The procedures manual of Exhibit 19.4, for example, was applauded by the new managers yet, once issued, would constrain further journeys round the learning loop.

■ Resistance

Stacey explains what happens when managers engage in budgetary control.[19] Performance variances from budgets are investigated and corrective action chosen. This, along with uncontrollable external changes, influences outcomes in the next accounting period. The process enables managers both to control and to *learn*. They are discovering the consequences of their actions and changing their behaviour as a result. They try harder but may not fundamentally question what they do. To them, the budget is fixed. Rhenman's example of two Swedish textile companies, given in Exhibit 19.5, compares a firm that tried harder and failed with another that tried *differently* and succeeded.[20]

Exhibit 19.5 Work harder or smarter?

Faced with pressure from competitors in low-cost countries, Company A automated much of its operations. In 10 years, productivity rose threefold. Yet, this was barely enough to counteract the unfavourable trend in prices and wages.

Starting from a similar base, Company B faced the threats differently. It changed direction by focusing on a specialised niche at the periphery of the traditional textile industry. Productivity increased only slightly, for the company had to reorganise its production frequently. Yet, the enhanced prices commanded by its products more than compensated for increased costs.

The more that managers share values, and hence share a mental model of the world, the more likely it is that they will resist change. Reasons for poor profit performance will be found within the shared view. This may blame external forces. One hears statements from, 'The government should do something about the strength of the currency', to, 'People are simply not buying enough'. Complex learning, on the other hand, involves challenging the mental model, as the managers of Company B did. It managed to 'break out' of its traditional ways. Two loops are working simultaneously in complex learning. The second, more difficult, loop means challenging the way things are, questioning paradigms and searching for solutions that are other than the obvious.

Why do people resist learning and change? Argyris argued that the answer lies in fear of breaking the mould. Part of this comes from difficulties with espoused models and models in use:

- *Espoused models* are the mental models we say we use. For instance, managers espouse rational decision making, open consultation, free access to information and the need to plan based on serious research. These models are usually easy to ascertain. They are found simply by asking the people concerned.

- *Models in use* are the models we actually use. So, while managers may espouse the above behaviour, they decide off the cuff, limit consultation for fear of 'leaks', and are often in so much hurry that they have little time to think. Since the models are often unconscious, managers find it difficult to clarify them.

(Note that we sometimes refer to the above concepts, not as models, but as *espoused theories* and *theories in use*.)

We often state one thing and do another. We may espouse commitment to equal opportunities yet may judge people according to the crudest stereotypes. Double-loop learning implies a challenge to the model in use. Yet, how can we challenge a view, such as a stereotype, that a person is hardly conscious of? It is no wonder that people avoid such issues and retreat into what Argyris calls defensive routines. Among his studies was a management consultancy firm, *see* Exhibit 19.6.[21]

Exhibit 19.6 Physician, heal thyself!

Seven partners had broken away from a large firm, hoping to avoid its wrangling and political games. Yet they were disappointed. Faced with threatening problems, they avoided challenging their theories in use. At partners' meetings, there always seemed to be one person unwilling to discuss an important issue. Outside the meetings, in the corridors and private offices, these questions were hotly debated.

This process built and reinforced divisions among the founders. The conflict habit soon spread to the rest of the firm.

Managers use many defensive routines to deflect challenges to their theories in use. Figure 19.7 is based on Argyris's explanation of how a manager overrules a decision. Espousing democratic ideals and wishing to bring out the best in each person, the boss seeks to save the disappointed employee's face. Yet, to tell someone you are doing so defeats its purpose. 'What you tell Fred is a fiction about the success of his own decision making and lie about your reasons for rescinding it. What's more, if Fred correctly senses the mixed message, he will almost certainly say nothing. The logic here, as in all organisational defensive routines, is unmistakable: send a mixed message.'[22] We also see here a conflict between open communication as an espoused theory and holding back, or deviousness, as a theory in use.

To understand this behaviour further, refer to the critique of the communication model near the end of Chapter 13.

Figure 19.7 **The mixed message mitigates misery**

■ How individuals learn

Ideas from core competence to knowledge management suggest a consensus that a key success factor for future organisations will be the ability to learn. Meanwhile, managers experience frustration at the complexity of the process and the resistance to the changes it inevitably brings. Schein, in his studies of culture, leadership and learning, shows how deeper understanding of how individuals learn, combined with studying how they might learn together, can underpin plans for sustaining learning.[23]

Two learning anxieties

Change through learning involves two kinds of anxiety. The first is the fear of the new. As Senge suggests in our opening quotation, most of us prefer to stay the same. We will accept change only when we feel most of our situation is stable. Commonly heard are statements such as: 'I will only take on the MBA when … my job prospects are clearer/ … I no longer work shifts/ … the children have started school/ … the kitchen is finished/ … I've given up football.'

Fear of the new also refers to the process itself. From the instructor observing naive keyboard errors to trepidation before the examination, there are threats to be avoided.

The second anxiety refers to being left out. In a changing world, we worry that our competences will date. Worse, we may realise our skills are already inadequate. Lawyers or accountants, for instance, must pass the professional examinations. But these are merely the first steps. Double-loop learning, learning how to maintain professional competence through careers, is coming more to the fore.

Schein argues that learning occurs when the pressure for change exceeds the pressure resisting it. In other words, $Anxiety_2 > Anxiety_1$. How does the instructor, teacher, coach or manager ensure that this occurs?

■ *Increase Anxiety$_2$*

Here, the manager or teacher increases the fear of not learning. A common tactic is to threaten the learner. This is the schoolteacher's cliché, 'If you don't learn this you won't get a job'. More seriously, a person may recognise that lack of information system skills prevents leadership or participation in new developments. Reason dictates that the person puts some time into bridging the gap.

Schein warns that we are not always so logical. High Anxiety$_1$ makes us defensive, misunderstand or deny reality, procrastinate and, in the end, fail. Then we blame others. No matter how much threatening or cajoling occurs, how much effort is put into creating a sense of incompetence, the individual resists. Is this the time to give up? Another way beckons.

■ *Reduce Anxiety$_1$*

Here, we focus on making the learner feel easier about the uncertainty associated with learning by providing an appropriate environment. The elements of fear abatement are set out in Exhibit 19.7.

Exhibit 19.7 Limiting learners' alarm

- *Psychological safety* – learning will occur with supportive encouragement.
- *A vision of a better future* – all can co-operate in creating a positive view of individuals, groups and the organisation.
- *Direction* – naive learners do not know what is possible. A map is helpful.
- *A practice ground* – time off the job to make mistakes and learn from them.
- *Opportunities for sharing* – group learning cuts the sense of incompetence and supports continuation.
- *Good coaching* – providing learning skills and feedback on progress.
- *Rewards* – rewards for progress are more effective than punishments for failure.
- *A supportive climate* – mistakes are for learning and are not to be hidden.

■ Developing the learning organisation

Schein extends the idea of anxiety to organisations. The pressure seems to be for them to learn new initiatives, ranging from TQM to OD, or reengineering to empowerment, with increasing speed. Anxiety$_2$ is, therefore, growing so managers need to work on Anxiety$_1$. In other words, how can they lead their organisations to reduce barriers and accept continuous learning? The answer lies in the *learning culture, see* Exhibit 19.8. Although others suggest varying elements, there is a consensus on participation, free flows of information, culture and self-development.[24]

Listing the features of a learning culture is easy compared with putting them into practice. Schein advocates removing barriers. Only when we can see our behaviour and ourselves as inhibitors of progress can progress begin. We can mention three cultural barriers: hierarchy, individualism and delusion. First, the traditional hierarchical model, which for many managers is the only one they have, blocks change. By implication, it requires managers to create self-images of omniscience, omnipotence, decisiveness and certainty. While many know of their weaknesses, the

> **Exhibit 19.8 Seven elements of Schein's learning culture**
>
> ■ Shared concern for all stakeholders – staff, customers, suppliers, owners, community.
>
> ■ Shared belief that all people can and will learn, matching McGregor's Theory Y.
>
> ■ Shared belief that the environment can be understood and changed. The organisation is in the hands of its members and therefore learning is worthwhile.
>
> ■ Diversity and slack – diversity among people, groups and sub-cultures offers creative tensions and alternatives. Slack allows people to have time to learn away from the total preoccupation with the here and now.
>
> ■ Open communication. While it should be the norm, not every issue, especially personal ones, should be known to all. Communication should support tasks. Practices such as withholding information, or using it in power games, make it impossible to learn.
>
> ■ Learning to include the ability to think *systemically*. This means recognising the organisation as an open system with its implications of interconnectedness and complexity.
>
> ■ Learning to support teamwork. There must be a shared belief that co-operation will be needed and that it will work.

dominant culture prevents them from admitting it. These feelings resist learning; it must start with managers admitting that they do not know everything.

The second inhibitor is individualism. Someone who reaches the top against the odds is often the hero. Meanwhile, the contented, dependable team player, while often loved and trusted, is neither so admired nor so rewarded. This means that teamwork, so often advocated, becomes a tedious necessity. Unless its benefits are demonstrable, it is not used. The effect of this bias is that competitiveness is regarded as the more natural behaviour. Few see teamwork as the 'normal' way of operating.

The third barrier returns us to espoused theories and theories in use. Most managers espouse support for the long-term development of people. Yet, they perceive their real task to be relating to the world through models, numbers, accounts and money. Such theory in use is also seen in business schools. Courses with high 'quantitative' content are regarded as superior, at least by those who take them. They look down on other students, who choose human relations supported by just enough 'quantitative methods' to achieve the approval of university authorities. Job advertisements frequently mention the ability to 'apply analytical skills', 'take personal responsibility' and 'work independently under pressure'. These are the values of the technocrat. Being able to handle the short-term reporting and control systems is more impressive than paying attention to morale or employee development. The latter are only turned to when budgetary issues have been settled. And they never are.

Change

Our path has taken us from control to change by presenting the latter, at least in its second-order form, as what is needed when the cybernetic process model no longer works. Learning, whether individual or organisational, gives this discussion a humanistic gloss, seeing the way people gradually adapt to new circumstances. Yet there are other views. Rather than wait for individuals and groups to adapt, managers want to force the pace. They seek to drive change, to create structures and process in anticipation of future needs.

This is a more deliberate and strategic approach. Earlier in the book, we have mentioned management actions such as 'implement plans', 'diversify', 'improve quality', 'adopt an ethical policy' and so on. Their common theme is change and we shall look at some ideas about how this may be achieved.

■ Growth and change

Clearly organisational growth demands change. In a well-known model, Greiner saw organisations passing through stages as they developed. Each stage has an ideal structure into which the organisation becomes locked for a time. Moving to the next, therefore, involves a period of transition or crisis as one structure is replaced by another, *see* Exhibit 19.9.[25]

Exhibit 19.9 Greiner's model of alternating growth and crisis

■ *Growth through creativity*
At birth, the founder-entrepreneur provides the creative drive to press forward. With increasing workload, however, the leader cannot cover every detail. This is the well-known *crisis of leadership*.

■ *Growth through direction*
The crisis fades as professional managers arrive to introduce formal procedures and departments. Specialists create problems, however, when their desire for greater self-direction is resisted by the managers who brought them in. This tension is the *crisis of autonomy*.

■ *Growth through delegation*
The crisis is resolved by delegating responsibility to capable staff. This implies looser control, however, and different divisions and functions pull in contrary directions. The organisation faces a *crisis of control*.

■ *Growth through co-ordination*
The crisis is overcome by new co-ordination structures and control processes. In many cases, these lead to the proliferation of management channels, groups and committees. The key problem becomes complexity and the organisation faces a *crisis of red tape*.

■ *Growth through collaboration*
Red tape is diminished by simplification of procedures and reliance on managerial clans. Structures are seen as not so important in this mature organisation.

Red tape

Throughout the United Kingdom and the Empire, it was traditional for administrators to tie bundles of documents with red tape. Hence this derogatory name for excessively bureaucratic methods.

Greiner invites us to think of alternate periods of stability and crisis as managers change the organisation. As a description of events, however, this is outdated. Greiner was writing well before the emergence of the virtual organisation; information systems had not been applied to horizontal control; and *downsizing* had not entered the managerial vocabulary. We should also beware of such generalisation. Many organisations do not follow the path. Most remain SMEs. Others start large, follow other paths or face different crises. Many have elements at different stages of development.

We should take from the model, however, the sense of intermittent change. A flourishing organisation creates structures and processes to maintain its vigour. Yet, their very success makes them resist change, thus delaying and amplifying subsequent crises.

▓ Forces and resistance

We can explore the nature of change through thinking about forces pressing against opposing resistance. As we shall see, the balance settles whether and how much change occurs.

Forces for change

Forces arise both outside and inside the organisation. For example, managers may be concerned by an emerging gap between what is wanted and forecasted outcomes. This performance gap was experienced at Bausch & Lomb, encouraging managers to diversify in attempts to maintain promised sales growth.

Nadler and Tushman[26] offer a typology to explore origins of change and responses to them. In the model shown in Figure 19.8, the vertical axis divides planned developments from unanticipated reactions after the event. Labelled *proactive* and *reactive* these separate the deliberate planners from those who survive through flexibility. Neither is superior. Planning suits larger organisations in relatively certain environments, while reaction is the habit of the entrepreneur.

The horizontal axis refers to the scope of change from incremental steps to major strategic changes. Again, neither is superior. Sometimes a series of minor adjustments may be appropriate. At other times, small steps may not be enough and major moves are required.

The model picks out four types of change:

▓ *Tuning* – incremental change anticipating future events – exemplified by *kaizen*, continuous operational improvement.

▓ *Adaptation* – incremental change responding to events – illustrated by entrepreneurial responses to rivals entering the market.

▓ *Reorientation* – strategic changes based on forecast environmental events – embodied in Hitachi's refocusing of its R&D effort to cover emerging technologies.

▓ *Re-creation* – unplanned change in response to unexpected events. Often involving a severe crisis, an example is Shell's struggle with rising pressure from environmentalists, *see* Chapter 5.

The four types are ranked in order of rising complexity, potential impact and risk. It will not be surprising, therefore, that they will be met with increasing degrees of resistance.

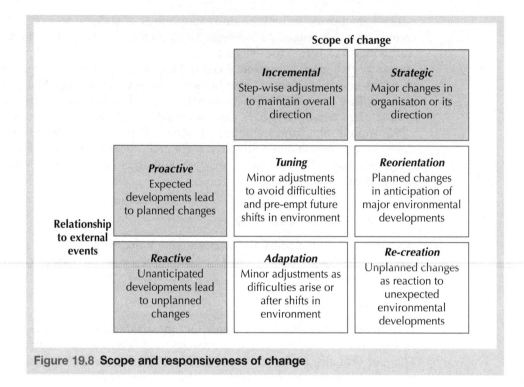

Figure 19.8 **Scope and responsiveness of change**

Resistance

Effective change management requires understanding resistance. Nicholson and West note, 'Uncertainty and danger constitute the darker opposite side to challenge and opportunity'.[27] Although this sounds neatly symmetrical, with a proponent for every opponent, Furnham argues that staff, and especially managers, prefer the status quo:

> *Small wonder that the management mantra for the 1990s is that 'the only constant is the need for change'. And even smaller wonder that staff at all levels appeal for 'a period of stability' following the last round of manoeuvres.*[28]

Some people are so wary of change that they go beyond acquiescence to opposition. To explain this we must look at causes, symptoms and forms of resistance.

■ *Causes of resistance*

Six common causes of resistance are given in Exhibit 19.10. Since resistance is personal, we must investigate each individual's point of view. Hultman proposed an analysis based on the following make-up of someone's state of mind:

■ *Facts* – statements that can be checked using evidence.

■ *Beliefs* – subjective assumptions, conclusions and predictions about the situation.

■ *Feelings* – senses of anger, relief, hope, frustration and other emotions that may be aroused by the change.

■ *Values* – convictions about what is important, the priorities we have and the criteria we use to compare them.

The comments in Exhibit 19.10 summarise how resistance can be better understood. Figure 19.9 shows typical questions to probe for the four factors. If we use

Exhibit 19.10 Causes of resistance to change

Cause of resistance	Beliefs, feelings and values behind them
My needs are already being met.	Without *feelings* of motivation, change is perceived negatively.
It will now be harder for me to meet my own (unstated) needs.	Facts may be less important than *values* (assumptions, predictions) that follow from them.
The risks outweigh the potential gains.	*Beliefs* about the risk will be subjective and may be wrong.
I think there is no justification for the change.	Leaders may use outside threats to disturb complacency but they may not be *believed, values* will be challenged and *feelings* of discontent may be aroused.
I don't like the way they propose to do it.	People may resist not so much the change itself as the means by which it is introduced. 'No consultation!' is an oft-heard cry when *feelings* are hurt.
I don't believe it will be carried through.	*Disbelieving* outcomes or the commitment of others to make the change will generate negative *feelings.*

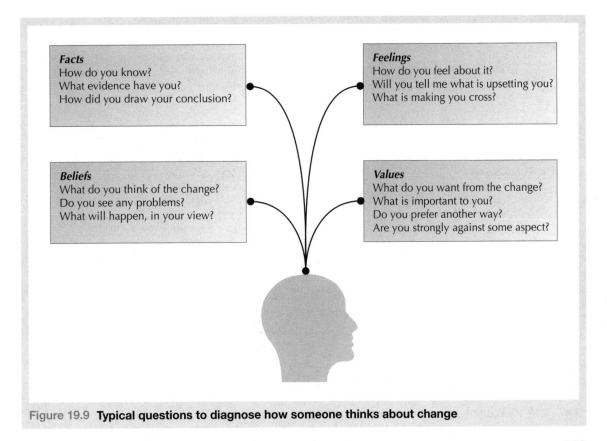

Facts
How do you know?
What evidence have you?
How did you draw your conclusion?

Feelings
How do you feel about it?
Will you tell me what is upsetting you?
What is making you cross?

Beliefs
What do you think of the change?
Do you see any problems?
What will happen, in your view?

Values
What do you want from the change?
What is important to you?
Do you prefer another way?
Are you strongly against some aspect?

Figure 19.9 Typical questions to diagnose how someone thinks about change

639

this model as a template, we can compare snapshots of each individual. A brief example of events at Daimler-Benz illustrates the point. Exhibit 19.11 has the background and Figure 19.10 offers a diagnosis of Dr Werner's resistance to change.[29]

Exhibit 19.11 Daimler-Benz loses a top manager

In early 1997, the supervisory board of Daimler-Benz introduced sweeping changes to streamline decision making. Observers suggested that €200 million could be saved each year by making the 23 divisions more responsive to their markets. At the time, it could take months for simple matters, such as the budget for one plant, to be decided.

The proposal by senior managers included removing one layer of management. This meant eliminating the two boards of subsidiary Mercedes-Benz. The semi-independence of Mercedes-Benz, lasting nine years, had been strongly defended by its chairman, Helmut Werner. He wished to safeguard the position of Europe's most profitable car maker, seeing the change as risky, unnecessary and unlikely to succeed. Yet, having lost the power struggle with group chief Jurgen Schrempp, Werner resigned.

At a press conference, Werner acknowledged that the reorganisation did make sense but he saw no role in it for himself. An amicable settlement, at least on the surface, was vital for both sides. Aged 60, Werner planned to refocus his energies on leading the Hanover World's Fair 2000. Continuing support of Daimler-Benz as sponsor and exhibitor was assured.

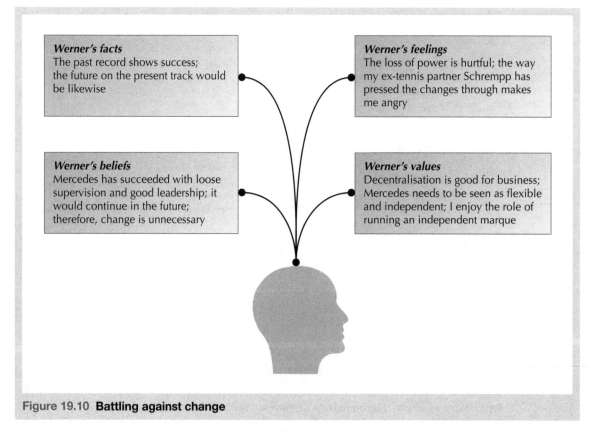

Werner's facts
The past record shows success; the future on the present track would be likewise

Werner's feelings
The loss of power is hurtful; the way my ex-tennis partner Schrempp has pressed the changes through makes me angry

Werner's beliefs
Mercedes has succeeded with loose supervision and good leadership; it would continue in the future; therefore, change is unnecessary

Werner's values
Decentralisation is good for business; Mercedes needs to be seen as flexible and independent; I enjoy the role of running an independent marque

Figure 19.10 **Battling against change**

Since we expect senior managers to share facts in this situation, we look for divergence on their interpretation. We also know that Werner did not share beliefs about the Mercedes-Benz company with his colleagues. His values in relation to business and his own role impeded agreement. For instance, in a letter to the board he had stressed how the company's image had already been damaged. Finally, we should not be surprised by the managers' emotional involvement. Although we do not have the inside story, reference to a power struggle gives us a hint of acrimonious debates, subtle manoeuvres and aroused indignation.

■ *Symptoms of resistance*

Resistance takes many forms, active and passive. Exhibit 19.12 suggests some examples. Recognising how people oppose change, and how these methods relate to their states of mind, offers clues on how to respond. For example, managers often diagnose lack of support as caused by staff not having the facts. So they stress communication to reach a common perspective. The resistance may run deeper, however. If value differences are the cause, then further fact sharing will bring no benefit. Instead of seeking a unitarist solution, managers should respond to the pluralist circumstances.

Exhibit 19.12 Active and passive resistance and states of mind

	Active resistance	Passive resistance
Facts	Distort or use facts selectively; produce more complex interpretations; bring in experts.	Withhold or delay information.
Beliefs	Argue; challenge interpretation.	Appear to agree but do nothing.
Feelings	Ridicule proponents; spread fear.	Withhold support; cold-shoulder.
Values	Advocate alternative values; start rumours.	Feign lack of interest.

A manager with a unitary perspective seeks alignment. Opposition is deviance, cured by information and persuasion. The pluralist approach, on the other hand, accepts that differences are normal and proceeds through negotiation. Change comes after bargaining. This was shown in the Daimler-Benz case. Clearly, the parties could not reach a working accommodation and the story ended with a negotiated settlement.

■ Force Field Analysis

Force Field Analysis was proposed by the pioneering behavioural scientist Kurt Lewin.[30] He argued that change occurs when *change drivers* collectively overcome *restraining forces*. The analysis can be used during the planning process or later, to investigate how to turn the plan into action. Often presented in a diagram, *see* Figure 19.11, the analysis simply summarises the forces, each with a score suggesting its strength.

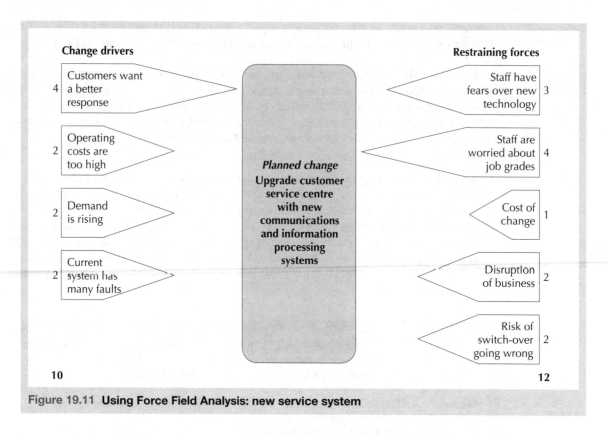

Figure 19.11 Using Force Field Analysis: new service system

In the example, although the scores offer only a rough guide, the 10–12 against should warn managers against pressing ahead. Clearly, some problems should have been foreseen at the planning stage. Yet, approval having been given, Force Field Analysis may improve chances of accomplishment. Figure 19.11 suggests two possibilities. First, introduce the change in stages, possibly with a pilot for one type of customer. Although this would delay the process and increase costs, it may have a favourable impact. Better and more interesting work offered with the new system may stimulate others to join. This adds a new change driver. Furthermore, the demonstration could ameliorate worries over new technology and cut the risk of failure. Therefore, restraining forces would weaken. The second approach uses bargaining to change the balance. For example, the staff worries over job grades could be countered by offering guarantees. A promise of higher pay for those who take on the new work may increase the demand for training and ease system introduction. In all, by changing the number and weighting of the forces on each side, the manager can build support for the change.

For others, adapting sub-systems will always be sub-optimal. Extending the tradition of systems and management science, they argue that the skills and tools are now available to cope with the complexity. It must be possible to make comprehensive changes. These counter-philosophies are exemplified by organisation development and reengineering.

Organisation development

Organisation development (OD) represents a long-term change to the organisation through interventions which involve collective action. As Grieves points out, it differs from training because, instead of producing knowledge and skill, the main aim is to change attitudes, behaviours, and performances of people.[31] Organisational learning is, therefore, a key component of any OD programme. OD is not a single technique but a family of approaches concerned with improvement through people. We shall define it as:

> *a planned, organisation-wide programme*
> *managed from the top*
> *to increase organisation effectiveness and future capability*
> *through specific interventions in the practices of the organisation*
> *which apply knowledge and techniques from behavioural science.*

Note the key features, one on each line. The programme applies across the whole organisation; it is run and supported by senior management; its purpose is effectiveness and capability in the long term; it identifies and uses specific interventions; these interventions are based on knowledge. In short, it is an informed approach to improving organisations through changing people.

Phases of the OD process

Since OD focuses on the people element of organisations, specialists appreciate that success is difficult. Lewin provides a process model of how to make change happen.[32] Three steps are illustrated in Figure 19.12.

Unfreezing

Unfreezing, or breaking the mould, makes change possible. First, there must be diagnosis of the need for change. We have already noted the possibility of a performance gap, although the need may also be discovered through deeper diagnosis

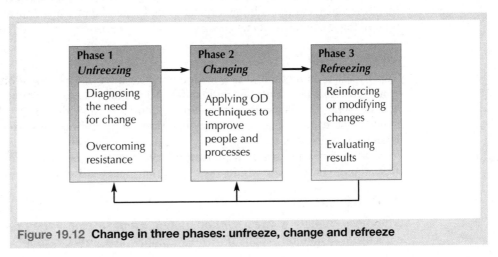

Figure 19.12 Change in three phases: unfreeze, change and refreeze

of the organisation's culture. Second, overcoming resistance to change comes early on Lewin's agenda. He advocated diagnosis to incorporate responses into any change plan.

Organisations must tolerate some level of dissatisfaction. This echoes Greiner's model of organisations alternating between stability and crisis. Continual change is ruled out because the small advantages of minor adaptations are outweighed by their costs. Beer showed how to decide whether a major change is desirable by comparing the gains from reaching the desired end state with the costs of the plan to get there.[33]

■ Changing

The change, according to OD practice, is a systematic attempt to correct diagnosed deficiencies. The plan may call for action in specific areas such as training, recruitment or communications. Otherwise, it may span the whole organisation, as with a major restructuring. Examples of what practitioners, echoing medical practice, call *interventions* appear in the next section.

■ Refreezing

The newly created structures, processes or techniques become the norm during the refreezing phase. Unless steps are taken to reinforce change, with minor adaptations in the light of experience, people return to old practices and arrangements. It is normal for OD specialists to monitor the effectiveness of their interventions so that, as with any properly managed activity, feedback can be used to adapt and learn.

Lewin's images encourage us to think of change as shifting from one stable state to another. Such thinking may create problems, however. Refreezing confirms the changes just introduced. Yet, if it confirms these too successfully, it builds strong resistance for the next time round. Refreezing becomes deep freezing. Lewin's view, therefore, is somewhat dated. Through the quality movement, Japanese engineers taught the world that change should be continuous. Chapter 6 shows how *kaizen* implies a stream of developments that are not seen as challenges to existing practices and relationships. No one remains happy with the status quo and all expect change.

■ OD techniques

Managers, supported by specialist advisers, select appropriate interventions. Many techniques can be assembled under the OD banner. Table 19.1 links a range of possibilities to sub-systems and levels in the organisation. We note that many appear in other chapters, so these comments focus on six examples of the people aspects of change.

Survey feedback

This widely used method uses questionnaires or interviews to monitor attitudes relevant to the diagnosed problems. It differs from conventional opinion surveys in two aspects: everyone is asked to participate, and all receive the results. This creates a sense of sharing of data and their interpretation, and enables free discussion in training and decision making.

Surveys can be carried out during the diagnostic phase. But they also mark the first step in change. The results facilitate other interventions.

Team building

The most commonly used method among groups, team building increases both effectiveness and job satisfaction. For example, in a project group, an OD specialist

Table 19.1 Examples of OD interventions linked to sub-systems and levels
I = individual, G = group, O = organisation

Sub-system	Intervention	Level	Chapter
Goals and values	Setting goals	I,O	8
	Planning	G,O	8
	Strategic change	O	8
Structural	Designing new structures	O	10
	Analysing roles	I,G,O	Here
	Creating flexible organisations	O	10
Socio-technical	Designing jobs	I,G	1 and 12
People	Arranging survey feedback	O	Here
	Building teams	G	Here and 12
	Life and career planning	I	Here
	Improving quality of work life	I,G,O	Here
	Counselling	I	Here
Management	Improving interdepartmental relations	O	10
	Designing reward systems	I,G,O	12 and 14
	Making decisions	I,G,O	9

has individual meetings to assess how each feels about the group. Then, in a meeting away from the workplace, discussions and exercises aim to iron out problems and improve relationships. Exhibit 19.13 shows the benefit of team building when there is a radical departure from previous practices.[34]

Exhibit 19.13 Team building in rebuilding a business

The twenty years before the fall of the Berlin wall in 1989 had seen little change at Automobilwerke Eisenach (AWE) in East Germany. Although AWE devoted some 10 000 workers to producing 100 000 Wartburg cars annually, the waiting list had risen to 17 years! After German unification, General Motors became the new owners, quickly converting the plant to Vectra assembly. Full production of Astra and Corsa models followed. GM moved away from traditional mass production techniques, placing people at the core of the new production system. With about 200 teams of between 6 and 8, a fifth of the previous personnel produced twice the output. Eisenach became one of the most productive plants in Europe and the model for GM developments worldwide.

Change was eased by people's disappointment with their recent past. They were ready for something new. Yet work teams do not build themselves. GM managers had to coach, advise and assist in times of difficulty. They built on the comradeship of AWE's former 'work brigades'. These, however, had tackled problems *after* they arose. Training in group problem analysis and decision making was crucial if problems with lean production and quality were to be prevented in advance. Efforts were made to foster group cohesion outside work. Company funds supported activities such as family days, hiking and children's parties.

Role analysis

At Eisenach, GM combined team building with other techniques. One was role analysis, the systematic clarification and allocation of roles among group members. The interdependence among tasks in, say, car assembly means doubts over responsibilities would immediately cause difficulties. The group, therefore, recognises what is required and develops means to allocate and rotate tasks.

Life and career planning

Training is often provided after analysis of a person's immediate job needs. In the broader OD context, however, specification of training needs might be one outcome of life and career planning. Here, people are encouraged to express personal goals and strategies for integrating them with those of the organisation.

Some think that such training is expensive and wasteful. People gaining better qualifications are poached by rivals. Yet Dearden and others found this to be a myth.[35] Employers who provide training, including that for qualifications not directly related to the current job, are slightly less likely to lose staff than employers who do not. Companies known for commitment to long-term staff development, such as the retailer John Lewis, train the people they want to keep and believe they stay because of it. It is the fear of poaching, rather than the fact of it, that restricts investment in non-specific training.

Quality of work life

There are links between quality of work life and career planning. Not a specific technique, it is a philosophy of improving the climate in which work occurs. It may identify the need for less conflict and greater job satisfaction through participation.

Counselling

Spotlighting the individual, counselling offers non-evaluative feedback. It improves a person's understanding of what it is like to work with them and, through this, assists them to attain their goals. As with other methods in the OD framework, it aims to enhance future performance.

■ Achieving success

According to one survey among 245 consultants, barely half of OD projects are successful.[36] French and Bell found that chances are improved by appointing an appropriate change agent who is backed by top management support, *see* Exhibit 19.14.[37] On the other hand, Buchanan and colleagues reported that, of 61 organisations, only 24 found external help useful.[38]

Reengineering

Managers sometimes perceive a need for change that is so urgent and radical that long-term, incremental programmes like OD are unsuitable. Such fundamental change has become known as *reengineering,* or, when aimed at process improvements, *business process reengineering* (BPR). As with OD, however, there is incomplete consensus of what BPR is, but the following features are commonly advanced:

■ practitioners take a process view;

■ in principle, they redesign from a 'clean sheet' and create the ideal;

Exhibit 19.14 Successful OD with an effective change agent

Conditions for success ...	... include the appointment of an outsider who ...
■ Support from top management and opinion leaders.	... reports to a senior person and is fully supported.
■ It is accepted that the system needs change.	... is chosen on the basis of relevant skills.
■ Early successes in the OD programme demonstrate that it is working.	... uses multiple interventions, probably in sequence.
■ No criticism of those who are expected to undergo 'improvement'.	... is discreet.
■ Proper co-ordination of the OD programme.	... has a high degree of access to people and resources.
■ Careful measurement of outcomes.	... shares results; admits and overcomes difficulties.

■ the whole system discards old habits and adopts new methods;

■ BPR sees stability as abnormal, continually seeking improvements;

■ 'stretch' targets are set, seeking major breakthroughs in factors such as performance, profit, quality and costs;

■ leaders seek ways of decentralising decision making and control;

■ teamwork among multi-skilled members is favoured.

The stress on process flow, cutting across conventional hierarchies, is central to the BPR ideal. Leading proponents Champy and Hammer[39] argue that the link between products and success needs to be turned round. Good products do not lead to success, they argue, but successful businesses deliver good products. Therefore, managers must get *processes* right. A detailed example is given in the closing case of this chapter.

Information technology has been an important influence. Drawing ideas from systems engineering, and supported by growth in systems capacity, reengineering has often concentrated on the 'hard' aspects of management. These are questions such as product and process design, work flow layout and control and work team organisation. 'Softer' aspects, such as attitudes, values and culture, are played down. These are expected to adjust to the new realities of whatever processes are devised.

Evaluation

We have argued that evaluation is a vital component of improvement, both to current programmes and to any that may follow. Results are mixed both in the directions they give for the techniques and in their general quality. We shall first look at evaluations of BPR and OD before reviewing some general difficulties of assessing change.

■ Does reengineering work?

One problem with reengineering is the language used by supporters. They prefer words and phrases such as fundamental, relentless, radical restructuring, dramatic improvements and discontinuous change. Hammer's often-quoted saying, 'Don't automate, obliterate',[40] epitomises the view that it is better to do without operations than to make them more efficient. Yet he also stressed the sense of urgency and use of power with phrases such as 'root out resistance', combatting those who do resist with the 'back of the hand' and 'shooting the dissenters'. This imagery presents BPR as best driven by aggressive managers riding roughshod over human sensitivities. Despite this, the revolutionary language is tempered by the espoused need to involve everyone. Hammer and Stanton admit that ignoring people's concerns is a common way to fail.[41]

So, what is the reality? Revolution or hyperbole? Crainer quotes several examples where figures are impressive. In one case, an insurance company cut costs by 40 per cent, reduced staff turnover by 58 per cent and shortened claims handling time from 28 to four days. In another, IBM saved £1.8 million.[42] Yet such selective cases can be misleading. The insurance company must have been very bad to start with; IBM's gain was mainly through automation, which could have happened without attaching the BPR label. Willcocks is more circumspect. Using Hammer and Champy's three measures of 'significant breakthrough' – 20 per cent gains in both profitability and revenue and 10 per cent cut in cost – he found only 18 per cent of a sample of 168 United Kingdom companies had succeeded in their interventions.[43] Yet, almost half had reported success in their own terms, suggesting considerably lower targets. Practice was much more pragmatic than that advocated by the champions.

Mumford and Hendricks, in what they call 'the story of the rise and fall of business process reengineering', recount 'a tale of fashion and fads, of unfulfilled promises and financial catastrophes'.[44] Under pressure to cut costs to meet competition from offshore manufacturers, struggling United States companies gladly grasped BPR. Even those doing well jumped on the 'downsizing' bandwagon. The authors chart a wave of uncritical enthusiasm followed by backlash and disillusionment. Belmiro and colleagues found interventions under the BPR banner did not address processes at all and these misconceptions led to unrealised expectations.[45]

While the main criticisms have been that people had been forgotten, proponents argue that critics arbitrarily select bad cases. When BPR is done well, and people are included, results are impressive. 'It is not something that happens to people – it is what they do.'[46] 'Reengineering is not dead. It just needs more professional engineers.'[47]

Many with experience share the pragmatic view. They regret that the language of revolution has 'oversold' the idea of total system change. It may have attracted too many who yearn for a return to the coercive excesses of Taylorism. The counterargument is that moderation and balance win in the end. Studies by Vakola show that the technical change process must be supported by good people management, allowing learning and adopting a continuous improvement approach.[48] Therefore, BPR may be seen as less than revolutionary and more a timely reminder of the need for a holistic approach to change.

■ Does OD work?

Porras and Berg summarised 35 published studies, a so-called *meta-analysis*, of OD.[49] Based on a wide range of both outcome measures (productivity, absenteeism, profit) and process measures (trust, leadership, motivation and decision making), the key results were:

- OD provided improvements. Output measures showed strongly at the group level while process measures suggested that individuals gain most often.
- Team building and survey feedback were the most successful techniques when looked at separately. More successful, however, were interventions that used four or more techniques in combination. Being prepared to use an *eclectic* approach is a key to success.

Despite the expectation that practitioners will report results in the most favourable light, there is general support for the idea that OD works. Yet does it work in all organisations? Practitioners display values favouring trust, openness and sharing. In those organisations already receptive to these notions, changes will be welcomed. The snag is that when there exists a high level of distrust and conflict, OD will be rejected. Thus, we meet another management paradox: in cases where OD would bring the greatest benefit, it is least likely to be used.

Difficulties with evaluation

Whatever change we are considering, reliable measurements are difficult to obtain. Vecchio points out three sources of difficulty, common to many aspects of management – experimental design, time span and measurement scales.[50]

Experimental design

There is only one organisation and only one set of interventions. The change programme is but a single case study. At the simplest level, a review follows the programme, collecting views on whether things have improved. It will be impossible to say whether and how far the change accounted for the reported observations. People may have simply become more optimistic.

A slightly superior design makes observations both before and after the change period. The baseline enables the post-event results to be compared. Yet difficulties remain: it is still not certain what caused the changes; the pre-tests may have changed participants' sensitivity to surveys and other changes; and, in the follow-up, respondents may feel they have to report improvements.

Such challenges suggest experimental designs that include the random assignment of people to groups. These are given various combinations of pre-test surveys and change programmes so that biases can be eliminated. In practice, however, these research designs are expensive. They are impossible when programmes span whole organisations.

Time span

Many interventions aim to improve long-term performance. This implies monitoring outcomes over a lengthy period, first to check that they occur, and second to ensure that things do not slip back to where they were before. Apart from obvious difficulties related to experimental design, the interval between intervention and survey raises two further problems. First, it will become progressively more difficult to link any outcome with the change programme. Second, if one purpose of monitoring is to improve the intervention, the information will be too late for anything to be done. As we saw in Chapter 18, feedback with a long delay can be useless.

Measurement scales

It seems a good idea to use the same attitude scale before and after an intervention. For instance, one question may be, 'Do colleagues in the finance department keep you well informed on budget matters?' A reply of 'Agree' followed by 'Strongly agree' implies an improvement. Or does it? The snag is that the 'tape measure' is both elastic and flexible. There are three possibilities:[51]

- *Alpha change* indicates that the scale remained stable and there was a favourable change.

- *Beta change* means that the respondent changed the length of the scale, that is the tape stretched or shrank. This could arise if, during the change, the person learned more about the finance department, recognising that it could do little more with its current resources. The prior 'Agree' may mean the same as the later 'Strongly agree (all things considered)'.

- *Gamma change* refers to shifts in the meaning of the scale itself. This may be caused, for example, by including finance training in the programme. The 'Agree' response may have assessed the quantity, frequency or timeliness of financial information. Later, 'Strongly agree' may have referred to which items were included and whether they were presented usefully. The attitude scale now measures a different construct and the results are no longer comparable. It is as though one gauges how much a child has grown by comparing the chest size one time with the arm length the next.

Given these difficulties, it is clear that evaluation is approximate and personal. Of course, if the aim is to help people to achieve personal fulfilment, personal assessments will be valid. Managers, however, want more than this. They are investing in development and want to measure the benefits.

Chaos and change

Conventional views of dynamic systems see them as dominated by either negative or positive feedback loops. Negative loops dampen disturbances and lead the system towards a stable state. We are used to this idea in control systems, whether it be in our blood temperature or a finance minister keeping inflation within targets. Positive feedback loops mean that disturbances build on themselves to generate explosive growth or rapid collapse. Human population or nuclear plant meltdowns are examples. In such cases, the concept of a stable state does not apply.

Bounded instability

Work on the theory of chaos has discovered a third possibility. As a negative feedback system is adapted to incorporate some positive feedback effects, it passes through an intermediate region in which the forces of stability and instability work together. Sometimes they balance; sometimes one gains the upper hand. This behaviour is called *bounded instability*. While the system remains mostly under the control of negative feedback loops, new patterns follow the tiniest disturbances. Predicting them is almost impossible.

Deterministic

In the zone of bounded instability, behaviour remains deterministic. This means it is subject to the laws of cause and effect, unlike stochastic behaviour that depends on chance. In the deterministic system, events cause events in a predictable ways. Because, however, overall behaviour emerges in so complex a manner, the individual links are lost.

For Stacey, such deterministic, non-linear feedback systems generate completely unpredictable behaviour in the long term.[52] The future of any such system is not merely difficult to predict, but *unknowable*. Behaviour is sensitive to changes too small to be measured accurately. Through cyclic repetition, they work through to become large changes. An often-quoted example of a real chaotic system governed by countless feedback loops is the weather, *see* Exhibit 19.15.

Exhibit 19.15 Wise about the weather

If you were asked to forecast the weather in your district one year ahead, you may reply, 'I haven't the foggiest idea!' On reflection, however, you may be persuaded to try harder. Depending on the season, you may estimate the noon-time temperature with a range (to be safe) of ±20 degrees. You may also observe, 'If it were sunny the previous day, the chances are that it will be fine'. This is because you know the weather follows patterns. In the United Kingdom at least, we tend to have wet and dry spells.

Weather is not random, although it appears to be. The system of moving air and water has patterns of behaviour that are remarkably stable although irregular in detail. The above statements recognised this. They appreciate the patterns and the seasons and that parameters are bounded. The 'rules' prevent snow in the Sahara or years of drought in Iceland. Given these limits, however, weather is unknowable.

Some have presented chaos theory in terms of the question, 'Can a butterfly taking off in a European garden cause a typhoon in Japan?' The theory of complex deterministic systems means that the answer is a qualified 'Yes'. The insect does not cause the typhoon on its own but may influence one in detail. The draught from its wings may be amplified through millions of loops, to which have been added all sorts of other behaviour, leading to the typhoon. We can never know. But we can say that trapping all butterflies will not prevent typhoons. They occur in any case as part of the general climate pattern.

■ Chaos and organisations

Stacey demonstrates the parallels between many organisations and those natural systems, such as the weather, that show chaotic behaviour. This is more than a weak analogy. He shows how the structure and processes of human systems make them work in the region of bounded instability. An organisation is a complex adaptive system. It evolves so that at least part of it operates within the chaotic region. Therefore, the theory is relevant. Having demonstrated this point, Stacey shows how it has profound significance for managers.

Unknowability has two implications. First, the bounded nature of system behaviour means that we can predict broad limits with some confidence. Second, chaos means that it is impossible to make any prediction within these limits. Therefore, leadership should not be about plotting and steering a detailed course. It is more like keeping afloat on a heavy sea. Being in control in the traditional sense means having the power to impose the targets and rules and to act based on monitored performance. Instability is different. As Stacey says:

> The perspective that predictability is possible leads to the view that surprise must be due to ignorance ... [yet] intelligent managers do the best they can and still the surprises come. ... Surprise is inevitable no matter how well informed, competent and well behaved everyone is.[53]

By now, we can make a connection with organisational learning. In the chaotic world, successful organisations face circumstances they cannot know in advance. Since the message for members is, 'Do not fool yourself into thinking the future is wholly knowable', they cannot be said to be 'in control' of it.[54] Nor can they subject it to any form of rational analysis or decision making. Therefore, continuing success depends on learning. This is, in Stacey's terms, 'a spontaneously self-organising process from which new strategic directions may emerge'.[55] For him, while the formal, espoused organisation may be some form of bureaucracy, working at the boundary of stability and chaos means that new forms will emerge to stand alongside or 'shadow' the formal system. He sees such developments as constructive, enabling the whole system to overcome the weaknesses of its formal arrangements. This means more than nourishing the grapevines of informal communications discussed in Chapter 13. Self-organising networks can act, and they can do so without formal authority from the centre.

In the emergence of today's *self-organising organisations*, we may be catching a glimpse of future forms. To describe them, Hock coined the word *chaord*, referring to order out of chaos. They are decentralised, non-hierarchical, evolving and self-regulating. He says, 'In chaordic systems, order emerges. Life is recognisable pattern within infinite diversity.'[56] Also, referring to the chaos theory, 'Small shifts in deeply held beliefs and values can massively alter behaviour and results.'[57] A notable chaordic organisation is the one Hock founded – Visa International, *see* Exhibit 19.16.[58]

Exhibit 19.16 Visa – a global chaord

Dee Hock is credited with inventing Visa International as a *chaord*, a chaotically organised complex system. Visa is not merely a co-operative, jointly owned by its 21 000 member banks. The governing body shapes the shared mission and common standards for operations, information systems and advertising. But it does not control members' businesses. Outside shared commitment to Visa, they compete as they have always done. Visa is a federation, with each region and board having substantial authority. Within global standards for the brand, regions vary slogans, advertising and so on. This reflects cultural differences. In mainland Europe, customers use debit cards, and then only for small transactions; those in the United States, where Visa's share is 80 per cent, use cards to borrow.

Member banks are united in wanting to keep their grip on money transactions. They charge retailers' banks a fee of about 1 per cent. Threats of 'disintermediation' arise from telecommunications companies and software houses. As well as joining Yahoo! on the Internet (another chaordic system), Visa sees 'Smart' cards as its answer to the threat led by Microsoft. In many nations, poor networks restrict use of both magnetic stripe card technology and the Internet. Smart cards allow retailers to authorise sales from the information carried on the chip.

Visa has been successful. It handles more than $1000 billion annually, some 57 per cent of all multipurpose card transactions. Europe accounts for a third of the turnover. There are some 84 million Visa cards in Europe, growing by 10 per cent each year. The largest cluster, about 25 million, is in the United Kingdom. Here, spending on credit and debit cards accounts for half of high street spending. It reached 20 per cent of GDP in 2001, twice the EU average.

Conclusion: the limits of control and change

Although control has operational applications and offers insights at all levels, defining it as a cybernetic process is too narrow. A structure with tight plan–act–monitor cycles only works in unchanging circumstances. We have seen how managers must think of control in relation to beliefs, boundaries and interactive systems. Outside the control model, the world is full of dilemmas.

The first is how to manage increasingly complex relationships through structures designed for simpler circumstances. We have seen how the work of Etzioni and Ouchi point us to links relying on other than hierarchy and rules.

Possibly a greater dilemma is how to introduce change without losing control. Managers often feel they have no choice, being pressed by superiors to 'tighten up'. They opt for top-down planning and enter the vicious circle of increasing fear and stringent controls. Advocates of the learning organisation offer hope. In exercising complex learning, an individual gathers not only know-how but also know-why. Argyris and Schon have extended this to organisational learning, suggesting how such double-loop learning can be disseminated. They suggest conditions that either encourage or restrain the growth of the learning organisation. Argyris, in particular, shows how managers call on defensive routines to stave off challenges to the status quo. Yet few studies suggest answers to the question, 'How can we change ourselves into a learning organisation?'

Greiner sees the change–control dilemma as a sequencing problem, arguing that managers prefer the stable state between periods of crisis when major changes occur. Lewin described how the moment for change could handled. Others, including the learning organisation advocates and some OD and BPR practitioners, see change as continuous. But this leads to our third dilemma, how to manage and change at the same time. In this view, rather than rely on external change agents, line managers have as much responsibility for innovation and improvement as for any other activities in their domain.

Change is also a process that can be managed well or badly. Lewin also gave us the force field model to be used in planning or implementation. We have seen how resistance arises from people's uncertainty, perceptions, emotions and values. Sensitive understanding and handling of these issues are skills in the management of change.

Of two examples of change methods that have received much attention, neither OD nor BPR is a technique. Both cover a range of interventions to be used singly or in combination. They may seem to embody the soft and hard approaches to change management. Yet, OD is often seen as a tool of management rather than a humanistic approach, while those experienced in BPR argue that it will not work unless the people issues are fully taken into account.

Whether we like it or not, change occurs and we must adapt to survive. As Nicholson put it,

> The riskiest thing of all is the no-change option. If you change, you may get it right, you may not get it right. If you don't change, that is bound to be wrong. A simple rule of thumb is that if it was working for you five years ago, whatever it is, assume that it can't be today, and certainly won't be tomorrow.[59]

Chaos theory gives us another angle. Authors argue that many parts of organisations should and do work in an intermediate zone between order and chaos. Stacey states they should not seek stability, but recognise the attraction of working far from equilibrium. Seeing the leader as the person 'in control' is false. Instead, leadership is not about omniscience and omnipotence. It is concerned with assuring and coaching members as they work at the edge of chaos. Together they create, discover and respond to the unforeseeable future.

QUICK CHECK

Can you ...

- State the control dilemma.
- Name Simons' control levers.
- Summarise Etzioni's power–involvement theory.
- Differentiate among Ouchi's types of control.
- Sketch single- and double-loop learning.
- Separate theory in use from espoused theory.
- List the key features of a learning organisation.
- Name the five steps of Greiner's growth model.
- Sketch the model of Nadler and Tushman on organisational change.

- List Hultman's four elements of someone's state of mind faced with change.
- Outline Force Field Analysis.
- Give six tactics for overcoming resistance.
- Define OD.
- Identify the steps of Lewin's change framework.
- Name five OD techniques for the 'people' sub-system.
- Summarise reasons for BPR failure.
- State the implications of chaos theory for control.

QUESTIONS

Chapter review

19.1 Explain Etzioni's power–involvement theory, illustrating its elements by reference to Bausch & Lomb.

19.2 Compare single- and double-loop learning, giving examples from your own experience.

19.3 What is meant by a bounded yet unknowable future?

19.4 Summarise, using a *rich picture* or otherwise, the ways in which managers can understand the forces restraining change in an organisation.

19.5 What tactics are available to a manager contemplating changing some aspect of the organisation? Give examples of the circumstances when each may be most appropriate.

19.6 Compare OD and BPR as means of carrying out change. Identify the strengths and weaknesses of each and relate them to situations in which they might be used.

Application

19.7 Illustrate Simons' control levers by applying them to Baring Brothers and Bausch & Lomb.

19.8 Using Ouchi's ideas, suggest why competitive tendering for complex contracts, such as large information systems, leads to problems.

Investigation

19.9 Investigate the function of procedures manuals and similar standing orders in an organisation to which you have access.

19.10 Do you think it is right for employees to resist change? Examine this question by a practical investigation, either based on reports of a dispute or by interviews.

Reengineering the Royal[60]

The Leicester Royal Infirmary is one of the United Kingdom's largest teaching hospitals. Its 4200 staff serve 400 000 outpatients, 103 000 inpatients and 120 000 in accident and emergency. Under the semi-independent status of a health trust, the hospital ranks among the nation's best. Radical change is difficult because: patients present a huge variety of demands; process responses to demands are fragmented; centres of power in hospitals are not well represented within formal structures; autonomy to make changes is limited by the government; and career structures are controlled by national conventions and agreements.

Despite the constraints, managers embarked on a radical rethink. Conversion to Trust status was a stimulus and the hospital was selected as a pilot site for the national 'whole hospital reengineering' programme. This looked to redesign for huge improvements in care, teaching and research. BPR champion Michael Hammer acted as unpaid adviser.

The programme started in September 1992 with five outpatients' services projects. Of these, three looked for improvements without fundamental change to system design. They were unsuccessful. Dramatic gains, however, came from the two investigations that redesigned processes from scratch. Managers perceived this was the only way to achieve significant improvements.

After the initial studies, some 50 change agents, drawn from the 'best and brightest' among the staff, were seconded to BPR teams, for between six and nine months. The chief executive devotes a considerable proportion of his time to BPR. Patients were involved, both in helping to redesign processes and, through a Patients' Council, in assessing the quality of the changes from a patient's point of view. Therefore, new processes were rigorously evaluated before implementation.

Four objectives were adopted:

- To realign key healthcare, teaching and research processes; to switch focus from managing inputs to managing outputs.

- To achieve unprecedented levels of service quality for patients, purchasers, students and researchers.

- To achieve unachieved levels of efficiency.

- To provide a working environment for staff to maximise the use of their abilities in delivering excellent healthcare.

The aim was to redesign all the main healthcare processes within two years. Themes selected included: 'entry', 'visit' and 'stay' of patients; clinical support functions such as 'medication' and 'diagnostic testing'; and operations management functions such as 'distribution' and 'stock management'.

In an early study of the neurology department, the aim was to achieve 'one-stop visits' for all tests and feedback of results to the patient. Time for procedures was cut from eight weeks to five hours, while administrative costs fell by 40 per cent. Supply time for hearing aids, from first notification of hearing loss to final fitting, was cut from 52 to four weeks. Routine outpatient tests yielded results in 40 minutes instead of 79 hours. Admission times for emergency patients were reduced by 70 per cent. Some groups of inpatients spent half the previous time in hospital.

A review in 1995, however, concluded that change was slower than expected and completion would stretch beyond the May 1996 target. Managers began to see that date not as the end, but as a stage in continuous process reengineering with a 10-year time scale. The experience of the first few years meant they shifted responsibility from a distinct group of change agents working within special teams to the line managers and clinicians supported by a few BPR specialists. The scope of each project was reduced from across the hospital to a focus within each speciality. Only then could flows across boundaries be incorporated.

Although it was already among the top teaching hospitals in England, the Royal improved its efficiency slightly faster than similar units did. Annual savings of about £$\frac{1}{2}$ million (from a budget of £100 million) were small yet significant. There were improvements in service quality in areas such as documentation and design of clinic, theatre, laboratory and supply chain processes. Reengineering has affected organisational structure and changed roles, for example the introduction of 'process managers'.

A review concluded that the changes in patient care processes were valuable and would last,

▶

CLOSING CASE

although the hoped-for cost improvements did not materialise. Transfer of the experience to other health service units would depend on several factors: whether BPR was applicable; the circumstances of the particular organisation; and its willingness and capacity to adapt techniques to local circumstances.

Hospital managers have always faced the problem of resolving, with professional bodies, who carries responsibility for standards and conduct. Reengineering challenged the relative certainty of traditional hierarchies with their accepted methods of control. It emphasised new roles in teamwork. Changes such as these are difficult, especially in an organisation that runs continuously. The question of managing today while inventing tomorrow was a significant one.

Questions

1 Examine the reasons for the claim made in the case that radical change is especially difficult in a National Health Service hospital.

2 Carry out a stakeholder analysis of the Leicester Royal Infirmary, bearing in mind that it is a teaching hospital. What impact might stakeholders have on changes to patient care processes such as those described here?

3 If you were advising the chief executive of the Royal on a Force Field Analysis, what issues would you include?

4 Why should 'managing today while inventing tomorrow' be so difficult?

Bibliography

The works of Argyris, Schon and Stacey, given in the reference list, offer scope for further study. All are difficult. Stacey has taken on the task of interpreting a new science. Argyris has a reputation for 'academic' thoroughness rather than populist exposition. Specialist books on managing change include Bernard Burnes' *Managing Change* (2nd edition, Hemel Hempstead: Financial Times Prentice Hall, 1996). It contains alternative approaches and case studies. For learning, Meinolf Dierkes and colleagues' *Handbook of Organizational Learning and Knowledge* (Oxford: Oxford University Press, 2003) is comprehensive. The Society for Organisational Learning has a website at **www.sol-ne.org/res/wp/index.html**.

References

1 Picken, Joseph C. and Dess, Gregory G. (1997) 'Out of (strategic) control', *Organizational Dynamics*, **25(1)**, Summer, 35–48; Sharpe, Rochelle (2000) 'Bausch & Lomb's blurry sales picture', *Business Week*, **3963**, 7 August, 87–8; Keenan, Faith and Roman, Monica (2001) 'The vision thing at Bausch & Lomb', *Business Week*, **3759**, 26 November, 51; Bausch & Lomb Inc. (2003) *2002 Annual Report*, 1–5; **www.bausch.com/us/vision/about/investor/profile. jsp**, accessed 11 April 2003.

2 Dunne, Helen and Pretzlik, Charles (1995) 'Wife of Baring's "rogue trader" held key post', *Daily Telegraph*, 1 March; Jones, George and Gribben, Roland (1995) 'Shock over bank man's £17 bn bet', *Daily Telegraph*, 2 March; Dunne, Helen (1995) 'The pleasant profits that broke Britain's blue-blooded bank', *Daily Telegraph*, 19 July, 1; Leeson, Nick (1996) *Rogue Trader*, Boston, Mass.: Little, Brown & Co.

3 Simons, Robert (1995) 'Control in the age of empowerment', *Harvard Business Review*, **73(2)**, March–April, 80–8.

4 Leifer, R. and Mills, P. (1996) 'An information processing approach for deciding upon control strategies and reducing control loss in emerging organizations', *Journal of Management*, **22(1)**, 113–37.

5 Etzioni, A. (1975) *A Comparative Analysis of Complex Organisations: On power, involvement and their correlates*, New York: Free Press.

6 Ouchi, William G. (1980) 'Markets, bureaucracies and clans', *Administrative Science Quarterly*, **25(1)**, 129–41.

7 Jones, T. Colwyn and Dugdale, David (1995) 'Manufacturing accountability', Chapter 19 in Berry, Anthony J., Broadbent, Jane and Otley, David (eds) *Management Control: Theories, issues and practices*, Basingstoke: Macmillan, 299–323.

8 *Ibid.*, 305.

9 Ferner, Anthony (2000) 'The underpinnings of "bureaucratic" control systems: HRM in European multinationals', *Journal of Management Studies*, **37(4)**, 521–40.

10 Ouchi, William G. (1979) 'A conceptual framework for the design of organisational control mechanisms', *Management Science*, **25(9)**, 833–49.

11 Budden, Robert (2003) 'Six broadband suppliers set to benefit from £1bn funding', *Financial Times*, 15 May, 6.

12 Stacey, Ralph D. (1996) *Strategic Management and Organisational Dynamics*, 2nd edition, London: Financial Times Pitman Publishing, 398.

13 Cohen, Claire (1995) 'Striving for seamlessness: Procedures manuals as a tool for organisational control', *Personnel Review*, **24(4)**, 50–7.

14 Stacey, Ralph D. (2003) *Strategic Management and Organisational Dynamics*, 4th edition, Harlow: Financial Times, Prentice Hall, 111–13.

15 Kim, Daniel H. (1993) 'The link between individual and organisational learning', *Sloan Management Review*, Fall, 37–50.

16 Argyris, Chris and Schon, Donald A. (1978) *Organisational Learning: A theory of action perspective*, Reading, Mass.: Addison-Wesley, 20

17 Tucker, Anita L., Edmondson, Amy C. and Spear, Steven (2002) 'When problem solving prevents organizational learning', *Journal of Organizational Change Management*, **15(2)**, 122–37.

18 Argyris, Chris and Schon, Donald A. (1996) *Organisational Learning II*, Reading Mass.: Addison-Wesley.

19 Stacey (2003) *op. cit.*, 111.

20 Rhenman, Eric (1973) *Organisation Theory for Long Range Planning*, London: John Wiley & Sons, 24.

21 Argyris, Chris (1993) *Knowledge for Action*, San Francisco, Cal.: Jossey-Bass; (1995) 'Action science and organisational learning', *Journal of Managerial Psychology*, **10(6)**, 20–6.

22 Pickard, Jane (1997) 'A yearning for learning', *People Management*, 6 March, 34–5.

23 Schein, Edgar H. (1992) *Organisational Culture and Leadership*, 2nd edition, San Francisco, Cal.: Jossey-Bass; (1993) 'How can organisations learn faster', *Sloan Management Review*, **34**, 85–92.

24 Burgoyne, John (1995) 'Feeding minds to grow the business', *People Management*, **1(19)**, 22–5; Leith, Clare, Harrison, Richard, Burgoyne, John and Blantern, Chris (1996) 'Learning organisations: the measurement of company performance', *Journal of European Industrial Training*, **20(1)**, 31–44.

25 Greiner, Larry E. (1972) 'Evolution and revolution as organisations grow', *Harvard Business Review*, **50(4)**, 37–46.

26 Nadler, David A. and Tushman, Michael L. (1990) 'Beyond the charismatic leader: Leadership and organisational change', *California Management Review*, **32(2)**; same authors (1989) 'Organizational frame bending: Principles for managing reorientation', *Academy of Management Executive*, **3(3)**, August, 194–204.

27 Nicholson, Nigel and West, Michael (1988) *Managerial Job Change*, Cambridge: Cambridge University Press, 5.

28 Furnham, Adrian (1995) 'Innovate and be damned', *Financial Times*, 7 September, 11.

29 Gray, Jeremy (1997) 'Daimler-Benz to profit by change', *The European*, 23 January, 15; *see also* **www.daimler-benz.com/index_e.htm**, accessed 26 June 2003.

30 Lewin, Kurt (1951) *Field Theory in Social Science: Selected theoretical papers*, New York: Harper.

31 Grieves, Jim (2000) 'Introduction: the origins of organizational development', *Journal of Management Development*, **19(5)**, 345–51.

32 Lewin, Kurt (1958) 'Group decision and social change', in Maccoby, E.E., Newcomb, T.M. and Hartley, E.L. (eds) *Readings in Social Psychology*, New York: Holt Rinehart and Winston, 197–211.

33 Beer, Michael (1980) *Organization Change and Development: A systems view*, Glenview, Ill.: Scott Foresman.

34 Haasen, Adolf (1996) 'Opel Eisenach GMBH – Creating a high-productivity workplace', *Organisation Dynamics*, Spring, 80–5; Kuryiko, Diana T. (1999) 'East German finds a future at Opel', *Automotive News*, **73**, 21 June; Morton, Ian (1999) 'GM to have Europe plants running lean this year', *Automotive News*, **74**, 11 October.

35 Dearden, Lorraine, Machin, Stephen, Reed, Howard and Wilkinson, David (1997) *Labour Turnover and Work-Related Training*, Institute of Fiscal Studies; *see also* **www1.ifs.org.uk**, accessed 26 June 2003.

36 Burke, W. Warner, Clark, Lawrence P. and Koopman, Cheryl (1984) 'Improve your OD project's chances of success', *Training and Development Journal*, **38**, September, 62–8.

37 French, W .I. and Bell, C. H. (1995) *Organization Development: Behavioural science interventions for organization improvement*, 5th edition, Englewood Cliffs, NJ: Prentice-Hall.

38 Buchanan, D., Claydon, D. and Doyle, M. (1999) 'Organisation development and change: the legacy of the nineties', *Human Resource Management Journal*, **9(2)**, 20–37.

39 Hammer, Michael and Champy, James (1993) *Reengineering the Corporation: A manifesto for business revolution*, London: Nicholas Brealey.

40 Hammer, Michael (1990) 'Reengineering work: Don't automate, obliterate', *Harvard Business Review*, **68**, 104–12.

41 Hammer, M. and Stanton, S. (1994) 'No need for excuses', *Financial Times*, 5 October, 20.

42 Crainer, Stuart (1996) *Key Management Ideas*, London: Financial Times Pitman Publishing, 155.

43 Willcocks, L. (1995) 'Does IT-enabled Business Process Reengineering pay off? Recent findings', Working Paper RDP95/4, Templeton College, Oxford Institute of Management.

44 Mumford, Enid and Hendricks, Rick (1996) 'Business process reengineering RIP', *People Management*, 2 May, 22–9.

45 Belmiro, Tânia R., Gardiner, Paul D., Simmons, John E.L. and Rentes, Antonio F. (2000) 'Are BPR practitioners really addressing business processes?' *International*

Journal of Operations and Production Management, **20(10)**, 1183–1201.

46 Lumb, Richard (1996) 'Case for the defence: 1 – Not a fad, not a failure', *People Management*, 2 May, 26.

47 Oram, Mike (1996) 'Case for the defence: 2 – Five stars guide the way forward', *People Management*, 2 May, 29.

48 Vakola, Maria (2000) 'Exploring the relationship between the use of evaluation in business process reengineering and organisational learning and innovation', *Journal of Management Development*, **19(10)**, 812–35.

49 Porras, J.I. and Berg, P.O. (1978) 'The impact of organisational development', *Academy of Management Review*, **3**, 248–66.

50 Vecchio, Robert (1995) *Organizational Behaviour*, 3rd edition, Fort Worth, Tex.: Dryden Press, 664–8.

51 Golembiewski, R.T., Billingsley, K. and Yeager, S. (1976) 'Measuring change and persistence in human affairs: Types of change generated by OD designs', *Journal of Applied Behavioural Science*, **12**, 133–57; Thompson, Richard C. and Hunt, James G. (1996) 'Inside the black box of Alpha, Beta and Gamma change: using a cognitive-processing model to assess attitude structure', *Academy of Management Review*, **21(3)**, July, 655–90.

52 Stacey (1996) *op. cit.*, 313.

53 Stacey (2003) *op. cit.*, 420.

54 Ballman, Paul C. (1969) 'Managing effectively in chaos', *Human Resource Planning*, **19(3)**, 11–14.

55 Stacey (1996) *op. cit.*, 349.

56 Durrance, Bonnie (1997) 'The evolutionary vision of Dee Hock: from chaos to chaords', *Training and Development*, **51(4)**, 24–31.

57 Hock, Dee (2000) 'Birth of the chaordic age', *Executive Excellence*, **17(6)**, June.

58 Croft, Jane (2003) 'Playing the Europe card: shoppers across the channel have not taken to the credit card as their US and UK counterparts have done', *Financial Times*, 29 April; Authers, John and Kehoe, Louise (1997) 'Visa links with Yahoo! on web directory', *Financial Times*, 30 July; 'Credit & Other Finance Cards', *Key Note Market Report*, December 1999.

59 Nicholson, John (1996) 'Thriving on change', *Making Sense of Management*, Programme 5, BBC1 Television, 3 November.

60 Bevan, H. (1996) 'Managing today while creating tomorrow: The paradox of a reengineering journey', Working Paper HWP 9630, Henley Management Group; Bowns, I.R. and McNulty, T. (2000) *Re-engineering Leicester Royal Infirmary: An Independent Evaluation of Implementation and Impact*, School of Health and Related Research, Warwick Business School, April.

INDEX

Note: to streamline the index, it includes only a few of the persons named in the text. These are listed either because their entries are extensive, they are mentioned more than once, or they have given their names to models or theories we have discussed.